4e

Research Methods
FOR THE
Behavioral Sciences

FREDERICK J GRAVETTER
State University of New York College at Brockport

LORI-ANN B. FORZANO
State University of New York College at Brockport

D1214921

Australia • Brazil • Japan • Korea • Mexico • Singapore • Spain • United Kingdom • United States

WADSWORTH
CENGAGE Learning

Research Methods for the Behavioral Sciences, 4th edition, International Edition
Frederick J Gravetter and Lori-Ann B. Forzano

Publisher: Linda Schreiber-Ganster

Acquisitions Editor: Tim Matray

Editorial Assistant: Lauren Moody

Media Editor: Mary Noel

Marketing Manager: Jessica Egbert

Marketing Assistant: Anna Andersen

Marketing Communications Manager: Laura Localio

Content Project Manager: Charlene M. Carpentier

Design Director: Rob Hugel

Art Director: Pamela Galbreath

Print Buyer: Rebecca Cross

Rights Acquisitions Specialist: Dean Dauphinais

Production Service: Graphic World Inc.

Text Designer: Lisa Henry

Photo Researcher: PreMediaGlobal

Text Researcher: Sarah D'Stair

Copy Editor: Graphic World Inc.

Illustrator: Graphic World Inc.

Cover/Interior Design: Natalie Hill

Cover image: © STILLFX/Shutterstock

Compositor: Graphic World Inc.

Library of Congress Control Number: 2010931693

International Edition:

ISBN-13: 978-1-111-34226-5

ISBN-10: 1-111-34226-1

Cengage Learning International Offices

Asia
www.cengageasia.com
tel: (65) 6410 1200

Australia/New Zealand
www.cengage.com.au
tel: (61) 3 9685 4111

Brazil
www.cengage.com.br
tel: (55) 11 3665 9900

India
www.cengage.co.in
tel: (91) 11 4364 1111

Latin America
www.cengage.com.mx
tel: (52) 55 1500 6000

UK/Europe/Middle East/Africa
www.cengage.co.uk
tel: (44) 0 1264 332 424

Represented in Canada by Nelson Education, Ltd.
tel: (416) 752 9100 / (800) 668 0671
www.nelson.com

Cengage Learning is a leading provider of customized learning solutions with office locations around the globe, including Singapore, the United Kingdom, Australia, Mexico, Brazil, and Japan. Locate your local office at: **www.cengage.com/global**

For product information: **www.cengage.com/international**
Visit your local office: **www.cengage.com/global**
Visit our corporate website: **www.cengage.com**

AVAILABILITY OF RESOURCES MAY DIFFER BY REGION. Check with your local Cengage Learning representative for details.

Printed in Canada
1 2 3 4 5 6 7 14 13 12 11 10

BRIEF CONTENTS

CONTENTS

For years we have watched students come into the psychology research methods course with a fundamental fear of science. Somewhere, these students seem to have developed the idea that psychology is interesting and fun, but science is tedious and difficult. Many students even resent the fact that they have to take a research methods course: "After all, I want to be a psychologist, not a scientist."

As the semester progresses, however, most of these students begin to lose their fears, and many of them actually begin to enjoy the course. Much of this change in attitude is based on a realization that science is simply the technique that psychologists use to gather information and to answer questions. As long as the questions are interesting, then the task of answering them should also be interesting.

When people watch a magician do an amazing trick, the common response is to ask, "How was that done?" In the same way, when you learn something interesting about human behavior, you ought to ask, "How do they know that?" The answer is that most of the existing knowledge in the behavioral sciences was gathered using scientific research methods. If you are really curious about human behavior, then you should also be curious about the process of studying human behavior.

This textbook has developed from years of teaching research methods. During that time, we would try different examples or different explanations in the classroom and watch the students' response. Over the years, the course evolved into a less intimidating and more interesting approach that seems to be very effective in getting students interested in research. Our students have been very helpful in this evolutionary process. Their feedback has directed our progress through the development of the research methods course and the writing of this book. In many respects they have been our teachers.

OVERVIEW OF TEXT

Research Methods for the Behavioral Sciences is intended for an undergraduate Research Methods course in Psychology or any of the behavioral sciences. We have organized the text according to the research process, making it appropriate for use in a lecture-only class or a class with a lab component. The text discusses in detail both experimental and nonexperimental research strategies. We use a rather informal writing style that emphasizes discussion and explanation of topics. Pedagogical aids include: preview outlines, chapter overviews, Learning Check questions throughout each chapter, a running glossary, chapter summaries, a list of Key Words for quick review at the end of each chapter, a set of end-of-chapter exercises and activities, and a Web Resources section that directs students to learning aids at a textbook companion website.

ORGANIZATION OF TEXT

Overall, the book is organized around the framework of the research process—from start to finish. This step-by-step approach emphasizes the decisions researchers must make at each stage of the process. The chapters of the text have been organized into five sections. Chapters 1 and 2 focus on the earliest considerations in the research process, presenting an overview of the scientific method and including tips for finding a new idea for research and developing a research hypothesis. Chapters 3 through 6 focus on the preliminary decisions in the research process, and include information on maintaining ethical responsibility throughout the process, measuring variables, selecting participants, and choosing a valid research strategy.

Chapters 7 and 8 present the descriptive and correlational research strategies. Chapters 9 through 11 introduce the experimental research strategy and provide the details of between-subjects and within-subjects experimental designs. Chapter 12 presents designs using nonexperimental and quasi-experimental strategies, and Chapter 13 introduces factorial designs using experimental and/or nonexperimental strategies. A review of statistical analyses for evaluating and interpreting research results is presented in Chapter 14. Chapter 15 introduces single-subject research designs, and Chapter 16 provides information on communicating and reporting research results.

Although the chapters are organized in a series that we view as appropriate for a one-semester research methods course, the order of chapters can be varied to meet the requirements of different course instructors. For example, the chapters on statistics and APA style can easily be presented much earlier in the course.

WRITING STYLE

We have attempted to use a rather informal, conversational style of writing that emphasizes discussion and explanation of topics rather than a simple "cookbook" presentation of facts. We have found this style to be very successful in our own classes and in Dr. Gravetter's co-authored textbook, *Statistics for the Behavioral Sciences*. Students find this style very readable and unintimidating. This style is particularly useful for material that students perceive as being difficult, including the topic of this text, research methodology.

PEDAGOGICAL AIDS

One item that has received particular attention as we developed this text is the use of a variety of pedagogical aids. Each chapter includes many opportunities for students to interact with the material, rather than simply be passively exposed to the material. In addition, the Learning Checks and the end-of-chapter exercises and activities may be used by the instructor as prepackaged assignments.

Each chapter contains the following pedagogical elements:

1. *Chapter Outline:* Each chapter begins with an outline of the material to be presented to help students see the organization of the material in the chapter.
2. *Chapter Overview:* A brief summary of the contents of the chapter is presented at the beginning of each chapter to prepare students for the material to come.
3. *Multiple sections:* Each chapter is divided into multiple sections and subsections that are clearly defined with headings to help break the material down into smaller, more manageable chunks.
4. *Definitions:* Each Key Word used in the text is first highlighted. At the end of the paragraph that contains a new Key Word, a clearly identified, concise definition is provided.
5. *Examples:* Numerous examples are used to illustrate concepts presented in the text. Some examples are hypothetical, but most are selected from current or classic studies in psychology.
6. *Boxes:* Boxed material, separate from the regular text, is used to offer additional, interesting information to help demonstrate a point.
7. *Figures:* When appropriate, diagrams or graphs are included to illustrate a point made in the text.
8. *Tables:* Occasionally, tables are used to present information that may best be depicted in a list format.
9. *Margin Notes:* Where appropriate, brief notes are presented in the margins of the text. These notes are used to offer reminders or cautions to the students.
10. *Learning Checks:* At the end of major sections within each chapter, a set of questions is provided to help students test how well they have learned the material.
11. *Chapter Summaries:* At the end of each chapter a general summary is presented to help students review the main points of the chapter.
12. *Key Words:* At the end of each chapter a list of the Key Words used in the chapter is presented. The Key Words are listed in their order of appearance in the chapter so that related terms are grouped together and so that students can spot parts of the chapter that they may need to review again.
13. *Exercises:* At the end of each chapter are questions and activities for students to answer and perform. The intent of the exercises is to help students test how well they have learned the material by having them apply what they have learned. Additionally, the instructor of the course can use the exercises as assignments.
14. *Learning Activities:* At the end of each chapter are one or two suggested activities that provide students with an additional learning opportunity to apply information presented in the text.

15. *Web Resources:* The final item in each chapter is a reminder about the learning resources available at the textbook companion website. The site contains flashcards with the new terms introduced in the chapter, a quiz covering the chapter content, access to workshops relevant to the chapter, and other learning aids.

NEW TO THIS EDITION

- Throughout the book, research examples have been updated and hypothetical results have been replaced with real research examples. Also, several Learning Checks as well as end-of-chapter exercises and activities have been revised or replaced.
- In Chapter 1, a new section on science and pseudoscience has been added. Also, we simplified the research process by separating the former step 1 into two separate steps. The distinction between the rational method and the empirical method was also clarified, and Figure 1.3 was revised to make it more compatible with the concepts of induction and deduction.
- In Chapter 2, we updated the text to be compatible with the changes to the research process in Chapter 1, and we updated the database information in Table 2.1 and Box 2.2. Tables 2.2 and 2.3 were revised to accommodate the guidelines from the new edition of the *APA Publication Manual* (6th ed.), and a new section on taking notes while conducting a literature search was added.
- In Chapter 3, the sections on ethical guidelines for research with humans and nonhumans were updated, and the discussion of plagiarism was greatly expanded, including examples of plagiarism in a new table.
- Material from the former Box 4.1 has been incorporated into a new section of text in Chapter 4 to emphasize its importance. Information was added to describe how validity and reliability can be established with consistent positive and negative relationships. A new subsection on artifacts, inducing experimenter bias and participant reactivity, was created by moving material from Chapter 6 of the 3rd edition.
- The introduction to Chapter 5 was edited to clarify the concept that sample selection can influence research results, and information about representativeness of the accessible population to the target population was added.
- In Chapter 6, the concept that different research questions can require different research strategies was clarified. We also made more consistent and more frequent cross-references to other chapters in which research strategies are discussed in more detail. The discussion of internal validity was edited to emphasize that threats are from different types of variables. The former section on validity and individual research strategies was edited drastically to minimize redundancy.
- Chapter 7 begins with updated examples of descriptive research in the introduction. Also, a new section discusses using the Internet to administer a survey.

- A new section in Chapter 8 introduces correlational research and identifies what it does and does not do using a study initially reported in Chapter 6. The description of positive and negative relationships was expanded, including revised figures to clarify directions of increasing and decreasing values. Also, we expanded the discussion concerning the evaluation of relationships for non-numerical data.
- Chapter 9 was edited to clarify the temporal nature of cause-and-effect relationships. Also, the text was simplified by deleting a redundant section on randomization.
- The first figure in Chapter 10 was revised to show how a between-subjects design begins with one sample of participants who are then divided into separate groups to be assigned to the separate treatment conditions. Also, the text was edited to simplify the discussion of variance and the discussion of problems related to studies using multiple treatment groups.
- In Chapter 11, the introduction of counterbalancing was expanded and a specific research example illustrating the counterbalancing procedure and its consequences was added. Figure 11.1, which illustrates the within-subjects design, was modified to be compatible with similar figures in Chapter 10.
- The Chapter 12 figures illustrating cross-sectional and longitudinal developmental designs were revised to be compatible with similar figures in Chapters 10 and 11. The developmental designs were also added to Table 12.2, which summarizes nonexperimental and quasi-experimental designs.
- In Chapter 13, major revisions throughout the introduction, discussion, and definition of interactions have produced a much simpler explanation of the concept.
- In Chapter 14 we revised the sections on measuring effect size to be in accord with the new emphasis on reporting effect size presented in the new *APA Publication Manual*. A new section describes how confidence intervals can provide an alternative method for measuring and reporting effect size. Another new section introduces post tests as a means for identifying significant and nonsignificant mean differences following an analysis of variance, and new text was added describing how effect size is measured for the chi-square test for independence.
- Edited text throughout Chapter 15 emphasizes that the power of a single-subject experimental design comes from replication, which involves repeatedly demonstrating the effect of the treatment. Throughout the chapter, updated research examples, including new figures, demonstrate different types of single-subject designs.
- Chapter 16 was revised throughout to be consistent with the new *APA Publication Manual* guidelines. A new sample research report provides examples of manuscript pages and is completely reproduced in Appendix D. A new table demonstrates a wide variety of citation styles, and a new section demonstrates how direct quotes should be used, formatted, and cited based on length of passage. Another new

table updates reference formats, emphasizing formats for referencing electronic sources.

- Appendix B updates statistics demonstrations to include measures of effect size to accompany each example of a hypothesis test.
- Appendix C updates examples for the current version of SPSS. Also, added notes explain how information from each hypothesis test output can be used to compute measures of effect size.
- Appendix D presents a new example of a research report demonstrating the revised APA-style guidelines.

ACKNOWLEDGMENTS

We appreciate the careful reading and thoughtful suggestions provided by the reviewers of this text:

Julie Slowiak	University of Minnesota
Mark Duva	Cerritos College
Jackie Braun	Ramapo College of New Jersey
Evelyn Marie Lyles	University of Maryland–Shady Grove
Jennifer Veilleux	University of Illinois at Chicago
Elizabeth Sheehan	Georgia State University
David W. Alfano	Community College of Rhode Island

We appreciate the hard work provided by the staff at Wadsworth Cengage Learning in the production of this text:

Linda Schreiber-Ganster, Publisher

Jon-David Hague, Executive Editor

Tim Matray, Acquisitions Editor

Rebecca Rosenberg, Assistant Editor

Alicia McLaughlin, Editorial Assistant

Mary Noel, Media Editor

Jessica Egbert, Marketing Manager

Anna Andersen, Marketing Coordinator

Talia Wise, Marketing Communications Manager

Vernon Boes, Senior Art Director

Special thanks also go to Mike Ederer at Graphic World Inc., who shepherded us through production.

Finally, our most heartfelt thanks go out to our spouses and children: Charlie Forzano, Ryan Forzano, Alex Forzano, Debbie Gravetter, Justin Gravetter, Melissa Monachino, and Megan Burke. This book could not have been written without their unwavering support and patience.

TO CONTACT US

Over the years our students have given us many helpful suggestions and we have benefited from their feedback. If you have any suggestions or comments about this book you can write to us at the Department of Psychology, The College at Brockport, SUNY, 350 New Campus Drive, Brockport, NY 14420. We can also be reached by e-mail at:

Lori-Ann B. Forzano   *Frederick J Gravetter*
lforzano@brockport.edu   fgravett@brockport.edu

FREDERICK J GRAVETTER is Professor Emeritus of Psychology at The College at Brockport, State University of New York. While teaching at Brockport, he specialized in statistics, research design, and cognitive psychology. Dr. Gravetter received his bachelor's degree in mathematics from M.I.T. and his Ph.D. in psychology from Duke University. In addition to publishing several research articles, Dr. Gravetter has co-authored *Statistics for the Behavioral Sciences* and *Essentials of Statistics for the Behavioral Sciences*.

LORI-ANN B. FORZANO is an Associate Professor of Psychology at The College at Brockport, State University of New York, where she has been teaching undergraduate and graduate courses in research methods since 1992. She earned a Ph.D. in experimental psychology from the State University of New York at Stony Brook in 1992, where she also received her B.S. in psychology. Dr. Forzano's research interests are in the area of conditioning and learning. Specifically, she studies self-control and impulsiveness in adults and young children. Her research has been published in the *Journal of the Experimental Analysis of Behavior, Learning and Motivation*, and *The Psychological Record*.

1

Methods for Acquiring Knowledge

CHAPTER OVERVIEW

In this chapter, we introduce the topic of this textbook: research methodology. To help you see the relevance of this material to your life, we begin with some comments about the usefulness of understanding research methodology. Then we discuss the many ways of acquiring knowledge or finding answers to questions, including the scientific method. Next, we provide a thorough discussion of the scientific method. The chapter ends with an outline of the research process, the way the scientific method is applied to answer a particular question. The research process provides the framework for the rest of the textbook.

1.1 | INTRODUCTION TO RESEARCH METHODOLOGY

1.2 | METHODS OF KNOWING AND ACQUIRING KNOWLEDGE

1.3 | THE SCIENTIFIC METHOD

1.4 | THE RESEARCH PROCESS

1.1 | INTRODUCTION TO RESEARCH METHODOLOGY

Consider the following questions.

> Are children of divorced parents less likely to commit to romantic relationships?
>
> Are girls more likely to cyberbully than boys are?
>
> Can parents' preoccupation with their own weight influence their children's dieting behavior?
>
> Are adolescents who play violent video games more aggressive than adolescents who do not play violent video games?
>
> How many hours of sleep are necessary to avoid a decline in mental alertness?
>
> Do children who grow up with brothers and sisters develop better social skills than children who grow up without brothers and sisters?

You might already know the answers to these questions, or you may know how to get the answers. However, there are many different ways to find answers to questions like these. In this book, we focus on the method that scientists use to answer questions: the scientific method. The scientific method is considered basic, standard practice in the world of science and students in the behavioral sciences (for example, psychology, sociology, or criminal justice) should understand how this process works and have some appreciation of its strengths and weaknesses.

Before we launch into our discussion of the specifics of the methods used in scientific research, we make a few preliminary comments about why an understanding of research methodology could be important to you. We hope these remarks pique your interest and, at minimum, open your mind to the idea that learning about research methodology will be useful to you.

Why Take a Research Methods Course?

Why are you taking this course and reading this textbook? The most straightforward answer is probably, "Because it's required." Nationwide, students take research methods courses because they have to. In addition, most students view the research methods course as largely irrelevant to their education and career goals. Psychology majors, for example, want to learn about people; however, Research Methods is not about people and it is not really about psychology. It is about science.

So why is Research Methods a required course? The simple answer is that professionals in the behavioral sciences rely on the methods of science to gather and interpret information. Suppose that a psychologist wanted to determine whether children raised by gay couples develop different characteristics than children raised by heterosexual couples. To answer this question, the psychologist would observe and compare children from families of both kinds. The psychologist would need to decide exactly what characteristics to observe. Self-esteem, relationships with friends, success in school, anxiety, depression, and parent/child attachment would be sensible choices. The psychologist would need to record objective measurements of these characteristics rather than rely on subjective interpretations or the potentially biased reports of friends and neighbors. This scenario is a simplified overview of scientific research. Our point is that science provides a carefully developed system for answering questions so that the answers we get are as accurate and complete as possible.

Other Reasons for Taking a Research Methods Course

Consider some of the other ways in which understanding research methodology can be useful to you.

Conducting a Study

A course in research methods will be most useful if you actually conduct a research study at some time in the future. Some of your undergraduate courses, including independent study and honors thesis classes, might involve conducting a study. In addition, if you plan to continue your education beyond the undergraduate degree, you probably will be expected to conduct research in graduate school. Incidentally, conducting your own research as an undergraduate enhances your marketability for admittance to a graduate program. Furthermore, you might pursue a job that involves conducting studies, perhaps as a research assistant.

Admittedly, however, most students are not planning to conduct research studies in the immediate future and, therefore, do not see a research methods course as meeting their immediate needs. In addition, many students never intend to conduct a study. Many psychology majors are interested in securing a position within the human services field after they complete their degrees. Therefore, many students do not see a research methods course as relevant to their career aspirations. However, a course in research methods can still be useful. To keep up to date in your profession, you will need to read and understand the most recent research publications.

Reading and Evaluating Other People's Studies

A grasp of research terminology and logic will allow you to read and understand research articles. Rather than reading a summary of someone else's research in a magazine, newspaper, or textbook, you can read the original article yourself and draw your own conclusions. A research methods course will help you read and critically evaluate journal articles detailing research studies. Many occupations use research findings. For example, if you were a residential counselor trying to settle a dispute between two roommates, you might review research articles that examine the effectiveness of different approaches to conflict resolution. Similarly, if you were an elementary school teacher trying to decide which teaching method is best for your students, you might review research articles that examine the effectiveness of different teaching methods. Reading and evaluating these articles would help you determine which treatments might work best with your roommate dispute and which teaching method might work best with your students. In addition, reading original sources of research is often required in other classes.

Understanding research methodology will also help you critically evaluate the research presented in journal articles. Many research articles jump from the results section (the section of the article that tells the reader what was discovered in the study) to the discussion section (the section of the article where the author interprets the results and draws conclusions). You must be able to analyze and evaluate that jump. You will need to determine to what extent the evidence supports the conclusions. A research methods course will, therefore, help you evaluate the research of others.

Understanding Brief Descriptions of Studies

A research methods course will also help you understand abbreviated descriptions of studies. In most of your other psychology courses and psychology textbooks, you are given abbreviated descriptions of studies as evidence supporting some conclusion or theory. For example, you could be told that a between-subjects design using a placebo control group was conducted with type of treatment as the independent variable and number of cigarettes smoked as the dependent variable, and that the researchers found that the nicotine patch significantly reduced the number of cigarettes smoked by heavy smokers. As you can see in this example, when a textbook or professor describes someone else's study, you are not told everything about the study. Instead, there is a style (a lingo, or vocabulary) that psychologists use to describe research. That style is determined by the principles of research methodology. This course will introduce you to the lingo of research methodology.

Some principles you will learn about in this textbook are so well known and basic that every research study follows them. Because all studies follow these principles, they are not mentioned in most research reports; it is assumed that the reader knows they were followed. Therefore, a research methods course will help you fill in the gaps in typical descriptions of studies. In addition, if you do not understand research methods, some features of experiments may seem strange, even nonsensical. For instance, in the previous example, why was it necessary for the study to include a group of smokers who wore patches that did not contain nicotine (the placebo control group)? A research methods course will help you better understand and remember studies. You will then be better able to master the material in your other courses.

Gathering and Evaluating Information in Your Daily Life

Every day, you are inundated with information. Web pages, magazines, television, and radio flood us with statements such as "Sexually abused children grow up to become sexual abusers as parents," "Drinking a glass of wine each day decreases a person's risk of heart disease," or "Hypnosis can be used to retrieve accurate memories of traumatic experiences." What do we do with this information? Is any of it even true? Should we take it to heart and modify our behaviors? For example, should child-custody decisions include a check into the parents' backgrounds to determine whether one parent experienced abuse as a child and, therefore, is likely to become an abuser? Should judges and juries consider testimony from a witness who has been hypnotized to be absolutely true? Should we all start drinking regularly? Or do we ignore the claims we read about and hear, and hope for the best? We need to be educated consumers of information. An understanding of research methodology will enable you to find and evaluate the original source of the information. A layperson who can think critically and logically can identify flaws in the methods used for collecting information. A course in research methods will make you aware of the logical constraints that apply to conducting research and interpreting the results, so you can tease apart the truth on your own and not be dependent solely on a supposed expert to do it for you, or rely on someone who may have a vested interest in having you buy a particular product. A research methods course will help you make educated decisions about the claims you encounter in everyday life.

You also can use the methods presented in this book to help make decisions in your own everyday life. Whether you are deciding which new car to buy, which job offer to accept, or which peanut butter is best, you should begin the decision process by gathering information. This is what Research Methods is all about; how to collect and interpret the information that you need to make the best possible decisions. As we discuss later, the scientific method is a procedure for acquiring knowledge and answering questions. It is a logical and objective method for obtaining information and making decisions based on that information. This way of thinking is not limited to scientific research but can be applied to all aspects of life. A research methods course will teach you to think like a scientist, which—we hope you will see—need not be restricted to the laboratory.

Summary

By discussing some of the ways a course in research methods can be of use to you, we have pointed out an alternative way to see the course as worthwhile in itself, and not just a course you have to take. We hope you are more open to the possibility that this course can be useful, interesting, and, perhaps, even enjoyable.

LEARNING CHECKS

Briefly summarize the different ways in which understanding research methodology can be useful.

Describe how you can use an understanding of research methodology when reading research claims in the newspaper.

1.2 | METHODS OF KNOWING AND ACQUIRING KNOWLEDGE

Terms printed in boldface are defined in the glossary. Some terms, identified as key words, are also defined in the text.

As we indicated at the beginning of this chapter, this textbook focuses on the use of the scientific method to answer questions. However, the methods used in scientific research are not the only ones available for answering questions, and they are not necessarily the most efficient. There are many different ways of knowing or finding answers to questions. In general, the different ways that people know, or the methods that people use to discover answers, are referred to as **methods of acquiring knowledge.** In this chapter, we examine several ways of knowing. Eventually, we describe the scientific method, the general approach used by the scientific community to obtain answers.

Methods of acquiring knowledge are ways in which a person can know things or discover answers to questions.

The rest of this chapter examines several established methods of knowing and acquiring knowledge. To appreciate the scientific method, we begin with five nonscientific approaches: the method of tenacity, the method of intuition, the method of authority, the rational method, and the method of empiricism. We conclude with a more detailed discussion of the scientific method. As you will see, the scientific method combines elements from each of the other methods to produce a general question-answering technique that avoids some of the limitations or pitfalls of other methods. Although the scientific method tends to be more complicated and more time consuming than the other methods, the goal is to obtain better-quality answers, or at least a higher level of confidence in the answers. Finally, we warn that the scientific method outlines a general strategy for answering questions; the specific details of applying the scientific method to particular problems form the content of the remainder of the book.

The Method of Tenacity

The **method of tenacity** involves holding on to ideas and beliefs simply because they have been accepted as facts for a long time or because of superstition. Therefore, the method of tenacity is based on habit or superstition. Habit leads us to continue believing something we have always believed. Often this is referred to as belief perseverance. For example, you've probably heard the clichés, "You cannot teach an old dog new tricks" and "Opposites attract." These statements have been presented over and over again, and they have been accepted as true. In general, the more frequently we are exposed to statements, the more we tend to believe them. Advertisers successfully use the method of tenacity, repeating their messages over and over, hoping consumers will accept them as true. An ad featuring milk-mustachioed celebrities is currently appearing in magazines everywhere—in the sponsor's hope that we get the message and ask ourselves the question, "got milk?"

DEFINITION In the **method of tenacity**, information is accepted as true because it has always been believed or because superstition supports it.

The method of tenacity also involves the persistence of superstitions, which represent beliefs reacted to as fact. For example, everyone "knows" that breaking a mirror will result in 7 years' bad luck, and that you should never walk under a ladder or let a black cat cross your path. Many sports figures will only play a game when wearing their lucky socks or jersey, and many students will not take an exam without their lucky pencil or hat.

One problem with the method of tenacity is that the information acquired might not be accurate. With regard to the statement about old dogs not being able to learn new tricks, the elderly can and do learn (O'Hara, Brooks, Friedman, Schroder, Morgan, & Kraemer, 2007). With regard to the statement that opposites attract, research shows that people are attracted to people who are like them (Klohnen & Luo, 2003). In addition, "getting milk" is not good advice for all people; many adults are lactose intolerant. Another pitfall of the method of tenacity is that there is no method for correcting erroneous ideas. Even in the face of evidence to the contrary, a belief that is widely accepted solely on the basis of tenacity is very difficult to change.

LEARNING CHECK   Describe how the cliché "You can lead a horse to water but you can't make it drink" can be used to explain a person's behavior.

The Method of Intuition

In the **method of intuition,** information is accepted as true because it "feels right." With intuition, a person relies on hunches and "instinct" to answer questions. Whenever we say we know something because we have a "gut feeling" about it, we are using the method of intuition. For example, at a casino, if someone puts his money on the number 23 at a roulette table because he "feels" it is going to come up, then that person would be using the method of intuition to answer the question of which number to play. For many questions, this method is the quickest way to obtain answers. When we have no information at all and cannot refer to supporting data or use rational justification, we often resort to intuition. For example, intuition provides answers when we are making personal choices between equally attractive alternatives such as: What should I have for dinner? Should I go out tonight or stay in? The ultimate decision is often determined by what I "feel like" doing. Many ethical decisions or moral questions are resolved by the method of intuition. For example, we know that it is wrong to do something because it does not "feel" right. Part of intuition is probably based on the subtle cues that we pick up from the people around us. Although we can't explain exactly how we know that a friend is having a bad day, something about the way she moves or speaks tells us that it is true. The predictions and descriptions given by psychics are thought to be intuitive. The problem with the method of intuition is that it has no mechanism for separating accurate from inaccurate knowledge.

DEFINITION   In the **method of intuition,** information is accepted on the basis of a hunch or "gut feeling."

LEARNING CHECK   Describe how one uses the method of intuition to find answers.

The Method of Authority

In the **method of authority,** a person finds answers by seeking out an authority on the subject. This can mean consulting an expert directly or going to a library or a website to read the works of an expert. In either case, you are relying on the assumed expertise of another person. Whenever you consult books, people, television, the Internet, or the newspaper to find answers, you use the method of authority. Some examples of experts are physicians, scientists, psychologists, professors, stockbrokers, and lawyers.

DEFINITION	In the **method of authority,** a person relies on information or answers from an expert in the subject area.

For many questions, the method of authority is an excellent starting point; often, it is the quickest and easiest way to obtain answers. Much of your formal education is based on the notion that answers can be obtained from experts (teachers and textbooks). However, the method of authority has some pitfalls. It does not always provide accurate information. For example, authorities can be biased. We have all seen examples of conflicting testimony by "expert witnesses" in criminal trials. Sources are often biased in favor of a particular point of view or orientation. For example, parents who are having a problem with their child's temper tantrums could seek help from an expert. If they were to ask a psychodynamic psychologist why their child was displaying this behavior, they would probably hear an explanation that involved a failure to meet the child's oral needs. In contrast, if the parents were to consult a behavioral psychologist, the child's tantrums might be explained as the result of the parents' reinforcing of the behavior by giving in to the demands of the child.

Another limitation of the method of authority is that the answers obtained from an expert could represent subjective, personal opinion rather than true expert knowledge. For example, one "expert" reviewer gives a movie a rating of "thumbs up" whereas another expert gives the same movie "thumbs down." Box 1.1 discusses a historical example of conflict between "expert" authorities.

An additional limitation of this method is that we assume, by virtue of the person's status as an authority, that expertise can be generalized to include the question we are asking. For example, advertisers often use the endorsements of well known personalities to sell their products. When a famous athlete appears on television telling you what soup is more nutritious, should you assume that being an outstanding football player makes him an expert on nutrition? The advertisers would like you to accept his recommendation on authority. Similarly, when Linus Pauling, a chemist who won the Nobel Prize for his work on the chemical bond, claimed that vitamin C could cure the common cold, many people accepted his word on authority. His claim is still widely believed, even though numerous scientific studies have failed to find such an effect.

Another pitfall of the method of authority is that people often accept an expert's statement without question. This acceptance can mean that people do not check the accuracy of their sources or even consider looking for a second opinion. As a result, false information is sometimes taken as truth. In some situations, the authority is accepted without question because the information appears to make sense, so there is no obvious reason to question it. We would all like to believe it when the doctor says, "That mole doesn't look cancerous," but you might be better protected by getting a second opinion.

People sometimes accept the word of an authority because they have complete trust in the authority figure. In this situation, the method of authority is

BOX **1.1**

Conflict Between Science and Authority

The method of authority has a long and, at times, colorful history in defining truth and disseminating knowledge. History is filled with instances of clashes between official authorities and scientists. Sometimes, theological authorities were involved and scientific pursuit was viewed as a threat to religious doctrine. Scientists were branded as heretics. For example, religious doctrine once held that Earth was at the center of the universe—that all heavenly bodies revolved around Earth. On the other hand, the seventeenth century astronomer Galileo supported the view of his predecessor Copernicus, that Earth revolved around the Sun (the heliocentric view). When Galileo discovered, with the aid of a new telescope, that Jupiter has its own moons that revolve around it, he knew that the religious doctrine was faulty. That is, not all objects revolve around Earth and, therefore, Earth was not the center of the universe. Needless to say, he continued to support the view of Copernicus. Consequently, in 1616, Galileo was condemned by the authorities of the Catholic Church and threatened with imprisonment if he ever espoused the heliocentric view again. Galileo's viewpoint was so opposed to the religious dogma of the time that many of his peers would not even look through his telescope. Lest you worry about Galileo's reputation, the Pope vindicated Galileo in an official statement—in 1992, more than 300 years after his condemnation. Although this is not a commentary on religious doctrine, it is an example of how differing values and differing views of truth and knowledge can clash. Resistance to scientific inquiry often results when science ventures into areas traditionally explained by other methods (authority, intuition, logic, and so on). It is also important to note that different methods of acquiring knowledge can lead to vastly different conclusions about the nature of the universe. Furthermore, conflict between science and authority is not limited to events that occurred 300 years ago. For example, today, there is considerable debate in science and society about the possible applications of cloning.

often called the **method of faith** because people accept on faith any information that is given. For instance, young children tend to have absolute faith in the answers they get from their parents. Another example of faith exists within religions. A religion typically has a sacred text and/or individuals (pastors, imams, priests, rabbis) who present answers that are considered the final word. The problem with the method of faith is that it allows no mechanism to test the accuracy of the information. The method of faith involves accepting another's view of the truth without verification.

DEFINITION The **method of faith** is a variant of the method of authority in which people have unquestioning trust in the authority figure and, therefore, accept information from the authority without doubt or challenge.

As a final pitfall of the method of authority, realize that not all "experts" are experts. There are a lot of supposed "experts" out there. Turn on the television to any daytime talk show. During the first 45 minutes of the show, in front of millions of viewers, people haggle with one another: women complain about their husbands, estranged parents and teenagers reunite, or two women fight over the same boyfriend. Then in the final 15 minutes, the "expert" comes out to discuss the situations and everyone's feelings. These "experts" are often people who lack the credentials, the experience, or the training to make the claims they are making. Being called an expert does not make someone an expert.

In conclusion, we should point out that there are ways to increase confidence in the information you obtain by the method of authority. First, you can evaluate the source of the information. Is the authority really an expert, and is the information really within the authority's area of expertise? Also, is the information an objective fact or is it simply a subjective opinion? Second, you can evaluate the information itself. Does the information seem reasonable? Does it agree with other information that you already know? If you have any reason to doubt the information obtained from an authority, the best suggestion is to get a second opinion. If two independent authorities provide the same answer, you can be more confident that the answer is correct. For example, when you obtain information from an Internet site you should be cautious about accepting the information at face value. Do you have previous experience with the site? Is it known to be reputable? If there is any doubt, it pays to check to see that other sites are providing the same information.

The methods of tenacity, intuition, and authority are satisfactory for answering some questions, especially if you need an answer quickly and there are no serious consequences for accepting a wrong answer. For example, these techniques are usually fine for answering questions about which shoes to wear or what vegetable to have with dinner. However, it should be clear that there are situations for which these uncritical techniques are not going to be sufficient. In particular, if the question concerns a major financial decision, or the answer could significantly change your life, you should not accept information as true unless it passes some critical test or meets some minimum standard of accuracy. The next two methods of acquiring knowledge (and the scientific method) are designed to place more demands on the information and answers they produce.

LEARNING CHECKS

Describe why you might be cautious about using the Internet to find answers to medical questions.

Describe situations in which you have used each method—tenacity, intuition, and authority—to know some information or to answer a question.

The Rational Method

The **rational method**, also known as **rationalism**, involves seeking answers by logical reasoning. We begin with a set of known facts or assumptions and use logic to reach a conclusion or get an answer to a question. Suppose a clinical psychologist wanted to know whether a client, Amy, had a fear of darkness. A simple example of reasoning that might be used is as follows:

All 3-year-old children are afraid of the dark.

Amy is a 3-year-old girl.

Therefore, Amy is afraid of the dark.

In this **argument,** the first two sentences are **premise statements.** That is, they are facts or assumptions that are known (or assumed) to be true. The final sentence is a logical conclusion based on the premises. If the premise statements are, in fact, true and the logic is sound, then the conclusion is guaranteed to be correct. Thus, the answers obtained by the rational method must satisfy the standards established by the rules of logic before they are accepted as true.

Notice that the rational method begins after the premise statements have been presented. In the previous argument, for example, we are not trying to determine whether all 3-year-old children are afraid of the dark; we simply accept this statement as true. Similarly, we are not concerned with proving that Amy is a 3-year-old girl; this statement is also accepted as a fact. Specifically, the rational method does not involve running around making observations and gathering information. Instead, you should think of the rational method as sitting alone, quietly in the dark, mentally manipulating premise statements to determine whether they can be combined to produce a logical conclusion.

DEFINITIONS	The **rational method,** or **rationalism,** seeks answers by the use of logical reasoning.
	In logical reasoning, **premise statements** describe facts or assumptions that are presumed to be true.
	An **argument** is a set of premise statements that are logically combined to yield a conclusion.

The preceding example (Amy and the dark) demonstrates the rational method for answering questions, and it also demonstrates some of the limitations of the rational method. Although the logic is sound, there is still a chance that the conclusion is not true; that is, the real-world child Amy might not be afraid of the dark. Unless both of the premise statements are true, the conclusion is not necessarily true, even in a valid logical argument. One obvious problem comes from the universal assumption expressed in the first premise statement, "All 3-year-old children are afraid of the dark." Although this statement might be accurate for most 3-year-olds, there is good reason to doubt that it is absolutely true for all 3-year-olds. Unless the premise statement is absolutely true, we cannot draw any conclusion about Amy. Also, it is possible that we have been misinformed about Amy's age. If she is actually 4 years old, then we cannot draw any logical conclusion about her fear of the dark. In general, the truth of any logical conclusion is founded on the truth of the premise statements. If any basic assumption or premise is incorrect, then we cannot have any confidence in the truth of the logical conclusion.

A common application of the rational method occurs when people try to think through a problem before they try out different solutions. Suppose, for example, that you have an exam scheduled, but when you are ready to leave for campus, you discover that your car will not start. One response to this situation is to consider your options logically:

1. You could call the AAA, but by the time they arrive and fix the car, you probably will have missed the exam.

2. You could take the bus, but you do not have the schedule, so you are not sure if the bus can get you to campus on time.
3. You could ask your neighbor to loan you her car for a few hours.

Notice that instead of actually doing something, you are considering possibilities and consequences to find a logical solution to the problem.

The following example is one of our favorite demonstrations of the rational method. As you read through the example, keep in mind that the entire process of trying to answer the question is based on logical reasoning.

Imagine that you are standing in the doorway of one building on campus and need to get to another building 100 yards away. Unfortunately, it is pouring rain, and you have no raincoat or umbrella. Before you step out into the storm, take a minute to figure out the best strategy to keep yourself as dry as possible. Specifically, should you (a) run as fast as you can from one building to the next, or (b) walk at a slow and steady pace?

Logically, as you move through the rain, there are two sources of getting wet:

1. The rain that is falling down on your head and shoulders
2. The rain in the air in front of you that you walk into as you move forward

Logically, the first source of wetness depends entirely on how long you are out in the rain. The more time you spend exposed, the more water will fall on you. On the other hand, the second source is independent of the length of time you are exposed. If you imagine the rain as suspended in the air, it is easy to see that your body will sweep a path or tunnel through the rain as you move from one shelter to another. The amount of rain contained in this tunnel determines how wet you will get as you move forward. However, this amount will be the same whether you zip along at 100 miles per hour or walk slowly at 1 mile per hour.

We can now construct a logical argument based on these facts to answer the original question:

- The faster you move, the less rain will fall on you (source 1).
- The amount of rain you walk into (source 2) will be the same whether you run or walk.
- The total amount of rain that hits you is the sum of the two sources.

Therefore, your best bet for keeping as dry as possible is to move as fast as you can.

In addition to demonstrating an application, the preceding example illustrates another limitation of the rational method. In the example, we assumed that there were only two sources of wetness. In fact, when you run through the rain, it is possible to get wet from splashing in puddles or slipping on a wet surface and falling. Because these possibilities were not considered, our conclusion might not be correct. In general, a logical conclusion is only valid for the specific situation described by the premise statements. If the premise statements are incomplete or do not totally represent the real-world situation, then the conclusion might not be accurate.

Another limitation of the rational method is that people are not particularly good at logical reasoning. Consider the following argument:

All psychologists are human.

Some humans are women.

Therefore, some psychologists are women.

Many people would view this as a sound, rational argument. However, this is not a valid argument; specifically, the conclusion is not logically justified by the premise statements. In case you are not convinced that the argument is invalid, consider the following argument, which has exactly the same structure but replaces psychologists and women with apples and oranges:

All apples are fruits.

Some fruits are oranges.

Therefore, some apples are oranges.

This time, it should be clear that the argument does not logically support the conclusion. The simple fact that most people have difficulty judging the validity of a logical argument means they can easily make mistakes using the rational method. Unless the logic is sound, the conclusion might not be correct.

In summary, the rational method is the practice of employing reason as a source of knowledge. Answers obtained using the rational method are not simply accepted as true without verification. Instead, all conclusions are tested by ensuring that they conform to the rules of logic. Because the rational method does not involve directly observing or actively gathering information, it has been said that logic is a way of establishing truth in the absence of evidence. As you will see in section 1.3, the rational method is a critical component of the scientific method. In the next section, we examine the opposite approach, in which we rely entirely on direct observation to obtain evidence to establish the truth.

 **LEARNING CHECK** Describe how the rational method can help you anticipate consequences before you actually make a decision.

The Empirical Method

The **empirical method,** also known as **empiricism,** attempts to answer questions by direct observation or personal experience. This method is a product of the empirical viewpoint in philosophy, which holds that all knowledge is acquired through the senses. Note that when we make observations, we use the senses of seeing, hearing, tasting, and so on.

DEFINITION The **empirical method,** or **empiricism,** uses observation or direct sensory experience to obtain knowledge.

Most of you know, for example, that children tend to be shorter than adults, that it is typically warmer in the summer than in the winter, and that a pound of steak costs more than a pound of hamburger. You know these facts from personal experience and from observations you have made.

Many facts or answers are available simply by observing the world around you: that is, you can use the empirical method. For example, you can check the oil level in your car by simply looking at the dipstick. You could find out the weight of each student in your class just by having each person step on a scale. In many instances, the empirical method provides an easy, direct way to answer questions. However, this method of inquiry also has some limitations.

It is tempting to place great confidence in our own observations. Everyday expressions such as, "I will believe it when I see it with my own eyes," reveal the faith we place in our own experience. However, we cannot necessarily believe everything we see, or hear and feel, for that matter. Actually, it is fairly common for people to misperceive or misinterpret the world around them. Figure 1.1 illustrates this point with the horizontal-vertical illusion. Most people perceive the vertical line to be longer than the horizontal line. Actually, they are exactly the same length. (You might want to measure them to convince yourself.) This illustration is a classic example of how direct sensory experience can deceive us.

Although direct experience seems to be a simple way to obtain answers, your perceptions can be drastically altered by prior knowledge, expectations, feelings, or beliefs. As a result, two observers can witness exactly the same event and yet "see" two completely different things. For most students,

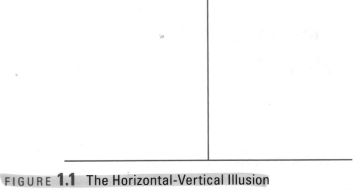

FIGURE **1.1** The Horizontal-Vertical Illusion
To most people, the vertical line appears to be longer, even though both lines are exactly the same length.

the following example provides a convincing demonstration that sensory experience can be changed by knowledge or beliefs.

> Suppose you are presented with two plates of snack food, and are asked to sample each and then state your preference. One plate contains regular potato chips and the second contains crispy, brown noodles that taste delicious. Based simply on your experience (taste), you have a strong preference for the noodles. Now suppose that you are told that the "noodles" are actually fried worms. Would you still prefer them to the chips? The problem here is that your sensory experience of good taste (the method of empiricism) is in conflict with your long-held beliefs that people do not eat worms (method of tenacity).

It also is possible to make accurate observations but then misinterpret what you see. For years, people watched the day-to-day cycle of the Sun rising in the east and setting in the west. These observations led to the obvious conclusion that the Sun must travel in a huge circle around Earth. Even today, people still speak of the "Sun rising" instead of saying the "Earth is turning toward the Sun."

Finally, the empirical method is usually time consuming and sometimes dangerous. When faced with a problem, for example, you could use the empirical method to try several possible solutions, or you could use the rational method and simply think about each possibility and how it might work. Often, it is faster and easier to think through a problem than to jump in with a trial-and-error approach. Also, it might be safer to use the rational method or the method of authority rather than experience something for yourself. For example, if I wanted to determine whether the mushrooms in my back yard are safe or poisonous, I would rather ask an expert than try the empirical method.

In summary, the empirical method is the practice of employing direct observation as a source of knowledge. In the empirical method, evidence or observations with one's senses is required for verification of information. Note that the observations can be casual and unplanned, such as when you are simply aware of the world around you. At the other end of the continuum, observations can be systematic and purposeful. As you will see in the next section, the planned and systematic application of the empirical method is a critical component of the scientific method.

Summary

As you have seen so far, the scientific method is not the only way to know the answers or find the answers to questions. The methods of tenacity, intuition, authority, rationalism, and empiricism are different ways of acquiring knowledge. Table 1.1 provides a summary of these five methods. We should point out that different people can use different methods to answer the same question and can arrive at different, or sometimes the same, answers. For example, if you wanted to know the weight of one of your classmates, you might have her step on a scale (empirical method), simply ask how much she weighs (method of authority), or compare her physical size to your own and calculate an estimated weight relative to how much you weigh (rational method).

TABLE **1.1**
Summary of Nonscientific Methods of Acquiring Knowledge

Method	Way of Knowing or Finding Answer
Tenacity	From habit or superstition
Intuition	From a hunch or feeling
Authority	From an expert
Rationalism	From reasoning; a logical conclusion
Empiricism	From direct sensory observation

LEARNING CHECKS

Describe how to find answers using the method of empiricism.

    Describe how the method of authority, the rational method, and the empirical method each could be used to determine whether mixing two chemicals together will cause an explosion.

1.3 | THE SCIENTIFIC METHOD

The **scientific method** is an approach to acquiring knowledge that involves formulating specific questions and then systematically finding answers. It is a method of acquiring knowledge—scientists seek answers to the questions they devise. The scientific method contains many elements of the methods previously discussed. By combining several different methods of acquiring knowledge, we hope to avoid the pitfalls of any individual method used by itself. The scientific method is a carefully developed system for asking and answering questions so that the answers we discover are as accurate as possible. In the following section, we describe the series of steps that define the scientific method.

The Steps of the Scientific Method

Step 1: Observe Behavior or Other Phenomena

The scientific method often begins with casual or informal observations. Notice that it is not necessary to start with a well-planned, systematic investigation. Instead, simply observe the world around you until some behavior or event catches your attention. The initial observations could be the result of your own personal experience (method of empiricism), and might involve watching the behavior of other people or monitoring your own behavior. For example, you might notice a group of strangers carefully avoiding eye contact as they share an elevator. Or you might sit in the back row of class one day and notice that you are surrounded by students who do not seem to be paying attention. Based on your observations, you begin to wonder why people do not look at each other in elevators or whether it is true that the better students tend to sit in the front of the class.

Perhaps your attention is caught by someone else's observations. For example, you might read a report of someone's research findings (the method of authority), or you might hear others talking about things they have seen or noticed. In any event, the observations catch your attention and begin to raise questions in your mind.

At this stage in the process, people commonly tend to generalize beyond the actual observations. The process of generalization is an almost automatic human response known as **induction**, or **inductive reasoning**. In simple terms, inductive reasoning involves reaching a general conclusion based on a few specific examples. For example, suppose that you taste a green apple and discover that it is sour. A second green apple is also sour, and so is the third. Soon, you reach the general conclusion that all green apples are sour. Notice that inductive reasoning reaches far beyond the actual observations. In this example, you tasted only three apples, and yet you reached a conclusion about the millions of other green apples that exist in the world.

DEFINITION	**Induction**, or **inductive reasoning**, involves using a relatively small set of specific observations as the basis for forming a general statement about a larger set of possible observations.

The following scenario combines observation and induction to demonstrate how the first stage of the scientific method can actually work. Suppose it is the third straight day of dark, cold, and dreary weather in late October, and you notice that you are feeling a bit depressed. It is not a serious clinical depression; you simply have realized that the carefree days of summer are definitely over and you are now facing several long months of cold and overcast winter days. As you mope through the day, you begin to wonder if others are sharing your feelings, and so you start watching your friends and colleagues. Soon, you reach the general conclusion that people seem to become sadder and more depressed during the winter than in the summer. At this point you could go to the library (either in person or on the Internet) to discover what other people have already learned about winter and depression. In most cases, you will find extensive information including theories, opinions, and actual research studies. The existing knowledge (method of authority) may provide an answer for your question and usually will give you a much better understanding of the issue. However, if you still have questions and are at all curious about the phenomenon, you are ready for the next step in the scientific method.

A detailed discussion of library research is presented in Chapter 2.

Step 2: Form a Tentative Answer or Explanation (a Hypothesis)

This step in the process usually begins by identifying other factors, or **variables**, that are associated with your observation. For example, what other variables are associated with winter and depression? You can identify variables based on common sense, or your background research in the library or on the Internet.

DEFINITION	**Variables** are characteristics or conditions that change or have different values for different individuals. For example, the weather, the economy, and your state of health can change from day to day. Also, two people can be different in terms of personality, intelligence, age, gender, self-esteem, height, weight, and so on.

The observed relationship between winter and depression might be associated with variables such as the weather and health. For example, winter weather tends to be cold, dark, and dreary, which could lead to depression. Also, people tend to be sick with colds and the flu in the winter, which could lead to depression. A quick library search (discussed in Chapter 2) reveals that atmospheric conditions, seasonal variations, and health are all variables that have been studied in relation to depression. Notice that we now have at least two possible explanations for the observation that people tend to be more depressed in the winter than in the summer:

> *Health:* People tend to catch colds and get the flu during the winter, and perhaps their illness leads to depression.

> *Weather:* Perhaps people become depressed in the winter because the weather is literally dark and depressing.

Next, you must select one of the explanations to be evaluated in a scientific research study. Choose the explanation that you consider to be most plausible or simply pick the one that you find most interesting. Remember, the other explanation is not discarded. If necessary, it can be evaluated later in a second study.

At this point, you have a **hypothesis,** or a possible explanation, for your observation. Note that your hypothesis is not considered to be a final answer. Instead, the hypothesis is a tentative answer that is intended to be tested and critically evaluated.

DEFINITION	In the context of science, a **hypothesis** is a statement that describes or explains a relationship between or among variables. A hypothesis is not a final answer but rather a proposal to be tested and evaluated. For example, a researcher might hypothesize that there is a relationship between personality characteristics and cigarette smoking. Or another researcher might hypothesize that a dark and dreary environment causes winter depression.

Step 3: Use Your Hypothesis to Generate a Testable Prediction

Usually, this step involves taking the hypothesis and applying it to a specific, observable, real-world situation. For example, if your hypothesis states that winter depression is the result of a darker environment, then a specific prediction is that decreasing the lighting on the third floor of a college dormitory should increase depression for the students living there (or increasing lighting should decrease depression). An alternative prediction is that there should be less depression in cities experiencing more sunshine than in cities with less

Weather information obtained from www .weatherbase.com.

sunshine. For example, Phoenix averages 211 clear days per year, receiving 86% of the possible sunshine, compared to Seattle, which has 71 clear days and 43% of the possible sunshine. Our hypothesis would predict a higher rate of depression in Seattle than in Phoenix.

Notice that a single hypothesis can lead to several different predictions, and that each prediction refers to a specific situation or an event that can be observed and measured.

Figure 1.2 shows our original hypothesis and the two predictions that we derived from it. Notice that we are using logic (rational method) to make the prediction. This time, the logical process is known as **deduction,** or **deductive reasoning.** We begin with a general (universal) statement and then make specific deductions. In particular, we use our hypothesis as a universal premise statement and then determine the conclusions or predictions that must logically follow if the hypothesis is true.

DEFINITION

Deduction, or **deductive reasoning,** uses a general statement as the basis for reaching a conclusion about specific examples.

Note that induction involves an *increase* from a few to many, and deduction involves a *decrease* from many to a specific few.
induction = increase
deduction = decrease

Induction and deduction are complementary processes. Induction uses specific examples to generate general conclusions or hypotheses, and deduction uses general conclusions to generate specific predictions. This relationship is depicted in Figure 1.3.

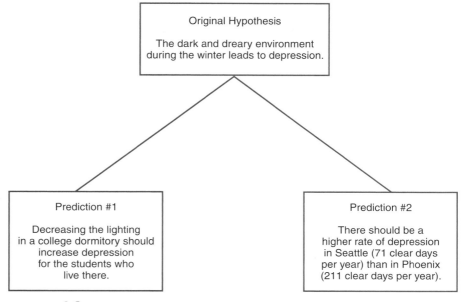

FIGURE **1.2** Two Testable Predictions Derived from a General Hypothesis

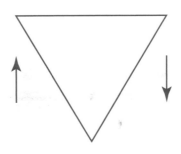

Set of All Possible Cases

INDUCTION

Generalize from a small
set of specific examples
to the complete set of all
possible examples.

I ate three green apples
and all were sour.
Therefore, all green
apples are sour.

DEDUCTION

Predict a small set of
specific examples from a
general statement about the
complete set of all possible
examples.

All green apples are sour.
Therefore, if I eat a green
apple it will be sour.

A Few Specific Cases

FIGURE **1.3** Examples of Induction and Deduction
Inductive reasoning uses a few limited observations to generate a general hypothesis. Deductive reasoning uses a general hypothesis or premise to generate a prediction
about specific observations.

Also notice that the predictions generated from a hypothesis must be
testable—that is, it must be possible to demonstrate that the prediction is
either correct or incorrect by direct observation. Either the observations will
provide support for the hypothesis or they will refute the hypothesis. For a
prediction to be truly testable, both outcomes must be possible.

Step 4: Evaluate the Prediction by Making Systematic, Planned Observations

After a specific, testable prediction has been made (the rational method), the next
step is to evaluate the prediction using direct observation (the empirical method).
This is the actual *research* or *data collection* phase of the scientific method. The
goal is to provide a fair and unbiased test of the research hypothesis by observing whether the prediction is correct. The researcher must be careful to observe
and record exactly what happens, free of any subjective interpretation or personal expectations. For example, a researcher could place 100-watt light bulbs in
all of the lamps on one floor of a college dorm and use only 60-watt bulbs on
another floor. After 6 weeks, all of the students are tested for depression and the
two groups of scores are compared to determine whether there is a relationship
between depression and the amount of light in the environment. Notice that the
research study is an empirical test of the research hypothesis.

Step 5: Use the Observations to Support, Refute, or Refine the Original Hypothesis

The final step of the scientific method is to compare the actual observations
with the predictions that were made from the hypothesis. To what extent do
the observations agree with the predictions? Some agreement indicates support

for the original hypothesis, and suggests that you consider making new predictions and testing them. Lack of agreement indicates that the original hypothesis was wrong or that the hypothesis was used incorrectly, producing faulty predictions. In this case, you might want to revise the hypothesis or reconsider how it was used to generate predictions. In either case, notice that you have circled back to Step 2; that is, you are forming a new hypothesis and preparing to make new predictions. Suppose, for example, that our researcher found lower depression scores for the students on the brightly lit dormitory floor than for those on the dimly lit floor. This result provides support for the original hypothesis and indicates that lighting is a factor to be considered in explaining winter depression. Suppose, however, that the results also show that some students with bright lights are still depressed and some students with dim lights show no signs of depression. This result indicates that lighting is not the entire answer. If the results show no difference between the two groups of students, then we must either conclude that lighting does not affect depression or that the difference in lighting was not big enough or did not last long enough to affect the students. In either case, other factors must be considered and other hypotheses must be tested before we can completely explain winter depression.

Notice that the scientific method continues the same series of steps over and over again. Observations lead to a hypothesis and a prediction, which leads to more observations, which lead to another hypothesis, and so on. Thus, the scientific method is not a linear process that moves directly from a beginning to an end, but rather is a circular process, or a spiral, that repeats over and over, moving higher with each cycle as new knowledge is gained (Figure 1.4).

DEFINITION	The **scientific method** is a method of acquiring knowledge that uses observations to develop a hypothesis, then uses the hypothesis to make logical predictions that can be empirically tested by making additional, systematic observations. Typically, the new observations lead to a new hypothesis, and the cycle continues.

LEARNING CHECKS

Describe the difference between inductive and deductive reasoning.

What variables influence whether you find someone to be attractive? Do you think that the same variables determine whether others find you attractive?

What are the five steps of the scientific method?

Other Elements of the Scientific Method

In addition to the basic process that makes up the scientific method, a set of overriding principles governs scientific investigation. Three important principles of the scientific method are: It is empirical, it is public, and it is objective.

Science Is Empirical

As you know, when we say that science is empirical, we mean that answers are obtained by making observations. Although preliminary answers or hypotheses may be obtained by other means, science requires empirical verification.

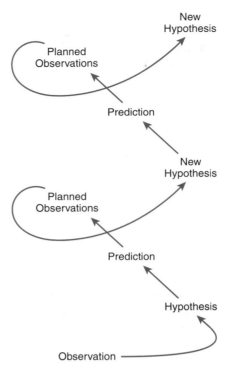

FIGURE **1.4** The Process of Scientific Inquiry

The scientific method can be viewed as a circular process or a spiral of steps. Initial observations lead to a hypothesis and a prediction, which leads to more observations and then to a new hypothesis. This never-ending process of using empirical tests (observations) to build and refine our current knowledge (hypothesis) is the basis of the scientific method.

An answer may be "obvious" by common sense, it might be perfectly logical, and experts in the field might support it, but it is not scientifically accepted until it has been empirically demonstrated.

However, unlike the method of empiricism we previously examined, the scientific method involves structured or systematic observation. The structure of the observations is determined by the procedures and techniques that are used in the research study. More specifically, the purpose of the observations is to provide an empirical test of a hypothesis. Therefore, the observations are structured so that the results either will provide clear support for the hypothesis or will clearly refute the hypothesis. Consider the following question: Do large doses of vitamin C prevent the common cold?

To answer this question, it would not be sufficient simply to ask people if they take vitamin C routinely and how many colds they get in a typical season. These observations are not structured, and no matter what responses are obtained, the results will not necessarily provide an accurate answer to the question. In particular, we have made no attempt to determine the dosage levels of the vitamin C that individuals have taken. No attempt was made to verify that the illnesses reported were, in fact, the common cold and not some type of influenza, pneumonia, or other illness. No attempt was made to take into account the age, general health, or lifestyle of the people questioned (maybe people who take vitamin C tend to lead generally healthy lives). We have made no attempt to reduce the possible biasing effect of people's beliefs about vitamins and colds on the answers they gave us. We have made no attempt to compare people who are receiving a specified daily dose of the vitamin with those who are not taking vitamin C or are getting a phony pill (a placebo). We could elaborate further, but you get the general idea.

In the scientific method, the observations are systematic in that they are performed under a specified set of conditions so that we can accurately answer the question we are addressing. That is, the observations—and indeed the entire study—are structured to test a hypothesis about the way the world works. If you want to know if vitamin C can prevent colds, there is a way to structure your observations to get the answer. Much of this book deals with this aspect of research and how to structure studies to rule out competing and alternative explanations.

Science Is Public

The scientific method is public. By this, we mean that the scientific method makes observations available for evaluation by others, especially other scientists. In particular, other individuals should be able to repeat the same step-by-step process that led to the observations so that they can replicate the observations for themselves. **Replication,** or repetition of observation, allows verification of the findings. Note that only public observations can be repeated, and thus only public observations are verifiable.

The scientific community makes observations public by publishing reports in scientific journals or presenting their results at conferences and meetings. This activity is important because events that are private cannot be replicated or evaluated by others. Research reports that appear in most journals have been evaluated by the researcher's peers (other scientists in the same field) for the rigor and appropriateness of methodology and the absence of flaws in the study. The report must meet a variety of standards for it to be published. When you read a journal article, one thing you will note is the level of detail used in describing the methodology of the study. Typically, the report has a separate "Method" section that describes in great detail the people or animals that were studied (the participants or subjects of the study, respectively), the instruments and apparatus used to conduct the study, the procedures used in applying treatments and making measurements, and so on. Enough detail should be provided so that anyone can replicate the same study exactly to verify the findings. The notions of replication and verification are important. They provide the checks and balances for research.

As we shall see, there is a multitude of ways—by error or chance—in which a study can result in an erroneous conclusion. Researchers can also commit fraud and deliberately falsify or misrepresent the outcome of research studies. As scientists, it is important that we scrutinize and evaluate research reports carefully, and maintain some skepticism about the results until more studies confirm the findings. By replicating studies and subjecting them to peer review, we have checks and balances against errors and fraud.

Science Is Objective

The scientific method is objective. That is, the observations are structured so that the researcher's biases and beliefs do not influence the outcome of the study. Science has been called "a dispassionate search for knowledge," meaning that the researcher does not let personal feelings contaminate the observations. What kind of biases and beliefs are likely to be involved? Often, bias comes from belief in a particular theory. A researcher might try to find evidence to support his theory. Because the researcher typically is testing a theory, he could have an expectation about the outcome of the study. In some cases, expectations can subtly influence the findings.

One way to reduce the likelihood of the influence of experimenter expectation is to keep the people who are making the observations uninformed about the details of the study. In this case, we sometimes say the researcher is *blind* to the details of the study. We discuss this type of procedure in detail later (see Chapter 4, p. 129).

Science versus Pseudoscience

By now it should be clear that science is intended to provide a carefully developed system for answering questions so that the answers we get are as accurate and complete as possible. Note that scientific research is based on gathering evidence from careful, systematic, and objective observations. This is one of the primary features that differentiates science from other, less rigorous disciplines known as **pseudoscience.** Pseudoscience is a system of ideas, often presented as science, but actually lacking some of the key components that are essential to scientific research. Theories such as aromatherapy, astrology, and intelligent design are examples of pseudoscience that are unsupported by empirical evidence. Pseudoscience is common among popular-psychology gurus who write self-help books and appear on TV talk shows presenting novel systems to solve your romantic relationship problems, end your episodes of depression, or help bring a normal life to your autistic child.

Although there is no universally accepted definition of pseudoscience, there is a common set of features that differentiate science and pseudoscience (Herbert et al., 2000; Lilienfeld, Lynn, & Lohr, 2004). The following list presents some of the more important differences.

1. The primary distinction between science and pseudoscience is based on the notion of testable and refutable hypotheses. Specifically, a theory is scientific only if it can specify how it could be refuted. That is, the theory must be able to describe exactly what observable findings would demonstrate that it is wrong. If a research study produces results that do not support a theory, the theory is either abandoned or, more commonly, modified to accommodate the new results. In either case, however, the negative results are acknowledged and accepted. In pseudoscience, on the other hand, the typical response to negative results is to discount them entirely or to explain them away without altering the original theory. For example, if research demonstrates that a particular therapy is not effective, the proponents of the therapy often claim that the failure

was caused by a lack of conviction or skill on the part of the therapist—the therapy is fine, it was simply the application that was flawed.

2. Science demands an objective and unbiased evaluation of all the available evidence. Unless a treatment shows consistent success that cannot be explained by other outside factors, the treatment is not considered to be effective. Pseudoscience, on the other hand, tends to rely on subjective evidence such as testimonials and anecdotal reports of success. Pseudoscience also tends to focus on a few selected examples of success and ignore instances of failure. In clinical practice, nearly any treatment shows occasional success, and hand-picking reports that demonstrate success does not provide convincing evidence for an effective treatment.

3. Science actively tests and challenges its own theories, and adapts the theories when new evidence appears. As a result, scientific theories are constantly evolving. Pseudoscience, on the other hand, tends to ignore nonsupporting evidence and treats criticism as a personal attack. As a result, pseudoscientific theories tend to be stagnant and remain unchanged year after year.

4. Finally, scientific theories are grounded in past science. A scientific system for teaching communication skills to autistic children is based on established theories of learning and uses principles that have solid empirical support. Pseudoscience tends to create entirely new disciplines and techniques that are unconnected to established theories and empirical evidence. Proponents of such theories often develop their own vaguely scientific jargon, or describe links to science that suggest scientific legitimacy without any real substance. Aromatherapy, for example is sometimes explained by noting that smells activate olfactory nerves, which stimulate the limbic system, which releases endorphins and neurotransmitters. Thus, smells affect your mind and emotions. Note that a similar argument could be used to justify a claim that clinical benefits are produced by looking at colored lights or listening to a bouncing tennis ball.

LEARNING CHECKS   Describe what it means to say that science is empirical, public, and objective, and explain why each of these principles is important.
Describe the differences between science and pseudoscience.

1.4 | THE RESEARCH PROCESS

The process of planning and conducting a research study involves using the scientific method to address a specific question. During this process, the researcher moves from a general idea to actual data collection and interpretation of the results. Along the way, the researcher is faced with a series of decisions about how to proceed. In this section, we outline the basic steps, or decision points, in the research process. The complete set of steps is also shown in Figure 1.5. Reading this section should give you a better understanding of the scientific method and how it is used, as well as an overview of the topics covered in the rest of the book. As a final note, remember that, although

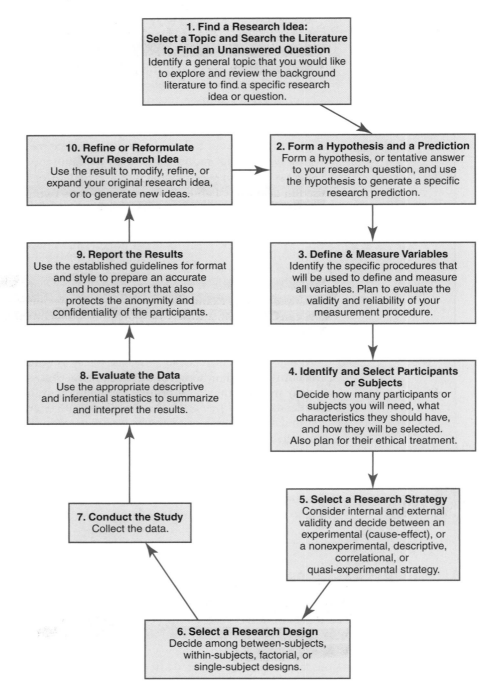

FIGURE **1.5** The Steps in the Research Process

research requires a decision about what to do at each stage in the process, there are no absolutely right or wrong decisions. Each choice you make along the way has disadvantages as well as advantages. Much of the material in the remainder of the book focuses on the kinds of decisions that need to be made during the research process, and examines the strengths and weaknesses of various choices.

Step 1: Find a Research Idea: Select a Topic and Search the Literature to Find an Unanswered Question

The first step in the research process is to find a research idea. This task, discussed in detail in Chapter 2, typically involves two parts:

1. Selecting a general topic area (such as human development, perception, social interaction, and so on).
2. Reviewing the literature in that area to identify the relevant variables and find an unanswered question.

You may decide, for example, that you are interested in the topic of obesity and want to examine the variables that contribute to overeating. Ideas for topics can come from a variety of sources including everyday experience, books, journal articles, or class work. It is important that a researcher be honestly interested in the chosen topic. The research process can be a long-term, demanding enterprise. Without intrinsic interest to sustain motivation, it is very easy for a researcher to get tired or bored, and give up before the research is completed.

Bear in mind that your general topic area is simply a starting point that eventually will evolve into a very specific idea for a research study. Your final research idea will develop as you read through the research literature and discover what other researchers have already learned. Your original topic area will guide you through the literature and help you to decide which research studies are important to you and which are not relevant to your interests. Eventually, you will become familiar with the current state of knowledge and can determine which questions are still unanswered. At this stage, you will be ready to identify your own research question. In Chapter 2, we discuss the task of searching through the research literature to find an idea for a research study.

As you become familiar with an area of research, you will learn the different variables that are being investigated and get some ideas about how those variables are related to each other. At this point, you should be looking for an unanswered research question.

Occasionally, finding an unanswered question is very easy. Published research reports often include suggestions for future research, or identify limitations of the studies they are reporting. You are welcome to follow the suggestions or try to correct the limitations in your own research. More often, however, the unanswered question is the result of critical reading. As you read a research report, ask yourself why the study was done a certain way. If the study only used participants from middle-class families, perhaps the researchers suspected that family income might influence the results. Ask what might happen if some characteristics of the study were changed. For example, if the study examined eating behavior in restaurants, would the same results apply to eating at home?

In some situations, the research question may simply ask for a description of an individual variable or variables. For example, a researcher might be interested in the sleeping habits of college students. How much sleep do college students typically get? What time do they get up each day? More often, however, the research question concerns a relationship between two or more variables. For example, a researcher may want to know whether there is a relationship between portion size and the amount of food that people eat. Does serving larger portions cause an increase in food consumption?

Step 2: Form a Hypothesis and a Prediction

If your unanswered question simply asks for a description of a variable or variables, you can skip this step and go directly to Step 3 of the research process. However, if your question concerns the relationship between variables, the next task is to form a hypothesis, or a tentative answer to the question. For example, if your question is whether serving larger portions leads to overeating, a hypothesis could be stated as follows: Increasing portion size will cause an increase in the amount of food eaten.

When you are selecting an answer to serve as your hypothesis, you should pick the answer that seems most likely to be correct. Remember, the goal of the research study is to demonstrate that your answer (your hypothesis) is correct. The likelihood of a hypothesis being correct is often based on previous research results. If similar research has demonstrated the importance of one specific variable, it is likely that the same variable will be important in your own study. It is also possible that you can develop a logical argument supporting your hypothesis. If you can make a reasonable argument for your hypothesis, then it is likely that the hypothesis is correct.

Because the hypothesis identifies the specific variables involved and describes how they are related, it forms the foundation for your research study. Conducting the study provides an empirical test of the hypothesis. The results of the study will either provide support for the hypothesis, or will refute the hypothesis. Although you will need to make additional decisions about the details of the study, the basic framework is established in the statement of the hypothesis. Therefore, it is essential that you develop a good hypothesis. The following four elements are considered to be important characteristics of a good hypothesis.

Logical

A good hypothesis is usually founded in established theories or developed from the results of previous research. Specifically, a good hypothesis should be the logical conclusion of a logical argument. Consider the following example:

Premise 1: Academic success is highly valued and respected in society (at least by parents and teachers).

Premise 2: Being valued and respected by others contributes to high self-esteem.

Conclusion (hypothesis): For a specific group of students, higher levels of academic success will be related to higher levels of self-esteem.

In this argument, we assume that the two premise statements are *facts,* or knowledge that has been demonstrated and reported in the scientific literature. Typically, these facts would be obtained from extensive library research. Library research acquaints you with the relevant knowledge that already exists: What other researchers have already done and what they have found. By knowing the basic facts, theories, predictions, and methods that make up the knowledge base for a specific topic area, you gain a clearer picture of exactly which variables are being studied and exactly which relationships are likely to exist. The logical argument provides a rationale or justification for your hypothesis, and establishes a connection between your research and the research results that have been obtained by others.

Testable

In addition to being logical, a good hypothesis must be **testable;** that is, it must be possible to observe and measure all of the variables involved. In particular, the hypothesis must involve real situations, real events, and real individuals. You cannot test a hypothesis that refers to imaginary events or hypothetical situations. For example, you might speculate about what might happen if the heat from the Sun gradually increased over the next 25 years, or you could debate what might have happened if JFK had not been assassinated. However, neither of these two propositions leads to a testable hypothesis. They cannot be observed and, therefore, are inappropriate as scientific hypotheses.

Refutable

One characteristic of a testable hypothesis is that it must be **refutable;** that is, it must be possible to obtain research results that are contrary to the hypothesis. For example, if the hypothesis states that the treatment will cause an increase in scores, it must be possible for the data to show no increase. A refutable hypothesis, often called a falsifiable hypothesis, is a critical component of the research process. Remember, the scientific method requires an objective and public demonstration. A nonrefutable hypothesis, one that cannot be demonstrated to be false, is inappropriate for the scientific method. For example, people occasionally claim to have miraculous or magical powers. However, they often add the stipulation that these powers can be seen only in the presence of true believers. When the miracles fail to occur under the watchful eye of scientists, the people simply state that the scientists are nonbelievers. Thus, it is impossible to prove that the claims are false. The result is a claim (or hypothesis) that cannot be refuted.

DEFINITIONS

A **testable hypothesis** is one for which all of the variables, events, and individuals are real, and can be defined and observed.

A **refutable hypothesis** is one that can be demonstrated to be false. That is, it is possible for the outcome to be different from the prediction.

Consider the following hypotheses that are not testable or refutable:

Hypothesis: The more sins a man commits, the less likely he is to get into heaven.

Hypothesis: If old dogs could talk, they would spend most of their time reminiscing about things they had smelled during their lives.

Hypothesis: If people could fly, there would be substantially fewer cases of depression.

Hypothesis: The human mind emits thought waves that influence other people, but that cannot be measured or recorded in any way.

Although you may find these hypotheses interesting, they cannot be tested or shown to be false and, therefore, are unsuitable for scientific research. In general, hypotheses that deal with moral or religious issues, value judgments, or hypothetical situations are untestable or nonrefutable. However, this does not mean that religion, morals, or human values are off-limits for scientific research. You could, for example compare personality characteristics or family backgrounds for religious and nonreligious people, or you could look for behavioral differences between pro-life individuals and pro-choice individuals. Nearly any topic can be studied scientifically if you take care to develop testable and refutable hypotheses.

Positive

A final characteristic of a testable hypothesis is that it must make a positive statement about the existence of something, usually the existence of a relationship, the existence of a difference, or the existence of a treatment effect. The following are examples of such hypotheses:

Hypothesis 1. For high school students, there is a relationship between intelligence and creativity.

Hypothesis 2. There is a difference between the verbal skills of 3-year-old girls and those of 3-year-old boys.

Hypothesis 3. The new therapy technique will produce significant improvement for severely depressed patients.

On the other hand, a prediction that denies existence is untestable. The following are examples of untestable predictions:

Hypothesis 4. For adults, there is no relationship between age and memory ability.

Hypothesis 5. There is no difference between the problem-solving strategies used by females and those used by males.

Hypothesis 6. The new training procedure has no effect on students' self-esteem.

The reason that a testable hypothesis must make a positive statement affirming existence is based on the scientific process that is used to test the prediction. Specifically, the basic nature of science is to assume that something does *not* exist until there is enough evidence to demonstrate that it actually does exist. Suppose, for example, that I would like to test the hypothesis that there is a relationship between creativity and intelligence. In this case, I begin with the assumption that a relationship does not exist, and the goal for my research study is to gather enough evidence (data) to provide a convincing demonstration that a relationship does exist. You may recognize this process as the same system used in jury trials: The jury assumes that a defendant is innocent until there is enough evidence to prove him guilty. The key problem with this system occurs when you fail to obtain convincing evidence. In a jury trial, if the prosecution fails to produce enough evidence, the verdict is *not guilty*. Notice that the defendant has *not* been proved innocent; there simply is not enough evidence to say that he is guilty. Similarly, if we fail to find a relationship in a research study, we cannot conclude that the relationship does not exist; we simply conclude that we failed to find convincing evidence.

Thus, the research process is structured to test for the existence of treatment effects, relationships, and differences; it is not structured to test a prediction that denies existence. For example, suppose I begin with a hypothesis stating that there is no relationship between creativity and IQ. (Note that this hypothesis *denies* existence and, therefore, is not testable.) If I do a research study that fails to find a relationship, have I proved that the hypothesis is correct? It should be clear that I have not proved anything; I have simply failed to find any evidence. Specifically, I cannot conclude that something does not exist simply because I failed to find it. As a result, a hypothesis that denies the existence of a relationship cannot be tested in a research study and, therefore, is not a good foundation for a study.

 **LEARNING CHECK**

Is the following hypothesis testable, refutable, and positive? Explain your answer.

Hypothesis: Married couples who regularly attend religious services have more stable relationships than couples who do not.

The second part of Step 2 in the research process is to use your general hypothesis to make a specific prediction about what will happen in the research study. The prediction should provide a general description of the individuals who will participate in the study, it should identify the variables that will be investigated, and it should describe the expected outcome of the study. For the hypothesis concerning portion size and food consumption, two possible predictions are as follows:

If a sample of college students is served the same meal with different portion sizes on two consecutive Friday nights, on average, they will eat more food for the meal with the larger portion sizes than for the meal with the smaller portion sizes.

If two elementary school cafeterias serve the same menu with two different portion sizes, the students who receive the larger portions will eat more food that the students who receive the smaller portions.

Note that each prediction simply applies the hypothesis to a concrete situation that can be observed. Creating this situation and observing the participants in it will become the research study that tests the hypothesis. The remaining steps in the research process will fill in the details for the research study and the interpretation and presentation of the results.

Step 3: Determine How You Will Define and Measure Your Variables

As part of making a specific prediction about the outcome of research study, you must also determine how you will define and measure your variables. Suppose, for example, that your hypothesis says that watching violence on television leads to more aggressive behavior. Also suppose that you have decided to evaluate this hypothesis using a group of preschool children as your participants. Thus, your hypothesis predicts that if we observe a group of preschool children, we should see that those who watch more television violence are more aggressive than those who watch less television violence. Before we can evaluate this prediction, however, we need to determine how we will distinguish between *more* and *less* television violence, and distinguish between *more* and *less* aggression. Specifically, we must decide exactly how we will define and measure *television violence*, and exactly how we will define and measure *aggressive behavior*. The variables identified in the research hypothesis must be defined in a manner that makes it possible to measure them by some form of empirical observation. These decisions are usually made after reviewing previous research and determining how other researchers have defined and measured their variables.

By defining our variables so that they can be observed and measured, we are continuing to transform the hypothesis (from Step 2 of the research process) into a specific, well-defined research study based on empirical observations. Notice that this step is necessary before we can evaluate the hypothesis by actually observing the variables. The key idea is to transform the hypothesis into an empirically testable form.

Note that the task of determining exactly how the variables will be defined and measured often depends on the individuals to be measured. For example, you would certainly measure the aggressive behavior of a group of preschool children very differently from the aggressive behavior of a group of adults. The task of defining and measuring variables is discussed in Chapter 4.

Step 4: Identify and Select the Participants or Subjects for the Study

To evaluate a hypothesis scientifically, we first use the hypothesis to produce a specific prediction that can be observed and evaluated in a research study. One part of designing the research study is to decide exactly what individuals will participate. If the individuals are human, they are called **participants**. Nonhumans are called **subjects**. It is the responsibility of the researcher to plan for the safety and well-being of the research participants and to inform them of all relevant aspects of the research, especially any risk or danger that may be involved. The issue of ethical treatment for participants and subjects is discussed in Chapter 3.

In addition, you must decide whether you will place any restrictions on the characteristics of the participants. For example, you may decide to use preschool children. Or you may be more restrictive and use only 4-year-old boys from two-parent, middle-income households who have been diagnosed with a specific learning disability. You also must determine how many individuals you will need for your research, and you must plan where and how to recruit them. Different ways to select individuals to participate in research are discussed in Chapter 5.

DEFINITION	

DEFINITION The individuals who take part in research studies are called **participants** if they are human, and **subjects** if they are nonhuman.

Notice that when you have completed Steps 3 and 4 you have moved closer to creating a specific research study that will evaluate the prediction from Step 2 and, ultimately, test the original hypothesis from Step 2 of the research process. Specifically, you have specified exactly how the variables will be defined and measured, and described exactly who will be observed and measured. Because the variables can usually be defined and measured several different ways for different groups of individuals, there are usually several different research studies that can be created to test one general hypothesis. Following are two examples of specific ideas for research studies intended to test the same general hypothesis.

General hypothesis: Sugar consumption is related to activity level. More sugar in the diet leads to higher activity levels and less sugar leads to lower activity levels.

Study #1: Preschool children who are given a high-sugar snack in the morning will display higher levels of activity during a 30-minute observation period than children who are given a low-sugar snack.

Study #2: Adolescents who are given soda with their school lunches will be more active than adolescents who are given water with their lunches. Activity will be measured by having each student wear a pedometer during the afternoon.

Note that each of these potential studies involves a specific event that can be observed. Ultimately, the research study will test the original hypothesis by actually making the observations.

Step 5: Select a Research Strategy

Choosing a research strategy involves deciding on the general approach you will take to evaluate your research hypothesis. General research strategies are introduced in Chapter 6 and discussed in Chapters 7, 8, 9, and 12. The choice of a research strategy is usually determined by one of two factors:

1. The type of question asked: Consider, for example, the following two research questions:

   Is there is a relationship between sugar consumption and activity level for preschool children?
   Will increasing the level of sugar consumption for preschool children cause an increase in their activity level?

At first glance, it may appear that the two questions are actually the same. In terms of research, however, they are quite different. They will require different research studies and may produce different answers. Consider the following two questions:

> Is there a relationship between intelligence and income for 40-year-old men? Will increasing the salary for 40-year-old men cause an increase in their IQ scores?

In this case, it should be clear that the two questions are not the same and may lead to different conclusions.

2. Ethics and other constraints: Often, ethical considerations, which are discussed in Chapter 3, or other factors such as equipment availability, limit what you can or cannot do in the laboratory. These factors often can force you to choose one research strategy over another.

Step 6: Select a Research Design

Selecting a research design involves making decisions about the specific methods and procedures you will use to conduct the research study. Does your research question call for the detailed examination of one individual, or would you find a better answer by looking at the average behavior of a large group? Should you observe one group of individuals as they experience a series of different treatment conditions, or should you observe a different group of individuals for each of the different treatments? Should you make a series of observations of the same individuals over a period of time, or should you compare the behaviors of different individuals at the same time? Answering these questions will help you determine a specific design for the study. Different designs and their individual strengths and weaknesses are discussed in Chapters 10, 11, 12, 13, and 15.

Step 7: Conduct the Study

Finally, you are ready to collect the data. But now you must decide whether the study will be conducted in a laboratory or in the field (in the real world). Will you observe the participants individually or in groups? In addition, you must now implement all your earlier decisions about manipulating, observing, measuring, controlling, and recording the different aspects of your study.

Step 8: Evaluate the Data

Once the data have been collected, you must use various statistical methods to examine and evaluate the data. This involves drawing graphs, computing means or correlations to describe your data, and using inferential statistics to help determine whether the results from your specific participants can be generalized to the rest of the population. Statistical methods are reviewed in Chapter 14.

Step 9: Report the Results

One important aspect of the scientific method is that observations and results must be public. This is accomplished, in part, by a written report describing what was done, what was found, and how the findings were interpreted. In Chapter 16, we review the standard style and procedures for writing research reports. Two reasons to report research results are: (1) the results become part of the general knowledge base that other people can use to answer questions or to generate new research ideas, and (2) the research procedure can be replicated or refuted by other researchers.

Step 10: Refine or Reformulate Your Research Idea

Most research studies generate more questions than they answer. If your results support your original hypothesis, it does not mean that you have found a final answer. Instead, the new information from your study simply means that it is now possible to extend your original question into new domains or make the research question more precise. Typically, results that support a hypothesis lead to new questions by one of the following two routes:

1. *Test the boundaries of the result:* Suppose your study demonstrates that higher levels of academic performance are related to higher levels of self-esteem for elementary school children. Will this same result be found for adolescents in middle school? Perhaps adolescents are less concerned about respect from their parents and teachers, and are more concerned about respect from peers. Perhaps academic success is not highly valued by adolescents. In this case, you would not necessarily expect academic success to be related to self-esteem for adolescents. Alternatively, you might want to investigate the relationship between self-esteem and success outside academics. Is there a relationship between success on the athletic field and self-esteem? Notice that the goal is to determine whether your result extends into other areas. How general are the results of your study?

2. *Refine the original research question:* If your results show a relationship between academic success and self-esteem, the next question is, "What causes the relationship?" That is, what is the underlying mechanism by which success in school translates into higher self-esteem? The original question asked, "Does a relationship exist?" Now you are asking, "Why does the relationship exist?"

Results that do not support your hypothesis also generate new questions. One explanation for negative results (results that do not support the hypothesis) is that one of the premises is wrong. Remember, for this example, we assumed that academic success is highly valued and respected. Perhaps this is not true. Your new research question might be, "How important is academic success to parents, to teachers, or to elementary school students?"

Notice that research is not a linear, start-to-finish process. Instead, the process is a spiral or a circle that keeps returning to a new hypothesis to start over again. The never-ending process of asking questions, gathering evidence, and asking new questions is part of the general scientific method. One characteristic of the scientific method is that it always produces tentative answers or tentative explanations. There are no final answers. Consider, for example, the theory of evolution: After years of gathering evidence, evolution is still called a "theory." No matter how much supporting evidence is obtained, the answer to a research question is always open to challenge and eventually may be revised or refuted.

■ CHAPTER SUMMARY

Most students enroll in a research methodology course because it is required. We hope, however, that you now see that understanding research methodology can be useful. For example, perhaps at some point in your future, you will conduct a study. In addition, understanding research methodology will help you understand and evaluate journal articles and descriptions of research. Furthermore, with so many research findings bombarding us daily, you will be able to make more informed decisions about those findings and how they may affect your life. Finally, the type of thinking that a scientist does can be used anywhere and at any time.

Although this textbook is devoted to discussing the scientific method, there are other ways of finding answers to questions. The methods of tenacity, intuition, authority, rationalism, and empiricism are different ways of acquiring knowledge. Each method has its strengths and limitations. The scientific method combines the various methods to achieve a more valid way of answering questions. The scientific method is empirical, public, and objective.

The scientific method consists of five steps: (1) observation of behavior or other phenomena; (2) formation of a tentative answer or explanation, called a hypothesis; (3) use of the hypothesis to generate a testable prediction; (4) evaluation of the prediction by making systematic, planned observations; and (5) use of the observations to support, refute, or refine the original hypothesis.

The research process is the way the scientific method is used to answer a particular question. The ten steps of the research process provide a framework for the remainder of this book.

KEY WORDS

(Defined in the chapter and in the Glossary)
methods of acquiring knowledge
method of tenacity
method of intuition
method of authority
method of faith

rational method, or rationalism
premise statements
argument
empirical method, or empiricism
induction, or inductive reasoning
variables
hypothesis

deduction, or deductive reasoning
scientific method
testable hypothesis
refutable hypothesis
participants
subjects

EXERCISES

1. In addition to the key words that were defined in the text, you should be able to define the following terms, which also appear in the Glossary:
   replication
   pseudoscience

2. Describe one way in which understanding research methodology will be useful in your life. Be specific.

3. Suppose that, after reading about a recent murder in your town, you want to learn more about what causes people to kill. You

go to the library and check out a book written by an expert in the field. Explain which method of inquiry you are using here.

4. Go through a current newspaper or magazine and cut out one article that describes the results of a study. Summarize the finding according to this article. Do you have any reason to doubt that this information is accurate?

5. Pessimists commonly claim that, if you drop a piece of buttered bread, it will probably land butter-side down. Identify the mode of inquiry (authority, rational, empirical) you would use to evaluate this claim, and briefly explain how you would go about it.

6. A European car company claims that its car provides greater protection from rear-end collisions than other manufacturers' cars. Identify the mode of inquiry (authority, rational, empirical) you would use to evaluate this claim, and briefly explain how you would go about it.

7. Describe a situation in which you or someone you know used the method of intuition to answer a question.

8. Make up an example of deduction or deductive reasoning. In deductive reasoning, if the premises or initial observations are true, does this guarantee that the conclusion is true? Explain why or why not.

9. Make up an example of induction or inductive reasoning. In inductive reasoning, if the premises or initial observations are true, does this guarantee that the conclusion is true? Explain why or why not.

10. Identify the six different methods of acquiring knowledge introduced in this chapter, and describe the limitations of each.

11. Determine whether each of the following hypotheses is testable and refutable; if not, explain why.
    a. A list of three-syllable words is more difficult to memorize than a list of one-syllable words.
    b. The color red as seen by males is different from the color red as seen by females.
    c. The incidence of paranoia is higher among people who claim to have been abducted by aliens than in the general population.
    d. If the force of gravity doubled over the next 50,000 years, there would be a trend toward the evolution of larger animals and plants, which could withstand the higher gravity.

LEARNING ACTIVITIES

1. The scientific method can be described as a circle or a spiral of steps that leads from an initial observation, to a hypothesis, to new observations, to a new hypothesis. For each of the following observations:
    a. State a hypothesis that offers a possible explanation for the observed behavior. Note that your hypothesis does not have to be some elaborate, sophisticated, scientific theory. Simply identify a variable that could possibly explain the differences in observed behavior. For example, I observe that some people seem to go through the entire winter without ever getting sick, whereas others seem to suffer constantly from a series of colds and flu. I hypothesize that the differences in winter health are determined by whether people get flu shots.
    b. Briefly explain how your hypothesis could be empirically tested. Specifically, use your hypothesis to predict what should be found if you made a set of systematic, planned observations. Again, you are not proposing a sophisticated experiment. Simply describe what you should find if your hypothesis is right. For example, at the end of the winter season, I will get a sample of 100 people, and for each

person I record (a) how many weeks during the winter they suffered from a cold or the flu, and (b) whether they got a flu shot. If my hypothesis is right, I should find fewer illnesses in the group that got the shots.

Observation #1: Some students consistently choose to sit in the front of the classroom and others sit in the rear.

Observation #2: In a learning course, each student is given a laboratory rat to train during the semester. Some students are very comfortable handling and working with their rats, and others are very uncomfortable.

Observation #3: Some students try to schedule most of their classes early in the day and other students avoid morning classes as much as possible.

2. Choose a theory presented in a self-help book. Investigate whether the theory is supported by science or is an example of pseudoscience.

3. In this chapter, we identified a variety of different methods for acquiring knowledge, including the method of authority, the rational method, and the empirical method. For each of the following questions, choose one of these three methods and describe how you could use it to answer the question. Can you describe an alternative method for finding the answer?

a. Pick a student in your class (not yourself). How old is he or she?

b. Was Henri Toulouse-Lautrec a painter, a musician, or a soccer player?

c. What is the average annual snowfall in Buffalo, New York?

d. The local music store is going out of business and is selling all CDs for $9.99. If you have exactly $42.05, how many CDs can you buy? (Assume that there is no tax.)

e. How many arms did the Roman Emperor Nero have?

f. Is your course instructor male or female?

g. Tommy is exactly 37 inches tall and a person must be at least 40 inches tall to ride the roller coaster at the local amusement park. Can Tommy ride the roller coaster?

WEB RESOURCES

Visit the Book Companion Website at **www .cengage.com/international** to access study tools including a glossary, flashcards, and web quizzing. You will also find a link to Statistics and Research Methods Workshops. For this chapter, we suggest you look at the following workshop:

What Is Science?

2

Finding Research Ideas

CHAPTER OVERVIEW

In this chapter, we discuss in detail the first and second steps of the research process: Step 1—finding a research idea (which involves selecting a topic and searching the literature to find an unanswered question), and Step 2—forming a hypothesis and a prediction. To get you started, we present some general pointers. To help you find a general topic area, we discuss sources of ideas and common mistakes to avoid. Then, we discuss how to find background literature on your topic, why a literature search is important, and how to conduct a literature search. Next, we include pointers for using background literature to find new research questions and for converting your general hypothesis into a specific research prediction. Finally, we discuss the task of reading and understanding a research article.

2.1 | GETTING STARTED

The first step in the research process is to find an idea for a research study, and for many students this seems like an intimidating task. How are you supposed to think of a good research idea? How do you even get started? Although finding research ideas is probably a new experience, it does not require extraordinary genius or monumental effort. Every year, thousands of people begin the research process for the first time. Following are a few suggestions that should help make getting started a little easier.

Pick a Topic in Which You Are Interested

Developing and conducting a research study involves work and definitely takes time. Working in an area that interests you will help you stay motivated, avoid burnout, and greatly increase your chances of seeing the research project through to the end. There are several different ways to define an interest area. Here are a few possibilities:

- a particular population or group of individuals; for example, preschool children, cats, single-parent families, grandmothers, or police officers
- a particular behavior; for example, language development, adolescent dating, math anxiety, honesty, overeating, or color preferences
- a general topic; for example, job stress, child abuse, aging, personality, learning, or motivation

The key is really wanting to learn more about the topic you select. Preparing, planning, and conducting research will provide you with a lot of information and answers. If the task is important to you personally, gathering and using this information will be fun and exciting. If not, your enthusiasm will fade quickly.

Do Your Homework

Many people think of research as collecting data in a laboratory, but this is only a small part of the total process. Long before actual data collection begins, most of your research time probably will be devoted to preparation. Once you have identified a research topic, collecting background information is the next essential step. Typically, this involves reading books and journal articles to make yourself more familiar with the topic: what is already known, what research has been done, and what questions remain unanswered. No matter what topic you select, it will soon become clear that there are hundreds of books and probably thousands of journal articles containing relevant background information. Do not panic; although the amount of printed material may appear overwhelming, keep these two points in mind:

1. You do not need to know everything about a topic, and you certainly do not need to read everything about a topic before you begin research. You should read enough to gain a solid, basic understanding of the current knowledge in an area, and this is fairly easy to attain. Later in this chapter (section 2.4), we provide some suggestions for doing library research.

2. You quickly will narrow your research topic from a general area to a very specific idea. For example, when reading a book on developmental psychology, one chapter on social development may capture your attention. Within that chapter, you become interested in the section on play and peer relations, and in that section you find a fascinating paragraph on the role of siblings in the development of a child's social skills. Notice that you have substantially narrowed your interest area from the broad topic of human development to the much more focused topic of siblings and social skills. You have also greatly reduced the amount of relevant background reading.

Keep an Open Mind

The best strategy for finding a research idea is to begin with a general topic area and then let your background reading lead you to a more specific idea. As you read or skim through material, look for items that capture your attention; then follow those leads. You need not start with a specific research idea in mind. In fact, beginning with a specific, preconceived research idea can be a mistake; you may find that your specific question has already been answered, or you might have difficulty finding information that is relevant to your preconceived notion. You may find that you do not have the necessary equipment, time, or participants to test your idea. So your best bet is to be flexible and keep an open mind. The existing knowledge in any topic area is filled with unanswered questions that provide the basis for future research.

Also, be critical; ask questions as you read: Why did they do that? Is this result consistent with what I see in my own life? How would this prediction apply to a different situation? Do I really believe this explanation? These questions, expanding or challenging current knowledge, can lead to good research ideas. Other suggestions for critical reading are presented in section 2.6.

As you move through the project, maintain a degree of flexibility. You may discover a new journal article or get a suggestion from a friend that causes you to revise or refine your original plan. Making adjustments is a normal part of the research process and usually improves the result.

Focus, Focus, Focus

Developing a single, specific research idea is largely a weeding-out process. You probably will find that 1 hour of reading leads you to a dozen legitimate research ideas. It is unlikely that you can answer a dozen questions with one research study, so you will have to throw out most of your ideas (at least temporarily). Your goal is to develop one research question and to find the background information that is directly relevant to that question. Other ideas and other background material may be appropriate for other research, but at this stage, will only complicate the study you are planning. Discard irrelevant items, and focus on one question at a time.

Take One Step at a Time

Like any major project, planning and conducting research can be a long and difficult process. At the beginning, contemplating the very end of a research project may lead you to feel that the task is impossibly large. Remember, you do not need to do the whole thing at once; just take it one step at a time. In this chapter, we move through the beginning steps of the research process. The remainder of the textbook continues that journey, step by step.

LEARNING CHECKS   Explain why it is important to choose a research topic in an area that is interesting to you.

Explain why it is not the best strategy to begin with a specific research idea.

2.2 | FINDING A GENERAL TOPIC AREA

All research begins with an idea. General ideas for research can come from many different sources. Unfortunately, beginning students often believe that getting an idea is very difficult, when, in fact, starting points for research are all around us. All that is really necessary is that you see the world around you from an actively curious perspective. Ask yourself why things happen the way they do or what would happen if things were different. Keep your eyes open! Any source can generate legitimate research ideas.

Common Sources of Research Topics

Personal Interests and Curiosities

Feel free to generate ideas for research based on your own interests and concerns. What interests you? What makes you curious? One way to find out is to think about the courses you have taken. Which courses were your favorites? Within courses, what were your favorite units or classes? Think about the people and behaviors that interest you. Think about the issues that concern you. A research project can be about anything, so choose a topic you would like to learn more about.

Casual Observation

Watching the behavior of people or animals you encounter daily can be an excellent source of ideas. If you simply watch, you will see people getting angry, laughing at jokes, lying, insulting each other, forming friendships and relationships, eating, sleeping, learning, and forgetting. Any behavior that attracts your attention and arouses your curiosity can become a good research topic. In addition, you can monitor your own behavior, attitudes, and emotions. Although casual observation probably will not lead to a precise research question, you can certainly identify a general topic for study, and you may develop your own hypotheses or ideas about why people act the way they do.

Practical Problems or Questions

Occasionally, ideas for research will arise from practical problems or questions you encounter in your daily life, such as issues from your job, your family relationships, your schoolwork, or elsewhere in the world around you. For example, you may want to develop a more efficient set of study habits. Should you concentrate your study time in the morning, in the afternoon, or at night?

Should you spend a 2-hour block of study time working exclusively on one subject, or should you distribute your time so that each of five different courses gets some attention? Or suppose that you want to simplify the audio controls in your car. What is the best placement of buttons and dials to minimize distraction while driving? Any of these problems could be developed into a research study.

Research that is directed toward solving practical problems is often classified as **applied research;** in contrast, studies that are intended to solve theoretical issues are classified as **basic research.** Although these different kinds of research begin with different goals, they are both legitimate sources of research ideas and, occasionally, they can overlap. For example, a school board may initiate an applied study to determine whether there is a significant increase in student performance if class size is reduced from 30 students to 25 students. However, the results of the study may have implications for a new theory of learning. In the same way, a scientist who is conducting basic research to test a theory of learning may discover results that can be applied in the classroom.

DEFINITION	**Applied research** is intended to answer practical questions or solve practical problems. Research studies intended to answer theoretical questions or gather knowledge simply for the sake of new knowledge are classified as **basic research.**

Vague and Fleeting Thoughts

Occasionally, ideas for research begin with flashes of inspiration. Your initial ideas may emerge at odd times and in a fleeting way. You may get a flash of creative thought while you are in the bathroom, in the midst of a conversation with a friend, crossing the street, or dreaming. For some people, research ideas just spontaneously "pop" into their minds. The history of science is filled with stories of famous researchers whose ideas first appeared as flashes of insight. For example, Archimedes (287–212 b.c.e) is said to have discovered the law of hydrostatics (buoyancy) while stepping into his bath. The story also claims that he then ran down the street shouting "Eureka!" (Greek for "I have found it"), still dressed for the bath. According to legend, Isaac Newton (1642–1727) first conceived of universal gravitation when he saw an apple fall to the ground. We do not suggest that you wait for something like this to happen to you. Instead, we suggest that you actively use one of the other potential sources for ideas, while keeping your mind open to the possibility that, along the way, a research idea could pop into your mind.

We do not want to leave you with the impression that research ideas are always found in such unsystematic, creative, and haphazard ways. Most research ideas are generated in a highly systematic fashion by using the theories and research of others.

Reading Reports of Others' Observations

The written reports of observations made by other people are another good source of research ideas. These can include informal sources such as newspaper and magazine reports and television programs. Research ideas do not come exclusively from serious reports. Gossip columns, personal ads, comics, political cartoons, and advertising can stimulate research questions. Keep in mind the fact that published information, especially in nonscientific sources, is not necessarily true, and does not always tell the whole story. Remember, you are looking for ideas—so read critically and ask questions.

Although informal sources can stimulate research questions, you are more likely to find good ideas in the formal research reports published in books and professional journals. In this same category is material you have encountered in previous academic courses or textbooks. These scholarly sources are definitely the best ones for identifying questions that researchers are asking and the techniques they use to find answers. As always, read critically and ask questions: Why did the study examine only 4-year-old boys? What would happen if the task were made more difficult? Would the scores have been higher if the participants had been motivated to try harder? Questions like these can lead to a modification or extension of an existing study, which is one pathway to creating new research.

Behavioral Theories

Watch for theories that offer explanations for behavior or try to explain why different environmental factors lead to different behaviors. In addition to explaining previous research results, a good theory usually predicts behavior in new situations. Can you think of a way to test the explanations or evaluate the predictions from a theory? Look closely at the different variables that are part of the theory (the factors that cause behavior to change), and ask yourself what might happen if one or more of those variables were manipulated or isolated from the others. Testing the predictions that are part of a theory can be a good source of research ideas. Occasionally, you will encounter two different theories that attempt to explain the same behavior. When two opposing theories make different predictions, you have found a good opportunity for research.

 **LEARNING CHECK**   Describe the six common sources of research topics identified in the text.

Common Mistakes in Choosing a Research Topic

Over the years, we have seen beginning students make many mistakes in trying to find a research topic. We mention these mistakes in the hope that you will either avoid them altogether, or recognize when you are making one and quickly shift gears.

The Topic Does Not Interest the Student

One very common mistake is choosing a topic that is not of interest to you. This seems like an easy enough mistake to avoid, so how do you think it could happen? Through procrastination! This mistake is often the result of putting off thinking about a choice of topic until the latest possible date. When pressed for time to select a topic, students often pick a topic that is only of marginal interest. Because interesting topics do not just pop into the mind, allow yourself plenty of time to discover a topic. As noted earlier, developing and conducting a research study involves work and time. Unless you are somewhat interested in the topic you pick, you will find this task extremely laborious. As a result, you are likely to lose motivation, and your research project will no doubt reflect this. Start looking for ideas now!

The Topic Is Too Safe or Too Easy

Another mistake is to pick a topic that is too safe or too easy. Often, students choose a topic with which they are quite familiar. Hoping to save time and effort, a student may pull out a paper written for another class and try to change it into an idea for a research project. However, the purpose of planning and conducting research is to teach you about the research process with the hope that, in your reading, you will learn something about a topic that is of interest to you.

The Topic Is Too Difficult

Just as problematic as selecting a topic that is too easy is choosing one that is too hard. When you begin your library research, you may find that all the articles on your topic are written in complex scientific jargon that you do not understand. If this happens, it is time to be flexible. When most of the literature in your chosen area is over your head, consider changing topics. The task you are taking on is challenging enough; do not bite off more than you can chew!

The Topic Is Too Broad

Choosing a research topic that is too broad is not a mistake if you are still in the early stages of searching for an idea. As we discussed in section 2.1, the best strategy for finding a research idea is to begin with a general topic area. However, as you skim material, you quickly need to home in on a single, very specific research idea. You cannot answer every question about a topic area with one research project. Your ultimate goal in choosing a topic is to let the background reading lead you to a very specific idea for a research hypothesis that can be tested in a research study.

Sticking With the First Topic That Comes to Mind

Another mistake that beginning research students often make is refusing to move away from their original research topic. If your first topic leads you to a good research idea, that is great. However, do not commit yet. When you read information on your topic, different and more interesting research ideas may come to light. For example, you might be reading research reports on the general topic of family relations when you come across a study examining step children. If the topic of step children is more interesting than the topic of family relations, you are certainly free to switch topics. Be open to this possibility. Second and third, sometimes fourth and fifth, research topics are usually more refined, simpler, and more manageable than first ones. Although you do not want to switch topic areas the day before you begin conducting your study, do not commit too quickly, either; give your ideas time to evolve.

Inadequate Literature on the Topic

What if you find nothing to read when you begin to search for published articles in a topic area? This can occur for several reasons. First, some of the potentially most interesting topics in psychology appear to have been little investigated. You may have stumbled on an area that no one has thought to investigate. On the one hand, you can be proud of yourself for this discovery; on the other, it will be difficult to develop a research project. Second, the topic may not lend itself to scientific investigation. For example, questions such as, "Is there a God?" "Do angels exist?" and "Is there an afterlife?" are very intriguing topic areas. However, as discussed in section 1.4, some of life's most interesting questions are unsuitable for scientific research because no testable and refutable hypotheses can be developed about them. Third, it may only appear that there is no material on your topic because you are not using the correct terms to search for information. In section 2.4, we discuss in detail how to conduct a literature search, including how to identify appropriate search terms. And fourth, it could appear that there is no material on your topic because you are not searching in the correct database. Most academic disciplines (criminal justice, psychology, social work) have their own specialized databases focusing on research in the discipline. If you are not finding material in one database, it may be wise to change to a different database in a related area. For example, if you are looking for literature on anti-oxidants and aging, you might be more successful searching in a medical database rather than one dedicated to psychology. Table 2.1 shows the basic characteristics of four databases commonly available through most college or university libraries.

LEARNING CHECKS

How will you know that your research topic is too difficult?
What are some reasons why you may not find literature for a particular topic area?

2.3 | FINDING AND USING BACKGROUND LITERATURE

Once you have settled on a general idea for a research study, the next step is to go to the library to gather background information on the topic you have identified. In addition to gaining general knowledge about your topic area, your goals are to determine the current state of knowledge and to become familiar with current research, in particular, to find a specific research question. Notice that we said "find" a question rather than "make up," or "create" one. Once you are familiar with what is currently known and what is currently being done in a research area, your task is simply to extend the current research one more step. Sometimes, this requires a bit of logic in which you combine two or more established facts to reach a new conclusion or prediction. Often, the authors of a research report literally give you ideas for new research. It is very common for researchers to include suggestions for future research in the discussion of their results. You are welcome to turn one of these suggestions into a research question. In section 2.5, we provide additional hints for

TABLE **2.1**
Information about Four Databases

PsycINFO contains 2.8 million citations and summaries of journal articles, book chapters, books, dissertations, and technical reports, all in the field of psychology. Journal coverage, which spans from 1872 to the present, includes international material selected from nearly 2,500 periodicals in more than 35 languages. The database is updated weekly and more than 60,000 records are added each year. It also includes information about the psychological aspects of related disciplines such as medicine, psychiatry, nursing, sociology, education, pharmacology, physiology, linguistics, anthropology, business, and law. Examples of the journals covered by PsycINFO include Autism Research, Behavior and Brain Functions, Behavior Genetics, Behavioral Disorders, Journal of Abnormal Child Psychology, Journal of Applied Social Psychology, Journal of Behavioral Medicine, Journal of Psychiatry & Neuroscience, Psychoanalytic Psychology, Psychological Assessment, and Psychological Medicine.

   PsycArticles is a definitive source of searchable full-text articles on current issues in psychology. The PsycArticles database covers general psychology and specialized, basic, applied, clinical, and theoretical research in psychology. The database contains more than 147,000 searchable full-text articles from 71 journals published by the American Psychological Association and 8 from allied organizations. It contains all journal articles, letters to the editor, and errata from each of the 79 journals. Examples of titles offered in PsycArticles include American Psychologist, Behavioral Neuroscience, Canadian Psychology/ Psychologie Canadienne, Developmental Psychology, Journal of Abnormal Psychology, Journal of Personality and Social Psychology, Psychoanalytic Psychology, and Psychotherapy: Theory/Research/Practice/ Training. Coverage for some journals spans from 1894 to the present.

   ERIC, the Educational Resource Information Center, is a national information system supported by the U.S. Department of Education, the National Library of Education, and the Office of Educational Research and Improvement. It provides access to more than 1.3 million records from journals and other education-related materials, and links to more than 317,000 full-text documents.

   Medline provides authoritative medical information on medicine, nursing, dentistry, veterinary medicine, the health care system, preclinical sciences, and much more. Created by the National Library of Medicine, Medline is a comprehensive source for life science and biomedical bibliographical information. Medline contains more than 11 million records from more than 4,800 indexed titles.

finding research ideas. For now, do not try to impose your own preconceived idea onto the literature. Instead, let the literature lead you to a new idea.

   In most college or university libraries, the books devoted to psychology occupy at least 100 feet of shelves. The psychology journals probably fill even more space. When you add related publications in the fields of education, sociology, criminal justice, social work, and so on, you are facing a vast amount of printed material. The items that exist in any one library are usually only a small fraction of the total amount that exists worldwide as a combination of printed pages and electronic files. This mass of published information is referred to as *the literature*. Your job is to search the literature to find a handful of items that are directly relevant to your research idea. This may, at first, appear to be an overwhelming task; fortunately, however, the literature is filled with useful aids to guide your search. Specifically, all the individual publications are interconnected by cross-referencing, and there are many summary guides providing overviews that can send you directly to specific topic areas. By following the guides and tracing the interconnections, it is possible to conduct a successful literature search without undue pain and suffering.

Primary and Secondary Sources

Before we discuss the actual process of a literature search, there are a few terms you should know. Individual items in the literature can be classified into two broad categories: primary sources and secondary sources. A **primary source** is a firsthand report in which the authors describe their own observations. Typically, a primary source is a research report, published in a scientific journal or periodical, in which the authors describe their own research study, including why the research was done, how the study was conducted, what results were found, and how those results were interpreted. Some examples of primary sources include (1) empirical journal articles, (2) theses and dissertations, and (3) conference presentations of research results. In contrast, a **secondary source** is a secondhand report in which the authors discuss someone else's observations. Some examples of secondary sources include (1) books and textbooks in which the author describes and summarizes past research, (2) review articles or meta-analyses, (3) the introductory section of research reports, in which previous research is presented as a foundation for the current study, and (4) newspaper and magazine articles that report on previous research.

> A meta-analysis is a review and statistical analysis of past research in a specific area that is intended to determine the consistency and robustness of the research results.

DEFINITIONS

A **primary source** is a firsthand report of observations or research results written by the individual(s) who actually conducted the research and made the observations.

A **secondary source** is a description or summary of another person's work. A secondary source is written by someone who did not participate in the research or observations being discussed.

Notice that the principal distinction between a primary source and a secondary source is firsthand versus secondhand reporting of research results. Students often confuse this distinction with the notion that anything published in a journal or periodical is automatically a primary source and that all other kinds of publications are secondary sources. This assumption is incorrect on several levels. The following are also possible:

- A journal article may not be a primary source. Instead, the article may be a review of other work (as in a review article or meta-analysis), a theoretical article that attempts to explain or establish relationships between several previous studies, or a historical summary of the research in a specific area. None of these is a primary source because none is a firsthand report of research results.
- A book or book chapter can be a primary source. Occasionally, an individual or a group of researchers will publish an edited volume that presents a series of interrelated research studies. Each chapter is written by the individual(s) who actually conducted the research and is, therefore, a primary source.
- A journal article may be a firsthand report of research results, yet sections of the article actually may be secondary sources. Specifically, most research reports begin with an introductory section that reviews

current research in the area and forms the foundation of the study being reported. This review of current research is secondary because the authors describe research conducted by others. Remember, to qualify as a primary source, the authors must describe their own research studies and results.

Both primary and secondary sources play important roles in the literature search process. Secondary sources can provide concise summaries of past research. A textbook, for example, often summarizes 10 years of research, citing several important studies, in a few paragraphs. A meta-analysis, for example, provides a great overview of an area by combining the results from a number of studies. Individual research reports that fill 10 to 15 pages in journals are often summarized in one or two sentences in secondary sources. Thus, secondary sources can save you hours of library research. However, you should be aware that secondary sources are always incomplete and can be biased or simply inaccurate. In a secondary source, the author has selected only bits and pieces of the original study; the selected parts might have been taken out of context and re-shaped to fit a theme quite different from what the original authors intended. In general, secondary sources tell only part of the truth and can, in fact, distort the truth. To obtain complete and accurate information, it is essential to consult primary sources. Reading primary sources, however, can be a tedious process because they are typically long, detailed reports focusing on a narrowly defined topic. Therefore, plan to use secondary sources to gain an overview and identify a few specific primary sources for more detailed reading. Secondary sources provide a good starting point for a literature search, but you must depend on primary sources for the final answers.

LEARNING CHECK   Define primary and secondary sources and explain how each plays a role in the process of finding a research idea.

The Purpose of a Literature Search

Research does not exist in isolation. Each research study is part of an existing body of knowledge, building on the foundation of past research and expanding that foundation for future research. Box 2.1 and Figure 2.1 explain how current knowledge grows, with each new piece of information growing out of an existing body of previous knowledge. As you read the literature and develop an idea for a research study, keep in mind that your study should be a logical extension of past research.

Ultimately, your goal in conducting a **literature search** is to find a set of published research reports that define the current state of knowledge in an area and to identify an unanswered question—that is, a gap in that knowledge base—that your study will attempt to fill. Eventually, you will complete your research study and write your own research report. The research report begins with an introduction that summarizes past research (from your literature search) and provides a logical justification for your study. Although we discuss the task of writing a research report later (in Chapter 16), the topic is introduced now as a means of focusing your literature search. Figure 2.2

BOX **2.1**

The Growth of Research

Throughout this chapter, we repeat the notion that each research study builds on previous knowledge and attempts to expand that knowledge base. With this thought in mind, it is possible to represent the existing knowledge base (the literature) as a tree-like structure that is continuously growing over time. Figure 2.1 is a graphic representation of this concept, with each point in the figure representing a single research study, and the branches representing the growth and development of the "knowledge tree." When you begin a literature search, you enter this tree and find your way along the branches. Your goal in conducting the search is twofold. First, you must work your way to the very tips of the highest branches and find a cluster of the most recent research studies. Your study will form a new branch coming out of this cluster. Second, you must search backward, down the tree, to identify the historically significant foundations of your work. You probably will find that most of the current research studies in an area cite the same classic studies as their foundations. These classics usually provide a broader perspective for your work, and will help you understand and explain the significance of your study as it relates to the more general tree of knowledge.

The tree metaphor is only a conceptual guide to help you visualize the process and the goals of a literature search—the concept of a tree greatly oversimplifies the process. For example, many good research studies involve establishing a connection between two previously unrelated branches of research. Nonetheless, the tree metaphor should help direct your literature search activities. You may, for example, find yourself with a cluster of recent articles that seem to be a dead end, offering no prospect for developing new research. If this happens, you can simply work back down the tree to an earlier branching point and branch off in a new direction without completely abandoning your original research topic.

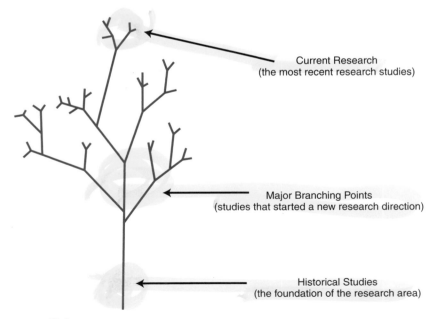

Current Research
(the most recent research studies)

Major Branching Points
(studies that started a new research direction)

Historical Studies
(the foundation of the research area)

FIGURE **2.1** How New Research Grows Out of Old
The tree-like structure emphasizes the notion that current research (the tips of the branches) is always based in previous research.

Why are we attracted to some individuals but not to others is one of the most fundamental human dilemmas and one of the most persistent questions in the study of close relationships, because these initial attractions are the basis for deciding with whom we develop long-term, committed relationships. The vast majority of research designed to address this age-old question has typically been framed in terms of similarity, with an emphasis on similarity in terms of attitudes, values, and beliefs (e.g. Berscheid, 1985). These studies have provided overwhelming evidence for the attractiveness of similarity, presumably because one's views of the world are validated, and because shared beliefs result in fewer disagreements and conflicts (e.g. Byrne, 1971). However, very few studies have assessed whether similarity in personality characteristics also leads to attraction, and the empirical evidence for this has been considerably weaker and mixed (e.g. Wetzel & Insko, 1982).

FIGURE **2.2** The Opening Paragraph of a Research Report by Klohnen and Luo, 2003.

presents the first paragraph of a journal article (Klohnen & Luo, 2003) as an example of the use of a literature review to introduce a topic area and provide a logical justification for a new study. The paragraph can be condensed into a simple, logical argument:

1. Research on interpersonal attraction has focused on similarity of attitudes, values, and beliefs.
2. Other types of similarity, such as similarity of personality, have been largely ignored or have produced mixed results.
3. Therefore, a reasonable research question is whether similar personalities play a role in determining when one person is attracted to another.

Although we have not described the research study, you should be able to predict the purpose of the study and should have some idea of what was done. Notice that the background literature is used to construct a logical argument that leads the reader directly to the research question for the proposed study. The purpose of your literature review is to provide the elements needed for an introduction to your own research study. Specifically, you need to find a set of research articles that can be organized into a logical argument supporting and justifying the research you propose to do.

Explain the purpose of a literature search.
   Explain what it means to say that a research study does not exist in isolation.

2.4 | CONDUCTING A LITERATURE SEARCH

Starting Points

Assume that you are starting your literature search with only a general idea for a research topic. Your purpose, therefore, is to narrow down your general idea to a specific research question, and to find all the published information necessary to document and support that question. As you will see, there are many ways to begin a search of the literature. In this section, we identify several different starting points and provide some suggestions to help you find one.

One of the best places to start is with a recently published secondary source, such as a textbook, in a content area appropriate for your idea (perhaps a developmental psychology or social psychology textbook). Use the chapter headings and subheadings in the text to help focus your search on a more narrowly defined area. In addition, make notes of the following items, each of which can serve as an excellent starting point when you begin to search for primary sources (empirical journal articles) relevant to your topic:

- Subject Words: Make a list of the correct terms, or **subject words,** used to identify and describe the variables in the study and the characteristics of the participants. Researchers often develop a specific set of terms to describe a topic area. It is much easier to locate related research articles if you use the correct terms. For example, you may have trouble finding articles on *foster homes* unless you use the accepted term, *foster care.*
- Author Names: Commonly, a small group of individual researchers is responsible for much of the work being done in a specific area. If you repeatedly encounter the same names, make a note of these individuals as the current leading researchers in the area.

As you develop your list of subject words and author names, keep in mind that any single secondary source is necessarily incomplete and probably selective. Thus, it is wise to repeat the list-making process with two or three different sources, then combine your lists. When you finish, you should have an excellent set of leads to help you move into the primary source literature.

Using Online Databases

Although there are thousands of research articles in psychology published every year, many tools are available to help you search through the publications to find the few that are directly relevant to your research topic. Most of these tools now exist as computer databases. A typical **database** contains about one million publications, or records, that are all cross-referenced by subject words and author names. You enter a subject word (or author name) as a search term and the database searches through all of its records and provides a list of the publications that are related to that subject (or author). Some databases are *full-text*, which means that each record is a complete, word-for-word copy of the original publication. Other databases provide only a brief summary of each publication. Typically, the summary includes the title, the authors, the name of the journal or book in which the publication appears, a list of the subject words that describe the publication, and an abstract. The **abstract** is a brief summary of the publication, usually about 100 words.

Because a full-text database requires more space to store each item, it often contains fewer items than other databases. Therefore, we generally recommend that students use a database that is not full-text to obtain more complete coverage of a topic area. For example, two databases that provide good coverage of psychology literature are **PsycINFO** (not full text) and **PsycArticles** (full text). These two databases are discussed further in Box 2.2.

LEARNING CHECK   How does a full-text database differ from other databases?

We warn that the process of searching the literature using a database like PsycINFO is very different from conducting a search on the Internet. Each month, the people at PsycINFO look through nearly 2,500 periodicals in the field of psychology, as well as a wide range of books and book chapters, to identify references to add to their database. All the references are selected

---

BOX **2.2**

Full-Text Databases

The value of a full-text database is that whenever you find a research article you would like to read, the entire article is immediately available right there on your computer screen. However, there is a price to pay for this convenience. Specifically, a full-text database must devote a lot of space to hold each publication. As a result, there is a limit to the number of publications it can hold. On the other hand, a database that is not full text needs only a small amount of space to hold each item, which means that it has room to hold a relatively large number of items. This relationship is demonstrated by comparing the full-text database PsycArticles with PsycINFO, which is not full text. PsycArticles contains about 147,000 items selected from 71 journals. By comparison, PsycINFO contains around 2.8 million items selected from nearly 2,500 periodicals.

Clearly, the full-text database contains only a small fraction of the psychology publications that are contained in PsycINFO. If you are conducting a literature search using PsycArticles, you probably will not find many relevant publications simply because they are not included in the database.

For most searches in psychology, we recommend using PsycINFO. If something is published in the field of psychology, it is almost guaranteed to be included in PsycINFO. Note, however, that this database provides only brief summaries of the items it references. To read the entire item, you must locate the original journal or book. Before using any database, quickly check the sources it reviews to be sure it provides good coverage of the area you would like to explore.

from reputable scientific publications, and most have been edited and reviewed by professional psychologists to ensure that they are legitimate and accurate contributions. This kind of professional screening does not usually exist on the Internet. For example, if you enter the subject word *amnesia* in PsycINFO, you will get a set of reputable scientific references. If you use the same subject word for an Internet search, you could obtain anybody's site with absolutely no guarantees about the quality or validity of the information. (One notable exception at the time of this writing is conducting a search with scholar .google.com, which does a good job of screening out the nonscientific items that normally clutter an Internet search.)

Using PsycINFO

In this section, we discuss the general process of conducting a literature search using PsycINFO. If you are using a different database or if you have a different version of PsycINFO, the specific suggestions and examples in this section may not apply directly to your search. However, the general process of conducting a literature search is fairly constant, and you should be able to adapt the tips and examples presented here to fit the characteristics of your specific database.

The process of getting into the PsycINFO database is different from one computer system to another. If you are unfamiliar with the system at your college or university, we suggest that you ask a teacher or a reference librarian to help you get started. Also, if you suspect that your research topic might be outside the field of psychology, you should also check with a librarian to determine whether a database other than PsycINFO would be better for your search.

Use the Advanced Search Option

The opening screen for PsycINFO will probably take you to the Basic Search option. This option provides only one box in which you can enter a subject term or an author name for your search. We suggest that you switch immediately to the Advanced Search option.

The Advanced Search gives you more control and more options for focusing your search. Figure 2.3 shows the opening screen for the Advanced Search option. (Note that this screen is an example; your version probably is slightly different.) Notice that you can enter up to three different search terms and you can specify exactly how each term should be interpreted (as an author's name, a word in the title, a subject term, and so on). The opening screen also presents a variety of other options for focusing and limiting your search. For example, you can limit the search to recent publications by specifying the range of years you would like to examine. We suggest that you make the following selections before clicking on the Search button to begin your search:

1. Limit the *Publication Type* to All Journals or Peer Reviewed Journal. This eliminates books and book chapters, which you probably do not want to read, and it eliminates dissertation abstracts that are produced by new Ph.D.s every year. Although the abstracts are available in

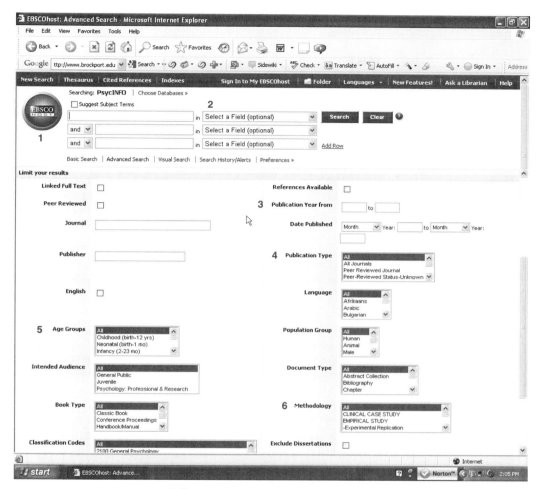

FIGURE 2.3 The Initial Screen for an Advanced Search in PsycINFO

Features of the screen are identified and numbered: (1) You can enter up to three search terms. (2) You can specify whether each term is a Subject, an Author, and so on. (3) You can limit the range of publication years. (4) You can specify the publication type. (5) You can select a specific age group. (6) You can select a research methodology.

Source: The PsycINFO ® Database screen shots are reproduced with permission of the American Psychological Association, publisher of the PsycINFO database, all rights reserved . No further reproduction or distribution is permitted without written permission from the American Psychological Association./ Image courtesy of EBSCO Publishing.

PsycINFO, you probably will never have access to the actual dissertation (the research report). Limiting the search to Peer Reviewed Journal adds another level of screening to ensure that the articles you find are legitimate and worthwhile contributions. All papers that appear in a peer-reviewed journal have been evaluated and approved by experts in the field before they are accepted for publication.

2. Limit the *Methodology* to Empirical Study. This focuses your search on research reports and eliminate essays, discussions, and general review articles.
3. If your research topic is focused on a specific *Age Group* or *Population Group*, you can also limit these areas.

Use the Thesaurus to Refine Your List of Search Terms

Begin your search with a list of terms you have identified as relevant or related to your topic. However, the words you have identified might not be identical to the official terms that are used by the American Psychological Association (APA). The official terms, known as subjects, are listed in the PsycINFO Thesaurus, which you can open by clicking on the Thesaurus tab, which is usually located at the top of the PsycINFO opening page. These subject terms are the specific words used to describe and categorize all of the publications included in the PsycINFO database. If you are not using one of the official subject words, you might not find all of the relevant publications. For example, suppose that you are interested in stress and teeth grinding. If you type these terms into the thesaurus, you will find that stress is an appropriate subject term, but that the correct term for teeth grinding is bruxism. We conducted a trial search using *stress* and *teeth grinding* as search terms and discovered 20 publications. When we changed *teeth grinding* to *bruxism,* the search revealed 33 publications. Using the official subject terms can make a big difference.

In addition to identifying official subject terms, the thesaurus often leads you to a set of related terms that can help you broaden or refine your search. For example, clicking on the term *family relations* in the thesaurus leads a list of broader terms, narrower terms, and related terms. Using one of the broader terms will expand your search, the narrower terms will limit your search to a smaller, more focused set of items, and it is possible that one of these related terms is more appropriate for your research interests than your original subject term. You can also use the Explode or the Major Concept options in the thesaurus to help broaden or narrow your search. Checking the Explode box before you click on Search broadens the search to include all references indexed to the search term as well as all references indexed to narrower terms. If you check the Major Concepts box before searching, the search will only retrieve records for which your search term is a major point of the article.

When you have identified a set of subject terms that accurately describes the research topic that you want to investigate, you can identify them as official subject terms in the search process. On the opening screen for an Advanced Search in PsycINFO, there are three boxes for entering search terms (see Figure 2.3). Beside each box is a default field in which you can specify how your search term should be used. One of the options in the default field is Subjects, which means that you want to identify your search term as an official APA subject term. On the other hand, if you are using a term that is not an official subject term (not included in the thesaurus), you should not select Subjects in the default field. Instead, you can simply leave it as Default or select Key Concepts, which are unofficial terms that have been identified as descriptive by the authors of the publication. If your research interest is directed toward a currently hot topic, the specific topic may not be recognized as an official subject by the APA. A good example is *road rage,* which is not yet (at the time of writing) an APA subject term, but is descriptive of some recent research. A quick check of the PsycINFO Thesaurus shows that the suggested official subject term is *aggressive driving behavior.*

Beginning a Literature Search

A literature search is usually begun by typing a subject word into a Search box on the opening page (see Figure 2.3). Suppose, for example, that you are interested in the topic of bulimia. You enter the term *bulimia* in the first of the three Advanced Search boxes. If you know that bulimia is an official subject word, you can also click on the default field box and select Subjects. When you click the Search button, PsycINFO searches through its two million entries and identifies all that have bulimia as a designated subject term. (If you did not select Subjects in the default field, PsycINFO looks for items that use the word bulimia in the title, the abstract, or as a descriptive word.) When the search is complete, the computer shows a numbered list of the first few items it found. Typically, PsycINFO presents 10 items on a page and you simply click to move to the next page and see the next 10 items. The total number of items found in the search is also reported at the top and bottom of each page. For example, the first page of a recent bulimia search showed items 1–10 out of 7,697. The items are listed in order of publication date, with the most recent publications reported first.

Figure 2.4 shows a few items, or records, as they appear in a PsycINFO list. Note that each record includes a basic description of the publication, including the title and the author(s). Reviewing the titles is the first level of screening journal articles. Most articles are discarded at this stage. When you find a title that is interesting to you, you can click on the title to obtain the detailed record, which contains additional information about the publication, including an abstract.

Figure 2.5 shows a detailed record. Within each detailed record you will find a number of fields, each containing specific information about the publication. The fields include:

Title

Author(s)

Keywords (unofficial terms describing the content)

Abstract

Subjects (official terms describing the content)

The full name of each field is included in Figure 2.5, but many systems include abbreviations. For example, author is abbreviated AU, title TI, source SO, and abstract AB. The two items in a detailed record that are most useful are the abstract and the list of subject terms (Subjects) that describe this specific publication. By reading the abstract, you can get a much better idea of what the article is about and decide whether you are

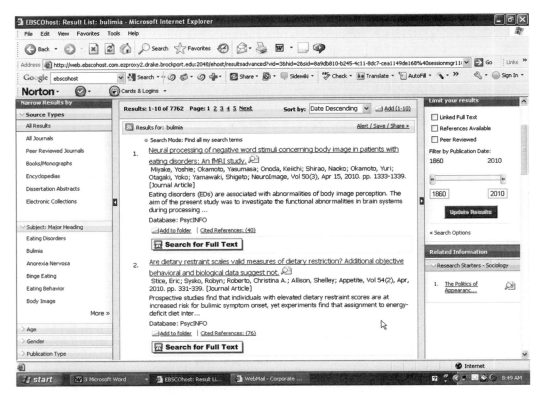

FIGURE **2.4** A Partial List of Records in PsycINFO

Source: The PsycINFO ® Database screen shots are reproduced with permission of the American Psychological Association, publisher of the PsycINFO database, all rights reserved . No further reproduction or distribution is permitted without written permission from the American Psychological Association./ Image courtesy of EBSCO Publishing.

still interested in reading the whole article. This is the second level of screening journal articles and many more will be discarded based on the content of the abstract. Immediately following the abstract is the list of subject terms. You should check the list to determine whether there are specific terms that could be used to improve your search. If you are still interested in the article, print out the detailed record and locate that journal article, chapter, or book in your library. If your library does not have an item you need, you may be able to request an interlibrary loan. Often, this involves clicking some additional keys for an online request or completing a form. In either case, your library will get that item for you—usually within days and often for free.

The Process of Conducting a Literature Search

In this section, we discuss using the library research tools we have described to help you find the journal articles that are directly relevant to your research study. The literature search process is likely to uncover hundreds of journal

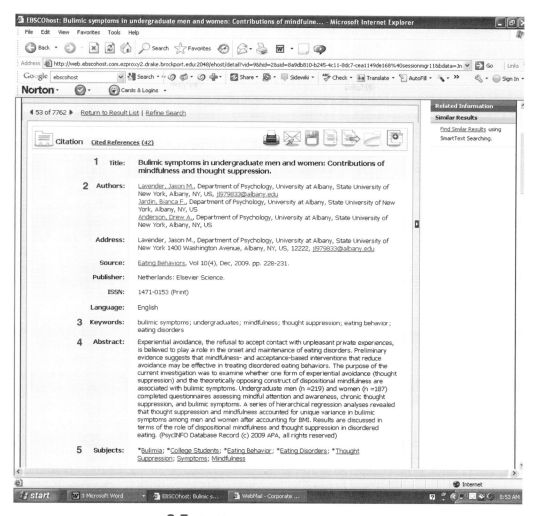

FIGURE **2.5** An Example of a Detailed Record in PsycINFO

Notice that the detailed record includes a variety of information about the publication, including (1) the Title, (2) the Author(s), (3) a list of Keywords, (4) the Abstract, and (5) a list of official Subject words.

Source: The PsycINFO ® Database screen shots are reproduced with permission of the American Psychological Association, publisher of the PsycINFO database, all rights reserved . No further reproduction or distribution is permitted without written permission from the American Psychological Association./ Image courtesy of EBSCO Publishing.

articles. And, although each of these articles is related to your topic, most of them probably are not directly related to the research you hope to do. Therefore, as you work through the literature search process, one of your main concerns is to weed out irrelevant material. There are no absolute criteria for determining whether an article is relevant or should be discarded; you must make your own decisions. However, here are some suggestions to help make the selection/weeding process more efficient:

1. Use the **title** of the article as your first basis for screening. You can find a title either in PsycINFO or at the beginning of the article itself. Based only on the titles, you probably can discard about 90% of the articles as not directly relevant or interesting.

2. Use the **abstract** of the article as your second screening device. If the title sounds interesting, read the abstract to determine whether the article itself is really relevant. Many of the articles that seemed interesting (from the title) get thrown out at this stage. You can find an abstract either in PsycINFO or at the beginning of the article itself.

3. If you are still interested after looking at the title and the abstract, go to the appropriate journal to find the article, or request an interlibrary loan if your library does not have that journal. Incidentally, when you retrieve a journal to look up a specific article, it is useful to review the contents of the rest of the journal. Occasionally, a journal devotes an entire issue to a single topic, and several other relevant works may surround your article. Also, the simple fact that the journal considers the topic of your article appropriate for its coverage means that it may publish other articles on the same topic. Once you find the article, first skim it, looking specifically at the introductory paragraphs and the discussion section.

4. If it still looks relevant, then read the article carefully and/or make a copy for your personal use. The process of reading and understanding a research article is discussed in section 2.6 at the end of this chapter. For now, we concentrate on those parts of the article that can help you with your literature search. First, you should notice that it is customary for a research article to be arranged into standard, distinct sections. Table 2.2 lists the sections in order and summarizes the content of each section. For your literature search, you should focus on the introduction, the discussion, and the references. The **introduction** discusses previous research that forms the foundation for the current research study and presents a clear statement of the problem being investigated. This can help you decide whether the article will be useful in the development of your research idea and may identify previous studies that may also be useful. Incidentally, the introduction is not labeled "Introduction." Instead, the text simply begins immediately after the abstract and continues until the next section, which is entitled "Method." The next two sections, the **method section** and the **results section,** present details of the research study and usually are not important for purposes of a literature search. Immediately following the results section is the discussion section, entitled "Discussion." In the **discussion section,** the authors often present ideas for future research. You are welcome to use one of these ideas as the basis for your new research study. Finally, the **reference section** at the end of the article lists all of the publications that were cited in the text. These publications can often lead to new subject terms or author names for your literature search.

TABLE **2.2**
Contents of Standard Sections of a Research Article

Introduction
Basic introduction to the topic area
Literature review
Research question, purpose, or hypothesis of the study
Brief outline of the methodology
Specific prediction of the study

Method
Participants/Subjects—description of the sample that participated in the study
Procedures—description of how the study was conducted, including a description of the questionnaires and equipment used in the study

Results
Findings
Statistical analyses
Figures and tables of data

Discussion
Conclusions
Applications of the research
Ideas for future studies

References
Bibliographic information for each item cited in the article

5. Use the references from the articles that you have already found to expand your literature search. Although the list of references will contain "old" research studies published years earlier, some of them may be directly relevant to your research idea. In this case, find the relevant articles and add them to your collection. As noted earlier, the references may contain terms that you can use as subjects for a new search, and the authors constitute a list of people who are doing research in the same area you have selected. You can enter these author names in PsycINFO and find the research reports that they have published recently. If people conducted research in a specific area 5 years ago, there is a good chance that they are continuing to do work in a related area today. In general, old references can be a good source for new research studies. Theoretically, you should continue using the old references to track down new material until you reach a point at which you no longer find any new items. Realistically, however, you must decide when to call off the search. At some point, you will realize you are not uncovering new leads and that you should proceed with the items you have found. Throughout the process, keep in mind that a literature search has two basic goals: (1) to gain a general familiarity with the current research in your specific area of interest, and (2) to find a small set of research studies that will serve as the basis for your own research idea. When you feel comfortable

that you are knowledgeable about the topic area and have found a few recent research studies that are particularly relevant to your own interests, then you have completed a successful search.

We are deliberately vague about how many articles form a good foundation for developing a new research idea. You may find two or three interrelated articles that all converge on the same idea, or you might find only one research study that appears to be directly relevant to your interests. In any event, the key criterion is that the study (or studies) you find provides some justification for new research. Even if you have only one study, remember that it cites other research studies that form a basis for the current research question. These same studies should be relevant to your research idea, and you are welcome to include them as part of the foundation for your own research.

Figure 2.6 summarizes the steps of a literature search.

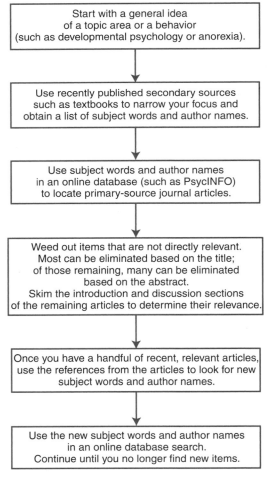

FIGURE **2.6** The Process of Conducting a Literature Search

LEARNING CHECKS

How can a database thesaurus help you refine your literature search?

List the five sections typically found in a research article, and describe briefly what each should contain.

The Web of Science combines several previous indexing systems, including the Science Citations Index and the Social Science Citations Index.

Searching Forward

Although a literature search typically begins with typing a subject word into the search box, there may be times when your starting point is an interesting article that was published years ago. In this case, your goal is to discover what, if any, current research is being done on the same topic. For example, in 1963 Stanley Milgram published a controversial study in which participants were willing to administer painful and dangerous electric shocks to other people when ordered to do so by an authority figure. (See page 74 for further discussion of Milgram's study.) If you are interested in Milgram's obedience study, you may want to know what current research exists in the same area. There are two very effective techniques to help you begin with an old publication and search forward to discover current research. The most direct method for conducting a forward search is to use a reference tool known as the Web of Science. If your library has access to this powerful indexing system, you can use it to conduct a cited-reference search by entering the citation for the old article and then searching for current studies that have cited this original source. For example, you could enter the citation for Milgram's obedience study and discover current publications that use Milgram's 1963 study as a reference. Presumably, current research that cites Milgram's study also is examining issues of obedience to authority. An alternative search method is to stay with a traditional database such as PsycINFO and use keywords from the original study as your search terms. For example, a recent search using *Milgram* and *obedience* as search terms produced 158 articles. When the search was limited to include only empirical studies, we still found 36 publications, 13 of which appeared in the past 10 years.

Taking Notes

As noted earlier, each time you find an article that is relevant to your research question, you should read the article carefully and either take notes or make a copy for future reference. If you are taking notes, which we recommend, there are a few points to keep in mind. First, be sure to get a complete reference for the article. This includes the author name(s), the year of publication, the title, and the source of the article. If the source is a print journal, get the name of the journal as well as the volume number and the page numbers. If the article is from an electronic source, you also should note the Digital Object Identifier (DOI), which is a unique code that provides continuous access to the article. If there is no DOI, make a note of the complete website address (URL) and the date that the article was retrieved. This information will be necessary for you and others to locate the article in the future and will appear in the list of references that goes in your research report. Second, it is best to summarize and describe the important aspects of the article in your own words. Avoid copying specific phrases or sentences used by the authors. By using your own words during note taking you are less likely to unintentionally plagiarize by incorporating words or ideas from other people into the research report that you write.

2.5 FINDING AN IDEA FOR A RESEARCH STUDY AND CONVERTING THE IDEA INTO A HYPOTHESIS AND A PREDICTION

Once you have located a set of recent and relevant articles, the final step is to use these research reports as the foundation for your research idea or research question (see Chapter 1, Step 1 of the research process). Earlier, we called this task "finding a research idea." When you are familiar with the current research in an area, the idea for the next study simply involves extending the current research one more step. However, discovering this next step might not be as simple as we have implied, and so we list a few suggestions here.

Find Suggestions for Future Research

The easiest way to find new research ideas is to look for them as explicit statements in the journal articles you already have. Near the end of the discussion section of most research reports is a set of suggestions for future research. In most cases, a research study actually generates more questions than it answers. The authors who are reporting their research results usually point out the questions that remain unanswered. You can certainly use these suggestions as ideas for your own research. Instead of specifically making suggestions for future research, authors occasionally point out limitations or problems with their own study. If you can design a new study that fixes the problems, you have found a new research idea.

Modify or Extend an Existing Study—Critical Reading

The task of reading and understanding a research article is discussed in section 2.6. However, reading critically can generate ideas for new research. Specifically, as you are reading, ask yourself how the study might be modified or expanded. Any study uses a specific set of instructions, stimuli, tests, and participants. What might happen if any of these were changed? For example, would a result obtained for 8-year-old boys also be obtained for adolescents? If a study demonstrates that a treatment is effective under specific circumstances, it is perfectly legitimate to ask whether the treatment would still be effective if the circumstances were changed. Please note that we are not suggesting that you can create good research ideas by simply changing variables randomly. There should be some reason, based on logic or other research results, to expect that changing circumstances might change results. In general, however, examining and questioning each element of an existing study can be an effective technique for creating new research ideas. If you are considering changing a variable in an existing study, it is usually wise to expand your literature search to include the new variable. Suppose for example, you used the search terms *competition* and *games* to find an interesting article on competitive behavior for 8-year-old boys. If you are thinking about modifying the study by using *adolescents,* you could add adolescents as a new search term (along with your original two terms) to see if there is additional research that might help you develop your idea.

Combine or Contrast Existing Results

Occasionally, it is possible to find a new research idea by combining two (or more) existing results. For example, one study reports that people who experience stressful events tend to have more illness and visit the doctor more often than people with relatively stress-free lives (Rahe & Arthur, 1978). Another study suggests that owning a pet can help people cope with stress (Broadhead et al., 1983). Given these two results, can you generate a hypothesis for a new study? (See Siegel, 1990, for one example.) Another possibility is that two research results seem to contradict each other. In this case, you could look for factors that differentiate the two studies and might be responsible for the different results.

In general, research is not static. Instead, it is constantly developing and growing as new studies spring from past results. New research ideas usually come from recognizing the direction in which an area of research is moving and then going with the flow.

LEARNING CHECK Describe the three ways identified in the text to find or develop a new research idea from existing research report(s).

Converting a Research Idea into a Hypothesis and Prediction

Typically, a research idea or a research question involves a general statement about the relationship between two variables. For example:

Visual imagery is related to human memory.

Stated as a question, this idea might become:

Is there a relationship between using visual images and human memory?

The next step in the research process (Step 2) is to transform your research idea into a hypothesis, which is simply a tentative answer to the question, and then use the hypothesis to make a logical prediction that can be tested empirically in a research study. For the imagery example, a possible hypothesis is as follows:

Hypothesis: The use of visual images is related to better memory performance.

To determine whether the hypothesis is true, we first use the hypothesis to make a logical prediction that can be empirically evaluated in a research study. If the prediction is confirmed by the results of the study, we have support for our hypothesis. If the results contradict the prediction, we must reject the hypothesis and make another attempt to answer the research question.

As we noted earlier, there are usually several different predictions that can come from one hypothesis, and there are usually dozens of possible studies that can be used to evaluate each prediction. The decisions you make at each step in the research process ultimately determine the specific research study that you do. For example, the participants in an imagery/memory study could be college students, elderly adults, or children. You could choose to measure memory using an immediate recall test, or by testing memory 2 months after the material was originally studied. Two possible predictions (research studies) for the imagery/memory hypothesis are as follows:

> College students who are instructed to form a mental image of the object represented by each word while studying a list of 40 words for 2 minutes will recall more words (on average) than college students who study the same words for 2 minutes but are not given instructions to form mental images.

> Ten-year-old children who view pictures of 20 items (for example, a table, a horse, and a tree) will recall more items, on average, than 10-year-old children who view a series of words representing the same 20 items (for example, *table, horse,* and *tree*).

In general, there are many different ways to convert a hypothesis into a specific prediction for a research study. The method you select depends on a variety of factors, including the set of individuals you want to study and the measurement techniques that are available. However, each of the many possible research studies should provide a direct test of the basic hypothesis.

As a final note, the fact that several different research studies can be created from the same general hypothesis gives you one more technique for creating a new research study. Specifically, you can take the general hypothesis from an existing study and develop your own new study. For example, we have presented two specific studies based on the general hypothesis that memory is related to images. If you can develop your own study by changing the group of participants, modifying the method for measuring memory, or finding another way to have people use images, then you will have produced your own research study.

LEARNING CHECK   Explain the basic difference between a hypothesis and a specific research prediction.

2.6 | READING AND UNDERSTANDING A RESEARCH ARTICLE

Although most of the research articles you encounter will be discarded after looking at the title, reading the abstract, or simply skimming the text, there will be some that are directly relevant to your research interests and deserve careful reading. In this section, we present some general suggestions to bear in mind when you are reading a research article.

In most situations, there are two general goals involved in reading a research article. First, you want to learn about the specific research study that is being reported. What was the purpose of the study? How was the study conducted? What result did the study produce? Typically, the goal is to be able to summarize the study in your own words. Second, you want to use the study as the starting point for a new research project of your own. What elements of the study might be modified to produce different results or to extend the results into a new area? What new questions does the study produce? Notice that both goals involve asking questions. This is the essence of critical reading: examine and question each part of the paper you are reading. Earlier, in Table 2.2 (p. 61), we identified the basic content of each section of an APA-style research report. In Table 2.3 we repeat the list of major sections

TABLE **2.3**
Critically Reading a Research Article

This table identifies the major elements that make up a research report and describes the kinds of questions you should ask for a critical evaluation of each element.

Introduction

Literature review
Is the literature review complete and up to date?
Are there relevant or related topics that are not covered?

Hypothesis or purpose for study
Is the hypothesis or purpose clearly stated?
Is the hypothesis directly related to the reviewed literature?

Specific prediction from hypothesis
Does the predicted outcome logically follow from the hypothesis?
Are there other specific predictions that can be made?

Method

Participants
Are the participants representative of the population being considered?
If restrictions were imposed on participants (e.g., males only), are they justified? Is there reason to predict different results if participants had different characteristics?

Procedure
Are the variables well defined, and are the measurement procedures reasonable?
Are there alternative methods for defining and measuring the same variables?
Are the procedures appropriate for answering the research question?
Are there alternative procedures that could be used?

Results

Statistics (significance and effect size)
Were the appropriate statistics and statistical tests used?
Do you understand exactly what is significant and what is not?
Are the treatment effects large enough to be meaningful?

Discussion

Results related to hypothesis
Do the results really support (or refute) the hypothesis?

Justified conclusions
Are the conclusions justified by the significance of the results?
Do the conclusions follow logically from the results?

Alternative explanations
Are there alternative conclusions or explanations for the results?
Are there any other variables that could affect the results?

Applications
Do the results have any real-world application?

Limits to generalization
Is there reason to suspect that the same results might not occur outside the lab?
Would the same results be expected with different participants or under different circumstances?

References

Is the list of references current and complete?

that typically make up a research report and list questions you should ask about each element. If you identify and question each element as you are reading an article, you should finish with a good understanding of the study and some ideas for the next step in the research process.

■ CHAPTER SUMMARY

Beginning the research process can seem intimidating, but keeping a few points in mind will make the task a little easier. First, pick a topic in which you have some real personal interest to help yourself stay motivated throughout the research process. Second, do your homework on your topic; collect and familiarize yourself with the background information in your area. Third, keep an open mind in settling on a research topic; let your background reading lead you to a specific idea. Fourth, after doing the background reading, focus specifically on one research question. Finally, break down the planning and conducting of your research into manageable steps, and take them one at a time.

All research begins with a topic area, and, fortunately, there are many places from which topics can come. Feel free to get topics for research from your own personal interests, your own casual observations, practical problems, flashes of inspiration, and reports of others' observations and theories. However you obtain your initial research topic, be wary of making these common mistakes: choosing a topic that does not interest you; picking a topic that is too easy or too difficult; picking a topic that is too broad; sticking with the first idea that comes to mind; or choosing a topic for which there is inadequate literature.

Once you settle on a general topic area, become familiar with the current research in that area. To find research journal articles in psychology, we recommend PsycINFO because this database provides extensive coverage of psychology literature. Consult your librarian to determine the appropriate databases for other academic disciplines. Based on their titles and abstracts, discard articles that are not directly relevant. As you read selected articles, you will "find" a new research idea. Finally, convert your research idea into a specific research study.

KEY WORDS

applied research	primary source	secondary source
basic research		

EXERCISES

1. In addition to the key words, you should be able to define each of the following terms:
   literature search
   subject words
   database
   abstract
   PsycINFO

   PsycArticles
   title
   introduction
   method section
   results section
   discussion section
   reference section

2. Find a research article and make a copy of its introduction. In two or three sentences, write out the simple, logical argument for the proposed study.

3. List five behaviors that you could observe in your day-to-day life. For each one, identify one or two variables that might influence the behavior. For example, falling asleep in class is a behavior that might be influenced by caffeine consumption or amount of sleep the night before.

4. Make a list of five general topic areas that interest you. For each, identify the source of ideas you used to come up with that topic.

5. Find the appropriate database at your library for searching the psychology literature. Get background information to determine what kinds of publications the database searches to obtain its references. How many periodicals are searched, and what other kinds of publications are considered? Does your database search the Journal of Abnormal Psychology? Does it search Behavioral Neuroscience?

6. Using the appropriate psychology database at your library, enter the subject words *short-term memory* and see how many references you obtain. Now enter the combination of *short-term memory* and *imagery* as subject words. By how much was the number of references reduced with this combination of subject words?

7. Using PsycINFO (or a similar database), find research articles on binge drinking in college students. Print out the Detailed Record (including the abstract) for one research article on this topic.

8. Using PsycINFO (or a similar database), find five articles on the topic of depression in young children. Print out a copy of the Record List page.

LEARNING ACTIVITIES

1. Ideas for future research studies often can be obtained from the discussion sections of research reports. Occasionally, the researchers provide explicit suggestions for new research studies. At other times, the suggestions for future research may be more subtle, often phrased in terms of self-criticism or shortcomings of the research study being reported. For example, a study may admit that the data were restricted to children living in a Western society. It should be clear that the authors are inviting future research to examine a more diverse group.

    Using a full-text database (like PsycArticles), find a journal article that reports on an empirical research study (a study with participants, measurements, statistics, and so on). In the discussion section, find a suggestion for future research. (Remember that you may find a very clear statement about future research or a more subtle hint.)

    a. Provide a complete citation for the article (authors, year, title, journal).
    b. Provide a photocopy of the suggestion for future research (or simply quote the section).
    c. Briefly describe how the future research study might be conducted (who would participate, what would be measured, and so on).

2. After you have identified a research topic that you find interesting and would like to explore, the next step is to visit the library to discover what researchers have already learned about the topic and what questions remain unanswered. In addition, you need to find out how researchers have defined and measured the variables they are investigating. For example, you may be interested in motivation or self-esteem, but can you provide a good definition for these two concepts and do you know how to measure them? Most library databases allow you to search for information using

specific terms. In PsycINFO, for example, these terms are called subject terms. When you enter a subject term, the database searches for all related publications. Select a subject term that is of interest to you and find three recent empirical articles dealing with the topic. For each article, provide:

- a complete citation (authors, date, title, journal)
- statement of the hypothesis or purpose
- summary of results

WEB RESOURCES

Visit the Book Companion Website at **www.cengage.com/international** to access study tools including a glossary, flashcards, and web quizzing. You will also find a link to Statistics and Research Methods Workshops.

For this chapter, we suggest you look at the following workshops:

Getting Ideas for a Study

Evaluating Published Research

Common Mistakes in Student Research

3

Research Ethics

CHAPTER OVERVIEW

Consideration of ethical issues is integral to the research process. Researchers have two basic categories of ethical responsibility: (1) responsibility to the individuals, both human and nonhuman, who participate in their research studies; and (2) responsibility to the discipline of science to be accurate and honest in the reporting of their research. We discuss each of these ethical issues in this chapter.

3.1 INTRODUCTION

3.2 ETHICAL ISSUES AND HUMAN PARTICIPANTS IN RESEARCH

3.3 ETHICAL ISSUES AND NONHUMAN SUBJECTS IN RESEARCH

3.4 ETHICAL ISSUES AND SCIENTIFIC INTEGRITY

3.1 │ INTRODUCTION

Ethical Concerns Throughout the Research Process

After you have identified a new idea for research, formed a hypothesis and prediction, and determined a method for defining and measuring variables, you may think, "Great! Now I'm really ready to begin research." We hope you are beginning to feel the excitement of starting a research project; however, we must now consider the fact that the research process includes an element of serious responsibility.

Up to this point, your research project has been entirely private and personal. You have been working on your own, in the library and on the Internet, gathering information and formulating an idea for a research study. Now, however, you have reached the stage where other individuals become involved with your research: first, the participants or subjects whose behaviors and responses you observe and measure during the course of the study; and then the people who will see (and, perhaps, be influenced by) your report of the study's results. All these individuals have a right to expect honesty and respect from you, and as you proceed through the following stages of the research process, you must accept the responsibility to behave ethically toward those who will be affected by your research. In general, **ethics** is the study of proper action (Ray, 2000). This chapter is devoted to the subject of **research ethics** in particular.

DEFINITION	**Research ethics** concerns the responsibility of researchers to be honest and respectful to all individuals who are affected by their research studies or their reports of the studies' results. Researchers are usually governed by a set of ethical guidelines that assist them to make proper decisions and choose proper actions. In psychological research, the American Psychological Association (APA) maintains a set of ethical principles for research (APA, 2002).

Caution! Research ethics is not an issue of morality; it concerns the proper conduct of researchers. Researchers have observed their own conduct and reached a consensus regarding acceptable conduct for all researchers.

Consider the following examples.

- Suppose that, as a topic for a research study, you are interested in brain injury that may result from repeated blows to the head such as those suffered by boxers and soccer players. For obvious ethical reasons (physical harm), you could not plan a study that involved injuring people's brains to examine the effects. However, you could compare two preexisting groups; for example, a group of soccer players who are regularly hit on the head with soccer balls, and a group of swimmers who are also athletes but are not routinely hit in the head (see Downs & Abwender, 2002, for a sample study).
- Suppose that you are interested in sexual behavior as a research topic. For obvious ethical reasons (privacy), you cannot secretly install video cameras in people's bedrooms. However, you could ask people to complete a questionnaire about their sexual behavior (see Page, Hammermeister, & Scanlan, 2000, for a sample study).

In research, ethical issues must be considered at each step in the research process. Ethical principles dictate (1) what measurement techniques may be used for certain individuals and certain behaviors, (2) how researchers select individuals to participate in studies, (3) which research strategies may be used with certain populations and behaviors, (4) which research designs may be used with certain populations and behaviors, (5) how studies may be carried out with individuals, (6) how data are analyzed, and, finally, (7) how results are reported. The issue of ethics is an overriding one and must be kept in mind at each step of the research process when you make decisions. Scientists' exploration is bounded by ethical constraints.

The Basic Categories of Ethical Responsibility

Researchers have two basic categories of ethical responsibility: (1) responsibility to ensure the welfare and dignity of the individuals, both human and nonhuman, who participate in their research studies, and (2) responsibility to ensure that public reports of their research are accurate and honest.

Any research involving humans or nonhumans immediately introduces questions of ethics. The research situation automatically places the scientist in a position of control over the individuals participating in the study. However, the researcher has no right to abuse this power or to harm the participants or subjects, physically, emotionally, or psychologically. On the contrary, the relative power of the researcher versus the participant or subject means that the researcher has a responsibility to ensure the safety and the dignity of the participants. Committees such as the Institutional Review Board (IRB), which reviews research involving human participants, and the Institutional Animal Care and Use Committee (IACUC), which reviews research with nonhuman subjects, assist researchers in meeting their ethical responsibilities. These committees examine all proposed research with respect to treatment of humans and nonhumans. Details concerning the safe treatment of humans and nonhumans in research are discussed in Sections 3.2 and 3.3, respectively.

Reporting of research also introduces questions of ethics. It is assumed that reports of research are accurate and honest depictions of the procedures used and results obtained in a research study. As we discussed in Chapter 1, the scientific method is intended to be a valid method of acquiring knowledge. Its goal is to obtain answers in which we are confident. Any reporting decision that jeopardizes this confidence is an ethical issue. Two of these issues, fraud and plagiarism, are discussed in Section 3.4.

3.2 | ETHICAL ISSUES AND HUMAN PARTICIPANTS IN RESEARCH

Historical Highlights of Treatment of Human Participants

Until the end of World War II, researchers established their own ethical standards and safeguards for human participants in their research. It was assumed that researchers, bounded by their own moral compasses, would protect their participants from harm. However, not all researchers were committed to the ethical treatment of human participants. The major impetus for a shift from individualized ethics to more formalized ethical guidelines was the uncovering of the brutal experiments performed on prisoners in Nazi concentration camps. A variety of sadistic "medical experiments" were conducted on unwilling participants. Some examples include breaking and rebreaking of bones (to see how many times they could be broken before healing failed to occur) and exposure to extremes of high altitude and freezing water (to see how long a person could survive). When these and other atrocities came to light, some of those responsible were tried for their crimes at Nuremberg in 1947. Out of these trials came the **Nuremberg Code,** a set of 10 guidelines for the ethical treatment of human participants in research. It is reprinted here in Table 3.1 (Katz, 1972). The Nuremberg Code laid the groundwork for the ethical standards that are in place today for both psychological and medical research. A similar set of ethical guidelines, known as the Declaration of Helsinki, was adopted by the World Medical Association in 1964, and provides an international set of ethical principles for medical research involving humans (available at www.wma.net).

Tragically, even after the development of the Nuremberg Code, researchers have not always ensured the safety and dignity of human participants. Since the late 1940s, there have been additional examples of maltreatment of human participants in biomedical research. In 1963, for example, it was revealed that unsuspecting patients had been injected with live cancer cells (Katz, 1972). In 1972, a newspaper report exposed a Public Health Service study, commonly referred to as the Tuskegee study, in which nearly 400 men had been left to suffer with syphilis long after a cure (penicillin) was available. The study began as a short-term investigation to monitor untreated syphilis, but continued for 40 years just so the researchers could examine the final stages of the disease (Jones, 1981).

Similar examples of the questionable treatment of human participants have been found in behavioral research. The most commonly cited example is the Milgram obedience study (Milgram, 1963). Milgram instructed participants to use electric shocks to punish other individuals when they made errors during a learning task. The intensity of the shocks was gradually increased until the participants were administering what appeared to be dangerously strong and obviously painful shocks. In fact, no shocks were used in the study (the "shocked" individuals were pretending); however, the participants (those who administered the shocks) believed that they were inflicting real pain and suffering. Although the participants in Milgram's study sustained no physical harm, they suffered shame and embarrassment for having behaved inhumanely toward their fellow human beings. The participants entered the study thinking that they were normal, considerate human beings, but they left with the knowledge that they could all too easily behave inhumanely.

It is important to note two things about these cases. First, although they constitute a very small percentage of all the research that is conducted, many examples of questionable treatment exist. Second, it is events like these that shaped the guidelines we have in place today. In the late 1960s, the U.S. Surgeon General required all institutions receiving federal funding for research from the Public Health Service to review proposed research to safeguard human participants. Because of growing concern about research ethics, in 1974 Congress passed the **National Research Act.** The Act mandated regulations for

TABLE **3.1**
10 Points of the Nuremberg Code

1. The voluntary consent of the human subject is absolutely essential. This means that the person involved should have legal capacity to give consent; should be so situated as to be able to exercise free power of choice, without the intervention of any element of force, fraud, deceit, duress, over-reaching, or other ulterior form of constraint or coercion; and should have sufficient knowledge and comprehension of the elements of the subject matter involved as to enable him to make an understanding and enlightened decision. This latter element requires that before the acceptance of an affirmative decision by the experimental subject there should be known to him the nature, duration, and purpose of the experiment; the method and means by which it is to be conducted; all inconveniences and hazards reasonably to be expected; and the effects upon his health or person which may possibly come from his participation in the experiment. The duty and responsibility for ascertaining the quality of the consent rests upon each individual who initiates, directs, or engages in the experiment. It is a personal duty and responsibility that may not be delegated to another with impunity.

2. The experiment should be such as to yield fruitful results for the good of society, un-procurable by other methods or means of study, and not random and unnecessary in nature.

3. The experiment should be so designed and based on the results of animal experimentation and a knowledge of the natural history of the disease or other problem under study that the anticipated results will justify the performance of the experiment.

4. The experiment should be so conducted as to avoid all unnecessary physical and mental suffering and injury.

5. No experiment should be conducted where there is an a priori reason to believe that death or disabling injury will occur; except, perhaps, in those experiments where the experimental physicians also serve as subjects.

6. The degree of risk to be taken should never exceed that determined by the humanitarian importance of the problem to be solved by the experiment.

7. Proper preparations should be made and adequate facilities provided to protect the experimental subject against even remote possibilities of injury, disability, or death.

8. The experiment should be conducted only by scientifically qualified persons. The highest degree of skill and care should be required through all stages of the experiment of those who conduct or engage in the experiment.

9. During the course of the experiment the human subject should be at liberty to bring the experiment to an end if he has reached the physical or mental state where continuation of the experiment seems to him to be impossible.

10. During the course of the experiment the scientist in charge must be prepared to terminate the experiment at any stage, if he has probable cause to believe, in the exercise of the good faith, superior skill, and careful judgment required of him that a continuation of the experiment is likely to result in injury, disability, or death to the experimental subject.

Source: From Katz, J. (1972). *Experimentation with human beings.* New York: Russell Sage Foundation.

the protection of human participants and had the Department of Health, Education, and Welfare create the National Commission for the Protection of Human Subjects of Biomedical and Behavioral Research (Dunn & Chadwick, 1999). In 1979 the National Commission published *The Belmont Report: Ethical Principles and Guideline for the Protection of Human Subjects of Research.* The **Belmont Report** summarizes the basic ethical principles identified by the National Commission, which are used as the foundation upon which the federal regulations for protecting human participants are based, even to this day (available at: www.hhs.gov/ohrp/humansubjects/guidance/belmont.htm).

The Belmont Report identifies three basic principles: (1) The principle of respect for persons requires that individuals should consent to participate in studies and those who cannot give their consent, such as children, people with diminished abilities, and prisoners, need to be protected; (2) The principle of beneficence requires that the researcher not harm the participants, minimize risks, and maximize possible benefits; (3) The principle of justice requires fairness in procedures for selecting participants (Gillespie, 1999).

Although the development of ethical guidelines may seem like ancient history to many of you in college today, you should realize that they were put in place just in time to protect your parents, who may have participated in research studies during their years in college. Before the 1970s, formal guidelines and standards were rare and researchers were generally left on their own to decide what procedures were proper and acceptable. The Milgram study, for example, may seem somewhat bizarre and inhumane, but it was preceded by other psychological research in which human participants actually were shocked for making errors (Crafts & Gilbert, 1934).

LEARNING CHECK

For each of the following, identify which of the three basic principles of the Belmont Report is being violated:

A researcher recruits poor minorities to be participants in a risky experiment.

A researcher tricks people into participating by suggesting that they might win a contest.

A researcher knows that people will feel ashamed after one part of the study.

American Psychological Association Guidelines
Ethical Guidelines for the Use and Treatment of Human Participants in Research

Around the same time that the federal government began to concern itself with protecting human participants in research, the American Psychological Association (APA) prepared its first set of now widely distributed and accepted guidelines (1973). The first APA committee on ethics was set up in 1952; however, it was not until the mid 1960s, in response to major criticisms of Milgram's now famous obedience study, that APA members began to discuss a formal code of ethics.

You may have noticed the term *guidelines*. Because it is impossible to anticipate every specific research situation, the guidelines are intended to identify general areas in which researchers should be cautious and aware of ethical concerns. The APA guidelines have been updated and expanded several times since they were first developed, and are periodically revised. The most recent version was published in 2002. The **APA Ethics Code** contains 10 ethical standards, and you should be completely familiar with all of them before beginning any research with human participants. (You can visit APA.org on the Internet for more information, or you can go directly to www.apa.org/ethics/code/index.aspx for the complete Ethics Code.) According to APA (2002), "This Ethics Code provides a common set of principles and standards upon which psychologists build their professional and scientific work. This Ethics Code is intended to provide specific standards to cover most situations encountered by psychologists. It has as its goals the welfare and protection of the individuals and groups with whom the psychologists work and the education of members, students, and the public regarding ethical standards of the discipline."

A summary of the most recent ethical guidelines concerning human participants in research (APA, 2002) is presented in Table 3.2. This summary is based on the *APA Ethical Principles of Psychologists and Code of Conduct* (APA, 2002), and includes the elements most relevant to the use and treatment of human participants in research (parts of Standards 2, 3, 4, 6, and 8). The APA guidelines are continually reviewed and revised—as are federal, state, and local regulations—so researchers always must check to make sure they are abiding by the current rules.

LEARNING CHECK   Although the APA guidelines and the Nuremberg Code have substantial overlap, there are three specific points that they share: No harm, competence, and informed consent. These are points 1, 4, and 6 in the APA Guidelines. What are the corresponding points in the Nuremberg Code?

Major Ethical Issues

Rather than discussing each of the guidelines point by point, we present in detail a few issues that are the most important for new researchers.

No Harm (Item 1, Table 3.2)   The researcher is obligated to protect participants from physical or psychological harm. The entire research experience should be evaluated to identify risks of harm, and when possible, such risks should be minimized or removed from the study. Any risk of harm must be justified. The justification may be that the scientific benefits of the study far outweigh the small, temporary harm that can result. Or it may be that greater harm is likely to occur unless some minor risk is accepted during the study. (Doctors and their patients face this concern when deciding whether to use a medication that has known side effects.) In any event, participants must be informed of any potential risks, and the researcher must take steps to minimize any harm that can occur. In the behavioral sciences, the risk of physical harm is relatively rare (except in areas in which psychology and medicine overlap). Psychological harm, on the other hand, is a common concern. During or after a study, participants may feel increased anxiety, anger, lower self-esteem, or mild depression, especially in situations in which they feel they have been cheated, tricked, deceived, or insulted. Occasionally researchers deliberately create these situations as an integral part of the study; for example, participants may be given an impossible task so the researcher can observe responses to failure (note that Item 9 in Table 3.2 allows deception). Often, participants

TABLE **3.2**

Selected Elements from the APA Ethical Guidelines Concerning
Human Participants in Research

This summary is based on the *APA Ethical Principles of Psychologists and Code of Conduct* (APA, 2002) and includes the elements most relevant to the use and treatment of human participants in research. The section numbers correspond to the standards referred to in the *APA Ethical Principles of Psychologists and Code of Conduct.*

1. No Harm (Sections 3.04 and 8.08)

Psychologists take reasonable steps to avoid harming their research participants, and to minimize harm where it is foreseeable and unavoidable.

When psychologists become aware that research procedures have harmed a participant, they take reasonable steps to minimize the harm.

2. Privacy and Confidentiality (Sections 4.01-4.05)

Psychologists have a primary obligation and take reasonable precautions to protect confidential information.

Psychologists discuss with persons the relevant limits of confidentiality.

Psychologists discuss confidential information only for appropriate scientific or professional purposes, and only with persons clearly concerned with such matters.

Psychologists may disclose confidential information with the appropriate consent of the individual or another legally authorized person on behalf of the participant, unless prohibited by law.

3. Institutional Approval (Section 8.01)

When institutional approval is required, psychologists provide accurate information about their research proposals and obtain approval prior to conducting the research. They conduct research in accordance with the approved research protocol.

4. Competence (Sections 2.01 and 2.05)

Psychologists conduct research with populations and in areas only within the boundaries of their competence.

Psychologists planning to conduct research involving populations, area, techniques, or technologies new to them undertake relevant education, training, supervised experience, consultation or study.

Psychologists who delegate work to research assistants take reasonable steps to authorize only those responsibilities that such persons can be expected to perform competently on the basis of their education, training, or experience, and see that such persons perform these services competently.

5. Record Keeping (Sections 6.01-6.02)

Psychologists create, and to the extent the records are under their control, maintain, disseminate, store, retain, and dispose of records and data relating to their scientific work in order to allow for replication of research design and analyses and meet institutional requirements.

Psychologists maintain confidentiality in creating, storing, accessing, transferring, and disposing of records under their control, whether these are written, automated, or in any other medium.

6. Informed Consent to Research (Sections 3.10 and 8.02-8.04)

When psychologists conduct research they obtain informed consent of the individual using language that is reasonably understandable to that person except when conducting such activities without consent.

For persons who are legally incapable of giving informed consent, psychologists nevertheless (1) provide an appropriate explanation, (2) seek the individual's assent, (3) consider such persons' preferences and best interests, and (4) obtain appropriate permission from a legally authorized person, if such substitute consent is permitted or required by law.

When obtaining informed consent, psychologists inform participants about:

a. the purpose of the research, expected duration, and procedures.

TABLE **3.2**

Selected Elements from the APA Ethical Guidelines Concerning
Human Participants in Research—cont'd

b. their right to decline to participate and to
   withdraw from the research once participation
   has begun.
c. the foreseeable consequences of declining or
   withdrawing.
d. reasonable foreseeable factors that may be
   expected to influence their willingness to
   participate (such as potential risks, discomfort,
   or adverse effects).
e. any prospective research benefits.
f. limits of confidentiality.
g. incentives for participation.
h. who to contact for questions about the research
   and research participants' rights.
   They provide opportunity for the prospective
participants to ask questions and receive answers.
   Psychologists conducting intervention research
involving the use of experimental treatments clarify
to participants at the onset of the research:
a. the experimental nature of the treatment.
b. the services that will or will not be available to
   the control group(s) if appropriate.
c. the means by which assignment to treatment and
   control groups will be made.
d. available treatment alternatives if an individual
   does not wish to participate in the research or
   wishes to withdraw once the study has begun.
e. compensation for or monetary costs of participating.
Psychologists obtain informed consent from
research participants prior to recording their voices
or images for data collection unless: (1) the research
consists solely of naturalistic observations in public
places, and it is not anticipated that the recording
will be used in a manner that could cause personal
identification or harm; or (2) the research design
includes deception, and consent for the use of the
recording is obtained during the debriefing (see also
Standard 8.07, Deception in Research).
   When psychologists conduct research with
students or subordinates as participants, psychologists take steps to protect the prospective participants from adverse consequences of declining or
withdrawing from participation.

When research participation is a course requirement or an opportunity for extra credit, the
prospective participant is given the choice of
equitable alternative activities.

7. Dispensing with Informed Consent (Section 8.05)

Psychologists may dispense with informed consent
only (1) where research would not reasonably be
assumed to create distress or harm, and involves:
a. the study of normal educational practices,
   curricula, or classroom management methods
   conducted in educational settings.
b. only anonymous questionnaires, naturalistic
   observations, or archival research for which
   disclosure of responses would not place participants at risk of criminal or civil liability or
   damage their reputation, and confidentiality is
   protected.
c. the study of factors related to job or organization
   effectiveness conducted in organizational
   settings for which there is no risk to participants'
   employability, and confidentiality is protected.
   or (2) where otherwise permitted by law or
   federal or institutional regulations.

8. Offering Inducements for Research Participation (Section 8.06)

Psychologists make reasonable efforts to avoid
offering excessive or inappropriate financial or
other inducements for research participation
when such inducements are likely to coerce
participation.

9. Deception in Research (Section 8.07)

Psychologists do not conduct a study involving
deception unless they have determined that the use
of deceptive techniques is justified by the study's
significant prospective scientific, educational, or
applied value, and that effective non-deceptive alternative procedures are not feasible.

Continued

TABLE **3.2**
Selected Elements from the APA Ethical Guidelines Concerning
Human Participants in Research—cont'd

	10. Debriefing (Section 8.08)
Psychologists do not deceive prospective participants about research that is reasonably expected to cause physical pain or severe emotional distress. Psychologists explain any deception that is an integral feature of the design and conduct of an experiment to participants as early as is feasible, preferably at the conclusion of their participation but no later than the conclusion of the data collection, and permit participants to withdraw their data (see also Standard 8.08, Debriefing).	Psychologists provide a prompt opportunity for participants to obtain appropriate information about the nature, results, and conclusions of the research, and then take reasonable steps to correct any misconceptions that participants may have of which the psychologists are aware. If scientific or humane values justify delaying or withholding this information, psychologists take reasonable measures to reduce the risk of harm.

Source: From Ethical Principles of Psychologists and Code of Conduct from *American Psychologist*, 2002, 57, 1060–1073. Copyright 2002 by the American Psychological Association. Reprinted with permission.

generate their own mental distress from imaginative speculation about the purpose of the research. In either case, researchers should reassure participants by explaining before the study exactly what will be done and why (insofar as possible), and by providing a complete explanation and justification for the research as soon as possible after the study is completed. The goal is for participants to leave the study feeling just as well as when they entered. (Deception and how to deal with it are covered in more detail in a later section.) Finally, research involving sensitive topics such as physical or sexual abuse and violence against women can produce serious ethical dilemmas for researchers who risk retraumatizing their participants by reawakening memories of prior traumas (Fontes, 2004).

One area of current debate concerning the issue of no harm is the topic of **clinical equipoise** (Young, 2002). The basic concept is that clinicians have an ethical responsibility to provide the best possible treatment for their patients. However, many research studies evaluate and compare different treatment options by randomly assigning patients to different treatments. If the clinician knows (or even believes) that one of the treatment conditions is inferior to the others, then some patients are being denied the best possible treatment and the ethical principle of no harm is being violated. The solution to this dilemma is to conduct studies that only compare equally preferred treatments; this is the principle of clinical equipoise. This means that a researcher can compare treatments when:

a. there is honest uncertainty about which treatment is best.
b. there is honest professional disagreement among experts concerning which treatment is best.

Note that universally adopting the principle of equipoise would effectively eliminate many common research studies such as those that involve a no-treatment control group or studies that compare an active drug with a placebo. It is unlikely that this will happen in the near future.

In general, the principle of no harm means that a researcher is obligated to anticipate and remove any harmful elements in a research study. During the study, a researcher also must monitor the well-being of the participants and halt the study at any sign of trouble. A classic example of monitoring wellbeing is a prison simulation study by Haney, Banks, and Zimbardo (1973). In this study, male undergraduates were randomly assigned to play the roles of prisoners and guards for a 1-week period. Except for prohibiting physical abuse, the participants did not receive any specific training. Within a few days, however, the prisoners began to display signs of depression and helplessness, and the guards showed aggressive and dehumanizing behavior toward the prisoners. Half of the prisoners developed severe emotional disturbances and had to be "released" for their own well-being. Ultimately, the entire study was stopped prematurely for the safety of the remaining participants. Although these results are somewhat extreme, they do demonstrate the need for continuous observation during the course of a research study to ensure that the no-harm principle is maintained throughout.

 **LEARNING CHECK** When is risk in a study justified?

Informed Consent (Item 6, Table 3.2)   The general concept of **informed consent** is that human participants should be given complete information about the research and their roles in it before agreeing to participate. They should understand the information and then voluntarily decide whether to participate. This ideal is often difficult to achieve. Here, we consider three components of informed consent and examine the problems that can exist with each.

1. *Information:* Often, it is difficult or impossible to provide participants with complete information about a research study prior to their participation. One common practice is to keep participants "blind" to the purpose of the study. If participants know that one treatment is supposed to produce better performance, they may adjust their own levels of performance in an attempt to satisfy the experimenter. To avoid this problem, researchers often tell participants exactly what will be done in the study but do not explain why. In situations in which the study relies on deception, disguised measurement, concealed observation, and so on, informing the participants would undermine the goals of the research. In clinical research, the outcome of an experimental therapy (risks and benefits) may not be known. In this case, a researcher may not be able to tell the participant exactly what will happen. Although some information may be disguised, concealed, or simply unknown, it is essential that participants be informed of any known potential risks.
2. *Understanding:* Simply telling participants about the research does not necessarily mean they are informed, especially in situations in which the participants may not be competent enough to understand. This problem occurs routinely with special populations such as young children,

developmentally disabled people, and psychiatric patients. In these situations, it is customary to provide information to the participant as well as to a parent or guardian who also must approve of the participation. With special populations, researchers occasionally speak of obtaining *assent* from the participants and *consent* from an official guardian. Even with regular populations, there may be some question about true understanding. Researchers must express their explanations in terms that the participants can easily understand and should give the participants ample opportunity to ask questions.

3. *Voluntary Participation:* The goal of informed consent is that participants should decide to participate of their own free will. Often, however, participants may feel coerced to participate or perceive that they have limited choice. For example, a researcher who is a teacher, professor, or clinician may be in a position of power or control over the potential participants who may perceive a threat of retribution if they do not cooperate. Suppose, for example, that your professor asked for volunteers from the class to help with a research project. Would you feel a little extra pressure to volunteer just to avoid jeopardizing your grade in the class? This problem is particularly important with institutionalized populations (prisoners, hospital patients, and so on) who must depend on others in nearly every aspect of their lives. In these cases, it is especially important that the researcher explain to the participants that they are completely free to decline participation or to leave the study at any time without negative consequences.

DEFINITION   The principle of **informed consent** requires the investigator to provide all available information about a study so that an individual can make a rational, informed decision to participate in the study.

The procedure for obtaining informed consent varies from study to study, depending in part on the complexity of the information presented and the actual degree of risk involved in the study. In most situations, researchers use a written consent form. A **consent form** contains a statement of all the elements of informed consent and a line for the participant's and/or guardian's signature. The form is provided before the study so the potential participants have all the information they need to make an informed decision regarding participation. Consent forms vary according to the specifics of the study but typically contain some common elements. Table 3.3 lists the common components of consent forms (Kazdin, 2003).

Although consent forms are very commonly used, in some situations involving minimal risk, it is possible to obtain verbal consent without a written consent form. And in some situations (such as the administration of anonymous questionnaires), it is permissible to dispense with informed consent entirely (see Item 7 in Table 3.2, and further discussion in the IRB section on page 90).

TABLE **3.3**
Components of Informed Consent Forms

Section of the Form	Purpose and Contents
Overview	Presentation of the goals of the study, why this study is being conducted, and who is responsible for the study and its execution.
Description of Procedures	Clarification of the experimental conditions, assessment procedures, and requirements of the participants.
Risks and Inconveniences	Statement of any physical and psychological risks and an estimate of their likelihood. Inconveniences and demands to be placed on the participants (e.g., how many sessions, requests to do anything, or contact at home).
Benefits	A statement of what the participants can reasonably hope to gain from participation, including psychological, physical, and monetary benefits.
Costs and Economic Considerations	Charges to the participants (e.g., in treatment) and payment (e.g., for participation or completing various forms).
Confidentiality	Assurances that the information is confidential and will only be seen by people who need to do so for the purposes of research (e.g., scoring and data analyses), procedures to assure confidentiality (e.g., removal of names from forms, storage of data). Also, caveats are included here if it is possible that sensitive information (e.g., psychiatric information, criminal activity) can be subpoenaed.
Alternative Treatments	In an intervention study, alternatives available to the client before or during participation are outlined.
Voluntary Participation	A statement that the participant is willing to participate and can decline participation now or later without penalty of any kind.
Questions and Further Information	A statement that the participant is encouraged to ask questions at any time and can contact one or more individuals (listed by name and phone number) who are available for such questions.
Signature Lines	A place for the participant and the experimenter to sign.

Source: From Kazdin, A. E., *Research Design in Clinical Psychology.* Copyright 2003 by Allyn & Bacon. Reprinted by permission.

 **LEARNING CHECK**   Explain the role of voluntary participation in informed consent.

Deception (Item 9, Table 3.2)   Often, the goal of a research study is to examine behavior under "normal" circumstances. To achieve this goal, researchers must sometimes use **deception.**

For example, if participants know the true purpose of a research study, they may modify their natural behaviors to conceal embarrassing secrets or to appear to be better than they really are. To avoid this problem, researchers sometimes do not tell participants the true purpose of the study. One technique is to use **passive deception,** or omission, and simply withhold information about the study. Another possibility is to use **active deception,** or commission, and deliberately present false or misleading information. In simple terms, passive deception is keeping secrets and active deception is telling lies.

In a classic study of human memory, for example, Craik and Lockhart (1972) did not inform the participants that they were involved in a study of memory (passive deception). Instead, the participants viewed words that were presented one at a time, and were asked to respond to the words in different ways. Some participants were asked to decide whether the word was printed in uppercase letters or lowercase letters. Others were asked to make judgments about the meaning of each word. After responding to a large number of words, the participants were given a surprise memory test and asked to recall as many of the words as possible. None of the participants were informed that the true purpose of the study was to test memory. In this case, the deception was necessary to prevent the participants from trying to memorize the words as they were presented.

Active deception can take a variety of forms. For example, a researcher can state an explicit lie about the study, give false information about stimulus materials, give false feedback about a participant's performance, or use **confederates** to create a false environment. Although there is some evidence that the use of active deception is declining (Nicks, Korn, & Mainieri, 1997), this technique has been standard practice in many areas of research, particularly in social psychology. For example, Asch (1956) told participants that they were in a perception study, and asked each individual in a group of eight to identify the stimulus line that correctly matched the length of a standard line. Seven of the eight individuals were confederates working with Asch. For the first few lines, the confederates selected the correct match, but on later trials, they unanimously picked what was obviously the wrong line. Although the real participants often appeared anxious and confused, nearly one-third of them conformed to the group behavior and also picked the obviously wrong line. Asch was able to demonstrate this level of social conformity by actively deceiving his participants. If individuals are simply asked whether they conform, the vast majority say no (Wolosin, Sherman, & Mynat, 1972).

In a more recent study examining the psychology of false confessions, Kassin and Kiechel (1996) were able to trick participants into accepting guilt for a crime they did not commit. The participants were told that they were in a reaction time experiment using a computer keyboard to record responses. In addition, they were warned not to press a specific key because it would damage the computer. After 60 seconds of the reaction time task, the computer suddenly quit and the participant was accused of hitting the wrong key. In some instances, a confederate also said that she saw the participant hit the wrong key. Although all the participants were truly innocent and initially denied the crime, many ultimately confessed and internalized guilt for damaging the computer. In this study, the researchers used active deception to generate an unusual behavior (false confessions) in a controlled laboratory situation where it could be examined scientifically.

> Confederates are people who pretend to be participants in a research study but actually work for the researcher.

DEFINITIONS

Deception occurs when a researcher purposefully withholds information or misleads participants with regard to information about a study. There are two forms of deception: passive and active.

Passive deception (or omission) is the withholding or omitting of information; the researcher intentionally does not tell participants some information about the study.

Active deception (or commission) is the presenting of misinformation about the study to participants. The most common form of active deception is misleading participants about the specific purpose of the study.

In any study involving deception, the principle of informed consent is compromised because participants are not given complete and accurate information. In these situations, a researcher has a special responsibility to safeguard the participants. The APA guidelines identify three specific areas of responsibility (see Item 9 in Table 3.2):

1. The deception must be justified in terms of some significant benefit that outweighs the risk to the participants. The researcher must consider all alternatives to deception and must justify the rejection of any alternative procedures.
2. The researcher cannot conceal from the prospective participants information about research that is expected to cause physical pain or severe emotional distress.
3. The researcher must debrief the participants by providing a complete explanation as soon as possible after participation is completed.

The first point, justification of the deception, obviously involves weighing the benefits of the study against the rights of the individual participants. Usually, the final decision is not left entirely to the researcher but requires review and approval by a group of individuals charged with the responsibility of ensuring ethical conduct in all human research (for example, the IRB, which is discussed later). This review group also can suggest alternative procedures not requiring deception, and the researcher must consider and respond to its suggestions (the review process is also discussed later).

The second point is that researchers definitely cannot use deception to withhold information about risk or possible harm. Suppose, for example, that a researcher wants to examine the influence of increased anxiety on performance. To increase anxiety, the researcher informs one group of participants that they may receive relatively mild electric shocks occasionally during the course of the study. No shocks are actually given, so the researcher is deceiving the participants; however, this type of deception involves no harm or risk, and probably would be considered acceptable. On the other hand, suppose that the researcher wants to examine how performance is influenced by sudden, unexpected episodes of pain. To create these episodes, the researcher occasionally administers mild shocks during the study without warning the participants. To ensure that the shocks are unexpected, the informed consent process does not include any mention of shocks. In this case, the researcher is withholding information about a potential risk, and this type of deception is not allowed.

The final point is that deceived participants must receive a **debriefing** that provides a full description of the true purpose of the study, including the use and purpose of deception, after the study is completed. The debriefing serves many purposes, including:

- conveying what the study was really all about, if deception was used
- counteracting or minimizing any negative effects of the study
- conveying the educational objective of the research (i.e., explaining the value of the research and the contribution to science of participation in the research)
- explaining the nature of and justification for any deception used
- answering any questions the participant has

DEFINITION	A **debriefing** is a post-experimental explanation of the purpose of a study that is given to a participant, especially if deception was used.

Overall, the intent of debriefing is to counteract or minimize harmful effects. Unfortunately, evidence suggests that debriefing may not always achieve its purpose. Although some studies show that debriefing can effectively remove harm and leave no lingering effects (Holmes, 1976a, 1976b; Smith & Richardson, 1983), other studies indicate that debriefing is not effective, is not believed, and may result in increased suspicion (Fisher & Fyrberg, 1994; Ring, Wallston, & Corey, 1970). Most of this work is based on studies in which participants were interviewed immediately after being debriefed. However, some researchers believe that participants may not truthfully reveal their reactions to debriefing, especially when the debriefing informs them of previous deception (Baumrind, 1985; Rubin, 1985). Finally, there is some evidence that debriefing only further annoys or embarrasses participants (Fisher & Fyrberg, 1994); not only were they deceived during the study, but also the researcher is forcing them to face that fact. Still, the participants deserve a full and complete explanation, and the researcher has an obligation to safeguard participants as much as possible. Some things that seem to influence a debriefing's effectiveness include:

- the participants' suspicions (how likely they are to think the debriefing is merely a continuation of the deception)
- the nature of the deception (whether it was passive or active; debriefing is less effective with active deception)
- the sincerity of the experimenter (the last thing a participant needs is a condescending experimenter)
- the time interval between the end of the study and the delivery of the debriefing (the sooner the better)

In some situations, the research design permits a researcher to inform participants that deception may be involved and to ask the participants for consent to be deceived. Drug research, for example, often involves comparison of one group of participants who receive the drug and a second group of participants who are given a **placebo** (an ineffective, inert substitute). At the beginning of the experiment, all participants are informed that a placebo group exists, but none know whether they are in the drug group or the placebo group. Thus, before they consent to participate, participants are informed that they may be deceived. This kind of prior disclosure helps minimize the negative effects of deception: that is, participants are less likely to become angry, or feel tricked or abused. On the other hand, when participants know that deception is involved, they are likely to become more defensive and suspicious of all aspects of the research. In addition, participants may adopt unusual responses or behaviors that can undermine the goals of the research. For example, in some studies that examined the effectiveness of experimental AIDS medications, groups of participants conspired to divide and share their medications, assuming that this strategy would ensure that everyone got at least some of the real drug (Melton, Levine, Koocher, Rosenthal, & Thompson, 1988).

Deception can also cause participants to become skeptical of experiments in general. Having been deceived, a person may refuse to participate in any future research or may enter future studies with a defensive or hostile attitude. Deceived participants may share their negative attitudes and opinions with their friends, and one deceptive experiment may contaminate an entire pool of potential research participants.

LEARNING CHECKS

Explain the difference between passive and active deception.

What limits are put on deception to minimize the contradiction between deception and the principle of informed consent?

What factors can influence the effectiveness of a debriefing?

Confidentiality (Item 2, Table 3.2)   The essence of research in the behavioral sciences is the collection of information by researchers from the individuals who participate in their studies. Although the specific information can vary tremendously from one study to another, the different types of information can be categorized as follows:

- attitudes and opinions; for example, politics and prejudices
- measures of performance; for example, manual dexterity, reaction time, and memory
- demographic characteristics; for example, age, income, and sexual orientation

The APA ethical guideline requiring that researchers ensure the confidentiality of their research participants is similar to the Health Insurance Portability and Accountability Act (HIPAA) of 1996 provision that addresses the security and privacy of health information.

Any of these items can be considered private and personal by some people, and it is reasonable that some participants would not want this information to be made public. Therefore, the APA ethical guidelines require that researchers ensure the confidentiality of their research participants (see Item 2 in Table 3.2). **Confidentiality** ensures that the information obtained from a research participant will be kept secret and private. The enforcement of confidentiality benefits both the participants and the researcher. First, participants are protected from embarrassment or emotional stress that could result from public exposure. Also, researchers are more likely to obtain willing and honest participants. Most individuals demand an assurance of confidentiality before they are willing to disclose personal and private information.

Although there are different techniques for preserving confidentiality, the basic process involves ensuring that participants' records are kept anonymous. **Anonymity** means that the information and measurements obtained from each participant are not referred to by the participant's name, either during the course of the study or in the written report of the research results.

DEFINITIONS

Confidentiality is the practice of keeping strictly secret and private the information or measurements obtained from an individual during a research study.

    Anonymity is the practice of ensuring that an individual's name is not directly associated with the information or measurements obtained from that individual.

To ensure the confidentiality of the data, usually, one of the following two strategies is used:

1. No names or other identification appear on data records. This strategy is used in situations in which there is no need whatsoever to link an individual participant to the specific information that she provides. For example, a study may involve participants completing a questionnaire concerning their attitudes about racial discrimination in the work place, or individuals may be observed in a campus café to record their recycling behavior. If participants are promised payment or extra credit, researchers often keep a separate list of the participants so that they can receive promised payment or extra credit, and so they can be contacted later if necessary. However, this list is completely separate from the data and is destroyed at the end of the study. There is no way that the researcher or anyone else can connect a specific set of responses to a specific participant.

2. Researchers use a coding system to keep track of which participant names go with which sets of data. This strategy is used in situations in which it is necessary to reconnect specific names with specific data at different times during a research study. For example, a study may involve measuring the same participants at different times under different conditions. In this case, the researcher wants to examine how each participant changes over time. When a participant shows up for the third stage of the study, the researcher must be able to retrieve the same participant's responses from the first two stages. Only the code name or code number identifies the actual data, and the researcher keeps a separate, secured list to connect the participants with the codes. Thus, anyone who has access to the data has only the codes and cannot associate a specific participant with any specific data. The secured list is used only to retrieve previous data from a particular participant, and the list is destroyed at the conclusion of the study.

In most research reports, the results are presented as average values that have been collapsed across a large group of individual participants, and there is no mention of any individual participants, code numbers, or code names. In situations in which a single participant is examined in great detail, researchers must take special care to preserve anonymity. In these situations, only the code name or code number is used to identify the participant, and any description of the participant is edited to eliminate unique characteristics that could lead to individual identification.

LEARNING CHECK   Explain how the enforcement of confidentiality benefits both the participants and the researcher.

The Institutional Review Board

Although the final responsibility for the protection of human participants rests with the researcher, most human–participant research must be reviewed and approved by a group of individuals not directly affiliated with the specific research study. As part of the guidelines for the protection of human participants, the U.S. Department of Health and Human Services (HHS) requires review of all human–participant research conducted by government agencies and institutions receiving government funds. This includes all colleges, universities, hospitals, and clinics, essentially every place that human-participant research takes place. This review is to assure compliance with all requirements of Title 45, Part 46 of the Code of Federal Regulations (45 CFR 46). The **Common Rule,** as it is typically referred to, published in 1991, is based on the principles of the Belmont Report and provides a common set of federal regulations for protecting human participants to be used by review boards (Dunn & Chadwick, 1999).

Each institution or agency is required to establish a committee called an **Institutional Review Board (IRB),** which is composed of both scientists and nonscientists. The IRB examines all proposed research involving human participants with respect to seven basic criteria. If the IRB finds that a proposed research study fails to satisfy any one of the criteria, the research project is not approved. In addition, the IRB can require a research proposal be modified to meet its criteria before the research is approved. Following is a listing and brief discussion of the seven basic IRB criteria (Maloney, 1984).

1. *Minimization of Risk to Participants.* The purpose of this criterion is to ensure that research procedures do not unnecessarily expose participants to risk. In addition to evaluating the degree of risk in a proposed study, the IRB reviews the research to ensure that every precaution has been taken to minimize risk. This may involve requiring the researcher to justify any component of the research plan that involves risk, and the IRB may suggest or require alternative procedures.
2. *Reasonable Risk in Relation to Benefits.* The IRB is responsible for evaluating the potential risks to participants as well as the benefits that result from the research. The benefits include immediate benefits to the participants as well as general benefits such as advanced knowledge.
3. *Equitable Selection.* The purpose of this criterion is to ensure that the participant selection process does not discriminate among individuals in

the population and does not exploit vulnerable individuals. For example, a researcher recruiting volunteers from the general community can inadvertently exclude the Spanish-speaking population if all the publicity soliciting participants is in English. The issue for the IRB is not to ensure a random sample (although this should benefit the researcher) but rather to ensure equal opportunity for all potential participants. The concern with vulnerability is that some individuals (children and people who are developmentally disabled, psychologically impaired, or institutionalized) might be easily tricked or coerced into "volunteering" without a complete understanding of their actions.

4. *Informed Consent.* The notion of informed consent is one of the basic elements of all ethical codes and is a primary concern for the IRB. The IRB carefully reviews and critiques the procedures used to obtain informed consent, making sure that the researcher provides complete information about all aspects of the research that might be of interest or concern to a potential participant. In addition, the IRB ensures that the information is presented in a form that participants can easily understand. For example, the information should be in everyday language and presented at a level appropriate for the specific participants (the presentation of information for college students would be different from the presentation for 6-year-old children). In addition, the IRB typically looks for a clear statement informing participants that they have the right to withdraw from the study at any time without penalty. The goal is to ensure that participants receive complete information and understand the information before they decide to participate in the research.

5. *Documentation of Informed Consent.* The IRB determines whether it is necessary to have a written consent form signed by the participant and the researcher.

6. *Data Monitoring.* During the course of the research study, the researcher should make provision for monitoring the data to determine whether any unexpected risks or causes of harm have developed. In some research situations, the researcher should monitor the testing of each individual participant so the procedure can be interrupted or stopped at the first indication of developing harm or danger.

7. *Privacy and Confidentiality.* This criterion is intended to protect participants from the risk that information obtained during a research study could be released to outside individuals (parents, teachers, employers, peers) where it might have embarrassing or personally damaging consequences. The IRB examines all record keeping within the study: How are participants identified? How are data coded? Who has access to participant names and data? The goal is to guarantee basic rights of privacy and to ensure confidentiality for the participants.

To implement the criteria for approval of human-participant research, the IRB typically requires that researchers submit a written research proposal that addresses each of the seven criteria. Often, the local IRB has forms that a researcher must complete. Research proposals are classified into three categories that determine how each proposal will be reviewed. A proposal fits in

Category I (Exempt Review) if the research presents no possible risk to adult participants. Examples of Category I proposals include anonymous, mailed surveys on innocuous topics and anonymous observation of public behavior. This research is exempt from the requirements of informed consent, and the proposal is reviewed by the IRB Chair. A proposal fits in Category II (Expedited Review) if the research presents no more than minimal risk to participants, and typically includes research on individual or group behavior of normal adults when there is no psychological intervention or deception. Research under this category does not require written documentation of informed consent, but oral consent is required. Category II proposals are reviewed by several IRB members. Also note that most often, classroom research projects fall into the expedited review category. Category III (Full Review) is used for research proposals that include any questionable elements such as special populations, unusual equipment or procedures, deception, intervention, or invasive measurements. A meeting of all of the IRB members is required, and the researcher must appear in person to discuss, explain, and answer questions about the research. During the discussion of Category III research, the IRB members may become active participants in the development of the research plan, making suggestions or contributions that modify the research proposal. Throughout the process, the primary concern of the IRB is to ensure the protection of human participants.

DEFINITION

The **Institutional Review Board (IRB)** is a committee that examines all proposed research with respect to its treatment of human participants. IRB approval must be obtained before any research is conducted with human participants.

 **LEARNING CHECK**

Describe in your own words the criteria that the IRB uses to evaluate proposed research.

3.3 | ETHICAL ISSUES AND NONHUMAN SUBJECTS IN RESEARCH

Thus far, we have considered ethical issues involving human participants in research. However, much research is conducted with nonhumans—animals—as subjects, and here, too, many ethical issues must be considered. For many people, the first ethical question is whether nonhuman subjects should be used at all in behavioral research. However, nonhuman subjects have been a part of behavioral science research for more than 100 years and probably will continue to be used as research subjects for the foreseeable future. Researchers who use nonhumans as subjects do so for a variety of reasons including: (1) to understand animals for their own sake; (2) to understand humans (many processes can be generalized from nonhumans to humans); and (3) to conduct research that is impossible to conduct using human participants. Two excellent articles that examine both sides of the animal rights issue appeared back to back in the 1993 Journal of Social Issues (Baldwin, 1993; Bowd & Shapiro, 1993). The animal research debate is also presented in a pair of articles in the February 1997 issue of Scientific American (Barnard & Kaufman, 1997; Botting & Morrison, 1997) and in Gluck and Bell (2003).

Historical Highlights of Treatment of Nonhuman Subjects

To protect the welfare of nonhumans, various organizations have been formed including the Society for the Prevention of Cruelty to Animals (SPCA), established in the United States in 1866 (Ray, 2000). More recent regulation of the use of nonhumans in research began in 1962, when the federal government first issued guidelines. In 1966, the Animal Welfare Act was enacted; it was most recently amended in 2007. The Animal Welfare Act deals with general standards for animal care. In addition, the U.S. Government Principles for the Utilization and Care of Vertebrate Animals Used in Testing, Research, and Training were incorporated into the Public Health Service (PHS) Policy on Humans and Use of Laboratory Animals in 1986, and continue to provide a framework for conducting research (Office of Laboratory Animal Welfare, 2002). Several organizations, including the American Association for Laboratory Animal Science (AALAS) and the American Association for Accreditation of Laboratory Animal Care (AAALAC), encourage monitoring the care of laboratory animals by researchers.

Today, the federal government regulates the use of nonhuman subjects in research. It requires researchers using nonhuman subjects to follow (1) the guidelines of the local IACUC (the review board for animal research, similar to the IRB, to be discussed later); (2) the U.S. Department of Agriculture's guidelines; (3) guidelines of state agencies; and (4) established guidelines within the academic discipline (for example, the APA guidelines in psychology). The U.S. Department of Agriculture's requirements for use of nonhumans in research can be found in the *Guide for the Care and Use of Laboratory Animals* (National Research Council, 1996). The PHS requires institutions to use the Guide for activities involving animals.

American Psychological Association Guidelines

Ethical Guidelines for the Use and Treatment of Nonhuman Subjects in Research

The APA has prepared a set of ethical guidelines for the use and treatment of nonhuman subjects that parallels the guidelines for human participants presented earlier. Table 3.4 lists the basic standards of the APA Ethics Code for the care and use of animal subjects (APA, 2002). In addition, the APA's Committee on Animal Research and Ethics (CARE) has prepared even more detailed guidelines for researchers working with nonhuman subjects (APA, 1996). This document, *Guidelines for Ethical Conduct in the Care and Use of Animals,* can be obtained from APA's website at www.apa.org/science/rcr/guidelines.pdf. Anyone planning to conduct research with nonhuman subjects should carefully review and abide by these guidelines. As is the case with human participants, the APA guidelines—as well as federal, state, and local regulations—are continually reviewed and revised; researchers should always check to make sure they are abiding by the current rules.

TABLE **3.4**
2002 APA Ethical Principles for the Humane Care and Use of Animals in Research

The following ethical standard is reprinted from the *Ethical Principles of Psychologists and Code of Conduct* (APA, 2002).

8.09 Humane Care and Use of Animals in Research

a. Psychologists acquire, care for, use, and dispose of all animals in compliance with current federal, state, and local laws and regulations, and with professional standards.
b. Psychologists trained in research methods and experienced in the care of laboratory animals closely supervise all procedures involving animals and are responsible for ensuring appropriate consideration of their comfort, health, and humane treatment.
c. Psychologists ensure that all individuals under their supervision who are using animals have received instruction in research methods and in the care, maintenance, and handling of the species being used, to the extent appropriate for their role.
d. Psychologists make reasonable efforts to minimize discomfort, infection, illness, and pain of animal subjects.
e. Psychologists use a procedure subjecting animals to pain, stress, or privation only when an alternative procedure is unavailable and the goal is justified by its prospective scientific, educational, or applied value.
f. Psychologists perform surgical procedures under appropriate anesthesia and follow techniques to avoid infection and minimize pain during and after surgery.
g. When it is appropriate that an animal's life be terminated, psychologists proceed rapidly, with an effort to minimize pain, and in accordance with accepted procedures.

Major Ethical Issues

The list in Table 3.4 includes many of the same elements contained in the human participants code. In particular, qualified individuals must conduct research, the research must be justified, and the researcher has a responsibility to minimize discomfort or harm. Because most research animals are housed in a laboratory setting before and after their research experience, the code also extends to the general care and maintenance of animal subjects. In particular, the code refers to federal, state, and local regulations that govern housing conditions, food, sanitation, and medical care for research animals.

The Institutional Animal Care and Use Committee

Institutions that conduct research with animals have an animal research review board called the **Institutional Animal Care and Use Committee (IACUC)**. The IACUC is responsible for reviewing and approving all research using animal subjects in much the same way that the IRB monitors research with humans. The purpose of the committee is to protect animal subjects by ensuring that all research meets the criteria established by the code of ethics. Researchers must submit proposals to the committee and obtain approval before beginning any research with animal subjects. According to the *Guide for the Care and Use of Laboratory Animals* (National Research Council, 1996), the committee must consist of a veterinarian, at least one scientist experienced in research involving animals, and one member of the public with no affiliation with the institution where the research is being conducted.

DEFINITION	The **Institutional Animal Care and Use Committee (IACUC)** is a committee that examines all proposed research with respect to its treatment of nonhuman subjects. IACUC approval must be obtained prior to conducting any research with nonhuman subjects.

3.4 | ETHICAL ISSUES AND SCIENTIFIC INTEGRITY

Thus far, we have discussed the ethical issues that researchers face when they make decisions about the individuals, both human and nonhuman, that participate in their research. Later in the research process, to make the research public, the investigator prepares a report describing what was done, what was found, and how the findings were interpreted (see Chapter 1, Step 9). Ethical issues can arise at this point as well. Here we consider two such issues: fraud and plagiarism. Two APA ethical standards (2002) relate to these issues:

8.10 Reporting of Research

    a. Psychologists do not fabricate data. (See also Standard 5.01, Avoidance of False or Deceptive Statements—Psychologists do not make false, deceptive, or fraudulent statements concerning their publications or research findings.)

    b. If psychologists discover significant errors in their published data, they take reasonable steps to correct such errors in a correction, retraction, erratum, or other appropriate publication means.

8.11 Plagiarism

    a. Psychologists do not present portions of another's work or data as their own, even if the other work or data source is cited occasionally.

From Ethical Principles of Psychologists and Code of Conduct from *American Psychologist*, 2002, 57, 1060–1073. Copyright 2002 by the American Psychological Association. Reprinted with permission.

Fraud in Science
Error Versus Fraud

It is important to distinguish between error and fraud. An error is an honest mistake that occurs in the research process. There are, unfortunately, many opportunities for errors to be made in research; for example, in collecting data, scoring measures, entering data into the computer, or in publication typesetting. Researchers are only human, and humans make mistakes. However, it is the investigator's responsibility to check and double-check the data to minimize the risk of errors. **Fraud,** on the other hand, is an explicit effort to falsify or misrepresent data. If a researcher makes up or changes data to make it support the hypothesis, this constitutes fraud. As you know, the essential goal of science is to discover knowledge and reveal truth, which makes fraud the ultimate enemy of the scientific process.

DEFINITION	**Fraud** is the explicit effort of a researcher to falsify or misrepresent data.

Why Is Fraud in Science Committed?

Although researchers know that their reputations and their careers will be seriously damaged if they are caught falsifying their data, on rare occasions, some researchers commit fraud. Why? The primary cause of fraud is the competitive nature of an academic career. You have probably heard the saying, "Publish or perish." There is strong pressure on researchers to have their research published. For example, tenure and promotion within academic departments are often based on research productivity. In addition, researchers must obtain significant findings if they hope to publish their research results or receive grants to support their research. Another possible motivator is a researcher's exceedingly high need for success and the admiration that comes along with it. Researchers invest a great deal of time and resources in conducting their studies, and it can be very disappointing to obtain results that cannot be published.

It is important to keep in mind that discussing possible reasons why a researcher may commit fraud in no way implies that we condone such behavior. There is no justification for such actions. We include this information only to make you aware of the forces that might influence someone to commit such an act.

Safeguards Against Fraud

Fortunately, several safeguards are built into the process of scientific research reporting to help keep fraud in check. First, researchers know that other scientists are going to read their reports and conduct further studies, including replications. The process of repeating a previous study, step by step, allows a researcher to verify the results. Recall from Chapter 1 that **replication** is one of the primary means of revealing error and uncovering fraud in research. The most common reason to suspect fraud is that a groundbreaking finding cannot be replicated.

DEFINITION	**Replication** is repetition of a research study using the same basic procedures used in the original. Either the replication supports the original study by duplicating the original results, or it casts doubt on the original study by demonstrating that the original result is not easily repeated.

A second safeguard against fraud is **peer review,** which takes place when a researcher submits a research article for publication. In a typical peer review process, the editor of the journal and a few experts in the field review the paper in extreme detail. The reviewers critically scrutinize every aspect of the research from the justification of the study to the analysis of data. The primary purpose of peer review is to evaluate the quality of the research study and the contribution it makes to scientific knowledge. The reviewers also are likely to detect anything suspect about the research or the findings.

The consequences of being found guilty of fraud probably keep many researchers honest. If it is concluded that a researcher's data are fraudulent, a number of penalties can result, including suspension or firing from a job, removal of a degree granted, cancellation of funding for research, and forced return of monies paid from grants.

LEARNING CHECK

What constitutes fraud, and what are some reasons for its occurrence?

Plagiarism

To present someone else's ideas or words as your own is to commit **plagiarism.** Plagiarism, like fraud, is a serious breach of ethics. Reference citations (giving others credit when credit is due) must be included in your paper whenever someone else's ideas or work has influenced your thinking and writing. Whenever you use direct quotations or even paraphrase someone else's work, you need to give them credit. If an idea or information you include in a paper is not originally yours, you must cite the source. For students, the penalties for plagiarism may include receipt of a failing grade on the paper or in the course, and expulsion from the institution. For faculty researchers, the penalties for plagiarism are much the same as those for fraud.

DEFINITION

Plagiarism is the representation of someone else's ideas or words as one's own, and it is unethical.

Plagiarism can occur on a variety of different levels. At one extreme, you can literally copy an entire paper word for word and present it as your own work or you can copy and paste passages from articles and sites found on the Internet. In these cases, the plagiarism is clearly a deliberate act committed with complete awareness, and is usually easy to identify, especially for faculty using programs such as TurnItIn. However, plagiarism can be much more subtle and even occur without your direct knowledge or intent. For example, while doing the background research for a paper, you may be inspired by someone's ideas or influenced by the phrases someone used to express a concept. After working on a project for an extended time, it can become difficult to separate your own words and ideas from those that come to you from outside sources. As a result, outside ideas and phrases can appear in your paper without appropriate citation, and you have committed plagiarism.

Fortunately, the following guidelines can help prevent you from plagiarizing (Myers & Hansen, 2006).

1. Take complete notes, including complete citation of the source. (For articles, include author's name, year of publication, title of the article, journal name, volume number, and page numbers. For books, also include the publisher's name and city.)
2. Within your paper, identify the source of any ideas, words, or information that are not your own.

3. Identify any direct quotes by quotation marks at the beginning and end of the quotes, and indicate where you got them.
4. Be careful about paraphrasing (restating someone else's words). It is greatly tempting to lift whole phrases or catchy words from another source. Use your own words instead, or use direct quotes. Be sure to give credit to your sources.
5. Include a complete list of references at the end of the paper. References should include all the information listed in Item 1.
6. If in doubt about whether a citation is necessary, cite the source. You will do no harm by being especially cautious.

There are occasions when your work is based directly on the ideas or words of another person and it is necessary to paraphrase or quote that person's work. For example, your research idea may stem from the results or claims made in a previously published article. To present the foundation for your idea, it is necessary to describe the previous work. In this situation, there are several points to keep in mind. First, you should realize that direct quotes are used very infrequently. They should be used only when it is absolutely necessary to capture the true essence of the statement (note that the author's original words are unlikely to be the only way to express the idea). The use of extensive quoting in a paper constitutes lazy writing. Second, when you paraphrase, you still must cite your source, because you always must give credit for presenting someone else's ideas or words. Third, paraphrasing consists of rewording the meaning or content of someone else's work—not simply repeating it. Paraphrasing is more than simply changing a word or two in each sentence. Table 3.5 shows some examples of plagiarism as well as an acceptable form of paraphrasing.

Throughout this book, we often use other people's ideas, figures, and passages (including the guidelines just stated), but note that we always acknowledge and cite the original authors, artists, and publishers. In an ironic example of failing to acknowledge sources, the University of Oregon handbook contains a section on plagiarism that is copied from the Stanford handbook (Posner, 2007). A lot of embarrassment could have been avoided by asking permission and citing their source.

 **LEARNING CHECK** Explain why plagiarism is unethical.

■ CHAPTER SUMMARY

Researchers have two basic categories of ethical responsibility: (1) responsibility to the individuals, both human and nonhuman, who participate in their research studies; and (2) responsibility to the discipline of science and to be accurate and honest in the reporting of their research. Researchers are responsible for ensuring the safety and well-being of their research participants and subjects, and must abide by all the relevant ethical guidelines when conducting research. Researchers are also obligated to present truthful and accurate

TABLE **3.5**
Examples of Plagiarism

Original text from Quirin, Kazén, and Kuhl (2009):
Are affective experiences like happiness, sadness, or helplessness always amenable to self-report? Whereas many individuals may be able to describe their affective states or traits relatively accurately, others may provide self reports that deviate from their automatic affective reactions.

(a)   Repeating large sections of text verbatim is clearly plagiarism, even with a citation.
Are people really in touch with their emotional responses? For example, are feelings like happiness, sadness, or helplessness always available for self-report? Whereas many individuals may be able to describe their feelings relatively accurately, others may provide self reports that deviate from their true reactions (Quirin, Kazén, & Kuhl, 2009).

(b)   Changing a few words is still plagiarism, even with a citation.
Are feelings like happiness, sadness, or helplessness always available for self-report? Whereas many individuals may be able to describe their feelings relatively accurately, others may provide self reports that deviate from their true reactions (Quirin, Kazén, & Kuhl, 2009).

(c)   Changing most of the wording but keeping the same structure and order of ideas is a step toward
*   paraphrasing but is still plagiarism, even with a citation.*
Is it easy for people to report their feelings? Although some people may be able to give accurate reports, others fail to provide accurate descriptions of how they feel (Quirin, Kazén, & Kuhl, 2009).

(d)   Rephrasing in your own words, using your own structure, and a citation for the original source is an
*   acceptable paraphrase (not plagiarism).*
It is difficult for many people to accurately describe their emotional responses (Quirin, Kazén, & Kuhl, 2009).

---

reports of their results and to give appropriate credit when they report the work or ideas of others.

Any research involving humans or nonhumans immediately introduces questions of ethics. Historical incidents in which human participants were injured or abused as part of a research study shaped the guidelines we have in place today. Psychological research using humans and nonhumans is regulated by the APA Ethics Code and by federal, state, and local guidelines. The primary goal of the APA Ethics Code is the welfare and protection of the individuals and groups with whom the psychologists work. Tables 3.2 and 3.4 provide summaries of the elements of the Ethics Code most relevant to the use and treatment of human participants and nonhuman subjects, respectively. The points that are most important for new researchers include the issues of no harm, informed consent, deception, and confidentiality. To assist researchers in protecting human participants and nonhuman subjects, IRBs and IACUCs examine all proposed research.

Reporting of research also introduces questions of ethics. It is assumed that reports of research are accurate and honest depictions of the procedures used and results obtained. In this chapter, we considered two reporting issues: fraud and plagiarism.

Ethics in research is an enormous topic. In this chapter, we considered the ethical decisions that researchers make when conducting research and when publishing their results. For more on the topic of research ethics, see Rosnow and Rosenthal, 1997; Sales and Folkman, 2000; and Stanley, Sieber, and Melton, 1996. In addition, if you are interested in reading a more detailed history of the development of current ethical standards, we suggest *Encyclopedia of Bioethics* (Reich, 1995).

KEY WORDS

research ethics
informed consent
deception
passive deception (omission)
active deception (commission)

debriefing
confidentiality
anonymity
Institutional Review Board
 (IRB)

Institutional Animal Care and
 Use Committee (IACUC)
fraud
replication
plagiarism

EXERCISES

1. In addition to the key words, you should also be able to define each of the following terms:
   ethics
   Nuremberg Code
   National Research Act
   Belmont Report
   APA Ethics Code
   clinical equipoise
   consent form
   confederate
   placebo
   Common Rule
   peer review
2. Summarize the major APA Ethical Principles concerning research with human participants.
3. In your own words, define the concept of informed consent and explain its purpose.
4. Describe the circumstances in which it is acceptable to conduct research without obtaining informed consent from human participants.
5. Describe one historical incident in which human participants were injured or abused as part of a research study. Describe how the injury or abuse would have been avoided if the researchers had followed today's ethical guidelines.
6. What are the safeguards against fraud in science?
7. Under what circumstances is it acceptable for a researcher to use deception in a study with human participants?
8. What does IRB stand for, and what is its purpose?
9. Describe the two strategies for maintaining participants' anonymity.
10. What kinds of information must be included accurately as part of the informed consent? (That is, what kinds of information are off limits for deception?)
11. Is it acceptable for researchers to justify the use of human participants in a study simply by saying that they are curious about what might happen? Why or why not?
12. What are some of the purposes of debriefing participants?

LEARNING ACTIVITIES

1. Although experiments typically manipulate some aspect of the environment to create different treatment conditions, it is also possible to manipulate characteristics of the participants. For example, researchers can give some participants a feeling of success and others a feeling of failure by giving false feedback about their performance or by rigging a task to make it easy or impossible (Thompson, Webber, & Montgomery, 2002). By manipulating the participants' experiences, it is possible to examine how people's performance and attitudes are influenced by success and failure.

   Other research has manipulated the participants' mood. Showing movies, playing music, or having participants read a series of positive (or negative) statements can induce different mood states (positive, negative, neutral). Being able to manipulate mood in the laboratory allows researchers to study how mood influences behaviors such as memory (Teasdale & Fogarty, 1979) or the ability to read emotions in facial expression (Bouhuys, Bloem, & Groothuis, 1995), and how other factors such as alcohol consumption affect mood (Van Tilburgh & Vingerhoets, 2002).

   Suppose you are planning a research study in which you intend to manipulate the participants' mood; that is, you plan to create a group of happy people and a group of sad people. For example, one group will spend the first 10 minutes of the experiment listening to upbeat, happy music, and the other group will listen to funeral dirges.

   a. Do you consider the manipulation of people's moods to be ethical? Explain why or why not.

   b. Would you tell your participants about the mood manipulation as part of the informed consent process before they begin the study? Explain why or why not.

   c. Assuming that you decided to use deception and not tell your participants that their moods are being manipulated, how would you justify this procedure to an IRB? What could you do to minimize the negative effects of manipulating people's moods (especially the negative mood group)?

   d. How could you determine whether the different kinds of music really influenced people's moods? (Note: This is called a manipulation check, and is discussed in Chapter 9

WEB RESOURCES

Visit the Book Companion Website at **www.cengage.com/international** to access study tools including a glossary, flashcards, and web quizzing. You will also find a link to Statistics and Research Methods Workshops. For this chapter, we suggest you look at the following workshops:

Ethical Issues

Effective Debriefing

4

Measuring Variables

CHAPTER OVERVIEW

In this chapter, we consider how researchers define and measure variables (Step 3 of the research process). Frequently, operational definitions are used to define and measure the variables. Two criteria used to evaluate the quality of a measurement procedure—validity and reliability—are discussed. We consider six methods of assessing the validity of measurement and three methods for assessing reliability, and follow with discussion of the scales of measurement, the modes of measuring, and other aspects of measurement.

4.1 | AN OVERVIEW OF MEASUREMENT

The first step in the research process is to find an unanswered question that will serve as a research idea. The second step involves forming a hypothesis, a tentative answer to the question, and using the hypothesis to make a prediction that can be empirically evaluated in a research study. If the results from the study support the prediction, we will have evidence that the hypothesis is correct. If the results refute the prediction, we must conclude that the hypothesis is wrong. The next steps in the research process involve developing a research study that empirically evaluates the prediction. To accomplish this goal, we begin by specifying how each of the variables will be measured.

In Chapter 1 (p. 18), we defined variables as characteristics or conditions that change or have different values for different individuals. Usually, researchers are interested in how variables are affected by different conditions or how variables differ from one group of individuals to another. For example, a clinician may be interested in how depression scores change in response to therapy, or a teacher may want to know how much difference there is in the reading scores for third-grade children versus fourth-grade children. To evaluate differences or changes in variables, it is essential that we are able to measure them. Thus, the next step in the research process (Step 3) is determining a method for defining and measuring the variables that are being studied.

Although we all measure things from time to time, the process of measurement in research can be complicated; it usually involves a number of decisions that have serious consequences for the outcome of a research study. Two aspects of measurement are particularly important when planning a research study or reading a research report:

1. Often, there is a not a one-to-one relationship between the variable being measured and the measurements obtained.
2. There are usually several different options for measuring any particular variable. The options chosen can influence the measurements and the interpretation of the variables.

As a more concrete example, suppose that an instructor evaluates a group of students. In this situation, the underlying variable is knowledge or mastery of subject matter, and the instructor's goal is to obtain a measure of knowledge for each student. However, it is impossible for the instructor to look inside each student's head to measure how much knowledge is there. Therefore, instructors typically give students a task (such as an exam, an essay, or a set of problems), then measure how well students perform the task. Although it makes sense to expect that performance is a reflection of knowledge, performance and knowledge are not the same thing. For example, physical illness or fatigue may affect performance on an exam, but they probably do not affect knowledge. There is not a one-to-one relationship between the variable that the instructor wants to measure (knowledge) and the actual measurements that are made (performance).

One common way instructors measure students' knowledge is to give exams and record a numerical score or a letter grade as the measurement for each student. This measurement procedure is so familiar that most students (and instructors) accept it without much thought. However, there are many options for administering and scoring exams. For example:

- The instructor may use a 100-question exam or a 10-question quiz.
- The instructor may decide to grade the students on an absolute basis or on a relative basis. Relative grading, for example, could involve ranking the exam scores from best to worst and awarding As to the top 20%, Bs to the next 20%, and so on. In this case, a grade depends on individual performance as well as on the performance of all the other students. Absolute grading might involve awarding As to everyone who scores more than 90%, Bs to everyone who scores more than 80%, and so on. In this case, your grade is determined entirely by your own performance and is not influenced by how well the other students do on the exam.
- The instructor could assign numerical grades based on the number of questions answered correctly or assign letter grades that group students into broad categories. Or the instructor could use a pass/fail grading system that simply places each student in one of two categories.

Obviously, the instructor has many different options for measuring the students' knowledge or mastery, and these different options have different consequences. For example:

- If each student receives a numerical grade for each exam, it is possible to compute an average for the course. Exam grades of 86, 92, and 74 result in an average score of 84. Letter grades, on the other hand, make determining an average more difficult; for example, what is the average of grades of A, B, and D on three exams?
- Scores from a 100-point exam provide better discrimination between students than a 10-point quiz. On the exam, for example, there is a 4-point difference between scores of 78 and 82. On the other hand, it is reasonable to expect that two students scoring 78 and 82 on the exam would both score 8 on a 10-point quiz (assuming that they each have learned about 80% of the material). Is there a real difference between the two individuals or should they both receive the same grade?
- The measurement (the exam grade) may not be an accurate reflection of the variable (knowledge). A student may learn most of the course material and then encounter an exam that focuses on one small section that he did not study. In this situation, the student ends up with a low score despite a high level of knowledge.

Thus, the selection of a measurement procedure involves decisions that can have consequences for the outcome of a research study. The remainder of this chapter deals with the general process of measurement, the different measurement options, and some of the consequences of each option.

Some variables, such as height, can be measured directly, and the measurement procedure is usually quite straightforward. Other variables—for example, hunger, motivation, or attitude about the death penalty—are more difficult to measure.
   a. Describe one procedure that might be used to measure hunger.
   b. Use the procedure you described in (a) to explain why there may not be a one-to-one relationship between a variable and the procedure used to measure it.

Choose another variable and identify different options for measuring it.

4.2 | CONSTRUCTS AND OPERATIONAL DEFINITIONS

Occasionally, a research study involves variables that are well defined, easily observed, and easily measured. For example, a study of physical development might involve the variables of height and weight. Both of these variables are tangible, concrete attributes that can be observed and measured directly. On the other hand, some studies involve intangible, abstract attributes such as motivation or self-esteem. Such variables are not directly observable, and the process of measuring them is more complicated.

Theories and Constructs

In attempting to explain and predict behavior, scientists and philosophers often develop **theories** that contain hypothetical mechanisms and intangible elements. Although these mechanisms and elements cannot be seen and are only assumed to exist, we accept them as real because they seem to describe and explain behaviors that we see. For example, a bright child does poor work in school because she has low "motivation." A kindergarten teacher may hesitate to criticize a lazy child because it may injure the student's "self-esteem." But what is motivation, and how do we know that it is low? Do we read the child's motivation meter? What about self-esteem? How do we recognize poor self-esteem or healthy self-esteem when we cannot see it in the first place? Many research variables, particularly variables of interest to behavioral scientists, are in fact hypothetical entities created from theory and speculation. Such variables are called **constructs**, or **hypothetical constructs.**

DEFINITIONS In the behavioral sciences, **theories** are statements about the mechanisms underlying a particular behavior. Theories help organize and unify different observations related to the behavior, and good theories generate predictions about the behavior.

   Constructs are hypothetical attributes or mechanisms that help explain and predict behavior in a theory.

Although constructs are hypothetical and intangible, they play very important roles in behavioral theories. In many theories, constructs can be influenced by external stimuli and, in turn, can influence external behaviors.

$$\text{External Stimulus} \rightarrow \text{Construct} \rightarrow \text{External Behavior}$$

For example, external factors such as rewards or reinforcements can affect motivation (a construct), and motivation can then affect performance. As another example, external factors such as an upcoming exam can affect anxiety (a construct) and anxiety can then affect behavior (worry, nervousness, increased heart rate, lack of concentration). Although researchers may not be able to observe and measure a construct directly, it is possible to examine the factors that theoretically influence a construct and study the behaviors that theoretically result from a construct.

 **LEARNING CHECK** | Identify another construct, such as mood (happy/sad) or fatigue (rested/tired), and describe how external factors influence it and how that influence affects behavior.

Operational Definitions

Although a construct itself cannot be directly observed or measured, it is possible to observe and measure the external factors and the behaviors that are associated with the construct. Researchers can measure these external, observable events as an indirect method of measuring the construct itself. Typically, researchers identify a behavior or a cluster of behaviors associated with a construct; the behavior is then measured, and the resulting measurements are used as a definition and a measure of the construct. This method of defining and measuring a construct is called an **operational definition.** Researchers often refer to the process of using an operational definition as *operationalizing* a construct.

DEFINITION | An **operational definition** is a procedure for measuring and defining a construct. An operational definition specifies a measurement procedure (a set of operations) for measuring an external, observable behavior, and uses the resulting measurements as a definition and a measurement of the hypothetical construct.

Probably the most familiar example of an operational definition is the IQ test, which is intended to measure intelligence. Notice that "intelligence" is a hypothetical construct; it is an internal attribute that cannot be observed directly. However, intelligence is assumed to influence external behaviors that can be observed and measured. An IQ test actually measures external behavior consisting of responses to questions. The test includes both elements of an operational definition: There are specific procedures for administering and scoring the test, and the resulting scores are used as a definition and a measurement of intelligence. Thus, although an IQ score is really a measure of intelligent behavior, we use the score both as a definition of intelligence and as a measure of it.

As another example, the construct "hunger" can be operationally defined in a variety of ways. It is possible to manipulate hunger by controlling the number of hours of food deprivation. In a research study, for example, one group could be tested immediately after eating a full meal, a second group could be tested 6 hours after eating, and a third group could be tested 12 hours after eating. In this study, we are comparing three different levels of hunger, which are defined by the number of hours without food. Alternatively, we could measure hunger for a group of rats by recording how much food each animal eats when given free access to a dish of rat chow. The amount that each rat eats defines how hungry it is.

Limitations of Operational Definitions

Although operational definitions are necessary to convert an abstract variable into a concrete entity that can be observed and studied, you should keep in mind that an operational definition is not the same as the construct itself. For example, we can define and measure variables such as intelligence, motivation, and anxiety, but in fact we are measuring external manifestations that (we hope) provide an indication of the underlying variables. As a result, there are always concerns about the quality of operational definitions and the measurements they produce.

First, it is easy for operational definitions to leave out important components of a construct. It is possible, for example, to define depression in terms of behavioral symptoms (social withdrawal, insomnia, and so on). However, behavior represents only a part of the total construct. Depression includes cognitive and emotional components that are not included in a totally behavioral definition. One way to reduce this problem is to include two or more different procedures to measure the same variable. Multiple measures for a variable are discussed in more detail on p. 126.

Second, operational definitions often include extra components that are not part of the construct being measured. For example, a self-report of depression in a clinical interview or on a questionnaire is influenced by the participant's verbal skills (ability to understand questions and express feelings and thoughts) as well as the participant's willingness to reveal personal feelings or behaviors that might be perceived as odd or undesirable. A person who is able and willing to describe her symptoms may appear to be more depressed than someone who withholds information because he is unable or unwilling to openly express himself.

Using Operational Definitions

Whenever the variables in a research study are hypothetical constructs, you must use operational definitions to define and measure the variables. Usually, however, this does not mean creating your own operational definition. The best method of determining how a variable should be measured is to consult previous research involving the same variable. Whether or not the variable is an operationally defined construct, reports of previous research describe in detail how each variable is defined and measured. By reading several research reports concerning the same variable, you typically can discover that a standard, generally accepted measurement procedure has already been developed. When you plan your own research, the best advice is to use the conventional

Authors typically describe how variables are defined and measured in the method section of a research report.

method of defining and measuring your variables. In this way, your results will be directly comparable to the results obtained in past research. However, keep in mind that any measurement procedure, particularly an operational definition, is simply an attempt to classify the variable being considered. Other measurement procedures are always possible and may provide a better way to define and measure the variable. In general, critically examine any measurement procedure and ask yourself whether a different technique might produce better measurements.

In the following section, we introduce the two general criteria used to evaluate the quality of any measurement procedure. In later sections, we examine some specific details of measurement that can influence whether a particular measurement procedure is appropriate for a particular research question. As you read through the following sections, keep in mind that the choice of a measurement procedure involves a number of decisions. Usually, there is no absolutely right or absolutely wrong choice; nonetheless, you should be aware that other researchers had options and choices when they decided how to measure their variables.

LEARNING CHECK

Briefly explain what an operational definition is and why operational definitions are sometimes necessary.

4.3 | VALIDITY AND RELIABILITY OF MEASUREMENT

In the previous section, we noted that several different methods are usually available for measuring any particular variable. How can we decide which method is best? In addition, whenever the variable is a hypothetical construct, a researcher must use an operational definition as a measurement procedure. In essence, an operational definition is an indirect method of measuring something that cannot be measured directly. How can we be sure that the measurements obtained from an operational definition actually represent the intangible construct? In general, we are asking how good a measurement procedure, or *measure,* is. Researchers have developed two general criteria for evaluating the quality of any measurement procedure: validity and reliability.

Validity of Measurement

The first criterion for evaluating a measurement procedure is **validity.** To establish validity, you must demonstrate that the measurement procedure is actually measuring what it claims to be measuring. Although the notion of validity may appear to be self-evident, there are circumstances in which legitimate questions can be asked about what really is being measured when a particular measurement procedure is used.

The question of validity is especially important whenever an operational definition is used to measure a hypothetical construct. For example, how do we measure intelligence? The answer is, we cannot. Intelligence is hypothetical and cannot be directly observed or measured. The best we can do is to measure intelligent behavior or some other external manifestation of intelligence. In the past, researchers have attempted to measure intelligence by measuring brain size (bigger brain equals greater intelligence) and bumps on the skull. Operationally, defining intelligence in terms of brain size or bumps probably seems silly, but at one time, these were viewed as valid measures of intelligence.

Similarly, we could question the validity of a standardized IQ test. Consider, for example, an absent-minded professor who has an IQ of 158 but is incredibly stupid in everyday life (constantly misplacing car keys, forgetting when and where classes are supposed to be, smoking three packs of cigarettes each day, carelessly burning holes in clothes). How intelligent is this person? Has the IQ score truly measured intelligence? Again, this is a question of validity: Does the measurement procedure accurately capture the variable that it is supposed to measure?

DEFINITION

The **validity** of a measurement procedure is the degree to which the measurement process measures the variable that it claims to measure.

Researchers have developed several methods for assessing the validity of measurement. Six of the more commonly used definitions of validity follow.

Face Validity

Face validity is the simplest and least scientific definition of validity. Face validity concerns the superficial appearance, or face value, of a measurement procedure. Does the measurement technique look like it measures the variable that it claims to measure? For example, an IQ test ought to include questions that require logic, reasoning, background knowledge, and good memory. Such questions appear to be appropriate for measuring intelligence and, therefore, have high face validity. Face validity is based on subjective judgment and is difficult to quantify. In addition, there are circumstances in which a high level of face validity can create problems. If the purpose of the measurement is obvious, the participants in a research study can see exactly what is being measured and may adjust their answers to produce a better self-image. For this reason, researchers often try to disguise the true purpose of measurement devices such as questionnaires, deliberately trying to create a measurement technique that has very little face validity.

Concurrent Validity

Often, the validity of a new measurement is established by demonstrating that the scores obtained from the new measurement technique are directly related to the scores obtained from another, better-established procedure for measuring the same variable. This is called **concurrent validity.** For example, if you had developed a new test to measure intelligence, you could demonstrate that your test really measures intelligence by showing that the scores from your test differentiate individuals in the same way as scores from a standardized IQ test. Basically, concurrent validity establishes consistency between two different procedures for measuring the same variable, suggesting that the two measurement procedures measure the same thing. Because one procedure is well established and accepted as being valid, we infer that the second procedure must also be valid. However, the simple fact that two sets of measurements are related does not necessarily mean that they are identical. For example, we could claim to measure people's height by having them step on a bathroom scale and recording the number that appears. Note that we claim to be measuring height, although we are actually measuring weight. However, we could provide support for our claim by demonstrating a reasonably strong relationship between our scores and more traditional measurements of height (taller people tend to weigh more; shorter people tend to weigh less). Although we can establish some degree of concurrent validity for our measurements, it should be obvious that a measurement of weight is not really a valid measure of height. In particular, these two measurements behave in different ways and are influenced by different factors. Manipulating diet, for example, influences weight but has little or no effect on height.

Consistency of a Relationship

Often, the validity (and reliability) of measurements can be established by demonstrating the consistency of a relationship between two different measurements. For example, concurrent validity requires that the scores obtained from a new measurement procedure are consistently related to the scores from a well-established technique for measuring the same variable. To show the amount of consistency, the two scores for each person (one score from the new measure and one score from a well-established measure) can be presented in a graph called a scatter plot. In a scatter plot, the two scores for each person are represented as a single point, with the horizontal position of the point determined by one score and the vertical position determined by the second score. Figure 4.1(a) shows an example of a consistent **positive relationship** between two measurements. The relationship is described as positive because the two measurements change together in the same direction so that people who score high on the first measurement (toward the right of the graph) also tend to score high on the second measurement (toward the top of the graph). Similarly, people scoring low on one measure also score low on the other. On the other hand, Figure 4.1(b) shows an example of a consistent **negative relationship.** This time the two measures change in opposite directions so that people who score high on one measure tend to score low on the other. For example, we could measure performance on a math test by counting the number of correct answers (measure 1) or by counting the number of errors (measure 2). These two measures should be negatively related. Finally, Figure 4.1(c) shows two measurements that are not consistently related. In this graph, some people who score high on one measurement also score high on the second, but others who score high on the first measurement now score low on the second. In this case there is no consistent, predictable relationship between the two measurements.

Often, the consistency of a relationship is determined by computing a correlation between the two measures (see Chapter 14, pp. 410–413). A consistent positive relationship like the one in Figure 4.1(a) produces a correlation near +1.00, a consistent negative relationship like the one in Figure 4.1(b)

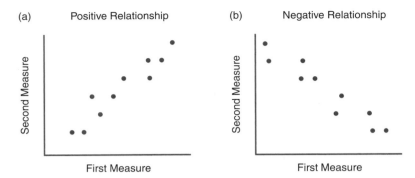

(a) Positive Relationship

(b) Negative Relationship

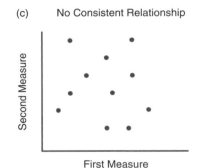

(c) No Consistent Relationship

FIGURE **4.1** Scatter Plots Showing Different Relationships

(a) a positive relationship, (b) a negative relationship, (c) no consistent relationship. Note: For the first measure, values increase from left to right. For the second measure, values increase from bottom to top.

produces a correlation near –1.00, and an inconsistent relationship like the one in Figure 4.1(c) produces a correlation near zero. The numerical value of the correlation (independent of the sign) describes the consistency of the relationship by measuring the degree to which the data points form a straight line. If the points fit perfectly on a line, the correlation is +1.00 or –1.00. If there is no linear fit whatsoever, the correlation is 0. Thus, correlations are often used to determine the degree of validity for a measurement procedure. Note that correlations are also commonly used to determine the degree of reliability for a measure.

Note that the reliability or validity of a measurement procedure is usually established with a consistent positive or a consistent negative relationship, depending on how the variables are defined and measured. For example, if a researcher develops a new timed test as a measure of intelligence, the concurrent validity of the test could be established by demonstrating that the scores from the test are consistently related to traditional IQ scores. If the researcher measures the number of items answered correctly on the test, then you would expect a consistent positive relationship between the test scores and traditional IQ scores (more correct answers go with higher IQs). However, if the researcher measures the amount of time each person needs to finish the test, you would expect a consistent negative relationship (needing more time is related to lower IQ). An inconsistent relationship, or a correlation near zero, is an indication that the measurement procedure is not valid.

Predictive Validity

Most theories make predictions about the constructs they contain. Specifically, theories predict how different values of a construct affect behavior. When the measurements of a construct accurately predict behavior (according to the theory), the measurement procedure is said to have **predictive validity.** For example, one characteristic that appears to differentiate people is need for achievement. Theoretically, need for achievement (abbreviated n-Ach) is a fundamental motivator that causes individuals to seek success in competitive and challenging situations. According to the theory, individuals with high n-Ach look for tasks that include reasonable levels of competition and challenge, and thus provide an opportunity to satisfy the need for achievement. On the other hand, individuals with low n-Ach are content with very easy tasks (offering no challenge) or with extremely difficult tasks for which success is very unlikely and probably a result of luck if it occurs at all. To evaluate this prediction, McClelland (1958) administered the n-Ach test to a group of kindergarten children and then presented the children with a ring-toss game. The goal was to toss a rope ring onto a peg. The children were allowed to choose how far from the peg they wanted to stand, and McClelland measured the distance for each child. As predicted, children with high n-Ach selected moderate distances that created a reasonably challenging game. The children with low n-Ach showed a tendency to stand very near the peg, where failure was impossible, or to stand very far from the peg, where success was very unlikely. Thus, the scores from the n-Ach test accurately predicted the behavior of the children, demonstrating predictive validity for the n-Ach test.

Construct Validity

For most variables that you are likely to encounter, numerous research studies probably already have examined the same variables. Past research has studied each variable in a variety of different situations, and has documented which factors influence the variable and how different values of the variable produce different kinds of behavior. In short, past research has demonstrated how the specific variable behaves. If we can demonstrate that measurements of a variable behave in exactly the same way as the variable itself, then we have established the **construct validity** of the measurement procedure. Suppose, for example, that you are examining a measurement procedure that claims to measure aggression. Past research has demonstrated a relationship between temperature and aggression: In the summer, as temperature rises, people tend to become more aggressive. To help establish construct validity, you would need to demonstrate that the scores you obtain from the measurement procedure are also related to temperature; that is, that the scores tend to increase as the temperature goes up. Note, however, that this single demonstration is only one small part of construct validity. To completely establish construct validity, you would need to examine all the past research on aggression and show that the measurement procedure produces scores that behave in accordance with everything that is known about the construct "aggression." Because new research results are reported every day, construct validity is never established absolutely. Instead, construct validity is an ideal or a goal that develops gradually from the results of many research studies that examine the measurement procedure in a wide variety of situations.

Earlier, we used the example of attempting to measure height by having people step on a bathroom scale. Because height and weight are related, the measurement that we obtain from the scale would be considered a valid measure of height, at least in terms of concurrent validity. However, the weight measurement is not a valid method of measuring height in terms of construct validity. In particular, height is not influenced by short periods of food deprivation. Weight measurements, on the other hand, are affected by food deprivation. Therefore, measurements of weight do not behave in accordance with what is known about the construct "height," which means that the weight measurement procedure does not have construct validity as a measure of height.

Convergent and Divergent Validity

One procedure that has been suggested as a method for establishing construct validity is to demonstrate a combination of convergent and divergent validity (Campbell & Fiske, 1959). In general terms, **convergent validity** involves creating two different methods to measure the same construct, then showing a strong relationship between the measures obtained from the two methods. The goal is to demonstrate that different measurement procedures "converge" on the same construct. **Divergent validity,** on the other hand, involves demonstrating that we are measuring one specific construct and not combining two different constructs in the same measurement process. The goal is to differentiate between two conceptually distinct constructs. The following scenarios illustrate the concepts of convergent and divergent validity.

Suppose you are interested in measuring aggressive behavior for preschool children. Your measurement procedure involves observing a group of children on a playground and recording their behaviors. However, you realize you are observing only a small part of the children's total environment, and you wonder whether you really have a valid measure of aggression. Therefore, you decide that you will also ask the children's teacher to provide a rating of aggression for each child. Notice that you have created two operational definitions of aggressive behavior; one based on your observations and one based on the teacher's perceptions. If there is a strong relationship between your observation scores and the teacher's ratings, you can be reasonably confident that you are obtaining a valid measure of aggression. Creating two different methods to measure the same variable, and then demonstrating a strong relationship (usually a correlation) between the two measures is an example of convergent validity (see Figure 4.1).

We should note that the distinction between convergent validity and concurrent validity can be confusing. Both attempt to establish the validity of a new measurement technique by demonstrating that it is strongly related to a second technique for measuring the same variable. However, convergent validity involves using two methods for measuring the variable, and concurrent validity involves using a well-established measurement procedure in addition to your new technique.

After you have established convergent validity, however, you may still question whether you are really measuring aggression and not some other variable. For example, your scores may actually reflect the general activity level of each child rather than the level of aggression. It is possible, for example, that very active children simply appear to be more aggressive than their less active peers. To resolve this problem, you need to demonstrate that the two constructs, "aggression" and "activity," are separate and distinct. Therefore, you now obtain measures of activity level by observing the children on the playground. Once again, you can check the validity of your measurements by asking the children's teacher for a rating of activity for each child. At this point, you have two different measurements (observation and rating) of two different constructs (aggression and activity), and you are ready to evaluate divergent validity.

The first step in establishing divergent validity is to demonstrate convergent validity for both constructs. For this example:

- There should be a strong relationship between the observational scores for aggression and the teacher's scores for aggression [see Figure 4.1(a)].
- There should be a strong relationship between the observational scores for activity and the teacher's scores for activity.

The second step is to demonstrate that the two constructs are separate and distinct. To accomplish this, you must demonstrate that:

- Relatively little relationship exists between the observational scores for aggression and the observational scores for activity [see Figure 4.1(c)].
- Relatively little relationship exists between the teacher's scores for aggression and the teacher's scores for activity.

By demonstrating that two different methods of measurement produce strongly related scores for the same construct (convergent validity), and by demonstrating that two distinct constructs produce unrelated scores (divergent validity), you can provide very strong and convincing evidence of validity. That is, there is little doubt that you are actually measuring the construct that you intend to measure.

DEFINITIONS

Face validity is an unscientific form of validity demonstrated when a measurement procedure superficially appears to measure what it claims to measure.

Concurrent validity is demonstrated when scores obtained from a new measure are directly related to scores obtained from an established measure of the same variable.

Predictive validity is demonstrated when scores obtained from a measure accurately predict behavior according to a theory.

Construct validity requires that the scores obtained from a measurement procedure behave exactly the same as the variable itself. Construct validity is based on many research studies that use the same measurement procedure and grows gradually as each new study contributes more evidence.

Convergent validity is demonstrated by a strong relationship between the scores obtained from two different methods of measuring the same construct.

Divergent validity is demonstrated by using two different methods to measure two different constructs. Then convergent validity must be shown for each of the two constructs. Finally, there should be little or no relationship between the scores obtained for the two different constructs when they are measured by the same method.

LEARNING CHECKS

A researcher evaluates a new growth hormone. One sample of rats is raised with the hormone in their diet and a second sample is raised without the hormone. After 6 months, the researcher weighs each rat to determine whether the rats in one group are significantly larger than the rats in the other group. A second researcher measures femininity for each individual in a group of 10-year-old girls who are all daughters of mothers who work outside of the home. These scores are then compared with corresponding measurements obtained from girls who are all daughters of mothers who work at home. The researcher hopes to show that one group is significantly more feminine than the other. Explain why the first researcher is probably not concerned about the validity of measurement, whereas the second researcher probably is. (Hint: What variable is each researcher measuring and how will it be measured?)

A researcher has developed a new test measuring social anxiety and would like to determine the validity of the test. The new test and an established measure of social anxiety are both administered to a sample of participants. Describe the pattern of results that would establish concurrent validity for the new test.

Describe how a researcher establishes construct validity for a measurement procedure.

Reliability of Measurement

The second criterion for evaluating the quality of a measurement procedure is called **reliability**. A measurement procedure is said to have reliability if it produces identical (or nearly identical) results when it is used repeatedly to measure the same individual under the same conditions. For example, if we use an IQ test to measure a person's intelligence today, then use the same test for the same person under similar conditions next week, we should obtain nearly identical IQ scores. In essence, reliability is the stability or the consistency of the measurements produced by a specific measurement procedure.

DEFINITION	The **reliability** of a measurement procedure is the stability or consistency of the measurement. If the same individuals are measured under the same conditions, a reliable measurement procedure produces identical (or nearly identical) measurements.

The concept of reliability is based on the assumption that the variable being measured is stable or constant. For example, your intelligence does not change dramatically from one day to another, but rather stays at a fairly constant level. However, when we measure a variable such as intelligence, the measurement procedure introduces an element of error. Expressed as an equation:

$$\text{Measured Score} = \text{True Score} + \text{Error}$$

For example, if we try to measure your intelligence with an IQ test, the score we get is determined partially by your actual level of intelligence (your true score), but also is influenced by a variety of other factors such as your current mood, your level of fatigue, your general health, how lucky you are at guessing on questions to which you do not know the answers, and so on. These other factors are lumped together as error and are typically a part of any measurement.

It is generally assumed that the error component changes randomly from one measurement to the next, raising your score for some measurements and lowering it for others. Over a series of many measurements, the increases and decreases caused by error should average to zero. For example, your IQ score is likely to be higher when you are well-rested and feeling good, and lower when you are tired and depressed. Although your actual intelligence has not changed, the error component causes your score to change from one measurement to another.

As long as the error component is relatively small, your scores will be relatively consistent from one measurement to the next, and the measurements are said to be reliable. If you are feeling especially happy and well rested, it may affect your IQ score by a few points, but it is not going to boost your IQ from 110 to 170.

On the other hand, if the error component is relatively large, you will find huge differences from one measurement to the next, and the measurements are, therefore, not reliable. A common example of a measurement with a large error component is reaction time. Suppose, for example, that we ask you to sit at a desk with your finger on a button and a light bulb in front of you. Your task is to press the button as quickly as possible when the light goes on. On some trials, you will be fully alert and focused on the light, with your finger tensed and ready to move. On other trials, you may be daydreaming or distracted, with your attention elsewhere, so that extra time passes before you can refocus on the task and respond. In general, it is quite common for reaction time on some trials to be twice as long as reaction time on other trials. When scores change dramatically from one trial to another, the measurements are said to be unreliable, and we cannot trust any single measurement to provide an accurate indication of an individual's true score. In the case of reaction time, most researchers solve the problem by measuring reaction times in several trials and computing an average. The average value provides a much more stable, more reliable measure of performance.

The inconsistency in a measurement comes from error. Error can come from a variety of sources. The more common sources of error are as follows:

- *Observer error:* The individual who makes the measurements can introduce simple human error into the measurement process. Imagine four people using handheld stopwatches to record the winner's time in a 100-meter dash. In this situation, it is highly likely that the four people will obtain four different times. To some extent, the time that each person records is influenced by that person's judgment of when the race started and ended, and that person's reflex time to push the buttons on the watch. Thus, each recorded time includes some error introduced by the observer.

- *Environmental changes:* Although the goal is to measure the same individual under identical circumstances, this ideal is difficult to attain. Often, there are small changes in the environment from one measurement to another, and these small changes can influence the measurements. There are so many environmental variables (such as time of day, temperature, weather conditions, and lighting) that it is essentially impossible to obtain two identical environmental conditions.

- *Participant changes:* The participant can change between measurements. As noted earlier, a person's degree of focus and attention can change quickly and can have a dramatic effect on measures of reaction time. Such changes may cause the obtained measurements to differ, producing what appear to be inconsistent or unreliable measurements. For example, hunger probably does not lower intelligence, but it can be a distraction that causes a lower score on an IQ test.

In summary, any measurement procedure involves an element of error and the amount of error determines the reliability of the measurements. When error is large, reliability is low, and when error is small, reliability is high.

LEARNING CHECKS

Exams given in college classes are intended to measure the knowledge of students.
a.   Identify one way that error might improve a student's exam score.
b.   Identify one way that error might lower a student's exam score.
Explain how a large error component can make a measurement procedure unreliable.

Types and Measures of Reliability

We have defined reliability in terms of the consistency between two or more separate measurements. Thus far, the discussion has concentrated on situations involving successive measurements. Although this is one common example of reliability, it also is possible to measure reliability for simultaneous measurements and to measure reliability in terms of the internal consistency among the many items that make up a test or questionnaire.

- *Successive measurements:* The reliability estimate obtained by comparing the scores obtained from two successive measurements is commonly called **test-retest reliability.** A researcher may use exactly the same measurement procedure for the same group of individuals at two different times. Or a researcher may use modified versions of the measurement instrument (such as alternative versions of an IQ test) to obtain two different measurements for the same group of participants. When different versions of the instrument are used for the test and the retest, the reliability measure is often called **parallel-forms reliability.** Typically, reliability is determined by computing a correlation to measure the consistency of the relationship between the two sets of scores (see Figure 4.1).

- *Simultaneous measurements:* When measurements are obtained by direct observation of behaviors, it is common to use two or more separate observers who simultaneously record measurements. For example, two psychologists may watch a group of preschool children and observe social behaviors. Each individual records (measures) what she observes, and the degree of agreement between the two observers is called **inter-rater reliability.** This topic is also discussed in Chapter 7. Inter-rater reliability can be measured by computing the correlation between the scores from the two observers (Figure 4.1 and Chapter 13, p. 198), or by computing a percentage of agreement between the two observers (see Chapter 14, pp. 444–446).

- *Internal consistency:* Often, a complex construct such as intelligence or personality is measured using a test or questionnaire consisting of multiple items. The idea is that no single item or question is sufficient to provide a complete measure of the construct. A common example is the use of multiple-exams to measure performance in an academic course. The final measurement for each individual is then determined by adding or averaging the responses across the full set of items. A basic assumption in this process is that each item (or group of items) measures a part of the total construct. If this is true, then there should be some consistency between the scores for different items or different groups of items. To measure the degree of consistency, researchers commonly split the set of items in half and compute a separate score for each half. The degree of agreement between the two scores is then evaluated, usually with a correlation (Ch. 14, p. 442). This general process results in a measure of **split-half reliability.** You should note that there are many different ways to divide a set of items in half prior to computing split-half reliability, and the value you obtain depends on the method you use to split the items. Cronbach's Alpha and the Kuder-Richardson formula are two statistical techniques for dealing with this problem and are discussed in Chapter 14 (pp. 443–444).

DEFINITIONS — **Test-retest reliability** is established by comparing the scores obtained from two successive measurements of the same individuals and calculating a correlation between the two sets of scores. If alternative versions of the measuring instrument are used for the two measurements, the reliability measure is called **parallel-forms reliability.**

Inter-rater reliability is the degree of agreement between two observers who simultaneously record measurements of the behaviors.

Split-half reliability is obtained by splitting the items on a questionnaire or test in half, computing a separate score for each half, and then calculating the degree of consistency between the two scores for a group of participants.

LEARNING CHECKS

Suppose that a researcher has developed a new 10-item questionnaire intended to measure honesty. Describe how you could evaluate the reliability of the questionnaire.

Explain how inter-rater reliability is established.

The Relationship Between Reliability and Validity

Although reliability and validity are both criteria for evaluating the quality of a measurement procedure, these two factors are partially related and partially independent. They are related to each other in that reliability is a prerequisite for validity; that is, a measurement procedure cannot be valid unless it is reliable. If we measure your IQ twice and obtain measurements of 75 and 160, not only are the measurements unreliable but we also have no idea what your IQ actually is. The huge discrepancy between the two measurements is impossible if we are truly measuring intelligence. Therefore, we must conclude that there is so much error in the measurements that the numbers themselves have no meaning.

On the other hand, it is not necessary for a measurement to be valid for it to be reliable. For example, we could measure your height and claim that it is a measure of intelligence. Although this is a foolish and invalid method for defining and measuring intelligence, it would be very reliable, producing consistent scores from one measurement to the next. Thus, the consistency of measurement is no guarantee of validity.

A measure cannot be valid unless it is reliable, but a measure can be reliable without being valid.

In situations in which there is an established standard for measurement units, it is possible to define the **accuracy** of a measurement process. For example, we have standards that define precisely what is meant by an inch, a pound, a mile, and a second. The accuracy of a measurement is the degree to which the measurement conforms to the established standard. Occasionally, a measurement procedure produces results that are consistently wrong by a constant amount. The speedometer on a car, for example, may consistently read 10 mph faster than the actual speed. In this case, the speedometer readings are not accurate but they are valid and reliable. When the car is traveling at 40 mph, the speedometer consistently (reliably) reads 50 mph, and when the car is actually going 30 mph, the speedometer reads 40 mph. Note that the speedometer correctly differentiates different speeds, which means that it is producing valid measurements of speed. (Note that a measurement process can be valid and reliable even if it is not accurate.) In the behavioral sciences, it is quite common to measure variables for which there is no established standard. In such cases, it is impossible to define or measure accuracy. A test designed to measure depression, for example, cannot be evaluated in terms of accuracy because there is no standard unit of depression that can be used for comparison. For such a test, the question of accuracy is moot, and the only concerns are the validity and the reliability of the measurements.

LEARNING CHECKS

Explain why we cannot establish the accuracy of certain measures.

A researcher claims that intelligence can be measured by measuring the length of a person's right-hand ring finger. Explain why this procedure is very reliable but probably not valid.

4.4 | SCALES OF MEASUREMENT

In very general terms, measurement is a procedure for classifying individuals. The set of categories used for classification is called the **scale of measurement.** Thus, the process of measurement involves two components: a set of categories and a procedure for assigning individuals to categories.

In this section, we focus on scales of measurement. Traditionally, researchers have identified four different types of measurement scales: nominal, ordinal, interval, and ratio. The differences among these four types are based on the relationships that exist among the categories that make up the scales.

The Nominal Scale

The categories that make up a **nominal scale** simply represent qualitative (not quantitative) differences in the variable measured. The categories have different names but are not related to each other in any systematic way. For example, if you were measuring academic majors for a group of college students, the categories would be art, chemistry, English, history, psychology, and so on. Each student would be placed in a category according to his major. Measurements from a nominal scale allow us to determine whether two individuals are different, but they do not permit any quantitative comparison. For example, if one individual is an art major and another is an English major, we can say that the two individuals have different majors, but we cannot determine the direction of the difference (is art "more than" English?), and we cannot determine the magnitude of the difference. Other examples of nominal scales include classifying people by race, gender, or occupation.

The Ordinal Scale

The categories that make up an **ordinal scale** have different names and are organized sequentially. Often, an ordinal scale consists of a series of ranks (first, second, third, and so on) like the order of finish in a horse race. Occasionally, the categories are identified by verbal labels such as small, medium, and large drink sizes at a fast-food restaurant. In either case, the fact that the categories form an ordered sequence means that there is a directional relationship between categories. With measurements from an ordinal scale, we can determine whether two individuals are different, and we can determine the direction of difference. However, ordinal measurements do not allow us to determine the magnitude of the difference between two individuals. For example, if Billy is placed in the low reading group and Tim is placed in the high reading group, we know that Tim is a better reader, but we do not know how much better.

Other examples of ordinal scales include socioeconomic class (upper, middle, lower) and T-shirt sizes (small, medium, large). In addition, ordinal scales are often used to measure variables for which it is difficult to assign numerical scores. For example, people can rank order their food preferences but might have trouble explaining how much they prefer steak to hamburger.

Interval and Ratio Scales

The categories on **interval** and **ratio scales** are organized sequentially and all categories are the same size. Thus, the scale of measurement consists of a series of equal intervals like the inches on a ruler. Other common examples of interval or ratio scales are the measures of time in seconds, weight in pounds, and temperature in degrees Fahrenheit. Notice that in each case, one interval (one inch, one second, one pound, one degree) is the same size, no matter where it is located on the scale.

The fact that the categories are all the same size makes it possible to determine the distance between two points on the scale. For example, you know that a measurement of 10 inches is larger than a measurement of 7 inches, and you know that it is exactly 3 inches larger.

The characteristic that differentiates interval and ratio scales is the zero point. The distinguishing characteristic of an interval scale is that it has an arbitrary zero point. That is, the value 0 is assigned to a particular location on the scale simply as a matter of convenience or reference. Specifically, a value of 0 does not indicate the total absence of the variable being measured. For example, a temperature of 0 degrees Fahrenheit does not mean that there is no temperature, and it does not prohibit the temperature from going even lower. Interval scales with an arbitrary zero point are fairly rare. The two most common examples are the Fahrenheit and Celsius temperature scales. Other examples include golf scores (above and below par) and relative measures, such as above and below average rainfall.

A ratio scale, on the other hand, is characterized by a zero point that is not an arbitrary location. Instead, the value 0 on a ratio scale is a meaningful point representing none (a complete absence) of the variable being measured. The existence of an absolute, non-arbitrary zero point means that we can measure the absolute amount of the variable; that is, we can measure the distance from 0. This makes it possible to compare measurements in terms of ratios. For example, an individual who requires 10 seconds to solve a problem (10 more than 0) has taken twice as much time as an individual who finishes in only 5 seconds (5 more than 0). With a ratio scale, we can measure the direction and magnitude of the difference between measurements and describe differences in terms of ratios. Ratio scales are quite common and include physical measures such as height and weight, as well as variables such as reaction time or number of errors on a test.

Remember, the difference between an interval scale and a ratio scale is the definition of the zero point. Thus, measurements of height in inches, or weight in pounds could be either interval or ratio depending on the location of zero.

For example, with traditional measurements of weight, zero corresponds to none (no weight whatsoever) and the measurements make up a ratio scale. In this case, an 80-pound child (80 pounds above 0) weighs twice as much as a 40-pound child (40 pounds above 0). However, you also could measure each child's weight relative to the average for the age group. Now, a child who is 12 pounds above average receives a score of +12 pounds. A child who is 4 pounds below average is assigned a score of −4 pounds. In this case the measurements make up an interval scale. In particular, a child who is 12 pounds above average (+12) does not weigh twice as much as a child who is 6 pounds above average (+6). Both scales, however, provide the same information about the distance between two measurements. For the ratio measurements, 84 pounds is 4 more than 80 pounds. For the interval measurements, a score of +8 pounds is 5 more than a score of +3 pounds. For most applications, the ability to measure distances is far more important than the ability to measure ratios. Therefore, in most situations, the distinction between interval and ratio scales has little practical significance.

Dealing with Equivocal Measurements

Although the distinction between interval and ratio scales has little practical significance, the difference between ordinal and interval or ratio scales can be enormous. Recall that ordinal scales do not provide any measure of distance. For example, a rank of 1st is better than a rank of 2nd, but you do not know how much better. Interval and ratio scales, on the other hand, do measure distance. For example, a measurement of 8 seconds is longer than a measurement of 3 seconds, and it is exactly 5 seconds longer. This difference between the scales of measurement has some important consequences. In particular, scores from an interval or ratio scale are compatible with basic arithmetic, but scores from an ordinal scale are not. To demonstrate this difference, consider the following data showing the estimated value of the top three major league baseball franchises according to *Forbes'* annual review (Badenhausen, Ozanian, & Settimi, 2010).

Rank	Value	Team
1	$1,600,000,000	New York Yankees
2	$870,000,000	Boston Red Sox
3	$858,000,000	New York Mets

For these data, the ranks form an ordinal scale and the dollar amounts form a ratio scale. Notice that if we calculate the average rank for the Yankees and the Mets (1st and 3rd), we obtain a value of 2. Because the value 2 is exactly halfway between 1 and 3, it is tempting to conclude that the Red Sox franchise, which is ranked 2nd, must have a value that is halfway between the Yankees and the Mets. However, this is clearly not true. Trying to do basic arithmetic with ordinal values can cause problems. Also notice that there is no problem doing arithmetic with scores from an interval or ratio scale. According to these data, the average value for the Yankees and the Mets is $1,229,000,000, which is exactly halfway between the value for the Yankees and the value for the Mets.

Because interval or ratio scale measurements are compatible with basic arithmetic and ordinal measurements are not, the different scales of measurement are also not equally compatible with many methods of statistical analysis. For example, measurements from interval or ratio scales can be used to compute means and variances, and they allow hypothesis testing with t tests or analysis of variance. Ordinal measurements, on the other hand, do not produce meaningful values for means and variances and are not appropriate for most commonly used hypothesis tests. Therefore, it can be critical to determine whether your measurements are from an ordinal scale or an interval/ratio scale.

Although many measurements are clearly classified as either ordinal or interval, there are others that are not obviously in one category or the other. IQ scores, for example, are numerical values that appear to form an interval scale. However, there is some question about the size of one point of IQ. Is the difference between an IQ of 85 and an IQ of 86 exactly the same as the difference between an IQ of 145 and an IQ of 146? If the answer is yes, then IQ scores form an interval scale. However, if you are not sure that one point is exactly the same everywhere on the scale, then IQ scores must be classified as ordinal measurements. It also is common for researchers in the behavioral sciences to measure variables using rating scales. For example, participants are asked to use a scale from 1 to 5 to rate the degree to which they agree (or disagree) with controversial statements. The five numerical values are often labeled, for example:

Strongly Agree	Somewhat Agree	Neutral	Somewhat Disagree	Strongly Disagree
1	2	3	4	5

Although the choices appear to form an interval scale with equal distance between successive numbers, is the distance between *Strongly Agree* and *Somewhat Agree* exactly equal to the distance between *Neutral* and *Somewhat Disagree*? Again, should the scale be treated as ordinal or interval?

Fortunately, the issue of distinguishing between ordinal and interval scales of measurement has been resolved. First, researchers have routinely treated scores from ambiguous scales, such as IQ scores and rating scales, as if they were from an interval scale. By tradition or convention, such scores have been added and averaged and multiplied as if they were regular numerical values. In addition, scientists have argued convincingly for over 50 years that this kind of mathematical treatment is appropriate for these types of ordinal data (Lord, 1953). For a recent review of the history of this issue, see Norman (2010).

Selecting a Scale of Measurement

One obvious factor that differentiates the four types of measurement scales is their ability to compare different measurements. A nominal scale can tell us only that a difference exists. An ordinal scale tells us the direction of the difference (which is more and which is less). With an interval scale, we can determine the direction and the magnitude of a difference. Measurements from a ratio scale allow us to determine the direction, the magnitude, and the ratio of the difference. The ability to compare measurements has a direct effect on the ability to describe relationships between variables. For example, when a research study involves measurements from nominal scales, the results of the study can establish the existence of only a qualitative relationship between variables. With nominal scales, we can determine whether a change in one variable is accompanied by a change in the other variable, but we cannot determine the direction of the change (increase or a decrease), and we cannot determine the magnitude of the change. An interval or a ratio scale, on the other hand, allows a much more sophisticated description of a relationship. For example, we could determine that a 1-point increase in one variable (such as drug dose) results in a 4-point decrease in another variable (such as heart rate).

LEARNING CHECK

Identify the scale of measurement that allows each of the following conclusions.
a. Tom's score is larger than Bill's, but we cannot say how much larger.
b. Tom's score is three times larger than Bill's.
c. Tom and Bill have different scores, but we cannot say which one is larger, and we cannot determine how much difference there is.

4.5 | MODALITIES OF MEASUREMENT

Although a construct such as motivation or intelligence is hypothetical and cannot be observed directly, the construct reveals itself in a variety of different external manifestations that can be observed and measured. One major decision for a researcher is which of these external manifestations provides the best indication of the underlying construct. The many different external expressions of a construct are traditionally classified into three categories that also define three different types, or modalities, of measurement. The three categories are self-report, physiological, and behavioral. Consider, for example, the hypothetical construct "fear," and suppose that a researcher would like to evaluate the effectiveness of a therapy program designed to reduce the fear of flying. This researcher must somehow obtain measurements of fear before the therapy begins, then compare them with measurements of fear obtained after therapy. Although fear is an internal construct that cannot be observed directly, it is possible to observe and measure external expressions of fear. For example, an individual may claim to be afraid (self-report), may have an increased heart rate (physiological), or may refuse to travel on an airplane (behavioral). One major decision in developing a measurement procedure (an operational definition) is to determine which type of external expression should be used to define and measure fear.

Self-Report Measures

One option for measuring, or operationalizing fear of flying is to ask each participant to describe or to quantify her own fear. The researcher could simply ask, "Are you afraid to fly?" Or participants could be asked to rate the amount of fear they are experiencing on a scale from 1 to 10. Or they could be given a comprehensive questionnaire about airline travel and the researcher could use the set of responses to obtain an overall score measuring fear of flying.

Self-report measures are discussed in more detail in Section 7.3, in which we present the survey research design.

The primary advantage of a **self-report measure** is that it is probably the most direct way to assess a construct. Each individual is in a unique position of self-knowledge and self-awareness; presumably, no one knows more about the individual's fear than the individual. Also, a direct question and its answer have more apparent validity than measuring some other response that theoretically is influenced by fear. On the negative side, however, it is very easy for participants to distort self-report measures. A participant may deliberately lie to create a better self-image, or a response may be influenced subtly by the presence of a researcher, the wording of the questions, or other aspects of the research situation. One phenomenon observed by clinical psychologists, called the hello–goodbye effect, is that patients tend to exaggerate their symptoms at the beginning of therapy and to minimize symptoms at the end, probably in an attempt to please the therapist. When a participant distorts self-report responses, the validity of the measurement is undermined.

LEARNING CHECK   What is the primary advantage of self-report measures? What is the primary disadvantage?

Physiological Measures

A second option for measuring a construct is to look at the physiological manifestations of the underlying construct. Fear, for example, reveals itself by increased heart rate and perspiration (measured by galvanic skin response, GSR). A researcher measuring "fear of flying" could attach electrodes to participants and monitor heart rates as they board a plane and during the flight. Or a researcher could ask participants to imagine a flight experience while GSR and heart rate are monitored in a laboratory setting.

Other **physiological measures** involve brain imaging techniques such as positron emission tomography (PET) scanning and magnetic resonance imaging (MRI). These techniques allow researchers to monitor activity levels in specific areas of the brain during different kinds of activity. For example, researchers studying attention have found specific areas of the brain where activity increases as the complexity of a task increases and more attention is required (Posner & Badgaiyan, 1998). Other research has used brain imaging to determine which areas of the brain are involved in different kinds of memory tasks (Wager & Smith, 2003) or in the processing of information about pain (Wager et al., 2004).

One advantage of physiological measures is that they are extremely objective. The equipment provides accurate, reliable, and well-defined measurements that are not dependent on subjective interpretation by either the researcher or the participant. One disadvantage of such measures is that they typically require equipment that may be expensive or unavailable. In addition, the presence of monitoring devices creates an unnatural situation that may cause participants to react differently than they would under normal circumstances. A more important concern with physiological measures is whether they provide a valid measure of the construct. Heart rate, for example, may be related to fear, but heart rate and fear are not the same thing. Increased heart rate may be caused by anxiety, arousal, embarrassment, or exertion as well as by fear. Can we be sure that measurements of heart rate are, in fact, measurements of fear?

 **LEARNING CHECK** | Describe the strengths and weaknesses of physiological measures.

Behavioral Measures

Constructs often reveal themselves in overt behaviors that can be observed and measured. The behaviors may be completely natural events such as laughing, playing, eating, sleeping, arguing, or speaking. Or the behaviors may be structured, as when a researcher measures performance on a designated task. In the latter case, a researcher usually develops a specific task in which performance is theoretically dependent on the construct being measured. For example, reaction time could be measured to determine whether a drug affects mental alertness; the number of words recalled from a list provides a measure of memory ability; and performance on an IQ test is a measure of intelligence. To measure the "fear of flying," a researcher could construct a hierarchy of potential behaviors (visiting an airport, walking onto a plane, sitting in a plane while it idles at the gate, riding in a plane while it taxies on a runway, actually flying) and measuring how far up the hierarchy an individual is willing to go.

Behavioral measures provide researchers with a vast number of options, making it possible to select the behavior(s) that seems to be best for defining and measuring the construct. For example, the construct "mental alertness" could be operationally defined by behaviors such as reaction time, reading comprehension, logical reasoning ability, or ability to focus attention. Depending on the specific purpose of a research study, one of these measures probably is more appropriate than the others. In clinical situations in which a researcher works with individual clients, a single construct such as depression may reveal itself as a separate, unique behavioral problem for each client. In this case, the clinician can construct a separate, unique behavioral definition of depression that is appropriate for each patient.

In other situations, the behavior may be the actual variable of interest and not just an indicator of some hypothetical construct. For a school psychologist trying to reduce disruptive behavior in the classroom, it is the actual behavior that the psychologist wants to observe and measure. In this case, the psychologist does not use the overt behavior as an operational definition of an intangible construct but rather simply studies the behavior itself.

On the negative side, a behavior may be only a temporary or situational indicator of an underlying construct. A disruptive student may be on good behavior during periods of observation or shift the timing of negative behaviors from the classroom to the school bus on the way home. Usually, it is best to measure a cluster of related behaviors rather than rely on a single indicator.

Behavioral measures are discussed in more detail in Section 7.2, in which we present the observational research design.

For example, in response to therapy, a disruptive student may stop speaking out of turn in the classroom but replace this specific behavior with another form of disruption. A complete definition of disruptive behavior would require several behavioral indicators.

LEARNING CHECKS

Explain why it might be easier to obtain a self-report measure than a behavioral measure for some behaviors.

Describe the advantages and disadvantages of behavioral measures.

4.6 | OTHER ASPECTS OF MEASUREMENT

Beyond the validity and reliability of measures, the scale of measurement, and the modality of measurement, several other factors should be considered when selecting a measurement procedure. The right decisions about each of these factors can increase the likelihood of success of a research study. In this section, we consider additional issues related to the measurement process: multiple measures, sensitivity of measurement and range effects, artifacts including experimenter bias and participant reactivity, and selection of a measurement procedure.

Multiple Measures

One method of obtaining a more complete measure of a construct is to use two (or more) different procedures to measure the same variable. For example, we could record both heart rate and behavior as measures of fear. The advantage of this multiple-measure technique is that it usually provides more confidence in the validity of the measurements. However, multiple measures can introduce some problems. One problem involves the statistical analysis and interpretation of the results. Although there are statistical techniques for evaluating multivariate data, they are complex and not well understood by many researchers. A more serious problem is that the two measures may not behave in the same way. A therapy program for treating fear, for example, may produce an immediate and large effect on behavior but no effect on heart rate. As a result, participants are willing to approach a feared object after therapy, but their hearts still race. The lack of agreement between two measures is called **desynchrony,** and it can confuse the interpretation of results (did the therapy reduce fear?). Desynchrony may be caused by the fact that one measure is more sensitive than the other, or it may indicate that different dimensions of the variable change at different times during treatment (behavior may change quickly, but the physiological aspects of fear take more time). One method for limiting the problems associated with multiple measures is to combine them into a single score for each individual.

Sensitivity and Range Effects

Typically, a researcher begins a study with some expectation of how the variables will behave, specifically the direction and magnitude of changes that are likely to be observed. An important concern for any measurement procedure is that the measurements are sensitive enough to respond to the type and magnitude of the changes that are expected. For example, if a medication is expected to have only a small effect on reaction time, then it is essential that time be measured in units small enough to detect the change. If we measure time in seconds and the magnitude of the effect is 1/100 of a second, then the change will not be noticed. In general, if we expect fairly small, subtle changes in a variable, then the measurement procedure must be sensitive enough to detect the changes, and the scale of measurement must have enough different categories to allow discrimination among individuals.

One particular sensitivity problem occurs when the scores obtained in a research study tend to cluster at one end of the measurement scale. For example, suppose that an educational psychologist intends to evaluate a new teaching program by measuring reading comprehension for a group of students before and after the program is administered. If the students all score around 95% before the program starts, there is essentially no room for improvement. Even if the program does improve reading comprehension, the measurement procedure probably will not detect an increase in scores. In this case, the measurement procedure is insensitive to changes that may occur in one direction. In general, this type of sensitivity problem is called a **range effect.** When the range is restricted at the high end, the problem is called a **ceiling effect** (the measurements bump into a ceiling and can go no higher). Similarly, clustering at the low end of the scale can produce a **floor effect.**

In general, range effects suggest a basic incompatibility between the measurement procedure and the individuals measured. Often, the measurement is based on a task that is too easy (thereby producing high scores) or too difficult (thereby producing low scores) for the participants being tested. Note that it is not the measurement procedure that is at fault but rather the fact that the procedure is used with a particular group of individuals. For example, a measurement that works well for 4-year-old children may produce serious range effects if used with adolescents. For this reason, it is advisable to pretest any measurement procedure for which potential range effects are suspected. Simply measure a small sample of representative individuals to be sure that the obtained values are far enough from the extremes of the scale to allow room to measure changes in either direction.

DEFINITIONS

A **ceiling effect** is the clustering of scores at the high end of a measurement scale, allowing little or no possibility of increases in value.

A **floor effect** is the clustering of scores at the low end of a measurement scale, allowing little or no possibility of decreases in value.

 **LEARNING CHECK**

What is a ceiling effect and why is it a problem?

Artifacts: Experimenter Bias and Participant Reactivity

An **artifact** is a nonnatural feature accidentally introduced into something being observed. In the context of a research study, an artifact is an external factor that may influence or distort the measurements. For example, a doctor who startles you with an ice-cold stethoscope is probably not going to get accurate observations of your heartbeat. An artifact can threaten the validity of the measurements because you are not really measuring what you intended, and it can be a threat to reliability. Although there are many potential artifacts, two deserve special mention: experimenter bias and participant reactivity.

Experimenter Bias

Typically, a researcher knows the predicted outcome of a research study and is in a position to influence the results, either intentionally or unintentionally. For example, an experimenter might be warm, friendly, and encouraging when presenting instructions to a group of participants in a treatment condition expected to produce good performance, and appear cold, aloof, and somewhat stern when presenting the instructions to another group in a comparison treatment for which performance is expected to be relatively poor. The experimenter is manipulating participant motivation, and this manipulation can distort the results. When researchers influence results in this way, the effect is called **experimenter bias.**

DEFINITION	**Experimenter bias** occurs when the measurements obtained in a study are influenced by the experimenter's expectations or personal beliefs regarding the outcome of the study.

Rosenthal and Fode (1963) identified a variety of ways that an experimenter can influence a participant's behavior:

- by paralinguistic cues (variations in tone of voice) that influence the participants to give the expected or desired responses
- by kinesthetic cues (body posture or facial expressions)
- by verbal reinforcement of expected or desired responses
- by misjudgment of participants' responses in the direction of the expected results
- by not recording participants' responses accurately (errors in recording of data) in the direction of the expected or desired results

In a classic example of experimenter bias, Rosenthal & Fode (1963) had student volunteers act as the experimenters in a learning study. The students were given rats to train in a maze. Half of the students were led to believe that their rats were specially bred to be "maze bright." The remainder were told that their rats were bred to be "maze dull." In reality, both groups of students received the same type of ordinary laboratory rat, neither bright nor dull. Nevertheless, the findings showed differences in the rats' performance between the two groups of experimenters. The "bright" rats were better at learning the maze. The student expectations influenced the outcome of the study. How did their expectations have this effect? Apparently there were differences in how the students in each group handled their rats, and the handling, in turn, altered the rats' behavior.

Note that the existence of experimenter bias means that the researcher is not obtaining valid measurements. Instead, the behaviors or measurements are being distorted by the experimenter. In addition, experimenter bias undermines reliability because the participants may produce very different scores if tested under the same conditions by a different experimenter.

One option for limiting experimenter bias is to standardize or automate the experiment. For example, a researcher could read from a prepared script to ensure that all participants receive exactly the same instructions. Or instructions could be presented on a printed handout, or by video or audio recording. In each case, the goal is to limit the personal contact between the experimenter and the participant. Another strategy for reducing experimenter bias is to use a "blind" experiment. If the research study is conducted by an experimenter (assistant) who does not know the expected results, the experimenter should not be able to influence the participants. This technique is called **single-blind** research. An alternative is to set up a study in which neither the experimenter nor the participants know the expected results. This procedure is called **double-blind** research and is commonly used in drug studies in which some participants get the real drug and others get a placebo. The double-blind study is structured so that neither the researcher nor the participants know exactly who is getting which drug until the study is completed.

DEFINITION

A research study is **single-blind** if the researcher does not know the predicted outcome.

A research study is **double-blind** if both the researcher and the participants are unaware of the predicted outcome.

 **LEARNING CHECK**

Explain how a single-blind study minimizes the potential for experimenter bias.

Demand Characteristics and Participant Reactivity

The fact that research studies involve living organisms, particularly humans, introduces another factor that can affect the validity and reliability of the measurements. Specifically, living organisms are active and responsive, and their actions and responses can distort the results. If we observe or measure an inanimate object such as a table or a block of wood, we do not expect the object to have any response such as "Whoa! I'm being watched. I had better be on my best behavior." Unfortunately this kind of reactivity can happen with human participants.

Participants who are aware they are being observed and measured may react in unpredictable ways. In addition, the research setting often creates a set of cues or demand characteristics that suggest what kinds of behavior are appropriate or expected. The combination of **demand characteristics** and participant **reactivity** can change participants' normal behavior and thereby influence the measurements they produce.

DEFINITIONS

The term **demand characteristics** refers to any of the potential cues or features of a study that (1) suggest to the participants what the purpose and hypothesis is, and (2) influence the participants to respond or behave in a certain way.

Reactivity occurs when participants modify their natural behavior in response to the fact that they are participating in a research study or the knowledge that they are being measured.

Orne (1962) describes participation in a research study as a social experience in which both the researcher and the participant have roles to play. In particular, the researcher is clearly in charge and is expected to give instructions. The participant, on the other hand, is expected to follow instructions. In fact, most participants strive to be a "good subject" and work hard to do a good job for the researcher. Although this may appear to be good for the researcher's study, it can create two serious problems. First, participants often try to figure out the purpose of the study and then modify their responses to fit their perception of the researcher's goals. Second, participants can become so dedicated to performing well that they do things in a research study that they would never do in a normal situation. To demonstrate this phenomenon, Orne (1962) instructed participants to complete a sheet of 224 addition problems. After finishing each sheet, the participant picked up a card with instructions for the next task. Every card contained the same instructions, telling the participants to tear up the sheet they just completed into at least 32 pieces and then go on to the next sheet of problems. The participants continued working problems and tearing them up over and over for hours without any sign of fatigue or frustration.

Clearly, this was a senseless task that no one would do under normal circumstances, yet the research participants were content to do it. Apparently, the act of participating in an experiment "demands" that people cooperate and follow instructions beyond any reasonable limit. However, because the participants are not acting normally, there is reason to question the validity and the reliability of the measurements they produce. When participants hide or distort their true responses, the researcher is not measuring what he intended to measure.

Although striving to be a responsible subject is the most common response, participants may adopt different ways of responding to experimental cues based on whatever they judge to be an appropriate role in the situation. These ways of responding are referred to as **subject roles,** or **subject role behaviors.** Four different subject roles have been identified (Weber & Cook, 1972):

1. The **good subject role.** These participants have identified the hypothesis of the study and are trying to produce responses that support the investigator's hypothesis. As good as this may sound, we do not want participants to adopt the good subject role because then we do not know if the results of the study extend to individuals who did not adopt such a role.
2. The **negativistic subject role.** These participants have identified the hypothesis of the study and are trying to act contrary to the investigator's hypothesis. Clearly, we do not want participants in our study to adopt this role.
3. The **apprehensive subject role.** These participants are overly concerned that their performance in the study will be used to evaluate their abilities or personal characteristics. They try to place themselves in a desirable light by responding in a socially desirable fashion instead of truthfully. Again, we do not want participants to adopt this role because they are not providing truthful responses.
4. The **faithful subject role.** These participants attempt to follow instructions to the letter and avoid acting on any suspicions they have about the purpose of the study. Two types of participants take on this role: those

who want to help science and know they should not allow their suspicions to enter into their responses, and those who are simply apathetic and do not give the study much thought. These are the participants we really want in our study.

Reactivity is especially a problem in studies conducted in a **laboratory,** where participants are fully aware that they are participants in a study. Although it is essentially impossible to prevent participants from noticing the demand characteristics of a study and adjusting their behaviors, there are steps to help reduce the effects of reactivity. Often, it is possible to observe and measure individuals without their awareness. For example, in a **field** study, participants are observed in their natural environment and are much less likely to know that they are being investigated, hence they are less reactive. Although this strategy is often possible, some variables are difficult to observe directly (for example, attitudes), and in some situations, ethical considerations prevent researchers from secretly observing people. An alternative strategy is to disguise or conceal the measurement process. The true purpose of a questionnaire can be masked by embedding a few critical questions in a larger set of irrelevant items or by deliberately using questions with low face validity. Another option is to suggest (subtly or openly) that the participant is performing one task when, in fact, we are observing and measuring something else. In either case, some level of deception is involved, which can raise a question of ethics (see Chapter 3). The most direct strategy for limiting reactivity is to reassure participants that their performance or responses are completely confidential and anonymous, and encourage them to make honest, natural responses. Any attempt to reassure and relax participants helps reduce reactivity.

DEFINITIONS

A **laboratory** is any setting that is obviously devoted to the discipline of science. It can be any room or any space that the subject or participant perceives as artificial.

A **field** setting is a place that the participant or subject perceives as a natural environment.

LEARNING CHECKS

What are demand characteristics, and how do they limit the validity of the measurements obtained in a research study?

Describe how the concept of participant reactivity might explain why a person's behavior during a job interview is very different from his behavior after he has been hired.

Explain (or give an example of) how participant reactivity can influence the measurements obtained in a research study.

Selecting a Measurement Procedure

As seen in the preceding sections, the choice of a measurement procedure involves several decisions. Because each decision has implications for the results of the study, it is important to consider all the options before deciding on a scheme for measurement for your own study or when critically reading a report of results from another research study.

The best starting point for selecting a measurement procedure is to review past research reports involving the variables or constructs to be examined. Most commonly used procedures have been evaluated for reliability and validity. In addition, using an established measurement procedure means that results can be compared directly to the previous literature in the area.

If more than one procedure exists for defining and measuring a particular variable, examine the options and determine which method is best suited for the specific research question. In particular, consider which measure has a level of sensitivity appropriate for detecting the individual differences and group differences that you expect to observe. Also decide whether the scale of measurement (nominal, ordinal, interval, ratio) is appropriate for the kind of conclusion you would like to make. Simply to establish that differences exist, a nominal scale may be sufficient. On the other hand, to determine the magnitude of a difference, you need either an interval or a ratio scale.

As noted in Chapter 2, critically examining and questioning a published measurement procedure can lead to new research ideas. As you read published research reports, always question the measurement procedures: Why was the variable measured as it was? Would a different scale have been better? Were the results biased by a lack of sensitivity or by range effects? What would happen if the variable(s) were defined and measured in a different way? If you can reasonably predict that a different measurement strategy would change the results, then you have the grounds for a new research study. Keep in mind, however, that if you develop your own operational definition or measurement procedure, you need to demonstrate validity and reliability, a task that is very detailed and time consuming. Some researchers dedicate their entire careers to developing a measure.

■ CHAPTER SUMMARY

In this chapter, we considered how a researcher defines and measures variables in a study. Because many research variables are hypothetical constructs and, hence, intangible, operational definitions are developed to define and measure the variables. Many measurement procedures are available for each variable. A researcher decides which procedure to use by evaluating the validity and reliability of the procedure. A valid measure truly measures the variable that it claims to measure. The six most commonly used measures of the validity of measurement are face, concurrent, predictive, construct, convergent, and divergent validity. A measure is reliable if it results in stable and consistent measurements. Three assessments of reliability are test-retest, interrater, and split-half reliability.

The process of measurement involves classifying individuals. The set of categories used for classification is called the scale of measurement. Four different types of measurement scales are nominal, ordinal, interval, and ratio. A major decision faced by researchers is which type, or modality, of measurement to use. The three modalities of measurement are self-report, physiological, and behavioral; each has certain advantages and disadvantages. Multiple measures, sensitivity of measurement, artifacts, and selection of a measurement procedure are also considered.

KEY WORDS

theories	divergent validity	double-blind research
constructs or hypothetical	reliability	demand characteristics
constructs	test-retest reliability	reactivity
operational definition	parallel-forms reliability	good subject role
validity	inter-rater reliability	negativistic subject role
face validity	split-half reliability	apprehensive subject role
concurrent validity	ceiling effect	faithful subject role
predictive validity	floor effect	laboratory
construct validity	experimenter bias	field
convergent validity	single-blind research	

EXERCISES

1. In addition to the key words, you should also be able to define each of the following terms:
   positive relationship
   negative relationship
   accuracy
   scale of measurement
   nominal scale
   ordinal scale
   interval scale
   ratio scale
   self-report measure
   physiological measure
   behavioral measure
   desynchrony
   range effect
   artifact
   subject roles or subject role behaviors
2. Pick a hypothetical construct. Describe external stimuli that influence the construct and external behaviors that are influenced by the construct.
3. Describe how a researcher establishes the predictive validity of a measure.
4. Describe how a researcher establishes the concurrent validity of a measure.
5. What are the limitations of operational definitions?

6. What is meant by the reliability of a measure?
7. What is meant by the validity of a measure?
8. Describe how split-half reliability is established.
9. Describe how test-retest reliability is established.
10. What is the advantage of using multiple measures for a single variable? What is the disadvantage?
11. Describe the concept of error in a measurement. How is error related to reliability?
12. Briefly explain how a ceiling effect (or floor effect) can affect the outcome of a research study.
13. Imagine that you are a participant in a research study. For each of the following scenarios, describe how you would probably react, and explain how your reactivity would influence your responses.
    a. A researcher tells you that the task you are about to perform is directly related to intelligence. Intelligent people usually find the task quite easy and perform very well.

b. A researcher tells you that the purpose of the study is to measure your attitudes and prejudices concerning race. First assume that the researcher intends to ask you questions in an interview. Then assume that the researcher hands you an anonymous questionnaire to fill out privately.

14. Which scale of measurement would probably be used for each of the following variables?
    a. occupation
    b. age
    c. gender
    d. socioeconomic class (upper, middle, or lower class)

LEARNING ACTIVITIES

1. For each of the following operational definitions, decide whether you consider it to be a valid measure. Explain why or why not. Decide whether you consider it to be a reliable measure. Explain why or why not.
   a. A researcher defines academic motivation in terms of the number of minutes a student spends working on class-related material outside of class during a 24-hour period from noon on Monday to noon on Tuesday.
   b. Reasoning that bigger brains require bigger heads, a researcher measures intelligence by measuring the circumference of each person's head (just above the ears).
   c. A sports psychologist measures physical fitness by measuring how far each person can throw a baseball.
   d. A professor classified students as either introverted or extroverted based on the level of participation in class discussions during the first week of class.

2. Select a subject and use a full-text database such as PsycArticles to locate an empirical journal article that reports the results of a research study examining your subject. Specifically, find an article in which the researchers obtained a sample of participants and then used some form of measurement. Once you have found your article, answer each of the following questions.
   a. What was measured and how was it measured? (If multiple variables were measured, select one.)
   b. Was the variable measured directly (like height or weight), or did the research use an operational definition to measure a hypothetical construct such as motivation?

   c. If an operational definition was used, what was the operational definition?
   d. What scale of measurement was used (nominal, ordinal, interval, or ratio)?
   e. Did the researchers use a physiological, a behavioral, or a self-report measure?

3. A researcher has developed a new test of personality. To evaluate the reliability of the test the researcher obtains a sample of $n = 8$ participants. Each individual takes the test on a Monday morning, then returns 2 weeks later to take the test again. The two scores for each individual are reported in the following table.

Participant	First Test	Second Test
A	13	15
B	5	4
C	12	13
D	11	11
E	9	10
F	14	13
G	8	8
H	8	6

Sketch a graph (a scatter plot) showing the relationship between the first and second test (see Figure 4.1). Just by looking at your graph, estimate the degree of test-retest reliability of the personality measure (i.e., is it high or low?).

4. Select one construct from the following list:
   self-esteem
   femininity/masculinity
   creativity
   hunger
   motivation
   fear

Briefly describe how it might be measured using:

a. an operational definition based on self-report (for example, a questionnaire).

b. an operational definition based on behavior (for example, what kinds of behavior would you expect to see from an individual with high self-esteem?)

WEB RESOURCES

Visit the Book Companion Website at **www.cengage.com/international** to access study tools including a glossary, flashcards, and web quizzing. You will also find a link to Statistics and Research Methods Workshops.

For this chapter, we suggest you look at the following workshops:

Specifying Constructs

Operational Definitions

Reliability and Validity

5

Sampling Techniques

CHAPTER OVERVIEW

In this chapter, we discuss the selection of individuals for participation in research studies, Step 4 of the research process outlined in Chapter 1. In any research study, only a small number of individuals actually participate. However, the researcher would like to generalize the results of the study beyond the small group of participants and, therefore, must develop a plan for selecting participants so that the individuals in the study constitute a reasonable representation of the broader population. The options for selecting individuals are presented here.

5.1 | INTRODUCTION

Beyond the research idea, hypothesis and prediction, and how you decide to define and measure your variables, one of the most critical issues in planning research is the selection of research participants (see Chapter 1, Step 4 of the research process). Suppose, for example, that you are interested in using a survey to study high school students' attitudes toward unrestricted searches of their lockers. Who will complete your questionnaire? All the high school students in the nation? Not likely—that would be an enormous and expensive undertaking. Instead, you will have to select a relatively small group of students to represent the entire group. Other practical constraints probably mean that you will be limited to selecting students from your own local region. As a result, a researcher who works in Los Angeles will probably select a very different group of students than would be selected by a researcher working in rural Kentucky. Because these two researchers will have very different participants, it also is likely that they will obtain very different results. The bottom line in any research study is that not everyone can participate, and the outcome of the study may depend on the way in which participants are selected.

Populations and Samples

In the terminology of research design, the large group of interest to a researcher is called the **population,** and the small set of individuals who participate in the study is called the **sample.** Figure 5.1 illustrates the relationship between a population and a sample. Typically, populations are huge, containing far too many individuals to measure and study. For example, a researcher may be interested in adolescents, preschool children, men, women, or humans. In each of these cases, the population is much too large to permit a researcher to study every individual. Therefore, a researcher must rely on a smaller group, a sample, to provide information about the population. A sample is selected from a population and is intended to represent that population. The goal of the research study is to examine the sample, then generalize the results to the entire population. Although several different researchers may begin with the same research question concerning the same population, each research study is a unique event that involves its own specific group of participants.

DEFINITIONS

A **population** is the entire set of individuals of interest to a researcher. Although the entire population usually does not participate in a research study, the results from the study are generalized to the entire population.

A **sample** is a set of individuals selected from a population and usually is intended to represent the population in a research study.

**LEARNING CHECK**

Explain the relationship between a population and a sample.

Before proceeding, we need to distinguish among different types of populations. A **target population** is the group defined by the researcher's specific interests. Individuals in a target population typically share one

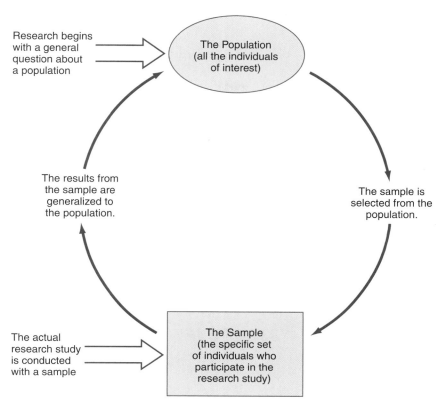

FIGURE **5.1** The Relationship Between a Population and a Sample

characteristic. All children of divorced parents, all elementary school–aged children, and all adolescents diagnosed with bulimia nervosa are examples of target populations. Usually, target populations are not easily available. For example, for a researcher interested in the treatment of bulimia nervosa in adolescents, the target population would be all of the adolescents in the world who are diagnosed with this disorder. Clearly, the researcher would not have access to most of these people to recruit as a sample of participants for the research study. However, a researcher would have access to the many local clinics and agencies that treat clients with eating disorders. These local clients (adolescents diagnosed with bulimia nervosa) become the **accessible population** from which the sample is selected. Most researchers select their samples from accessible populations. Therefore, we not only need to be cautious about generalizing the results of a study to the accessible population but we must also always be extremely cautious about generalizing the results of a research study to the target population. Figure 5.2 depicts the relationship among target populations, accessible populations, and samples. For the remainder of the book, we use the term *population* to mean the target population.

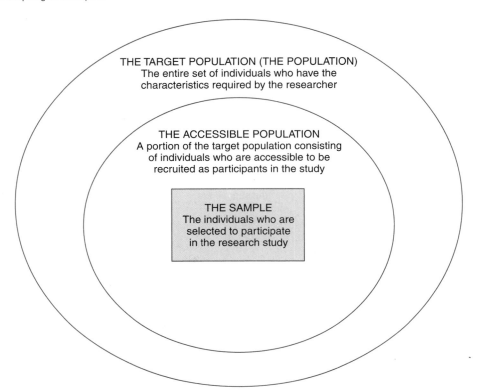

FIGURE **5.2** The Relationship Among the Target Population, the Accessible
Population, and the Sample

Representative Samples

We have said that the goal of a research study is to examine a sample and then
generalize the results to the population. How accurately we can generalize the
results from a given sample to the population depends on the **representativeness** of the sample. The degree of representativeness of a sample refers to how
closely the sample mirrors or resembles the population. Thus, one problem
that every researcher faces is how to obtain a sample that provides a reasonable representation of the population. To generalize the results of a study to a
population, the researcher must select a **representative sample.**

Before even beginning to select a sample, however, you must consider how
well the accessible population represents the target population. Specifically, the
group of participants who are available for selection may not be completely representative of the more general population. For example, the elderly adults in the
southeastern United States will have a unique cultural background that may differentiate them from other elderly adults throughout the world. Thus, the ability to generalize the results from a research study may be limited by the specific
characteristics of the accessible population. Often, the most a researcher can
hope for is to select a sample that is representative of the accessible population.

The major threat to selecting a representative sample is bias. A **biased sample** is one that has characteristics noticeably different from those of the population. If the individuals in a sample are smarter (or older or faster) than the individuals in the population, then the sample is biased. A biased sample can occur simply by chance; for example, tossing a balanced coin can result in heads 10 times in a row. It is more likely, however, that a biased sample is the result of **selection bias** (also called **sampling bias**), which means that the sampling procedure favors the selection of some individuals over others. For example, if the population we are interested in is adults and we recruit our sample from the students enrolled at a university, we are likely to obtain a sample that is smarter, on average, than the individuals in the entire population. If we recruit from Facebook, our sample is likely to be younger than the population. In general, the likelihood of the sample being representative depends on the procedure that is used to select participants. In this chapter, we consider two basic approaches to sampling, and examine some of the common strategies or techniques for obtaining samples.

DEFINITIONS

The **representativeness** of a sample refers to the extent to which the characteristics of the sample accurately reflect the characteristics of the population.

A **representative sample** is a sample with the same characteristics as the population.

A **biased sample** is a sample with different characteristics from those of the population.

Selection bias or **sampling bias** occurs when participants or subjects are selected in a manner that increases the probability of obtaining a biased sample.

 **LEARNING CHECKS**

A researcher studying cyberbullying among middle school students interviews a group of students from a local middle school about their cyberbullying experiences. For this study, identify the target population, the accessible population, and the sample.

Describe why it is important to obtain a representative sample.

Sample Size

As we noted, research studies typically use the results from a relatively small sample as the basis for answering questions about a relatively large population. The goal is to obtain a sample that is representative of the population. One fundamental question in reaching this goal is determining how large the sample should be to be representative. Unfortunately, there is no simple answer to this question, but there are some general guidelines that can help you choose a sample size.

The first principle is the simple observation that a large sample is probably more representative than a small sample. In the field of statistics, this principle is know as the **law of large numbers** and states that the larger the sample size, the more likely it is that values obtained from the sample are similar to the actual values for the population. In simple terms, the bigger the sample is, the more accurately it represents the population. Although large samples are good, there is also a practical limit to the number of individuals it is reasonable to use in a research study. As a result, researchers typically must compromise between the advantages of a really large sample and the demands of recruiting and testing a really large group of participants. One aid in determining a compromise number is the statistical observation that the discrepancy between a sample and its population tends to decrease in relation to the square root of the sample size. For example, Figure 5.3 shows how the average difference between a sample mean and the population mean decreases as the sample size increases. Notice that the sample becomes a more accurate representative of the population as the size of the sample increases. Also notice that accuracy improves rapidly as the sample size is increased from 4 to 16 to 25, but the improvement in accuracy slows dramatically once the sample size is around 30. Because there is only a limited benefit from increasing sample size beyond 25 or 30, researchers often use this sample size as a goal when planning research.

Although a sample size of 25 or 30 individuals for each group or each treatment condition is a good target, other considerations may make this sample size unreasonably large or small. If, for example, a research study is comparing 10 or 15 different treatment conditions, a separate group of 25 individuals in each condition would require a total sample of 250 to 375 participants. In many situations it could be difficult or impossible to recruit that many individuals, and researchers might have to settle for samples of only 10 or 12 in each condition. At the other extreme, researchers often begin a research study with a specific target for the level of accuracy. For example, a political poll may want an accuracy of $\pm 5\%$ in determining voters' preferences between two candidates. In this situation, it can be computed that the sample must have at least 384 individuals to be confident that the preferences observed in the sample are within 5% of the corresponding population preferences.

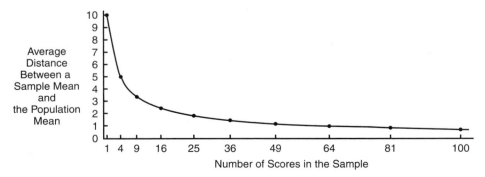

FIGURE **5.3** The Average Distance Between a Sample Mean and the Population Mean as a Function of Sample Size

Note that the larger the sample, the more accurately the sample represents the population. However, representativeness increases in relation to the square root of the sample size.

In general, there is no simple solution to determining how many individuals should be in a sample. One helpful guide is to review published reports of similar research studies to see how many participants they used, keeping in mind that a larger sample tends to be more representative and increases your chances for a successful study.

Sampling Basics

The process of selecting individuals for a study is called **sampling.** Researchers have developed a variety of different **sampling methods** (also called **sampling techniques** or **sampling procedures**). Sampling methods fall into two basic categories: probability sampling and nonprobability sampling.

In **probability sampling,** the odds of selecting a particular individual are known and can be calculated. For example, if each individual in a population of 100 people is equally likely to be selected, then the probability of selection is 1/100 for each person. Probability sampling has three important conditions:

1. The exact size of the population must be known and it must be possible to list all of the individuals.
2. Each individual in the population must have a specified probability of selection.
3. When a group of individuals are all assigned the same probability, the selection process must be unbiased so that all group members have an equal chance of being selected. Selection must be a **random process,** which simply means that every possible outcome is equally likely. For example, each time you toss a coin, the two possible outcomes (heads and tails) are equally likely.

In **nonprobability sampling,** the odds of selecting a particular individual are not known because the researcher does not know the population size and cannot list the members of the population. In addition, in nonprobability sampling, the researcher does not use an unbiased method of selection. For example, a researcher who wants to study the behavior of preschool children may go to a local child-care center where a group of preschool children are already assembled. Because the researcher does not ensure that all preschool children have an equal chance of being selected, this sample has an increased chance of being biased. For example, if the child-care center includes only white, middle-class children, then the sample definitely does not represent the target population of preschool children. In general, nonprobability sampling has a greater risk of producing a biased sample than does probability sampling.

Notice that probability sampling requires extensive knowledge of the population. Specifically, we must be able to list all of the individuals in the population. In most situations, this information is not available to a researcher. As a result, probability sampling is rarely used for research in the behavioral sciences. Nonetheless, this kind of sampling provides a good foundation for introducing the concept of representativeness and demonstrating how different sampling techniques can be used to help ensure a representative sample.

DEFINITIONS

Sampling is the process of selecting individuals to participate in a research study.

In **probability sampling,** the entire population is known, each individual in the population has a specifiable probability of selection, and sampling occurs by a random process based on the probabilities.

A **random process** is a procedure that produces one outcome from a set of possible outcomes. The outcome must be unpredictable each time, and the process must guarantee that each of the possible outcomes is equally likely to occur.

In **nonprobability sampling,** the population is not completely known, individual probabilities cannot be known, and the sampling method is based on factors such as common sense or ease, with an effort to maintain representativeness and avoid bias.

In the following sections, we discuss five probability sampling methods (simple random, systematic, stratified, proportionate stratified, and cluster sampling) and two nonprobability sampling methods (convenience and quota sampling). For each method, the general goal is to obtain a sample that is representative of the population from which it is taken. For different kinds of research, however, the definition of representative varies; hence, there are several well-defined sampling procedures that attempt to produce a particular kind of representation.

LEARNING CHECK

A researcher plans to select a sample from each of the following populations. Which would probably be a probability sample and which would probably be a nonprobability sample?

a. The population consists of the class of entering freshmen at a local college.

b. The population consists of 12-month-old infants.

5.2 | PROBABILITY SAMPLING METHODS

Simple Random Sampling

The starting point for most probability sampling techniques is **simple random sampling.** The basic requirement for random sampling is that each individual in the population has an equal chance of being selected. Equality means that no individual is more likely to be chosen than another. A second requirement that is sometimes added is that each selection is independent of the others. Independence means that the choice of one individual does not bias the researcher for or against the choice of another individual.

Suppose a researcher is interested in a population defined as all the adults who live in a particular city. To obtain a sample, the researcher opens a city phone book at random, plunks down a finger on someone's name, and selects that person to be in the sample. The researcher then turns to the next page and plunks a finger on the next name to be included. This process of turning pages and picking names continues until the complete sample is obtained. Is this an example of simple random sampling? No, because the requirement of equality is violated; not everyone in the population has an equal chance of being selected. Some people in the population have no chance of being selected because their names are not in the phone book (for example, people who have unlisted phone numbers, phone numbers under other people's names, or only use cell phones). In addition, the names are not selected independently. Because the researcher picks only one name from each page, all the other names on that page are excluded from the sample. Thus, selecting one name produces a bias (zero probability) against all the other names on the same page.

The obvious goal of a simple random sample is to ensure that the selection procedure cannot discriminate among individuals and thereby result in a non-representative sample. The two principal methods of random sampling are:

1. *Sampling with replacement:* This method requires that an individual selected for the sample be recorded as a sample member, and then returned to the population (replaced) before the next selection is made. This procedure ensures that the probability of selection remains constant throughout a series of selections. For example, if we select from a population of 100 individuals, the probability of selecting any particular individual is 1/100. To keep this same probability (1/100) for the second selection, it is necessary to return the first individual to the pool before the next is selected. Because the probabilities stay constant, this technique ensures that the selections are independent.
2. *Sampling without replacement:* As the term indicates, this method removes each selected individual from the population before the next selection is made. Although the probability of being selected changes with each selection, this method guarantees that no individual appears more than once in a single sample. Because the probabilities change with each selection, this technique does not produce independent selections; the probability that you will be selected increases each time another person is selected and removed from the population.

Sampling with replacement is an assumption of many of the mathematical models that form the foundation of statistical analysis. In most research, however, individuals are not actually replaced because then one individual could appear repeatedly in the same sample. If we conduct a public opinion survey, for example, we would not call the same person 10 times and then claim that we had a sample of 10 individuals. Most populations are so large that the probabilities remain essentially unchanged from one selection to the next, even when we do not replace individuals. For example, the difference between a probability of 1/1,000 and 1/999 is negligible. By using large populations, researchers can sample without replacement, which ensures that individuals are not repeated in one sample, and still satisfy the mathematical assumptions needed for statistical analysis.

The process of simple random sampling consists of the following steps:

1. Clearly define the population from which you want to select a sample.
2. List all the members of the population.
3. Use a random process to select individuals from the list.

Often, each individual is assigned a number, and then a random process is used to select numbers. For example, suppose a researcher has a population of 100 third-grade children from a local school district, from which a sample of 25 children is to be selected. Each child's name is put on a list, and each child is assigned a number from 1 to 100. Then the numbers 1 to 100 are written on separate pieces of paper and shuffled. Finally, the researcher picks 25 slips of paper and the numbers on the paper determine the 25 participants.

As noted above, researchers typically use some random process such as a coin toss or picking numbers from a hat to guide the selection. But what if, in picking the numbers from a hat, the size of the papers is different or the slips of paper are not shuffled adequately? The researcher could select individuals with larger slips of paper or individuals at the end of the list whose slips of paper are at the top of the pile. A more unbiased random process involves using the random number table for selection of participants. Appendix A contains a table of random numbers and a step-by-step guide for using it.

The logic behind simple random sampling is that it removes bias from the selection procedure and should result in representative samples. However, note that simple random sampling removes bias by leaving each selection to chance. In the long run, this strategy generates a balanced, representative sample. If we toss a coin thousands of times, eventually, the results will be 50% heads and 50% tails. In the short run, however, there are no guarantees. Because chance determines each selection, it is possible (although usually unlikely) to obtain a very distorted sample. We could, for example, toss a balanced coin and get heads 10 times in a row. Or we could get a random sample of 10 males from a population that contains an equal number of men and women. To avoid this kind of nonrepresentative sample, researchers often impose additional restrictions on the random sampling procedure; these are presented later in the sections on stratified and proportionate stratified random sampling.

LEARNING CHECK Explain how it is possible to obtain a biased sample with simple random sampling.

Systematic Sampling

Systematic sampling is a type of probability sampling that is very similar to simple random sampling. Systematic sampling begins by listing all the individuals in the population, then randomly picking a starting point on the list. The sample is then obtained by moving down the list, selecting every *n*th name. Note that systematic sampling is identical to simple random sampling (i.e., follow the three steps) for selection of the first participant; however, after the first individual is selected, the researcher does not continue to use a random process to select the remaining individuals for the sample. Instead, the researcher systematically selects every *n*th name on the list following the first selection. The size of *n* is calculated by dividing the population size by the desired sample size. For example, suppose a researcher has a population of 100 third-grade students and would like to select a sample of 25 children. Each child's name is put on a list and assigned a number from 1 to 100. Then, the researcher uses a random process such as a table of random numbers to select the first participant; for example, participant number 11. The size of n in this example is 4 (100/25). Therefore, every fourth individual after participant 11 (15, 19, 23, and so on) is selected.

This technique is truly less random than simple random sampling because the principle of independence is violated. Specifically, if we select participant number 11, we are biased against choosing participants number 12, 13, and 14, and we are biased in favor of choosing participant number 15. However, as a probability sampling method, this method ensures a high degree of representativeness.

Stratified Random Sampling

A population usually consists of a variety of identifiable subgroups. For example, the population of registered voters in California can be subdivided into men and women, Republicans and Democrats, different ethnic groups, different age groups, and so on. The different subgroups can be viewed as different layers or strata like the layers of rock on a cliff face (Figure 5.4). Often, a researcher's goal for a *representative sample* is to ensure that each of the different subgroups is adequately represented. One technique for accomplishing this goal is to use **stratified random sampling**. To obtain this kind of sample, we first identify the specific subgroups (or strata) to be included in the sample. Then we select equal-sized random samples from each of the pre-identified subgroups, using the same steps as in simple random sampling. Finally, we combine the subgroup samples into one overall sample. For example, suppose that we plan to select 50 individuals from a large introductory psychology class and want to ensure that men and women are equally represented. First, we select a random sample of 25 men from the males in the class and then a random sample of 25 women from the females. Combining these two subgroup samples produces the desired stratified random sample.

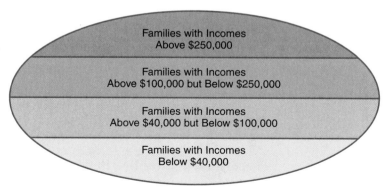

FIGURE **5.4** The Population of a Major City Shown as Different Layers, or Strata, Defined by Annual Income

Stratified random sampling is particularly useful when a researcher wants to describe each individual segment of the population or wants to compare segments. To do this, each subgroup in the sample must contain enough individuals to adequately represent its segment of the population. Consider the following example.

> A sociologist conducts an opinion survey in a major city. Part of the research plan calls for describing and comparing the opinions of four different ethnic groups: African Americans, Hispanics, Asians, and Whites. If the researcher uses simple random sampling to select 300 individuals, the sample might contain only a few individuals from one (or more) of these groups. With only a handful of representatives of a particular group, the researcher could not make any definite statements about that group's opinion, and could not make any meaningful comparisons with other ethnic groups. A stratified random sample avoids this problem by ensuring that each subgroup contains a predetermined number of individuals (set by the researcher). For a total sample of 300, the researcher selects 75 representatives of each of the four predetermined subgroups.

The main advantage of a stratified random sample is that it guarantees that each of the different subgroups will be well represented with a relatively large group of individuals in the sample. Thus, this type of sampling is appropriate when the purpose of a research study is to examine specific subgroups and make comparisons between them. However, stratified random sampling also has some negative consequences. First, stratified random sampling tends to produce a distorted picture of the overall population. Suppose, for example, that we are taking a stratified random sample of 50 people (25 men and 25 women) from a population consisting of 50 men and 250 women. In this case, men and women are represented equally in the sample but are not equal in the population. Men, for example, represent less than 17% of the population but make up 50% of the sample. Also, you should notice that stratified random sampling is not equivalent to simple random sampling. Specifically, every individual in the population does not have an equal chance of being selected. In our example, the probability of selecting any individual man is 25/50, or 1 out of 2, and the probability of selecting any specific woman is 25/250, or 1 out of 10. Although all the women have an equal chance of selection (1/10) and all the men have an equal chance (1/2), it is not the case that men and women are equally likely to be selected. The next sampling method does produce a true random sample by using a different definition of a *representative* sample.

LEARNING CHECK Explain the advantage of using stratified random sampling instead of simple random sampling.

Proportionate Stratified Random Sampling

Occasionally, researchers try to improve the correspondence between a sample and a population by deliberately ensuring that the composition of the sample matches the composition of the population. As with a stratified sample, we begin by identifying a set of subgroups or segments in the population.

Next, we determine what proportion of the population corresponds to each subgroup. Finally, a sample is obtained such that the proportions in the sample exactly match the proportions in the overall population. This kind of sampling is called **proportionate stratified random sampling**, or simply **proportionate random sampling**.

For example, suppose that we want our sample to accurately represent gender in the population. If the overall population contains 75% females and 25% males, then the sample is selected so that it, too, contains 75% females and 25% males. First, determine the desired size of the sample, then randomly select from the females in the population until you have a number corresponding to 75% of the sample size. Finally, randomly select from the males in the population to obtain the other 25% of the sample. Proportionate random sampling is used commonly for political polls and other major public opinion surveys in which researchers want to ensure that a relatively small sample provides an accurate, representative cross-section of a large and diverse population. The sample can be constructed so that several variables such as age, economic status, and political affiliation are represented in the sample in the same proportions in which they exist in the population.

Depending on how precisely we want sample proportions to match population proportions, the proportionate stratified sample can create a lot of extra work. Obviously, we must first determine the existing population proportions, which may require a trip to the library or another research center; then we must find individuals who match the categories we have identified. One strategy is to obtain a very large sample (much bigger than ultimately needed), measure all of the different variables for each individual, then randomly select those who fit the criteria (or randomly weed out the extras who do not fit). This process requires a lot of preliminary measurement before the study actually begins, and it discards many of the sampled individuals. In addition, a proportionate stratified sample can make it impossible for a researcher to describe or compare some subgroups or strata that exist within the population. For example, if a specific subgroup makes up only 1% of the population, they also make up only 1% of the sample. In a sample of 100 individuals, this means that there is only one person from the subgroup. It should be clear that you cannot rely on one person to adequately represent the entire subgroup.

LEARNING CHECKS

Explain the advantage of using stratified random sampling instead of proportionate stratified random sampling.

Explain the advantage of using proportionate stratified random sampling instead of stratified random sampling.

Cluster Sampling

All of the sampling techniques we have considered so far are based on selecting individual participants, one at a time, from the population. Occasionally, however, the individuals in the population are already clustered in preexisting groups, and a researcher can randomly select groups instead of selecting individuals. For example, a researcher may want to obtain a large sample of third-grade students from the city school system. Instead of selecting 300 students one at a time, the researcher can randomly select 10 classrooms (each with about 30 students) and still end up with 300 individuals in the sample. This procedure is called **cluster sampling** and can be used whenever well-defined clusters exist within the population of interest. This sampling technique has two clear advantages. First, it is a relatively quick and easy way to obtain a large sample. Second, the measurement of individuals can often be done in groups, which can greatly facilitate the entire research project. Instead of selecting an individual and measuring a single score, the researcher can often test and measure the entire cluster at one time, and walk away with 30 scores from a single experimental session.

The disadvantage of cluster sampling is that it can raise concerns about the independence of the individual scores. A sample of 300 individuals is assumed to contain 300 separate, individual, and independent measurements. However, if one individual in the sample directly influences the score of another individual, then the two scores are, in fact, related and should not be counted as two separate individuals. As an extreme example, suppose one child completes a research questionnaire and a second child simply copies all the answers. Clearly, the two questionnaires should not be treated as two separate individuals. If the individuals within a cluster share common characteristics that might influence the variables being measured, then a researcher must question whether the individual measurements from the cluster actually represent separate and independent individuals.

LEARNING CHECK Describe the problem associated with cluster sampling.

Combined-Strategy Sampling

Occasionally, researchers combine two or more sampling strategies to select participants. For example, a superintendent of schools may first divide his district into regions (e.g., north, south, east, and west), which involves stratified sampling. From the different regions, the superintendent may then select two third-grade classrooms, which involves cluster sampling. Selection strategies are commonly combined to optimize the chances that a sample is representative of a widely dispersed or broad-based population such as in a wide market survey or a political poll.

A Summary of Probability Sampling Methods

Probability sampling techniques have a very good chance of producing a representative sample because they tend to rely on a random selection process. However, as we noted earlier, simple random sampling by itself does not guarantee a high degree of representativeness. To correct this problem, researchers often impose restrictions on the random process. Specifically, stratified random sampling can be used to guarantee that different subgroups are equally represented in the sample, and proportionate stratified sampling can be used to guarantee that the overall composition of the sample matches the composition of the population. However, probability sampling techniques can be extremely time consuming and tedious (that is, obtaining a list of all the members of a population and developing a random, unbiased selection process). These techniques also require that the researcher "know" the whole population and have access to it. For these reasons, probability sampling techniques are rarely used except in research involving small, contained populations (for example, students at a school or prisoners at one correctional facility) or large-scale surveys.

5.3 | NONPROBABILITY SAMPLING METHODS

Convenience Sampling

Convenience sampling is also known as *accidental sampling*, or *haphazard sampling*.

The most commonly used sampling method in behavioral science research is probably **convenience sampling.** In convenience sampling, researchers simply use as participants those individuals who are easy to get. People are selected on the basis of their availability and willingness to respond. Examples include conducting research with students from an Introductory Psychology class or studying the children in a local daycare center. A researcher who teaches at The College at Brockport, State University of New York and uses college students as participants is likely to use students enrolled at that college. A researcher at the University of California, Berkeley, is likely to use students enrolled there.

Convenience sampling is considered a weak form of sampling because the researcher makes no attempt to know the population or to use a random process in selection. The researcher exercises very little control over the representativeness of the sample and, therefore, there is a strong possibility that the obtained sample is biased. This is especially problematic when individuals actively come forward to participate as with phone-in radio surveys or mail-in magazine surveys. In these cases, the sample is biased because it contains only those individuals who listen to that station or read that magazine, and feel strongly about the issue being investigated. These individuals are probably not representative of the general population.

Despite this major drawback, convenience sampling is probably used more often than any other kind of sampling. It is an easier, less expensive, more timely technique than the probability sampling techniques, which involve identifying every individual in the population and using a laborious random process to select participants.

Finally, although convenience sampling offers no guarantees of a representative and unbiased sample, you should not automatically conclude that this type of sampling is hopelessly flawed. Most researchers use two strategies to help correct most of the serious problems associated with convenience sampling. First, researchers try to ensure that their samples are reasonably representative and not strongly biased. For example, a researcher may select a sample that consists entirely of students from an Introductory Psychology class at a small college in Atlanta. However, if the researcher is careful to select a broad cross-section of students (males and females, different ages, different levels of academic performance, and so on), it is sensible to expect this sample to be reasonably similar to any other sample of college students that might be obtained from other academic departments or other colleges around the country. Unless the research study involves some special skill such as surfing or winter driving, it usually is reasonable to assume that a sample from one location is just as representative as a sample from any other location. The students in a state college in Florida are probably quite similar to the students in a state college in Idaho, and the children in a Seattle child-care center are probably similar to the children in a St. Louis child-care center. The exception to this simple concept occurs whenever a convenience sample is obtained from a location with unusual or unique characteristics such as a music school for extremely talented students or a private child-care center for child geniuses.

The second strategy that helps minimize potential problems with convenience sampling is simply to provide a clear description of how the sample was obtained and who the participants are. For example, a researcher might report that a sample of 20 children aged 3 to 5 was obtained from a child-care center in downtown Houston. Or a research report may state that a sample of 100 students, 67 females and 33 males, all between the ages of 18 and 22, was obtained from the Introductory Psychology class at a large midwestern state university. Although these samples may not be perfectly representative of the larger population and each may have some biases, at least everyone knows what the sample looks like and can make their own judgments about representativeness.

LEARNING CHECK   Describe the advantages and disadvantages of convenience sampling.

Quota Sampling

One method for controlling the composition of a convenience sample is to use some of the same techniques that are used for probability sampling. In the same way that we used stratified sampling to ensure that different subgroups are represented equally, **quota sampling** can ensure that subgroups are equally represented in a convenience sample. For example, a researcher can guarantee equal groups of boys and girls in a sample of 30 preschool children by establishing quotas for the number of individuals to be selected from each subgroup. Rather than simply taking the first 30 children, regardless of gender, who agree to participate, you impose a quota of 15 girls and 15 boys. After the quota of 15 boys is met, no other boys have a chance to participate in the study. In this example, quota sampling ensures that specific subgroups are adequately represented in the sample.

A variation of quota sampling mimics proportionate stratified sampling. Specifically, a researcher can adjust the quotas to ensure that the sample proportions match a predetermined set of population proportions. For example, a researcher could ensure that a sample contained 30% males and 70% females to match the same proportions that exist in a specific population. We should note that quota sampling is not the same as stratified and proportionate stratified sampling because it does not randomly select individuals from the population. Instead, individuals are selected on the basis of convenience within the boundaries set by the quotas.

Finally, there is not unanimous agreement about the terminology used to designate the different types of samples. For example, we recently read an article about a study that used "convenience stratified sampling" to create three groups of participants (McMahon, Rimsza, & Bay, 1997). In this study, the groups were obtained by convenience sampling, with the restriction that half of the participants in each group spoke Spanish only and the other half spoke both Spanish and English. We would call this a "quota sample," but the term "convenience stratified sample" also provides a sensible description of what was done. In general, you should rely on the description of the sampling technique rather than the name applied to it.

It also is possible for a convenience sample to use techniques borrowed from systematic sampling or cluster sampling. For example, a researcher who is sampling shoppers at a local mall could systematically select every fifth person who passes by. This technique can help ensure that the researcher gets a broadly representative sample and does not focus on one particular subgroup of people who appear to be more approachable. Also, a researcher who is selecting children from the local school (because it is convenient) could still select classroom clusters rather than individual students.

Different sampling techniques, including probability and nonprobability sampling, are summarized in Table 5.1.

TABLE **5.1**
Summary of Sampling Methods

Type of Sampling	Description	Strengths and Weaknesses
Probability Sampling		
Simple Random	A sample is obtained using a random process to select participants from a list containing the total population. The random process ensures that each individual has an equal and independent chance of selection.	The selection process is fair and unbiased, but there is no guarantee that the sample is representative.
Systematic	A sample is obtained by selecting every nth participant from a list containing the total population, after a random start.	An easy method for obtaining an essentially random sample, but the selections are not really random or independent.
Stratified Random	A sample is obtained by dividing the population into subgroups (strata) and then randomly selecting equal numbers from each of the subgroups.	Guarantees that each subgroup will have adequate representation, but the overall sample is usually not representative of the population.
Proportionate Stratified	A sample is obtained by subdividing the population into strata and then randomly selecting from each strata a number of participants so that the proportions in the sample correspond to the proportions in the population.	Guarantees that the composition of the sample (in terms of the identified strata) will be perfectly representative of the composition of the population, but some strata may have limited representation in the sample.

Continued

TABLE **5.1**
Summary of Sampling Methods—cont'd

Type of Sampling	Description	Strengths and Weaknesses
Cluster	Instead of selecting individuals, a sample is obtained by randomly selecting clusters (preexisting groups) from a list of all the clusters that exist within the population.	An easy method for obtaining a large, relatively random sample, but the selections are not really random or independent.
Nonprobability Sampling		
Convenience	A sample is obtained by selecting individual participants who are easy to get.	An easy method for obtaining a sample, but the sample is probably biased.
Quota	A sample is obtained by identifying subgroups to be included, then establishing quotas for individuals to be selected through convenience from each subgroup.	Allows a researcher to control the composition of a convenience sample, but the sample probably is biased.

■ CHAPTER SUMMARY

The goal of the research study is to measure a sample and then generalize the results to the population. Therefore, the researcher should be careful to select a sample that is representative of the population. This chapter examines some of the common strategies for obtaining samples.

The two basic categories of sampling techniques are probability and non-probability sampling. In probability sampling, the odds of selecting a particular individual are known and can be calculated. Types of probability sampling are simple random sampling, systematic sampling, stratified sampling, proportionate stratified sampling, and cluster sampling. In nonprobability sampling, the probability of selecting a particular individual is not known because the researcher does not know the population size or the members of the population. Types of nonprobability sampling are convenience and quota sampling. Each sampling method has advantages and limitations, and differs in terms of the representativeness of the sample obtained.

KEY WORDS

population
sample
representativeness
representative sample

biased sample
selection bias, or sampling
  bias
sampling

probability sampling
random process
nonprobability sampling

EXERCISES

1. In addition to the key words, you should also be able to define each of the following terms:
   target population
   accessible population
   law of large numbers
   sampling methods, or sampling techniques, or sampling procedures
   simple random sampling
   systematic sampling
   stratified random sampling
   proportionate stratified random sampling
   cluster sampling
   convenience sampling
   quota sampling
2. Explain the difference between probability and nonprobability sampling.
3. What is the problem with a biased sample?
4. Explain the difference between target and accessible populations.
5. Dr. Kim wants to conduct a study on memory in nursing home residents. He contacts local nursing homes and selects 50 residents from their resident lists to participate in his study.
   a. What is the target population?
   b. What is the accessible population?
   c. What is the sample?
6. For each of the following scenarios, identify which sampling method is used:
   a. The State College is conducting a survey of student attitudes and opinions. The plan is to use the list of all registered students and randomly select 50 freshmen, 50 sophomores, 50 juniors, and 50 seniors to make up the sample.
   b. An educational psychologist selects a sample of 40 third-grade children from the local public school, ensuring that the sample is divided evenly with 20 boys and 20 girls.
   c. The County Democratic Committee would like to determine which issues are most important to registered Democrats in the county. Using the list of registered Democrats, the committee selects a random sample of 30 for telephone interviews.
   d. A second option for the college survey (in part a) is based on the observation that the college accepts a large number of transfer students each year. As a result, the junior and senior classes are twice as large as the freshman and sophomore classes. To ensure that the sample reflects this difference in class size, the alternative plan is to determine the number of students in each class, then select a sample so that the number for each class in the sample is in direct relation to the number in each class for the entire college.
   e. A faculty member in the Psychology Department posts notices in classrooms and buildings on campus, asking for volunteers to participate in a human memory experiment. Interested students are asked to leave their names and telephone numbers.
7. Explain how the ability to generalize a study's results is affected by the sampling method used.

LEARNING ACTIVITIES

1. A population consists of only four individuals identified as A, B, C, and D. Your job is to select a random sample of two individuals from this population.
   a. Assuming that you are using *sampling without replacement,* list all of the possible random samples that could be obtained. (Hint #1: List the samples

systematically; for example, begin with all of the samples with individual A as the first person selected. Hint #2: If the same people are selected in two different orders, it counts as two different samples. For example, if A is selected first, then B, it is a different sample than if B were selected first, then A. Hint #3: You should obtain 12 different samples.)

b. Assuming that you are using *sampling with replacement,* list all of the possible random samples that could be obtained. Note: The same hints apply as in part a, except that you should now obtain 16 different samples.

WEB RESOURCES

Visit the Book Companion Website at **www .cengage.com/international** to access study tools including a glossary, flashcards, and web quizzing. You will also find a link to

Statistics and Research Methods Workshops. For this chapter, we suggest you look at the following workshop:

Sampling Methods

6

Approaches to Research: Internal and External Validity

CHAPTER OVERVIEW

In this chapter, we discuss research strategy selection as well as validity, an issue central to research strategy and design. Both internal and external validity are described, as are the principal threats to each. Research strategies are distinguished from designs and procedures.

6.1 | QUANTITATIVE AND QUALITATIVE RESEARCH

The primary purpose for this chapter is to introduce research strategies and the concept of validity for research. Before we begin that task, however, we should make a distinction between quantitative and qualitative research. Throughout this book, including the remainder of this chapter, we focus on **quantitative research.** The term *quantitative* refers to the fact that this type of research examines variables that typically vary in quantity (size, magnitude, duration, or amount). In Chapter 4, we examined different methods for measuring variables to determine how much, how big, or how strong they are. The results, or data, obtained from these measurements are usually numerical scores that can be summarized, analyzed, and interpreted using standard statistical procedures.

There is, however, an alternative approach to gathering, interpreting, and reporting information. The alternative is known as **qualitative research.** The primary distinction between quantitative and qualitative research is the type of data they produce. As noted, quantitative research typically produces numerical scores. The result of qualitative research, however, is typically a narrative report (that is, a written discussion of the observations). Qualitative research involves careful observation of participants (often including interaction with participants), usually accompanied by extensive note taking. The observations and notes are then summarized in a narrative report that attempts to describe and interpret the phenomenon being studied. A qualitative researcher studying depression in adolescents would simply talk with adolescents, asking questions and listening to answers, then prepare a written narrative describing the behaviors and attitudes that had been observed. On the other hand, a quantitative researcher would probably develop a test to measure depression for each participant and then compute an average score to describe the amount of depression for different subgroups of adolescents.

DEFINITIONS

Quantitative research is based on measuring variables for individual participants to obtain scores, usually numerical values, that are submitted to statistical analysis for summary and interpretation.

 Qualitative research is based on making observations that are summarized and interpreted in a narrative report.

Qualitative research is commonly used by social anthropologists, who often immerse themselves in a foreign culture to observe patterns of behavior that help them to understand and describe the social structure and customs of a different civilization. Other examples of qualitative research include Dian Fossey's observations of mountain gorillas (reported in *Gorillas in the Mist,* 1983), Thigpen and Cleckley's detailed description of a woman with multiple-personality disorder (reported in *The Three Faces of Eve,* 1957), and Jean Piaget's observations of his own children, which formed the basis for his theories of child development. None of these researchers measured individual scores but rather made more holistic observations of behavior that resulted in a detailed narrative rather than an average number.

As a final note, we should warn you that the distinction between quantitative and qualitative research is not as simple as numbers versus no numbers. In fact, the scores obtained in quantitative research occasionally are qualitative values. Recall from Chapter 4 that scores measured on a nominal scale do not differentiate degrees of quantity. Instead, nominal measurements simply classify individuals into separate, qualitatively different categories. For example, a researcher examining the relationship between gender and color blindness would classify participants according to gender (male/female) and color blindness (yes/no). Notice that these variables do not produce quantitative measurements—both are qualitative. However, the measurements ultimately are transformed into numbers by computing the percentage of males who are color blind and comparing that number with the percentage for females. As a result, this study would be classified as quantitative research.

6.2 | STRATEGIES FOR QUANTITATIVE RESEARCH

After you have identified a new idea for research, formed a hypothesis and a prediction, decided how to define and measure your variables, and determined which individuals should participate in the study and how to treat them ethically, the next step is to select a research strategy (Step 5 in the research process; see Section 1.4). The term **research strategy** refers to the general approach and goals of a research study. The selection of a research strategy is usually determined by the kind of question you plan to address and the kind of answer you hope to obtain—in general terms, what you hope to accomplish. For example, consider the following three research questions.

1. What is the average number of words a typical 2-year-old can say?
2. Is there a relationship between the quality of a child's breakfast and the level of the child's academic performance?
3. Do changes in breakfast quality cause changes in academic performance for children?

Notice that the first question is asking about a single variable (the number of words). The second question is asking about a relationship between two variables (quality of breakfast and academic performance). Specifically, this question is asking whether a relationship exists. The third question is also asking whether a relationship exists, however, this question asks for an *explanation* for the relationship. In this form, the question is asking whether differences in breakfast quality help explain why children have different levels of academic performance. These three different questions would require different research strategies. In this chapter, we introduce five research strategies that are intended to answer different types of research questions.

DEFINITION A **research strategy** is a general approach to research determined by the kind of question that the research study hopes to answer.

As noted earlier, this book focuses on quantitative research, which involves measuring variables to obtain scores. The five strategies we introduce in this chapter are all intended to examine measurements of variables and relationships between variables, and are presented as they apply to quantitative research. Nonetheless, some components of quantitative and qualitative research overlap and some of the methods and strategies we discuss can be used with either type of research. For example, observational research is discussed in Chapter 7 as it is used in quantitative research. However, this same procedure also forms the foundation for many qualitative research studies.

The Descriptive Research Strategy

This strategy is intended to answer questions about the current state of individual variables for a specific group of individuals. For example, for the students at a specific college, what is the typical number of text messages received each day? What is the average number of hours of sleep each day? What percentage voted in the latest presidential election? To answer these questions, a researcher could measure text messages, sleep time, and voting history for each student, and then calculate an average or percentage for each variable. Note that the **descriptive research strategy** is not concerned with relationships between variables but rather with the description of individual variables. The goal of the descriptive strategy is to obtain a snapshot (a description) of specific characteristics of a specific group of individuals. In Chapter 7 the details of the descriptive research strategy are discussed.

Relationships Between Variables

Descriptive research studies are conducted simply to describe individual variables as they exist naturally. Most research, however, is intended to examine the relationships between variables. For example, is there a relationship between the quality of breakfast and academic performance for elementary school children? Is there a relationship between the number of hours of sleep and grade point average (GPA) for college students? There are many different techniques for examining relationships and the four remaining research strategies presented in this chapter are intended to identify and describe relationships between variables.

A relationship between variables simply means that changes in one variable are consistently and predictably accompanied by changes in another variable. For example, Figure 6.1(a) shows the general relationship between self-esteem and gender for adolescents; when gender changes from male to female, self-esteem also changes from relatively high to relatively low (Kling, Hyde, Showers, & Buswell, 1999). In this example, only one of the two variables (self-esteem) is measured with numerical scores. In other situations, when both variables are measured using numbers or ranks, a variety of terms can be used to classify the relationships. For example, Figures 6.1(b) and 6.1(c) show **linear relationships** because the data points produced by the changing values of the two variables tend to form a straight-line pattern. Figures 6.1(d) shows an example of a **curvilinear relationship.** Again, there is a consistent, predictable relationship between the two variables, but now the pattern is a curved line. As we noted in Chapter 4 (p. 109), Figure 6.1(b) and 6.1(d) are examples of **positive relationships** because increases in one variable tend to be accompanied by increases in the other. Conversely, Figure 6.1(c) shows an example of a **negative relationship,** in which increases in one variable are accompanied by decreases in the other. Finally, recall that the terms describing relationships only apply when both variables consist of numbers or ranks. For example, Figure 6.1(a) shows a consistent and predictable relationship between gender and self-esteem; however, the relationship cannot be classified as linear, curvilinear, positive, or negative.

To establish the existence of a relationship, researchers must make observations—that is, measurements of the two variables. Depending on how the measurements are used, two distinct data structures can be produced. The two data structures also help to classify the different research strategies.

The Correlational Research Strategy: Measuring Two Variables for Each Individual

One technique for examining the relationship between variables is to observe the two variables as they exist naturally for a set of individuals. That is, simply measure the two variables for each individual. For example, researchers have found a relationship between GPA and sleep habits, specifically, wake-up time, for college students (Trockel, Barnes, & Egget, 2000). Figure 6.2 shows an example of the kind of data found in the study.

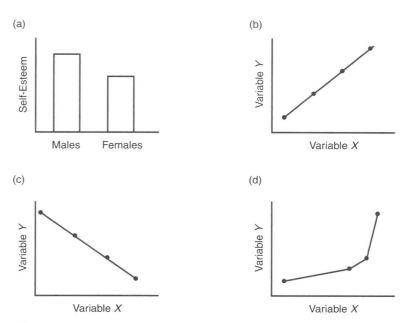

FIGURE **6.1** Examples of Different Types of Relationships Between Variables

(a) a general relationship (b) positive linear (c) negative linear (d) positive curvilinear. For graphs (b), (c) and (d), values for variable *X* increase from left to right and values for variable *Y* increase from bottom to top.

(a)

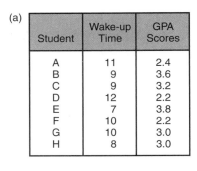

(b)

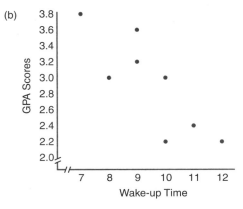

FIGURE **6.2** An Example of Data from a Correlational Study

Wake-up time and GPA scores were measured for each individual in a group of eight college students. (a) The resulting scores are listed in the table on the left-hand side of the figure. (b) The same scores are shown in a scatter plot on the right-hand side of the figure. Note that the data show a tendency for the GPA scores to decrease as wake-up time increases.

From Gravetter, *Essentials of Statistics for the Behavioral Sciences,* 7th ed., Fig. 1.4. Copyright © 2011 Wadsworth, a part of Cengage Learning. Reproduced with permission.

Consistent patterns in the data are often easier to see if the scores are presented in a graph. The right-hand side of Figure 6.2 shows the wake-up time and GPA scores in a graph called a *scatter plot*. In the scatter plot, each individual is represented by a point so that the horizontal position corresponds to the wake-up time and the vertical position corresponds to the student's GPA. The scatter plot shows a clear relationship; as wake-up time increases, GPA tends to decrease.

A research study that simply measures two variables for each individual and produces the kind of data shown in Figure 6.2, in which each variable is measured with numerical scores, is an example of the **correlational research strategy.** Note that the correlational strategy only attempts to describe the relationship (if one exists); it is not trying to explain the relationship. For example, although there may be a relationship between wake-up time and GPA, this does not mean that waking students earlier in the day would cause them to get better grades. The details of the correlational research strategy are discussed in Chapter 8.

Comparing Two or More Sets of Scores: The Experimental, Quasi-Experimental, and Nonexperimental Research Strategies

The second technique for examining the relationship between two variables involves comparing two or more groups of scores. In this situation, one of the variables is used to differentiate the groups. For example, one group of students is selected from high-income families and a second group is selected from low-income families. The second variable, each student's grade average, is then measured to obtain a score for each individual. An example of the resulting data is shown in Table 6.1. Note that the researcher compares the

TABLE **6.1**
High School Grades for Students from High-
and Low-Income Families

High-Income		Low-Income
72		83
86		89
81		94
78		90
85		97
80		89
91		95
Mean = 81.9	Compare the two groups	Mean = 91.0

scores for the high-income group with the scores for the low-income group. A systematic difference between the two groups of scores provides evidence of a relationship between family income and academic performance.

There are three different research strategies that examine relationships between variables using the kind of data shown in Table 6.1. The differences among the three strategies are based on the questions that they address and their ability to produce unambiguous answers.

The Experimental Research Strategy

The **experimental research strategy** is intended to answer cause-and-effect questions about the relationship between two variables. For example, are increases in exercise responsible for causing decreases in cholesterol level? To answer the question, a researcher could create two treatment conditions by changing the amount of exercise from low in one condition to high in the other. Then, one group of individuals is assigned to the low-exercise condition and a similar group is assigned to the high-exercise condition. Cholesterol is measured for each group and the scores in the low-exercise condition are compared with the scores in the high-exercise condition to determine whether changes in the level of exercise cause changes in cholesterol (Table 6.2a). Note that the purpose of the experimental research strategy is to explain the relationship by determining the underlying cause. An experimental study is conducted with rigorous control to help ensure an unambiguous demonstration of a cause-and-effect relationship. In Chapter 9 the details of the experimental research strategy are discussed.

The Quasi-Experimental Research Strategy

Although this strategy usually attempts to answer cause-and-effect questions about the relationship between two variables, it can never produce an unambiguous explanation. For example, a researcher would like to determine

TABLE **6.2**

Examples of Data for Experimental, Quasi-Experimental, and Nonexperimental Research Studies

a. Experimental		b. Quasi-Experimental		c. Nonexperimental	
Low Exercise	High Exercise	Without Treatment	With Treatment	Girls	Boys
168	122	still smoking	quit	27	14
196	210	still smoking	still smoking	30	16
175	130	quit	quit	19	18
210	124	still smoking	quit	27	15
226	146	still smoking	quit	24	21
183	133	still smoking	quit	23	23
142	158	quit	still smoking	18	18
198	122	quit	quit	15	14
207	140	still smoking	still smoking	29	21
195	135	still smoking	quit	28	20
Compare cholesterol scores		Compare smoking behaviors		Compare verbal scores	

whether a specific treatment program causes a reduction in cigarette smoking. Attempting to answer this question, a researcher could select a group of individuals who have signed up for the stop-smoking program and measure the smoking behavior for each individual before and after the program. The scores for this group could then be compared with those obtained for another group of individuals who are also trying to quit smoking but did not join the treatment program (see Table 6.2b). The **quasi-experimental research strategy** uses some of the rigor and control that exist in experiments; however, quasi-experimental studies always contain a flaw that prevents the research from obtaining an absolute cause-and-effect answer. For example, although people who joined the treatment program may be more successful at quitting, you cannot conclude that the treatment *caused* greater success. It may be that the treatment has no effect and the smokers who were more successful simply were more motivated. As the name implies, quasi-experimental studies are almost, but not quite, experiments. In Chapter 12 the details of the quasi-experimental research strategy are discussed.

The Nonexperimental Research Strategy

The **nonexperimental research strategy** is intended to demonstrate a relationship between variables but it does not attempt to explain the relationship. In particular, this strategy does not try to produce cause-and-effect explanations. For example, a researcher would like to determine whether the verbal skills for 6-year-old girls are different from those for 6-year-old boys. (Is there a relationship between verbal skills and gender?) To answer this question, a researcher could measure verbal skills for each individual in a group of boys and in a group of girls, then compare the two sets of scores (see Table 6.2c). Nonexperimental studies do not use the rigor and control that exist in experiments and in quasi-experimental studies, and do not produce cause-and-effect explanations. For example, a study may demonstrate that girls have higher verbal skills than boys, but it does not explain *why* the girls' scores are higher. Nonexperimental studies demonstrate the existence of relationships but do not explain relationships. In Chapter 12 the details of the nonexperimental research strategy are discussed.

Research Strategy Summary

The five research strategies are summarized in Table 6.3. For organizational purposes we group the five research strategies into three broad categories:

1. Strategies that examine individual variables instead of relationships between variables.
2. Strategies that examine relationships between variables by measuring two (or more) variables for each participant.
3. Strategies that examine relationships between variables by comparing two (or more) groups of scores.

Note that the three research strategies in Category 3 form a hierarchy in terms of their ability or interest in explaining relationships between variables. Experiments are designed to demonstrate cause-and-effect relationships. That is, experimental studies produce unambiguous explanations by demonstrating that changes in one variable are responsible for causing changes to occur in a second variable. Quasi-experimental studies would like to demonstrate cause-and-effect relationships but fall short of achieving this goal. Finally, nonexperimental research simply attempts to demonstrate that a relationship exists, and makes no attempt to explain why the two variables are related. Also notice that although the correlational and nonexperimental strategies use different data, they have the same purpose and produce the same kind of conclusion.

LEARNING CHECKS   How do the experimental, quasi-experimental, and nonexperimental strategies differ in terms of rigor and control?

How is the descriptive strategy different from the other four research strategies?

Data Structures and Statistical Analysis

Experimental, quasi-experimental, and nonexperimental studies all involve comparing groups of scores (see Table 6.2). Usually, the comparison involves looking for mean differences or differences in proportions. For example:

- The average cholesterol score is 142 for people in the high-exercise group compared to an average of 190 for people in the low-exercise group.
- Of the individuals who joined the treatment program, 70% quit smoking compared with only 30% of those who did not join.

TABLE **6.3**
Five Research Strategies Organized by the Data Structures They Use

Category 1: Strategies that examine individual variables.

Descriptive
Purpose: Produce a description of individual variables as they exist within a specific group.
Data: A list of scores obtained by measuring each individual in the group being studied.
Example: On average, students at the local college spend 12.5 hours studying outside of class each week and get 7.2 hours of sleep each night.

Category 2: Strategies that examine relationships between variables by measuring two (or more) variables for each participant.

Correlational
Purpose: Produce a description of the relationship between two variables but do not attempt to explain the relationship.
Data: Measure two variables (two scores) for each individual in the group being studied (see Figure 6.2).
Example: There is a relationship between wake-up times and grade point averages for college students, but we don't know why.

Category 3: Strategies that examine relationships between variables by comparing two (or more) groups of scores.

Experimental
Purpose: Produce a cause-and-effect explanation for the relationship between two variables.

Data: Create two treatment conditions by changing the level of one variable. Then measure a second variable for the participants in each condition (see Table 6.2a).
Example: Increasing the amount of exercise causes a decrease in cholesterol levels.

Quasi-Experimental
Purpose: Attempt to produce a cause-and-effect explanation, but fall short.
Data: Measure before/after scores for one group that receives a treatment and for a different group that does not receive the treatment (see Table 6.2b).
Example: The treatment may cause a reduction in smoking behavior but the reduced smoking may be caused by something else.

Nonexperimental
Purpose: Produce a description of the relationship between two variables but do not attempt to explain the relationship.
Data: Measure scores for two different groups of participants or for one group at two different times (see Table 6.2c).
Example: There is a relationship between gender and verbal ability. Girls tend to have higher verbal skills than boys, but we don't know why.

- The average verbal score for the girls is 24, compared with an average score of 18 for the boys.

Because these three strategies produce similar data, they also tend to use similar statistical techniques. For example, *t* tests and analysis of variance are used to evaluate mean differences and chi-square tests are used to compare proportions.

Correlational studies do not involve comparing different groups of scores. Instead, a correlational study measures two different variables (two different scores) for each individual in a single group and then looks for patterns within

Statistical techniques are discussed in Chapter 14.

the set of scores (see Figure 6.2). If a correlational study produces numerical scores, the data are usually evaluated by computing a correlation (such as the Pearson correlation). If the data consist of nonnumerical classifications, the statistical evaluation is usually a chi-square test.

Descriptive studies are intended to summarize single variables for a specific group of individuals. For numerical data, the statistical summary usually consists of a mean, or average, score. If the data are nonnumerical classifications, the summary is typically a report of the proportion (or percentage) associated with each category. For example, the average student sleeps 7 hours a day and eats two pizzas a week. Or, 58% of the students report having failed at least one course.

Summary

Different research strategies are available to address the variety of questions with which research can begin. Each strategy is directed toward different types of questions, and each strategy has its own strengths and limitations. Although we have identified five research strategies, another common method differentiates only two: experimental research and nonexperimental, or nonmanipulative, research. The rationale for this two-way classification is that only the experimental strategy can establish the existence of cause-and-effect relationships; other strategies cannot.

 **LEARNING CHECK**   Which research strategies involve comparing groups of scores?

6.3 | INTERNAL AND EXTERNAL VALIDITY

In later chapters, we examine each of the research strategies in detail. For now, however, we focus on a more fundamental issue: How well does the research study actually answer the question it was intended to answer? This is a question concerning the **validity** of the research study. The dictionary defines validity as "the quality or state of being true." In the context of a research study, validity is concerned with the truth of the research or the accuracy of the results. In general, validity is the standard criterion by which researchers judge the quality of research. You probably have heard people talk about research studies that are "flawed," studies that are "poorly designed," or studies that produce "limited or non-applicable results." These are examples of research studies that lack validity. In this chapter, we examine how scientists define validity and how the concept of validity applies to different kinds of research. The goal is for you to learn how to design a valid research study and how to recognize validity (or the lack of it) in other people's research.

DEFINITION   The **validity** of a research study is the degree to which the study accurately answers the question it was intended to answer.

There is some potential for confusion about the use of the word validity. In Chapter 3, we introduced the concept of validity as it applies to measurement; the validity of a measurement procedure refers to whether the procedure actually measures the variable that it claims to measure. Here, however, we introduce the concept of validity as it applies to an entire research study. Specifically, we examine the quality of the research process, and the accuracy of the results. The same word, validity, applies to both contexts. Therefore, we are careful to distinguish between the validity of a research study and the validity of measurement, and you should be careful to separate the two concepts in your own mind.

Any researcher's goal is to be able to summarize a research study by stating, "This is what happened and this is what it means." Any factor that raises doubts about the limits of research results or about the interpretation of the results is a **threat to validity.**

DEFINITION Any component of a research study that introduces questions or raises doubts about the quality of the research process or the accuracy of the research results is a **threat to validity.**

Although there are many approaches to defining validity, questions about the validity of research are traditionally grouped into two categories: questions about external validity and questions about internal validity.

External Validity

Every research study is conducted at a specific time and place with specific participants, instructions, measurement techniques, and procedures. Despite the unique nature of the study itself, researchers usually assume that the obtained results are not unique but can be generalized beyond that study. **External validity** concerns the extent to which the results obtained in a research study hold true outside that specific study. Can the results of the study be generalized to other populations, other settings, or other measurements? For example, Strack, Martin, and Stepper (1988) conducted a study showing that people rate cartoons as funnier when holding a pen in their teeth (which forced them to smile) than when holding a pen in their lips (which forced them to frown). Although this study was done in 1988 using undergraduate students from the University of Illinois, it seems reasonable to assume that the results are still valid today. That is, if the same study were conducted with today's undergraduate students from a different university, it would be reasonable to expect essentially the same results.

External validity focuses on any unique characteristics of the study that may raise questions about whether the same results would be obtained under different conditions. Any factor that limits the ability to generalize the results from a research study is a **threat to external validity.** For example, the results obtained from a group of 50-year-old males do not necessarily generalize to females or to other age groups. In this case, the limited range of participant characteristics is a threat to the external validity of the study.

DEFINITIONS **External validity** refers to the extent to which we can generalize the results of a research study to people, settings, times, measures, and characteristics other than those used in that study.

A **threat to external validity** is any characteristic of a study that limits the ability to generalize the results from a research study.

There are at least three different kinds of generalization, and each can be a concern for external validity.

1. *Generalization from a sample to the general population.* Most research questions concern a large group of individuals known as a population. For example, a researcher may be interested in preschool children or adults with an eating disorder. In each case, the population contains millions of individuals. However, the actual research study is conducted with a relatively small group of individuals known as a sample. For example, a researcher may select a sample of 50 preschool children to participate in a study. One concern for external validity is that the sample is representative of the population so that the results obtained for the sample can be generalized to the entire population. If, for example, a researcher finds that television violence influences the behavior of preschool children in a sample, the researcher would like to conclude that television violence affects the behavior of preschool children in general.

2. *Generalization from one research study to another.* As we noted earlier, each research study is a unique event, conducted at a specific time and place using specific procedures with a specific group of individuals. One concern for external validity is that the results obtained in one specific study will also be obtained in another similar study. For example, if I conduct a study with a specific group of 25 college students, will I obtain the same (or similar) results if I repeat the study 2 years later with a different group of students? If I do my study in New York, will another researcher using the same procedures obtain the same results in California? If I measure IQ scores with the Stanford Binet Intelligence Scales, will another researcher get the same results measuring IQ with the Wechsler Adult Intelligence Scale–IV(WAIS–IV)?

3. *Generalization from a research study to a real world situation.* Most research is conducted under relatively controlled conditions with individuals who know that they are participating in a research study. One concern for external validity is whether the results obtained in a relatively sterile research environment will also be obtained out in the real world. For example, a researcher may find that a new computer program is very effective for teaching mathematics to third-grade children. However, will the results obtained in the laboratory study also be found in a real third-grade classroom?

Internal Validity

For research studies using the experimental strategy, the goal is to obtain a cause-and-effect explanation for the relationship between two variables, and many other research studies hope to produce some support for a cause-and-effect explanation. For example, consider the following research questions:

- Does increased exercise cause a decrease in cholesterol level?
- Does this particular therapy cause a reduction in depression?
- Does this particular teaching technique cause an improvement in students' academic performance?

In each case, a valid research study would have to demonstrate that changes in one variable (for example, the amount of exercise) are followed by changes in the other variable (cholesterol level), and that no other variable provides an alternative explanation for the results. This kind of validity is called **internal validity.** Internal validity is concerned with factors in the research study that raise doubts or questions about the interpretation of the results. A research study is said to have internal validity if it allows one and only one explanation of the results. Any factor that allows an alternative explanation for the results is a **threat to internal validity.** For example, suppose a clinician obtains a group of depressed clients and measures the level of depression for each individual. The clinician then begins therapy with the clients and measures depression again after 3 weeks. If there is a substantial decline in depression, the therapist would like to conclude that the therapy caused a reduction in depression. However, suppose that the weather was cold and miserable when the study began, and changed to bright and sunny when the study ended 3 weeks later. In this case, the weather provides an alternative explanation for the results. Specifically, it is possible that the improved weather caused the reduction in depression. In this example, the weather is a threat to the internal validity of the research study.

DEFINITIONS	A research study has **internal validity** if it produces a single, unambiguous explanation for the relationship between two variables. Any factor that allows for an alternative explanation is a **threat to internal validity.**

LEARNING CHECKS	A researcher finds that college students are more anxious near final exams in December than at the beginning of the semester in September. However, it is not clear whether the anxiety is caused by exams or by the change in season. Does this study have a problem with internal validity or external validity? A researcher conducts a study with 6-year-old children at a summer computer camp for gifted children. However, the researcher suspects that different results would be obtained if the study were conducted with regular 6-year-old children. Does this study have a problem with internal validity or external validity?

Validity and the Quality of a Research Study

The value or quality of any research study is determined by the extent to which the study satisfies the criteria of internal and external validity. The general purpose of a research study is to answer a specific research question. A well-designed study produces results that accurately represent the variables being examined and justify a conclusion that accurately answers the original question. Any factor that generates doubts about the accuracy of the results or raises questions about the interpretation of the results is a threat to validity.

A good researcher is aware of these threats while planning a research study. Anticipating threats to validity allows a researcher to incorporate elements into a research design that eliminate or minimize threats to validity before the research is actually conducted. In this section, we identify and briefly describe some general threats to internal and external validity. In later chapters, we present a variety of different research designs and consider the specific threats to validity associated with each design. In addition, we identify methods of modifying or expanding each design to limit specific threats to validity.

One final caution: It is essentially impossible for a single research study to eliminate all threats to validity. Each researcher must decide which threats are most important for the specific study and then address those threats. Less-important threats can be ignored or treated casually. In fact, design changes that eliminate one threat may actually increase the potential for another threat; thus, each research study represents a set of decisions and compromises about validity. Although researchers typically try to make the best decisions and produce the best possible studies, most still contain some flaws. This basic "fact of life" has two implications:

1. Research studies vary in terms of validity. Some studies have strong internal and external validity and their results and conclusions are highly respected. Other studies have only moderate validity, and some have little or no validity. Never accept a research result or conclusion as true simply because it is said to have been "scientifically demonstrated."
2. Being aware of threats to validity can help you critically evaluate a research study. As you read research reports, mentally scan the list of threats and ask yourself whether each one applies. A major learning objective of this book is to make you an informed consumer of research, capable of making your own decisions about its validity and quality.

6.4 | THREATS TO EXTERNAL VALIDITY

As discussed previously, external validity refers to the extent to which the results of the study can be generalized. That is, will the same (or similar) results be obtained with other populations, conditions, experimenters, other measurements, and so forth? When research findings can be generalized outside the confines of the specific study, the research is said to have external validity. Any characteristic of the study that limits the generality of the results is a threat to external validity. Some of the more common threats to external validity follow, grouped into three major categories.

Category 1: Generalizing Across Participants or Subjects

The results of a study are demonstrated with a particular group of individuals. One question of external validity is, "To what extent can research results be generalized to individuals who differ from those who actually participated in the study?"

1. *Selection bias:* In Chapter 5 we defined a biased sample as one that has characteristics that are noticeably different from those of the population. A

biased sample is usually the result of **selection bias,** which means that the sampling procedure favors the selection of some individuals over others. It should be obvious that selection bias is a threat to external validity. Specifically, if a sample does not accurately represent the population, then there are serious concerns that the results obtained from the sample will not generalize to the population. The question of external validity is always raised when a researcher selects participants based on convenience rather than using an unbiased selection process. Selection of research participants is discussed in detail in Chapter 5, but for now, consider this common situation. Most researchers are interested in a broadly defined population such as adolescents in the United States; however, because of cost considerations, such a researcher is likely to obtain local adolescents. Therefore, a researcher in San Francisco, California, is likely to solicit participants from San Francisco Bay Area high schools, whereas a researcher in Kansas City, Missouri, is likely to solicit participants from Kansas City high schools. The issue here is whether the results obtained with west coast adolescents can be generalized to adolescents in the Midwest or other parts of the country. Research results obtained with participants from one geographic region or setting may contain selection bias and, hence, may not generalize to people in other regions or settings (urban, suburban, rural).

2. *College students:* The undergraduate shares with the laboratory rat the status of the most easily available and, therefore, most favored participant in behavioral research. However, evidence is accumulating to suggest that many of the characteristics of college students limit the ability to generalize the results to other adults. For example, Sears (1986) demonstrated that college students are likely to have a less formulated sense of self, a stronger tendency to comply with authority, less stable peer relationships, and higher intelligence than noncollege adults. We need to be cautious about generalizing research results obtained with this highly select group to adults in general.

3. *Volunteer bias:* In most cases, someone who participates in research has volunteered for it. As noted in Chapter 3, the APA guidelines for human research require (in most cases) that research participants be volunteers. This creates a basic problem for researchers known as **volunteer bias** because volunteers are not perfectly representative of the general population. The question of external validity is, "To what extent can we generalize results obtained with volunteers to individuals who may not volunteer to participate in studies?"

In an extensive study of volunteer participants, Rosenthal and Rosnow (1975) identified a number of characteristics that tend to differentiate individuals who volunteer from those who do not. Table 6.4 presents a list of some of the characteristics they examined. Note that none of the individual characteristics is a perfectly reliable predictor of volunteerism, and some are better predictors than others. After an extensive review of previous research, Rosenthal and Rosnow grouped the items into categories based on the amount of evidence supporting the notion that these characteristics are, in fact, associated with volunteering.

TABLE **6.4**
Participant Characteristics Associated with Volunteering

The characteristics are grouped according to the degree of confidence that the items are indeed related to volunteerism.

Maximum Confidence

Volunteers are more educated.
Volunteers are from a higher social class.
Volunteers are more intelligent.
Volunteers are more approval motivated.
Volunteers are more sociable.

Considerable Confidence

Volunteers are more arousal-seeking.
Volunteers are more conventional.

Volunteers are more likely to be female than male.
Volunteers are more nonauthoritarian.
Volunteers are more likely to be Jewish than Protestant and more likely Protestant than Catholic.
Volunteers are more nonconforming.

Some Confidence

Volunteers are from smaller towns.
Volunteers are more interested in religion.
Volunteers are more altruistic.
Volunteers are more self-disclosing.
Volunteers are more maladjusted.
Volunteers are more likely to be young than old.

From Rosenthal and Rosnow (1975).

As you read through the list in Table 6.4, try to classify yourself and determine your own likelihood of volunteering. You probably will find that some of the characteristics describe you perfectly, some are completely wrong, and some do not seem to apply at all. Although you may be educated and intelligent (suggesting that you would volunteer), you may not be an arousal-seeking individual (suggesting that you would not). This is part of the reason that it is impossible to predict perfectly who will volunteer and who will not. Another complicating factor is the type of research being considered. For example, females are more likely to volunteer in general, but for studies involving stress, males tend to be the most likely volunteers. Similarly, high intelligence is related to volunteering in general but not if the research involves unusual experiences such as hypnosis, sensory isolation, or sex research (Rosenthal & Rosnow, 1975).

Thus, the items in Table 6.4 should be viewed as general characteristics of volunteers; they are not intended to apply to each individual or to every situation. Nonetheless, the data clearly indicate that, on the average, volunteers are different from nonvolunteers, which raises questions about the external validity of research conducted with volunteer participants.

4. _Participant characteristics:_ Another threat to external validity occurs whenever a study uses participants who share similar characteristics. Demographic characteristics such as gender, age, race, ethnic identity, and socioeconomic status can limit the ability to generalize the results. For example, a study done in a Republican, suburban community with preschoolers may not generalize to other populations. You certainly would not expect to generalize the results to urban, Democratic young adults. It is always possible that the results of a study may be specific to

participants with a certain set of characteristics and may not extend to participants with different characteristics.

5. *Cross-species generalizations:* External validity is also in question when research is conducted with nonhumans and presumed to be readily applicable to humans. Before we can consider whether the results obtained with one species can be generalized to another species, we must note the parallels and differences between the two species on the mechanism or process of interest. For example, rats are an excellent species to use for research on eating. Rat eating is similar to human eating both physically and behaviorally (rats and humans have similar digestive systems, eating patterns, and food preferences). As a result, researchers can confidently generalize the results of research with rats to humans. In contrast, the blowfly is not a good species to use to generalize results to humans' eating because, unlike that of humans, the blowfly's eating behavior is purely reflexive and not learned (Logue, 1991). All of this is not to imply that nonhuman research is worthless and not applicable to humans; many major scientific advances in understanding humans have been made from research conducted with nonhumans. We must be careful not to presume, however, that all nonhuman research is directly applicable to humans.

 **LEARNING CHECK** Explain how selection bias may limit the external validity of a study's findings.

Category 2: Generalizing Across Features of a Study

In addition to the fact that each research study is conducted with a specific group of individuals, the results of a study are demonstrated with a specific set of procedures. Another question of external validity is, "To what extent can the results of the study be generalized to other procedures for conducting the study?"

1. _Novelty effect_: Participating in a research study is a novel, often exciting or anxiety-provoking experience for most individuals. In this novel situation, individuals may perceive and respond differently than they would in the normal, real world. This is called the **novelty effect.** In addition, the treatment(s) administered are typically clearly defined and unusually salient to the participants. Thus, the behavior (scores) of individuals participating in a research study may be quite different from behavior (scores) they would produce in other, more routine, situations in everyday life.

2. *Multiple treatment interference:* When individuals are tested in a series of treatment conditions, participation in one condition may have an effect on the participants that carries over into the next treatment and influences their performance or behavior. Common examples are **fatigue** and **practice** effects. With fatigue, participants become tired in one condition, which causes their performance to deteriorate in the following treatment. With practice, participants gain experience in one condition that leads to improved performance in the following condition. In

either case, participation in a previous treatment can be a threat to external validity. Specifically, the results obtained from individuals who have participated in previous conditions may not generalize to individuals who do not have the same previous experience. Again, any factor that limits the ability to generalize results in a threat to external validity. In this case, the potential influence of experience in earlier treatments is called **multiple treatment interference.**

3. *Experimenter characteristics:* As we have noted, each research study is conducted with a specific group of participants and a particular set of procedures. In addition, the results of a study are demonstrated with a specific experimenter conducting the study. The question of external validity is, "To what extent can the results of the study be generalized to other experimenters?"

   Experimenter characteristics can be a threat to external validity. The results of a study can be specific to an experimenter with a certain set of characteristics. Both demographic and personality characteristics of the experimenter can limit the generality of the results. Demographic characteristics can include gender, age, race, and ethnic identity; personality characteristics can include degree of friendliness, prestige, anxiety, and hostility. For example, a study conducted by a hostile experimenter is likely to produce different results from a study conducted by a kind experimenter.

Category 3: Generalizing Across Features of the Measures

As we have noted, each research study is conducted with a specific group of participants, a particular set of procedures, and a specific experimenter. In addition, the results of a study are demonstrated with a specific set of measurements. Another question of external validity is, "To what extent can the results of the study be generalized to other ways of measuring in the study?"

1. *Sensitization:* Occasionally, the process of measurement, often called the assessment procedure, can alter participants so that they react differently to treatment. This phenomenon is called **sensitization, or assessment sensitization.** Sensitization is a threat to external validity because it raises the question of whether the results obtained in a research study using assessment are different from results in the real world, where the treatment is used without assessment. For example, a self-esteem program for school children might be tested in a study in which self-esteem is actually measured, but then the program is applied throughout the school district without any measurement. Assessment sensitization commonly occurs in studies in which participants' behavior is measured before they are given a treatment, and they are measured again after treatment. The concern with regard to external validity is that the pretest (the before-treatment measurement) may in some way sensitize the participants so that they become more aware of their own attitudes or behaviors. The increased awareness may cause the participants to be affected differently by the treatment. This threat to external validity is also known as **pretest sensitization.**

Assessment sensitization also commonly occurs in studies that use self-monitoring as a means of measuring scores. Harmon, Nelson, and Hayes (1980) demonstrated that the process of self-monitoring significantly reduced depression. That is, depressed patients who simply observed and recorded their own behavior showed significant improvement without any clinical treatment or therapy. Again, this is an example of a measurement procedure (not a treatment) affecting scores. You may recognize the self-monitoring effect as a common component of diet plans and smoking cessation programs in which simply observing habits sensitizes people to their behavior and thereby changes it.

2. *Generality across response measures:* Many variables can be defined and measured in different ways. The variable fear, for example, can be defined in terms of physiological measures (for example, heart rate), self-report measures, or behavior. In a research study, a researcher typically selects one definition and one measurement procedure. In this case, the results of the study may be limited to that specific measurement and may not generalize to other definitions or other measures. For example, a study may find that a particular therapy is effective in treating phobias when fear is defined and measured by heart rate. In actual practice, however, the therapy may not have any effect on phobic patients' behaviors.

3. *Time of measurement:* In a research study, the scores for individuals are measured at a specific time after (or during) the treatment. However, the actual effect of the treatment may decrease or increase with time. For example, a stop-smoking program may appear to be very successful if the participants are measured immediately after the program, but may have a much lower rate of success if participants are measured 6 months later. Thus, the results obtained in a research study in which responses are measured at a specific time may differ from the results obtained when measured at a different time.

LEARNING CHECK   Describe two ways in which measurement issues can threaten the external validity of research findings.

Table 6.5 provides a summary of the three major categories of threats to the external validity of research results.

6.5 | THREATS TO INTERNAL VALIDITY

Extraneous Variables

A typical research study concentrates on two variables and attempts to demonstrate a relationship between them. For example, Hallam, Price, and Katsarou (2002) conducted a research study examining the effects of background music (variable #1) on task performance (variable #2) for primary school students. The results showed that calming and relaxing music led to better performance on an arithmetic task when compared to a no-music condition. Although the study focuses on two variables, there are countless other

TABLE **6.5**
General Threats to the External Validity of a Research Study

Source of the Threat	Description of the Threat
Participants	Characteristics that are unique to the specific group of participants in a study may limit ability to generalize the results of the study to individuals with different characteristics. For example, results obtained from college students may not generalize to noncollege adults.
Features of the Study	Characteristics that are unique to the specific procedures used in a study may limit ability to generalize the results to situations in which other procedures are used. For example, the results obtained from participants who are aware that they are being observed and measured may not generalize to situations in which the participants are not aware that measurement is occurring. Also, results obtained with one experimenter might not generalize to a different experimenter.
Measurements	Characteristics that are unique to the specific measurement procedure may limit ability to generalize the results to situations in which a different measurement procedure is used. For example, the results obtained from measurements taken immediately after treatment may not generalize to a situation in which measurements are taken 3 months after treatment.

elements that vary within the study; that is, there are many additional variables (beyond the two being studied) that are part of every research study. Some of these extra variables are related to the individuals participating. For example, different students enter the study with different personalities, different IQs, different genders, different skills and abilities, and so on. Other variables involve the study's environment—for example, some participants may be tested in the morning and others in the afternoon; or part of the study may be conducted on a dark and dreary Monday and another part on a sunny Tuesday. The researcher is not interested in differences in IQ or weather, but these factors are still variables in the study. Additional variables that exist in a research study but are not directly investigated are called **extraneous variables,** and every research study has thousands of them.

DEFINITION   Any variable in a research study other than the specific variables being studied is an **extraneous variable.**

Confounding Variables

Occasionally, an extraneous variable is allowed to creep into a study in a way that can influence or distort the results. When this happens, there is a risk that the observed relationship between two variables has been artificially produced by the extraneous variable. Consider the following scenario in which the researcher is attempting to demonstrate a relationship between background music and student performance.

Suppose the research study starts with a group of students in a room with calm and relaxing background music for one treatment condition; later, the music is turned off to create a second treatment condition. In each condition, the students are given arithmetic problems to solve and their performance is measured. The results show that performance declines after the music is turned off. Although it is possible that the music is influencing performance, it also is possible that the participants are just getting tired. They do well on the first set of problems (with music) but are wearing down by the time they get to the second set (with no music). In this scenario, the observed decline in performance may be explained by fatigue. We now have an alternative explanation for the observed result: The decline in problem-solving performance may be explained by the removal of the music or it may be explained by fatigue. Although the results of the study are clear, the interpretation of the results is questionable.

Recall that any factor allowing an alternative explanation for the results is a threat to internal validity. In this example, a third variable—fatigue—might explain the observed relation between background music and problem-solving performance. A third variable of this sort is called a **confounding variable.**

DEFINITION	A **confounding variable** is an extraneous variable (usually unmonitored) that changes systematically along with the two variables being studied. A confounding variable provides an alternative explanation for the observed relationship between the two variables and, therefore, is a threat to internal validity.

Whenever three variables all change together systematically, it is impossible to reach a simple, clear conclusion about the relationship between any two of them. Thus, whenever a confounding variable exists, internal validity is threatened. One more look at the music and problem-solving study should illustrate this point. This time, suppose that one group of individuals is given a problem-solving task in a room with background music at nine o'clock in the morning. A second group is given the problem-solving task in a room with no music at four o'clock in the afternoon. Finally, suppose that the results show much better performance for the first group than for the second group. Note that this study involves three variables and that all three variables change together systematically: As the background changes from music to no-music, the time of day also changes from morning to afternoon, and the students' performance changes from good to bad.

The researcher would like to explain the results by saying that there is a relationship between background music and performance:

Changing the background from music to no-music caused a decrease in performance from good to bad.

However, the time of day (morning or afternoon) is an extraneous variable that has turned into a confounding variable and provides an alternative explanation for the results. Specifically, it is possible to explain the results by saying that there is a relationship between time of day and performance:

Changing the time of day from morning to afternoon caused a decrease in performance from good to bad.

Again, a confounding variable is a threat to internal validity. Remember, any factor that allows an alternative explanation for the results from a research study threatens the internal validity of the study.

Extraneous Variables, Confounding Variables, and Internal Validity

For a research study to have internal validity, there must be one, and only one, explanation for the research results. If a study includes a confounding variable, then there is an alternative explanation and the internal validity is threatened. Therefore, the key to achieving internal validity is to ensure that no extraneous variable is allowed to become a confounding variable. Because every research study involves thousands of extraneous variables, avoiding a confounding variable can be quite a task. Fortunately, however, confounding variables can be classified in a few general categories that make it somewhat easier to monitor them and keep them out of a research study. Before we examine the different categories of confounding variables, we look more closely at the general structure of a research study for which internal validity is a concern.

When the goal of a research study is to explain the relationship between two variables, it is common practice to use one of the variables to create different *treatment conditions* and then measure the second variable to obtain a set of *scores* within each condition. For example, Hallam, Price, and Katsarou (2002) conducted a second study in which they created three background conditions by playing pleasant, calming music in one room, unpleasant, aggressive music in one room, and no music in one room. The researchers then measured problem-solving performance (variable #2) for a group of students in each of the three rooms. Because they found differences in the problem-solving scores from one room to another, the researchers successfully demonstrated that problem solving depends on background music; that is, there is a relationship between the two variables. The general structure of this study is shown in Figure 6.3.

To ensure the internal validity of the study, it is essential that the only difference between the treatment conditions is the single variable that was used to define the conditions. In Figure 6.3, for example, the only difference between the three rooms is the background music. If there is any other factor that differentiates the treatment conditions, then the study has a confounding variable and the internal validity is threatened. For example, if the pleasant and calming music room is painted green, the no-music room yellow, and the unpleasant and aggressive music room red, then the study is confounded. In this case, the color of the room is a confounding variable. Specifically, any differences in performance from one room to another may be explained by the music but they also may be explained by room color. In the following sections, we identify three different ways that internal validity can be threatened. That is, we examine three different categories of confounding variables: environmental variables, individual differences, and time-related variables.

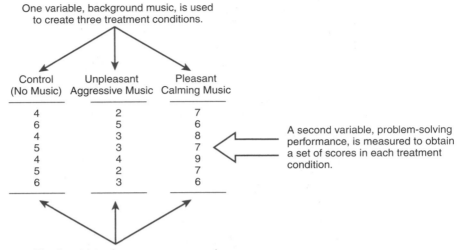

One variable, background music, is used
to create three treatment conditions.

Control (No Music)	Unpleasant Aggressive Music	Pleasant Calming Music
4	2	7
6	5	6
4	3	8
5	3	7
4	4	9
5	2	7
6	3	6

A second variable, problem-solving
performance, is measured to obtain
a set of scores in each treatment
condition.

The three sets of scores are compared.
Consistent differences between treatments provide
evidence for a relationship between background
music and problem-solving performance.

F I G U R E **6.3** The Structure of a Research Study Designed to Explain
the Relationship Between Variables

In this example, the goal of the study is to demonstrate that changes in the background
music produce changes in problem-solving performance.

**LEARNING
CHECKS**

Suppose that you wake up in the morning with all the symptoms of a head
cold. You take a cold pill and eat a big bowl of your mother's chicken soup.
By midday, your cold symptoms are gone and you are feeling much better.
Can you conclude that the chicken soup cured your cold? Explain why or
why not.

Describe how a confounding variable threatens internal validity.

Environmental Variables: General Threats to Internal Validity for All Studies

It is possible that variables in the general environment of the study such as size
of room, time of day, or gender of the experimenter can become threats to
internal validity. If one treatment is administered in a large, cheerful room
and another treatment is administered in a small, dreary room, it is possible
that the type of room (and not the treatment) is responsible for any differences
between the scores in the two treatment conditions. Another example of this
type of problem is a taste-test study that compared consumer preference for
Coca-Cola versus Pepsi-Cola. In this study, individuals were asked to taste the
colas in two different glasses and identify the one they preferred. The participants were not told which cola was in each glass but the glasses were marked

with a Q and an M so that the researcher could record the responses. However, the glass containing Coca-Cola was always marked with the letter Q, and the Pepsi-Cola glass was always marked with the letter M. Although the results indicated that people prefer Pepsi, an alternative explanation is that people prefer the glass labeled with the letter M (Huck & Sandler, 1979). In this study, the identifying letter was allowed to vary systematically with the brand of cola, so the letters M and Q became a confounding variable. To avoid confounding variables and ensure the internal validity of a research study, it is necessary that there are no systematic differences in the general environment from one treatment condition to another. Whenever a difference exists, there is an alternative explanation for the results and the internal validity of the study is threatened.

Individual Differences: Threats to Internal Validity for Studies Comparing Different Groups

Personal characteristics that can differ from one individual to another are known as **individual differences.** Examples include differences in height, weight, gender, age, IQ, and personality. Because no two people (or animals) are identical, individual differences are a part of every research study. For research studies that use a different group of individuals for each of the treatment conditions being compared, the concern is that there may be individual differences between groups. For example, if you select two individuals and measure reaction time, one person will be faster and one will be slower; if you measure age, one person will be older and one will be younger; and so on. However, if individuals are assigned to treatment conditions so that the faster people are consistently assigned to one treatment and the slower people are consistently assigned to another, then you have a problem. The problem is called **assignment bias,** and is a threat to internal validity because it allows two alternative explanations for any differences observed between the treatments. Specifically, it is possible that the scores in one treatment are higher than the scores in another treatment because there are real differences between the treatments, or it is possible that the differences in scores are caused by the fact that the participants in one treatment are faster (or smarter or older or more motivated) than the participants in the other treatment.

DEFINITION

Assignment bias occurs when the process used to assign different participants to different treatments produces groups of individuals with noticeably different characteristics.

Time-Related Variables: Threats to Internal Validity for Studies Comparing One Group over Time

An alternative to having a different group in each treatment condition is to have the same group of individuals participate in all of the different treatments. In Figure 6.3, for example, the researcher could test the same group of people in all three of the background-music conditions. The basic problem with this type of research is that it not only compares scores obtained in different treatments, but also compares scores obtained at different times. For example, a group of students could be tested in the pleasant and calming music room on Monday, in the unpleasant and aggressive music room on Tuesday, and then brought back to be tested again in the no-music room on Wednesday. Although the background music changes from day to day, there are a number of other variables that also change as time goes by. It is possible that these other **time-related variables** could be confounding variables. That is, during the time between the first treatment condition and the final treatment condition, individual participants or their scores may be influenced by factors other than the treatments. Any factor affecting the data other than the treatment is a threat to the internal validity of the study. Note that time-related variables can be environmental, such as the weather or time of day, and they can be participant variables, such as mood or physical state. In this section, we identify five time-related threats to internal validity.

1. *History:* The term **history** refers to environmental events other than the treatment that change over time and may affect the scores in one treatment differently than in another treatment. Events that occur in participants' lives at home, in school, or at work may affect their performance or behavior in different sections of the research study. For example, suppose a group of students serves as participants in a research study that extends over several days with a different treatment condition each day. If there is an outside event that is likely to affect many of the students on one particular day, but not on another day, then the event may provide an explanation for unusual performance on that particular day. For example, suppose that in the middle of this study a fire alarm sounds in the main campus dormitory just after midnight, and the students are left standing outdoors for hours. When the students are tested later in the day, they are likely to show poor memory scores, not because of the treatment condition but because they are all exhausted from missing sleep the night before.

DEFINITION When a group of individuals is being tested in a series of treatment conditions, any outside event(s) that influences the participants' scores in one treatment differently than in another treatment is called a history effect. **History** is a threat to internal validity because any differences that are observed between treatment conditions may be caused by history instead of by the treatments.

Note that history effects are usually events that occur during the course of the research study. However, a study can be influenced by an event that occurs prior to it. Earlier, we discussed the effect of a midnight fire alarm on the participants' performance the following day. If the fire alarm sounded on the night before the study started, then it could affect performance on the first day of the study but not on subsequent days. In this case, the event is still a threat to internal validity, even though it occurred prior to the start of the study. To be a confounding variable, history effects must influence at least one treatment condition differently and influence enough of the participants to have an influence on the overall group performance.

2. *Maturation:* Any systematic changes in participants' physiology or psychology that occur during a research study and affect the participants' scores are referred to as **maturation**. Maturation effects are of particular concern when the research participants are young children or elderly adults. Young children, for example, can gather new knowledge and skills or simply grow bigger and stronger in a relatively short time. As a result, their performance at the end of a series of treatment conditions may be very different from their performance at the beginning, and the change in performance may not have been caused by the treatments but instead by maturation. With elderly participants, maturation effects often have a detrimental effect. As people age, they may experience losses in vision or hearing that could affect their performance in a research study. In general, maturation threatens the internal validity of a research study conducted over time because it weakens our confidence that the different treatment conditions are responsible for observed changes in the participants' scores. Maturation is a particular concern in research situations in which the series of treatments extends over a relatively long time.

DEFINITION

When a group of individuals is being tested in a series of treatment conditions, any physiological or psychological change that occurs in participants during the study and influences the participants' scores is called **maturation**. Maturation is a threat to internal validity because observed differences between treatment conditions may be caused by maturation instead of by the treatments.

3. *Instrumentation:* The term **instrumentation** (sometimes called **instrumental bias** or **instrumental decay**) refers to changes in a measuring instrument that occur over time. For example, a scale used to weigh participants may gradually wear out during the course of the study. In this case, the measurements change during the study, not because of the different treatments but because of the changes in the scale. Behavioral observation measures (discussed in Chapter 4 and Chapter 7) are much more subject to instrumentation than other types of measures. For example, from one testing to the next, the researcher doing the observing may become more proficient in making the observations, change the standards on which the observations are based, or become more skilled or fatigued, and as a result, judge the same behavior differently at different times. Notice that the changes in the participants' scores are not caused by the treatment but instead by a change in the measurement instrument (the researcher). Like history and maturation, instrumentation is a particular concern in research situations in which the series of treatments extends over a relatively long time.

DEFINITION	**Instrumentation** refers to changes in the measuring instrument that occur during a research study in which participants are measured in a series of treatment conditions. Instrumentation is a threat to internal validity because any observed differences between treatment conditions may be caused by changes in the measuring instrument instead of the treatments.

4. *Testing effects (practice, fatigue, and carry-over effects):* Earlier, we identified multiple treatment interference as a potential threat to external validity (p. 174). The idea behind multiple treatment interference is that when individuals are tested in a series of treatment conditions, participation in one treatment may have an influence on the participants' scores in the following treatments. For example, becoming fatigued in one treatment may lead to poorer performance in the next treatment. You should realize that this problem can also be viewed as a threat to internal validity. Specifically, the experience of being tested in one treatment may explain why the participants' scores are different in the following treatment. Remember, an alternative explanation for an observed difference is a threat to internal validity. In this case, the researcher does not know whether the observed change in performance is caused by the different treatments or by fatigue. Any possible change in performance caused by participation in a previous treatment is called a **testing effect** and is a threat to internal validity because it provides an alternative explanation for the results.

It also is possible that a specific treatment causes changes in the participants so that the lingering aftereffects of the treatment carry over into the next treatment (or treatments) and alter the participants' scores. For example, participants in a memory study may learn a new rehearsal strategy in one treatment condition, and continue to use the strategy to help improve their memory scores when participating in later treatment conditions. Appropriately, these effects are called **carry-over effects.** Notice that a testing effect, such as fatigue, comes from general experience in the research study, whereas carry-over effects are caused by experiencing a specific treatment.

Whenever participants go through a series of treatments in order, their performance in one treatment may be influenced by experience from a treatment earlier in the series. For this reason, testing effects and carry-over effects are often grouped together under the general term **order effects.**

DEFINITION	**Testing effects,** also known as **order effects,** occur when the experience of being tested in one treatment condition (participating and being measured) has an influence on the participants' scores in a later treatment condition(s). Testing effects threaten internal validity because any observed differences between treatment conditions may be caused by testing effects rather than the treatments.

5. *Regression toward the mean:* **Statistical regression,** or **regression toward the mean,** refers to the tendency for extreme scores on any measurement

to move toward the mean (regress) when the measurement procedure is repeated. Individuals who score extremely high on a measure during the first testing are likely to score lower on the second testing, and, conversely, individuals who score extremely low on a measure during the first testing are likely to score higher on the second testing.

Statistical regression occurs because an individual's score is a function both of stable factors such as skill and of unstable factors such as chance. Although the stable factors remain constant from one measurement to another, the unstable factors can change substantially. Your grade on an exam, for example, is based on a combination of knowledge and luck. Some of the answers you really know, others you guess. The student who gets the highest score on the first exam probably combines knowledge and good luck. On the second exam, this student's knowledge is still there, but luck is likely to change; thus, the student will probably score lower on the second exam. This is regression toward the mean.

In research, regression is a concern whenever participants are selected for their exceptionally high (or low) scores. Suppose a clinical psychologist is examining how a specific treatment influences the social skills of autistic children. A sample of autistic children is selected because a preliminary test indicates that they have exceptionally poor social skills. The psychologist administers the treatment and then once again measures social skills. Because of the children's extremely low scores on social skills at the beginning of the study, it is possible that the children's scores improve, not because of the treatment but because their scores regress toward the mean. In general, statistical regression threatens the internal validity of a research study because it creates the possibility that the observed changes in the participants' scores are caused by regression instead of by the treatments. Threats to internal validity are summarized in Table 6.6.

DEFINITION	**Statistical regression**, or **regression toward the mean**, is a mathematical phenomenon in which extreme scores (high or low) on one measurement tend to be less extreme on a second measurement. Regression is a threat to internal validity because changes that occur in participants' scores from one treatment to the next can be caused by regression instead of the treatments.

 LEARNING CHECKS	What is the primary threat to internal validity for a study that compares different groups of participants? What are the five primary threats to internal validity for a study that compares the same group of participants at different times?

6.6 | MORE ABOUT INTERNAL AND EXTERNAL VALIDITY

The obvious goal of any research study is to maximize internal and external validity; that is, every researcher would like to be confident that the results of a study are true, and that the truth of the results extends beyond the

TABLE **6.6**
General Threats to the Internal Validity of a Research Study

Source of the Threat	Description of the Threat
	General Threats for All Designs
Environmental Variables	If two treatments are administered in noticeably different environments, then the internal validity of the study is threatened. For example, if one treatment is administered in the morning and another at night, then any difference obtained may be explained by the time of day instead of treatment.
	Participant-Related Threats For Designs that Compare Different Groups
Assignment Bias	If the participants in one treatment condition have characteristics that are noticeably different from the participants in another treatment, then the internal validity of the study is threatened. For example, if the participants in one treatment are older than the participants in another treatment, then any difference between the treatments may be explained by age instead of the treatment.
	Time-Related Threats for Designs that Compare One Group over Time
History	If outside events influence the participants differently in one treatment than in another, then the internal validity is threatened. Any difference between treatments could be explained by the outside events instead of the treatment.
Maturation	If participants experience physiological or psychological changes between treatments, then the internal validity is threatened. Any differences between treatments could be explained by the changes instead of the treatment.
Instrumentation	If the measurement instrument changes from one treatment to another, then the internal validity is threatened. Any differences between treatments could be explained by the measuring instrument instead of the treatment.
Testing Effects	If the experience of being in one treatment influences the participants' scores in another treatment, then the internal validity is threatened. Any differences between treatments could be explained by the prior experience instead of the current treatment.
Statistical Regression	If participants have extreme scores (high or low) in the first treatment, then the internal validity is threatened. A change toward more average scores in later treatments could be explained by regression instead of the treatment.

particular individuals, conditions, and procedures used in the study. However, it is almost impossible to design and conduct a perfect research study. In fact, the steps taken to reduce or eliminate one threat to validity often increase others. As a result, designing and conducting research is usually a balancing act filled with choices and compromises that attempt to maximize validity and provide the best possible answer to the original research question. As we introduce specific research designs in later chapters, we discuss in more detail the choices and consequences involved in developing a research study. In particular, we consider the specific threats to internal and external validity associated with specific designs. For now, we outline some of the general constraints on validity to consider when planning or reading research, and discuss some of the necessary trade-offs between internal and external validity.

Balancing Internal and External Validity

To gain a high level of internal validity, a researcher must eliminate or minimize confounding variables. To accomplish this, a study must be tightly controlled so that no extraneous variables can influence the results. However, controlling a study may create a research environment that is so artificial and unnatural that results obtained within the study may not occur in the outside world. Thus, attempts to increase internal validity can reduce external validity. In general, the results from a tightly controlled research study should be interpreted as demonstrating what can happen but not necessarily what will happen in an outside environment where other variables are free to operate.

On the other hand, research that attempts to gain a high level of external validity often creates a research environment that closely resembles the outside world. The risk in this type of research comes from the fact that the real world is often a chaotic jumble of uncontrolled variables, especially in comparison with the highly regulated environment of a controlled study. Thus, striving for increased external validity can allow extraneous variables (potentially confounding variables) into a study and thereby threaten internal validity.

In very general terms, there tends to be a trade-off between internal and external validity. Research that is very strong with respect to one kind of validity often tends to be relatively weak with respect to the second type. This basic relationship must be considered in planning a research study or evaluating someone else's work. Usually the purpose or goals of a study help you decide which type of validity is more important and which threats must be addressed.

Artifacts: Threats to Both Internal and External Validity

In Chapter 4 (pp. 127–131) we described an **artifact** as an external factor that may influence or distort measurements. Because an artifact can threaten the validity and reliability of measurements, it also can threaten both the internal and external validity of the research study. Experimenter bias and participant reactivity are two of the many potential artifacts.

Experimenter Bias

Experimenter bias occurs when the findings of a study are influenced by the experimenter's expectations or personal beliefs regarding the outcome of the study. Experimenter bias threatens external validity because the results obtained in a study may be specific to the experimenter who has the expectations. The results may not be the same with an experimenter who did not have such a bias. Experimenter bias also threatens internal validity because the data may show a pattern that appears to be a real treatment effect but was actually caused by the experimenter's influence. As discussed in Chapter 4 (p. 129) single-blind and double-blind studies minimize the potential for experimenter bias.

Demand Characteristics and Participant Reactivity

Also discussed in Chapter 4 (pp. 129–131), the combination of **demand characteristics** and participant **reactivity** can change a participant's normal behavior and thereby influence the outcome of the study. Recall that **demand characteristics** refer to any of the potential cues or features of a study that (1) suggest to the participants what the purpose and hypothesis is, and (2) influence the participants to respond or behave in a certain way. Also recall that **reactivity** occurs when participants modify their natural behavior in response to the fact that they are participating in a research study or the knowledge that they are being measured. Some participants may assume *subject roles* becoming overly cooperative or uncooperative, and some may become defensive. Additional discussion of the subject roles adopted by research participants is presented in Chapter 4 (p. 130). If the participants are not acting normally, the internal validity of the study is threatened because the obtained results can be explained by participant reactivity instead of the different treatment conditions. Also, demand characteristics and reactivity can threaten the external validity of the study because the results obtained under the influence of demand characteristics may not generalize to a new situation where the environmental demands are different. Recall also from Chapter 4 that reactivity is particularly a problem in studies conducted in a **laboratory** setting, where participants are fully aware that they are participating in a study. In contrast, in a **field** study individuals are observed in their natural environment and are much less likely to know that they are being investigated. Laboratories and field studies are discussed in more detail in Chapter 9 section 9.6 (pp. 272–274). Steps to help reduce the effects of reactivity are discussed in Chapter 4 (p. 131).

LEARNING CHECKS

Describe how experimenter bias can be a threat to internal validity; that is, how can experimenter bias provide an explanation for the scores in one condition being higher than the scores in a second condition?

Describe how participant reactivity can be a threat to external validity; that is, how can participant reactivity limit the ability to generalize research results?

Exaggerated Variables

Most research is undertaken in the hope of demonstrating a relationship between variables. To accomplish this goal, a research study often maximizes the differences for one of the variables to increase the likelihood of revealing a relationship with a second variable. In particular, researchers often exaggerate the differences between treatment conditions to increase the chance that the scores obtained in one treatment are noticeably different from the scores obtained in another treatment. To evaluate the effects of temperature on learning, for example, a researcher probably would not compare a 70-degree room and a 72-degree room. The study has a greater chance of success if it involves comparison of 70 degrees and 90 degrees. Although the larger temperature difference is likely to reveal a relationship between temperature and learning, the researcher should be cautious about generalizing the result to a normal classroom situation in which 20-degree temperature changes are unlikely.

Validity and Individual Research Strategies

Because different research strategies have different goals, they tend to have different levels of internal validity and external validity. For example, descriptive, correlational, and nonexperimental studies tend to examine variables in their natural, real-world settings and, therefore, tend to have relatively good external validity. On the other hand, experimental research tends to be rigorously controlled and monitored and, therefore, has high internal validity. Quasi-experimental studies tend to fall somewhere in between; they attempt to mimic the control of true experiments, which helps internal validity, and they tend to take place in applied, real-world situations, which helps external validity.

6.7 | RESEARCH STRATEGIES, RESEARCH DESIGNS, AND RESEARCH PROCEDURES

The process of developing a research study can be broken down into three distinct stages: determining a research strategy, determining a research design, and determining research procedures. Although these three terms are often used interchangeably without much regard for precise definitions, we introduce them here as a means of differentiating the separate stages of research development and identifying the choices and decisions that comprise each stage.

Research Strategies

The term *research strategy* refers to the general approach and goals of a research study (see section 6.2). Research strategy is usually determined by the kind of question you plan to address and the kind of answer you hope to obtain. The five basic research strategies are the experimental strategy, the quasi-experimental strategy, the nonexperimental strategy, the correlational strategy, and the descriptive strategy. In general terms, a research strategy is concerned with what you hope to accomplish in a research study. Chapters 7, 8, 9, and 12 provide more details about these different approaches.

Research Designs

The next step, the research design, addresses how to implement the strategy. Determining a **research design** requires decisions about three basic aspects of the research study:

1. *Group versus individual.* Will the study examine a group of individuals, producing an overall description for the entire group, or should the

study focus on a single individual? Although group studies tend to have higher external validity (results from a large group can be more confidently generalized than results from a single individual), the careful examination of a single individual often can provide detail that is lost in averaging a large group.

2. *Same individuals versus different individuals.* Some research examines changes within the same group of individuals as they move from one treatment to the next. Other research uses a different group of individuals for each separate treatment and then examines differences between groups. Each design has advantages and disadvantages that must be weighed in the planning phase.

3. *The number of variables to be included.* The simplest study involves examining the relationship between two variables. However, some research involves three or more variables. For example, a researcher may be interested in multiple relationships, or a study may focus on two variables but ask how their relationship is affected by other variables. Thus, one factor in determining a research design is deciding how many variables will be observed, manipulated, or regulated.

A research design is a general framework for conducting a study. Different designs and their individual strengths and weaknesses are discussed in Chapters 7, 10, 11, 12, 13, and 15.

DEFINITION	A **research design** is a general plan for implementing a research strategy. A research design specifies whether the study will involve groups or individual participants, will make comparisons within a group or between groups, and how many variables will be included in the study.

Research Procedures

The next stage in developing a research study involves filling in the details that precisely define how the study is to be done. This final, detailed stage is called the **research procedure**. It includes a precise determination of:

- exactly how the variables will be manipulated, regulated, and measured.
- exactly how many individuals will be involved.
- exactly how the individual participants or subjects will proceed through the course of the study.

The procedure contains the final decisions about all choices still open after the general design is determined. The task of defining and measuring variables is discussed in Chapter 4; different ways of selecting individuals to participate in a study are discussed in Chapter 5. For each completed study, a description of the research procedure is typically presented in the method section of the research report, which is discussed briefly in Table 2.2 (p. 61) and in Chapter 16.

DEFINITION	A **research procedure** is an exact, step-by-step description of a specific research study.

In summary, research strategies are broad categories that classify research according to the type of question the research study addresses. Research designs are general categories that classify research according to how the study is conducted. Notice that several different research studies can all have the same strategy and different studies can all share the same design. Research procedures, on the other hand, are unique to the specific study being considered. Occasionally, a researcher deliberately copies the procedures from another study. This kind of direct replication is relatively rare and usually is done only when there is some doubt that the two "identical" studies will produce the same results. Normally, each study has its own unique procedures.

LEARNING CHECK Explain the difference among the terms research strategy, design, and procedure.

■ CHAPTER SUMMARY

There are five general categories of research strategies: experimental, quasi-experimental, nonexperimental, correlational, and descriptive. The experimental strategy assesses whether there is a causal relationship between two variables. The quasi-experimental strategy attempts to obtain evidence for a causal relationship between two variables, but this strategy cannot unambiguously demonstrate cause and effect. The nonexperimental strategy examines relationships between variables by demonstrating differences between groups or treatment conditions. The correlational strategy determines whether there is a relationship or association between two variables by measuring both variables for each individual. The descriptive strategy assesses the variables being examined as they exist naturally.

Central to selecting a research strategy and design is validity, which is concerned with the truth of the research or the accuracy of the results. Any factor that raises doubts about the research results or the interpretation of the results is a threat to validity. Questions about the validity of research are traditionally grouped into two general categories: external validity and internal validity. A study has external validity if the results of the study can be generalized to people, settings, times, measures, and characteristics other than those in the study. The generality of a study's findings may be a function of virtually any characteristic of the study, including the participants or subjects, the features of the study, and the features of the measures. A research study has internal validity if it produces a single, unambiguous explanation for the relationship between variables. Any factor that allows for an alternative explanation of the relationship is a threat to the internal validity of the research. Confounding variables are the most common threats to internal validity. Artifacts threaten both internal and external validity.

There tends to be a trade-off between internal and external validity. Research that is very strong with respect to one kind of validity is often relatively weak with respect to the second type. This basic relationship must be considered in planning a research study or evaluating someone else's work. Research strategies also vary in terms of validity. Descriptive, correlational, and nonexperimental studies tend to have high external validity and relatively low internal validity; experiments tend to have high internal validity and relatively low external validity. Quasi-experimental studies tend to fall in between. Research strategy refers to the general approach of a research study. Research design addresses the question of how to implement the strategy. A research procedure is an exact, step-by-step description of a specific research study.

KEY WORDS

quantitative research
qualitative research
research strategy
validity
threat to validity
external validity
threat to external
   validity
internal validity

threat to internal validity
extraneous variable
confounding variable
assignment bias
history
maturation
instrumentation, or instrumental bias, or instrumental
   decay

testing effects, or order
   effects
statistical regression, or
   regression toward the
   mean
research design
research procedure

EXERCISES

1. In addition to the key words, you should also be able to define each of the following terms:
   descriptive research strategy
   linear relationship
   curvilinear relationship
   positive relationship
   negative relationship
   correlational research strategy
   experimental research strategy
   quasi-experimental research strategy
   nonexperimental research strategy
   selection bias
   volunteer bias
   novelty effect
   multiple treatment interference
   sensitization, or assessment sensitization, or
      pretest sensitization
   individual differences
   time-related variables
   fatigue
   practice
   carry-over effects

   artifact
   experimenter bias
   single-blind
   double-blind
   demand characteristics
   reactivity
   laboratory
   field

2. Describe the purpose of each of the five different research strategies.

3. For each of the following scenarios, identify which research strategy is used: descriptive, correlational, experimental, or nonexperimental. (Note: For now, do not differentiate between nonexperimental and quasi-experimental studies. The distinction between them is discussed in Chapter 10.)

   a. Dr. Jones conducts a study examining aggressive behavior of 5-year-old boys. Each afternoon for 1 week, a group of boys in a child-care center is observed during a 30-minute period while they play outdoors. Aggressive behaviors are recorded during the 30-minute period.

b. Dr. Jones conducts a study examining the relationship between viewing violent television and aggressive behavior of 5-year-old boys. Television preferences are obtained by interviewing each child. Based on the interview results, the boys are divided into two groups: those who prefer violent television and those who prefer nonviolent television. Then aggressive behavior is measured by observing the children during an outdoor play period to determine if there is any difference between the two groups.

c. Dr. Jones conducts a study examining the relationship between viewing violent television and aggressive behavior of 5-year-old boys. Television preferences are obtained by interviewing each child and aggressive behavior is measured by observing the children during an outdoor play period.

d. Dr. Jones conducts a study examining the relationship between viewing violent television and aggressive behavior of 5-year-old boys. A group of boys is randomly separated; half the boys are shown violent television programs for 30 minutes before play time and the other half of the boys are shown nonviolent television programs during the same period. Aggressive behavior is then measured by observing the children during an outdoor play period to determine if

there is any difference between the two groups.

4. What is the novelty effect, and how does it affect a study's external validity?

5. How does sensitization threaten the external validity of research findings?

6. Explain how using college students as participants in a study may limit the external validity of a study's research findings.

7. Imagine that you are a participant in a research study. For each of the following scenarios, describe how you would probably react, and explain how your reactivity would influence your responses.

a. A researcher tells you that the purpose of the study is to measure your attitudes and prejudices concerning race. First assume that the researcher intends to ask you questions in an interview. Then assume that the researcher hands you a questionnaire to fill out privately.

b. A researcher tells you that the task you are about to perform is directly related to intelligence. Intelligent people usually find the task quite easy and perform very well.

8. Describe one way in which the experimenter may threaten the external validity of the results of a study.

9. Develop an example of a research study that contains a confounding variable.

LEARNING ACTIVITIES

1. At the first meeting of an American History class for new freshmen, the professor identifies 10 students who appear to be the most anxious individuals in the class. Based on their observed behaviors, the professor rates each student's anxiety level on a 10-point scale. After class, the 10 students are approached and offered an opportunity to participate in a 2-week massage therapy program free of charge. All 10 students accept the offer. At the first class meeting after the massage program, the professor again observes the 10 students and rates each individual's level of anxiety. The results indicate a significant decrease in

anxiety following the 2-week massage therapy program. The professor would like to conclude that the massage program caused a reduction in anxiety.

a. Briefly describe how *history* might provide an alternative explanation for the reduction in anxiety.

b. Briefly describe how *regression* toward the mean might provide an alternative explanation for the reduction in anxiety.

c. Briefly describe how *instrumentation* might provide an alternative explanation for the reduction in anxiety.

WEB RESOURCES

Visit the Book Companion Website at **www.cengage.com/international** to access study tools including a glossary, flashcards, and web quizzing. You will also find a link to Statistics and Research Methods Workshops. For this chapter, we suggest you look at the following workshop:

Confounds—Threats to Validity

7

Descriptive Research

CHAPTER OVERVIEW

In this chapter, we discuss the details of the descriptive research strategy. The goal of descriptive research is to describe individual variables as they exist. Three descriptive research designs are considered: the observational research design, the survey research design, and the case study research design.

7.1 | AN INTRODUCTION TO DESCRIPTIVE RESEARCH

In Chapter 6, we identified five basic research strategies for investigating variables and their relationships: experimental, nonexperimental, quasi-experimental, correlational, and descriptive. In this chapter, we present the details of the **descriptive research strategy.** (The experimental strategy is discussed in Chapter 9, the nonexperimental and quasi-experimental strategies are discussed in Chapter 12, and details of the correlational strategy are discussed in Chapter 8.)

Descriptive research typically involves measuring a variable or set of variables as they exist naturally. The descriptive strategy is not concerned with relationships between variables but rather with the description of individual variables. The goal is to describe a single variable or to obtain separate descriptions for each variable when several are involved. This strategy is extremely useful as preliminary research (that is, in the early stages of research) and in its own right. The first step in understanding a new phenomenon is to gain some idea of the variable of interest as it naturally exists. In addition, the results from descriptive research can help us capture interesting, naturally occurring behavior.

Before we begin our formal discussion of descriptive research, look briefly at the following items, each of which appeared in our local newspaper or on the Internet in the spring of 2010:

The Pew Research Center reports that half of American teenagers, ages 12 through 17, send 50 or more text messages a day and that one third send more than 100 a day.

Survey results show that 61% of the adults in the United States currently drink alcohol.

Facebook has replaced Google as the number one website in the United States.

The Kaiser Family Foundation reports that Americans between the ages of 8 and 18 average 7 1/2 hours a day using some sort of electronic device, such as smart phones, MP3 players, and computers.

The suicide rate for college students is about 7.5 a year per 100,000 students.

Although none of these reports is particularly earthshaking or insightful (we are not even sure that they are really true), they are good examples of descriptive research. In each case, the intent of the study is simply to describe a phenomenon. The studies do not try to explain what is related to these things, why these things happen, or identify the underlying causes. Although these newspaper and Internet reports appear to be somewhat trivial, this kind of research plays a very important role in the behavioral sciences. Much of what we know about human and animal behavior is based on descriptions of variables.

In the following sections, three descriptive research designs are considered: observational research, survey research, and case study research. In the observational research design, we describe observations of behaviors as they occur in natural settings. In survey research design, we describe people's responses to questions about behavior and attitudes. In case studies, we describe a single individual in great detail.

7.2 | THE OBSERVATIONAL RESEARCH DESIGN

In the **observational research design,** the researcher observes and systematically records the behavior of individuals for the purpose of describing behavior; for example, the mating behavior of birds, parent–child interactions on a playground, or the shopping behavior of adolescents in a mall. In Chapter 4, we discussed behavioral observation (that is, the observation and recording of behavior) as a technique for measuring variables. As a measurement technique, behavioral observation can be used in a variety of research strategies including experimental and correlational designs. However, a study using behavioral observation simply for descriptive purposes is classified as an observational research design. Following are details of the process of behavioral observation.

DEFINITION	In the **observational research design,** the researcher observes and systematically records the behavior of individuals to describe the behavior.

LEARNING CHECK

What is the difference between behavioral observation and the observational research design?

Behavioral Observation

The process of **behavioral observation** simply involves the direct observation and systematic recording of behaviors, usually as the behaviors occur in a natural situation. For example, a researcher may observe children on a playground or tropical birds in a rain forest. This measurement technique, however, introduces two special measurement problems.

Caution! Many students assume all research studies that use behavioral observation are observational research designs. However, observation can be used to measure variables in a variety of different designs. The defining element of an observational research design is that the results of the observations are used simply to describe the variable being studied.

1. Because the goal is to observe natural behavior, it is essential that the behaviors are not disrupted or influenced by the presence of an observer. This raises the question of demand characteristics and reactivity (see Chapter 4, pp. 129–131).
2. Observation and measurement require at least some degree of subjective interpretation by the observer. If we observe two preschool children bumping into each other, we must decide whether the contact was accidental or deliberate, and if it was deliberate, which child initiated the contact and whether it was aggression or simply play. The fact that the measurements are based, in part, on a subjective judgment, raises the question of reliability (see Chapter 4, pp. 114–118); that is, would two different occurrences of the same behavior be judged in the same way?

The first problem can be addressed by concealing the observer so that the individuals do not know that their behaviors are being observed and recorded. As long as we observe public behaviors in public places, there is no ethical problem with this technique. An alternative procedure is to habituate the participants to the observer's presence. **Habituation** requires repeated exposure until the observer's presence is no longer a novel stimulus. For example, an observer might sit in a classroom for an hour every day for a week before the actual observation begins. On the first day or two, the observer is a novel event and the children modify their behaviors. After a few days, however, the children become accustomed to the observer's presence (like a piece of furniture) and return to their normal behaviors.

To address the second problem, subjectivity, researchers typically employ three interrelated devices to help ensure the objectivity of their behavioral observations. First, they develop a list of well-defined categories of behavior; next, they use well-trained observers; and finally, they use multiple observers to assess inter-rater reliability. As noted, the first step in the process is to prepare a list of behaviors called **behavior categories.** Developing a set of behavior categories means that before observation begins, we identify the categories of behavior we want to observe (such as group play, play alone, aggression, or social interaction) and then list exactly which behaviors count as examples of each category. A preexisting list enables observers to know exactly what to look for and how to categorize each behavior. For example, observers do not have to make a subjective decision about whether an observed behavior is aggressive; they simply need to decide whether the observed behavior is on the preexisting list of aggressive behaviors. In addition, a set of pre-established behavior categories provides a clear operational definition of each construct being examined. (For example, aggression is defined as the occurrence of any of the specific behaviors identified on the list.)

During the observation period, normally only one individual observes and records behaviors using the set of behavioral categories as a guide. To establish reliability, however, two or more individuals must observe and record simultaneously for some of the observation periods (see Chapter 4, pp. 114–118). The degree of agreement between the two observers is then computed either by computing a correlation between the scores for the two observers (Chapter 4 and Figure 4.1) or by computing a proportion of agreement (see Chapter 14, pp. 444–446), ranging from 1.00, perfect agreement, to 0, no agreement, as a measure of **inter-rater reliability.**

Quantifying Observations

Behavioral observation also involves converting the observations into numerical scores that can be used to describe individuals and groups. The creation of numerical values is usually accomplished by one of three techniques:

1. The **frequency method** involves counting the instances of each specific behavior that occur during a fixed time observation period. For example, the child committed three aggressive acts during the 30-minute period.

2. The **duration method** involves recording how much time an individual spends engaged in a specific behavior during a fixed-time observation period. For example, the child spent 18 minutes playing alone during the 30-minute period.

3. The **interval method** involves dividing the observation period into a series of intervals and then recording whether a specific behavior occurs during each interval. For example, the 30-minute observation period is divided into 30 1-minute intervals. The child was observed in group play during 12 of the intervals.

The first two techniques are often well suited for specific behaviors but can lead to distorted measurements in some situations. For example, a bird that sings continuously for the entire 30-minute observation period would get a *frequency* score of only 1. Another bird that sings 25 times with each song lasting 2 seconds, would get a *duration* score of only 50 seconds. In such situations, the *interval method* provides a way to balance frequency and duration to obtain a more representative measurement.

Sampling Observations

When an observer is confronted with a complex situation, it can be impossible to observe many different individuals and record many different behaviors simultaneously. One solution is to record the situation so the scene can be replayed repeatedly to gather observations. A second solution is to take a sample of the potential observations rather than attempt to watch and record everything. The first step in the process of sampling observations is to divide the observation period into a series of time intervals. The sampling process then consists of one of the following three procedures:

1. **Time sampling** involves observing for one interval, then pausing during the next interval to record all the observations. The sequence of observe-record-observe-record is continued through the series of intervals.

2. **Event sampling** involves identifying one specific event or behavior to be observed and recorded during the first interval; then the observer shifts to a different event or behavior during the second interval, and so on, for the full series of intervals.

3. **Individual sampling** involves identifying one participant to be observed during the first interval, then shifting attention to a different individual for the second interval, and so on.

LEARNING CHECKS

Briefly explain why it is important to determine a set of behavior categories before making behavioral observations.

Under what circumstances is it necessary to use sampling (time, event, or individual) during behavioral observation?

Content Analysis and Archival Research

The same techniques that are used in behavioral observation can be applied to other situations that do not involve the direct observation of ongoing behaviors. For example, it is possible to measure behaviors that unfold in movies or books, and it is possible to study documents recording behaviors that occurred long ago. Thus, researchers can measure and record incidences of violence in movies or television programs, and they can look into the past to see whether adults with personality disorders displayed any evidence of abnormal behavior as children. When researchers measure behaviors or events in books, movies, or other media, the measurement process is called **content analysis.** Perhaps the most familiar application of content analysis is the examination of violence on television. For example, studies find more aggressive acts on Saturday morning cartoons than any other programs (Jeffres, 1997). Recording behaviors from historical records is called **archival research.** For example, Jones, Pelham, Carvallo, and Mirenberg (2004) used a series of four archival studies to demonstrate that people tend to marry individuals whose first or last names resemble their own significantly more often than would be expected by randomly pairing names. The data for all four studies were obtained from Internet sites containing birth records (parents' names), marriage records, and joint telephone listings.

DEFINITIONS

Content analysis involves using the techniques of behavioral observation to measure the occurrence of specific events in literature, movies, television programs, or similar media that present replicas of behaviors.

Archival research involves looking at historical records (archives) to measure behaviors or events that occurred in the past.

To ensure that the measurements are objective and reliable, the processes of content analysis and archival research follow the same rules that are used for behavioral observation. Specifically, the measurement process involves the following:

1. Establishing behavioral categories to define exactly which events are included in each category being measured; for example, a list of specific examples is prepared to define television violence.
2. Using the frequency method, the duration method, or the interval method to obtain a numerical score for each behavioral category; for example, an observer records how many examples of violence are seen in a 30-minute television program or how many disciplinary actions appear on an individual's school records.
3. Using multiple observers for at least part of the measurement process to obtain a measure of inter-rater reliability.

Types of Observation and Examples

Ethologists (researchers who study nonhumans in their natural environment) and researchers interested in human behavior commonly use the observational research design. There are three basic kinds of observation: naturalistic observation, participant observation, and contrived observation.

Naturalistic Observation

When a researcher observes and records behavior in a natural setting without intervening in any way, it is called **naturalistic observation, or nonparticipant observation.** A natural setting is one in which behavior ordinarily occurs and that has not been arranged in any way for the purpose of modifying behavior. In naturalistic observation, researchers try to be as inconspicuous and unobtrusive as possible, passively recording whatever occurs.

DEFINITION

In **naturalistic observation, or nonparticipant observation,** a researcher observes behavior in a natural setting as unobtrusively as possible.

Naturalistic observation could be used to describe any behavior; for example, the behavior of children in a classroom, the behavior of protestors in a riot, or the behavior of patrons at a bar. A classic example of naturalistic observation used to describe nonhuman behavior is Jane Goodall's research (1971, 1986). Goodall lived with a colony of chimpanzees in Gombe, Tanzania, for a number of years during the 1960s and observed behaviors in chimps never before recorded (for example, tool use in nonhumans). She observed chimpanzees stripping leaves off twigs, inserting the twigs into a termite hill, then withdrawing the twigs and licking off the termites that clung to them.

Naturalistic observation is particularly useful in providing insight into real-world behavior. The results of studies using naturalistic observation also have high degrees of external validity because the behavior is examined in real-world settings as opposed to laboratories. Furthermore, naturalistic observation is useful for examining behaviors that, for practical or ethical reasons, cannot be manipulated by the researcher. For example, a researcher interested in investigating spanking behavior in parents obviously could not make parents spank their children for the purposes of scientific exploration. A researcher could, however, stroll through public places such as malls and watch parents disciplining their children.

One limitation of naturalistic observation is the time needed to conduct this type of research. To observe the mating behavior of a particular species of bird, for example, a researcher would need to wait until two opposite sex members of that species appeared. In addition, both birds would need to be sexually ready before a researcher could observe their courtship and mating behaviors. Similarly, using naturalistic observation of parent–child interactions on a playground means waiting for a parent with a child of the appropriate age and gender to arrive at the playground, then engage in the behavior the researcher wants to observe. A second problem with naturalistic observation is that the observer must take extra care not to disrupt or influence the behavior being observed because the goal is to observe natural behavior.

LEARNING CHECK

Describe what a researcher attempts to do in naturalistic observation.

Participant Observation

In **participant observation,** a researcher does not observe from afar as in naturalistic observation. Instead, the researcher interacts with the participants and becomes one of them to observe and record behavior. This type of observation is needed in situations in which inconspicuous observation is not possible. For example, researchers certainly could not set up observation in the middle of a cult or gang meeting and expect that no one would notice them, that their presence would not alter behavior, or that the observed behaviors would be at all natural.

DEFINITION   In **participant observation,** the researcher engages in the same activities as the people being observed in order to observe and record their behavior.

A great example of participant observation is Rosenhan's (1973) research investigating the experiences of mental patients and patient–staff interactions in psychiatric hospitals. In this research, Rosenhan had eight individuals misrepresent their names and occupations, and claim they heard voices in order to be admitted to various mental hospitals. All eight individuals were admitted. The pseudopatients observed hospital conditions, their own treatment, and the behaviors of staff and patients. The eight researchers were admitted to 12 different hospitals, and apparently no hospital staff realized that they were not real patients.

Participant observation allows researchers to observe behaviors that are not usually open to scientific observation—for example, occult activities—and to get information that may not be accessible to outside observation. Additionally, by having the same experiences as the participants in the study, the observer gains a unique perspective, obtaining insight into behavior not obtainable by observing from afar. The results of participant-observation studies have high external validity because the behaviors are examined in real-world settings, not laboratories.

There are several limitations of this type of observation. It is extremely time consuming; for example, the observers' stays in the mental hospitals in the Rosenhan study ranged from 7 to 52 days. In addition, participant observation is potentially dangerous for the observer. Furthermore, the observer may inadvertently alter participants' behavior by directly interacting with them; and, finally, by interacting with the participants and identifying closely with the individuals in the study, an observer may lose objectivity.

 **LEARNING CHECK**   Describe the situations in which participant observation may be particularly useful.

Contrived Observation

Another type of observation is **contrived observation,** or **structured observation.** In contrast to observing behavior in natural settings, the observer sets up a situation that is likely to produce the behaviors to be observed so that it is not necessary to wait for them to occur naturally. The purpose of contrived observation is to precipitate a behavior that occurs naturally but infrequently, to create a situation wherein a natural behavior will probably occur and be observed in a more timely fashion.

DEFINITION Observation of behavior in settings arranged specifically to facilitate the occurrence of specific behaviors is known as **contrived observation,** or **structured observation.**

Often, such studies are conducted in laboratory settings. For example, if a researcher wants to observe parent–child interactions, the parents and children could be brought into a laboratory and given a task to perform while being observed or videotaped. This process is much quicker than waiting for parents and children to show up at a playground and interact with one another, which is how natural observation would proceed. To observe disruptive behavior, for example, Hughes, et al. (2002) had pairs of children play a competitive card game that was rigged to ensure that each child would experience a losing streak. Within 5 minutes, the researchers were able to observe behavioral responses to the anger and frustration produced by losing.

Developmental psychologists frequently use structured observation. The most notable example is Jean Piaget (1896–1980). In many of Piaget's studies, a child is given a problem to solve (for example, which cylinder contains more water), and the researcher observes and records how the child solves the problem. These descriptions have provided a wealth of information regarding children's cognitive abilities and are the basis for Piaget's stage theory of cognitive development.

Contrived observation may also take place in a natural but "set up" arena: a field setting (which the participant perceives as a natural environment) arranged by the researcher for the purposes of observing and recording a behavior. For example, to observe the eating behaviors of birds, a researcher could set up a bird feeder. Structured observation is a compromise between the purely descriptive naturalistic observation discussed earlier and manipulative field experiments (discussed in Chapter 9). Ethologists frequently use contrived observation to study animals' responses. For example, Nobel Prize-winning ethologist Konrad Lorenz discovered the phenomenon of imprinting by observing the behavior of graylag goslings. Imprinting is the establishment of a strong, stable preference for or attachment to an object when that object is encountered during a sensitive period in an animal's life; normally, a gosling imprints on its parent immediately after hatching. Lorenz discovered imprinting by naturalistic observation when the goslings pursued him as if he were their parent! He and others then used contrived observation to see if the young goslings would imprint on other models as well. (Indeed they will; graylag goslings will imprint on almost any moving object in the environment.)

An advantage of contrived observation over both natural and participant observation is that researchers do not have to wait for behaviors to occur naturally. Instead, the environment is structured in such a way that the desired behaviors are more likely to occur. However, a disadvantage of contrived observation is that, because the environment is less natural, the behavior may be as well.

LEARNING CHECK What are the advantages and disadvantages of contrived observation compared to naturalistic observation?

Strengths and Weaknesses of Observational Research Designs

The strengths and weaknesses of the three types of observation are summarized in Table 7.1. Here, we discuss some additional strengths and weaknesses of observational research designs in general. A major strength of observational research is that the researcher observes and records actual behavior; in contrast, survey research, for example, relies on the participants' *reports* of their behavior. Participants can distort or conceal the accuracy or truthfulness of their responses, and thus not reflect their actual behavior. Observational research results often have high external validity as well. With the exception of contrived observation in a laboratory, most observational research is conducted in a field setting, and field research tends to have higher external validity. Another strength of observational research is its flexibility. A researcher can complete a comprehensive observation of antecedents, behaviors, and consequences of the behaviors, whereas other studies examine a single, discrete behavior.

A potential problem with observational research is the ethical concern about spying on people. If participants are not aware that their behavior is being observed, the researcher may be violating a person's privacy and right to choose to participate in the study. (In Chapter 3, we discussed when it is not necessary to obtain informed consent before individuals participate in a research study.) Finally, a general weakness of the descriptive research strategy and, therefore, of all observational research designs, is that they simply describe behavior and do not examine its causes.

TABLE **7.1**
A Summary of the Strengths and Weaknesses of the Observational Research Design

Research Design	Strengths	Weaknesses
Naturalistic Observation	Behavior observed in the real world.	Time-consuming.
	Useful for nonmanipulated behaviors.	Potential for observer influence.
	Actual behaviors observed and recorded.	Potential for subjective interpretation.
Participant Observation	When natural observation is impossible.	Time consuming.
	Get information not accessible otherwise.	Potential for loss of objectivity.
	Participation gives unique perspective.	Increased chance for observer influence.
Contrived Observation	Do not have to wait for behaviors to occur.	Less natural.

7.3 | THE SURVEY RESEARCH DESIGN

Caution! The survey is used as a measurement technique in a variety of different research designs. Simply because a study uses a survey does not mean that it is a survey research design. The defining element of the survey research design is that the results of the survey are used simply to describe the variables being studied.

Surveys and questionnaires are used extensively in the behavioral sciences as relatively efficient ways to gather large amounts of information. By presenting people with a few carefully constructed questions, it is possible to obtain self-reported answers about attitudes, opinions, personal characteristics, and behaviors. The simple notion behind a survey is that it is not necessary to observe directly where people shop or what foods they prefer, or how many hours they sleep each night; instead, we simply ask. With a survey, a researcher does not have to wait until a behavior or response occurs; for example, it is not necessary to wait until after an election to discover people's attitudes about candidates or issues; we can ask at any time. Although surveys can be used to obtain scores for a variety of different research designs, a survey often is conducted simply to obtain a description of a particular group of individuals. A study using the results from a survey simply for descriptive purposes is classified as a **survey research design**.

| DEFINITION | A research study that uses a survey to obtain a description of a particular group of individuals is called a **survey research design**. |

The goal of the survey research design is to obtain an accurate picture of the individuals being studied. The survey provides a "snapshot" of the group at a particular time. Sometimes, survey research focuses on a specific characteristic such as eating behavior or political attitudes; other survey research may seek a more complex picture of a variety of behaviors and opinions. For example, a researcher could use a survey to investigate alcohol use at a local high school. Depending on the questions asked, the results could provide a description of how many students drink alcohol, how much they drink, and when and where. Other questions could yield a description of student attitudes toward alcohol use among their peers.

A common application of survey research is by companies to obtain more accurate descriptions of their customers. When you buy any electronic device, for example, a warranty registration card usually accompanies it. In addition to your name and address and the serial number of the product, other demographic questions are usually asked:

What is your age?

What is your occupation?

What is your income?

How did you hear about our product?

Clearly, the purpose of these questions is to obtain the demographic characteristics of customers; that is, to put together a description of the people who are likely to buy this product so that the company can do a better job of targeting its advertising.

Conducting survey research presents researchers with four issues that must be addressed for the results to be accurate and meaningful. First, survey questions must be developed. Second, the questions must be assembled and organized to produce a well-constructed survey. Third, a selection process must be developed to determine exactly who will participate in the survey and who will not; survey participants must be representative of the general group to be studied. Finally, researchers must determine how the survey will be administered. Will participants receive printed surveys through the mail; will the survey questions be read to people over the telephone; or will participants complete the questions online in an Internet survey, or in person? These four issues are discussed in the following sections.

Types of Questions

There are different ways to ask participants for self-report information. Sometimes, you may be satisfied with a simple yes or no answer (Have you ever...), but in other circumstances, you may want a quantitative answer (how much, how often). Different types of questions encourage different types of responses. Also, different types of questions permit different degrees of freedom in the participants' answers. For example, a question may severely restrict response options (Which of the following three flavors of ice cream do you prefer?), or a question may give each participant complete freedom in choosing a response (What is your favorite ice cream flavor?). The wording of a question also can introduce bias into participants' answers (Are you one of those bland, unimaginative people who prefer vanilla ice cream?). Finally, different types of questions permit different types of statistical analysis and interpretation. If answers are limited to non-numerical categories on a nominal scale, for example, you cannot compute a group average. In this section, we consider three general types of self-report questions. Each type has its own individual strengths and weaknesses, and is designed to obtain specific information.

Open-Ended Questions

An open-ended question simply introduces a topic and allows participants to respond in their own words. For example:

1. What do you think about the current availability of food on this campus?
2. In your view, what are the most important factors in choosing a college or university?

The primary advantage of an open-ended question is that it allows an individual the greatest flexibility in choosing how to answer. An open-ended question imposes few restrictions on the participant and, therefore, is likely to reveal each individual's true thoughts or opinions. Although the question may lead the participant in a particular direction or suggest a specific point of view, individuals are free to express their own thoughts. However, this can also be a major disadvantage. For example, different participants may approach the question from entirely different perspectives, leaving you with answers that are impossible to compare or summarize. To the question about food on the college campus, for example, one individual may respond with a list of food suggestions, another may suggest new locations for selling food, and a third participant may state simply that the current situation is "okay." All three answers may be useful, but they are clearly not compatible with each other and they may be very different from the issue you had in mind when the original question was written.

A second disadvantage of open-ended questions is that the answers are often difficult to summarize or analyze with conventional statistical methods. As with the food question, different participants may provide responses that are difficult to group together or to average in any meaningful way. Often, the researcher must impose some subjective interpretation on the answer, such as classifying a rambling response as generally positive or generally negative. Finally, the responses to open-ended questions may be limited by a participant's ability or willingness to express his thoughts. Inarticulate or tired people may give very brief answers that do not completely express the true breadth of their thinking.

Restricted Questions

A restricted question presents the participant with a limited number of response alternatives, thereby restricting the response possibilities. Like a multiple-choice question, a restricted question typically asks the participant to select the best or most appropriate answer in a series of choices. For example:

1. If the election were held today, which of the following candidates would receive your vote?
   a. Mr. Jones
   b. Ms. Smith
   c. Mr. Johnson
2. Which of the following alternatives is the best description of your current occupation?
   a. Blue collar
   b. White collar (sales/service)
   c. Professional
   d. Managerial
   e. Student
   f. Unemployed

Because these questions produce a limited and predetermined set of responses, they are easy to analyze and summarize. Typically, the data are tabulated and reported as percentages or proportions of participants selecting each alternative.

It also is possible to obtain quantitative information from restricted questions by using an ordered set of response alternatives. For example:

1. During a typical week, how often do you eat at a fast-food restaurant?
   a. Not at all
   b. Once
   c. Twice
   d. Three times
   e. Four times or more

With this type of question, it often is possible to compute some kind of average response for a group of participants.

Finally, an element of open-endedness can be allowed in a restricted question by including a blank category where participants are free to fill in their own responses. For example:

1. Which of the following is your favorite local department store?
   a. Jones & Bederman
   b. Macy's
   c. Marx
   d. McReynold's
   e. Other (please specify) _____

LEARNING CHECK   Briefly identify the relative strengths and weaknesses of open-ended and restricted questions.

Rating-Scale Questions

A rating-scale question requires a participant to respond by selecting a numerical value on a predetermined scale. Movie critics often use this type of scale to evaluate films with a number from 1 to 10. The numerical scale that accompanies each question typically presents a range of response alternatives from very positive to very negative. A common example uses a 5-point scale on which individuals rate their level of agreement or disagreement with a simple statement:

1. Strongly disagree
2. Disagree
3. Neither agree or disagree
4. Agree
5. Strongly agree

The rating scale is usually presented as a horizontal line divided into categories so that participants can simply circle a number or mark an X at the location corresponding to their response (Figure 7.1). This type of rating-scale question is often called a **Likert scale** (or a Likert-type scale) after Rensis Likert, who developed the 5-point response scale as part of a much more sophisticated scaling system (Likert, 1932). Notice that the scale is presented with equal spacing between the different response choices. The idea is to simulate an interval scale of measurement, and the responses from rating scales are usually treated as interval measurements. Thus, the distance between agree and strongly agree is treated as a 1-point distance that is equivalent to any other 1-point difference on the scale.

There is no absolute rule for determining the number of categories for a rating-scale question; however, researchers commonly use from 5 to 10 numerical values. The reasoning behind this range of values is based on two observations:

1. Participants tend to avoid the two extreme categories at the opposite ends of the scale, especially if they are identified with labels that indicate extreme attitudes or opinions. Thus, the actual scale is effectively reduced by two categories.

Questionnaire

Use the following scale (numbers 1 through 5) to describe how you feel about each of the
statements below. For each statement, circle the number that gives the best description
of how you feel.

Strongly Disagree	Disagree	Undecided	Agree	Strongly Agree
1	2	3	4	5

1. I have a natural talent for mathematics. 1 2 3 4 5

2. I am a good math student. 1 2 3 4 5

3. I like mathematics. 1 2 3 4 5

4. Math is easier for me than it is for most students. 1 2 3 4 5

5. I probably will use mathematics in my future job. 1 2 3 4 5

FIGURE **7.1** A Likert-Type Rating Scale and a Series of Questions
Examining Elementary School Students' Attitudes about Mathematics
The participants' responses consist of numerical ratings for each of the five questions.
The numbers can be added and averaged, and are compatible with most standard
statistical procedures.

2. Participants have trouble discriminating among more than 9 or
10 different levels. If the scale offers more than 10 options, the
participants usually blend categories and effectively create their
own 10-point scale.

There also is no absolute rule for labeling the categories. Typically, the
opposite extremes are identified with verbal labels called **anchors** that establish the endpoints of the scale. In addition, the central category is often
labeled, especially if it represents a neutral response. Beyond the endpoints
and the middle, however, labeling categories is optional.

One criticism of rating-scale questions is that whenever questions in a
series all have the same choices for responding, participants tend to use the
same response to answer all (or most) of the questions. This tendency is called
a **response set.** With a Likert-type scale, for example, some participants use
the neutral (#3) answer for everything. One rationalization is that they really
do not feel strongly about any of the items so they really are neutral. (A more
likely explanation is that they simply want to finish quickly.) Another possibility is that a participant may use the agree category for all responses except
to those few items where there is serious disagreement. To minimize this
problem, it is recommended that the items include a mixture of positive and

negative statements, including some alternate phrasing of the same item. For example, one item might be:

Today's teenagers are rude and disrespectful.

Later in the series, an alternate item might be:

Today's teenagers are polite and courteous.

The intent is to force respondents to move back and forth between opposite sides of the scale so that they cannot fall into a single response set for answering the questions.

Another common scale, called the **semantic differential,** presents pairs of bipolar adjectives (such as happy—sad, boring—exciting), and asks each participant to identify the location between the two adjectives that best describes a particular individual. For example, one item might be:

neat ———————————— messy
  1   2   3   4   5

The primary advantage of rating-scale questions is that they produce numerical values that can be treated as measurements from an interval scale. (Recall from Chapter 4 that an interval scale consists of a series of equal-sized categories, which makes it possible to measure distances on the scale.) Using the five items in Figure 7.1 as an example, each participant receives a total score obtained by adding the responses from the five items. A participant who answered 1 (strongly disagree) to all five items would have a total score of 5. Someone who answered 5 (strongly agree) to all five items would have a total score of 25. Thus, we can position each individual on a scale that represents attitudes toward mathematics. This way, we can compare different individuals and compute means to describe different groups of participants. In general, it is very easy to use standard statistical procedures to summarize and interpret the results from a rating-scale question.

A secondary advantage of rating-scale questions is that participants usually find them easy to understand and easy to answer. Because the scale permits different degrees of response, participants are not forced into an absolute yes or no, all-or-none choice. Instead, they can qualify their answers by indicating degrees of agreement or approval. It also is easy for participants to breeze through a long series of questions after the rating scale has been introduced at the beginning of the survey. Thus, it is possible to collect a lot of data on a variety of different topics in a single, relatively efficient survey.

LEARNING CHECK What is the main advantage of using a rating scale compared to other types of self-report questions?

Constructing a Survey

Once the survey questions are determined, the next step is to organize the questions into a coherent survey that participants can easily understand and complete. The details of constructing a survey are beyond the scope of this text, but there are a few general guidelines for creating a well-organized survey.

1. Demographic questions (such as age, gender, level of education) should be placed at the end of the survey. These items are considered boring, and you do not want participants to quit because they are bored by the first few questions. In addition, identifying age, race, or gender first may influence how the participant answers survey questions that relate to these variables.

2. Sensitive questions or items that may cause embarrassment or discomfort should be placed in the middle of the survey. By the time participants encounter these items, they are more likely to have warmed up to the topic and become committed to completing the survey.

3. Questions dealing with the same general topic should be grouped together. Also, questions in the same format should be grouped together; for example, all rating-scale questions should be grouped together. Grouping questions simplifies the survey so participants do not have to jump from one topic to another or switch from one type of question to another.

4. If participants are going to read the survey, the format for each page should be relatively simple and uncluttered. Questions that are crammed together and seem to fill every square inch of the page create an overwhelming appearance that can intimidate participants.

5. Finally, vocabulary and language style should be easy for participants to understand. A survey with language appropriate for college students probably would not be appropriate for elementary school students.

These guidelines address only a few of the considerations involved in designing a survey. If you plan to construct your own survey, you probably should seek more detailed guidance. Two excellent sources are Rea and Parker (2005) and Dillman, Smyth, and Christian (2009).

Selecting Relevant and Representative Individuals

Researchers typically want to generalize their results from the study's sample to the target population. (See Chapter 5 for information about selecting a sample.) In addition, the external validity of a research study is limited, in part, by the representativeness of the sample to the population (see Chapter 6). The survey research design introduces a few additional concerns regarding sample selection. First, many surveys address a specific issue that is relevant to only a small subset of the general population. For such a survey, care must be taken to select survey participants to whom the questions are relevant. For a survey about childcare issues, for example, participants should be parents with small children. A sensible strategy might be to hand out surveys to parents as they pick up their children at childcare centers around the city. Or you might obtain mailing lists from the different childcare centers. Similarly, participants for a shopping survey might be selected from the people in a shopping mall, and participants for an education survey could come from the parents of children in the local school district.

Second, although some surveys focus on a specific topic or group of people, some surveys seek to describe a broad cross-section of the general population.

In this case, the sample of survey participants must not be too restricted. For example, administering surveys to the students in a psychology class would not result in an accurate description of the political attitudes of people in the community. A researcher should take some time to identify the group to be described, then make an effort to select individuals who accurately represent the group. This often means that the individuals who participate in the survey are not necessarily the ones who are easiest or most convenient to obtain.

Occasionally, individual researchers seek professional help preparing surveys and identifying participants. In most major metropolitan areas, there are several research companies that design, administer, and analyze surveys. These companies usually have access to specialized mailing lists that can focus on a specific, well-defined population. Typically, a researcher supplies specific demographic characteristics, and the computer generates a list of individuals who meet the criteria; for example, single mothers between the ages of 20 and 29 who have an annual income greater than $35,000. Focusing a survey in this way can increase the chances of obtaining a reasonable number of useful responses.

Administering a Survey

Once you have developed the survey questions, constructed the survey, and identified the participants, the next step is to distribute the survey to the individuals you would like to investigate. There are a number of options for administering a survey, each of which has advantages and disadvantages. In this section we examine some of the most common methods for administering surveys: by mail, by telephone, and in person. It is also increasingly common to administer surveys on the Internet.

Mail Surveys

One common method of administration is to mail the survey to a large sample of individuals. For individual participants, a mailed survey is very convenient and nonthreatening. Individuals can complete the survey at their own convenience, and can be relatively confident that responses are anonymous and confidential. On the other hand, the fact that the survey is anonymous means that a researcher can never be sure exactly who in the household completed and returned the survey.

Mailing surveys is usually a relatively simple and easy process, although printing a large number of surveys, addressing them, and paying postage can be expensive and time consuming. The expense is compounded by the fact that response rates tend to be very low for mailed surveys. A response rate of 10% to 20% is fairly typical. This means that you need to distribute at least five times the number of surveys you hope to have returned.

In addition to the costs of a low response rate, there may be a bias differentiating those who do and those who do not return surveys. One obvious possibility is that people who are most interested in the survey topic (those with the most intense feelings) are most likely to complete and return the survey. This trend creates what is called a **nonresponse bias** in the sample: The individuals who return surveys are usually not representative of the entire group who receives them. Imagine, for example, a survey about blocking Internet sites on the computers at a public library. Although the surveys are mailed to all library patrons, they are most likely to be completed by people who are passionate about free speech and those who are paranoid about pornography. Neither group accurately represents the people who typically use the library. As a result, nonresponse bias can limit your ability to generalize survey results and poses a threat to the external validity of your study.

Although it is impossible to eliminate nonresponse bias completely, several actions can increase the overall response rate for a mail survey and thereby reduce the bias. First, response rates can be significantly improved if a good cover letter accompanies the survey. A cover letter should introduce the survey and ask for participation, and include the following elements:

1. An explanation of why the topic is important. For a survey on television program preferences, for example, you should point out the major role that television plays in the entertainment and education of most people.
2. An explanation of the usefulness of the results. Usually, the results of a survey are used in future planning or to help determine a future course of action. This should be explained in the cover letter so that participants know that the information they are providing may actually influence them in the future.
3. An emphasis on the importance of each individual response. The intent is to encourage all people to respond, whether or not they feel strongly about the issues in the survey. The cover letter should point out the importance of results that represent the entire population (not just a small group with special interests) and that it is, therefore, especially important that each person respond.
4. A contact person (name, address, and telephone number) whom participants can call or write to if they have any questions or comments. Participants rarely contact this person, but a real name and address help personalize the survey.
5. The signature of a person who is recognized and respected by individuals in the sample. People are more likely to respond if they are asked to by someone they know and like.

A second technique for improving response rates is to include a gift or token of appreciation with each survey (James & Bolstein, 1992). Common examples include a pen ("Please use this pen to fill out the survey, then keep the pen as our gift to you.") or money. Some surveys arrive with a dollar taped to the top and a note suggesting that the recipient use the money to buy a cup of coffee ("Sit back and enjoy your coffee while you complete the survey.")

Finally, it is possible to increase response rates by giving participants advance warning of the survey, then providing a follow-up reminder after the survey has been received (Dillman, Clark, & Sinclair, 1995). Typically, participants are notified by mail or by telephone, about 1 week before the survey is mailed, that they have been selected to participate. The advance warning helps make the individuals feel special (they are a select group) and helps ensure that they will be watching for the survey in the mail. Approximately 1 week after the surveys have been received, a follow-up call or postcard is used to remind each person to complete and return the survey (if they have not done so already), and to thank each person for participating. Essentially, the advance notice and reminder provide a polite way to add an extra please and thank you to the recruitment process, and can significantly increase the response rate.

Telephone Surveys

A second method of administering a survey is to contact individuals by telephone. However, administering a survey by telephone can be incredibly time consuming. The obvious problem with a telephone survey is that there is a direct, one-to-one relationship between the time spent by the researcher and the time spent by the participants; to get 100 minutes of survey responses, a researcher must spend 100 minutes on the telephone. Therefore, most telephone surveys are restricted to situations in which a large number of researchers or assistants can share the telephone assignments.

Administering a survey by telephone does have some advantages. First, the survey can be conducted from home or office. If several people place the calls and the survey is relatively brief, it is possible to contact a fairly large number of participants in only a few days. If you are considering a telephone survey, here are a few important notes for improving your chances for success.

1. Keep the questions short and use a small number of response alternatives. With a telephone survey, the participants do not have a written copy for reference, so you must depend on the listener's memory. If a participant gets confused or lost in the middle of a long, complicated question, you may not get a sensible response.
2. Practice reading the survey aloud. Listening to a question can be different from reading a question. On the telephone, participants cannot see the punctuation and other visual cues that help communicate the content of a written question. A good strategy is to pretest your survey questions by reading them to a set of friends. Be sure that your listeners understand the questions as you intended.
3. Beware of **interviewer bias.** Whenever a researcher has direct contact with participants, even over the telephone, there is a risk that the researcher will influence their natural responses. On the telephone, the primary problem is exerting influence by tone of voice or by rephrasing questions. The standard solutions are to practice reading the survey questions in a consistent, neutral tone, and never to alter a survey question. If a participant does not understand a question and asks for clarification, your only option is to reread the question. If you paraphrase a question or try to explain what it means, then you have changed the question and maybe even changed the participant's answer. Consider the following two versions of the same question. The first uses neutral wording and focuses on the library hours. The second question is phrased in a leading way; that is, it appears to be an invitation for the participant to join a happy little group (especially if the question is read in a very friendly tone of voice).

Do you think there should be an increase in the hours that the library is open on weekends?

Don't you think we should increase the hours that the library is open on weekends?

4. Begin by identifying yourself and your survey. People are constantly bombarded by "junk" telephone calls and are inclined to hang up whenever a stranger calls. You can help avoid this problem if you immediately identify yourself and your topic, and make it clear that you are conducting a survey and not trying to sell anything. Your first few sentences on the telephone are similar to the cover letter for a mail survey, and should contain the same elements (see p. 213).

LEARNING CHECK Outline the advantages and disadvantages of using telephone surveys as compared to mail surveys.

Internet Surveys

More often surveys are being administered over the Internet. Occasionally, you will find links to surveys on existing websites of businesses or organizations. Commonly, people are sent an email or other invitation asking them to visit the survey website. Today, setting up a survey on a website is relatively easy and fast. There are a number of survey authoring software packages and online survey services available (Wright, 2005). SurveyMonkey is one popular example of a company that, for a monthly fee, provides software to create and conduct a survey. The survey is housed on their server and they provide additional support as well.

Internet surveys provide an economical and efficient medium for reaching a large number of potential respondents. A related advantage of Internet surveys is that a researcher has greater access to participants with a particular characteristic (McKenna & Bargh 2000; Wright, 2005). It is easier to find people who share a specific interest, belief, or characteristic, than asking many more people by mail or on the phone. Hence there is a saving of time, as well as the cost of printing surveys, postage, and phone bills.

Another advantage of an Internet survey is the flexibility in presenting questions and response alternatives. For example, if a survey question asks whether you have flown on a commercial airline during the past 7 months, it is possible to select the next question(s) based on an individual's response. For individuals who answer no, the survey can jump immediately to the next topic and skip all the other questions about airline travel. For individuals who answer yes, the survey can move to a series of questions concerning the travel experience. For example, the next question might be "On what airline did you travel?" accompanied by a drop box that presents 20 response choices. The ability to skip irrelevant questions, or move to a set of related questions, based on an individual's responses, makes it possible to individualize a survey to obtain the maximum amount of information from each individual. In addition, the ability to control response alternatives with pop-ups and drop down boxes increases the options for types of questions.

However, administering a survey on the Internet has numerous disadvantages related to issues of the sample. Because participants are often recruited from users of newsgroups, chatrooms, or other specific sites, participants in the sample may differ from Internet users in general and other people who are not on the Internet. Internet surveys, similarly to mail surveys, are also subject to nonresponse bias (Wright, 2005). Furthermore, it can be difficult to control the sample of respondents. For example, there is no simple system for organizing email addresses. Many households have several computers with several different users, all of whom have different email addresses. In addition, many people have more than one email address. This makes it difficult to identify and select a sample of individuals or households who will be asked to participate in the survey.

Internet surveys are controlled best when they are administered to a closed group of email users such as a university or other organization with a common address. For example, emails directing people to a survey website can be sent to all the students at a university by using the university list serve. If a link to a survey is simply posted on an existing website, you have no idea who might visit the site and decide to participate in the survey. Although people who visit a website are likely to be interested in the content, and therefore a relevant sample, you have no ability to control or even determine the composition of the sample.

In-Person Surveys and Interviews

Probably the most efficient method for administering a survey is to assemble a group of participants and have all of them complete the survey at the same time. You can ask people to sign up for predetermined meeting times, or simply ask for volunteers to gather at a specific time and place. Another possibility is to approach preexisting groups such as those in school classrooms or workplace lunchrooms. By having participants volunteer before the survey is presented, you guarantee a 100% response rate. The efficiency comes from the fact that you give instructions once to the entire group and then collect a whole set of completed surveys in the time it takes one participant to finish.

It also is possible to administer a survey in person to a single participant. In this case, the survey becomes a one-on-one interview. Although this appears to be a very inefficient method of collecting information, an interview can be quite valuable. Usually, interviews are reserved for a very small group of specially selected individuals, often called key informants. Typically, these are people who have unique perspectives on the issues or unique access to information (such as a college president, a chief of police, or a mayor). Interviews are also useful in situations in which you are willing to accept the limitations of a small group of participants in exchange for the in-depth information that can come from a detailed interview. An interview provides an opportunity for follow-up questions, and it is possible to explore complex issues more fully than could be done with a few isolated paper-and-pencil questions. Finally, interviews allow you to gather information from individuals who are unable to read and answer printed questions such as young children, people who cannot read, and people with low IQs.

A major concern with the interview is that interviewer bias can distort the results. For example, a participant may perceive a smile or nod from the researcher as a sign of approval or encouragement to continue on the current topic. Thus, the participant's response may be influenced by subtle actions on the part of the interviewer. Although it is impossible to completely eliminate this problem, it can be limited if the interviewer maintains a consistent attitude throughout the entire interview. A common strategy is to adopt a universal, mildly positive response to anything the participant says.

Strengths and Weaknesses of Survey Research

Table 7.2 summarizes the strengths and weaknesses of each method for administering a survey. In general, one of the real strengths of survey research is its flexibility. Surveys can be used to obtain information about a wide variety of different variables including attitudes, opinions, preferences, and behaviors. In fact, some of these variables are very difficult to describe in any other way. In addition, surveys typically provide a relatively easy and efficient means of gathering a large amount of information.

We have already noted some of the disadvantages of survey research, such as low response rates and nonresponse bias. Responses to survey questions can also be difficult to analyze or summarize. This problem is especially important with open-ended questions, to which participants are allowed to respond in their own words. For example, if you ask students to identify what they consider the best things about their college or university, you probably would obtain a wide variety of answers that would be difficult to classify or categorize in any systematic manner. A final concern about survey research is

TABLE **7.2**
A Summary of the Strengths and Weaknesses of the Survey Research Design

Survey Type	Strengths	Weaknesses
Mail Surveys	Convenient and anonymous. Nonthreatening to participants. Easy to administer.	Can be expensive. Low response rate and nonresponse bias. Unsure exactly who completes the survey.
Telephone Surveys	Can be conducted from home or office. Participants can stay at home or office.	Time consuming. Potential for interviewer bias.
Internet surveys	Efficient to administer to a large number of participants. Access to large number of individuals with common characteristics. Survey can be individualized based on participant's responses.	Initial expense for site. Sample may not be representative. Cannot control composition of the sample.
In-Person Surveys	Efficient to administer with groups. 100% response rate. Flexible (groups or individual interviews).	Time consuming with individual interviews. Risk of interviewer bias.

that the information obtained is always a self-report. Ultimately, the quality of a survey study depends on the accuracy and truthfulness of the participants. It is certainly possible that at least some participants will distort or conceal information, or simply have no knowledge about the topic when they answer certain questions. Therefore, if your survey results show that 43% of the high school students use alcohol at least once a month, keep in mind that the results actually show that 43% of the students *report* using alcohol at least once a month.

LEARNING CHECK   What is the general advantage of using the survey research design instead of the observational design? In the same context, what is the disadvantage of survey research?

7.4 | THE CASE STUDY DESIGN

Research in the behavioral sciences tends to emphasize the study of groups rather than single individuals. By focusing on groups, researchers can observe the effects of a treatment across a variety of different personal characteristics and form a better basis for generalizing the results of the study. At the same time, however, some fields within the behavioral sciences are more concerned with individual behavior than with group averages. This is particularly true in the field of clinical psychology, in which clinicians concentrate on treatments and outcomes for individual clients. For clinicians, research results averaged over a large group of diverse individuals may not be as relevant as the specific result obtained for an individual client. In fact, it has been argued that intensive study of individuals (called the **idiographic approach**) is just as important as the study of groups (called the **nomothetic approach**) for clinical research (Allport, 1961).

Although it is possible to conduct experimental research with individual participants (see Chapter 15), most individual-participant research studies can be classified as case studies. A **case study design** is a study of a single individual for the purpose of obtaining a description of the individual. The description is typically prepared as a report, usually containing a detailed description of observations and experiences during the diagnosis and treatment of a specific clinical client, including a detailed description of the unique characteristics and responses of the individual. If no treatment is administered to the individual being studied, the term **case history** often is used instead of case study. The information included in a case study can be obtained in a variety of ways, such as interviews with the client and/or close relatives, observation of the client, surveys, and archival data.

Caution! Other types of research, too, involve the detailed study of single individuals (see Chapter 15). The defining element of a case study design is that its goal is simply to obtain a description of the individual.

DEFINITIONS   The **case study design** involves the in-depth study and detailed description of a single individual (or a very small group). A case study may involve an intervention or treatment administered by the researcher. When a case study does not include any treatment or intervention, it often is called a **case history**.

 **LEARNING CHECK** Identify the advantages of conducting a research study with a single individual instead of a group of participants.

Applications of the Case Study Design

The case study design is most commonly used in clinical psychology. However, the case study has a long history of successful application throughout the behavioral sciences. Although group studies probably offer a more direct path to discovering general laws of behavior, it can also be argued that group studies are necessarily limited because they overlook the importance of the individual. By highlighting individual variables, case studies can offer valuable insights that complement and expand the general truths obtained from groups. In some instances, case studies can lead directly to general laws or theories. The developmental theories of Jean Piaget, for example, are largely based on detailed observations of his own children. The following sections identify specific applications of the case study design.

Rare Phenomena and Unusual Clinical Cases

The case study design is often used to provide researchers with information concerning rare or unusual phenomena such as multiple personality, a dissociative disorder in which two or more distinct personalities exist within the same individual. Although multiple personality is fairly common in television and popular fiction, it is actually an extremely rare condition. With a disorder this rare, it is essentially impossible to gather a group of individuals to participate in any kind of experimental investigation. As a result, most of what is known about multiple personality and its treatment comes from case studies. One of the most famous cases involved a relatively quiet and humble 25-year-old woman (Eve White) who also exhibited a more playful and mischievous personality (Eve Black), as well as a more mature and confident personality (Jane) (Thigpen & Cleckley, 1954, 1957). You may recognize this highly publicized case study by the title of the 1957 publication, *Three Faces of Eve.*

Unique or unusual examples of individuals with brain injuries are often used to help identify the underlying neurological mechanisms for human memory and mental processing. A classic example is the case study of a patient identified as H. M. (Scoville & Milner, 1957). In an attempt to control severe epileptic seizures, H. M.'s hippocampus was surgically severed in both the left and right hemispheres of the brain. After surgery, H. M. had normal memory of events that occurred prior to surgery and his overall intelligence was unchanged. In addition, his immediate memory (short-term memory) also appeared to function normally. For example, he could repeat a string of digits such as a telephone number. However, H. M. had lost the ability to permanently store any new information in memory. You could introduce yourself and talk briefly with H. M., then leave the room while he was occupied with some other task; when you returned to the room after only a few minutes, H. M. would have no memory of ever having met you and no memory of your conversation. In general, H. M. was unable to learn any new information presented to him after the surgery. This remarkable case study completely changed the way psychologists think about memory. Prior to the H. M. case, psychologists tended to view memory as a location in the brain. Now, memory is viewed as a process. H. M.'s injury did not destroy any specific memories; instead it seems to have disrupted a process. As a consequence of the study of H. M.'s case, evidence was provided that the hippocampus appears to play a crucial role in the process by which our current experiences are transformed into permanent memories. Finally, we should note that the initials H. M. were used in research reports to protect the identify of Henry Molaison, whose name was revealed when he died in December of 2008 (Bhattacharjee, 2008). Over a period of more than 50 years, Mr. Molaison participated in hundreds of research studies examining human learning and memory.

Case Studies as Counterexamples

Another application of the case study design is to use the detailed description of a single individual to demonstrate an exception to the rule. Although a single case study is usually not sufficient to demonstrate that a treatment is universally effective, it is possible to use a single case study to show that the treatment does not always work.

One case study used in this manner exposed the flaws in a controversial method of treating phobias. The initial study (Valins & Ray, 1967) claimed to have demonstrated a new therapy technique called cognitive desensitization. The technique essentially tricks clients into thinking that their phobias have been cured. The idea is that clients who believe that they are cured develop new thinking patterns that eventually lead to a real cure. The study examined a group of individuals with fear of snakes. The treatment involved having the participants view pictures of snakes while listening to their own heartbeats played over a loudspeaker. However, the researchers actually presented false heart rates that appeared to show participants that they no longer experienced fear when shown the snake pictures. A follow-up study (Kent, Wilson, & Nelson, 1972) disputed the effectiveness of the treatment by clearly demonstrating that the treatment simply did not work. In addition to the experimental demonstration, the follow-up report presented a case study as a clinical addendum. The case study described a 24-year-old woman, Miss H., who had a phobia of spiders. She was given the false-feedback "therapy" using pictures of spiders instead of snakes. After treatment, Miss H. stated that her fear of spiders was in no way altered or reduced. Although she accepted the false feedback as her own heart rate, she stated that she was still "paralyzed by fear" and that she would prefer to avoid such therapy sessions in the future.

Strengths and Weaknesses of the Case Study Design

One of the primary strengths of a case study is the intense detail that is typically included. A case study exposes a wide variety of different variables, events, and responses that would probably be overlooked or deliberately eliminated (controlled) in an experiment. Thus, a case study can identify or suggest new variables that might account for a particular outcome, and can thereby generate hypotheses for future research.

As we saw in the false heart rate study cited earlier (Kent, Wilson, & Nelson, 1972), case studies also can be used to demonstrate exceptions to the rule. It takes only one negative demonstration, a single counterexample, to show that a general "law" of behavior is not always true. Case studies provide researchers with a good opportunity to identify special situations or unique variables that can modify a general treatment effect. Although this type of case study can be used to destroy or discredit a theory, usually counterexamples serve as constructive criticism. They allow theories to expand and develop by introducing new variables, and they can help establish the boundaries or limitations of a treatment application. There are very few absolute laws of behavior; most have exceptions, limitations, and qualifications, and often the qualifiers are discovered in case studies.

The false heart rate study (Kent, Wilson, & Nelson, 1972) also demonstrates one final strength of the case study strategy: Case studies can be extremely powerful and convincing. The detailed description in a case study tends to make it more personal, more vivid, and more emotional than the "cold" facts and figures that result from a traditional laboratory study. These factors have all been demonstrated to have a strong, positive effect on memory (Tversky & Kahneman, 1973), suggesting that case studies may be more memorable and have a greater effect than experiments. As an analogy, consider your own response to witnessing an automobile accident versus reading an article on accident statistics. Witnessing one accident usually has more influence than reading a statistical summary of all the accidents across the state during the past year. In addition, case studies are typically descriptions of the everyday work of clinicians. This fact gives a case study a sense of realism that can be lacking in an "artificial" laboratory study. As a result, case studies often have an appearance of credibility and a degree of acceptance that far exceed a more objective evaluation of their true levels of internal and external validity.

Like all descriptive designs, the case study is necessarily limited because it simply describes and does not attempt to identify the underlying mechanisms that explain behavior. For example, a case study can provide a detailed description of the individual participant's characteristics (age, gender, family background, and the like), but it provides no means of determining how these variables influence the participant's response to treatment. A case study can tell how a specific individual with specific characteristics responded to a specific treatment, but it cannot explain why. Although a case study may offer an explanation for the observed results, alternative explanations are always possible. In research terminology, case studies lack internal validity.

In addition to lacking internal validity, case studies also tend to be weak in external validity. Because a case study reports results for a single individual in a specific situation, it is difficult to justify generalizing the results to other individuals in other situations. It is always possible that a case study concerns a unique event in the life of a unique person, and there is no reason to expect the same outcome outside the confines of the study. Again, this threat can be tempered by the extent and detail of description within the study. If the study describes a relatively typical client and a relatively straightforward treatment procedure, there is good reason to expect the results to generalize to a broader population. On the other hand, if the case includes odd or unusual circumstances, a strange historical background, bizarre behaviors, or a uniquely individualized treatment program, it is less likely that the results will generalize beyond the specific case being described.

Finally, case studies can suffer from bias that distorts or obscures the results and interpretations, and thus, threaten internal validity. First, there is always a degree of selective bias that determines which cases are reported and which are not. Obviously, a researcher is likely to report the most successful or dramatic case. It is unlikely that a researcher would write a detailed report (and that a journal would publish the report) of an elaborate new treatment that has absolutely no effect. More subtle biases can operate within a reported case study. Remember, a case study consists of observations made by the researcher. These observations are subject to interpretations, impressions, and inferences. In general, the reports of participants are filtered through the researcher who decides what is important and what is not. In addition, the client may provide a biased or falsified report. Clients may exaggerate, minimize, lie about, or simply imagine events that are reported to a clinician/researcher.

Although case studies are exposed to serious threats to both internal and external validity and are subject to bias, many of these problems are reduced by replication. A case study rarely exists by itself but rather is accompanied by several similar reports. Repeated examples of the same basic finding by different researchers with different clients clearly helps bolster the validity and the credibility of the results. Table 7.3 summarizes the strengths and weaknesses of the case study research design.

 **LEARNING CHECK**   Discuss how internal validity and external validity are both threatened in a case study design.

TABLE **7.3**

A Summary of the Strengths and Weaknesses of the Case Study Research Design

Strengths	Weaknesses
Not averaged over a diverse group	Limited generalization
Detailed description	Potential for selective bias
Vivid, powerful, convincing	Potential for subjective interpretation
Compatible with clinical work	
Can study rare and unusual events	
Can identify exceptions to the rule	

■ CHAPTER SUMMARY

The goal of the descriptive research strategy is to describe the variables being examined as they exist naturally. Three different types of descriptive research designs were discussed: observational research, survey research, and case study research.

In the observational research design, researchers observe and describe behaviors as they occur in natural settings. There are three kinds of observation. In naturalistic observation, a researcher tries as unobtrusively as possible to observe behavior in a natural setting. Although the results of naturalistic observation have high external validity, a major weakness is the time it takes to conduct such research. Participant observation is used in situations in which inconspicuous observation is not possible; instead, the researcher interacts with the participants to observe and record behaviors. Participant observation allows researchers to observe behaviors not usually open to scientific observation; however, it, too, is time-consuming. In contrived observation, the observer sets up a situation that is likely to produce the behaviors to be observed. A major strength of the observational research design is that the researcher observes and records actual behaviors.

In the survey research design, we describe people's responses to questions about behaviors and attitudes. The four most common methods for administering a survey are mail surveys, telephone surveys, Internet surveys, and in-person surveys and interviews; each has strengths and weaknesses. Surveys are relatively easy to administer and can be used to obtain information about a wide variety of different variables. However, major weaknesses of survey research include low response rates, nonresponse bias, and the self-report nature of the design.

In case study research, a single individual is described in great detail. Case studies can be used to provide information about rare and unusual behaviors, and to demonstrate exceptions to the rule. Furthermore, case studies can suggest new variables that might account for a particular outcome and thereby generate hypotheses for future research. However, case studies tend to be weak in both internal and external validity.

Overall, the descriptive research strategy is extremely useful as preliminary research and is valuable in its own right as a source of basic knowledge. However, the strategy is simply intended to provide a description of behavior and does not examine causal factors.

KEY WORDS

observational research design
content analysis
archival research
naturalistic observation, or
   nonparticipant observation

participant observation
contrived observation
   or structured
   observation

survey research design
case study design
case history

EXERCISES

1. In addition to the key words, you should also be able to define each of the following terms:

   descriptive research strategy
   behavioral observation
   habituation
   behavior categories
   inter-rater reliability
   frequency method
   duration method
   interval method
   time sampling
   event sampling
   individual sampling
   Likert scale
   anchors
   response set
   semantic differential
   nonresponse bias
   interviewer bias
   idiographic approach
   nomothetic approach

2. What is the general characteristic that differentiates descriptive research designs from other types of research? For example, what differentiates the survey research design from other research that uses surveys to obtain measurements?

3. Describe each of the three types of descriptive research designs.

4. Compare and contrast the three types of observation, identifying the advantages and disadvantages of each.

5. Most descriptive research designs gather information from a group of participants. However, the case study design focuses on a single individual. What are the advantages and disadvantages of describing a single individual as compared to describing a group?

6. For each of the following research goals, identify which of the descriptive research designs would be most appropriate:

   a. To describe how peer counseling affects a severely depressed teenager.

   b. To describe the social interactions among a group of preschool children while they play in a city park.

   c. To describe the study habits of students at a state college.

LEARNING ACTIVITIES

1. Each of the following research studies uses a survey as a method for collecting data. However, not all of the studies are examples of the *survey research design*. Based on the information provided for each study, indicate (a) whether it is or is not an example of the survey research design, and (b) briefly explain the reason for your answer.

   a. Based on a survey of 12,344 U.S. college students and 6,729 Canadian college students, Kuo, Adlaf, Lee, Gliksman, Demers, and Wechsler (2002) report that alcohol use is more common among Canadian than U.S. students, but heavy drinking (five or more drinks in a row for males, four or more for females) is significantly higher among U.S. students than Canadian students.

   b. To examine adolescent substance abuse, Li, Pentz, and Chou (2002) surveyed 1,807 middle school students from 57 schools. The results showed that a greater risk of adolescent substance abuse was associated with increasing numbers of parents and friends who were substance abusers. However, friends' use did not affect adolescent substance abuse when parents were nonusers.

   c. Wolak, Mitchell, and Finkelhor (2002) used a survey of 1,501 adolescents to examine online relationships. The results showed that 14% reported close online friendships during the past year, 7% reported face-to-face meetings with online friends, and 2% reported romantic online relationships.

2. Two studies (Hughes, Cutting, & Dunn, 2001; Hughes et al., 2002) have demonstrated a new observational technique for assessing disruptive behavior in young children. The technique involves observing disruptive behaviors that are triggered while the children play a competitive card game (SNAP) that is rigged to ensure that they experience a losing streak. The situation is contrived to produce frustration (the kids cannot win), which often leads to a disruptive outburst.

a. Briefly explain the difference between *naturalistic* observation and *contrived* observation. Is the SNAP technique an example of naturalistic or contrived observation? What is the major advantage of contrived observation?

b. Prepare a list of five specific behaviors that you would consider to be examples of disruptive behavior for children in the SNAP game.

WEB RESOURCES

Visit the Book Companion Website at **www.cengage.com/international** to access study tools including a glossary, flashcards, and web quizzing.

8

The Correlational Research Strategy

CHAPTER OVERVIEW

In this chapter, we discuss the details of the correlational research strategy. The goal of correlational research is to describe the relationship between variables and to measure the strength of the relationship. Applications, strengths, and weaknesses of this strategy are discussed.

8.1 | AN INTRODUCTION TO CORRELATIONAL RESEARCH

In Chapter 6, we identified five basic research strategies for investigating variables and their relationships: experimental, nonexperimental, quasi-experimental, correlational, and descriptive. In this chapter, we deal with the details of the **correlational research strategy.** (The experimental strategy is discussed in Chapter 9, the nonexperimental and quasi-experimental strategies are discussed in Chapter 12, and details of the descriptive strategy are discussed in Chapter 7.)

The goal of the correlational research strategy is to examine and describe the associations and relationships between variables. More specifically, the purpose of a correlational study is to establish that a relationship exists between variables and to describe the nature of the relationship. Notice that the correlational strategy does not attempt to explain the relationship and makes no attempt to manipulate, control, or interfere with the variables.

> A correlational study can involve measuring more than two variables but usually involves relationships between two variables at a time.

The data for a correlational study consist of two or more measurements, one for each of the variables being examined. Usually, the scores are obtained from the same individual. For example, a researcher might record IQ and measure creativity for each person in a group of college students. Or a researcher could record food consumption and activity level for each animal in a colony of laboratory rats. Measurements can be made in natural surroundings or the individuals can be measured in a laboratory setting. The important factor is that the researcher simply measures the variables being studied. The measurements are then examined to determine whether they show any consistent pattern of relationship. The statistical procedures that are used to measure the strength or consistency of a relationship are discussed in Chapter 14 (pp. 439–441).

DEFINITION	In the **correlational research strategy,** two or more variables are measured to obtain a set of scores (usually two scores) for each individual. The measurements are then examined to identify any patterns of relationship that exist between the variables and to measure the strength of the relationship.

For example, in Chapter 6 we described a correlational study by Trockel, Barnes, and Egget (2000) examining the relationship between grade point average and sleep habits, specifically wake-up time, for college students (pp. 161–162). The researchers measured the grade point average and wake-up time for each individual in a group of college students and found that earlier wake-up times were consistently related to higher grade point averages. Although the study demonstrated a relationship between the two variables, it does not explain why the relationship exists. Specifically, the results do not justify a conclusion that waking earlier causes higher grades (or that higher grades cause students to wake earlier).

In the definition of correlational research, we state that a correlational study usually obtains two or more scores for each individual. Usually, the word *individual* refers to a single person. However, the individual is intended to be a single source, not necessarily a single person. For example, a researcher could use a correlational study to examine the relationship between parents' IQ scores and the IQ scores of their children. The researcher could select a group of high school students and record each student's IQ score and the IQ score for the student's mother. Note that the researcher has two different scores for each student, however one score comes from the mother and one from the child. In this case, each *individual* is a family rather than a single person.

LEARNING CHECKS

Explain how the purpose of a correlational study differs from the purpose of an experimental study.

In a correlational research study, how many different variables are measured for each individual?

8.2 | THE DATA FOR A CORRELATIONAL STUDY

A correlational research study produces two or more scores for each individual. However, researchers are usually interested in the relationship between two variables at a time. Therefore, multiple scores are typically grouped into pairs for evaluation. In this section, we focus on relationships between pairs of scores. Relationships among multiple variables are discussed in section 8.5.

Traditionally, the scores in each pair are identified as X and Y. The data can be presented in a list showing the two scores for each individual or the scores can be shown in a graph known as a **scatter plot.** In the scatter plot, each individual is represented by a single point with a horizontal coordinate determined by the individual's X score and the vertical coordinate corresponding to the Y value. Figure 8.1 shows hypothetical data from a correlational study presented as a list of scores and as a scatter plot. The benefit of a scatter plot is that it allows you to see the characteristics of the relationship between the two variables.

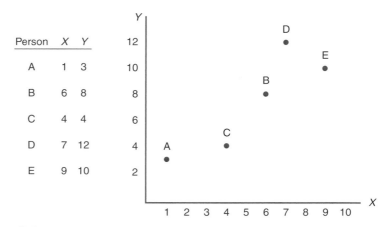

FIGURE **8.1** Data from a Correlational Study

Two scores, X and Y, for each of five people are shown in a table and in a scatter plot.

Measuring Relationships

Researchers typically calculate a numerical value known as a **correlation,** or a **correlation coefficient,** to measure and describe the relationship between two variables. A correlation describes three characteristics of a relationship.

1. *The direction of the relationship.* In Figure 8.1, there is a clear tendency for individuals with larger X values to also have larger Y values. Equivalently, as the X values get smaller, the associated Y values also tend to get smaller. A relationship of this type is called a **positive relationship.** For example, there is a positive relationship between height and weight for college students; taller students also tend to weigh more. Positive relationships are indicated by positive values (greater than zero) for the correlation. In a scatter plot, a positive relationship is indicated by data points that cluster around a line that slopes up to the right. On the other hand, a relationship in which X and Y tend to change in opposite directions (as X increases, Y decreases) is called a **negative relationship.** On most performance tasks, for example, there is a negative relationship between speed and accuracy; going faster tends to result in lower accuracy. Negative relationships are indicated by negative values (less than zero) for the correlation. In a scatter plot, a negative relationship is indicated by data points that cluster around a line that slopes down to the right.

DEFINITIONS In a **positive relationship,** there is a tendency for two variables to change in the same direction; as one variable increases, the other also tends to increase.
    In a **negative relationship,** there is a tendency for two variables to change in opposite directions; increases in one variable tend to be accompanied by decreases in the other.

---

2. *The form of the relationship.* Typically, researchers are looking for a pattern in the data that suggests a consistent and predictable relationship between the two variables. In most situations, researchers look for a **linear relationship,** in which the data points in the scatter plot tend to cluster around a straight line. In a positive linear relationship, for example, each time the X variable increases by 1 point, the Y variable also increases, and the size of the increase is a consistently predictable amount. Figure 8.2a shows an example of a positive linear relationship. However, it is possible for a relationship to be consistent and predictable, but not linear. For example, there tends to be a consistent relationship between practice and performance; for most skills, increased practice leads to improved performance. However, the amount of improvement is not constant from one week to another, so the relationship is not linear. During the first few weeks of practice, the increases in performance are large. However, after years of practice, one more week produces a hardly noticeable change in performance. A relationship that is consistently one-directional, either consistently positive or consistently negative, is called a **monotonic relationship.** In a

positive monotonic relationship, for example, increases in one variable tend to be accompanied by increases in the other variable. However, the amount of increase need not be constantly the same size. Figure 8.2b shows an example of a positive monotonic relationship similar to the practice and performance example.

Different kinds of correlations are used to measure different kinds of relationships. For example, a **Pearson correlation** measures linear relationships and a **Spearman correlation** is used to measure monotonic relationships (see Chapter 14, pp. 410–411). Finally, we should remind you that most correlational studies are looking for linear relationships, and Pearson correlations, measuring linear relationships, are by far the most commonly used correlations in behavioral science research. If you see a correlation in a research report, you can safely assume it is a Pearson correlation unless the report specifically identifies it as something else.

3. *The consistency or strength of the relationship.* You may have noticed that the data points presented in Figure 8.2 do not form perfectly linear or perfectly monotonic relationships. In Figure 8.2a, the points are not perfectly on a straight line and in Figure 8.2b, the relationship is not perfectly one directional (there are reversals in the positive trend). In fact, perfectly consistent relationships are essentially never found in real behavioral sciences data. Instead, real data show a degree of consistency. In correlational studies, the consistency of a relationship is typically measured and described by the numerical value obtained for a correlation coefficient. A correlation of +1.00 (or −1.00) indicates a perfectly

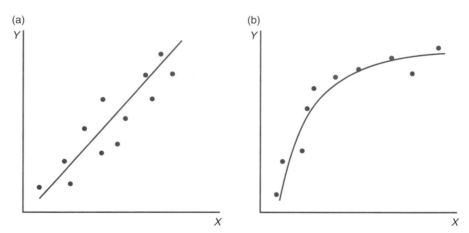

FIGURE **8.2** Linear and Monotonic Relationships
(a) An example of a linear relationship. The data points cluster around a straight line.
(b) An example of a monotonic relationship. The data points show a one-directional trend; as the *X* values increase from left to right, the *Y* values also tend to increase from bottom to top.

consistent relationship, and a value of zero indicates no consistency whatsoever. Intermediate values indicate different degrees of consistency. For example, a Pearson correlation coefficient of 0.8 (or −0.8) indicates a nearly perfect linear relationship in which the data points cluster closely around a straight line. Each time the value of X changes, the value of Y also changes by a reasonably predictable amount. By contrast, a correlation of 0.2 (or −0.2) describes a relationship in which there is only a weak tendency for the value of Y to change in a predictable manner when the value of X changes. In this case, the data points are widely scattered around a straight line. Note that the sign of the correlation (+ or −) and the numerical value are independent. A correlation of +0.8 has the same degree of consistency as a correlation of −0.8, and both correlations indicate that the data points cluster closely around a straight line; the lines simply tilt in different directions. Figure 8.3 shows a series of scatter plots demonstrating different degrees of linear relationship and the corresponding correlation values. As a final point, we should note once again that a correlation coefficient simply *describes* the consistency or strength of a relationship between variables. Even the strongest correlation of 1.00 (or −1.00) does not imply that there is a cause-and-effect relationship between the two variables.

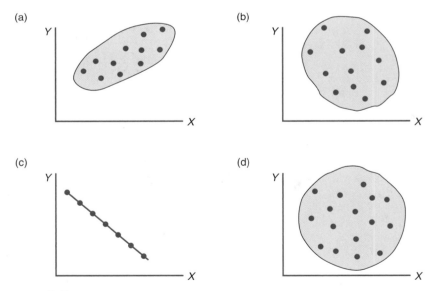

FIGURE **8.3** Examples of Different Degrees of Linear Relationship

(a) shows a strong positive correlation, approximately +0.90; (b) shows a relatively weak negative correlation, approximately −0.40; (c) shows a perfect negative correlation, −1.00; (d) shows no linear trend, a correlation of 0. In all graphs, the X values increase from left to right and the Y values increase from bottom to top.

DEFINITION	A **correlation**, or **correlation coefficient**, is a numerical value that measures and describes the relationship between two variables. The sign of the correlation (+/–) indicates the direction of the relationship. The numerical value of the correlation (0.0 to 1.0) indicates the strength or consistency of the relationship. The type of correlation (Pearson or Spearman) indicates the form of the relationship.

LEARNING CHECKS	Describe the pattern that would appear in a scatter plot showing the data points for each of the following correlations: $r = -0.9$ and $r = +0.3$. Explain the difference between a linear relationship and a monotonic relationship.

Evaluating Relationships for Non-numerical Scores

Occasionally a correlational research study produces two or more scores for each individual with at least one score that does not consist of numerical values. For example, a researcher may be interested in the relationship between gender (male/female) and success on a problem-solving task (succeed/fail). In this case, there are two measurements for each individual but neither is a numerical score suitable for computing a correlation. In this situation, there are several alternatives for evaluating the relationship.

1. If one of the scores is numerical, like IQ, and the other is non-numerical, like gender, the most common strategy is to use the non-numerical variable to organize the scores into separate groups. For this example, the data would consist of a group of IQ scores for the males and a group of scores for the females. The two groups are then compared using an independent-measures t test (for two groups) or an analysis of variance (for more than two groups). These hypothesis tests are discussed in Chapter 14 (see pp. 433–435). Note that when the data are organized into groups of scores, the research strategy is generally considered to be differential rather than correlational (see Chapter 12, p. 340).

   If the non-numerical variable consists of exactly two categories, it is also possible to calculate a correlation. First, the two categories are numerically coded as 0 and 1. For example, male = 0 and female = 1. The data then consist of two scores per person, an IQ score and a coded score for gender, and the Pearson correlation can be computed for the coded data. The resulting correlation is called a *point-biserial* correlation. The numerical value of the correlation is a measure of the strength or consistency of the relationship; however, the sign of the correlation is meaningless (because 0 and 1 are assigned arbitrarily).

2. If both variables are non-numerical, the relationship is typically evaluated by organizing the data in a matrix with the categories of one variable forming the rows and the categories of the second variable forming the columns. Each cell of the matrix shows the frequency or number of individuals in that cell and the data are evaluated using a chi-square hypothesis test (see Chapter 14, p. 441). Figure 8.4 shows an example of

Outcome

	Succeed	Fail
Male	12	8
Female	17	3

FIGURE **8.4** Hypothetical Data Showing Results from a Study Examining the Relationship between Gender and Success on a Problem-Solving Task

The values are the number of individuals in each category; for example, 12 of the males successfully completed the task and eight failed.

data from a study examining the relationship between gender and success on a problem-solving task.

If the two non-numerical variables both consist of exactly two categories, each can be numerically coded as 0 and 1. For example, male = 0 and female = 1; failure = 0 and success = 1. If the Pearson correlation is computed for the coded data, the result is known as the *phi-coefficient.* The numerical value of the correlation measures the strength or consistency of the relationship but the sign of the correlation and the concept of a linear relationship are not meaningful.

Comparing Correlational, Experimental, and Differential Research

The goal of an experimental study is to demonstrate a cause-and-effect relationship between two variables. To accomplish this goal, an experiment requires the manipulation of one variable to create treatment conditions and the measurement of the second variable to obtain a set of scores within each condition. All other variables are controlled. The researcher then compares the scores from each treatment with the scores from other treatments. If there are differences between treatments, the researcher has evidence of a causal relationship between variables. Specifically, the researcher can conclude that manipulating one variable causes changes in the second variable. Note that an experimental study involves measuring only one variable and looking for differences between two or more groups of scores.

A correlational study, on the other hand, is intended to demonstrate the existence of a relationship between two variables. Note that a correlational study is not trying to explain the relationship. To accomplish its goal, a correlational study does not involve manipulating, controlling, or interfering with variables. Instead, the researcher simply measures two different variables for each individual. The researcher then looks for a relationship within the set of scores.

In Chapter 12 (p. 340), we noted that differential research, an example of a nonexperimental design, is very similar to correlational research. The difference between these two research strategies is that a correlational study views the data as two scores, *X* and *Y*, for each individual, and looks for patterns within the pairs of scores to determine whether there is a relationship. A differential design, on the other hand, establishes the existence of a relationship by demonstrating a difference between groups. Specifically, a differential design uses one of the two variables to create groups of participants and then measures the second variable to obtain scores within each group. For example, a researcher could divide a sample of students into two groups corresponding to high and low self-esteem, and then measure academic performance scores in each group. If there is a consistent difference between groups, the researcher has evidence for a relationship between self-esteem and academic performance. A correlational study examining the same relationship would first measure a self-esteem score and an academic performance score for each student, and then look for a pattern within the set of scores. Note that the correlational study involves one group of participants with two scores for each individual. The primary focus of the correlational study is on the relationship between the two variables. The differential study involves two groups of scores and focuses on the difference between groups. However, both designs are asking the same basic question: "Is there a relationship between self-esteem and academic performance?"

 **LEARNING CHECK** Although correlational research and differential research have the same purpose, they use different data. Identify the purpose for both types of research and explain the difference between the two types of data.

8.3 | APPLICATIONS OF THE CORRELATIONAL STRATEGY

As noted earlier, the correlational design is used to identify and describe relationships between variables. Following are three examples of how correlational designs can be used to address research questions.

Prediction

One important use of correlational research is to establish a relationship between variables that can be used for purposes of prediction. For example, research shows a good positive relationship between SAT scores and future grade point average in college (Camera & Echternacht, 2000; Geiseer & Studley, 2002). College administrators can use this relationship to help predict which applicants are most likely to be successful students. High school students who do well on the SAT are likely to do well in college, and those who have trouble with the SAT are likely to have difficulty in college classes.

The use of correlational results to make predictions is not limited to predictions about future behavior. Whenever two variables are consistently related, it is possible to use knowledge of either variable to help make predictions about the other. For example, because there is a consistent, positive relationship between parents' IQs and their children's IQs, we can use either score to predict the other. Specifically, parents with above-average IQs are likely to have children with above-average IQs. Often, one of the two variables is simply easier to measure or more readily available than the other. In these situations, it is possible to use the available knowledge of one variable to predict the value of the unavailable variable. By establishing and describing the existence of a relationship, correlational studies provide the basic information needed to make predictions.

Within a correlational study, the two variables being examined are essentially equivalent. Nonetheless, correlational studies often identify one variable as the **predictor variable** and the second variable as the **criterion variable.** In a correlational study used for prediction, the designation of the two variables is usually quite clear. University admissions offices occasionally use the graduate record exam (GRE) scores to predict graduate school success. In this situation, the GRE scores are the predictor variable and graduate performance is the criterion variable. Clearly, one variable (the predictor) is used to predict the other (the criterion).

The statistical process for using one variable to predict another is called **regression.** Typically, the goal is to find the equation that produces the most accurate predictions of Y (the criterion variable) for each value of X (the predictor variable). For example, Ng and Jeffery (2003) used regression to predict health behaviors for working adults using stress as the predictor variable. The results showed that higher levels of stress predicted a higher-fat diet and more cigarette smoking. However, stress was not a significant predictor of alcohol use.

In situations in which a correlational study is not used for prediction, researchers still tend to refer to a predictor and a criterion variable. In these situations, the labels are usually determined by the purpose of the study. Typically, a correlational study begins with one of the two variables relatively known or understood, and the second variable is relatively unknown. Thus, the purpose of the study is to gain a better understanding of the unknown variable by demonstrating that it is related to an established, known variable. In this situation, the known variable is designated as the predictor and the unknown variable as the criterion. For example, researchers have found a positive relationship between IQ and processing speed in a variety of perceptual and cognitive tasks (Eysenck, 1999). In this research, IQ would be the predictor variable and speed would be the criterion variable.

DEFINITIONS When a correlational study demonstrates a relationship between two variables, it allows researchers to use knowledge about one variable to help predict or explain the second variable. In this situation, the first variable is called the **predictor variable** and the second variable (being explained or predicted) is called the **criterion variable.**

 **LEARNING CHECK** Suppose that there is a negative relationship between grade point average and the number of hours spent playing video games for high school boys. What grades would you predict for boys who spend more than the average amount of time playing video games?

Reliability and Validity

In Chapter 4 (p. 107), the concepts of reliability and validity were introduced as the two basic criteria for evaluating a measurement procedure. In general terms, reliability evaluates the consistency or stability of the measurements, and validity evaluates the extent to which the measurement procedure actually measures what it claims to be measuring. Both reliability and validity are commonly defined by relationships that are established using the correlational research design. For example, test-retest reliability is defined by the relationship between an original set of measurements and a follow-up set of measurements. If the same individuals are measured twice under the same conditions, and there is a consistent relationship between the two measurements, then the measurement procedure is said to be reliable.

The concurrent validity of a measurement procedure can also be defined in terms of a relationship (see Ch. 4, p. 108). If a new test is developed to detect early-stage Alzheimer's disease, for example, the validity of the test can be established by demonstrating that the scores from the test are strongly related to scores from established tests. This is exactly what was done by Ijuin et al. (2008) to validate a relatively new 7-minute test that was developed as an alternative to other commonly used screening tests for Alzheimer's. Correlations were computed to measure the relationship between the scores from the 7-Minute Screen and the scores from each of the three established cognitive tests for Alzheimer's. The researchers obtained correlations around 0.70 for each test, indicating a strong positive relationship and high concurrent validity between the 7-Minute Screen and established screening tests.

 **LEARNING CHECK**   Describe how the reliability of a personality test could be established using the results from a correlational study.

Evaluating Theories

Many theories generate research questions about the relationships between variables that can be addressed by the correlational research design. A good example comes from the age-old nature/nurture question as it applies to intelligence: "Is intelligence primarily an inherited characteristic, or is it primarily determined by environment?" A partial answer to this question comes from correlational studies examining the IQs of identical twins separated at birth and placed in different environments. Because these twins have identical heredity and different environments, they provide researchers with an opportunity to separate the two factors. The original work in this area, conducted by British psychologist Cyril Burt, showed a strong relationship between the twins' IQs, suggesting that hereditary factors overwhelmed environment (Burt, 1972). However, later evidence showed that Burt probably falsified much of his data (Kamin, 1974). Nonetheless, correlational results suggest a strong relationship between twins' IQs. Note that the correlational research design is being used to address a theoretical issue.

Interpreting a Correlation

The numerical value of a correlation, ranging from 0.00 to 1.00, describes the consistency of the relationship with 1.00 (or −1.00) indicating a perfectly consistent relationship and 0.00 indicating a complete lack of consistency. However, there are two additional factors that must be considered when interpreting the strength of a relationship. One is the coefficient of determination, which is obtained by squaring the correlation, and the other is the significance of the correlation. Each of these factors is discussed in the following sections.

The Strength of a Relationship

The most common technique for measuring the strength of the relationship between two variables is to compute the **coefficient of determination,** which is obtained by squaring the numerical value of the correlation. Because a correlation is typically identified by the letter r, the coefficient of determination is r^2. This coefficient measures how much of the variability in one variable is predictable from its relationship with the other variable. For example, if two college students are randomly selected, they will almost certainly have different grade point averages. Although there are many explanations for different grades, one possibility is that the two students have different IQs. In general, there is a tendency for higher IQs to correlate with higher grades. If the correlation between IQ and grade point average is calculated and then squared, the result provides a measure of how much of the differences in grade point averages can be predicted by IQ scores. A correlation of $r = 0.80$ would mean that $r^2 = 0.64$ (or 64%) of the differences in grade point average can be predicted by difference in IQ. A correlation of $r = 0.30$ would mean that only 0.09 (9%) of the differences are predictable.

DEFINITION	The squared value of a correlation is called the **coefficient of determination** and measures the percentage of variability in one variable that is determined, or predicted, by its relationship with the other variable.

In the behavioral sciences, the differences that exist from one individual to another tend to be large and are usually difficult to predict or explain. As a result, the ability to predict only a small portion of the differences in behavior is typically considered a major accomplishment. With this in mind, the guidelines in Table 8.1 are commonly used to interpret the strength of the relationship between two variables (Cohen, 1988).

We should note that the values in Table 8.1 are a general guide for interpreting the correlations obtained in most behavioral science research. There are some situations, however, in which a correlation of 0.50 would not be considered to be large. For example, when using correlations to measure

TABLE **8.1**
Guidelines for Interpreting the Strength of a Correlation

Degree of Relationship	Value of the Correlation Coefficient, or Coefficient of Determination
Small	$r = 0.10$ or $r^2 = 0.01$ (1%)
Medium	$r = 0.30$ or $r^2 = 0.09$ (9%)
Large	$r = 0.50$ or $r^2 = 0.25$ (25%)

the reliability of measurement, researchers usually look for large values, typically much greater than $r = 0.50$. Similarly, a research study that finds a theoretically important relationship between two variables might view a "small" correlation of $r = 0.10$ as a substantial relationship.

The Significance of a Relationship

The **statistical significance of a correlation** is the second important factor for interpreting the strength of a correlation. In the context of a correlation, the term *significant* means that a correlation found in the sample data is very unlikely to have been produced by random variation. Instead, whenever a sample correlation is found to be significant, you can reasonably conclude that it represents a real relationship that exists in the population.

With a small sample, it is possible to obtain what appears to be a very strong correlation when, in fact, there is absolutely no relationship between the two variables being examined. For example, with a sample of only two individuals, there are only two data points and they are guaranteed to fit perfectly on a straight line. Thus, with a sample of two individuals, you will always obtain a perfect correlation of 1.00 (or −1.00) no matter what variables you are measuring. As the sample size increases, it becomes increasingly more likely that the sample correlation accurately represents the real relationship that exists in the population. A correlation found in a relatively large sample is usually an indication of a real, meaningful relationship and is likely to be significant. You should be warned, however, that a statistically significant correlation does not necessarily mean that the correlation is large or strong. With a very large sample, for example, it is possible for a correlation of $r = 0.10$ or smaller to be statistically significant. Clearly, this is not a strong correlation.

8.4 | STRENGTHS AND WEAKNESSES OF THE CORRELATIONAL RESEARCH STRATEGY

The correlational research strategy is often used for the preliminary work in an area that has not received a lot of research attention. The correlational design can identify variables and describe relationships between variables that might suggest further investigation using the experimental strategy to determine cause-and-effect relationships. In addition, the correlational research design allows researchers an opportunity to investigate variables that would be impossible or unethical to manipulate. For example, a correlational study could investigate how specific behaviors or skills are related to diet deficiencies or exposure to pollution. Although it is possible and ethical to record diet deficiencies and environmental pollution as they exist naturally, it would not be ethical to create these conditions in the laboratory. Countless other variables such as family size, personality, alcohol consumption, level of education, income, and color preferences can be interesting topics for behavioral research but cannot be manipulated and controlled in an experimental research study. However, these variables can be easily measured and described in correlational research.

One of the primary advantages of a correlational study is that the researcher simply records what exists naturally. Because the researcher does not manipulate, control, or otherwise interfere with the variables being examined or with the surrounding environment, there is good reason to expect that the measurements and the relationships accurately reflect the natural events being examined. In research terminology, correlational studies tend to have high external validity. In general, a correlational study can establish that a relationship exists and it can provide a good description of the relationship. However, a correlational study usually does not produce a clear and unambiguous explanation for the relationship. In research terminology, correlational studies tend to have low internal validity. In particular, two limitations arise in explanations of results from a correlational study.

The third-variable and directionality problems are discussed in more detail in Chapter 9, pp. 251–252.

1. *The third-variable problem.* Although a correlational study may establish that two variables are related, it does not mean that there must be a direct relationship between the two variables. It is always possible that a third (unidentified) variable is controlling the two variables and is responsible for producing the observed relation. As noted in Chapter 9 (p. 252), this is known as the **third-variable problem**. A recent television news program, for example, reported that higher participation in a company's fitness training program was associated with higher employee productivity and lower absenteeism. However, the company cannot conclude that their fitness program is causing benefits to the company; it may be that the employees who regularly participate were already healthier and had a higher level of fitness than those who rarely participate. Thus, a third variable (preexisting health) may be controlling both participation and productivity, resulting in the observed relationship (Figure 8.5).

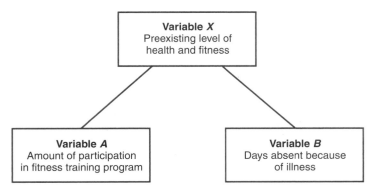

FIGURE **8.5** The Third-Variable Problem

Although participation in the fitness training program (Variable *A*) and absenteeism (Variable *B*) appear to vary together, there is no direct connection between these two variables. Instead, both are influenced by a third variable. In this example, an employee's level of health and fitness (Variable *X*) influences the employee's amount of participation in the fitness program. In addition, an employee's level of health influences the number of days that the employee is likely to be absent due to illness.

2. *The directionality problem.* A correlational study can establish that two variables are related; that is, that changes in one variable tend to be accompanied by changes in the other variable. However, a correlational study does not determine which variable is the cause and which is the effect. As noted in Chapter 9 (p. 252), this is known as the **directionality problem**. For example, a recent study has found a relationship between exposure to sexual content on television and sexual behavior among adolescents (Collins, Elliott, Berry, Kanouse, Kunkel, Hunter, & Miu, 2004). Given this relationship, it is tempting to conclude that watching sex on television causes adolescents to engage in sexual behavior. However, it is possible that the true causal relationship is in the opposite direction. Adolescents who tend to be sexually active could simply choose to watch television programs that are consistent with their own behaviors. In this case, sexual behavior causes the teenager to prefer television programs with sexual content (Figure 8.6).

The study linking sexual content on television and sexual behavior provides one more opportunity to discuss the fact that the correlational research strategy does not establish the existence of cause-and-effect relationships. The study consisted of a survey of 1,792 adolescents, 12 to 17 years of age, who reported their television viewing habits and their sexual behaviors. Notice that this is a correlational study; specifically, there is no manipulated variable. The title of the research report correctly states that watching sex on television *predicts* adolescent sexual behavior. However, when the study was presented in newspaper articles, it often was interpreted as a demonstration that sex on television *causes* adolescent sexual behavior. It was even suggested that reducing the sexual content of television shows could substantially reduce adolescent sexual behavior. As an analogy, consider the fact that the beginning of football season *predicts* the onset of fall and winter. However, no reasonable person would suggest that we could substantially postpone the change of seasons by simply delaying the opening day of football.

Table 8.2 summarizes the strengths and weaknesses of the correlational research design.

LEARNING CHECK   Describe how the third-variable problem and the directionality problem limit the interpretation of results from correlational research designs.

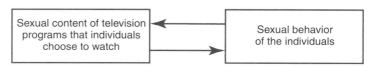

FIGURE **8.6** The Directionality Problem

Although a correlational study can demonstrate a relationship between the sexual content of television programs that adolescents watch and their sexual behaviors, the study cannot determine if the television content is influencing behavior or whether the behavior is influencing the choice of television programs.

TABLE **8.2**
A Summary of the Strengths and Weaknesses of the Correlational
Research Design

Strengths	Weaknesses
Describes relationships between variables	Cannot assess causality
Nonintrusive—natural behaviors	Third-variable problem
High external validity	Directionality problem
	Low internal validity

8.5 | RELATIONSHIPS WITH MORE THAN TWO VARIABLES

Thus far, we only have considered correlational research in which the investigators are examining relationships between two variables. In most situations, however, an individual variable, especially a behavior, is related to a multitude of other variables. For example, academic performance is probably related to IQ as well as to a number of other cognitive variables such as motivation, self-esteem, social competence, and a variety of other personal characteristics. One commonly used technique for studying multivariate relationships is a statistical procedure known as **multiple regression.** The underlying concept is that one criterion variable such as academic performance can be explained or predicted from a set of predictor variables such as IQ and motivation. IQ predicts part of academic performance, but you can get a better prediction if you use IQ and motivation together. For example, Collins and Ellickson (2004) evaluated the ability of four psychological theories to predict smoking behavior for adolescents in 10th grade. Although all four theories were good independent predictors, an integrated model using multiple regression to combine predictors from all four theories was more accurate than any of the individual models.

One interesting use of multiple regression is to examine the relationship between two specific variables while controlling the influence of other, potentially confounding variables. By adding predictor variables one at a time into the regression analysis, it is possible to see how each new variable adds to the prediction after the influence of the earlier predictors has already been considered. Earlier, we discussed a correlational study examining the relationship between adolescents' sexual behavior and the sexual content of the television programs they watch (Collins, Elliott, Berry, Kanouse, Kunkel, Hunter, & Miu, 2004). Because the age of the participants ranged from 12 to 17 years, the researchers were aware that participant age could create a third-variable problem. Specifically, the older the participants are, the more likely it is that they watch television programs with sexual content and that they engage in sexual behaviors. Thus, the participants' age can create an artificial relationship between sexual content and sexual behavior; individuals who watch less sexual content tend to engage in less sexual behavior (the younger participants), and individuals who watch more sexual content tend to engage in more sexual behavior (the older participants). However, the researchers were able to use multiple regression to eliminate this problem. Sexual content of the television programs was entered into the regression equation after the effects of age (and other variables) had been removed. The results indicated that sexual content still was a significant predictor of adolescent sexual behavior.

As a final note, we should warn you that the language used to discuss and report the results from a multiple regression can be misleading. For example, you will occasionally see reports that the predictor variables *explained* the observed differences in the criterion variable. For example, a report might say that regression has demonstrated that variables such as intelligence, personality, and work drive *explain* differences in student grades. The truth is that the predictor variables only *predict* student grades; they do not really explain them. To get a cause-and-effect explanation, you must use the experimental research strategy. Unless a research study is using the experimental strategy (including manipulation and control), the best you can do is to describe relationships, not explain them.

■ CHAPTER SUMMARY

The goal of the correlational research strategy is to examine the relationship between variables and to measure the strength of the relationship. The data typically consist of measurements of two different variables for each individual. A graph of the data provides an opportunity to see the characteristics of the relationship (if one exists). Typically, researchers examine three characteristics of a relationship: the direction, the form, and the degree of consistency.

Correlational research can be used for prediction, to establish validity and reliability, and to evaluate theories. However, because of the third-variable and directionality problems, correlational research cannot be used to determine the causes of behavior.

The correlational research strategy is extremely useful as preliminary research and valuable in its own right as a source of basic knowledge. However, this strategy simply describes relationships between variables, and does not explain the relationships or determine their underlying causes.

KEY WORDS

correlational research strategy	correlation, or correlation coefficient	criterion variable
positive relationship		coefficient of
negative relationship	predictor variable	determination

EXERCISES

1. In addition to the key words, you should also be able to define each of the following terms:
   scatter plot
   linear relationship
   monotonic relationship
   Pearson correlation
   Spearman correlation
   regression
   statistical significance of a correlation
   third-variable problem
   directionality problem
   multiple regression

2. Each of the following studies examines the relationship between the quality of breakfast and academic performance for third-grade children. Identify which is correlational, which is experimental, and which is nonexperimental.

   Study 1: A researcher obtains a sample of 100 third-grade children. Each child is interviewed to determine his typical breakfast, and the child is assigned a score describing the nutritional value of his breakfast. Also, the child's level of academic performance is obtained from school records. The results show that higher academic performance tends to be associated with a higher level of breakfast nutrition.

   Study 2: A researcher obtains a sample of 100 third-grade children. The children are randomly assigned to two groups. On arriving at school each morning, one group is given a nutritious breakfast and the other group is given a breakfast relatively low in nutritional value. After 6 weeks, each child's level of academic performance is measured. On average, the children in the nutritious breakfast group had a higher level of academic performance than the children in the low-nutrition group.

   Study 3: A researcher obtains a sample of 100 third-grade children. Based on school records, the children are divided into two groups corresponding to high and low academic performance. The children are then interviewed and each child is given a score describing the nutritional value of her typical breakfast. On average, the children in the high academic performance group ate a more nutritious breakfast than the children in the low academic performance group.

3. For the correlational study described in Problem 2, describe how a third variable, such as family income or parents' educational level, might explain the relationship between academic performance and breakfast quality. Explain why this third-variable is not a problem in the experimental study.

4. One advantage of displaying correlational data in a scatter plot is that you can literally see the relationship in the graph.
   a. In a scatter plot, what pattern of points would indicate a positive relationship between variables?
   b. What pattern would indicate a negative relationship?

LEARNING ACTIVITIES

1. The following list contains several variables that differentiate college students.
   a. Select one variable from the list and then think of a second variable (on the list or one of your own) that should be positively related to the one you selected. Briefly describe how you would do a correlational study to evaluate the relationship.
   b. Select another variable from the list and then think of a second variable that should be negatively related to the one you selected. Briefly describe how you would do a correlational study to evaluate the relationship.

   physical attractiveness
   intelligence
   alcohol consumption
   shyness
   exam anxiety
   hours of sleep per night
   hours of television per week
   alphabetical position of last name
      (A = 1, B = 2, and so on)

2. Select one of your correlational studies from activity #1 and describe how the same relationship could be examined using a nonexperimental, differential research study (see Chapter 12, p. 312).

WEB RESOURCES

Visit the Book Companion Website at **www .cengage.com/international** to access study tools including a glossary, flashcards, and web quizzing.

9

True Experiments

CHAPTER OVERVIEW

In this chapter, we discuss details of the experimental research strategy. The goal of experimental research is to establish and demonstrate a cause-and-effect relationship between two variables. To accomplish this goal, an experiment must manipulate one of the two variables and isolate the two variables being examined from the influence of other variables. Manipulation and control are considered here.

9.1 | CAUSE-AND-EFFECT RELATIONSHIPS

In Chapter 6, we identified five basic strategies for investigating variables and their relationships: descriptive, correlational, experimental, quasi-experimental, and nonexperimental. In this chapter, we discuss details of the experimental research strategy. (The nonexperimental and quasi-experimental strategies are discussed in Chapter 12, the correlational strategy is discussed in Chapter 8, and details of the descriptive strategy are discussed in Chapter 7.)

More complex experiments may involve several variables. In its simplest form, however, an experiment focuses on only one variable that may cause changes in one other variable.

The goal of the **experimental research strategy** is to establish the existence of a cause-and-effect relationship between two variables. Note that it is possible for two variables to be related, yet the relationship is merely coincidental. For example, in a group of children who are 6 to 12 years old, there will be a strong relationship between the children's weights and their mathematics ability; as weight increases from child to child, ability also tends to increase. However, this does not mean that increasing weight causes an increase in mathematics ability. Instead, it is probably age, and not weight, that is responsible for the increase in mathematics ability. An **experiment,** often called a **true experiment,** attempts to establish a cause-and-effect relationship by demonstrating that changes in one variable are directly responsible for changes in another variable. To accomplish this goal, an experimental study contains the following four basic elements, which are also shown in Figure 9.1:

1. *Manipulation.* The researcher manipulates one variable by changing its value to create a set of two or more treatment conditions.
2. *Measurement.* A second variable is measured for a group of participants to obtain a set of scores in each treatment condition.
3. *Comparison.* The scores in one treatment condition are compared with the scores in another treatment condition. Consistent differences between treatments are evidence that the manipulation has caused changes in the scores (See Box 9.1).
4. *Control.* All other variables are controlled to be sure that they do not influence the two variables being examined.

For example, Cialdini, Reno, and Kallgren (1990) conducted a series of experiments to examine how perceived social norms affect people's littering behavior. In one study, they first created a set of treatment conditions by preparing a parking garage so that the floor was completely cleaned or heavily littered. Notice that the researchers are *manipulating* the variable by changing from clean to littered. Their goal was to create one environment in which littering appears to be acceptable and one in which it is not. They then observed the behavior of people who returned to their cars to find a handbill tucked under the driver's side windshield wiper. The handbill announced: THIS IS AUTOMOBILE SAFETY WEEK. PLEASE DRIVE CAREFULLY. The handbill was large enough to obscure the driver's vision and had to be removed before the car could be driven away. Because there were no trashcans in the area, drivers were forced to drop the handbill on the garage floor or take it with them in the car. The researchers *measured* whether the driver littered. Littering was operationally defined as

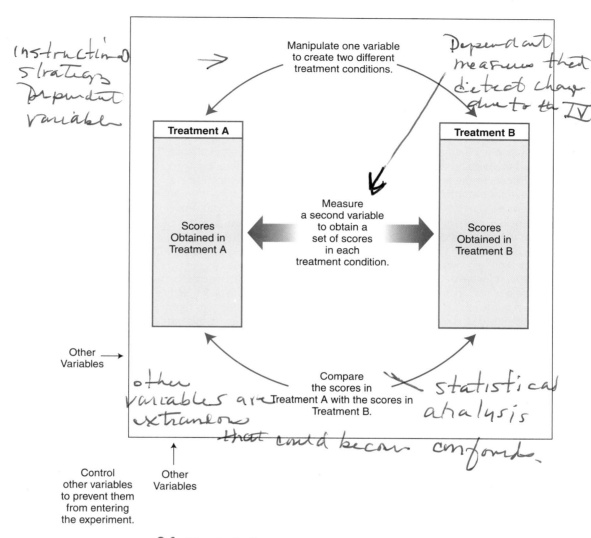

[Handwritten annotations: "Instructional strategies Dependent variable" (top left); "Dependent measures that detect change due to the IV" (top right); "other variables are extraneous" and "that could become confounds." (bottom left); "statistical analysis" (bottom right)]

Manipulate one variable to create two different treatment conditions.

Treatment A

Scores Obtained in Treatment A

Measure a second variable to obtain a set of scores in each treatment condition.

Treatment B

Scores Obtained in Treatment B

Other Variables

Compare the scores in Treatment A with the scores in Treatment B.

Control other variables to prevent them from entering the experiment.

Other Variables

FIGURE **9.1** The Basic Components of an Experimental Research Study

An experiment involves manipulating one variable, measuring a second variable, comparing the scores between treatments, and controlling all other variables.

dropping the handbill on the garage floor. Littering behavior in the clean environment was then *compared* with behavior in the already littered environment. During the study, the researchers *controlled* other variables by alternating between clean and littered conditions every 2 hours and randomly picking which condition would start each day to ensure that outside factors were balanced across the two conditions. The results showed more littering behavior in the already-littered environment than in the clean environment.

BOX **9.1**

Statistical Significance

Whenever you compare two sets of scores that were obtained at different times or came from different people, the two sets will never be *exactly* the same. Small differences from one person to another (or from one time to another) always produce small differences between the two sets of scores. As long as the differences are small and random (one set does not have consistently larger scores than the other), they probably are meaningless and can be attributed to chance. For example, if you drew a line through the center of your classroom and compute the average age for students on the right side and for students on the left side, the two averages would be different. However, the age difference is simply the result of chance and should not be interpreted as evidence for some mysterious force that causes older students to gravitate toward one side of the room.

In an experiment, the scores in one treatment condition are compared with the scores in another condition. If there is a difference between the scores, however, you cannot automatically conclude that the treatments have *caused* a difference. As we noted earlier, the difference may simply be the result of chance. Before you can interpret the difference as a cause-and-effect relationship, you must conduct a hypothesis test and demonstrate that the difference is statistically significant. A significant result means that the difference is large enough and consistent enough for a hypothesis test to rule out chance as a plausible explanation, and thereby conclude that the difference must have been caused by the treatments. Chapter 15 presents a detailed presentation of hypothesis testing and statistical significance. For now, you should realize that any difference between treatment conditions must be evaluated statistically before you can conclude that the difference was caused by the treatments.

Terminology for the Experimental Research Strategy

In an experiment, the variable that is manipulated by the researcher is called the **independent variable.** Typically, the independent variable is manipulated by creating a set of **treatment conditions.** The specific conditions that are used in the experiment are called the **levels** of the independent variable. The variable that is measured in each of the treatment conditions is called the **dependent variable.** All other variables in the study are **extraneous variables.** For the littering example, the independent variable is the amount of litter on the garage floor, and there are two levels: clean and heavily littered. The dependent variable is the littering behavior observed in each treatment condition. Other variables, such as the participants' age, gender, and personality, as well as environmental variables, such as the season and the weather conditions, are extraneous.

DEFINITIONS

The purpose of the **experimental research strategy** is to establish the existence of a cause-and-effect relationship between two variables. To accomplish this goal, an experiment manipulates one variable while a second variable is measured and other variables are controlled.

An **experiment** attempts to show that changes in one variable are directly responsible for changes in a second variable.

In an experiment, the **independent variable** is the variable manipulated by the researcher. In behavioral research, the independent variable usually consists of two or more treatment conditions to which participants are exposed.

In an experiment, a **treatment condition** is a situation or environment characterized by one specific value of the manipulated variable. An experiment contains two or more treatment conditions that differ according to the values of the manipulated variable.

The different values of the independent variable selected to create and define the treatment conditions are called the **levels** of the independent variable.

The **dependent variable** is the variable that is observed for changes to assess the effects of manipulating the independent variable. The dependent variable is typically a behavior or a response measured in each treatment condition.

All variables in the study other than the independent and dependent variables are called **extraneous variables**.

Caution! Not all research studies are experiments!

Finally, you should note that in this book, we use the terms *experiment* and *true experiment* in a well-defined technical sense. Specifically, a research study is called an experiment only if it satisfies the specific set of requirements that are detailed in this chapter. Thus, some research studies qualify as true experiments whereas other studies, such as correlational studies, do not. In casual conversation, people tend to refer to any kind of research study as an experiment. ("Scientists" do "experiments" in the "laboratory.") Although this casual description of research activity is acceptable in some contexts, we are careful to distinguish between experiments and other research studies. Therefore, whenever the word experiment is used in this text, it is in this more precise, technical sense. This chapter introduces the characteristics that differentiate a true experiment from other kinds of research studies.

Causation and the Third-Variable Problem

One problem for experimental research is that variables rarely exist in isolation. In natural circumstances, changes in one variable are typically accompanied by changes in many other related variables. For example, in the littering experiment described earlier (p. 248), the researchers manipulated the amount of litter in the garage. Under normal circumstances, however, the amount of litter on a garage floor is related to the time of day, the location of the garage, and the characteristics of the patrons using the garage. As a result, in natural circumstances researchers are often confronted with a tangled network of interrelated variables. Although it is relatively easy to demonstrate that one variable is related to another, it is much more difficult to establish the underlying cause of the relationship. To determine the nature of the relationships among variables, particularly to establish the causal influence of one event on another, it is essential that an experiment separate and isolate the specific variables being studied. The task of teasing apart and separating a set of naturally interconnected variables is the heart of the experimental strategy. The following example illustrates one basic problem with interrelated variables.

Ronald Freedman and his colleagues examined trends in family planning, birth control, and economic development through the 1960s and 1970s in Taiwan. In the course of their studies, they recorded data on a wide range of behavioral and environmental variables. The purpose of this research was to identify the factor or factors that determine how people set preferences for family size, and whether they use birth control. The researchers evaluated the relationship between birth control practices and each of the behavioral and environmental variables. Although the research identified many variables related to family planning, the results clearly showed a strong relationship between the number of radios in the population and birth control practices (Freedman, Coombs, & Chang, 1972). Over the years, as the number of radios increased, the use of contraception also increased and the ideal number of children desired by families decreased. Although the results of the study establish that the number of radios is related to family planning, you probably are not willing to conclude that it is a causal relationship; that is, putting radios in people's homes probably does not cause them to increase their use of contraception or lower the number of children they would like to have. Clearly, other variables such as age, household income, and education are involved. The existence of a relationship—even a strong one—is not sufficient to establish cause and effect.

This example is a demonstration of the **third-variable problem.** Although a study may establish that two variables are related, it does not necessarily mean that there is a direct (causal) relationship between the two variables. It is always possible that a third (unidentified) variable is controlling the two variables and is responsible for producing the observed relation. For example, although the researchers demonstrated a relation between contraception use and radios, common sense suggests that this is not a causal relationship. A more reasonable interpretation of the results is that other, unidentified variables, such as household income, are responsible for causing simultaneous increases in birth control and the number of radios in the population.

Causation and the Directionality Problem

A second problem for researchers attempting to demonstrate cause-and-effect relationships is demonstrated in the following example.

Although it is reasonable to assume that children who are naturally aggressive choose to watch violent TV, the experimental research on this topic indicates that viewing violent TV causes aggressive behavior (Wood, Wong, & Chachere, 1991).

Many researchers have investigated the relationship between exposure to violence on TV and aggressive behavior for children. The results from these studies indicate that children who see more violent TV programs also tend to exhibit more aggressive behaviors. Based on the consistency of the relationship and on common sense, it is tempting to conclude that there is a causal relation between watching TV violence and behaving aggressively. Specifically, it appears that exposure to TV violence *causes* children to behave aggressively. However, it is equally reasonable to assume that children who are naturally aggressive and violent simply choose to watch TV programs that are consistent with their personalities; that is, an aggressive personality *causes* children to watch more TV violence.

This example is a demonstration of the **directionality problem.** Although a research study may establish a relationship between two variables, the problem is determining which variable is the cause and which is the effect.

Controlling Nature

The preceding examples demonstrated that we cannot establish a cause-and-effect relationship by simply observing two variables. In particular, the researcher must actively unravel the tangle of relationships that exists naturally. To establish a cause-and-effect relationship, an experiment must control nature, essentially creating an unnatural situation wherein the two variables being examined are isolated from the influence of other variables and wherein the exact character of a relationship can be seen clearly.

We acknowledge that it is somewhat paradoxical that experiments must interfere with natural phenomena to gain a better understanding of nature. How can observations made in an artificial, carefully controlled experiment reveal any truth about nature? One simple answer is that the contrived character of experiments is a necessity: To see beneath the surface, it is necessary to dig. A more complete answer, however, is that there is a difference between the conditions in which an experiment is conducted and the results of the experiment. Just because an experiment takes place in an unnatural environment does not necessarily imply that the results are unnatural.

For example, you are probably familiar with the law of gravity, which states that all objects fall at the same rate independent of mass. You are, no doubt, equally familiar with the "natural" fact that if you drop a brick and a feather from the roof of a building, they will not fall at the same rate. Other factors in the natural world, such as air resistance, conceal the true effects of gravity. To demonstrate the law of gravity, we must create an artificial, controlled environment (specifically, a vacuum) wherein forces such as air resistance have been eliminated. This fact does not invalidate the law of gravity; the law accurately describes the underlying force of gravity and explains the behavior of falling objects, even though natural conditions may conceal the basic principle. In the same way, the goal of any experiment is to reveal the natural underlying mechanisms and relationships that may be otherwise obscured. Nonetheless, there is always a risk that the conditions of an experiment are so unnatural that the results are questionable. To use the terminology presented in Chapter 6, an experimenter can be so intent on ensuring internal validity that external validity is compromised. Researchers are aware of this problem and have developed techniques to increase the external validity (natural character) of experiments. We discuss some of these techniques in section 9.6.

 **LEARNING CHECKS**

It has been demonstrated that students with high self-esteem tend to have higher grades than students with low self-esteem. Does this relationship mean that higher self-esteem causes better academic performance? Does it mean that better academic performance causes higher self-esteem? Explain your answer, and identify the general problem that can preclude a cause-and-effect explanation.

A researcher would like to compare two methods for teaching math to third-grade students. Two third-grade classes are obtained for the study. Mr. Jones teaches one class using method A, and Mrs. Smith teaches the other class using method B. At the end of the year, the students from the method-B class have significantly higher scores on a mathematics achievement test. Does this result indicate that method B causes higher scores than method A? Explain your answer, and identify the general problem that precludes a cause-and-effect explanation.

9.2 | DISTINGUISHING ELEMENTS OF AN EXPERIMENT

The general purpose of the experimental research strategy is to establish a cause-and-effect relationship between two variables. That is, an experiment attempts to demonstrate that changing one variable (the independent variable) causes changes in a second variable (the dependent variable). This general purpose can be broken down into two specific goals.

1. The first step in demonstrating a cause-and-effect relationship is to demonstrate that the "cause" happens before the "effect" occurs. In the context of an experiment, this means that you must show that a change in the value of the independent variable is followed by a change in the dependent variable. To accomplish this, a researcher first manipulates the independent variable and then observes the dependent variable to see if it also changes.
2. To establish that one specific variable is responsible for changes in another variable, an experiment must rule out the possibility that the changes are caused by some other variable.

Earlier, we described the experimental research strategy as consisting of four basic elements: manipulation, measurement, comparison, and control. Two of these elements, measurement and comparison, are also components in a number of other research strategies. The two elements that are unique to experiments and distinguish experimental research from other strategies are manipulation of one variable and control of other, extraneous variables. These two unique elements of experimental research are discussed in the following sections.

Manipulation

A distinguishing characteristic of the experimental strategy is that the researcher manipulates one of the variables under study. **Manipulation** is accomplished by first deciding which specific values of the independent variable you would like to examine. Then you create a series of treatment conditions corresponding to those specific values. As a result, the independent variable changes from one treatment condition to another. For example, if you wanted to investigate the effect of temperature (independent variable) on appetite (dependent variable), you would first determine which levels of temperature you wanted to study. Assuming that 70 degrees Fahrenheit is a "normal" temperature, you might want to compare 60 degrees, 70 degrees, and 80 degrees to see how warmer- or colder-than-normal temperatures affect appetite. You would then set the room temperature to 60 degrees for one treatment condition, change it to 70 degrees for another condition, and change it again to 80 degrees for the third condition. A group of participants or subjects is then observed in each treatment condition to obtain measurements of appetite.

In an experiment, **manipulation** consists of identifying the specific values of the independent variable to be examined and then creating a set of treatment conditions corresponding to the set of identified values.

Manipulation and the Directionality Problem

The primary purpose of manipulation is to allow researchers to determine the direction of a relationship. Suppose, for example, there is a systematic relationship between temperature and ice-cream sales at major-league baseball stadiums, so that temperature and ice-cream sales rise and fall together. This relationship is shown in Figure 9.2. As we have noted, however, simply observing that a relationship exists does not explain the relationship and certainly does not identify the direction of the relationship. One technique for determining the direction of a relationship is to manipulate one of the variables (cause it to increase and decrease) and watch the second variable to determine whether it is affected by the manipulation. We could, for example, select enclosed baseball stadiums and use the heating/cooling system to manipulate the temperature while monitoring ice-cream consumption. In this situation, it is reasonable to expect that increasing the temperature would produce an increase in ice-cream consumption. On the other hand, we could manipulate ice-cream consumption (hand out free ice cream) and

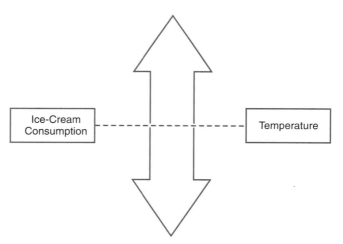

FIGURE **9.2** Using Manipulation to Determine the Direction of a Cause-and-Effect Relationship

Ice-cream consumption and temperature rise and fall together. Manipulating temperature (increasing or decreasing) causes a corresponding change in ice-cream consumption. However, increasing ice-cream consumption by handing out free ice cream has no influence on temperature.

monitor temperature. In this case, it is unlikely that more ice-cream consumption would result in higher temperatures. Note that manipulation of the individual variables allows us to demonstrate the direction of the relationship: changes in temperature are responsible for causing changes in ice-cream consumption, not the other way around. In general, whenever there is a relationship between two variables, a researcher can use manipulation to determine which variable is the cause and which is the effect.

For an example more closely related to psychology, consider the relationship between depression and insomnia. It has been observed repeatedly that people suffering from depression also tend to have problems sleeping. However, the observed relationship does not answer the causal question, "Does depression cause sleep problems, or does the lack of sleep cause depression?" Although it may be difficult to manipulate depression directly, it certainly is possible to manipulate the amount of sleep. One group of individuals, for example, could be allowed only 4 hours of sleep each night and a comparison group allowed 8 hours. After a week, depression scores could be obtained and compared for the two groups. If the 4-hour group is more depressed, this is evidence that a lack of sleep causes depression.

> Note that the researcher manipulates only the independent variable. Although we hope that this manipulation also will cause changes in the dependent variable, we are not directly manipulating the dependent variable.

Manipulation and the Third-Variable Problem

A second purpose for manipulation is to help researchers control the influence of outside variables. In an experiment, researchers must actively manipulate the independent variable rather than simply waiting for the variable to change by itself. If you let variables change on their own, it is always possible that other variables are also changing, and these other variables may be responsible for the relationship you are observing. Earlier, we speculated about a relationship between ice-cream consumption and temperature: increasing temperature is related to increased ice-cream consumption. Similarly, there is a relationship between temperature and crime (Cohn & Rotton, 2000). These two relationships are shown together in Figure 9.3. Notice that increasing temperature is related to both an increase in ice-cream consumption and an increase in crime. If a researcher simply observed ice-cream consumption and crime rates, the results would indicate a strong relationship; increases in ice cream consumption are accompanied by increases in crime. However, the existence of a relationship does not necessarily mean that there is a direct connection between the two variables. As in Figure 9.3, it is possible that a third, outside variable is responsible for the apparent relationship. The lack of any direct connection between variables can be demonstrated using manipulation. In this example, we could manipulate ice-cream consumption (hand out free ice cream) and monitor crime rates. Presumably, increasing ice-cream consumption would have no influence on crime rates. Similarly, we could manipulate crime rates (start a massive police initiative) and monitor ice-cream consumption. Again, it is unlikely that changing the crime rate would have any effect on ice-cream consumption. Notice that we are using manipulation to show that there is not a direct cause-and-effect relationship between crime and ice-cream consumption. Specifically, you can manipulate either crime rate or ice-cream consumption and it will have no effect on the other variable.

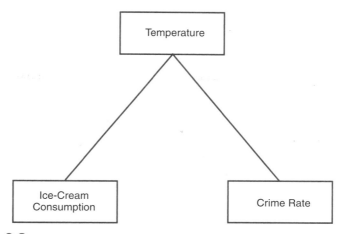

FIGURE **9.3** Manipulation and the Third-Variable Problem
Ice-cream consumption and crime rate rise and fall together as temperature increases
and decreases. However, there is not a direct connection between ice-cream consumption and crime rate. Manipulating either of the two variables will have no influence on
the other.

In an experiment, the researcher is responsible for causing the independent variable to change by direct manipulation. In this way, the researcher can
be confident that changes in the independent variable are not being caused by
some outside variable (a third variable) that could influence the outcome of the
study. Thus, the act of manipulation helps eliminate one aspect of the third-
variable problem in an experiment.

Control

The second distinguishing characteristic of an experiment is control of other
variables; that is, those other than the independent and dependent variables.
To accurately evaluate the relationship between two specific variables, a
researcher must ensure that the observed relationship is not contaminated by
the influence of other variables.

Control and the Third-Variable Problem

In general, the purpose of an experiment is to show that the manipulated
variable is responsible for the changes observed in the dependent variable.
To accomplish this, an experiment must rule out any other possible explanation for the observed changes; that is, eliminate all **confounding variables.**
In Chapter 6 (p. 178) we defined a confounding variable as a third variable
that is allowed to change systematically along with the two variables being
studied. In the context of an experiment, the particular concern is to identify and control any third variable that changes systematically along with
the independent variable and has the potential to influence the dependent
variable.

A confounding variable and the need for control are illustrated in a study examining the role of humor in memory. In 1994, Schmidt conducted a series of experiments investigating the effects of humor on memory. He first generated pairs of humorous and nonhumorous sentences that had the same basic content. For example:

Humorous: If at first you don't succeed, you are probably not related to the boss.

Nonhumorous: People who are related to the boss often succeed the very first time.

Participants were then presented with lists of sentences followed by a memory test to determine how many sentences they could recall. In general, the results showed that participants recalled more humorous sentences than nonhumorous sentences. However, the study contained a third, potentially confounding variable. Schmidt was concerned that the positive effects of humor may have been caused by surprise. Specifically, participants may be surprised to find humorous material in the middle of a boring memory experiment, and the surprise may cause them to pay more attention to the humorous sentences. Thus, the level of surprise varies systematically with the level of humor, and may be a confounding variable. In this experiment, it is impossible to tell whether the differences in sentence recall were caused by humor or by surprise. The structure of this study, including the confounding variable, is shown in Figure 9.4.

To establish an unambiguous causal relationship between humor and memory, it is necessary to eliminate the possible influence of the confounding variable. Schmidt (1994) chose to eliminate the surprise variable altogether. Before the sentences were presented, the participants were warned that half of the sentences would be humorous and half would be nonhumorous. In addition, participants were told that each sentence would be labeled humorous or nonhumorous so they would know what to expect before reading a sentence. The structure of the controlled experiment is shown in Figure 9.5. In the controlled experiment, the confounding variable has been eliminated, and the true relation between humor and memory performance can be observed.

The Schmidt study provides an opportunity to make another important point. Specifically, the independent variable in an experiment is determined by the hypothesis. Because Schmidt was studying the effects of humor on memory, the independent variable was the level of humor. On the other hand, if Schmidt had been studying the effects of surprise on memory, then the independent variable would be the level of surprise. In a study in which surprise was the independent variable, the humor level of the sentences could become a confounding variable. The classification as an independent variable or a confounding variable depends on the hypothesis.

LEARNING CHECKS

Identify the two characteristics needed for a research study to qualify as an experiment.

In an experiment examining human memory, two groups of participants are used. One group is allowed 5 minutes to study a list of 40 words and

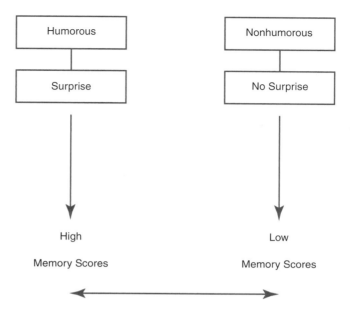

Is the difference in memory caused by the change from humorous to nonhumorous, or by the change from surprise to no surprise?

FIGURE **9.4** Confounding Variables

Because the level of humor and the level of surprise vary together systematically, they are confounded, and it is impossible to determine which variable is responsible for the differences in memory scores.

the second group is given 10 minutes of study time for the same list of words. Then, both groups are given a memory test, and the researcher records the number of words correctly recalled by each participant. For this experiment, identify the independent variable and the dependent variable.

9.3 | DEALING WITH EXTRANEOUS VARIABLES

The intent of an experiment is to focus on two specific variables: the independent variable and the dependent variable. However, within every experiment, there are thousands of other factors—variables—that are constantly changing or have different values. Different individuals enter the experiment with different backgrounds, ages, genders, heights, weights, IQs, personalities, and the like. As time passes, room temperature and lighting fluctuate, weather changes, people get tired or bored or excited or happy, they forget things or remember things, and develop itches or aches and pains that distract from the task at hand. Beyond the independent and dependent variables, all these other variables are called *extraneous variables,* and every experiment is filled with them.

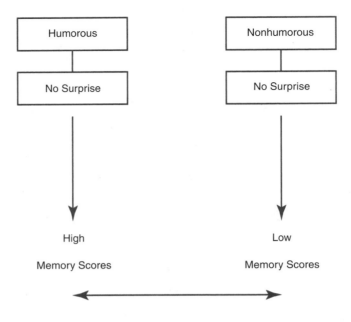

Because the level of surprise does not change, it cannot be responsible for causing the difference in memory scores.

FIGURE **9.5** Eliminating a Confounding Variable

Because the level of surprise does not change systematically with the level of humor, the two variables are not confounded. In this study, you can be confident that the level of humor (not surprise) is responsible for the differences in memory scores.

An experimental researcher must prevent any extraneous variable from becoming a confounding variable. This is the basic purpose of *control* within an experiment. With thousands of potentially confounding variables, however, the problem of controlling (or even monitoring) every extraneous variable appears insurmountable. Close inspection of the definition of a confounding variable, however, reveals some hints. Note that a confounding variable has two important characteristics:

1. First, an extraneous variable becomes a confounding variable only if it influences the dependent variable. Something totally unrelated to the dependent variable is not a threat. In Schmidt's humor-and-memory experiment, for example, individuals probably entered the experiment wearing different types of shoes (sneakers, flats, heels, loafers, or sandals); however, it is unlikely that the type of shoe has any influence on memory performance. Thus, it was not necessary to take any steps to control the shoe variable (Schmidt did not even mention shoes in his report).

2. Second, a confounding variable must vary systematically with the independent variable. A variable that changes randomly, with no relation to the independent variable, is not a threat. The concept of random versus systematic change is an important part of control.

The first step in controlling extraneous variables is to identify those variables most likely to influence the dependent variable. This identification process is based primarily on common sense, simple logical reasoning, and past experience in controlling extraneous variables. For example, if you are measuring memory performance, IQ is a reasonable choice as a potentially confounding variable. If very young and/or very old participants are used, then age is also a variable that could reasonably affect memory performance. If memory performance is being measured in different settings or at different times, these variables also could influence performance. (A loud, busy room can create distractions that lower performance, as opposed to a quiet, empty room.) The variables you identify at this step merit special attention to ensure control. Other variables are not ignored, but are handled more casually. When identifying extraneous variables, recall from Chapter 6 (p. 179–185) that they can be classified into three general categories:

1. *Environmental Variables.* Participants may be observed in different environments at different times of day, in different rooms, by different experimenters, under different lighting conditions, and at different temperatures.
2. *Individual Differences.* The individuals who participate in a research study differ from one another in a variety of ways such as gender, age, IQ, educational background, and number of siblings.
3. *Time-Related Variables.* When participants are observed in a series of treatment conditions over time, factors other than the treatments also change as time goes by. Factors such as weather changes from day to day, or people becoming fatigued or more experienced can become confounding variables because they may influence the scores obtained in the study.

Control by Holding Constant or Matching

Once a limited set of specific variables with real potential as confounding variables is identified, it is possible to exercise some control over them. There are three standard methods for controlling extraneous variables. Two involve actively intervening to control variables by holding the variable constant or by matching values across the treatment conditions. The third method is randomization, which is discussed in the next section. For now, we focus attention on the two active methods for controlling extraneous variables.

Holding a Variable Constant

An extraneous variable can be eliminated completely by holding it constant. For example, all individuals in the experiment could be observed in the same room, at the same time of day, by the same researcher. Because these factors are the same for every observation, they are not variables and, therefore, cannot be confounding. By standardizing the environment and procedures, most environmental variables can be held constant. This technique can also be used with participant variables. For example, by selecting only 6-year-old males to participate in an experiment, age and gender are held constant.

Often, it is unreasonable to hold a variable completely constant. For example, it would not be practical to hold IQ constant by requiring all participants to have IQs of exactly 109. Similarly, it would be a bit overzealous to hold age constant by requiring all participants to have been born on June 13, 1992. Instead, researchers often choose to restrict a variable to a limited range instead of holding it absolutely constant. For example, a researcher may require participants to be between 18 and 21 years of age and to have IQ scores between 100 and 110. Although age and IQ are not perfectly constant here, the restricted range should ensure that the participants in one treatment are not noticeably older or smarter than the participants in another treatment.

Holding a variable constant eliminates its potential to become a confounding variable. However, this method also may have negative consequences because it can limit the external validity of an experiment. For example, if an experiment is conducted exclusively with females (holding gender constant) the results cannot be generalized to males. Recall from Chapter 6 that any factor limiting the generalization of research results is a threat to external validity.

Matching Values Across Treatment Conditions

Control over an extraneous variable can also be exercised by matching the levels of the variable across treatment conditions. For example, 10 males and 20 females could be assigned to each separate treatment condition. Gender still varies within treatment conditions, but it is now balanced and does not vary across treatments. Another common form of matching is to ensure that the average value is the same (or nearly the same) for all treatments. For example, participants could be assigned so that the average age is the same for all of the different treatment conditions. In this case, age is balanced across treatments and, therefore, cannot be a confounding variable. Matching can also be used to control environmental variables. For example, a study using two different rooms could match the rooms across treatment conditions by measuring half of the participants in one room and the other half in the other room for every treatment condition. Finally, matching can be used to control time-related factors. By varying the order of two treatments, I and II, some participants experience treatment I early in the series and others experience the same treatment later. In the same way, some participants experience treatment II early and others later. In this way, the treatment conditions are matched with respect to time. The process of matching treatment conditions over time is called *counterbalancing* and is discussed in detail in Chapter 11.

Typically, controlling a variable by matching or holding constant requires some time and effort from the researcher, and can intrude on the experimental participants. Matching individuals for IQ, for example, requires the researcher to obtain an IQ score for each participant before the experiment can begin. Although it is possible to control a few variables by matching or holding constant, the demands of these control techniques make them impractical or impossible to use to control all extraneous variables. Therefore, active control by matching or holding constant is recommended for a limited set of specific variables identified as potentially serious threats to an experiment.

LEARNING CHECK   Identify the two active methods of preventing extraneous variables from becoming confounding variables.

Control by Randomization

Because it is essentially impossible to actively control the thousands of extraneous variables that can intrude on an experiment, researchers usually rely on a simpler, more passive control technique known as **randomization**. The principle underlying randomization is the disruption of any systematic relation between extraneous variables and the independent variable, thereby preventing the extraneous variables from becoming confounding variables.

Randomization involves using an unpredictable and unbiased procedure (such as a coin toss) to distribute different values of each extraneous variable across the treatment conditions. The procedure that is used must be a **random process,** which simply means that all the different possible outcomes are equally likely. For example, when we toss a coin, the two possible outcomes—heads and tails—are equally likely (see Chapter 5, p. 144).

One common use of randomization is **random assignment**, in which a random process such as a coin toss or a random number table (see Appendix A) is used to assign participants to treatment conditions. For an experiment comparing two treatment conditions, a researcher could use a coin toss to assign participants to treatment conditions. Because the assignment of participants to treatments is based on a random process, it is reasonable to assume that individual participant variables (such as age, gender, height, IQ, and the like) are also distributed randomly across treatment conditions. Specifically, the use of random assignment should ensure that the participant variables do not change systematically from one treatment to another and, therefore, cannot be confounding variables.

DEFINITIONS   **Randomization** is the use of a random process to help avoid a systematic relationship between two variables.

Random assignment is the use of a random process to assign participants to treatment conditions.

Randomization can also be used to control environmental variables. If the research schedule requires some observations in the morning hours and some in the afternoon, a random process can be used to assign treatment conditions to the different times. For example, a coin is tossed each day to determine whether treatment I or treatment II is to be administered in the morning. In this way, a morning hour is equally likely to be assigned to treatment condition I or treatment condition II. Thus, time of day is randomly distributed across treatments and does not have a systematic effect on the outcome.

Randomization is a powerful tool for controlling extraneous variables. Its primary advantage is that it offers a method for controlling a multitude of variables simultaneously and does not require specific attention to each extraneous variable. However, randomization does not guarantee that extraneous variables are really controlled; rather, it uses chance to control variables. If you toss a coin 10 times, for example, you expect to obtain a random mixture of heads and tails. This random mixture is the essence of randomization. However, it is possible to toss a coin 10 times and obtain heads every time; chance can produce a biased (or systematic) outcome. If you are using a random process (such as a coin toss) to assign people to treatment conditions, it is still possible for all the high-IQ individuals to be assigned to the same condition. In the long run, with large numbers (that is, a large sample), a random process guarantees a balanced result. In the short run, however, especially with small numbers (that is, a small sample), there is a chance that randomization will not work. Because randomization cannot be relied on to control extraneous variables, specific variables that have been identified as having high potential for influencing results should receive special attention and be controlled by matching or holding constant. Then, other variables can be randomized with the understanding that they probably will be controlled by chance, but with the risk that randomization may not succeed in providing adequate control.

LEARNING CHECK

Define a random process, and explain how this process is used for random assignment of participants to treatment conditions.

Explain how the process of randomly assigning participants to treatment conditions should prevent a participant variable such as age or gender from becoming a confounding variable.

Comparing Methods of Control

The goal of an experiment is to show that the scores obtained in one treatment condition are consistently different from the scores in another treatment, and that the differences are caused by the treatments. In the terminology of the experimental design, the goal is to show that differences in the dependent variable are caused by the independent variable. In this context, the purpose of control is to ensure that no other variable (other than the independent variable) could be responsible for causing the scores to be different.

We have examined three different methods for controlling extraneous variables, and each is shown in Table 9.1. The table shows how participant gender can be a confounding variable and how the three methods are used to prevent confounding.

a. Column A shows two treatment conditions with 10 participants in each treatment. In this column, gender (M and F) is confounded with the treatments; 80% of the participants in treatment I are females, but in

TABLE **9.1**
A Confounding Variable and Three Methods to Prevent Confounding

(A) Gender Confounded		(B) Gender Held Constant		(C) Gender Matched		(D) Gender Randomized	
Treatment		Treatment		Treatment		Treatment	
I	II	I	II	I	II	I	II
M	M	F	F	M	M	M	F
M	M	F	F	M	M	F	M
F	M	F	F	M	M	F	F
F	M	F	F	M	M	M	F
F	M	F	F	F	F	F	M
F	M	F	F	F	F	M	M
F	M	F	F	F	F	M	F
F	M	F	F	F	F	F	F
F	F	F	F	F	F	M	M
F	F	F	F	F	F	F	M

treatment II, only 20% are females. If this study found differences between the scores in treatment I and treatment II, the differences in scores could have been caused by the differences in gender.

b. In column B, gender is held constant. All the participants in treatment I are female, and all the participants in treatment II are female. In this case, there is absolutely no gender difference between the two treatments, so gender cannot be responsible for causing differences in the scores.

c. In column C, gender is matched across the treatments. In treatment I, 40% are males, and in treatment II, 40% are males. Again, the two groups are balanced with respect to gender, so any differences in scores for the two treatments cannot be caused by gender.

d. Finally, in column D, gender is randomized across treatments. By using a random process to assign males and females to the treatment conditions, it is reasonable to expect that gender will be balanced across treatments. If there are no substantial gender differences between treatments, then gender cannot cause the scores in one treatment to be different from the scores in the other treatment.

Advantages and Disadvantages of Control Methods

The two active methods of control (holding constant and matching) require some extra effort or extra measurement and, therefore, are typically used with only one or two specific variables identified as real threats for confounding. In addition, holding a variable constant has the disadvantage of limiting generalization (external validity). On the other hand, randomization has the advantage of controlling a wide variety of variables simultaneously. However, randomization is not guaranteed to be successful; chance is trusted to balance the variables across the different treatments. Nonetheless, randomization is the primary technique for controlling the huge number of extraneous variables that exist within any experiment.

9.4 | CONTROL GROUPS

An experiment always involves comparison. The experimental strategy requires comparing observations of the dependent variable across different levels of the independent variable. In general terms, an experiment compares observations across different treatment conditions. However, sometimes a researcher wishes to evaluate only one treatment rather than compare a set of different treatments. In this case, it is still possible to conduct an experiment. The solution is to compare the treatment condition with a baseline "no-treatment" condition. In experimental terminology, the treatment condition is called the **experimental group,** and the no-treatment condition is called the **control group.** The term group is somewhat misleading. It is possible, for example, to observe the same set of individuals in both the treatment and the no-treatment conditions. In this type of design, only one "group" of subjects is used to generate two "groups" of scores for comparison. Although it might be less confusing to speak of a control condition, we use the more conventional term, control group.

DEFINITIONS

The term **experimental group** refers to the treatment condition in an experiment.

The term **control group** refers to the no-treatment condition in an experiment.

The variety of different ways to construct a control group for an experiment can be classified into two general categories: no-treatment control groups and placebo control groups.

No-Treatment Control Groups

As the name implies, a **no-treatment control group** is simply a treatment condition in which the participants do not receive the treatment being evaluated. The purpose of the no-treatment control is to provide a standard of normal behavior, or baseline, against which the treatment condition can be compared. To evaluate the effects of a drug, for example, an experiment could include one condition in which the drug is administered and a control condition in which there is no drug. To evaluate the effectiveness of a training procedure, the experimental group receives the training and the control group does not.

DEFINITION

In an experiment, a **no-treatment control group** is a condition in which the participants do not receive the treatment being evaluated.

At first glance, it may appear that a treatment versus no-treatment experiment eliminates the independent variable. However, the researcher still creates treatment conditions by manipulating different values of the treatment variable; the no-treatment condition is simply a zero-value of the independent variable. Thus, the experiment compares one condition having a "full amount" of the treatment with a second condition having a "zero amount" of the treatment. The independent variable still exists, and its two levels now consist of treatment and no-treatment control.

Placebo Control Groups

A **placebo** is an inert or innocuous medication, a fake medical treatment such as a sugar pill or a water injection that, by itself, has absolutely no medicinal effect. Although there is no biological or pharmacological reason for a placebo to be effective, nonetheless, a placebo can have a dramatic effect on health and behavior (Shapiro & Morris, 1978). The **placebo effect** is believed to be psychosomatic: The mind (psyche), rather than the placebo itself, has an effect on the body (somatic). The fact that an individual thinks or believes a medication is effective can be sufficient to cause a response to the medication.

DEFINITION	The **placebo effect** refers to a response by a participant to an inert medication that has no real effect on the body. The placebo effect occurs simply because the individual thinks the medication is effective.

In psychotherapy, the term nonspecific is often used in place of placebo to refer to the elements of therapy that are not specifically therapeutic.

Although the concept of the placebo effect originated in medical research, it has been generalized to other situations in which a supposedly ineffective treatment produces an effect. Common examples in behavioral research include the use of inactive drugs (especially when participants believe they are receiving psychotropic drugs), nonalcoholic beverages (when participants are expecting alcohol), and nonspecific psychotherapy (therapy with the therapeutic components removed).

In the context of experimental research, the placebo effect can generate serious questions about the interpretation of results. When a researcher observes a significant difference between a treatment condition and a no-treatment control condition, can the researcher be sure that the observed effect is really caused by the treatment, or is part (or all) of the effect simply a placebo effect? The importance of this question depends on the purpose of the experimental research. Investigators often differentiate between outcome research and process research.

1. *Outcome research* simply investigates the effectiveness of a treatment. The goal is to determine whether a treatment produces a substantial or clinically significant effect. It is concerned with the general outcome of the treatment rather than identifying the specific components that cause the treatment to be effective.
2. *Process research*, on the other hand, attempts to identify the active components of the treatment. In process research, it is essential that the placebo effect be separated from other, active components of the treatment.

To separate placebo effects from "real" treatment effects, researchers include one or more **placebo control groups** in an experiment. The placebo control is simply a treatment condition in which participants receive a placebo instead of the actual treatment. Comparison of the placebo control condition with the treatment condition reveals how much treatment effect exists beyond the placebo effect. It is also common to include a third, no-treatment control group. Comparison of the placebo control with the no-treatment condition reveals the magnitude of the placebo effect. In situations in which it is possible to identify several different elements of a treatment, researchers may conduct a component analysis, or dismantling of the treatment, using multiple control groups in which selected elements (or combinations of elements) are included or excluded in each condition.

DEFINITION	A **placebo control group** is a condition in which participants receive a placebo instead of the actual treatment.

As a final word of caution, you should recognize that using a control group and the control of extraneous variables are two completely different aspects of an experiment. Control of extraneous variables is an essential component of all experiments, and is required to prevent extraneous variables from becoming confounding variables and threatening the internal validity of the study. However, a control group is an optional component that is used in some experiments but certainly not all. In particular, a research study does not need a control group to qualify as a true experiment.

 **LEARNING CHECKS**

What is the reason for controlling extraneous variables? What is the purpose of a control group?

Can a research study be an experiment without a control group? Can a study be an experiment without controlling extraneous variables?

9.5 | MANIPULATION CHECKS

In an experiment, a researcher always manipulates the independent variable. Although this manipulation and its results are obvious to the researcher, occasionally, there is some question about the effect of the manipulation on the participants. Specifically, are the participants even aware of the manipulation and, if so, how do they interpret it? When these questions are important to the results or interpretation of an experiment, researchers often include a **manipulation check** as part of the study. A manipulation check directly measures whether the independent variable had the intended effect on the participant.

DEFINITION	A **manipulation check** is an additional measure to assess how the participants perceived and interpreted the manipulation and/or to assess the direct effect of the manipulation.

There are two ways to check the manipulation. First, a manipulation check may be an explicit measure of the independent variable. Suppose, for example, a researcher wants to examine the effects of mood on performance. The study involves manipulating people's mood (that is, mood is the independent variable). The researcher may include a mood measure to make sure that happy and sad moods were actually induced.

A second way to check the manipulation is to embed specific questions about the manipulation in a questionnaire that participants complete after their participation in the experiment. For example, participants may be given an exit questionnaire that asks for their responses to the experiment:

Did you enjoy participating?

How long did the experiment seem to take?

Were you bored?

What do you think was the purpose of the experiment?

Did you suspect that you were being deceived?

Embedded in the questionnaire are specific questions that address the manipulation. Participants can be asked directly whether they noticed a manipulation. For example, if the room lighting was adjusted during the experimental session, you could simply ask, "Did you notice that the lights were dimmed after the first 15 minutes?" Or, "Did you notice any change in the lights during the experiment?" In an experiment in which the researcher manipulates "praise" versus "criticism" by making verbal comments to the participants, she might ask, "How did the researcher respond when you failed to complete the first task?" Notice that the intent of the manipulation-check questions is to determine whether the participants perceived the manipulation and/or how they interpreted the manipulation.

Although a manipulation check can be used with any study, it is particularly important in four situations.

1. *Participant Manipulations.* Although researchers can be confident of the success of environmental manipulations (such as changing the lighting), there often is good reason to question the success of manipulations that are intended to affect participants. For example, a researcher who wanted to examine the effects of frustration on task performance might try to induce a feeling of frustration by giving one group of participants a series of impossible tasks to perform. To determine whether the participants actually are frustrated, the researcher might include a measure of frustration as a manipulation check.

2. *Subtle Manipulations.* In some situations, the variable being manipulated is not particularly salient and may not be noticed by the participants. For example, a researcher might make minor changes in the wording of instructions or in affect (smiling versus not smiling). Small changes from one treatment condition to another might be overlooked completely, especially when participants are not explicitly told that changes are being made.

3. *Simulations.* In simulation research, the researcher attempts to create a real world environment by manipulating elements within the experimental

situation. The effectiveness of the simulation, however, depends on the participants' perception and acceptance. A manipulation check can be used to assess how participants perceive and respond to an attempted simulation.

4. *Placebo Controls.* As with a simulation, the effectiveness of a placebo depends on its credibility. It is essential that participants believe that the placebo is real; they must have no suspicion that they are being deceived. A manipulation check can be used to assess the realism of the placebo.

 **LEARNING CHECK**   What is the general purpose of a manipulation check?

9.6 | INCREASING EXTERNAL VALIDITY: SIMULATION AND FIELD STUDIES

Once again, the goal of the experimental strategy is to establish a cause-and-effect relationship between two variables. To do this, an experiment creates an artificial, controlled environment in which the two variables being studied are isolated from outside influences. As a result, experiments are commonly conducted in a laboratory setting. A controlled environment increases the internal validity of the research (see Chapter 6). However, by creating an artificial environment, experimenters risk obtaining results that do not accurately reflect events and relations that occur in a more natural, real-world environment. As we discussed in Chapter 6, in research terminology, this risk is a threat to external validity. One example of this problem occurs when demand characteristics are present. Recall that demand characteristics are cues given to the participant that may influence the participant to behave in a certain way. Demand characteristics, as well as reactivity, are much more likely to be problems in experiments conducted in a laboratory setting. For some research questions, a threat to external validity can be extremely serious. In particular, when research seeks cause-and-effect explanations for behavior in real-world situations, it is essential that the experimental results generalize outside the confines of the experiment. In these situations, researchers often attempt to maximize the realism of the experimental environment to increase the external validity of the results. Two standard techniques are used to accomplish this: simulation and field studies.

Simulation

Simulation is the creation of conditions within an experiment that simulate or closely duplicate the natural environment being examined. The term natural environment is used in a very broad sense to mean the physical characteristics of the environment, and more important, its atmosphere or mood. Most people are familiar with flight simulators that duplicate the cockpit of an airplane and allow pilots to train and be tested in a safe, controlled environment. In the same way that a flight simulator duplicates the natural environment of an airplane, researchers often use simulation so they can control the "natural environment" and observe how people behave in real-world situations.

DEFINITION

A **simulation** is the creation of conditions within an experiment that simulate or closely duplicate the natural environment in which the behaviors being examined would normally occur.

Researchers often differentiate between mundane realism and experimental realism in the context of simulation (Aronson & Carlsmith, 1968). **Mundane realism** refers to the superficial, usually physical, characteristics of the simulation, which probably have little positive effect on external validity. For example, converting a research laboratory into a mock singles bar probably would not do much to promote "natural" behavior of participants. In fact, most participants would probably view the situation as phony and respond with artificial behaviors. **Experimental realism,** on the other hand, concerns the psychological aspects of the simulation; that is, the extent to which the participants become immersed in the simulation and behave normally, unmindful of the fact that they are involved in an experiment. Obviously, a successful simulation is far more dependent on experimental realism than on mundane realism, and often the more mundane aspects of a simulation can be minimized or eliminated.

One of the most famous and most detailed simulation experiments was conducted in 1973 by researchers at Stanford University (Haney, Banks, & Zimbardo, 1973). The intent of the research was to study the development of interpersonal dynamics and relationships between guards and inmates in a prison. An actual prison, consisting of three barred cells, a solitary confinement facility, guards' quarters, and an interview room was built in the basement of the psychology building. A sample of 24 normal, mature, emotionally stable male college students was obtained. On a random basis, half were assigned the role of "guard" and half were assigned the role of "prisoner." The guards were issued khaki uniforms, nightsticks, and sunglasses. The prisoners' uniforms were loose smocks with ID numbers on the front and back. The prisoners were publicly arrested, charged, searched, handcuffed, and led off to jail where they were fingerprinted, photographed, stripped, sprayed with a delousing preparation, and finally given uniforms and locked up. Except for an explicit prohibition against physical punishment or aggression, little specific instruction was given to the guards or the prisoners. Almost immediately, the prisoners and guards became immersed in their roles. The interactions became negative, hostile, dehumanizing, and impersonal. Five prisoners had to be released because they developed extreme depression, crying, rage, and anxiety. When the experiment was stopped prematurely after only 6 days, the remaining prisoners were relieved, but the guards were distressed at the idea of giving up the control and power that had been part of their roles. Clearly the simulation was successful; perhaps too much so.

The Stanford prison study is an extreme example of a simulation experiment involving role-playing and a detailed simulated environment. However, this degree of detail is not always necessary for a successful simulation. Bordens and Horowitz (1983) investigated the decision process by which trial jurors reach their verdicts by having college students participate as jurors in a mock trial. The study did not attempt to recreate a detailed simulation of a real criminal trial but rather had participants base their verdicts on an audiotaped summary of a trial. Although the study made some effort to duplicate a real courtroom environment, the emphasis was on experimental realism rather than mundane realism.

Both the prison study and the mock trial study attempted to simulate a specific real-world situation, and both involved some degree of mundane realism. It is possible, however, for a simulation experiment to create a general atmosphere rather than a specific situation, and completely ignore the concept of mundane realism. The many studies using the "prisoner's dilemma" game provide good examples of this type of simulation research. The prisoner's dilemma game is based on a hypothetical situation in which two individuals have been arrested and are being interrogated by the police. Imagine that you and a partner have committed a crime and have both been arrested. The police have no real evidence against you and are relying on a confession to make their case. You and your partner are being held incommunicado so you have no idea what your partner is saying or doing. The rules of the game are as follows: If both suspects confess, then both will be convicted, but if both deny the crime, then both will be set free. However, if only one confesses and implicates his partner, then the confessor will be set free and will be rewarded for turning state's evidence. Note that your highest personal gain comes when you confess and your partner denies the crime. But the highest mutual gain comes when you both deny the crime. The dilemma is deciding what to do: Do you choose to behave in a cooperative manner and deny the crime, or do you behave in a conflicting manner and confess?

The prisoner's dilemma game is used in laboratory research to create a situation of interpersonal conflict, simulating real-life situations in which people must choose between cooperation and conflict based on the consequences of reward or punishment. In the laboratory, the two options of cooperation or conflict typically result in monetary consequences; for example, both players win 2 dollars if both cooperate, both lose 2 dollars if both conflict, and if they make opposite responses, the "conflictor" wins 5 dollars, whereas the "cooperator" loses 1 dollar. Notice that the prisoner's dilemma game is a generic simulation that is used to create a general atmosphere of competition. Nonetheless, it can be used to duplicate a variety of real-world conflict situations. For example, it has been used successfully to investigate racial prejudice (Tyson, Schlachter, & Cooper, 1987), gender stereotyping (Ferguson & Schmitt, 1988), and employee conflict/cooperation in the business world (Tomer, 1987).

 **LEARNING CHECK** Define and differentiate experimental realism and mundane realism.

Field Studies

A simulation experiment can be viewed as an effort to bring the real world into the laboratory to increase the external validity of experimental results. An alternative procedure that seeks the same goal is to take the laboratory into the real world. Research studies conducted in a real-world environment are called **field studies,** and researchers often speak of "going into the field" as a euphemism for taking research outside the laboratory. Field settings were discussed briefly in Chapters 3 and 6 and are detailed here.

DEFINITION	The term **field study** refers to research conducted in a place that the participant or subject perceives as a natural environment.

Not all studies conducted in the field are experiments. For example, observational research is often conducted in a field setting.

Although it can be difficult to maintain the necessary control of a true experiment in a field study, it is possible to conduct field study experiments. Many of the more famous field study experiments involve the investigation of helping behavior or "bystander apathy" in emergency situations. In these studies, the researchers create an emergency situation, then manipulate variables within the emergency and observe bystander responses. Research has used a variety of staged emergencies such as a flat tire (Bryan & Test, 1967), a lost wallet (Hornstein, Fisch, & Holmes, 1968), and a collapsed victim (Piliavin, Rodin, & Piliavin, 1969). A representative study involves a victim with a cane collapsing in a Philadelphia subway car (Piliavin & Piliavin, 1972). In one treatment condition, the victim "bled" from the mouth; in the second condition, there was no bleeding. The results show that help was significantly slower and less frequent for the bloody victim.

Cialdini, Reno, and Kallgren (1990) conducted a series of field experiments examining the natural phenomenon of littering and the theoretical issue of social conformity. They wanted to determine whether a person's tendency to litter depended on the social norm established by the amount of litter already in the area. Individuals were observed in a variety of natural settings including a parking garage, an amusement park, a library parking lot, and the mail box area of a college dorm. In each case the researchers manipulated the amount of preexisting litter in the area and removed all waste containers. Individuals entering each area were presented with a handbill and were then observed to determine whether they discarded the handbill as litter. The results indicated that behavior is influenced by social norms: People are significantly more likely to litter when a large amount of existing litter implies social acceptability.

 **LEARNING CHECK**

What is the general purpose for using a simulation or a field study for experimental research?

Advantages and Disadvantages of Simulation and Field Studies

Although simulation and field studies can be used to increase the realism of experiments, there are risks as well as advantages to these techniques. The obvious advantage of both procedures is that they allow researchers to investigate behavior in more life-like situations and, therefore, should increase the chances that the experimental results accurately reflect natural events. The disadvantage of both procedures is that allowing nature to intrude on an experiment means that the researcher often loses some control over the situation and risks compromising the internal validity of the experiment. This problem is particularly important for field experiments. In the "bloody victim" experiment, for example, the researchers had no control over who was riding in the subway car or how many passengers were present. Although it is reasonable that random variation of the "blood" versus "no-blood" conditions should have randomized participant variables across conditions, there is no guarantee.

It is conceivable, for example, that the 4 o'clock subway was filled with business commuters but the 2 o'clock subway had only three or four people. This type of unpredictable and uncontrolled variation could have significantly influenced the results. Simulation experiments, on the other hand, do provide researchers with the opportunity to control the assignment of participants to treatment conditions. However, simulation experiments are totally dependent on the participants' willingness to accept the simulation. No matter how realistic the simulation, participants still know that it is only an experiment and they know that their behaviors are being observed. This knowledge could influence behavior and compromise the experimental results.

■ CHAPTER SUMMARY

The goal of the experimental research strategy is to establish a cause-and-effect relationship between two variables. To accomplish this goal, an experiment must manipulate one of the two variables and create a situation in which the two variables being examined are isolated from the influence of other variables. In this chapter, manipulation and control are considered.

In general, an experiment attempts to demonstrate that changes in one variable are directly responsible for changes in a second variable. The two basic characteristics that distinguish the experimental research strategy from other research strategies are (1) manipulation of one variable while measuring a second variable, and (2) control of extraneous variables. In an experiment, the independent variable is manipulated by the researcher, the dependent variable is measured for changes, and all other variables are controlled to prevent them from influencing the results.

To establish an unambiguous causal relationship between the independent and dependent variables, it is necessary to eliminate the possible influence of a confounding variable. Extraneous variables become confounds when they change systematically along with the independent variable. After identifying a short list of extraneous variables that have the potential to become confounding variables, it is possible to actively or passively control these variables. The two standard methods of active control are (1) holding a variable constant, and (2) matching values across the treatment conditions. The method for passive control is to randomize these variables across the treatment conditions.

An experiment always involves comparison of measures of the dependent variable across different levels of the independent variable. To accomplish this, a treatment condition (an experimental group) and a no-treatment condition (a control group) often are created. The no-treatment condition serves as a baseline for evaluating the effect of the treatment. There are two general categories of control groups: (1) the no-treatment control group, a condition that involves no treatment whatsoever (participants receive a zero level of the independent variable); and (2) the placebo control group, a condition that involves the appearance of a treatment but from which the active, effective elements have been removed.

In an experiment, a researcher always manipulates the independent variable. Occasionally, a researcher may include a manipulation check to assess whether the participants are aware of the manipulation. A manipulation check is an additional measure to assess whether the manipulation was successful. It is particularly useful to use a manipulation check when participant manipulations, subtle manipulations, simulations, or placebo control conditions are used.

To establish a cause-and-effect relationship between two variables, an experiment necessarily creates an artificial, controlled environment in which the two variables being studied are isolated from outside influences. This high level of control required by an experiment can be a threat to external validity. To gain higher external validity, a researcher may use a simulation or a field study. A simulation involves creating a real-world atmosphere in a laboratory to duplicate a natural environment or situation; a field study involves moving an experiment from the laboratory into the real-world environment.

KEY WORDS

experimental research strategy	extraneous variable	no-treatment control group
experiment, or true experiment	manipulation	placebo effect
independent variable	randomization	placebo control group
treatment condition	random assignment	manipulation check
levels	experimental group	simulation
dependent variable	control group	field study

EXERCISES

1. In addition to the key words, you should also be able to define the following terms:
   third-variable problem
   directionality problem
   confounding variable
   random process
   placebo
   mundane realism
   experimental realism

2. Dr. Jones conducted a study examining the relationship between the amount of sugar in a child's diet and the activity level of the child. A sample of thirty 4-year-old children from a local preschool was used in the study. Sugar consumption was measured by interviewing the parents about each child's diet. Based on the result of the interview, each child was then placed into one of two groups: high sugar consumption and low sugar consumption. Activity level was measured by observing the children during a regular preschool afternoon. Finally, Dr. Jones compared the activity level for the high-sugar group with the activity level for the low-sugar group. Explain why Dr. Jones' study is not an example of the experimental research strategy.

3. Define or describe the third-variable problem and the directionality problem. Explain the actions used in an experiment to avoid these two problems.

4. Dr. Jones conducts an experiment investigating the effects of distraction on memory. A list of 40 two-syllable words is prepared. Dr. Jones obtains a sample of 50 students, all between the ages of 18 and 22, and presents the list of words to the entire group. Then each individual is randomly assigned to one of two groups. One group of participants is given a memory test for the list of words in a quiet room, and the second group is tested

in a room with loud construction noises (hammering, sawing, and so on) in the background.

a. Identify the independent variable and the dependent variable in this study.

b. Explain why Dr. Jones can be reasonably confident that the participants' age is not a confounding variable. That is, explain why it is unlikely that one group does better on the memory task because they are substantially older than the other group.

c. Although personality varies from one participant to another, Dr. Jones is probably not worried about personality as a confounding variable. Explain why not.

5. For each of the following research studies, explain why it is or is not an example of the experimental research strategy.

a. To evaluate the relationship between stress and general health, a researcher selects a random sample of 50-year-old men. For 2 months, each man is asked to keep a daily journal recording stressful events (such as a fight with his wife, an argument with his boss, or an automobile accident). After 2 months, a doctor examines each man and records an overall health rating. The goal of the study is to determine whether there is a relationship between the total amount of stress and overall health of the men.

b. In a study examining the relationship between self-esteem and dishonest behavior, college students were first given a self-esteem questionnaire to classify them into high and low self-esteem groups. At a later time, cheating behavior was measured while the students corrected their own exams. The goal of the study is to find a difference between the two groups.

c. In a study examining the relationship between dietary fiber and cholesterol, a sample of 50-year-old men is randomly separated into two groups. Each group eats exactly the same diet for 2 months, except that one group also gets 2 cups of oatmeal every day. At the end of 2 months, the cholesterol level is measured for each man. The researcher hopes to find a difference between the two groups.

6. In an experiment, participants are usually assigned to treatments using a random assignment procedure. Explain why random assignment is used.

7. Define extraneous variable and confounding variable. Describe two methods used to prevent extraneous variables from becoming confounding variables.

8. Describe and differentiate a no-treatment control group and a placebo control group.

9. Read the following example and answer the questions that follow it.

Dr. Jones conducts a research study investigating the effects of a new drug that is intended to reduce the craving for alcohol. A group of alcoholics who are being treated at a clinic is selected for the study. Half of the participants are given the drug along with their regular treatment, and the other half receives a placebo. Dr. Jones records whether each individual is still sober after 6 months.

a. Identify the dependent variable in this study.

b. Identify the independent variable in this study.

c. Identify the number of levels of the independent variable.

d. Assuming that the study includes participants ranging in age from 18 to 62 years of age, then which of the following most accurately describes the age variable in the study? (independent, dependent, extraneous, confounding)

e. If the participants in the drug group are noticeably older (on average) than the individuals in the placebo group, then which of the following most accurately describes the age variable in the study? (independent, dependent, extraneous, confounding)

10. Explain why simulations and field studies are used.

LEARNING ACTIVITIES

1. A researcher examines the relationship between the quality of breakfast and academic performance for a group of elementary-school children. For each child, the researcher interviews the parents to obtain information about the child's typical breakfast, and uses school records to obtain a measure of academic performance.

   a. Explain why this study is not a true experiment.

   b. Describe how the study could be modified to make it into an experiment that investigates whether the quality of breakfast has a direct effect on academic performance for elementary-school children. (Note: Your experiment may raise ethical questions that would make it very unlikely that the study could actually be conducted.)

2. To qualify as a true experiment, a research study requires the manipulation of at least one variable. The fact that some variables cannot (or should not) be manipulated limits the topics that can be investigated easily with an experimental study. If you were conducting a PsycINFO search for each of the following subjects, indicate which subjects are more likely to produce examples of true experiments and which are less likely. In each case, explain your answer.

   a. mathematics instruction

   b. alcohol and academic performance

   c. anorexia treatment

   d. adolescent self-esteem

WEB RESOURCES

Visit the Book Companion Website at **www .cengage.com/international** to access study tools including a glossary, flashcards, and web quizzing. You will also find a link to Statistics and Research Methods Workshops. For this chapter, we suggest you look at the following workshops:

Experimental Methods

True Experiments

Manipulation Checks in Experimental Research

Controls

10

The Between-Subjects Experimental Design

CHAPTER OVERVIEW

Step 6 of the research process involves selecting a research design. In this chapter, we discuss in detail one type of experimental research design: the between-subjects design. The advantages, disadvantages, and different versions of between-subjects designs are considered.

10.1 | INTRODUCTION TO BETWEEN-SUBJECTS EXPERIMENTS

Review of the Experimental Research Strategy

In Chapter 9, we introduced the experimental research strategy, as well as its major goal, which is to demonstrate a cause-and-effect relationship between two variables. To accomplish this goal, the experimental strategy requires several basic characteristics: (1) manipulation of one variable to create a set of two or more treatment conditions; (2) measurement of a second variable to obtain a set of scores within each treatment condition; (3) comparison of the scores between treatments; and (4) control of all other variables to prevent them from becoming confounding variables.

At the end of the study, the researcher compares the scores from each treatment with the scores from every other treatment. If there are consistent differences between treatments, the researcher can conclude that the differences have been *caused* by the treatment conditions. For example, a researcher may compare memory scores for a list of one-syllable words with scores for a list of two-syllable words. By showing that there are consistent differences between the two groups of scores, the researcher can demonstrate that memory is related to the number of syllables in the words (that is, the number of syllables causes differences in memory).

Two basic research designs are used to obtain the groups of scores that are compared in an experiment:

1. The different groups of scores all can be obtained from the same group of participants. For example, one group of individuals is given a memory test using a list of one-syllable words, and the same set of individuals is also tested using a list of two-syllable words. Thus, the researcher gets two sets of scores, both obtained from the same sample. This strategy is called a **within-subjects design** and is discussed in Chapter 11.
2. An alternative strategy is to obtain each of the different groups of scores from a separate group of participants. For example, one group of individuals is given a list of one-syllable words to memorize and a separate group receives a list of two-syllable words. This type of design, comparing scores from separate groups, is called a **between-subjects design.** We examine the characteristics of a between-subjects research design in this chapter.

Characteristics of Between-Subjects Designs

The defining characteristic of a between-subjects design is that it compares different groups of individuals. In the context of an experiment, a researcher manipulates the independent variable to create different treatment conditions, and a separate group of participants is assigned to each of the different conditions. The dependent variable is then measured for each individual, and the researcher examines the data, looking for differences between the groups (Figure 10.1).

This chapter focuses on the **between-subjects experimental design;** that is, the between-subjects design as it is used in *experimental* research, wherein

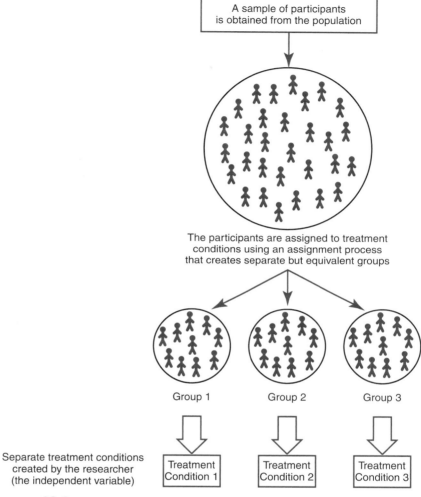

A sample of participants
is obtained from the population

The participants are assigned to treatment
conditions using an assignment process
that creates separate but equivalent groups

Group 1   Group 2   Group 3

Separate treatment conditions
created by the researcher
(the independent variable)

| Treatment Condition 1 | Treatment Condition 2 | Treatment Condition 3 |

FIGURE **10.1** The Structure of a Between-Subjects Experiment
The key element is that separate groups of participants are used for the different treatment conditions.

a researcher manipulates an independent variable. The general goal of a between-subjects experiment is to determine whether differences exist between two or more treatment conditions. For example, a researcher may want to compare two teaching methods (two treatments) to determine whether one is more effective than the other. In this case, two separate groups of individuals would be used, one for each of the two teaching methods. We should note, however, that between-subjects designs are commonly used for other research strategies, such as nonexperimental and quasi-experimental designs. The other strategies are examined in Chapter 12.

Independent Scores

One additional characteristic of the between-subjects design deserves special mention. A between-subjects design allows only one score for each participant. Every individual score represents a separate, unique participant. If a between-subjects experiment produces 30 scores in treatment A and 30 scores in treatment B, then the experiment must have employed a group of 30 individuals in treatment A and a separate group of 30 individuals in treatment B, for a total of 60 participants. In the terminology of experimental research, a between-subjects experimental design uses a different group of participants for each level of the independent variable, and each participant is exposed to only one level of the independent variable.

Occasionally, a researcher may combine several measurements for each individual into a single score. In particular, when the variable being measured is not particularly stable (for example, reaction time), a researcher may choose to measure the variable several times and then average the measurements to produce a single, more reliable score. However, the net result is always one score per individual participant.

DEFINITION	A **between-subjects experimental design,** also known as an **independent-measures experimental design,** requires a separate, independent group of individuals for each treatment condition. As a result, the data for a between-subjects design contain only one score for each participant. To qualify as an experiment, the design must satisfy all other requirements of the experimental research strategy, such as manipulation of an independent variable and control of extraneous variables.

 **LEARNING CHECK**   Identify the basic features of a between-subjects research design.

Advantages and Disadvantages of Between-Subjects Designs

A main advantage of a between-subjects design is that each individual score is independent from the other scores. Because each participant is measured only once, the researcher can be reasonably confident that the resulting measurement is relatively clean and uncontaminated by other treatment factors. For this reason, a between-subjects design is often called an **independent-measures design.** In an experiment comparing performance under different temperature conditions, for example, each participant is exposed to only one treatment condition. Thus, the participant's score is not influenced by such factors as:

- practice or experience gained in other treatments.
- fatigue or boredom from participating in a series of different treatments.
- contrast effects that result from comparing one treatment to another (a 60-degree room might feel cold after a 70-degree room, but the same 60-degree room might feel warm after a 50-degree room).

In addition, between-subjects designs can be used for a wide variety of research questions. For any experiment comparing two (or more) treatment conditions, it is always possible to assign different groups to the different treatments; thus, a between-subjects design is always an option. It may not always be the best choice, but it is always available.

One disadvantage of between-subjects designs is that they require a relatively large number of participants. Remember, each participant contributes only one score to the final data. To compare three different treatment conditions with 30 scores in each treatment, the between-subjects design requires 90 participants. This can be a problem for research involving special populations in which the number of potential participants is relatively small. For example, a researcher studying preschool children with a specific learning disability might have trouble finding a large number of individuals to participate.

Individual Differences

The primary disadvantage of a between-subjects design stems from the fact that each score is obtained from a unique individual who has personal characteristics that are different from all of the other participants. Consider the following descriptions of two individuals participating in the same research study.

John	Mary
John is a 21-year-old white male. He is 5′ 10″ tall, weighs 180 pounds, has blue eyes, blonde hair, and an IQ of 110. He comes from a middle-class family with one older sister. John is a chemistry major and was awake until 2:00 a.m. this morning after celebrating his success on a chemistry exam. He comes to the experiment with only 4 hours of sleep, suffering from a mild hang-over.	Mary is a 20-year-old black female. She is 5′ 3″ tall, has brown eyes, black hair, and an IQ of 142. Her mother and father are both doctors, and she is an only child. Mary is a history major with a minor in psychology. She had a head cold yesterday and went to bed at 8:00 p.m. She arrived at the experiment well-rested and feeling much better. However, she skipped breakfast and is hungry.

Clearly, these two individuals differ on a variety of dimensions. It should also be clear that we have identified only a few of the countless variables that differentiate the two people. Differences (such as gender, age, personality, and family background) that exist between participants at the beginning of an experiment are called preexisting individual differences, or simply **individual differences**. The concern with individual difference is that they can provide an explanation for why two different individuals produce two different scores in a research study.

DEFINITION　Personal characteristics that can differ from one participant to another are called **individual differences**.

Occasionally, research is designed with the intention of examining a specific individual difference; for example, a study may be designed to compare behavior or attitudes for males and females. (This type of research is discussed in Chapter 12.) Most of the time, however, individual differences are simply extraneous variables that are not directly addressed in the research design. For a between-subjects experimental design, individual differences are a particular concern and can create serious problems. The two major concerns are:

1. Individual differences can become confounding variables (see Chapter 6, p. 181). Suppose that a researcher finds that the participants in treatment A have higher scores than the participants in treatment B. The researcher would like to conclude that the higher scores were caused by the treatment. However, individual differences may also provide an explanation for the difference in the scores. Although you always expect individual differences between two specific participants, problems can develop if the assignment of individuals to treatment conditions produces individual differences between groups. As discussed in Chapter 6, this is a threat to internal validity and is called assignment bias (p. 181).

2. Individual differences can produce high variability in the scores, making it difficult to determine whether the treatment has any effect. The unpredictable variability caused by individual differences can obscure patterns in the data and cloud a study's results.

The problems of confounding variables and high variability are discussed in detail in the following sections. However, one more look at our two hypothetical participants, John and Mary, further illustrates the problems that individual differences can cause. Suppose John is assigned to treatment A, where he produces a score of 45, and Mary is assigned to treatment B and has a score of 51. The researcher has found a 6-point difference between the two scores. The researcher must determine what caused the difference. Notice that the difference in scores could be caused by the different treatment conditions. However, the difference could also be explained by the obvious fact that John and Mary are different people with different characteristics. You do not expect two different people to have exactly the same scores. Thus, the 6-point difference in scores could be caused by individual differences.

LEARNING CHECK In a between-subjects design, each individual score is obtained from a separate participant.
a. Briefly explain why this is an advantage.
b. Briefly explain why this is a disadvantage.

10.2 | INDIVIDUAL DIFFERENCES AS CONFOUNDING VARIABLES

In a between-subjects design, each level of the independent variable (each treatment condition) is represented by a separate group of participants. In this situation, a primary concern is to ensure that the different groups are as similar as possible except for the independent variable used to differentiate the groups. Any extraneous variable that systematically differentiates the groups is a confounding variable. For example, in a between-subjects experiment comparing two treatments (I and II), one group of participants is assigned to treatment I and a separate group to treatment II. If the participants in one group are generally older (or smarter, or taller, or faster, etc.) than the participants in the other group, then the experiment has a confounding variable.

Figure 10.2 shows an example of an experiment in which the participants' age is a confounding variable. In the Figure, the two groups of participants are differentiated by treatment (I versus II) and age (one group is older than the other). If the results from this example showed that the scores in one group were consistently higher than scores in the other group, it would be impossible to determine whether treatment or age is responsible for causing the difference between groups. Because the experiment is confounded, it is impossible to draw any clear conclusions. In Chapter 6, we identified this problem as **assignment bias** and noted that it applies exclusively to research designs comparing different groups; that is, between-subjects designs. Whenever the process of assigning participants to treatment conditions produces groups with different characteristics, the internal validity of the study is threatened.

Other Confounding Variables

In addition to the threat of assignment bias, a between-subjects design must also be concerned with threats to internal validity from environmental variables that can change systematically from one treatment to another (Chapter 6, p. 180). Thus, there are two major sources of confounding that exist in a between-subjects design.

1. *Confounding from individual differences, which is called assignment bias.* Individual differences are any participant characteristics that can differ from one participant to another. If these characteristics are different from one group to another, then the experiment is confounded

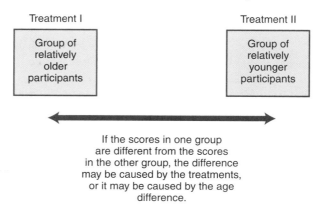

FIGURE **10.2** An Experiment in Which Individual Difference (Participant Age) Is a Confounding Variable

by assignment bias. For example, the participants in one group may be older, smarter, taller, or have higher socio-economic status than the participants in another group. One group may have a higher proportion of males or a higher proportion of divorced individuals than another group. Any of these variables may produce differences between groups that can compromise the research results.

2. *Confounding from environmental variables.* Environmental variables are any characteristics of the environment that may differ. If these variables are different between groups, then the experiment is confounded by environmental variables. For example, one group may be tested in a large room and another group in a smaller room. Or one group may be measured primarily during the morning and another group during the afternoon. Any such variable may cause differences between groups that cannot be attributed to the independent variable.

Equivalent Groups

In Chapter 9, we identified three general techniques for controlling confounding variables: randomization, matching, and holding constant. These techniques can be used to protect a study from confounding from environmental variables. With a between-subjects design, however, a researcher must also protect the study from assignment bias. Fortunately, with a between-subjects experimental design, the researcher has control over the assignment of individuals to groups. Thus, the researcher has both the opportunity and the responsibility to create groups that are equivalent. Specifically, the separate groups must be:

1. *Created equally.* The process used to obtain participants should be as similar as possible for all of the groups.
2. *Treated equally.* Except for the treatment conditions that are deliberately varied between groups, the groups of participants should receive exactly the same experiences.
3. *Composed of equivalent individuals.* The characteristics of the participants in any one group should be as similar as possible to the characteristics of the participants in every other group.

The techniques available for establishing equivalent groups of participants are discussed in the following section.

 **LEARNING CHECK** Briefly explain how a participant characteristic such as personality could be a confounding variable in a between-subjects experiment.

10.3 | LIMITING CONFOUNDING BY INDIVIDUAL DIFFERENCES

The first step in conducting a between-subjects experiment is to assign participants to different groups corresponding to the treatment conditions. If the assignment process is biased so that the groups have different characteristics, then the study is confounded from individual differences. Specifically, any difference in the scores from one group to another may be caused by assignment bias instead of the treatments. Therefore, the initial groups must be as similar as possible. To accomplish this, researchers typically use one of the following three procedures to set up groups for a between-subjects experimental study. The three procedures are the same methods that were identified for controlling potentially confounding variables in an experiment (Chapter 9).

Random Assignment (Randomization)

Probably the most common method of establishing groups of participants is random assignment. Recall from Chapter 9 that the term **random assignment** simply means that a random process (such as a coin toss) is used to assign participants to groups. The goal is to ensure that all individuals have the same chance of being assigned to a group. Because group assignment is based on a random process, it is reasonable to expect that characteristics such as age, IQ, and gender are also distributed randomly across groups. Thus, we minimize the potential for confounding because it is unlikely that any group is systematically older, or smarter, or more feminine than another.

It should be obvious that assigning participants with a simple random process such as a coin toss or drawing numbers out of a hat is likely to create groups of different sizes. If it is desirable to have all groups the same size (equal ns), the process can be modified to guarantee equal-size groups. To divide 90 participants into three equal groups, for example, the researcher could start with 90 slips of paper, 30 with #1, 30 with #2, and 30 with #3, and then draw one slip for each individual to determine the group assignment. In this case, the process is a **restricted random assignment;** the restriction is that the groups must be equal in size.

DEFINITION	In **restricted random assignment,** the group assignment process is limited to ensure predetermined characteristics (such as equal size) for the separate groups.

The advantage of using a random process to establish groups is that it is fair and unbiased. Just as football teams use a coin toss to determine who receives the opening kickoff, random assignment eliminates prejudice from the decision process. However, a random process does not guarantee a perfectly balanced outcome. When tossing a coin, for example, we can expect an equal, "50–50," distribution of heads and tails in the long run (with a large sample). However, in the short run (with a small sample), there are no guarantees. A sample of only $n = 10$ tosses, for example, can easily contain eight or nine heads and only one or two tails. With any random process, we trust chance to create a balanced outcome. In the long run, chance proves to be fair, but in the short run, anything can happen by chance. Specifically, there is always a possibility that random assignment will produce groups that have different characteristics and thus confound the experiment. Because pure chance is not a dependable process for obtaining balanced and equivalent groups, researchers often modify random processes by placing some limitations on or exerting some control over the outcomes. One such modification, restriction of equal group sizes, has been discussed; two additional techniques follow.

Briefly explain how random assignment attempts to keep participant characteristics such as age or gender from becoming confounding variables in a between-subjects experiment.

Explain why random assignment is not always successful at preventing individual differences from becoming confounding variables.

Matching Groups (Matched Assignment)

This section and Chapter 9 discuss methods of creating *matched groups;* that is, constructing groups so that, on average, one group of participants is equivalent to another group. An alternative matching process is one in which each participant in one group is matched one-to-one with an "equivalent" participant in another group. The process of matching individuals is called matching subjects (as opposed to matching groups). Technically, a *matched-subjects* design is not considered to be a between-subjects design and is discussed separately in Chapter 11.

In many situations, a researcher can identify a few specific variables that are likely to influence the participants' scores. In a learning experiment, for example, it is reasonable to expect that intelligence is a variable that can influence learning performance. In this case, it is important that the researcher not allow intelligence to become a confounding variable by permitting one group of participants to be noticeably more intelligent than another group. Instead of hoping that random assignment produces equivalent groups, a researcher can use **matching** to guarantee that the different groups of participants are equivalent (or nearly equivalent) with respect to intelligence.

For example, a researcher comparing two different methods for teaching fifth-grade math wants to be sure that the two groups of participants are roughly equivalent in terms of IQ. School records are used to determine the IQs of the participants, and each student is classified as high IQ, medium IQ, or low IQ. The high-IQ participants are distributed equally between the two groups; half is assigned to one group and the other half is assigned to the second group using restricted random assignment. The medium-IQ participants and the low-IQ participants are evenly distributed between the two groups in the same way. The result is two separate groups of participants with roughly the same level of intelligence on average.

A similar matching process can be used to equate groups in terms of proportions. If a sample consists of 60% males and 40% females, restricted random assignment could be used to distribute the males equally among the different groups. The same process is then used to distribute the females equally among the groups. The result is that the groups are matched in terms of gender, with each group containing exactly 60% males and 40% females. Notice that the matching process requires three steps.

1. Identification of the variable (or variables) to be matched across groups
2. Measurement of the matching variable for each participant
3. Assignment of participants to groups by means of a restricted random assignment that ensures a balance between groups

DEFINITION

Matching involves assigning individuals to groups so that a specific variable is balanced, or matched, across the groups. The intent is to create groups that are equivalent (or nearly equivalent) with respect to the variable matched.

Matching groups of participants provides researchers with a relatively easy way to ensure that specific variables do not become confounding variables. However, there is a price to pay for matching, and there are limitations that restrict the usefulness of this process. To match groups with respect to a specific variable, the researcher first must measure the variable. The measurement procedure can be tedious or costly, and always adds another level of work to the study. In addition, it can be difficult or impossible to match groups on several different variables simultaneously. To match groups in terms of intelligence, age, and gender could require some fairly sophisticated juggling to achieve the desired balance of all three variables. Finally, groups cannot be matched on every single variable that might differentiate participants. Therefore, researchers typically use matching only for variables that are judged to have strong potential to be confounding. In a learning experiment, for example, intelligence is a variable that is likely to affect learning performance, but eye color is a variable that probably has little to do with learning. In this case, it would make sense to match groups for intelligence but not for eye color.

Holding Variables Constant or Restricting Range of Variability

Another method of preventing individual differences from becoming confounding variables is simply to hold the variable constant. For example, if a researcher suspects that gender differences between groups might confound a research study, one solution is to eliminate gender as a variable. By using only female participants, a researcher can guarantee that all of the groups in a study are equivalent with respect to gender; all groups are all female.

An alternative to holding a variable completely constant is to restrict its range of values. For example, a researcher concerned about potential IQ differences between groups could restrict participants to those with IQs between 100 and 110. Because all groups have the same narrow range of IQs, it is reasonable to expect that all groups would be roughly equivalent in terms of IQ.

Although holding a variable constant (or restricting its range) can be an effective way to prevent the variable from confounding a research study, this method has a serious drawback. Whenever a variable is prevented from reaching its natural range of variation, the external validity of the research is limited. A research study that uses only females, for example, cannot be generalized to the entire population of males and females. Similarly, results obtained for participants within a narrow range of IQs cannot be generalized to the whole population. As we noted in Chapter 6, attempting to improve internal validity by exercising control within a research study can threaten external validity, or the ability to generalize the results.

Summary and Recommendations

Assignment bias (individual differences between groups) is always a potential confounding variable in a between-subjects design. Therefore, it is important for researchers to create groups of participants that are as equivalent as possible at the beginning of a research study. Most of the time, researchers attempt to create equivalent groups by using random assignment because it is relatively easy, and does not require any measurement or direct control of extraneous variables. The number of variables (individual differences) that could produce differences between groups is essentially infinite, and random assignment provides a simple method of balancing them across groups without addressing each individual variable. However, random assignment is not perfect and cannot guarantee equivalent groups, especially when a small sample is used. Pure chance is not a dependable process for obtaining balanced equivalent groups.

When one or two specific variables can be identified as likely to influence the dependent variable, these variables can be controlled either by matching groups or by holding the variable constant. However, matching requires pretesting to measure the variable(s) being controlled, and it can become difficult to match several variables simultaneously. Holding a variable constant guarantees that the variable cannot confound the research, but this process limits the external validity of the research results.

LEARNING CHECK   Briefly explain how holding a variable constant attempts to keep individual differences from becoming confounding variables in a between-subjects experiment.

10.4 | INDIVIDUAL DIFFERENCES AND VARIABILITY

In addition to becoming confounding variables, individual differences have the potential to produce high variability in the scores within a research study. As we noted earlier, high variability can obscure any treatment effects that may exist and therefore can undermine the likelihood of a successful study. In general, the goal of most research studies is to demonstrate a difference between two or more treatment conditions. For example, a study may be designed to show that one therapy technique is more effective than another. To accomplish this goal, it is essential that the scores obtained in one condition are noticeably different (higher or lower) than the scores in a second condition. Usually, the difference between treatments is described by computing the average score for each treatment, then comparing the two averages. However, simply comparing two averages is not enough to demonstrate a noticeable difference. The problem comes from the fact that in some situations, a 10-point difference is large, but in other circumstances, a 10-point difference is small. The absolute size of the difference must be evaluated in relation to the *variance* of the scores. Variance is a statistical value that measures the size of the differences from one score to another (see Chapter 14, p. 403). If the scores all have similar values, then the variance is small; if there are big differences from one score to the next, then variance is large. The following example demonstrates how individual differences influence variance, and how variance can influence the interpretation of research results.

We begin with two distinct populations, one in which the individual differences are relatively small and one in which the individual differences are large. The two populations are shown in Table 10.1. In the table, each number represents the score for a single individual. Notice that in population A, the numbers are all very similar, indicating that the individual differences (the differences from one person to another) are relatively small and the variance is

TABLE **10.1**
Two Simulated Populations

In population A the individual differences are relatively small, and in population B the individual differences are relatively large.

Population A					Population B				
42	39	41	39	39	32	48	28	24	20
41	40	41	41	40	24	32	56	60	44
40	38	38	40	40	44	20	40	52	40
42	39	40	41	40	44	36	36	48	60
40	42	40	38	39	36	56	56	52	28
38	41	40	39	38	56	32	60	24	28
38	42	41	42	39	36	52	48	40	20
41	38	42	39	40	48	28	20	60	40
40	39	41	40	40	40	44	32	24	48
41	40	40	42	39	40	32	36	44	52

small. In population B, the differences among the numbers are large, indicating large individual differences and large variance. We then conduct the following hypothetical research study, first with population A and then with population B.

1. We select a random sample of 20 individuals (numbers) from the population and randomly divide the sample into two groups with 10 in each group.
2. One group is then assigned to a control condition that has no effect whatsoever on the participants' scores. The second group is assigned to a treatment that increases each participant's score by 10 points. To simulate this treatment effect, we simply add 10 points to the original score for each individual.

For population A, the results of this hypothetical research study are shown as a table and as a graph in Figure 10.3. From either the numbers in the table or the piles of scores in the graph, it is easy to see the 10-point difference between the two conditions. Remember, in population A, the individual differences are small, which means that the variance of the scores is small. With small variance, the 10-point difference between treatments shows up clearly.

Next, we repeat the study using participants (numbers) selected from population B. The results of this simulation are shown in Figure 10.4. This time, it is very difficult to see any difference between the two conditions. With the large individual differences in population B, the variance is large and the 10-point treatment effect is completely obscured. Although Figures 10.3 and 10.4 illustrate the effects of increasing (or decreasing) variance, you should realize that variance also has a dramatic influence on the statistical

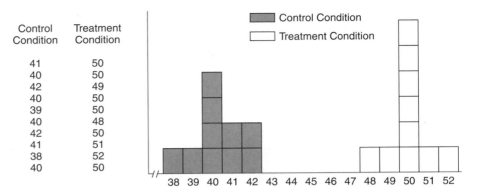

Control Condition	Treatment Condition
41	50
40	50
42	49
40	50
39	50
40	48
42	50
41	51
38	52
40	50

FIGURE **10.3** Results from a Simulated Experiment Comparing Two Conditions Using Participants Selected from a Population in Which Individual Differences Are Relatively Small

When the individual differences are small, the variance is also small, and it is easy to see the 10-point treatment effect.

interpretation of the results. Specifically, the difference between treatments in Figure 10.3 is statistically significant but the difference in Figure 10.4 is not significant.

It may be helpful to think of the variance within each group as analogous to interference for a cell phone or radio signal. When there is a lot of interference, it is difficult to get a clear signal. Similarly, when a research study has a lot of variance, it is difficult to see a real treatment effect. In between-subjects research, much of the variance is caused by individual differences. Remember,

The term *significant* means that it is very unlikely that the difference would occur if there was not a consistent difference between the treatment conditions (see Box 9.1, p. 250).

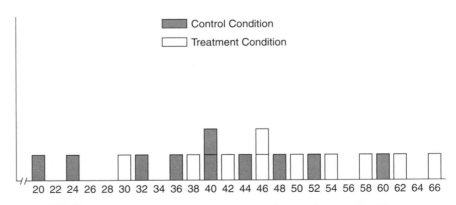

Control Condition	Treatment Condition
40	46
36	58
52	66
44	38
48	62
40	46
60	30
24	42
32	50
20	54

FIGURE **10.4** Results from a Simulated Experiment Comparing Two Conditions Using Participants Selected from a Population in Which Individual Differences Are Relatively Large

When the individual differences are large, the variance is also large, and it is not at all easy to see the 10-point treatment effect.

each individual score represents a different individual. Whenever there are large differences between individuals, there is large variance.

Differences Between Treatments and Variance Within Treatments

In general, the goal of a between-subjects research study is to establish the existence of a treatment effect by demonstrating that the scores obtained in one treatment condition are significantly different (higher or lower) than the scores in another treatment condition. For example, if we can demonstrate that people in a bright yellow room are consistently happier and have more positive moods than people in a dark brown room, then we have reason to conclude that room color (the treatment) has an effect on mood. Thus, big differences *between* treatments are good because they provide evidence of differential treatment effects. On the other hand, big differences *within* treatments are bad. Differences that exist inside the treatment conditions determine the variance of the scores, and, as we demonstrated in Figure 10.4, large variance can obscure patterns in the data.

Notice that we are distinguishing differences *between treatments* and variance (differences) *within treatments*. Researchers typically try to increase the differences between treatments and to decrease the variance within treatments. For example, if we were examining the effects of room color on mood, it would not be wise to compare two rooms that were slightly different shades of green. With only a subtle difference between the two colors, we would be unlikely to find a noticeable difference in mood. Instead, the best strategy would be to maximize the difference between room colors to increase our chances of finding a large difference in mood between treatments. Again, the goal is to increase the difference between treatments. At the same time, however, we would like to decrease the **variance within treatments.** Because a between-subjects design has a separate group of participants for each treatment condition, the variance within treatments is also the **variance within groups.** In the following section, we examine some of the methods that can be used to reduce or minimize the variance within treatments. In addition, we consider some of the design decisions that a researcher must make when developing a between-subjects research study, and look at how those decisions affect variance within treatments.

Minimizing Variance Within Treatments

As we have noted, large individual differences can lead to large variance within treatments, which can undermine the potential success of a between-subjects research study. Therefore, researchers are well-advised to take whatever steps are possible to reduce the variance inside each of the treatment conditions. The following options provide some ways to accomplish this.

Standardize Procedures and Treatment Setting

In a between-subjects design, each group of participants represents a single treatment condition. One obvious way to help minimize the variability within each group is to be sure that all participants within a group are treated exactly the same. Although existing individual differences are not reduced, at least care is taken not to increase them. Thus, researchers should avoid making any changes in the treatment setting or the procedures that are used from one individual to another. Whenever two individuals are treated differently, there is a chance that differences between their scores will be increased, thus increasing the variance within the group. In general, if two participants are in the same group (the same treatment condition), a researcher should not do anything that might cause their scores to be different. Standardizing procedures also makes it easier for other researchers to understand exactly how your study was done and makes it possible for them to replicate your study in their own research facility.

Limit Individual Differences

In Section 10.3, we suggested that holding a participant variable constant or restricting its range could be used as effective techniques for limiting the differences between groups of participants (see p. 289). This technique also reduces the variance within a group of participants. If it is known, for example, that gender is a variable related to the participants' scores (for example, females tend to have higher scores than males), then a mixed group of males and females will have higher variance than a group consisting of only males. In the mixed group, the gender differences (male versus female) will contribute to the variance within the group. By holding gender constant (males only), gender differences are eliminated and the variance within the group is reduced.

In the same way, restricting a participant variable to a narrow range of values creates a more homogeneous group and, therefore, can reduce the variability in the scores. For example, if the participants within a group are limited to those between the ages of 18 and 20, then age differences between participants contribute little to the variance of scores within the group. In general, any attempt to minimize the differences between participants within a group tends to reduce the variance within the group.

Random Assignment and Matching

In Section 10.3, we also suggested that random assignment or matching groups could be used to help minimize differences between groups. However, these techniques have no effect on the variance within groups. If we randomly assign males and females to each group, for example, then we can expect relatively little gender difference between groups, but we still have a mixture of males and females (gender differences) within groups. In the same way, matching groups so that each group has exactly 50% males does not eliminate or reduce the gender differences within each group.

Sample Size

Although sample size does not affect individual differences or variance directly, using a large sample can help minimize the problems associated with high variance. Sample size exerts its influence in the statistical analyses such that some of the negative effects of high variance can be statistically overcome by use of a very large sample. However, this technique has limitations because the influence of sample size occurs in relation to the *square root* of the sample size. The square-root relationship means that it takes a dramatic increase in sample size to have a real effect. To reduce the effects of high variance by a factor of four, for example, the sample size must be increased by a factor of 16; a sample of 20 would need to be increased to a sample of 320. Usually, it is much more efficient to control variance by either standardizing procedures or directly limiting individual differences.

Summary and Recommendations

The best techniques for minimizing the negative consequences of high variance are to standardize treatments and to minimize individual differences between participants. Both of these techniques help eliminate factors that can cause differences between scores and therefore can reduce the variance within treatments. The technique of minimizing individual differences by holding a variable constant or restricting its range has two advantages:

1. It helps create equivalent groups, which reduces the threat of confounding variables.
2. It helps reduce the variance within groups, which makes treatment effects easier to see.

As we noted earlier, however, limiting individual differences has the serious disadvantage of limiting external validity. (An alternative method for reducing individual differences without threatening external validity is presented in Chapter 13, wherein we introduce factorial research designs.)

 **LEARNING CHECK**   Briefly explain why large variance within treatments is a problem in a between-subjects experiment.

10.5 | OTHER THREATS TO INTERNAL VALIDITY OF BETWEEN-SUBJECTS DESIGNS

Remember that the goal of the between-subjects experimental design is to look for differences between groups on the dependent variable, and to demonstrate that the observed differences are caused by the different treatments (that is, by the manipulation of the independent variable). If the differences between the groups can be attributed to any factor other than the treatments, the research is confounded and the results cannot be interpreted without some ambiguity. Also recall from Chapter 6 that any factor that allows for an alternative explanation for the research results is a threat to internal validity. Earlier in this chapter, we discussed the two major threats that can undermine the internal validity of a between-subjects study: assignment bias and confounding from environmental variables. Now, we consider additional potential confounds that are specifically related to between-subjects designs.

Differential Attrition

The term *attrition* refers to participant withdrawal from a research study before it is completed. As long as the rate of attrition is fairly consistent from one group to another, it usually is not a threat to internal validity. However, big differences in attrition rates between groups can create problems. The different groups are initially created to be as similar as possible; if large numbers of individuals leave one group, the group may no longer be similar to the others. Again, whenever the groups of participants are noticeably different, the research is confounded. **Differential attrition** refers to differences in attrition rates from one group to another and can threaten the internal validity of a between-subjects experiment.

For example, a researcher may want to test the effectiveness of a dieting program. Using a between-subjects design, the researcher forms two groups of participants with approximately equal characteristics (weight, gender, dieting history). Next, one group of participants begins the 10-week dieting program and the other group receives no treatment (this group, recall from Chapter 9, is the no-treatment control group). At the end of the 10 weeks, the weights of the two groups are compared. During the course of the 10 weeks, however, it is likely that some participants will drop out of the study. If more participants drop out of one group than the other, there is a risk that the two groups will no longer be similar. For example, some of the individuals in the dieting program may decide that it is too demanding and withdraw from the study. As a result, only the most motivated participants stay in the diet program. Although the study started with two equivalent groups, the individuals who are left in the program at the end have a higher level of motivation than those in the control group. In this case, the difference in dropout rate between the groups could account for the obtained differences in mean weight. Differential attrition is a threat to internal validity because we do not know whether the obtained differences between treatment conditions are caused by the treatments or by differential attrition. Whenever participants drop out of a study, a researcher must be concerned about differential attrition as an alternative explanation for treatment effects.

Communication Between Groups

Whenever the participants in one treatment condition are allowed to talk with the participants in another condition, there is the potential for a variety of problems to develop. For example, a researcher may want to test the effectiveness of a new treatment for depression. Using a between-subjects design, the researcher randomly assigns half the clients of an inpatient facility to receive the new treatment and half to receive the standard treatment for depression. If the participants talk to each other, however, then those individuals receiving the old treatment may learn about the new treatment and may begin to use some elements from the new treatment. **Diffusion** refers to the spread of the treatment effects from the experimental group to the control group, which tends to reduce the difference between the two conditions. This is a threat to the internal validity of a between-subjects design because the true effects of the treatment can be masked by the shared information (that is, it appears that there is no difference between the groups because both groups are actually getting much of the same treatment).

Another risk is that an untreated group learns about the treatment being received by the other group, and demands the same or equal treatment. This is referred to as **compensatory equalization.** For example, in a study examining the effects of violent television viewing on boys in a residential facility, one team of researchers faced this problem. The boys in the nonviolent television group learned that those in the violent television group were allowed to watch the television series *Batman* and demanded the right to watch it, too (Feshbach & Singer, 1971). This threat commonly occurs in medical and clinical studies when one group receives a treatment drug and another does not. A similar problem arises when researchers try to assess the effectiveness of large-scale educational enrichment programs (involving such improvements as computers in the classrooms). Parents and teachers of the classes or schools that do not receive the enrichment (the control group) hear about the special program other classes or schools (the experimental group) receive, and demand that their children receive the same program or something equal in value. If the demand is met, the research study no longer has a no-treatment condition for comparison. Again, this is a threat to the internal validity of a between-subjects design because it can wipe out the true effects of the treatment (that is, make it look like there are no differences between the groups on the dependent variable).

Finally, problems can occur when participants in an untreated group change their normal behavior when they learn about a special treatment that is given to another group. One possibility is that the untreated groups works extra hard to show that they can perform just as well as the individuals receiving the special treatment. This is referred to as **compensatory rivalry.** In this case, the performance observed by the researcher is much higher that would normally occur. It is also possible that the participants in an untreated group simply give up when they learn that another group is receiving special treatment. This is referred to as **resentful demoralization.** In this case, the untreated group becomes less productive and less motivated because they resent the expected superiority of the treated group. As a result, the effect of the treatment appears to be much greater that it really is.

In each case, internal validity is threatened because the observed difference between groups can be explained by factors other than the effects of the treatment. The best way to minimize each of these threats to internal validity resulting from communication between the groups is to separate the groups of participants as much as possible and keep them from being aware of one another. Notice that these problems are exclusive to between-subjects experimental designs in which different groups of participants are used to compare different treatment conditions.

LEARNING CHECK   Describe some of the problems that can arise when the participants in one treatment condition of a between-subjects experiment are allowed to communicate with participants in a different condition.

10.6 | APPLICATIONS AND STATISTICAL ANALYSES OF BETWEEN-SUBJECTS DESIGNS

Two-Group Mean Difference

The simplest version of a between-subjects experimental design involves comparing only two groups of participants: the researcher manipulates one independent variable with only two levels. This design is often referred to as the single-factor two-group design or simply the two-group design. This type of design can be used to compare treatments, or to evaluate the effect of one treatment by comparing a treatment group and a control group. When the measurements consist of numerical scores, typically, a mean is computed for each group of participants, and then an independent-measures t test is used to determine whether there is a significant difference between the means (see Chapter 14).

The primary advantage of a two-group design is its simplicity. It is easy to set up a two-group study, and there is no subtlety or complexity when interpreting the results; either the two groups are different or they are not. In addition, a two-group design provides the best opportunity to maximize the difference between the two treatment conditions; that is, you may select opposite extreme values for the independent variable. For example, in a study comparing two types of therapy, the two therapies can be structured to maximize or even exaggerate the differences between them. Or, in a research study comparing a treatment and a no-treatment control, the treatment group can be given the full-strength version of the treatment. This technique increases the likelihood of obtaining noticeably different scores from the two groups, thereby demonstrating a significant mean difference.

The primary disadvantage of a two-group design is that it provides relatively little information. With only two groups, a researcher obtains only two real data points for comparison. Although two data points are sufficient to establish a difference, they often are not sufficient to provide a complete or detailed picture of the full relationship between an independent and a dependent variable. Figure 10.5 shows a hypothetical relationship between dosage levels for a drug (independent variable) and activity (dependent variable). Notice that the complete set of five data points, representing five different drug doses, gives a good picture of how drug dosage affects behavior. Now, consider the limited data that would be available if the researcher had used only two different drug doses. If, for example, the researcher had used only a 0-dose and

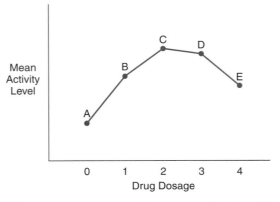

FIGURE **10.5** Hypothetical Data Showing a Relationship Between Activity Level and Drug Dosage for Five Different Levels of Drug Dosage

a 1-dose group (points A and B in the figure), the data would seem to indicate that increasing the drug dose produces an increase in activity. However, a researcher comparing a 2-dose versus a 4-dose group (points C and E) would reach exactly the opposite conclusion. Although both of the two-group studies are accurate, neither provides a complete picture. In general, several groups (more than two) are necessary to obtain a good indication of the functional relationship between an independent and a dependent variable.

A two-group study also limits the options when a researcher wishes to compare a treatment group and a control group. Often, it is necessary to use several control groups to obtain a complete picture of a treatment's effectiveness. As we noted in Chapter 9, two common controls that often are used together are a no-treatment control and a placebo control. With these two control groups, researchers can separate the real treatment effects from the placebo effects that occur simply because participants think that they are receiving treatment. However, as we noted in Chapter 3 (p. 80), there is some ethical concern regarding the use of no-treatment or placebo groups in clinical research. Rather than denying treatment to some participants, it is suggested that an established, standard therapy be used for the control comparison (LaVaque & Rossiter, 2001).

LEARNING CHECK   Describe the advantages of a two-group design compared to an experiment with more than two groups.

Comparing Means for More Than Two Groups

As noted in the previous section, research questions often require more than two groups to evaluate the functional relation between an independent and a dependent variable, or to include several different control groups in a single study. In these cases, a **single-factor multiple-group design** may be used. For example, a researcher may want to compare driving performance under three telephone conditions: while talking on a cell phone, while texting on a cell phone, and without using a phone. Another researcher may want to examine five different dosages of a drug to evaluate the relation between dosage and activity level for laboratory rats. In the first example, the independent variable is the telephone condition with three levels compared. In the second example, the researcher compares five levels of drug dosage. For either study, the mean is computed for each group of participants, and a single-factor analysis of variance (ANOVA) (independent measures) is used to determine whether there are any significant differences among the means (see Chapter 14). When the ANOVA concludes that significant differences exist, some form of post hoc test or posttest is used to determine exactly which groups are significantly different from each other.

In addition to revealing the full functional relationship between variables, a multiple-group design also provides stronger evidence for a real cause-and-effect relationship than can be obtained from a two-group design. With a multiple-group design, the researcher changes the treatment conditions (independent variable) several times across several groups, demonstrating differences in performance for each different treatment condition. By contrast, a two-group design changes the treatment condition only once and observes only one difference in performance.

A Word of Caution About Multiple-Group Designs

Although a research study with more than two groups can give a clear and convincing picture of the relationship between an independent and a dependent variable, it is possible to have too many groups in a research design. One advantage of a simple, two-group design is that it allows the researcher to maximize the difference between treatments by selecting opposite extremes for the independent variable. The mirror image of this argument is that a design with more than two groups tends to reduce or minimize the difference between treatments. At the extreme, there is a risk of reducing the differences between treatments so much that the differences are no longer significant. Therefore, when designing a single-factor multiple-group research study, be sure that the levels used for the independent variable are sufficiently different to allow for substantial differences for the dependent variable.

LEARNING CHECK   Identify the advantages of using multiple groups in a between-subjects experiment.

Comparing Proportions for Two or More Groups

Often, the dependent variable in a research study is measured on a nominal or ordinal scale. In this case, the researcher does not have a numerical score for each participant, and cannot calculate and compare averages for the different groups. Instead, each individual is simply classified into a category, and the data consist of a simple frequency count of the participants in each category on the scale of measurement. Examples of nominal scale measurements are:

- gender (male, female)
- academic major for college students
- occupation

Examples of ordinal scale measurements are:

- college class (freshman, sophomore, and so on)
- birth order (first born, second born)
- high, medium, or low performance on a task

Because you cannot compute means for these variables, you cannot use an independent-measures t test or an ANOVA (F test) to compare means between groups. However, it is possible to compare proportions between groups using a chi-square test for independence (see Chapter 14, p. 438). As with other between-subjects experiments, the different groups of participants represent different treatment conditions (manipulated by the researcher). For example, Loftus and Palmer (1974) conducted a classic experiment demonstrating how language can influence eyewitness memory. A sample of 150 students watched a film of an automobile accident and were then questioned about what they saw. One group was asked, "About how fast were the cars going when they smashed into each other?" Another group received the same question except that the verb was changed to "hit" instead of "smashed into." A third group served as a control and was not asked any question about the speed of the two cars. A week later, the participants returned and were asked a number of questions about the accident, including whether they remembered seeing any broken glass in the accident. (There was no broken glass in the film.) Notice that the researchers are manipulating the form of the initial question and then measuring a yes/no response to a follow-up question 1 week later. Figure 10.6 shows the structure of this design represented by a matrix with the independent variable (different groups) determining the rows of the matrix and the two categories for the dependent variable (yes/no) determining the columns. The number in each cell of the matrix is the frequency count showing how many participants are classified in that category. For example, of the 50 students who heard the word *smashed*, there were 16 (32%) who claimed to remember seeing broken glass even though there was none in the film. By comparison, only 7 out of 50 (14%) of the students who heard the word *hit* claimed to have seen broken glass. The chi-square test compares the proportions across one row of the matrix (one group of participants) with the proportions across other rows. A significant outcome means that the proportions in one row are different from the proportions in another row, and the difference is more than would be expected if there was not a systematic treatment effect. Loftus and Palmer found that participants who had been asked a leading question about the cars smashing into each other were significantly more likely to recall broken glass than participants who were not asked a leading question.

	Response to the Question Did You See Any Broken Glass?	
	Yes	No
Smashed into	16	34
Hit	7	43
Control (Not Asked)	6	44

Verb Used to Ask About the Speed of the Cars

FIGURE **10.6** Results from an Experiment Comparing Three Different Questions Asked of Witnesses About the Speed of Cars They Observed in a Collision (Loftus & Palmer, 1974)

The dependent variable is the participants' response to a question about whether they recall seeing any broken glass. Note that the dependent variable is not a numerical score so you cannot compute a mean score for each treatment condition.

■ CHAPTER SUMMARY

In this chapter, we examined the characteristics of the between-subjects experimental research design. The general goal of a between-subjects experiment is to determine whether differences exist between two or more treatment conditions. The defining characteristic of a between-subjects design is that different but equivalent groups of individuals are compared.

The primary advantage of a between-subjects design is the fact that each individual score is independent of the other scores because each participant is measured only once. The primary disadvantage of a between-subjects design is individual differences. In between-subjects designs, individual differences can become confounding variables and produce high variance.

The potential confounding influence of individual differences is a particular problem for between-subjects designs. Because a between-subjects design compares different groups of individuals, there is always the possibility of assignment bias; that is, the characteristics of one group can be substantially different from the characteristics of another group. Techniques for establishing equivalent groups of participants include random assignment, matched assignment, and holding variables constant. Individual differences also have the potential to produce high variance in the scores within each group or treatment condition. High variance within groups can obscure any treatment effects that may exist. Several methods that can be used to minimize the variance (differences) within treatments are discussed.

In addition to individual differences, there are other threats to the internal validity of between-subjects designs. Each of these potential confounds is also discussed in this chapter. Finally, different applications of the between-subjects design are considered along with the appropriate statistical analysis.

KEY WORDS

between-subjects experimental design, or independent-measures experimental design	individual differences restricted random assignment	matching

EXERCISES

1. In addition to the key words, you should also be able to define the following terms:
   within-subjects design
   between-subjects design
   independent-measures design
   assignment bias
   random assignment
   variance within treatments, or variance within groups

   differential attrition
   diffusion
   compensatory equalization
   compensatory rivalry
   resentful demoralization
   single-factor two-group design, or two-group design
   single-factor multiple-group design

2. Describe the advantages of the between-subjects design.
3. Describe the disadvantages of the between-subjects design.
4. How can individual differences create problems in a between-subjects design?
5. Describe the fundamental difference between a within-subjects design and a between-subjects design for an experiment comparing three treatment conditions.
6. Explain how the process of matching attempts to keep participant characteristics from becoming confounding variables in a between-subjects design.
7. Why is it so important in between-subjects designs to keep the different groups of participants as similar as possible?
8. Describe how each of the following factors threatens the internal validity of between-subjects designs: compensatory equalization, compensatory rivalry, and resentful demoralization.
9. Describe the advantages and disadvantages of the single-factor multiple-group design in comparison to a design with only two groups.
10. Describe how external validity can be limited when a researcher holds participant variables constant to prevent them from becoming confounding variables in a between-subjects experiment.
11. Describe the advantages and disadvantages of the single-factor two-group design in comparison to a design with more than two groups.
12. What steps can a researcher take to limit the variability within treatments?

LEARNING ACTIVITIES

1. A recent survey at a major corporation found that employees who regularly participated in the company fitness program tended to have fewer sick days than employees who did not participate. However, because the study was not a true experiment, you cannot conclude that regular exercise causes employees to have fewer sick days.
   a. Identify another factor (a confounding variable) that might explain why some employees participated in the fitness program and why those same employees have fewer sick days.
   b. Describe the design for a between-subjects experiment that would determine whether participation in the exercise program *caused* fewer sick days.
   c. Describe how the factor you identified in Part a is controlled in your experiment.
2. A researcher has a sample of 30 rats that are all cloned from the same source. The 30 rats are genetically identical and have been raised in exactly the same environment since birth. The researcher conducts an experiment, randomly assigning 10 of the clones to Treatment A, 10 to Treatment B, and the other 10 to Treatment C. Explain why the clone experiment is better than a between-subjects study using 30 regular rats that are randomly assigned to the three treatments. In other words, explain how the clone experiment eliminates the basic problems with a between-subjects study.

WEB RESOURCES

Visit the Book Companion Website at **www .cengage.com/international** to access study tools including a glossary, flashcards, and web quizzing. You will also find a link to Statistics and Research Methods Workshops. For this chapter, we suggest you look at the following workshop:

Between Versus Within Designs

11

The Within-Subjects Experimental Design

CHAPTER OVERVIEW

Step 6 of the research process involves selecting a research design. In this chapter, we discuss in detail another type of experimental research design: the within-subjects design. The advantages, disadvantages, and different versions of within-subjects designs are considered.

11.1 | INTRODUCTION TO WITHIN-SUBJECTS EXPERIMENTS

Characteristics of Within-Subjects Designs

In the preceding chapter, we described the basic elements of the between-subjects experimental research design. Recall that the defining characteristic of a between-subjects experiment is that it requires separate but equivalent groups of participants for the different treatment conditions compared. In this chapter, we introduce an alternative research procedure: the **within-subjects design.** The defining characteristic of a within-subjects design is that it uses a single group of participants, and tests or observes each individual in all of the different treatments being compared. Thus, in a within-subjects study, the sample is not separated into several groups but rather exists as a single group that participates in every treatment condition. Using the terminology of experimental research, in a within-subjects experimental design the same group of individuals participates in every level of the independent variable so that each participant experiences all of the different levels of the independent variable.

In one sense, a within-subjects study is the ultimate in equivalent groups because the group in one treatment condition is absolutely identical to the group in every other condition. In the context of statistical analysis, a within-subjects design is often called a **repeated-measures design** because the research study repeats measurements of the same individuals under different conditions (Figure 11.1).

In this chapter, we examine the **within-subjects experimental design;** that is, the within-subjects design as it is used in *experimental* research comparing different treatment conditions. However, the within-subjects design is also well suited to other, nonexperimental types of research that investigate changes occurring over time. For example, studies in human development often observe a single group of individuals at different ages to monitor development over time. Examples of nonexperimental within-subjects designs are examined in Chapter 12.

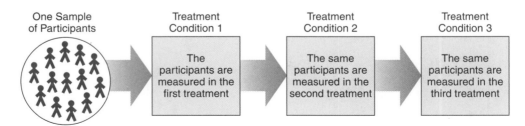

FIGURE **11.1** The Structure of a Within-Subjects Design

The same group of individuals participates in all of the treatment conditions. Because each participant is measured in each treatment, this design is sometimes called a repeated-measures design. Note: All participants go through the entire series of treatments but not necessarily in the same order.

DEFINITION

A **within-subjects experimental design,** also known as a **repeated-measures experimental design,** compares two or more different treatment conditions (or compares a treatment and a control) by observing or measuring the same group of individuals in all of the treatment conditions being compared. Thus, a within-subjects design looks for differences between treatment conditions within the same group of participants. To qualify as an experiment, the design must satisfy all other requirements of the experimental research strategy, such as manipulation of an independent variable and control of extraneous variables.

 **LEARNING CHECK**

Identify the basic features of a within-subjects research design.

Advantages of Within-Subjects Designs

One advantage of a within-subjects design is that it requires relatively few participants in comparison to between-subjects designs. For example, to compare three different treatment conditions with 30 participants in each treatment, a between-subjects design requires a total of 90 participants (three separate groups with 30 participants in each). A within-subjects design, however, requires only 30 participants (the same group of 30 participants is used in all three conditions). Because a within-subjects study requires only one group, it is particularly useful in situations in which participants are difficult to find. For example, it might be difficult to recruit a large sample of people for a study examining twins who are at least 80 years old.

The primary advantage of a within-subjects design, however, is that it essentially eliminates all of the problems based on individual differences that are the primary concern of a between-subjects design. Recall from Chapter 8 that in a between-subjects design, individual differences can create two major problems for research:

1. Individual differences between groups can become a confounding variable. If the individuals in one treatment condition are noticeably different from the individuals in another treatment (for example, smarter, faster, bigger, or older), the individual differences, rather than the treatments, may explain any observed differences.
2. The individual differences within each treatment condition can create high variance, which can obscure any differences between treatments.

These problems are reduced or eliminated in a within-subjects design. First, obviously, a within-subjects design has no individual differences between groups because there is only one group of participants. The group in one treatment is exactly the same as the group in every other treatment, which means that there are no individual differences between groups to confound the study. Second, because each participant appears in every treatment condition, each individual serves as his own control or baseline. This makes it possible to measure and remove the variance caused by individual differences. The following example demonstrates how the problems associated with individual differences are reduced in a within-subjects design.

Table 11.1 shows two sets of hypothetical data. The first set is from a typical between-subjects experiment and the second set represents a within-subjects experiment. Each score is labeled with the participant's name so that we can examine the effects of individual differences. For the between-subjects data, every score represents a different person. For the within-subjects data, on the other hand, the same people are measured in all three treatment conditions. The difference between the two designs has some important consequences:

1. Both research studies have exactly the same scores and both show the same differences between treatments. In each case, the researcher would like to conclude that the differences between treatments were caused by the treatments. However, with the between-subjects design (see Table 11.1a), the participants in treatment I may have characteristics that make them different from the participants in treatment II. For example, the four individuals in treatment II may be more intelligent than the participants in treatment I, and their higher intelligence may have caused their higher scores. This problem disappears in the within-subjects design (see Table 11.1b); the participants in one treatment

TABLE **11.1**
Hypothetical Data Showing the Results from a Between-Subjects Experiment and a Within-Subjects Experiment.

The two sets of data use exactly the same numerical scores.

(a) Between-Subjects Experiment—Three Separate Groups

Treatment I		Treatment II		Treatment III	
(John)	20	(Sue)	25	(Beth)	30
(Mary)	31	(Tom)	36	(Bob)	38
(Bill)	51	(Dave)	55	(Don)	59
(Kate)	62	(Ann)	64	(Zoe)	69
Mean =	41	Mean =	45	Mean =	49

(b) Within-Subjects Experiment—One Group in all Three Treatments

Treatment I		Treatment II		Treatment III	
(John)	20	(John)	25	(John)	30
(Mary)	31	(Mary)	36	(Mary)	38
(Bill)	51	(Bill)	55	(Bill)	59
(Kate)	62	(Kate)	64	(Kate)	69
Mean =	41	Mean =	45	Mean =	49

cannot differ from the participants in another treatment because the same individuals are used in all the treatments.

2. Although the two sets of data contain exactly the same scores, they differ greatly in the way that the individual differences contribute to the variance. For the between-subjects experiment, the individual differences and the treatment effects are tied together and cannot be separated. To measure the difference between treatments, we must also measure the differences between individuals. For example, John scored 5 points lower than Sue, but it is impossible to determine whether this 5-point difference is caused by the treatments or is simply a matter of individual differences (John is different from Sue). Individual differences are an integral part of a between-subjects design, and they are automatically a part of the variance in the scores. For the within-subjects data, however, the treatment effects are not connected to the individual differences. To evaluate the difference between treatments I and II, for example, we never compare John to Mary. Instead we compare John (in treatment I) to John (in treatment II), and we compare Mary (in treatment I) to Mary (in treatment II). Because the treatment effects and individual differences are not connected, we can separate the individual differences from the rest of the variance in a within-subjects design.

Once again, consider the within-subjects experiment (see Table 11.1b). Although individual differences are part of the variance in the data (for example, John's scores are different from Mary's scores), we can determine how much of the variance is caused by the individual differences. For these data, for example, there is a consistent difference of about 10 points between John and Mary in each of the three treatments. Similarly, there is a 30-point difference between John and Bill, and a 40-point difference between John and Kate. Whenever the individual differences are reasonably consistent across treatment conditions, they can be measured and separated from the rest of the variance. Thus, in a within-subjects design:

> It is possible to measure the differences between treatments without involving any individual differences. Because the same participants are in every treatment condition, the treatment effects and the individual differences are not linked.

> It is possible to measure the differences between individuals. When the individual differences are consistent across treatments, they can be measured and removed from the rest of the variance in the data. This can greatly reduce the negative effects of large variance.

To demonstrate the actual process of separating the individual differences from the rest of the variance, consider once again the within-subjects data in Table 11.1b. For these data, Kate consistently has the highest score in each treatment. Specifically, the average score for the four participants across all three treatments is 45, however the average score for Kate is 65. This is an example of an individual difference; clearly, Kate is different from the other participants. However, we can eliminate this difference by simply subtracting 20 points from each of Kate's scores. As a result, Kate becomes a more "normal" participant.

Similarly, John's average score is 20 points lower than the group average, so we can make John "normal" by adding 20 points to each of his scores. Finally, we subtract 10 points from each of Bill's scores and then add 10 points to each of Mary's scores. The resulting data are shown in Table 11.2. Notice that we have removed the individual differences by making the four individuals equal (all four participants now have an average score of 45) but we have not changed any of the treatment effects. For example, John's score still increases by 5 points as he goes from treatment I to treatment II, and increases another 5 points as he goes from treatment II to treatment III. Also, all of the treatment means are exactly the same as they were before we started adding and subtracting. Thus, the newly created scores preserve all of the important characteristics of the original scores. That is, the changes (treatment effects) that occur for the participants, individually and collectively, are the same as in the original data. However the big differences from one participant to another in Table 11.1b are now gone, and the resulting scores show only a 1- or 2-point difference between individuals. Removing the individual differences drastically reduces the variance of the scores and makes the 4-point mean differences from treatment to treatment much easier to see. Figure 11.2 shows the original within-subjects data from Table 11.1b and the adjusted data from Table 11.2. When the individual differences are removed, the treatment effects are much easier to see.

By measuring and removing individual differences, the within-subjects design reduces variance and reveals treatment effects that might not be apparent in a between-subjects design. In statistical terms, a within-subjects design is generally more powerful than a between-subjects design; that is, a

TABLE **11.2**
Removing Individual Differences from Within-Subjects Data

This table shows the same data from Table 11.1b, except that we have eliminated the individual differences from the data. For example, we subtracted 20 points from each of Kate's scores to make her more "average," and we added 20 points to each of John's scores to make him more "average." This process of eliminating individual differences makes the treatment effects much easier to see.

Treatment I		Treatment II		Treatment III	
(John)	40	(John)	45	(John)	50
(Mary)	41	(Mary)	46	(Mary)	48
(Bill)	41	(Bill)	45	(Bill)	49
(Kate)	42	(Kate)	44	(Kate)	49
Mean =	41	Mean =	45	Mean =	49

(a) Data Including Individual Differences (From Table 11.1)

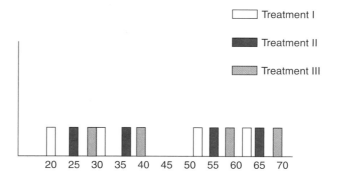

(b) Data with Individual Differences Removed (From Table 11.2)

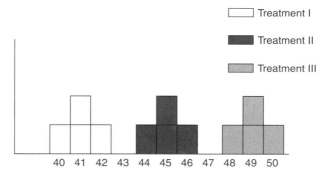

FIGURE **11.2** Removing Individual Differences from Within-Subjects Data

(a)   The original data, which include the individual differences among the four participants.

(b)   The individual differences have been removed by adjusting each participant's scores. When the individual differences are removed, it is much easier to see the differences between treatments.

within-subjects design is more likely to detect a treatment effect than a between-subjects design.

In the preceding example, we removed the individual differences by equalizing all the participants. In a normal research situation, this equalizing process is accomplished by statistical analysis (instead of manipulation of the data). However, the result is the same: The variance caused by individual differences is removed. The statistical removal of individual differences is demonstrated in Box 11.1. Finally, we should note that you cannot use this equalizing process to remove the individual differences from the data in a between-subjects design. In between-subjects data, every score is from a separate individual and an attempt to equalize the participants as in Table 11.2 would simply change *all* the scores to the same value, which would also eliminate the treatment effects.

BOX **11.1**

Statistical Consequences of Removing Individual Differences in a Within-Subjects Design

As we noted in the text, the process of removing individual differences from the variance in a within-subjects design is accomplished during the statistical analysis. To demonstrate this phenomenon, we consider the statistical evaluation for the two sets of data shown in Table 11.1. Both sets of data contain exactly the same scores and produce exactly the same means: the mean for treatment I is 41, for treatment II the mean is 45, and for treatment III the mean is 49. The purpose for the statistical analysis is to determine whether these mean differences are statistically significant; that is, are the differences large enough to conclude that they are very unlikely to have occurred by chance alone, and probably represent real differences between the treatments (see Box 9.1, p. 250).

With three treatment conditions, the appropriate statistical procedure is an analysis of variance (ANOVA). The analysis first computes a variance that measures the size of the actual mean differences; the bigger the differences, the bigger the variance. The analysis then computes a second variance, called the error variance, which estimates the size of the mean differences that would be expected if there were no treatment effects. This second variance, the error variance, is the one that is influenced by individual differences. Finally, the analysis compares the two variances to determine whether the actual

mean differences (variance 1) are significantly bigger than the mean differences that would be expected without any treatment effects (variance 2).

For the data in Table 11.1, both designs, between-subjects and within-subjects, have exactly the same mean differences and produce exactly the same value for variance 1, $V_1 = 64$. For the between-subjects design, the error variance includes individual differences and the data in Table 9.1 produce a value of $V_2 = 334$. In this case, the actual mean differences ($V_1 = 64$) are definitely not bigger that would be expected if there were no treatment effects ($V_2 = 334$), and we conclude that there are no significant differences. For the within-subjects design, however, the individual differences are eliminated from the error variance. As a result, the size of the error variance (V_2) is substantially reduced. For the data in Table 11.1, the error variance is $V_2 = 1$. For the within-subjects design, the actual mean differences ($V_1 = 64$) are substantially bigger than would be expected without any treatment effects ($V_2 = 1$), and we conclude that there are significant mean differences.

Once more, the general point from this demonstration is that a within-subjects design removes the individual differences from the data, which reduces the variance and can greatly increase the likelihood of detecting significant differences between treatment conditions.

LEARNING CHECKS

Explain why individual differences such as age or gender cannot become confounding variables in a within-subjects design comparing two treatment conditions.

What is the advantage of removing the variability caused by individual differences in a within-subjects design?

Disadvantages of Within-Subjects Designs

Although a within-subjects design has some definite advantages relative to a between-subjects design, it also has some disadvantages. The primary disadvantage comes from the fact that each participant usually goes through a series of treatment conditions with each treatment administered at a different time. Whenever the treatments occur at different times, there is an opportunity for time-related factors, such as fatigue or the weather, to influence the participants' scores. For example, if a participant's performance steadily declines over a series of treatment conditions, you cannot determine whether the decline is being caused by the different treatments or is simply an indication that the participant is getting tired. You should recognize this problem as an example of a confounding variable that threatens the internal validity of the experiment. Specifically, whenever there is an alternative explanation for the results, the experiment is confounded. In Chapter 6 (pp. 181–185) we introduced a set of time-related factors that can threaten the internal validity of a within-subjects experiment. These time-related factors, which are discussed again in the following section, are the major disadvantage of a within-subjects experimental design.

Caution: In Chapter 8 we discussed differential attrition as a threat to internal validity for between-subjects experiments. The attrition discussed here simply means the loss of participants from a research study.

Another potential problem for the within-subjects design is **participant attrition**. In simple terms, some of the individuals who start the research study may be gone before the study is completed. Because a within-subjects design usually requires repeated measurements under different conditions for each individual, some participants may be lost between the first measurement and the final measurement. This problem is especially serious when the study extends over a period of time and participants must be called back for additional observation. Participants may forget appointments, lose interest, quit, move away, or even die. In addition to shrinking the sample size, the attrition problem may exaggerate volunteer bias if only the most dedicated volunteers continue from start to finish. As noted in Chapter 6, volunteer bias can threaten the external validity of a research study.

In situations in which participant attrition is anticipated, it is advisable to begin the research study with more individuals than are actually needed. In this way, the chances are increased of having a reasonable number of participants left when the study ends.

11.2 | THREATS TO INTERNAL VALIDITY FOR WITHIN-SUBJECTS DESIGNS

A within-subjects experimental study must be concerned with threats to internal validity from environmental variables that may change systematically from one treatment to another, and from time-related factors that may influence the participants' scores (Chapter 6, pp. 181–185). Thus, there are two major sources of potential confounding for a within-subjects design.

1. *Confounding from environmental variables.* Environmental variables are characteristics of the environment that may change from one treatment condition to another. For example, one treatment may be evaluated during the morning and another treatment during the afternoon. Or two different treatments may be administered in two different rooms. Any such variable may cause differences in scores from one treatment to another, and therefore provides an alternative explanation for the differences between treatments.

2. *Confounding from time-related factors.* A serious concern of within-subjects designs comes from the fact that the design usually requires a series of measurements made over time. During the time between the first measurement and the final measurement, the participants may be influenced by a variety of factors other than the treatments being investigated, and these other factors may affect the participants' scores. If this occurs, then the internal validity of the study is threatened because a change in a participant's score from one treatment to the next could be caused by an outside factor instead of the different treatments. In Chapter 6, we identified five time-related factors that can threaten the internal validity of a within-subjects experimental design. Briefly reviewing, they are:

    • **History.** Scores may be affected by changing events outside the study.
    • **Maturation.** Scores may be affected by physiological or psychological changes in the participants.
    • **Instrumentation.** Scores may by affected by changes in the measuring instrument.
    • **Testing effects.** Scores may be affected by experience in prior treatment conditions.
    • **Statistical Regression.** Extreme scores may become less extreme as a result of statistical regression.

Separating Time-Related Factors and Order Effects

Although the time-related threats to internal validity are commonly grouped together in one category, researchers occasionally distinguish between those that are related exclusively to time and those that are related to previous experience within the research study. Specifically, threats from history, maturation, instrumentation, and regression are related exclusively to time, and are not directly connected to experience in a previous treatment. On the other hand, testing effects are directly related to experience obtained by participating in previous treatment conditions. For example, participants may learn new skills in one treatment that can influence future behavior, or become fatigued from participation in one treatment, which then affects their scores in later treatments. Based on this distinction, researchers often separate testing effects from the other time-related factors. In this context, the testing effects are often called **order effects** to emphasize that the participants go through a series of treatments in order, and that performance in any treatment may be influenced by treatments that occurred earlier in the order.

When an order effect is caused by a specific previous treatment, it is often called a **carryover effect.** This term comes from the idea that one treatment condition may produce a lasting change that carries over into the next treatment, where it affects the participant's performance or behavior. For example, a drug administered in the first treatment lingers in a participant's system when the individual enters the second treatment. In this case, the drug from the first treatment could influence the participant's score in the second treatment. Another common example of carryover is a **contrast effect,** in which the subjective perception of a treatment condition is influenced by its contrast with the previous treatment. For example, participants entering a room with moderate lighting for their second treatment may perceive it as dark if they are coming from a brightly lit room for their first treatment. However, the same moderately lit room may be perceived as bright if participants are coming from a dimly lit room.

Other order effects may not be directly related to a specific treatment, but rather are dependent on general experience accumulated during the study. Such changes are called **progressive error.** Common examples of progressive error are **practice** effects (progressive improvement in performance as a participant gains experience through the series of treatment conditions) and **fatigue** (a progressive decline in performance as a participant works through the series of treatment conditions). In each case, the research results are confounded because the researcher does not know whether performance changes in the second treatment are caused by the different treatments or by fatigue or practice.

Technically, carryover effects and progressive error are two different phenomena. Carryover effects are changes in a participant that can be attributed directly to the lingering aftereffects of an earlier treatment (or treatments). On the other hand, progressive error is a change in the participant that can be attributed to general experience rather than a specific treatment. However, both progressive error and carryover effects can be viewed as aspects of the same basic problem: Participants' scores are influenced by factors other than the immediate treatment. To simplify future discussion, we combine carryover effects and progressive error into the general category of order effects.

DEFINITIONS	Whenever individuals participate in a series of treatment conditions and experience a series of measurements, their behavior or performance at any point in the series may be influenced by experience that occurred earlier in the sequence. Such influences are called **order effects,** and include carryover effects and progressive error.

Carryover effects are changes in behavior or performance that are caused by the lingering aftereffects of an earlier treatment condition. Carryover effects exist whenever one treatment condition produces a change in the participants that affects their scores in subsequent treatment conditions.

Progressive error refers to changes in a participant's behavior or performance that are related to general experience in a research study but not related to a specific treatment or treatments. Common examples of progressive error are practice effects and fatigue.

Order Effects as a Confounding Variable

Order effects can produce changes from one treatment condition to another that are not caused by the treatments and can confound the results of a research study. To demonstrate this confounding effect, we examine a hypothetical experiment in which a researcher uses a within-subjects design to compare two treatment conditions with a sample of eight participants. We also assume that there is no difference between the two treatments; on average, the scores in treatment I are the same as the scores in treatment II. Results for this hypothetical study are shown in Table 11.3a. Notice that some individual participants show a small increase or decrease between treatment conditions, representing error that can occur in any measurement process (see the discussion of reliability in Chapter 4). However, on average, there is no difference between the treatment conditions; both produce an average score of 20.

Now, consider the data shown in Table 11.3b. For these data, we assume that each participant started the experiment in treatment I and then was moved to treatment II. In addition, we assume that participation in treatment I produces an order effect that changes each participant so that subsequent measurements show scores that are 5 points higher than they would be normally. Thus, we have added a 5-point order effect to each participant's score in treatment II. Notice that the 5-point increase is not caused by the second treatment but is rather an order effect resulting from earlier participation in treatment I. The resulting data in Table 11.3b illustrate two important points:

1. The order effect varies systematically with the treatments; that is, it always contributes to the second treatment but never to the first. Whenever something changes systematically with the independent variable, it is a confounding variable. Thus, the results of this study are confounded by the order effects.

2. In this example, the confounding from the order effects makes the data look like there is a 5-point difference between the treatments. With the help of order effects, the individual participants and the group mean show consistently higher scores in the second treatment. These data could lead the researcher to conclude that there is a significant difference between the treatments when, in fact, no such difference exists (remember, we constructed the original data so there is no difference between

TABLE **11.3**
Hypothetical Data Showing How Order Effects Can Distort
the Results of a Research Study

(a) Original Scores with No Order Effect		(b) Modified Scores with a 5-Point Order Effect	
Treatment I	Treatment II	Treatment I	Treatment II
20	21	20	26 (21 + 5)
23	23	23	28 (23 + 5)
25	23	25	28 (23 + 5)
19	20	19	25 (20 + 5)
26	25	26	30 (25 + 5)
17	16	17	21 (16 + 5)
14	14	14	19 (14 + 5)
16	18	16	23 (18 + 5)
Mean = 20	Mean = 20	Mean = 20	Mean = 25

treatments). Thus, order effects, like any confounding variable, can distort the results of a research study. In this example, the order effect creates what looks like a treatment effect but actually is just an order effect. In other situations, order effects can diminish or exaggerate a real effect, thereby posing a real threat to the internal validity of the research.

LEARNING CHECK | Briefly explain how an order effect such as fatigue can be a confounding variable in a within-subjects design.

11.3 | DEALING WITH TIME-RELATED THREATS AND ORDER EFFECTS

Within-subjects designs can control environmental threats to internal validity using the same techniques that are used in between-subject designs. Specifically, environmental factors such as the room, the experimenter, or the time of day, can be controlled by (1) randomization, (2) holding them constant, or (3) matching across treatment conditions. Time-related factors and order effects, on the other hand, require special attention and new strategies for control.

Because within-subjects designs can have significant advantages in comparison to between-subjects designs, they are often preferred as a method for addressing research questions. At the same time, however, order effects and time-related threats to internal validity can be serious problems whenever a within-subjects design is selected. Therefore, researchers have developed a variety of ways to control these potential threats. In this section, we examine some of the methods for dealing with order effects and time-related threats to gain the full benefit of within-subjects designs.

Controlling Time

The possibility that a research study will be affected by a time-related threat such as history or maturation is directly related to the length of time required to complete the study. For example, if participants go through a series of two or three treatment conditions in a single 45-minute laboratory session, it is very unlikely that time-related threats will have any influence on the results. On the other hand, if the different treatment conditions are scheduled over a period of weeks, the chances greatly increase that an outside event (history), maturation, or change in the measurement instrument will have an influence on the results. By controlling the time from one treatment condition to the next, a researcher has some control over time-related threats to internal validity.

Although shortening the time between treatments can reduce the risk of time-related threats, this technique can often increase the likelihood that order effects will influence the results. For example, in situations in which order effects are expected to be temporary, one strategy is to increase the time between treatment conditions so the order effects can dissipate. Fatigue, for example, is less likely to be a problem if participants are allowed ample opportunity to rest and recover between treatments. As we have noted, however, increasing the time between treatments increases the risk of time-related threats to internal validity.

Switch to a Between-Subjects Design

Often, researchers begin a research study with some knowledge or expectation of the existence and magnitude of order effects. For example, if the study involves measuring skill or performance over a series of treatment conditions, it is reasonable to assume that practice gained in the early treatments is likely to affect performance in later treatments. If the study involves a tedious or boring task repeated under different conditions, the researcher can expect fatigue or boredom to develop during the course of the study. In some situations, order effects are so strong and so obvious that a researcher probably would not even consider using a within-subjects design. For example, a within-subjects design is a poor choice for a study comparing two methods of teaching reading to first-grade children. After the children have been taught with method I, they are permanently changed. You cannot erase what they have learned and try to teach them again with method II. In this extreme case, the obvious strategy for avoiding order effects is to use a between-subjects design with a separate group for each of the two teaching methods. Usually, a between-subjects design (with a separate group for each treatment) is available as an alternative and completely eliminates any threat of confounding from order effects. Although the potential for order effects is not always as severe as with learning to read, a between-subjects design is often the best strategy whenever a researcher has reason to expect substantial order effects.

Counterbalancing: Matching Treatments with Respect to Time

In Chapter 9 (p. 262) we discussed the technique of matching variables across treatments to prevent the variables from becoming threats to internal validity. At that time, we also mentioned that a similar process could be used to help control time-related threats. The process of matching treatments with respect to time is called **counterbalancing.** In counterbalancing, different participants undergo the treatment conditions in different orders so that every treatment has some participants who experience the treatment first, some for whom it is second, some third, and so on. As a result, the treatments are matched, or balanced, with respect to time. With two treatments, for example, half of the participants begin in treatment I, and then move to treatment II. The other half begin in treatment II, then receive treatment I. As a result, the two treatments are matched; in both treatments, 50% of the participants experience the treatment first and 50% experience the treatment second. This procedure disrupts any systematic relationship between time and the order of treatment conditions, and thereby eliminates potential confounding from time-related threats or order effects.

For example, Stephens, Atkins, and Kingston (2009) used a counterbalanced, repeated-measures design to examine the effect of swearing in response to pain. Although swearing is a common response to pain, the question was whether swearing focuses attention on the pain and, thereby, increased its intensity, or serves as a distraction that reduces pain. Participants were asked to place their hands in icy water for as long as they could bear the pain. Half the participants were told to repeat their favorite swear words for as long as their hands were in the water. The other half repeated a neutral word. After a brief rest, the two groups switched words and repeated the ice water plunge. Thus, both groups experienced both conditions (curse and neutral), with half swearing on their first plunge and half on their second. The results clearly showed that swearing increased the amount of time people could tolerate the pain and reduced their ratings of pain intensity.

DEFINITION

Counterbalancing a within-subjects design involves changing the order in which treatment conditions are administered from one participant to another so that the treatment conditions are matched with respect to time. The goal is to use every possible order of treatments with an equal number of individuals participating in each sequence. The purpose of counterbalancing is to eliminate the potential for confounding by disrupting any systematic relationship between the order of treatments and time-related factors.

To better understand the effects of counterbalancing, first consider a situation in which the order of treatments is not counterbalanced. Without counterbalancing, all the participants begin in treatment I and then move to treatment II. Note that treatment II always occurs after treatment I. In this case, a time-related threat such as history or instrumentation influences only the scores in treatment II. An order effect, too, influences only the scores in treatment II. Thus, without counterbalancing, the scores in treatment II may be influenced by factors other than the treatment, and the study is confounded. With counterbalancing, however, a time-related threat would affect half of the participants in treatment II, but it would also affect the other half in treatment I. Thus, the effect is distributed evenly, balanced between the two treatments. Because the outside factor does not cause a difference between the two treatments, it is no longer a threat to internal validity.

You may have noticed that counterbalancing requires separate groups of participants, with each group going through the series of treatments in a different order. The existence of separate groups may appear to contradict the basic definition of a within-subjects design. The solution to this apparent contradiction is based on the observation that although the groups go through the treatments in different orders, they all receive the full set of treatments. Thus, we still have a within-subjects design, with one combined group of individuals participating in all of the different treatment conditions. In Chapter 13 (p. 386) we return to this issue when we re-examine a counterbalanced study as a combination of a within-subjects design (with one group in all the treatments) and a between-subjects design (with different groups receiving the treatments in different orders).

Counterbalancing and Order Effects

Although counterbalancing has exactly the same effect on time-related threats and order effects, the process of counterbalancing is usually discussed in terms of order effects. Therefore, throughout the rest of this section, we focus on counterbalancing and order effects. Keep in mind, however, that counterbalancing is just as effective for controlling factors such as history and maturation as for controlling order effects.

The hypothetical data in Table 11.4 provide a numerical demonstration of counterbalancing and how it controls threats to validity. The table shows the results from an experiment in which a researcher uses a within-subjects design to compare two treatments. The design is counterbalanced with four of the eight participants starting in treatment I and ending with treatment II, and the other four participants receiving the treatments in the reverse order. Table 11.4a shows scores as they would appear if there were no order effects.

The data have been constructed to produce a 6-point difference between the two treatment conditions (Mean I = 20 versus Mean II = 26). The modified scores in Table 11.4b show how order effects influence the data. For this example, we assume that experience in one treatment condition produces an order effect that causes a 5-point increase in scores for the next treatment.

Because the design is counterbalanced, the first four participants begin the experiment in treatment I, and the 5-point order effect adds to their scores in treatment II. The remaining four participants receive the treatments in the opposite order, so the order effect adds to their scores in treatment I. Notice that the result of the counterbalancing is to distribute the order effects evenly between the two treatments; that is, the order effects are balanced across the treatment conditions. Although the treatment means are affected by the order effects, they are affected equally. As a result, there is still a 6-point difference between the two treatment means, exactly as it was without any order effects. The point of this demonstration is to show that order effects

TABLE **11.4**
Hypothetical Data Showing How Counterbalancing Distributes
Order Effects Evenly between the Treatment Conditions

(a) Original Scores with No Order Effect		(b) Modified Scores with a 5-Point Order Effect		
Treatment I	**Treatment II**	**Treatment I**		**Treatment II**
20	27	20	— order ——>	32 (27 + 5)
23	29	23	——————>	34 (29 + 5)
25	29	25	——————>	34 (29 + 5)
19	26	19	——————>	31 (26 + 5)
26	31	(25 + 5) 31	<— order —	31
17	22	(17 + 5) 22	<—————	22
14	20	(14 + 5) 19	<—————	20
16	24	(16 + 5) 21	<—————	24
Mean = 20	Mean = 26	Mean = 22.5		Mean = 28.5

can change individual scores and can change means, but when a design is counterbalanced, the changes do not influence the mean differences between treatments. Because the treatment differences are not affected, the order effects do not threaten the internal validity of the study.

The value of counterbalancing a within-subjects design is that it prevents any order effects from accumulating in one particular treatment condition. Instead, the order effects are spread evenly across all the different conditions so that it is possible to make fair, unbiased comparisons between treatments (no single treatment has any special advantage or disadvantage). On the other hand, counterbalancing does not eliminate the order effects; they are still embedded in the data. Furthermore, the order effects are hidden in the data so that a researcher cannot see whether they exist or how large they are. In Table 11.4, we identify and expose hypothetical order effects to demonstrate how they influence a counterbalanced design. In real life, however, all you see are the final scores, which may or may not include order effects.

 **LEARNING CHECKS**   Explain how order effects such as fatigue cannot become confounding variables if a researcher uses a between-subjects design.

Describe the process of counterbalancing and the benefits of using it in a within-subjects design.

Limitations of Counterbalancing

As demonstrated in Table 11.4, counterbalancing can be used to prevent order effects (or other time-related effects) from confounding the results of a within-subjects research study. In the same way that random assignment is a routine technique for maintaining validity in between-subjects research, counterbalancing is a routine technique used in within-subjects research. However, this apparently simple and effective technique has some limitations.

Counterbalancing and Variance

The purpose of counterbalancing is to distribute order effects evenly across the different treatment conditions. However, this process does not eliminate the order effects. In particular, the order effects are still part of the data, and they can still create problems. One is that they can distort the treatment means. In Table 11.4, the order effects are present in both treatments and inflate both of the treatment means. Usually, this kind of distortion is not important because researchers typically are interested in the amount of difference between treatments rather than the absolute magnitude of any specific mean. When counterbalancing works as intended, the differences between means are not changed. However, in situations in which the absolute level of performance (the true mean) is important, the process of counterbalancing can disguise the true value of a treatment mean.

A more serious problem is that counterbalancing adds the order effects to some of the individuals within each treatment but not to all of the individuals. In the example shown in Table 11.4, some of the individuals in treatment

I receive an extra 5 points and some do not. As a result, the differences between scores are increased within each treatment, which adds to the variance within treatments. Recall from Chapter 10 (p. 293) that large variance within treatments can obscure treatment effects. In statistical terms, high variance within treatments decreases the likelihood that a research study will obtain significant differences between treatments. Thus, in situations in which order effects are relatively large, the process of counterbalancing can undermine the potential for a successful experiment.

Asymmetrical Order Effects

In Chapter 13 (p. 386), we present a method that allows researchers to measure and evaluate order effects.

In Table 11.4, we use exactly the same 5-point order effect whether participants started in treatment I or in treatment II. That is, we assume that the order effects are symmetrical. This assumption of symmetry is not always justified. It is definitely possible that one treatment might produce more of an order effect than another treatment. For example, one treatment condition might provide more opportunity for practice than the other conditions. Or one treatment might be more demanding and create more fatigue than the other treatment conditions. In such situations, the order effects are not symmetrical, and counterbalancing the order of treatments does not balance the order effects.

Counterbalancing and the Number of Treatments

To completely counterbalance a series of treatments, it is necessary to present the treatments in every possible sequence. The idea behind **complete counterbalancing** is that a particular series of treatment conditions may create its own unique order effect. For example, treatments II and III, in sequence, may produce a unique effect that carries over into the next treatment. Treatments I and III, in sequence, may produce a different order effect. To completely balance these combined effects, the research design should use every possible ordering of treatment conditions.

With only two treatment conditions, complete counterbalancing is easy: There are only two possible sequences. However, as the number of treatments increases, complete counterbalancing becomes more complex. If the number of different treatment conditions is identified as n, then the number of different sequences is $n!$ (n factorial).

$$n! = n\,(n-1)(n-2)(n-3)\ldots(1)$$

For example, with four treatment conditions, there are $4! = 4 \times 3 \times 2 \times 1 = 24$ different sequences. If the four treatments are identified as A, B, C, and D, the 24 sequences can be listed as follows:

ABCD	BACD	CABD	DABC	Note that the sequence ABCD indicates
ABDC	BADC	CADB	DACB	that treatment A is first, B is second, C is
ACBD	BCAD	CBAD	DBAC	third, and D is fourth.
ACDB	BCDA	CBDA	DBCA	
ADBC	BDAC	CDAB	DCAB	
ADCB	BDCA	CDBA	DCBA	

To completely counterbalance a within-subjects experiment with four treatment conditions, the researcher must divide the participants into 24 equal sized groups and assign one group to each of the 24 different sequences. Obviously, this study would require at least 24 participants (one per group), which may be more than the researcher needs or wants. With even more treatments, the demands of complete counterbalancing can become outrageous. With $n = 6$ treatments, for example, there are $6! = 720$ different treatment sequences, which means that the study would require a minimum of 720 participants.

One solution to this problem is to use what is known as **partial counterbalancing.** Instead of every possible sequence, partial counterbalancing simply uses enough different orderings to ensure that each treatment condition occurs first in the sequence for one group of participants, occurs second for another group, third for another group, and so on. With four treatments, for example, this requires only four different sequences, such as: ABCD, CADB, BDAC, DCBA. To conduct a partially counterbalanced study with four treatments, a researcher needs to divide the participants into four equal sized groups and assign one group to each of the four sequences. One group of participants receives treatment A first, one group has A second, one has A third, and one has A fourth. Similarly, each of the other treatments appears once in each ordinal position.

Because partial counterbalancing does not use every possible sequence of treatment conditions, one problem is to decide exactly which sequences to select. A simple and unbiased procedure for selecting sequences is to construct a Latin square. To create a **Latin square** for four treatment conditions, start with a 4 × 4 matrix and fill it in with the letters A, B, C, and D, as follows:

> List the letters ABCD in order in the top row of the matrix. To create the next row, simply move the last letter in line to the beginning. This creates DABC for the second row. Continue moving the last letter to the beginning of the line to create each new row. The result is the following Latin square:

A	B	C	D	By definition, a Latin square is a matrix of n elements (letters)
D	A	B	C	where each element appears exactly once in each column
C	D	A	B	and in each row.
B	C	D	A	

Each row in the square provides a sequence of treatment conditions for one group of participants. For this example, the first group receives the four treatments in the order ABCD. A second group receives the order DABC, and so on.

The Latin square in the preceding paragraph is not a particularly good example of partial counterbalancing because it does not balance every possible sequence of treatment conditions. For example, the first three groups all receive treatment A followed immediately by treatment B. On the other hand, no one receives treatment B followed by treatment A. Whenever possible, a Latin square should ensure that every possible sequence of treatments is represented. One method for improving the square is to use a random process to rearrange the columns (for example, a coin toss to decide whether or not each column is moved), then use a random process to rearrange the rows. The resulting rows in the square should provide a better set of sequences for a partially counter-balanced research study.

LEARNING CHECKS

Describe what is meant by *asymmetrical order effects* and explain why such effects create a problem for counterbalancing.

Explain why partial counterbalancing is sometimes necessary.

11.4 | APPLICATIONS AND STATISTICAL ANALYSES OF WITHIN-SUBJECTS DESIGNS

Within-subjects designs usually involve computing means and evaluating mean differences between treatment conditions. In an experiment, the researcher manipulates an independent variable to create two or more treatment conditions, and then observes the same group of individuals in all of the conditions. The mean score for the group is then computed for each treatment condition and the means are compared for significant differences.

Commonly, a within-subjects design is preferred to a between-subjects design to take advantage of one or more of the special characteristics of this type of research. For example:

1. Because the within-subjects design requires only one group, it often is used when obtaining a large group of research participants is difficult or impossible. If a researcher studies a population with a rare characteristic (Olympic athletes, people with multiple-personality disorder, or women taller than 7 feet), then a within-subjects design is more efficient because it requires fewer participants.

2. We have noted repeatedly that one big advantage of a within-subjects design is that it reduces or eliminates variability caused by individual differences. Whenever a researcher anticipates that the data will show large variability caused by differences between participants, a within-subjects design is the preferred choice.

Two-Treatment Designs

The simplest application of a within-subjects design is to evaluate the difference between two treatment conditions. The two-treatment within-subjects design has many of the same advantages and disadvantages as the two-group between-subjects design discussed in Chapter 10 (see pp. 297–299). On the positive side, the design is easy to conduct and the results are easy to understand. With only two treatment conditions, a researcher can easily maximize the difference between treatments by selecting two treatment conditions that are clearly different. This usually increases the likelihood of obtaining a significant difference. In addition, with only two treatment conditions, it is very easy to counterbalance the design to minimize the threat of confounding from time-related factors or order effects. On the negative side, a study with only two treatments provides only two data points. In this situation, it is possible to demonstrate a difference between conditions, but the data do not provide any indication of the functional relationship between the independent and dependent variables. That is, we cannot determine how the dependent variable would respond to small, gradual changes of the independent variable.

With data measured on an interval or ratio scale, the most common strategy for data analysis is to compute a mean score for each treatment condition. The means are used to describe (summarize) the individual treatments, and the difference between means is used to describe the differential effects of the treatments. With two treatment conditions, a repeated-measures *t* or a single-factor ANOVA (repeated measures) can be used to evaluate the statistical significance of the mean difference; that is, to determine whether the obtained mean difference is greater than what would be reasonably expected from sampling error (see Chapter 14). If the data do not permit the calculation of treatment means, there are alternative methods for statistically evaluating the difference between treatments. If the data are measured on an ordinal scale (or can be rank ordered), a Wilcoxon test can be used to evaluate significant differences. Occasionally, a within-subjects study comparing two treatments produces data that show only the direction of difference between the two treatments. For example, a therapist may be able to classify individual clients as showing improvement or showing decline after treatment. In this situation, the data can be statistically evaluated using a sign test to determine whether the changes are consistently in one direction (enough to satisfy statistical significance).

Multiple-Treatment Designs

As we discussed in Chapter 10, the primary advantage of using more than two treatment conditions is that the data are more likely to reveal the functional relationship between the two variables being studied (see Figure 10.5, p. 298). A researcher can create a series of conditions (independent variable), and then observe how the participants' behavior (dependent variable) changes as they move through the series of treatments. A multiple-treatment design also produces a more convincing demonstration of a cause-and-effect relationship than is provided by a two-treatment design. Demonstrating repeatedly that a dependent variable responds each time an independent variable is changed produces compelling evidence that the independent variable is responsible for causing changes in the dependent variable.

The disadvantages of using multiple treatments in a within-subjects design include the same basic problem introduced in Chapter 10 (see p. 300). If a researcher creates too many treatment conditions, the distinction between treatments may become too small to generate significant differences in behavior. In addition, multiple treatments for a within-subjects design typically increase the amount of time required for each participant to complete the full series of treatments. This can increase the likelihood of participant attrition. Finally, the ability to completely counterbalance a design becomes more difficult as the number of treatment conditions increases.

With data measured on an interval or ratio scale, the typical statistical analysis consists of computing a mean for each treatment condition, then using a repeated-measures ANOVA to test for any significant differences among the treatment means (see Chapter 14). For more complex within-subjects designs, consult an advanced statistics text to verify that an appropriate analysis technique exists before beginning the research study.

 **LEARNING CHECK**   Describe the advantages of a two-treatment design.

11.5 | COMPARING WITHIN-SUBJECTS AND BETWEEN-SUBJECTS DESIGNS

By now, it should be clear that a within-subjects design has some distinct advantages and some unique disadvantages compared to a between-subjects design. It should also be clear that the advantages of one design are essentially the same as the disadvantages of the other. Three factors that differentiate the designs are:

1. *Individual differences.* The prospect that individual differences may become confounding variables or increase variance is a major disadvantage of between-subjects designs. However, these problems are eliminated in a within-subjects design. Because the within-subjects design reduces variance, it is generally more likely to detect a treatment effect (if one exists) than is a between-subjects design. If you anticipate large individual differences, it is usually better to use a within-subjects design.

2. *Time-related factors and order effects.* There is usually the potential for factors that change over time to distort the results of within-subjects designs. However, this problem is eliminated in a between-subjects design, in which each individual participates in only one treatment and is measured only once. Thus, whenever you expect one (or more) of the treatment conditions to have a large and long-lasting effect that may influence the participants in future conditions, it is better to use a between-subjects design.

3. *Fewer participants.* Although it is a relatively minor advantage, we should note once again that a within-subjects design typically requires fewer participants. Because a within-subjects design obtains multiple scores for each individual, it can generate a lot of data from a relatively small set of participants. A between-subjects design, on the other hand, produces only one score for each participant and requires a lot of participants to generate a lot of data. Whenever it is difficult to find or recruit participants, a within-subjects design is a better choice.

Also, the choice between a within-subjects design and a between-subjects design can be influenced by the specific research question being asked. For example, Schmidt (1994) used both within-subjects and between-subjects designs to examine how humor affects human memory. He first prepared a set of sentences with a humorous and a nonhumorous version for each. For example,

Humorous: I got a bill for my surgery—now I know why the doctors were wearing masks.

Nonhumorous: I got a bill for my surgery—those doctors were like robbers with the prices they charged.

In the within-subjects version of the study, each participant was presented a list containing a mix of 10 humorous and 10 nonhumorous sentences. They were given 10 seconds to study each sentence. After the final sentence, the participants were given a distraction task (arithmetic) for 5 minutes, and then asked to recall as many sentences as they could. The data consisted of two scores for each person: (1) the number of humorous sentences recalled and (2) the number of nonhumorous sentences recalled. The results showed that the participants recalled significantly more humorous sentences than nonhumorous sentences. However, Schmidt noted that there are two possible interpretations for this result:

1. Humorous sentences are simply easier to remember than nonhumorous sentences.
2. The two types of sentence are competing for limited memory space. Because the humorous sentences are more fun and interesting, they are chosen to go into memory at the expense of the nonhumorous sentences.

To differentiate between these two interpretations, Schmidt switched to a between-subjects design. In this part of the experiment, one group of participants saw a set of exclusively humorous sentences and a second group viewed a set of nonhumorous sentences. Notice that these participants see only one type of sentence and are not allowed to choose which type they prefer to remember. Both groups were then given the distraction task followed by a recall test. This time, the results showed no difference in memory for the two types of sentences. Apparently, humorous material is not easier to remember, but if you are given a choice, it is preferred over nonhumorous material.

Schmidt's humorous sentence study provides an opportunity to make one more point about within-subjects experiments. Repeatedly, we have said that a within-subjects study *usually* involves a series of treatment conditions spaced over time, which creates the potential for confounding from time-related factors. However, the treatment conditions are not always separated in time. In Schmidt's experiment, for example, the two treatment conditions were presented simultaneously. Specifically, the humorous and nonhumorous sentences were mixed randomly in a single list that participants studied in a single 200-second period. In this type of study there is no potential for order effects or time-related factors to influence the data, and there is no need for conventional counterbalancing. Effectively, the treatments are automatically counterbalanced because the two types of sentence (the treatments) are mixed randomly.

Matched-Subjects Designs

Occasionally, researchers attempt to approximate the advantages of within- and between-subjects designs by using a technique known as a **matched-subjects design.** A matched-subjects design uses a separate group for each

In Chapter 10 (p. 288), we discussed matching groups as a technique for ensuring that the different groups in a between-subjects design all have essentially the same characteristics. Now, we are matching subjects, one-to-one, as an attempt to simulate a within-subjects design.

treatment condition, but each individual in one group is matched one-to-one with an individual in every other group. The matching is based on a variable considered to be particularly relevant to the specific study. Suppose, for example, that a researcher wants to compare different methods for teaching mathematics in the third grade. For this study, the researcher might give a mathematics achievement test to a large sample of students, then match individuals based on their test scores. Thus, if Tom and Bill have identical math achievement scores, these two students can be treated as a matched pair with Tom assigned to one teaching method and Bill assigned to the other. If the study compares three treatments, then the researcher needs to find triplets of matched individuals. Although a matched-subjects study does not have exactly the same individuals in each treatment condition (like a within-subjects design), it does have equivalent (matched) individuals in each treatment.

DEFINITION

In a **matched-subjects design,** each individual in one group is matched with a participant in each of the other groups. The matching is done so that the matched individuals are equivalent with respect to a variable that the researcher considers to be relevant to the study.

The goal of a matched-subjects design is to duplicate all the advantages of within- and between-subjects designs without the disadvantages of either one. For example, a matched-subjects design attempts to mimic a within-subjects design by having "equivalent" participants in all of the treatment conditions. In a within-subjects design the equivalent participants are literally the same people, and in a matched-subjects design the equivalent participants are matched sets of people. Thus, a researcher does not need to worry that the participants in one treatment are noticeably different from the participants in another treatment. In addition, the statistics used to evaluate a matched-subjects design are the same as those used for within-subjects designs. In both designs, the variance caused by individual differences is measured and removed. The matched-subjects design also mimics a between-subjects design by using a separate group for each treatment condition with each individual measured only once. Thus, there is no chance for the scores to be influenced by time-related factors or order effects.

It is possible to match participants on more than one variable. For example, a researcher could match participants on the basis of age, gender, race, and IQ. In this case, for example, a 22-year-old White female with an IQ of 118 who was in one group would be matched with another 22-year-old White female with an IQ of 118 in another group. Note, however, that matching can become extremely difficult as the number of matched variables increases and the number of different groups increases.

In general, a matched-subjects design attempts to eliminate the problems associated with between-subjects experiments (individual differences) and the problems associated with within-subjects experiments (order effects). However, this type of design can never match subjects perfectly. At best, a matched-subjects design achieves a degree of match that is limited to the variable(s) used for the matching process. Matching on only one or two variables is a crude approximation to the perfect match that exists in a real within-subjects design. Simply because two individuals have the same IQ is no guarantee that they are also the same or even similar on other variables. Thus, matched-subjects designs are not nearly as effective at removing individual differences as are within-subjects designs.

 **LEARNING CHECKS**

Describe how individual differences can create problems for a between-subjects design and how order effects can create problems for a within-subjects design.

Explain how a within-subjects design avoids the problems created by individual differences and how a between-subjects design avoids the problems created by order effects.

■ CHAPTER SUMMARY

This chapter examined the characteristics of the within-subjects experimental design. The general goal of a within-subjects experiment is to determine whether differences exist between two or more treatment conditions. The defining characteristic of a within-subjects design is that it uses a single group of individuals, and tests or observes each individual in all of the different treatments being compared.

The primary advantage of a within-subjects design is that it essentially eliminates all the problems based on individual differences that are the primary concern of a between-subjects design. First, a within-subjects design has no individual differences between groups. There is only one group of participants, so the group of individuals in treatment I is exactly the same as the group of individuals in treatment II; hence, there are no individual differences between groups to confound the study. Second, because each participant appears in every treatment condition, each individual serves as his own control or baseline. This makes it possible to measure and remove the variance caused by individual differences.

The primary disadvantage of a within-subjects design is that the scores obtained in one treatment condition are directly related to scores in every other condition. The relationship between scores across treatments creates the potential for the scores in one treatment to be influenced by previous treatments, previous measurements, or previous experience.

This general problem is called an order effect because the current scores may have been affected by events that occurred earlier in the order of treatments. Order effects can be a confounding variable in a within-subjects design. Two kinds of order effects are carryover effects and progressive error. A technique for dealing with such problems is to counterbalance the conditions.

In addition to order effects, other threats to the internal validity of within-subjects designs are discussed, as are different versions of the within-subjects design.

KEY WORDS

within-subjects experimental
  design or repeated-measures
  experimental design

order effects
carryover effects
progressive error

counterbalancing
matched-subjects design

EXERCISES

1. In addition to the key words, you should
   also be able to define the following
   terms:
   within-subjects design
   repeated-measures design
   participant attrition
   history
   maturation
   instrumentation
   testing effects
   statistical regression
   contrast effect
   practice
   fatigue
   complete counterbalancing
   partial counterbalancing
   Latin square
2. Describe the major difference between
   within-subjects and between-subjects
   designs.
3. Describe the disadvantages of the
   within-subjects design.

4. Describe the advantages of the
   within-subjects design.
5. Explain how a matched-subjects design
   attempts to achieve all the advantages of
   both between-subjects and within-subjects
   designs.
6. Explain how statistical regression
   and instrumentation threaten the
   internal validity of within-subjects
   designs.
7. Explain how the process of
   counterbalancing attempts to
   keep order effects from becoming a
   confounding variable in a within-subjects
   design.
8. Explain how order effects can create
   problems in a within-subjects
   design.
9. Describe the disadvantages of a
   multiple-treatment design, compared
   to a two-treatment design, for a
   within-subjects experiment.

LEARNING ACTIVITIES

1. In a Latin square, each treatment condition
   occurs first one time, second one time,
   third one time, and so on. Ideally, every
   possible sequence of two treatments should
   also occur exactly one time. For example, if
   two treatments are identified as A and B,
   then the sequence AB and the sequence
   BA should each occur one time in the
   square.
2. A researcher has a sample of 30 rats that
   are all cloned from the same source. The
   30 rats are genetically identical and have

been raised in exactly the same environment since birth. The researcher conducts
an experiment, randomly assigning 10 of
the clones to treatment A, 10 to treatment
B, and the other 10 to treatment C.
Explain why the clone experiment is better
than a within-subjects study using 10
regular rats that are tested in each of the
three treatments. In other words, explain
how the clone experiment eliminates the
basic problems with a within-subjects
study.

a. Try to construct an ideal Latin square for an experiment with four treatment conditions identified as A, B, C, and D. This may take a little time, but it can be done.

b. Now, try to construct an ideal Latin square for an experiment with three treatment conditions. You should quickly find that it is impossible.

WEB RESOURCES

Visit the Book Companion Website at **www .cengage.com/international** to access study tools including a glossary, flashcards, and web quizzing. You will also find a link to Statistics and Research Methods Workshops.

For this chapter, we suggest you look at the following workshop:

Between Versus Within Designs

12

The Nonexperimental and Quasi-Experimental Research Strategies

CHAPTER OVERVIEW

Research studies that are similar to experiments but fail to satisfy the strict requirements of a true experiment are generally called quasi-experimental or nonexperimental. The distinction between these two research strategies is that quasi-experimental studies make some attempt to minimize threats to internal validity, whereas nonexperimental studies typically do not. Because these two research strategies do not completely eliminate threats to internal validity, they cannot establish unambiguous cause-and-effect relationships. In this chapter, we discuss details of the quasi-experimental and nonexperimental strategies, as well as different types of quasi-experimental and nonexperimental designs. Developmental designs, which are closely related to nonexperimental designs, are also presented.

12.1 | NONEXPERIMENTAL AND QUASI-EXPERIMENTAL RESEARCH STRATEGIES

In Chapter 6, we identified five basic research strategies: experimental, nonexperimental, quasi-experimental, correlational, and descriptive. In this chapter, we discuss the details of the nonexperimental and quasi-experimental strategies. (The experimental strategy is discussed in Chapter 9, the correlational strategy is discussed in Chapter 8, and the details of the descriptive strategy are discussed in Chapter 7.) The experimental research strategy was introduced in Chapter 9 as a means for establishing a cause-and-effect relationship between variables. Recall that the experimental strategy is distinguished from other research strategies by two basic requirements: manipulation of one variable and control of other, extraneous variables.

In many research situations, however, it is difficult or impossible for a researcher to satisfy completely the rigorous requirements of an experiment. This is particularly true for applied research in natural settings such as educational research in the classroom and clinical research with real clients. In these situations, a researcher can often devise a research strategy (a method of collecting data) that is similar to an experiment but fails to satisfy at least one of the requirements of a true experiment. Such studies are generally called nonexperimental or quasi-experimental research studies. Although these studies resemble experiments, they always contain a confounding variable or other threat to internal validity that is an integral part of the design and simply cannot be removed. The existence of a confounding variable means that these studies cannot establish unambiguous cause-and-effect relationships and, therefore, are not true experiments.

The distinction between the **nonexperimental research strategy** and the **quasi-experimental research strategy** is the degree to which the research strategy limits confounding and controls threats to internal validity. If a research design makes little or no attempt to minimize threats, it is classified as nonexperimental. A quasi-experimental design, on the other hand, makes some attempt to minimize threats to internal validity and approaches the rigor of a true experiment. As the name implies, a quasi-experimental study is almost, but not quite, a true experiment. In this chapter, we introduce several different nonexperimental designs and some closely related quasi-experimental designs. In each case, we discuss the aspect of the design that prevents it from being a true experiment. The fact that quasi-experimental and nonexperimental studies are not true experiments does not mean that they are useless or even second-class research studies. Both of these research strategies serve a real purpose and are the only option available for certain questions.

At the end of this chapter, we examine developmental research, which includes research designs intended to investigate how age is related to other variables. Because age is a variable that cannot be manipulated, developmental designs are not true experiments and can be included in other categories of nonexperimental research. However, developmental designs are generally presented as a separate group of research designs with their own terminology. As we introduce the basic developmental research designs, we discuss how they are related to other types of nonexperimental research.

 **LEARNING CHECK**   Why are studies that examine the effects of aging not considered true experiments?

The Structure of Nonexperimental and Quasi-Experimental Designs

The term *significant* means that it is very unlikely that the difference between the groups of scores would occur if there were no corresponding difference in the population. (see Box 9.1, p. 250).

Nonexperimental and quasi-experimental studies often look like experiments in terms of the general structure of the research study. In an experiment, for example, a researcher typically creates treatment conditions by manipulating an independent variable, and then measures participants to obtain a set of scores within each condition. If the scores in one condition are significantly different from the scores in another condition, the researcher can conclude that the two treatment conditions have different effects (Figure 12.1). Similarly, a nonexperimental or quasi-experimental study also produces groups of scores to be compared for significant differences. One variable is used to create the groups or conditions, and then a second variable is measured to obtain a set of scores within each condition. In nonexperimental and quasi-experimental studies, however, the different groups or conditions are not created by manipulating an independent variable. Instead, the groups are usually defined in terms of a specific participant characteristic (for example, male/female) or in terms of time (for example, before and after treatment). These two methods of defining groups produce two general categories of nonexperimental and quasi-experimental designs.

1. Between-subjects designs, also known as nonequivalent group designs
2. Within-subjects designs, also known as pre–post designs.

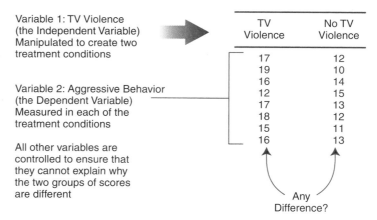

FIGURE **12.1** The Structure of an Experiment

An independent variable (in this case, violence on TV) is manipulated to create treatment conditions. Participants are then measured to obtain scores within each condition. Here, participants are observed during a free period at school and the score for each participant is a measure of aggressive behaviors. If there is a consistent difference between the scores in one condition and the scores in another condition, the difference is attributed to the treatment. In this case, a consistent difference would indicate that TV violence has an effect on aggressive behavior.

The two general types of nonexperimental and quasi-experimental research are shown in Figure 12.2 and are discussed in the following sections.

DEFINITIONS

Like true experiments, the **nonexperimental research strategy** and the **quasi-experimental research strategy** typically involve comparison of scores from different groups or different conditions. However, these two strategies use a nonmanipulated variable to define the groups or conditions being compared. The nonmanipulated variable is usually a participant characteristic (such as male versus female) or a time variable (such as before versus after treatment). The distinction between the two strategies is that nonexperimental designs make little or no attempt to control threats to internal validity, whereas quasi-experimental designs actively attempt to limit threats to internal validity.

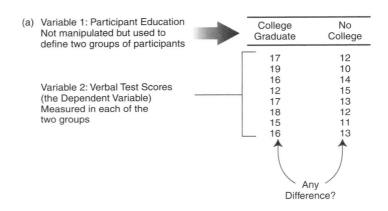

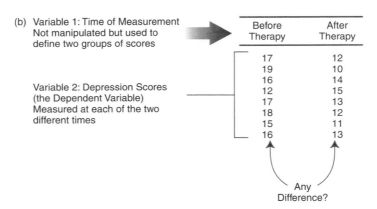

FIGURE **12.2** Two Examples of Nonexperimental or Quasi-Experimental Studies

(a) A preexisting participant variable (education) is used to define two groups, and then a dependent variable (verbal test score) is measured in each group.

(b) The two groups of scores are defined by the time of measurement, and a dependent variable (depression) is measured at each of the two times.

LEARNING CHECK   Explain why we cannot be as confident about causal relationships between variables when a nonexperimental design is used instead of a true experiment.

12.2 | BETWEEN-SUBJECTS NONEXPERIMENTAL AND QUASI-EXPERIMENTAL DESIGNS: NONEQUIVALENT GROUP DESIGNS

In Chapter 10, we introduced the between-subjects experimental design as a method of comparing two or more treatment conditions using a different group of participants in each condition. A common element to between-subjects experiments is the control of individual differences by assigning participants to specific treatment conditions. The goal is to balance or equalize the groups by using a random assignment process or by deliberately matching participants across treatment conditions. Note that the researcher attempts to create equivalent groups of participants by actively assigning which individuals go into which groups. There are occasions, however, when a researcher must examine preexisting groups. For example, a researcher may want to evaluate a teen pregnancy prevention program by comparing the pregnancy rates in a high school where the program is used with pregnancy rates in a high school that does not use the program. In this study, the researcher does not have control over which individuals are assigned to which group; the two groups of participants already exist. Because the researcher cannot use random assignment or matching to minimize the individual differences between groups, there is no assurance that the two groups are equivalent. In this situation, the research study is called a **nonequivalent group design.**

DEFINITION   A **nonequivalent group design** is a research study in which the different groups of participants are formed under circumstances that do not permit the researcher to control the assignment of individuals to groups, and the groups of participants are, therefore, considered nonequivalent. Specifically, the researcher cannot use random assignment to create groups of participants.

Threats to Internal Validity for Nonequivalent Group Designs

A general example of a nonequivalent group design is shown in Figure 12.3. Notice that the groups are differentiated by one specific factor that identifies the groups. In the teen pregnancy example, the differentiating factor was the pregnancy prevention program: one high school received the program and one did not. Typically, the purpose of the study is to show that the factor that differentiates the groups is responsible for causing the participants' scores to differ from one group to the other. For example, in the teen pregnancy study, the goal is to show that the pregnancy prevention program is responsible for the different pregnancy rates in the two schools.

However, a nonequivalent group design has a built-in threat to internal validity that precludes an unambiguous cause-and-effect explanation. That threat was introduced in Chapter 6 as **assignment bias.** Recall that assignment bias occurs whenever the assignment procedure produces groups that have

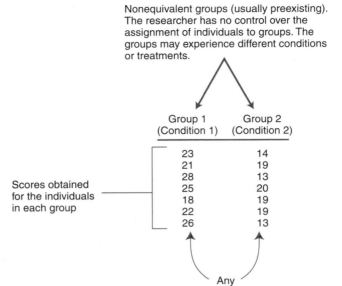

Nonequivalent groups (usually preexisting).
The researcher has no control over the
assignment of individuals to groups. The
groups may experience different conditions
or treatments.

Group 1   Group 2
(Condition 1)   (Condition 2)

Scores obtained
for the individuals
in each group

Group 1 (Condition 1)	Group 2 (Condition 2)
23	14
21	19
28	13
25	20
18	19
22	19
26	13

Any
Difference?

FIGURE **12.3** The General Structure of a Nonequivalent Group Study

different participant characteristics. For example, the two high schools in the teen pregnancy study may differ in terms of student IQs, socioeconomic background, racial mixture, student motivation, and so on. These variables are all potentially confounding variables because any one of them could explain the differences between the two groups. Because the assignment of participants is not controlled in a study using nonequivalent groups, this type of research always is threatened by assignment bias. You may recognize that a nonequivalent groups study is similar to the between-subjects experimental design presented in Chapter 10. However, the experimental design always uses some form of random assignment to ensure equivalent groups. In a nonequivalent groups design, there is no random assignment and there is no assurance of equivalent groups.

In this section, we consider three common examples of nonequivalent group designs: (1) the differential research design, (2) the posttest-only nonequivalent control group design, and (3) the pretest–posttest nonequivalent control group design. The first two are research designs that make no attempt to control or minimize assignment bias, and, as a result, do not approach the rigor of a true experiment; they are nonexperimental designs. The third design is classified as quasi-experimental because it does attempt to minimize the threat of assignment bias.

The Differential Research Design

In most between-subjects research, individual differences are considered to be a problem that must be controlled by random assignment, matching groups, or some other process. However, there are research studies for which individual differences are the primary interest. For example, researchers are often interested in how behavior is influenced by gender differences, or how performance is influenced by age differences. In these situations, researchers deliberately create separate groups of participants based on a specific individual difference such as gender or age. Note that these studies involve no manipulation but simply attempt to compare preexisting groups that are defined by a particular participant characteristic. For example, a researcher may want to compare self-esteem scores for children from two-parent households with children from single-parent households. Note that the researcher does not control the assignment of participants to groups; instead, the participants are automatically assigned to groups based on a preexisting characteristic. For this example, the children are assigned to groups based on the number of parents in the household. Although this type of study compares groups of participants (like a between-subjects experiment), the researcher does not manipulate the treatment conditions and does not have control over the assignment of participants to groups. Again, this is not a true experiment.

A research study that simply compares preexisting groups is called a **differential research design** because its goal is to establish differences between the preexisting groups. This type of study often is called ex post facto research because it looks at differences "after the fact;" that is, at differences that already exist between groups. Because the differential research design makes no attempt to control the threat of assignment bias, it is classified as a nonexperimental research design. For example, a study by InsuranceHotline.com (Romanov, 2006) found significant differences in the number of car accidents and tickets for people with different astrological signs. Libras and Aquarians were the worst offenders, while Leos and Geminis had the best overall records. Clearly, people who have different astrological signs form preexisting groups that were not manipulated or created by the researchers. In another somewhat bizarre study, DeGoede, Ashton-Miller, Liao, & Alexander (2001) swung a pendulum at their participants and measured how quickly the participants moved their hands to intercept the approaching object. This study examined gender differences and age differences, once again comparing preexisting groups.

Many research questions in social psychology and personality theory are focused on differences between groups or categories of people. Personality theorists, for example, often classify people according to attachment style, and then examine differences between individuals with different styles. Many research studies have demonstrated that the style of mother/child attachment formed in infancy persists as an individual develops and is related to adult intimacy and romantic relationships (Brennan & Morris, 1997; Feeney, 2004).

DEFINITION

A research study that simply compares preexisting groups is called a **differential research design**. A differential study uses a participant characteristic such as gender, race, or personality to automatically assign participants to groups. The researcher does not randomly assign individuals to groups. A dependent variable is then measured for each participant to obtain a set of scores within each group. The goal of the study is to determine whether the scores for one group are consistently different from the scores of another group. Differential research is classified as a nonexperimental research design.

Differential Research and Correlational Research

Many researchers place differential research in the same category as correlational research. In many ways, differential research is similar to the correlational research strategy (introduced in Chapter 6 and discussed in Chapter 8). In differential and correlational studies, a researcher simply observes two naturally occurring variables without any interference or manipulation. The subtle distinction between differential research and correlational research is whether one of the variables is used to establish separate groups to be compared. In differential research, participant differences in one variable are used to create separate groups, and measurements of the second variable are made within each group. The researcher then compares the measurements for one group with the measurements for another group, typically looking at mean differences between groups (Figure 12.4a). A correlational study, on the other hand, treats all the participants as a single group and simply measures the two variables for each individual (Figure 12.4b). Although differential research and correlational research produce different kinds of data and involve different statistical analyses, their results should receive the same interpretation. Both designs allow researchers to establish the existence of relationships and to describe relationships between variables, but neither design permits a cause-and-effect explanation of the relationship.

 **LEARNING CHECK** A researcher measures personality characteristics for a group of participants who successfully lost weight in a diet program, and compared their scores with a second group consisting of individuals who failed to lose weight in the program. Is this study a differential design? Explain your answer.

The Posttest-Only Nonequivalent Control Group Design

Nonequivalent groups are commonly used in applied research situations in which the goal is to evaluate the effectiveness of a treatment administered to a preexisting group of participants. A second group of similar but nonequivalent participants is used for the control condition. Note that the researcher uses preexisting groups and does not control the assignment of participants to groups. In particular, the researcher does not randomly assign individuals to groups.

For example, Skjoeveland (2001) used a nonequivalent group study to examine the effects of street parks on social interactions among neighbors. Parks were constructed in one area, and the people living in that neighborhood were compared with two control groups that did not get new parks. Similarly, Goldie, Schwartz, McConnachie, & Morrison (2001) evaluated a new ethics course for medical students by comparing the group of students who took the new course with a nonequivalent group who did not take the course. This type of research is called a **nonequivalent control group design**.

(a) A differential study examining the relationship between self-esteem and academic performance.

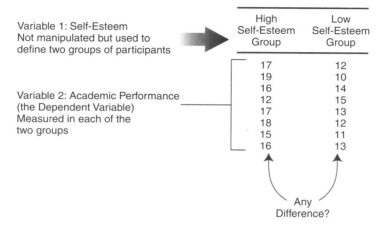

(b) A correlational study examining the relationship between self-esteem and academic performance.

Participant	Variable 1 Self-Esteem	Variable 2 Academic Performance
A	84	16
B	72	10
C	90	19
D	68	13
E	77	16
F	81	12
G	85	17
H	76	13

FIGURE **12.4** Comparison of Differential Research and Correlational Research

(a) The structure of a differential study examining the relationship between self-esteem and academic performance. Note that one of the two variables (self-esteem) is used to create groups, and the other variable (academic performance) is measured to obtain scores within each group.

(b) The structure of a correlational study examining the relationship between self-esteem and academic performance. Note that there is only one group of participants with two scores (self-esteem and academic performance) measured for each individual.

DEFINITION   A **nonequivalent control group design** uses preexisting groups, one of which serves in the treatment condition and the other in the control condition. The researcher does not randomly assign individuals to the groups.

One common example of a nonequivalent control group design is called a **posttest-only nonequivalent control group design.** This type of study is occasionally called a *static group comparison*. In this design, one group of participants is given a treatment and then is measured after the treatment (this is the posttest). The scores for the treated group are then compared with the scores from a nonequivalent group that has not received the treatment (this is the control group). This design can be represented schematically using a series of Xs and Os to represent the series of events experienced by each group. In this notation system, developed by Campbell and Stanley (1963), the letter X corresponds to the treatment, and the letter O corresponds to the observation or measurement. Thus, the treatment group experiences the treatment first (X) followed by observation or measurement (O). The control group does not receive any treatment but is simply observed (O). The two groups are represented as follows:

X   O   (treatment group)

O   (nonequivalent control group)

If a design includes random assignment of participants to groups in the study, an R is placed as the first symbol in each line of notation. The absence of an R in this schematic reflects the use of preexisting groups, as in a nonequivalent control group design.

DEFINITION

A **posttest-only nonequivalent control group design** compares two nonequivalent groups of participants. One group is observed (measured) after receiving a treatment, and the other group is measured at the same time but receives no treatment. This is an example of a nonexperimental research design.

The posttest-only nonequivalent control group design is commonly used when a treatment is given to a well-defined, isolated cluster of individuals, such as the students in a classroom or the patients in a clinic. In these situations, a separate cluster (for example, another classroom or another clinic) is often selected as the nonequivalent control group. The teen pregnancy program discussed earlier is a good example of this type of study. The program is administered at one high school, and a second high school that does not receive the program serves as a nonequivalent control group. Note that the purpose of the study is to show that the program has an effect by demonstrating a difference in pregnancy rates between the two schools.

Although this kind of research design appears to ask a cause-and-effect question (Does the treatment cause a difference?), the research design does not protect against assignment bias. As we noted earlier, the students at the two schools could differ on a variety of variables (in addition to the pregnancy program), and any of these other variables could be responsible for the difference in pregnancy rates. Because the posttest-only nonequivalent control group design does not address the threat of assignment bias, it is considered a nonexperimental design.

LEARNING CHECK

Earlier, we described a study in which Skjoeveland (2001) examined the effect of street parks on social interactions (p. 340). Although the results clearly showed greater social interaction in neighborhoods in which parks were built, the study does not justify a conclusion that building parks causes an increase in social interaction. Explain why the conclusion is not justified.

The Pretest–Posttest Nonequivalent Control Group Design

A much stronger version of the nonequivalent control group design is often called a **pretest–posttest nonequivalent control group design** and can be represented as follows:

O   X   O   (treatment group)

O   O   (nonequivalent control group)

In this case, the first step is to observe (measure) both groups. The treatment is then administered to one group, and, following the treatment, both groups are observed again.

The addition of the pretest measurement allows researchers to address the problem of assignment bias that exists with all nonequivalent group research. Specifically, the researcher can now compare the observations before treatment to establish whether the two groups really are similar. If the groups are found to be similar before treatment, the researcher has evidence that the participants in one group are not substantially different from the participants in another group, and the threat of assignment bias is reduced. Note, however, that the pretest scores simply allow the researcher to ensure that the two groups are similar with respect to one specific variable. Other potentially important variables are not measured or controlled. Thus, the threat of assignment bias is reduced, but it is certainly not eliminated.

This type of design also allows a researcher to compare the pretest scores and posttest scores for both groups to help determine whether the treatment or some other, time-related factor is responsible for changes. In Chapter 6, we introduced a set of time-related factors such as history and maturation that can threaten internal validity. In the pretest–posttest nonequivalent groups design, however, these time-related threats are minimized because both groups are observed over the same time period and, therefore, should experience the same time-related factors. If the participants are similar before treatment but different after treatment, the researcher can be more confident that the treatment has an effect. On the other hand, if both groups show the same degree of change from the pretest to the posttest, the researcher must conclude that some factor other than the treatment is responsible for the change. Thus, the pretest–posttest nonequivalent control group design reduces the threat of assignment bias, limits threats from time-related factors, and can provide some evidence to support a cause-and-effect relationship. As a result, this type of research is considered quasi-experimental.

DEFINITION

A **pretest–posttest nonequivalent control group design** compares two nonequivalent groups. One group is measured twice, once before a treatment is administered and once after. The other group is measured at the same two times but does not receive any treatment. Because this design attempts to limit threats to internal validity, it is classified as quasi-experimental.

Threats from Differential Effects

Although the addition of a pretest to the nonequivalent control group design reduces some threats to internal validity, it does not eliminate them completely. In addition, the fact that the groups are nonequivalent and often are in separate locations creates the potential for other threats. Specifically, it is possible for a time-related threat to affect the groups differently. For example, one group may be influenced by outside events that are not experienced by the other group. The students in one high school may be enjoying a winning football season whereas students in another school may be depressed because their team is losing every game. In Chapter 6 we identified the influence of outside events as history effects. When history effects differ from one group to another, they are called differential history effects. The **differential effects** can be a confounding variable because any differences observed between the two groups may be explained by their different histories. In a similar way other time-related influences such as maturation, instrumentation, testing effects, and regression may be different from one group to another, and these differential effects can threaten the internal validity of a nonequivalent group study.

LEARNING CHECKS

Explain how the pretest helps minimize the threat to internal validity from assignment bias in a pretest–posttest nonequivalent control group design.

Describe how differential history effects can threaten the internal validity of a pretest–posttest nonequivalent control group design.

12.3 | WITHIN-SUBJECTS NONEXPERIMENTAL AND QUASI-EXPERIMENTAL DESIGNS: PRE–POST DESIGNS

The second general category of quasi-experimental and nonexperimental designs consists of studies in which a series of observations is made over time. Collectively, such studies are known as **pre–post designs**. In a typical pre–post study, one group of participants is observed (measured) before and after a treatment or event. The goal of the pre–post design is to evaluate the influence of the intervening treatment or event by comparing the observations made before treatment with the observations made after treatment.

You may have noticed that a pre–post design is similar to the pretest-posttest nonequivalent control group design discussed earlier. However, a pre–post design has no control group. In addition, the primary focus of a pretest–posttest nonequivalent control group design is to compare the treatment group and the control group, not to compare the pretest scores with the posttest scores. As a result, the pretest–posttest nonequivalent control group design is primarily a nonequivalent group design and we have classified it in that category.

Threats to Internal Validity for Pre–Post Designs

Whenever the same group of individuals is observed repeatedly over time, time-related factors can threaten internal validity. As we noted in Chapter 6 and Chapter 11, the five categories of time-related threats are **history, instrumentation, testing effects, maturation,** and **statistical regression.** Clearly, pre–post studies are vulnerable to these threats; any differences found between the pretreatment observations and the posttreatment observations could be explained by history, instrumentation, testing effects, maturation, or regression. You may recognize that a pre–post design is similar to the within-subjects experimental design presented in Chapter 11. However, the experimental design uses counter-balancing to control order effects and other time-related threats to internal validity. In a pre–post design, it is impossible to counterbalance the order of treatments. Specifically, the before-treatment observations (pretest) must always precede the after-treatment observations (posttest).

In general, the internal validity of a pre–post study is threatened by a variety of factors related to the passage of time. During the time between the first observation and the last observation, any one of these factors could influence the participants and cause a change in their scores. Unless these factors are controlled or minimized by the structure of the research design, a pre–post study cannot approach the internal validity of a true experiment. In this section, we introduce two examples of pre–post studies: the one-group pretest–posttest design and the time-series design. The first of these designs makes no attempt to control the threats to internal validity and, therefore, is classified as nonexperimental. The second design manages to minimize most threats to internal validity and is classified as quasi-experimental.

The One-Group Pretest–Posttest Design

The simplest version of the pre–post design consists of only one observation for each participant made before the treatment or event, and only one observation made after it. Schematically, this simple form can be represented as follows:

$$O \quad X \quad O$$

This type of study is called a **one-group pretest–posttest design.** For example, a political consultant could evaluate the effectiveness of a new political television commercial by assessing voters' attitudes toward a candidate before and after they view the commercial. The results from this study may demonstrate a change in attitude. However, because this design makes no attempt to control the many threats to internal validity, the study cannot conclude that the change was caused by the intervening commercial. Because the one-group pretest–posttest study precludes a cause-and-effect conclusion, this type of research is classified as nonexperimental.

DEFINITION

In the **one-group pretest–posttest design,** each individual in a single group of participants is measured once before treatment and once after treatment. This type of research is classified as a nonexperimental design.

The Time-Series Design

A **time-series design** requires a series of observations for each participant before and after a treatment or event. It can be represented as follows:

$$O \quad O \quad O \quad X \quad O \quad O \quad O$$

The intervening treatment or event (X) may or may not be manipulated by the researcher. For example, a doctor may record blood pressure for a group of executives before and after they complete relaxation training. Or, a researcher may evaluate the effect of a natural disaster such as earthquake or flood on the wellbeing of a group of students by recording visits to the school nurse for the months before and after the disaster. In one case the researcher is manipulating a treatment (the relaxation training) and in the other case the researcher is studying a non-manipulated event (an earthquake). A study in which the intervening event is not manipulated by the researcher is sometimes called an **interrupted time-series design.**

Occasionally, a time-series study is used to investigate the effect of a predictable event such as a legal change in the drinking age or speed limit. In this case, researchers can begin collecting data before the event actually occurs. However, it often is impossible to predict the occurrence of an event such as an earthquake, so it is impossible for researchers to start collecting data just before one arrives. In this situation, researchers often rely on archival data such as police records or hospital records to provide the observations for the time-series study.

DEFINITION

A **time-series design** has a series of observations for each participant before a treatment or event and a series of observations after the treatment or event. A treatment is a manipulation administered by the researcher and an event is an outside occurrence that is not controlled or manipulated by the researcher.

LEARNING CHECK

What characteristic differentiates a one-group pretest–posttest design from a time-series design?

In a time-series design, the pretest and posttest series of observations serve several valuable purposes. First, the pretest observations allow a researcher to see any trends that may already exist in the data before the treatment is even introduced. Trends in the data are an indication that the scores are influenced by some factor unrelated to the treatment. For example, practice or fatigue may cause the scores to increase or decrease over time before a treatment is introduced. Similarly, instrumentation effects, maturation effects, or regression should produce noticeable changes in the observations before treatment. On the other hand, if the data show no trends or major fluctuations before the treatment, the researcher can be reasonably sure that these potential threats to internal validity are not influencing the participants. Thus, the series of observations allows a researcher to minimize most threats to internal validity. As a result, the time-series design is classified as quasi-experimental.

It is possible for an external event (history) to be a threat to internal validity in time-series designs, but only if the event occurs simultaneously with the treatment. If the outside event occurs at any time other than the introduction of the treatment, it should be easy to separate the history effects from the treatment effects. For example, if the participants are affected by an outside event that occurs before the treatment, the effect should be apparent in the observations that occur before the treatment. Figure 12.5 shows three possible

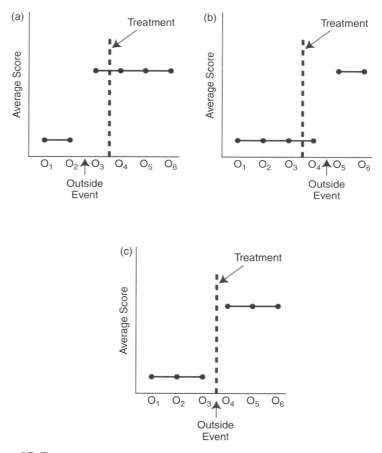

FIGURE 12.5 How Data in a Time-Series Study Might Be Affected by an Outside Event

(a) The event occurs and influences scores before the treatment is introduced.
(b) The event occurs and influences scores after the treatment.
(c) The event and the treatment occur simultaneously, and it is impossible to determine which is influencing the scores.

outcomes in which the treatment has no effect but instead the participants are influenced by an outside event. Notice that a problem occurs only when the treatment and the outside event coincide perfectly. In this case, it is impossible to determine whether the change in behavior was caused by the treatment or by the outside event. Thus, history effects (outside events) are a threat to validity only when there is a perfect correspondence between the occurrence of the event and the introduction of the treatment. Suppose, for example, that a clinical researcher uses a time-series design to evaluate a treatment for depression. Observations are made for a group of depressed clients for a week before therapy begins, and a second series of observations is made for a week after therapy. The observations indicate significant improvement after therapy. However, suppose that, by coincidence, there is an abrupt change in the weather on the same day that therapy starts; after weeks of cold, dark, rainy days, it suddenly becomes bright, sunny, and unseasonably warm. Because the weather changed at the same time as the treatment, it is impossible to determine what caused the clients' improvement. Was the change caused by the treatment or by the weather?

The series of observations after the treatment or event also allows a researcher to observe any posttreatment trends. For example, it is possible that the treatment has only a temporary effect that quickly fades. Such a trend would be seen in the series of posttreatment observations. Figure 12.6 demonstrates how a series of observations can be more informative than single observations made before and after treatment. The figure shows a series of scores that are consistently increasing before treatment and continue to increase in an uninterrupted pattern after treatment. In this case, it does not appear that the treatment has any effect on the scores. However, if the

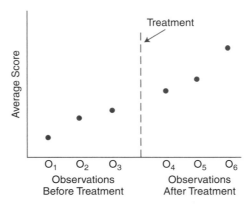

FIGURE **12.6** A Time Series Study with Multiple Observations Before and After Treatment

The series of observations makes it possible to see the trend in the data that existed before the treatment was administered and that continues after the treatment.

study included only one observation before treatment and only one observation after treatment (O3 and O4), the results would indicate a substantial increase in scores following the treatment, suggesting that the treatment did have an effect.

Single-Case Applications of Time-Series Designs

The time-series design was introduced as a research study that involves observing a group of participants at several different times. However, this design is often applied to single individuals or single organizations. For example, a high school could evaluate the effects of an anger-management program by monitoring the number of fights at the school for 3 months before the program is enacted and for 3 months afterward. This is an example of a time-series design but it involves measurements for one high school, not for individual participants. Similarly, a therapist could monitor instances of compulsive behavior in one client for 3 weeks before therapy and for 3 weeks after. This is an example of a time-series design applied to a single individual. Research designs that focus on a single case, rather than a group of participants, are occasionally called single-case time-series designs but are more often classified as **single-subject** or **single-case designs**. Single-subject designs are discussed in Chapter 15.

12.4 | DEVELOPMENTAL RESEARCH DESIGNS

Developmental research designs are another type of nonexperimental research that can be used to study changes in behavior that relate to age. The purpose of developmental research designs is to describe the relationship between age and other variables. For example, if a researcher is interested in how language ability changes with age, a developmental research design would be appropriate.

DEFINITION　**Developmental research designs** are used to examine changes in behavior related to age.

Two basic types of developmental research designs are the cross-sectional design and the longitudinal design. Each has its strengths and weaknesses.

The Cross-Sectional Developmental Research Design

The **cross-sectional developmental research design** is a between-subjects design that uses a separate group of participants for each of the ages being compared. A dependent variable is measured for the individuals in each group and the groups are compared to determine whether there are age differences. For example, a researcher who wants to examine the relationship between IQ and aging could select three different groups of people—40 year olds, 60 year olds, and 80 year olds—and could then measure IQ for each group. See Figure 12.7.

DEFINITION　The **cross-sectional developmental research design** uses different groups of individuals, each group representing a different age. The different groups are measured at one point in time and then compared.

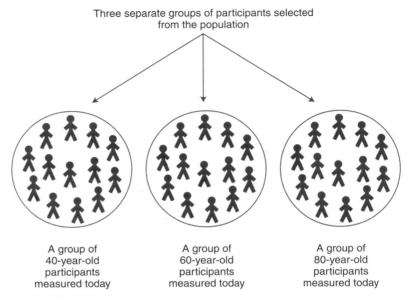

Three separate groups of participants selected
from the population

A group of
40-year-old
participants
measured today

A group of
60-year-old
participants
measured today

A group of
80-year-old
participants
measured today

FIGURE **12.7** The Structure of a Cross-Sectional Developmental
Research Design
Three separate groups of participants are selected to represent three different ages

The term *cross-sectional* is also used to describe surveys that classify people into different categories or subgroups. Here, we are discussing cross-sectional developmental designs.

For example, Oppenheimer (2006) used a cross-sectional study to examine changes in people's belief in a just and orderly world as they mature from 12 to 22 years of age. Comparing results from six age groups of students from secondary school through college, the study found that belief in a just world declined as the students age increased.

A cross-sectional design is an example of a between-subjects nonexperimental design; specifically, a nonequivalent group design. The different groups of participants are not created by manipulating an independent variable; instead, the groups are defined by a preexisting participant variable (age). Also, the researcher does not randomly assign participants to groups; instead, group assignment is predetermined by each participant's age. Earlier in this chapter, we defined this kind of study as differential research. However, when a study evaluates differences related to age, the design is typically called a cross-sectional study.

Strengths and Weaknesses of the Cross-Sectional Developmental Design

One obvious advantage of the cross-sectional design is that a researcher can observe how behavior changes as people age without waiting for a group of participants to grow older. The example in Figure 12.7 shows that we do not need to follow a group of people over the next 40 years to observe the differences that occur during 40 years of aging. With the cross-sectional design, data can be collected in a short period of time. In addition, cross-sectional research does not require long-term cooperation between the researcher and the participant; that is, the researcher does not have to incur the time and expense of tracking people down for 40 years and encouraging them to continue in the research.

The cross-sectional research design is not without its weaknesses. One weakness is that a researcher cannot say anything about how a particular individual develops over time because individuals are not followed over years. A more serious problem is that factors other than age may differentiate the groups. For example, 40-year-old women not only are younger than 80-year-old women, but also grew up in very different environments. Opportunities for education, employment, and social expectations were very different for these two groups of women. In general, individuals who are the same age and have lived in similar environments are called **cohorts**. For example, today's preschool children, today's adolescents, and today's college students would be three sets of cohorts. In addition to being different ages, these three groups have also experienced different social and cultural environments. The environmental factors that differentiate one age group from another are called **cohort effects,** or **generation effects,** and they may be responsible for differences observed between the groups instead of age. As a result, generation effects are a threat to internal validity for a cross-sectional design. Specifically, in a cross-sectional study, the generation of the participants changes from one group to another so that the apparent relationship between age and other variables may actually be caused by generation differences. For example, suppose that you compared computer literacy for three groups; one with 40-year-olds, one with 60-year-olds, and one with 80-year-olds. Almost certainly, the data would show a decline in literacy as the participants grow older. However, you should not assume that this difference should be attributed to age. Specifically, you should not conclude that losing computer literacy is a consequence of aging. The 80-year-old participants did not lose computer literacy as they aged; instead, they spent most of their lives in an environment without computers and never had computer literacy to start with.

DEFINITION	Individuals who were born at roughly the same time and grew up under similar circumstances are called **cohorts.** The terms **cohort effects** and **generation effects** refer to differences between age groups (or cohorts) caused by unique characteristics or experiences other than age.

A great example of how cohort effects can influence the results of research comes from studies on the relationship between IQ and age (Baltes & Schaie, 1974). Many research studies show that IQ declines between the ages of 20 and 50. On the other hand, a separate group of studies shows little or no decline in IQ between the ages of 20 and 50. How can these two sets of data be so completely different? One answer lies in the designs of the studies. The data that show IQ declining with age are generally obtained with cross-sectional studies. The problem with cross-sectional designs is that the results may be influenced by cohort effects because the groups being compared are not only different in age but also lived in different decades. The fact that the groups grew up and lived in different environments could affect their IQ scores and be the source of the IQ differences between the groups. Cohort effects are more problematic the more years there are between the groups. The second set of studies, showing stable IQ, monitored the same set of people over a long period of time. This type of research design is called the longitudinal research design and is discussed next. Incidentally, other researchers have raised serious questions about this interpretation of the aging and IQ relationship (Horn & Donaldson, 1976).

LEARNING CHECK   Why is the cohort effect a problem in the cross-sectional design?

The Longitudinal Developmental Research Design

The **longitudinal developmental research design** involves measuring a variable in the same group of individuals over a period of time (typically every few months or every few years). The individuals are usually cohorts, roughly the same age, who have grown up in similar circumstances. Several measurements of a particular variable are made in the same individuals at two or more times in their lives to investigate the relationship between age and that variable. For example, to examine IQ and age using the longitudinal approach, a researcher might measure IQ in a group of 40 year olds and then measure the same individuals again at ages 60 and 80 (Figure 12.8).

DEFINITION   The **longitudinal developmental research design** examines development by observing or measuring a group of cohorts over time.

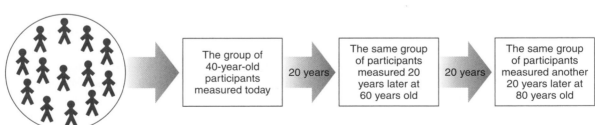

FIGURE **12.8** The Structure of a Longitudinal Developmental Research Design

One group of participants is measured at different times as the participants age.

A longitudinal study is an example of a within-subjects nonexperimental design; specifically, a one-group pretest–posttest design. In a longitudinal design, however, no treatment is administered; instead, the "treatment" is age. That is, a longitudinal study can be described as a set of observations followed by a period of development or aging, then another set of observations. The differences between the initial observations and the final observations define the effects of development. Thus, longitudinal studies can be viewed as a kind of pretest–posttest study. However, when this type of research is used to evaluate development or the effects of age, the design is typically called a longitudinal study.

The distinction between a longitudinal design and a time-series design is not always clear. For example, Sun (2001) examined the wellbeing of a group of adolescents for an extended period before and after their parents' divorces. This can be viewed as a longitudinal study because it examined the changes that occur over time for a group of participants. However, it also can be viewed as a pre–post time-series study that compared a series of observations made before an event (the divorce) with a series of observations made after the event.

Strengths and Weaknesses of the Longitudinal Developmental Design

A major strength of the longitudinal research design is the absence of cohort effects because the researcher examines one group of people over time rather than comparing groups that represent different ages and come from different generations. Second, with longitudinal research, a researcher can discuss how a single individual's behavior changes with age. However, longitudinal research is extremely time consuming, both for the participants (it requires a big commitment to continue in the study) and the researcher (the researcher must stay interested in the research and wait for years to see the final results). In addition, these designs are very expensive to conduct because researchers need to track people down and persuade them, when necessary, to come back to participate in the study. If the study spans many years, there is the additional expense of repeatedly training experimenters to conduct the study. Furthermore, these designs are subject to high dropout rates of participants. People lose interest in the study, move away, or die. When participants drop out of a study, it is known as **participant attrition** (or **participant mortality**), and it may weaken the internal validity of the research. Specifically, if the participants who drop out are systematically different from those who stay, the group at the end of the study may have different characteristics from the group at the beginning. For example, if the less-motivated individuals drop out, then the group at the end is more motivated than the group at the beginning. The higher level of motivation (rather than age) may explain any changes that are observed over time. (The issue of participant attrition is discussed in more detail in Chapter 11.) A final weakness of the longitudinal research design is that the same individuals are measured repeatedly. It is possible that the scores obtained late in the study are partially affected by previous experience with the test or measurement procedure. (In Chapter 6, we discussed testing effects as a threat to internal validity.)

Table 12.1 summarizes the strengths and weaknesses of cross-sectional and longitudinal developmental research designs.

**LEARNING
CHECKS**

Longitudinal research can be very time consuming, however, this is not a problem with cross-sectional research. Explain why not.

Although the cohort effect can be a serious problem for cross-sectional research, it is not a problem for longitudinal designs. Explain why not.

Cross-Sectional Longitudinal Designs

Although the term cross-sectional longitudinal design may appear to be internally contradictory, there are research studies for which this label is appropriate. Specifically, many research studies compare the results obtained from separate samples (like a cross-sectional design) that were obtained at different times (like a longitudinal design). Typically, this type of research is examining the development of phenomena other than individual aging. For example, Pope, Ionescu-Pioggia, and Pope (2001) examined how drug use and lifestyle have changed over the past 30 years by returning to the same college every 10 years to measure freshman attitudes and behaviors. Because Pope and his colleagues measured different individuals every 10 years, this research combines elements of cross-sectional and longitudinal designs. In a similar study, Mitchell, Wolak, and Finkelhor (2007) examined trends in youth reports of unwanted exposure to pornography on the Internet. This study compared results from a survey of 10- through 17-year-old Internet users in the year 2000 with an equivalent survey of a different sample in the year 2005. Although both of these studies are examining development (or social evolution) over time, neither is a purely longitudinal or a purely cross-sectional design. Nonetheless, you are likely to find this type of research is occasionally described as longitudinal and it is occasionally described as cross-sectional. Because the design is not clearly one or the other, we hedge a little and classify this research *cross-sectional longitudinal*.

The complete set of quasi-experimental and nonexperimental research designs, including developmental designs, is summarized in Table 12.2.

TABLE **12.1**
Strengths and Weaknesses of Cross-Sectional and Longitudinal Developmental Research Designs

	Longitudinal Research	Cross-Sectional Research
Strengths	No cohort or generation effects Assesses individual behavior changes	Time efficient No long-term cooperation required
Weaknesses	Time consuming Participant dropout may create bias Potential for practice effects	Individual changes not assessed Cohort or generation effects

TABLE **12.2**
Quasi-Experimental and Nonexperimental Research Designs

Between-Subjects Nonequivalent Group Designs		
Design Name	**Description**	**Classification**
Differential research	Compares preexisting groups	Nonexperimental
Posttest-only nonequivalent control group design	Compares preexisting groups after one group receives a treatment	Nonexperimental
Pretest–posttest nonequivalent control group design	Compares preexisting groups before and after one group receives a treatment	Quasi-experimental
Cross-sectional developmental design	Compares preexisting groups of different ages	Nonexperimental
Within-Subjects Pre–Post Designs		
Design Name	**Description**	**Classification**
One-group pretest–posttest design	Compares one observation before treatment (pretest) and one observation after treatment (posttest) for a single group of participants	Nonexperimental
Time-series design	Compares a series of observations before a treatment with a series of observations after the treatment	Quasi-experimental
Longitudinal developmental design	Observes one group of participants at different points in time	Nonexperimental

LEARNING CHECKS

For each of the following, indicate whether it is a typical longitudinal or cross-sectional study, or a combination of the two designs. In each case, a researcher examines changes in child discipline.

a. Every 3 years, the researcher contacts the local schools to obtain a sample of newly registered kindergarten students. The students' families are contacted and asked to complete a questionnaire describing the kinds of discipline they use and how often they discipline their children.

b. The researcher contacts the local schools to obtain a sample of newly registered kindergarten students. The students' families are contacted and asked to complete a questionnaire describing the kinds of discipline they use and how often they discipline their children. Every 3 years, the researcher returns to the families and asks them to complete the questionnaire again.

c. A researcher obtains a sample of newly registered kindergarten students, a sample of second-grade students, and a sample of fourth-grade students. The students' families are contacted and asked to complete a questionnaire describing the kinds of discipline they use and how often they discipline their children.

12.5 | TERMINOLOGY IN NONEXPERIMENTAL, QUASI-EXPERIMENTAL, AND DEVELOPMENTAL DESIGNS

In a true experiment, the researcher manipulates an independent variable to create treatment conditions and then measures a dependent variable (scores) in each condition; scores in one condition are compared with the scores obtained in another condition. In nonexperimental and quasi-experimental research, no independent variable is manipulated. Nonetheless, nonexperimental studies do involve comparing groups of scores. In nonequivalent group studies, for example, the scores from one group of participants are compared with the scores from a different group. In pre–post studies, the scores obtained before the treatment are compared with the scores obtained after the treatment. In general, the variable that differentiates the groups (or sets of scores) is similar to the independent variable in an experiment and is often called an independent variable. However, this variable is more accurately referred to as a **quasi-independent variable.** As in an experiment, the score obtained for each participant is called the **dependent variable.**

DEFINITIONS

Within the context of nonexperimental and quasi-experimental research, the variable that is used to differentiate the groups of participants or the groups of scores being compared is called the **quasi-independent variable,** and the variable that is measured to obtain the scores within each group is called the **dependent variable.**

In nonequivalent control group studies, for example, one group receives the treatment and one does not. The group difference, treatment versus nontreatment, determines the quasi-independent variable. In time-series studies, the researcher compares one set of observations (scores) before treatment with a second set of observations after treatment. For these studies, the quasi-independent variable is defined as "before versus after treatment."

Note that the same terminology is used for nonexperimental research as well as quasi-experimental studies. In differential research, for example, the participant variable used to differentiate the groups is called the quasi-independent variable. In a differential study comparing self-esteem scores for children from two-parent and single-parent homes, the number of parents is the quasi-independent variable, and self-esteem is the dependent variable. In a developmental study (either longitudinal or cross-sectional) examining changes in memory that occur with aging, the different ages are the quasi-independent variable and the memory scores are the dependent variable.

 **LEARNING CHECK**

The college offers all students an optional seminar on note taking and study skills. Suppose that a researcher compares personality scores for students who elected to take the seminar with the scores for students who did not. Identify the quasi-independent variable and the dependent variable for this study.

CHAPTER SUMMARY

In many research situations, it is difficult or impossible for a researcher to satisfy completely the rigorous requirements of an experiment, particularly when doing applied research in natural settings. In these situations, a researcher may use the quasi-experimental or the nonexperimental research strategy. Quasi-experimental and nonexperimental studies always contain a threat to internal validity that is integral to the design and cannot be removed. As a result, these two research strategies cannot establish unambiguous cause-and-effect explanations. Quasi-experimental studies make some attempt to control threats to internal validity but nonexperimental studies typically do not.

Quasi-experimental and nonexperimental studies often look like experiments because they involve comparing groups of scores. Unlike experiments, however, the different groups are not created by manipulating an independent variable; instead, the groups are defined in terms of a preexisting participant characteristic (for example, male/female) or defined in terms of time (for example, before and after treatment). These two methods for defining groups produce two general categories of quasi-experimental and nonexperimental designs: nonequivalent group designs and pre–post designs.

In nonequivalent group designs, the researcher does not control the assignment of individuals to groups because the two groups already exist. Therefore, there is no assurance that the two groups are equivalent in terms of extraneous variables and internal validity is threatened by assignment bias. Three types of nonequivalent group designs are discussed: (1) the differential research design, (2) the posttest-only nonequivalent control group design, and (3) the pretest–posttest nonequivalent control group design. The first two designs make no attempt to limit the threat of assignment bias and are classified as nonexperimental. The pretest–posttest design does reduce the threat of assignment bias and is classified as quasi-experimental.

The second general category is the pre–post design. The goal of a pre–post design is to evaluate the influence of the intervening treatment or event by comparing the observations before treatment with the observations made after treatment. Two examples of pre–post designs are considered: (1) the one group pretest–posttest design, and (2) the time-series design. The first design makes no attempt to control time-related threats and is classified as nonexperimental. The second is quasi-experimental.

Developmental research designs are another type of nonexperimental research. The purpose of developmental designs is to describe the relationship between age and other variables. There are two types of developmental research designs. The cross-sectional research design compares separate groups of individuals with each group representing a different age. The obvious advantage of this design is that the researcher need not wait for participants to age to examine the relationship between a variable and age. However, the cohort or generation effect is a major weakness. In the longitudinal research design, the same group of individuals is followed and measured at different points in time; hence, cohort effects are not a problem. However, longitudinal research is extremely time consuming for participants and researchers, and participant dropout can create a biased sample.

KEY WORDS

nonexperimental research
    strategy
quasi-experimental research
    strategy
nonequivalent group
    design
differential research design
nonequivalent control group
    design

posttest-only nonequivalent
    control group design
pretest–posttest nonequivalent
    control group design
one-group pretest–posttest
    design
time-series design
developmental research
    designs

cross-sectional developmental
    research design
cohorts
cohort effects, or generation
    effects
longitudinal developmental
    research design
quasi-independent variable
dependent variable

EXERCISES

1. In addition to the key words, you should
   also be able to define the following terms:
   assignment bias
   differential effects
   pre–post designs
   history
   instrumentation
   testing effects
   maturation
   statistical regression
   interrupted time-series designs
   single-subject, or single-case designs
   participant attrition, or participant mortality
2. Give an example of a situation (aside from
   gender) in which a researcher must examine
   preexisting groups.
3. Experimental studies are similar to
   nonexperimental and quasi-experimental
   studies because they all compare groups of
   scores. Describe the major difference
   between the experimental and the
   nonexperimental or quasi-experimental
   research strategy.
4. What names are used to identify
   between-subjects and within-subjects
   developmental research designs?
   Explain why each design is considered
   to be nonexperimental.
5. What is the purpose of developmental
   research designs?
6. Describe the basic problem that threatens
   internal validity for nonequivalent group
   designs.

7. Give an example of a between-subjects
   nonexperimental design and a
   between-subjects quasi-experimental
   design. Explain why one is considered
   nonexperimental and the other is
   quasi-experimental.
8. Explain how a time-series design minimizes
   most threats to internal validity from
   time-related variables.
9. For each of the following research goals,
   assume that the experimental,
   correlational, and descriptive strategies
   are not being used, and identify which
   nonexperimental or quasi-experimental
   research design(s) would be most
   appropriate. (Note that there may be
   more than one design available for
   each goal.)
   a. Describe possible gender differences for
      the social interactions that occur within
      a group of preschool children while they
      play in a city park.
   b. Describe how fine motor skills change
      as a group of infants ages from 12 to
      18 months.
   c. Describe the effectiveness of a new
      program (compared to the old program)
      for teaching reading to elementary
      school students.
   d. Describe the relationship between
      alcohol consumption and grade point
      average for college students.

LEARNING ACTIVITIES

1. Make a list of some of the factors in your life that change from one day to the next. Possible examples include your mood, health, environment, schedule, obligations, successes and failures, and the quality of your social interactions. Now, imagine that you are in a pre–post study examining how your sense of humor is affected by an acupuncture treatment. The pretest is given one afternoon, the treatment is the next morning, and the posttest is in the afternoon following the treatment.

   a. Pick two items from your list of the factors that change from one day to the next, and describe how these changing factors could influence your scores in the research study.

   b. Explain why the research study cannot conclude that acupuncture causes changes in a person's sense of humor.

2. All of us have a tendency to categorize people into stereotypic groups. If you look around at the students on campus, you will see science geeks, artsy freaks, jocks, wallflowers, cheerleaders, and party animals, just to mention a few. Part of stereotyping is to assume that all the individuals in a particular category share some common characteristics that make them different from the rest of us. These assumed differences can be the basis for a research study.

   a. Identify a stereotype that describes one group of college students and list one characteristic that presumably makes them different from other students.

   b. Describe a research study that could be used to determine whether the stereotype is accurate. That is, describe a research study that would determine whether the characteristic you identified really is different for the stereotypic group.

   c. How would you classify your research study? Is it experimental, quasi-experimental, or nonexperimental? Be as specific as possible.

3. Use PsycInfo or a similar database to find a quasi-experimental or nonexperimental research study. (Note: Try using a specific term such as nonequivalent control group or cross-sectional as a search term. Or look for a topic that involves comparing different populations of participants. For example, using gender differences as a search term should lead you to studies comparing males and females.) Once you have located an article, answer each of the following questions.

   a. Describe the structure of the research study. For example, what variables are measured? How many groups are involved? Are the participants measured several times or only once?

   b. Does your study fit into one of the general categories of quasi-experimental research discussed in this chapter? If so, which one? (Warning: You may find that your study is much more complex than the examples discussed in the text. In this case, it may be that a simple quasi-experimental study is one small part of a more complicated design. If you have a complex design, try to identify the part of the study that corresponds to a quasi-experimental design.)

   c. Identify one factor in the study that prevents it from being a true experiment. That is, why are the researchers unable to say that changes in one variable are unquestionably responsible for changes in another variable?

WEB RESOURCES

Visit the Book Companion Website at **www .cengage.com/international** to access study tools including a glossary, flashcards, and web quizzing. You will also find a link to

Statistics and Research Methods Workshops. For this chapter, we suggest you look at the following workshop:

Nonexperimental Approaches

13

Factorial Designs

CHAPTER OVERVIEW

Step 6 of the research process involves selecting a research design. Often, a research question requires a design that is more complex than the relatively simple experimental, quasi-experimental, and nonexperimental designs presented in Chapters 10, 11, and 12. In this chapter, we introduce factorial designs that allow experiments to have more than one independent variable, and permit nonexperimental and quasi-experimental studies to have more than one quasi-independent variable. In addition, we introduce the possibility of combining experimental and nonexperimental strategies or mixing between-subjects and within-subjects designs in one study. The unique information provided by factorial designs is considered as well as various applications of this research design.

13.1 | INTRODUCTION TO FACTORIAL DESIGNS

In most research situations, the goal is to examine the relationship between two variables by isolating those variables within the research study. The idea is to eliminate or reduce the influence of any outside variables that may disguise or distort the specific relationship under investigation. For example, experimental research (discussed in Chapters 9, 10, and 11) typically focuses on one independent variable (which is expected to influence behavior) and one dependent variable (which is a measure of the behavior). Similarly, the nonexperimental and quasi-experimental designs described in Chapter 12 usually investigate the relationship between one quasi-independent variable and one dependent variable. For example, developmental studies typically examine how a behavior (dependent variable) is related to age (quasi-independent). In real life, however, variables rarely exist in isolation. That is, behavior usually is influenced by a variety of different variables acting and interacting simultaneously. For example, academic performance may be related to IQ, motivation, parents' level of education, health, and a variety of other variables. To examine these more complex, real-life situations, researchers often design research studies that include more than one independent variable (or quasi-independent variable). These studies are called factorial designs.

> Recall from Chapter 12 (p. 356) that in nonexperimental and quasi-experimental research, the variable that differentiates the groups of participants or the groups of scores is called the quasi-independent variable.

Experimental Factorial Designs

To simplify our discussion of factorial designs, we begin by looking exclusively at experimental studies; that is, studies that involve the manipulation of two or more independent variables. However, it is also possible for factorial designs to involve variables such as age or gender that are not manipulated and, therefore, are quasi-independent variables. For example, a researcher could examine work proficiency for males and females (factor A) under different temperature conditions (factor B). In this case, gender is a factor, but it is not manipulated. Factorial studies involving quasi-independent variables are discussed in Section 13.4. The following example introduces experimental factorial designs.

> It is common practice for a host to serve coffee at the end of a party at which the guests have been drinking alcohol. Presumably, the caffeine counteracts some of the effects of the alcohol so that the guests are more mentally alert when they head out for the trip home. Most of us believe that we have a good understanding of the effects of caffeine and alcohol on mental alertness. For many people, the first cup of coffee each morning is necessary to get started; on the other hand, many people have a glass of wine in the evening to help them relax and unwind at the end of a busy day. But do we really know how these substances influence our ability to react in an emergency situation? Does that cup of coffee at the end of the party really improve response time? These questions were addressed in a study by Liguori and Robinson (2001). They designed an experiment in which both alcohol and caffeine consumption were manipulated within the same study. They observed how quickly participants with different levels of alcohol and caffeine could apply the brakes in a simulated driving test. Figure 13.1 shows the general structure of this experiment. Notice that the study involves two independent variables: Alcohol consumption is varied by having

	No Caffeine	200 Mg Caffeine	400 Mg Caffeine
No Alcohol	Response time scores for a group of participants who received no alcohol and a 0-mg dose of caffeine	Response time scores for a group of participants who received no alcohol and a 200-mg dose of caffeine	Response time scores for a group of participants who received no alcohol and a 400-mg dose of caffeine
Alcohol	Response time scores for a group of participants who received alcohol and a 0-mg dose of caffeine	Response time scores for a group of participants who received alcohol and a 200-mg dose of caffeine	Response time scores for a group of participants who received alcohol and a 400-mg dose of caffeine

F I G U R E **13.1** The Structure of a Two-Factor Experiment in Which Alcohol Consumption (Factor A) and Caffeine Consumption (Factor B) Are Manipulated in the Same Study

The purpose of the experiment is to examine how different combinations of alcohol and caffeine affect response time in a simulated emergency driving situation.

the participants drink either a placebo (no alcohol) or a beverage containing 0.6 grams of ethanol per kilogram of body weight (roughly 8 ounces of wine per 100 pounds of body weight). Caffeine consumption is varied from no caffeine, to 200 mg, to 400 mg. The two independent variables create a matrix with the different values of caffeine defining the columns and the different levels of alcohol defining the rows. The resulting 2 × 3 matrix shows six different combinations of the variables, producing six treatment conditions to be examined. The dependent variable for each of the six conditions was a measure of the response time to apply the brakes in a simulated driving emergency.

Nonexperimental studies using quasi-independent variables as factors are discussed in section 13.4.

To simplify further discussion of this kind of research study, some basic terminology and definitions are in order. When two or more independent variables are combined in a single study, the independent variables are commonly called **factors.** For the study in our example, the two factors are alcohol consumption and caffeine consumption. A research study involving two or more factors is called a **factorial design.** This kind of design is often referred to by the number of its factors, such as a two-factor design or a three-factor design. Our example is a **two-factor design.** A research study with only one independent variable is often called a **single-factor design.**

Generically, each factor is denoted by a letter (A, B, C, and so on). In addition, factorial designs use a notation system that identifies both the number of factors and the number of values or **levels** that exist for each factor (see Chapter 9, p. 251). The previous example has two levels for the alcohol factor (factor A) and three levels for the caffeine factor (factor B), and can be described as a 2 × 3 (read as "two by three") factorial design with 2 indicating two levels of the first factor (alcohol) and 3 symbolizing three levels of the second factor (caffeine). The total number of treatment conditions can be determined by multiplying the levels for each factor. For example, a 2 × 2 factorial design (the simplest factorial design) would represent a two-factor design with two levels of the first factor and two levels of the second, with a total of four treatment conditions; and a $2 \times 3 \times 2$ design would represent a **three-factor design** with two, three, and two levels of each of the factors, respectively, for a total of 12 conditions. Factorial designs including more than two independent variables are discussed in Section 13.4.

DEFINITIONS	In an experiment, an independent variable is often called a **factor**, especially in experiments that include two or more independent variables.

A research design that includes two or more factors is called a **factorial design**.

As we have noted, one advantage of a factorial design is that it creates a more realistic situation than can be obtained by examining a single factor in isolation. Because behavior is influenced by a variety of factors usually acting together, it is sensible to examine two or more factors simultaneously in a single study. At first glance, it may appear that this kind of research is unnecessarily complicated. Why not do two separate, simple studies looking at each factor by itself? The answer to this question is that combining two (or more) factors within one study provides researchers with an opportunity to see how each individual factor influences behavior and how the group of factors, acting together, can influence behavior. Returning to the alcohol and caffeine example, a researcher who manipulated only alcohol consumption would observe how alcohol affects behavior. Similarly, manipulating only caffeine consumption would demonstrate how caffeine affects behavior. However, combining the two variables permits researchers to examine how changes in caffeine consumption can influence the effects of alcohol on behavior. The idea that two factors can act together, creating unique conditions that are different from either factor acting alone, underlies the value of a factorial design.

 **LEARNING CHECK**

Suppose a researcher is interested in examining the effects of mood and food deprivation on eating. Female participants listen to one of two types of music to induce either a happy or a sad mood, following either 19 hours of food deprivation (breakfast and lunch are skipped) or no deprivation. The participants are then given free access to food in a controlled laboratory setting, and the amount of food consumed is measured for each individual.
a. How many independent variables or factors does this study have? What are they?
b. Describe this study using the notation system that indicates factors and numbers of levels of each factor.

13.2 | MAIN EFFECTS AND INTERACTIONS

The primary advantage of a factorial design is that it allows researchers to examine how unique combinations of factors acting together influence behavior. To explore this feature in more detail, we focus on designs involving only two factors; that is, the simplest possible factorial design. In Section 13.4, we look briefly at more complex situations involving three or more factors.

The structure of a two-factor design can be represented by a matrix in which the levels of one factor determine the columns and the levels of the second factor determine the rows (see Figure 13.1). Each cell in the matrix corresponds to a specific combination of the factors; that is, a separate treatment condition. The research study would involve observing and measuring a group of individuals under the conditions described by each cell.

 **LEARNING CHECK** Use a matrix to diagram the study examining the effects of mood and food deprivation on eating described in the previous Learning Check.

The data from a two-factor study provide three separate and distinct sets of information describing how the two factors independently and jointly affect behavior. To demonstrate the three kinds of information, the general structure of the alcohol and caffeine study is repeated in Table 13.1, with hypothetical data added showing the mean response time (in milliseconds) for participants in each of the cells. The data provide the following information:

1. Each column of the matrix corresponds to a specific level of caffeine consumption. For example, all of the participants tested in the first column (both sets of scores) were measured with no caffeine. By computing the mean score for each column, we obtain an overall mean for each of the three different caffeine conditions. The resulting three column means provide an indication of how caffeine consumption affects behavior. The differences among the three column means are called the **main effect** for caffeine. In more general terms, the mean differences among the columns determine the main effect for one factor. Notice that the calculation of the mean for each column involves averaging

TABLE **13.1**

Hypothetical Data Showing the Treatment Means for a Two-Factor Study Examining How Different Combinations of Alcohol and Caffeine Affect Response Time (in Milliseconds) in a Simulated Emergency Driving Situation

The data are structured to create main effects for both factors but no interaction.

	No Caffeine	200 Mg Caffeine	400 Mg Caffeine	
No Alcohol	M = 625	M = 600	M = 575	Overall M = 600
Alcohol	M = 675	M = 650	M = 625	Overall M = 650
	Overall M = 650	Overall M = 625	Overall M = 600	

both levels of alcohol consumption (half the scores were obtained with no alcohol and half were obtained with alcohol). Thus, the alcohol consumption is balanced or matched across all three caffeine levels, which means that any differences obtained between the columns cannot be explained by differences in alcohol.

For the data in Table 13.1, the participants in the no-caffeine condition have an average score of 650 milliseconds. This column mean was obtained by averaging the two groups in the no-caffeine column (Mean = 625 and Mean = 675). In a similar way, the other column means are computed as 625 and 600. These three means show a general tendency for faster response times as caffeine consumption increases. This relationship between caffeine consumption and response time is the main effect for caffeine. Finally, note that the mean differences among columns simply describe the main effect for caffeine. A statistical test is necessary to determine whether the mean differences are significant.

> For response time, smaller numbers indicate faster responses.

2. Just as we determine the overall main effect for caffeine by calculating the column means for the data in Table 13.1, we can determine the overall effect of alcohol consumption by examining the rows of the data matrix. For example, all of the participants in the top row were tested with no alcohol. The mean score for these participants (all three sets of scores) provides a measure of response time without any alcohol. Similarly, the overall mean for the bottom row describes response time when alcohol is given. The difference between these two means is called the main effect for alcohol. As before, notice that the process of obtaining the row means involves averaging all three levels of caffeine. Thus, each row mean includes exactly the same caffeine conditions. As a result, caffeine is matched across rows and cannot explain the mean differences between rows. In general terms, the differences between the column means define the main effect for one factor, and the differences between the row means define the main effect for the second factor.

For the data shown in Table 13.1, the overall mean for the first row (no alcohol) is 600 milliseconds. This mean is obtained by averaging the three treatment means in the top row (625, 600, and 575). Similarly, the overall mean response time for participants in the alcohol condition is 650 milliseconds. The 50 millisecond difference between the two row means (600 and 650) describes the main effect for alcohol. In this study, alcohol consumption increases (slows) response time by an average of 50 milliseconds.

3. A factorial design allows researchers to examine how combinations of factors working together affect behavior. In some situations, the effects of one factor are completely independent of the levels of the second factor. In this case, neither factor has a direct influence on the other. For the alcohol/caffeine study, independent factors would mean that the effect of alcohol on reaction time does not depend on the amount of caffeine you have consumed. In this case, the man effect for alcohol (the 50-point increase in reaction time) applies equally to all three caffeine conditions. In other situations, however, one factor does have a direct

influence on the effect of a second factor, producing an **interaction between factors,** or simply an **interaction.** For the alcohol/caffeine example, an interaction would mean that the effect of alcohol on reaction time depends on the amount of caffeine you have consumed. In this case, the main effect for alcohol does not apply equally across the different caffeine conditions, and the data will contain mean differences that are not explained by the main effects. Probably the most familiar example of an interaction between factors is a drug interaction, in which one drug modifies the effects of a second drug. In some cases, one drug can exaggerate the effects of another, and, in other cases, one drug may minimize or completely block the effectiveness of another. In either case, the effect of one drug is being modified by a second drug and there is an interaction.

DEFINITIONS

The mean differences among the levels of one factor are called the **main effect** of that factor. When the research study is represented as a matrix with one factor defining the rows and the second factor defining the columns, then the mean differences among the rows define the main effect for one factor, and the mean differences among the columns define the main effect for the second factor. Note that a two-factor study has two main effects; one for each of the two factors.

An **interaction between factors** (or simply an **interaction**) occurs whenever two factors, acting together, produce mean differences that are not explained by the main effects of the two factors. On the other hand, if the main effect for either factor applies equally across all levels of the second factor, then the two factors are independent and there is no interaction.

Identifying Interactions

To identify an interaction in a factorial study, you must compare the mean differences between cells with the mean differences predicted from the main effects. If there is no interaction, the combination of the two main effects completely explains the mean differences between cells. On the other hand, an interaction between factors produces "extra" mean differences between cells that cannot be explained by the main effects. To demonstrate this concept, we first consider the data in Table 13.1, for which there is no interaction. The data show a 50-point main effect for alcohol; the overall mean for the bottom row is 50 milliseconds higher than the mean for the top row. Note that this 50-point difference is consistent across all three caffeine conditions. In the first column, with no caffeine, the mean with no alcohol is $M = 625$ and increases to $M = 675$ with alcohol. In the second column, with 200 mg of caffeine, the mean increases from $M = 600$ to $M = 650$ with alcohol. The third column, with 400 mg of caffeine, shows the same 50-point increase from the no-alcohol to the alcohol condition. In this case, all the mean differences in the data are consistent with the main effects, and there is no interaction between factors.

Now, consider the relationship between main effects and cell differences when there is an interaction between factors. To demonstrate this situation, we have created a new set of data, shown in Table 13.2. These data have exactly the same main effects that existed in Table 13.1. Specifically, the main effect for alcohol is to increase response time by 50 milliseconds (+50) and the main effect for caffeine is to reduce response time by 25 milliseconds (–25) each time the caffeine dose is increased. For these data, however, we have modified the individual cell means to create an interaction between factors. Now, the main effects do not explain the differences between the cell means. For example, the participants with no caffeine (first column) show an 80-point mean difference between alcohol and no alcohol ($M = 610$ versus $M = 690$). This 80-point mean difference is not consistent with the 50-point main effect for alcohol, and indicates an interaction between factors.

Thus, the main effects from a two-factor design reveal how each of the factors affects behavior, and the interaction reveals how the two factors operating together can affect behavior. For the data in Table 13.2, the main effect for alcohol consumption describes the general effect of alcohol on response time, averaged across three levels of caffeine consumption. The main effect for caffeine consumption describes the general effect of caffeine on response time, averaged over two levels of alcohol consumption. Finally, the existence of an interaction indicates that the combined effect of caffeine and alcohol acting together is not the same as the effect of alcohol acting alone. Specifically, the effect of alcohol on response time depends on the amount of caffeine consumed. Equivalently, the effect of caffeine on response time depends on the amount of alcohol consumed.

In general, when the data from a two-factor study are organized in a matrix as in Tables 13.1 and 13.2, the mean differences between the columns describe the main effect for one factor and the mean differences between rows describe the main effect for the second factor. The main effects reflect the results that would be obtained if each factor were examined in its own separate experiment. The extra mean differences that exist between cells in the

TABLE **13.2**

Hypothetical Data Showing the Treatment Means for a Two-Factor Study Examining How Different Combinations of Alcohol and Caffeine Affect Response Time (in Milliseconds) in a Simulated Emergency Driving Situation

The data are structured to create the same main effects as in Table 13.1, but the cell means have been adjusted to produce an interaction.

	No Caffeine	200 Mg Caffeine	400 Mg Caffeine	
No Alcohol	$M = 610$	$M = 600$	$M = 590$	Overall $M = 600$
Alcohol	$M = 690$	$M = 650$	$M = 610$	Overall $M = 650$
	Overall $M = 650$	Overall $M = 625$	Overall $M = 600$	

matrix (differences that are not explained by the overall main effects) describe the interaction and represent the unique information that is obtained by combining the two factors in a single study.

LEARNING CHECK

The following data show the pattern of results that was obtained in the study by Liguori and Robinson (2001). The means show the average response time in milliseconds for different combinations of alcohol and caffeine. For these data:

a. Is there a main effect for alcohol?
b. Is there an interaction?
c. Does caffeine improve response time (produce faster times) for people who have consumed alcohol?
d. Does caffeine eliminate the effect of alcohol on response time?

	No Caffeine	200 Mg Caffeine	400 Mg Caffeine	Overall
No Alcohol	$M = 620$	$M = 600$	$M = 590$	$M = 603$
Alcohol	$M = 720$	$M = 700$	$M = 690$	$M = 703$
Overall	$M = 670$	$M = 650$	$M = 640$	

13.3 | MORE ABOUT INTERACTIONS

The previous section introduced the concept of an interaction as unique mean differences that are not explained by the main effects of the two factors. Now, we define an interaction more formally and look in detail at this unique component of a factorial design. For simplicity, we continue to examine two-factor designs and postpone discussion of more complex designs (and more complex interactions).

Alternative Definitions of an Interaction

A slightly different perspective on the concept of an interaction focuses on the notion of independence, as opposed to interdependency, between the factors. More specifically, if the two factors are independent so that the effect of one is not influenced by the other, then there is no interaction. On the other hand, if the two factors are interdependent so that one factor does influence the effect of the other, then there is an **interaction**. The notion of interdependence is consistent with our earlier discussion of interactions; if one factor does influence the effects of the other, then unique combinations of the factors produce unique effects.

DEFINITION

When the effects of one factor depend on the different levels of a second factor, then there is an **interaction** between the factors.

This alternative definition of an interaction uses different terminology but is equivalent to the first definition (p. 367). When the effects of a factor vary depending on the levels of another factor, the two factors are combining to produce unique effects. For the data in Table 13.2, notice that the size of the alcohol effect (top row versus bottom row) depends on the level of caffeine. With no caffeine, for example, the effect of adding alcohol is to increase response time by 80 milliseconds. However, the alcohol effect is reduced to 50 milliseconds with 200 mg of caffeine, and decreases further to only 20 milliseconds when the caffeine level is 400 mg. Again, the effect of one factor (alcohol) depends on the levels of the second factor (caffeine), which indicates an interaction. By contrast, the data in Table 13.1 show that the effect of alcohol is independent of caffeine. For these data, the alcohol increases response time by 50 milliseconds for all three levels of caffeine. Thus, the alcohol effect does not depend on caffeine and there is no interaction.

A second alternative definition of an interaction focuses on the pattern that is produced when the means from a two-factor study are presented in a graph. Figure 13.2 shows the original data from Table 13.1, for which there is no interaction. To construct this figure, one of the factors was selected as the independent variable to appear on the horizontal axis; in this case, the different levels of caffeine are displayed. The dependent variable—response time—is shown on the vertical axis. Notice that the figure actually contains two separate graphs; the top line shows the relationship between caffeine and reaction time when alcohol is given, and the bottom line shows the relationship when no alcohol is given. In general, the graph matches the structure of the data matrix; the columns of the matrix appear as values along the X-axis, and each row of the matrix appears as a separate line in the graph.

For this particular set of data (see Figure 13.2), notice that the lines in the graph are parallel. As you move from left to right, the distance between the lines is constant. For these data, the distance between the lines corresponds to the alcohol effect; that is, the mean difference in response times with alcohol and without alcohol. The fact that this difference is constant indicates that the alcohol effect does not depend on caffeine and there is no interaction between factors.

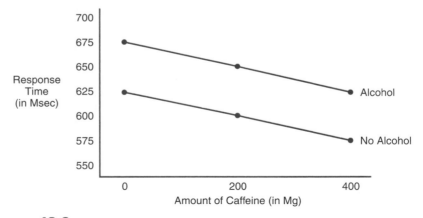

FIGURE **13.2** A Line Graph of the Data from Table 13.1

The hypothetical data are structured to show main effects for both factors but no interaction.

Now consider data for which there is an interaction between factors. Figure 13.3 shows the data from Table 13.2. In this case, the two lines are not parallel. The distance between the lines changes as you move from left to right, indicating that the alcohol effect changes from one level of caffeine to another. For these data, the alcohol effect does depend on caffeine and there is an **interaction** between factors.

> When the results of a two-factor study are graphed, the existence of nonparallel lines (lines that cross or converge) is an indication of an **interaction** between the two factors. (Note that a statistical test is needed to determine whether the interaction is significant.)

LEARNING CHECK

Evaluate the means in the following matrix.

	Treatment I	Treatment II
Males	$M = 10$	$M = 30$
Females	$M = 20$	$M = 50$

a. Is there evidence of a main effect for the treatment factor?
b. Is there evidence of a main effect for the gender factor?
c. Is there evidence of an interaction? (Hint: Sketch a graph of the data.)

Interpreting Main Effects and Interactions

As we have noted, the mean differences between columns and between rows describe the main effects in a two-factor study, and the extra mean differences between cells describe the interaction. However, you should realize that these

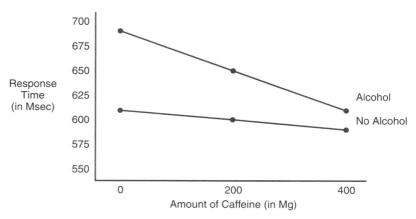

FIGURE **13.3** A Line Graph of the Data from Table 13.2

The hypothetical data are structured to show main effects for both factors and an interaction.

mean differences are simply descriptive and must be evaluated by a statistical hypothesis test before they can be considered significant. That is, the obtained mean differences may not represent a real treatment effect but rather may be caused by chance or error. Until the data are evaluated by a hypothesis test, be cautious about interpreting any results from a two-factor study (see Box 9.1, p. 250).

When a statistical analysis does indicate significant effects, you must still be careful about interpreting the outcome. In particular, if the analysis results in a significant interaction, then the main effects, whether significant or not, may present a distorted view of the actual outcome. Remember, the main effect for one factor is obtained by averaging all the different levels of the second factor. Because each main effect is an average, it may not accurately represent any of the individual effects that were used to compute the average. To illustrate this point, Figure 13.4 presents the general results from research examining the relationship between the TV viewing habits of 5-year-old children and their future performance in high school.

In general, research results indicate that 5-year-old children who watched a lot of educational programming such as Sesame Street and Mr. Rogers had higher high-school grades than their peers (Anderson, Huston, Wright, & Collins, 1998). The same study reported that 5-year-old children who watched a lot of noneducational TV programs had relatively low high-school grades compared to their peers. Figure 13.4 shows a data matrix and a graph presenting this combination of results. Notice that the data show no main effect for

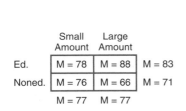

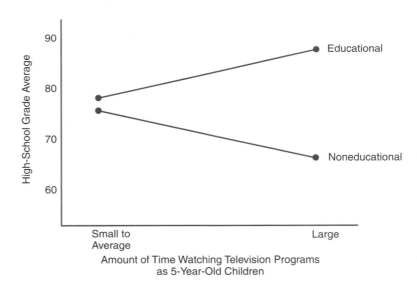

FIGURE **13.4** The Relationship between the TV Viewing Habits of 5-Year-Old Children and Their Future High-School Grades

Based on results from Anderson, Huston, Wright, and Collins (1998).

the factor representing the amount of time that the children watched TV. Overall, the grades for students who watched a lot of TV as children are the same as the grades for students who watched a small or moderate amount of TV. However, the lines in the graph show an interaction, suggesting that the effect of watching a lot of TV depends on the type of programs the children are watching. Educational programs are related to an increase in grades and noneducational programs are related to a decrease. Averaging these two results produces the zero value for the main effect. However, the main effect does not accurately describe the results. In particular, it would be incorrect to conclude that there is no relationship between the amount of time spent watching TV as a child and future high-school grades.

In general, the presence of an interaction can obscure or distort the main effects of either factor. Whenever a statistical analysis produces a significant interaction, you should take a close look at the data before giving any credibility to the main effects.

Independence of Main Effects and Interactions

The two-factor study allows researchers to evaluate three separate sets of mean differences: (1) the mean differences from the main effect of factor A, (2) the mean differences from the main effect of factor B, and (3) the mean differences from the interaction between factors. The three sets of mean differences are separate and completely independent. Thus, it is possible for the results from a two-factor study to show any possible combination of main effects and interaction.

The data sets in Figure 13.5 show several possibilities. To simplify discussion, the two factors are labeled A and B, with factor A defining the rows of the data matrix and factor B defining the columns.

Figure 13.5a shows data with mean differences between levels of factor A, but no mean differences for factor B and no interaction. To identify the main effect for factor A, notice that the overall mean for the top row is 10 points higher than the overall mean for the bottom row. This 10-point difference is the main effect for factor A, or, simply, the A effect. To evaluate the mean effect for factor B, notice that both columns have exactly the same overall mean, indicating no difference between levels of factor B; hence, no B effect. Finally, the absence of an interaction is indicated by the fact that the overall A effect (the 10-point difference) is constant within each column; that is, the A effect does not depend on the levels of factor B. (Alternatively, the data indicate that the overall B effect is constant within each row.)

Figure 13.5b shows data with an A effect and a B effect, but no interaction. For these data, the A effect is indicated by the 10-point mean difference between rows, and the B effect is indicated by the 20-point mean difference between columns. The fact that the 10-point A effect is constant within each column indicates no interaction.

Finally, Figure 13.5c shows data that display an interaction but no main effect for factor A or for factor B. For these data, note that there is no mean difference between rows (no A effect) and no mean difference between columns (no B effect). However, within each row (or within each column) there

(a) Data showing a main effect for factor A but no main effect for factor B and no interaction

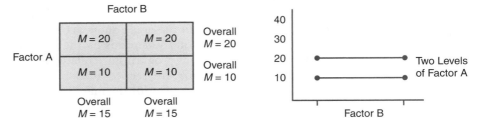

(b) Data showing main effects for both factor A and factor B but no interaction

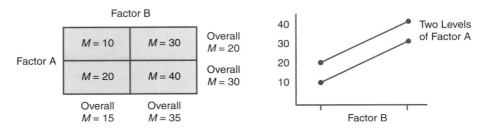

(c) Data showing no main effect for either factor, but an interaction

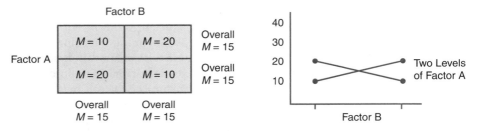

FIGURE **13.5** Three Possible Combinations of Main Effects and Interactions in a Two-Factor Experiment

are mean differences. The "extra" mean differences within the rows and columns cannot be explained by the overall main effects and, therefore, indicate an interaction.

13.4 | TYPES OF FACTORIAL DESIGNS

Thus far, we have examined only one version of all of the many different types of factorial designs. In particular:

- All of the designs that we have considered use a separate group of participants for each of the individual treatment combinations or cells.

In research terminology, we have looked exclusively at between-subjects designs.

- All of the previous examples use factors that are true independent variables. That is, the factors are manipulated by the researcher so that the research study is an example of the experimental strategy.

Although it is possible to have a separate group for each of the individual cells (a between-subjects design), it is also possible to have the same group of individuals participate in all of the different cells (a within-subjects design). In addition, it is possible to construct a factorial design in which the factors are not manipulated but rather are quasi-independent variables (see Chapter 12, p. 356). Finally, a factorial design can use any combination of factors. As a result, a factorial study can combine elements of experimental and nonexperimental research strategies, and it can combine elements of between-subjects and within-subjects designs within a single research study. A two-factor design, for example, may include one between-subjects factor (with a separate group for each level of the factor) and one within-subjects factor (with each group measured in all the different treatment conditions). The same study could also include one experimental factor (with a manipulated independent variable) and one nonexperimental factor (with a preexisting, nonmanipulated variable). The ability to mix designs within a single research study provides researchers with the potential to blend several different research strategies within one study. This potential allows researchers to develop studies that address scientific questions that could not be answered by any single strategy. In the following sections, we examine some of the possibilities for factorial designs.

Between-Subjects and Within-Subjects Designs

It is possible to construct a factorial study that is purely a between-subjects design; that is, a study in which there is a separate group of participants for each of the treatment conditions. As we noted in Chapter 10, this type of design has some definite advantages as well as some disadvantages. A particular disadvantage for a factorial study is that a between-subjects design can require a large number of participants. For example, a 2×4 factorial design has eight different treatment conditions. A separate group of 30 participants in each condition requires a total of 240 (8×30) participants. As noted in Chapter 10, another disadvantage of between-subject designs is that individual differences (characteristics that differ from one participant to another) can become confounding variables and increase the variance of the scores. On the positive side, a between-subjects design completely avoids any problem from order effects because each score is completely independent of every other score. In general, between-subjects designs are best suited to situations in which a lot of participants are available, individual differences are relatively small, and order effects are likely.

At the other extreme, it is possible to construct a factorial study that is purely a within-subjects design. In this case, a single group of individuals participates in all of the separate treatment conditions. As we noted in Chapter 11, this type of design has some definite advantages and disadvantages.

A particular disadvantage for a factorial study is the number of different treatment conditions that each participant must undergo. In a 2×4 design, for example, each participant must be measured in eight different treatment conditions. The large number of different treatments can be very time consuming, which increases the chances that participants will quit and walk away before the study is ended (participant attrition). In addition, having each participant undergo a long series of treatment conditions can increase the potential for testing effects (such as fatigue or practice effects) and make it more difficult to counterbalance the design to control for order effects. Two advantages of within-subjects designs are that they require only one group of participants and eliminate or greatly reduce the problems associated with individual differences. In general, within-subjects designs are best suited for situations in which individual differences are relatively large, and there is little reason to expect order effects to be large and disruptive.

Mixed Designs: Within- and Between-Subjects

Often, a researcher encounters a situation in which the advantages or convenience of a between-subjects design apply to one factor but a within-subjects design is preferable for a second factor. For example, a researcher may prefer to use a within-subjects design to take maximum advantage of a small group of participants. However, if one factor is expected to produce large order effects, then a between-subjects design should be used for that factor. In this situation, it is possible to construct a **mixed design,** with one between-subjects factor and one within-subjects factor. If the design is pictured as a matrix with one factor defining the rows and the second factor defining the columns, then the mixed design has a separate group for each row with each group participating in all of the different columns.

DEFINITION	A factorial study that combines two different research designs is called a **mixed design.** A common example of a mixed design is a factorial study with one between-subjects factor and one within-subjects factor.

Figure 13.6 shows a mixed factorial design in a study examining the relationship between mood and memory. The typical result in this research area is that people tend to recall information that is consistent with their current mood. Thus, people remember happy things when they are happy and remember sad things when they are sad. In a study like the one shown in Figure 13.6, Clark and Teasdale (1985) first showed participants a list containing a mixture of pleasant words (such as helpful, kind, beauty, and hope) and unpleasant words (such as rude, cruel, war, and misery). Because each participant saw all the words, the type of word (pleasant versus unpleasant) is a within-subjects factor corresponding to the two columns in Figure 13.6. The researchers then manipulated mood by having one group of participants listen to happy music for 7 minutes and another group listen to sad music. Each participant was also asked to get into a mood consistent with the music. Thus, the researchers created a between-subjects factor consisting of a happy-mood group and a sad-mood group. In Figure 13.6, the two groups correspond to the two rows in the matrix.

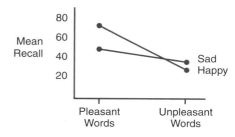

	Pleasant Words	Unpleasant Words
Happy Mood	Mean recall $M = 70$	Mean recall $M = 23$
Sad Mood	Mean recall $M = 48$	Mean recall $M = 35$

Groups

FIGURE **13.6** Results from a Mixed Two-Factor Study that Combines One Between-Subjects Factor and One Within-Subjects Factor

The graph shows the pattern of results obtained by Clark and Teasdale (1985). The researchers showed participants a list containing a mixture of pleasant and unpleasant words to create a within-subjects factor (pleasant/unpleasant). The researchers manipulated mood by dividing the participants into two groups and having one group listen to happy music and the other group listen to sad music, creating a between-subjects factor (happy/sad). Finally, the researchers tested memory for each type of word.

After listening to the music, the participants were asked to recall as many words as they could. For each participant, the researchers recorded how many pleasant words were recalled and how many unpleasant words were recalled.

 **LEARNING CHECKS**

For a two-factor research study with three levels for factor A and two levels for factor B, how many participants are needed to obtain five scores in each treatment condition for each of the following situations?
a. Both factors are between-subjects.
b. Both factors are within-subjects.
c. Factor A is a between-subjects factor and factor B is a within-subjects factor.

   A researcher would like to use a factorial study to compare the service provided by two different cell phone companies. Participants will be asked to rate the quality of service provided for basic phone calls (talking and texting) and for Internet access. Thus, the two cell phone companies make up one factor, the two types of service make up the second factor, and the participants' ratings are the dependent variable. For this study, which factor(s) should be between-subjects and which should be within-subjects? Explain your answer.

Experimental and Nonexperimental or Quasi-Experimental Research Strategies

As we demonstrated with the alcohol and caffeine example at the beginning of this chapter, it is possible to construct a factorial study that is a purely experimental research design. In this case, both factors are true independent variables that are manipulated by the researcher. It also is possible to construct a factorial study for which all the factors are nonmanipulated, quasi-independent variables. For example, Bahrick and Hall (1991) examined the permanence of memory by testing recall for high school algebra and geometry. The study compared two groups of participants; those who had taken college-level math courses and those who had no advanced math courses in college. Note that these groups were not created by manipulating an independent variable; instead, they are preexisting, nonequivalent groups, and, therefore, form a quasi-independent variable. The second factor in the study was time. The researchers tested recall at different time intervals ranging from 3 years up to 55 years after high school. Again, note that time is a nonmanipulated variable and hence another quasi-independent variable. Thus, the study contains no manipulated variables and is a purely nonexperimental design. We should note, however, that the two nonmanipulated variables are still called factors. Incidentally, the group with no advanced college math showed a systematic decline in mathematics knowledge over time, but the group with college math showed excellent recall of mathematics, even decades after their high school courses.

Combined Strategies: Experimental and Quasi-Experimental or Nonexperimental

In the behavioral sciences, it is common for a factorial design to use an experimental strategy for one factor and a quasi-experimental or nonexperimental strategy for another factor. This type of study is an example of a **combined strategy.** This kind of study involves one factor that is a true independent variable consisting of a set of manipulated treatment conditions, and a second factor that is a quasi-independent variable that typically falls into one of the following categories.

1. The second factor is a preexisting participant characteristic such as age or gender. For example, a researcher may want to determine whether the set of treatment conditions has the same effect on males as on females, or the question is whether the treatment effects change as a function of age. Note that preexisting participant characteristics create nonequivalent groups; thus, this factor is a quasi-independent variable. Occasionally, designs that add a participant characteristic as a second factor are called *person-by-environment* (P × E) designs or *person-by-situation* designs.

2. The second factor is time. In this case, the concern of the research question is how the different treatment effects persist over time. For example, two different therapy techniques may be equally effective immediately after the therapy is concluded, but one may continue to have an effect over time, whereas the other loses effectiveness as time passes. Note that time is not controlled or manipulated by the researcher, so this factor is a quasi-independent variable.

DEFINITION	A **combined strategy** study uses two different research strategies in the same factorial design. One factor is a true independent variable (experimental strategy) and one factor is a quasi-independent variable (nonexperimental or quasi-experimental strategy).

For example, Shrauger (1972) examined how the presence or absence of an audience can influence people's performance. Half of the research participants worked alone (no audience) on a concept-formation task, and half of the participants worked with an audience of people who claimed to be interested in observing the experiment. Note that the audience versus no-audience variable is manipulated by the researcher, so this factor is a true independent variable. The second factor in Shrauger's study was self-esteem. In each of the audience groups, participants were divided into high self-esteem and low self-esteem groups. Note that the second factor, self-esteem, is a preexisting participant variable and, therefore, a quasi-independent variable. The structure of this study, including results similar to Shrauger's actual data, is shown in Figure 13.7.

Notice that the results show an interaction between the two factors. Specifically, the presence of an audience had a large effect on participants with low self-esteem, but the audience had essentially no effect on those with high self-esteem.

 **LEARNING CHECKS**

A researcher would like to compare two therapy techniques for treating depression. One technique is suspected to have only temporary effects, and the other is expected to produce permanent or long-lasting effects. Describe a factorial research study that would compare the effectiveness of the two techniques and answer the question about the duration of their effectiveness. Identify which factor is an independent variable and which is quasi-independent.

A researcher would like to compare two therapy techniques for treating depression. One technique is expected to be very effective for patients with relatively mild depression, and the other is expected to be more effective for treating moderate to severe depression. Describe a

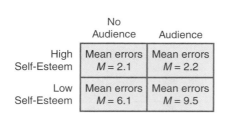

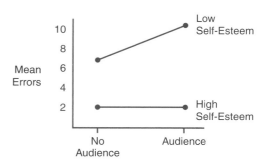

FIGURE **13.7** Results from a Two-Factor Study that Combines One Experimental Factor and One Nonexperimental Factor

The researchers manipulated whether the participants performed in front of an audience. This is an independent variable (audience versus no audience). Within each experimental condition, two nonequivalent groups of participants were observed (high versus low self-esteem). The level of self-esteem is a nonmanipulated, quasi-independent variable. The dependent variable is the number of errors committed by each participant.

factorial research study that would compare the effectiveness of the two techniques and answer the question about which is better for different levels of depression. Identify which factor is an independent variable and which is quasi-independent.

Pretest–Posttest Control Group Designs

In Chapter 12, we introduced a quasi-experimental design known as the pretest–posttest nonequivalent control group design (p. 343). This design involves two separate groups of participants. One group—the treatment group—is measured before and after receiving a treatment. A second group—the control group—also is measured twice (pretest and posttest) but does not receive any treatment between the two measurements. Using the notation introduced in Chapter 12, this design can be represented as follows:

O X O   (treatment group)

O   O   (nonequivalent control group)

Each O represents an observation or measurement, and the X indicates a treatment. Each row corresponds to the series of events for one group.

You should recognize this design as an example of a two-factor mixed design. One factor—treatment/control—is a between-subjects factor. The other factor—pretest–posttest—is a within-subjects factor. Figure 13.8 shows the design using the matrix notation customary for factorial designs.

Finally, the design introduced in Chapter 12 was classified as quasi-experimental because it used nonequivalent groups (for example, students from two different high schools or clients from two different clinics). On the other hand, if a researcher has one sample of participants and can randomly assign them to the two groups, then the design is classified as a combined strategy with one experimental factor (treatment/control) and one

	Pretest	Posttest
Treatment Group	Pretest scores for participants who receive the treatment	Posttest scores for participants who receive the treatment
Control Group	Pretest scores for participants who do not receive the treatment	Posttest scores for participants who do not receive the treatment

FIGURE **13.8** The Structure of a Pretest-Posttest Control Group Study Organized as a Two-Factor Research Design
Notice that the treatment/control factor is a between-subjects factor and the pre-post factor is a within-subjects factor.

nonexperimental factor (pre–post). This version of the pretest–posttest control group design can be represented as follows:

R   O   X   O   (treatment group)

R   O   O   (control group)

The letter R symbolizes random assignment, which means that the researcher has control over assignment of participants to groups and, therefore, can create equivalent groups.

Higher-Order Factorial Designs

The basic concepts of a two-factor research design can be extended to more complex designs involving three or more factors; such designs are referred to as **higher-order factorial designs.** A three-factor design, for example, might look at academic performance scores for two different teaching methods (factor A), for boys versus girls (factor B), and for first-grade versus second-grade classes (factor C). In the three-factor design, the researcher evaluates main effects for each of the three factors, as well as a set of two-way interactions: $A \times B$, $B \times C$, and $A \times C$. In addition, the extra factor introduces the potential for a three-way interaction: $A \times B \times C$.

The logic for defining and interpreting higher-order interactions follows the pattern set by two-way interactions. For example, a two-way interaction such as $A \times B$ indicates that the effect of factor A depends on the levels of factor B. Extending this definition, a three-way interaction such as $A \times B \times C$ indicates that the two-way interaction between A and B depends on the levels of factor C. For example, two teaching methods might be equally effective for boys and girls in the first grade (no two-way interaction between method and gender), but in the second grade, one of the methods works better for boys and the other method works better for girls (an interaction between method and gender). Because the method-by-gender pattern of results is different for the first graders and the second graders, there is a three-way interaction. Although the general idea of a three-way interaction is easily grasped, most people have great difficulty comprehending or interpreting a four-way (or higher) interaction. Although it is possible to add factors to a research study without limit, studies that involve more than three factors can produce complex results that are difficult to understand and, therefore, often have limited practical value.

13.5 | APPLICATIONS OF FACTORIAL DESIGNS

Factorial designs provide researchers with a tremendous degree of flexibility and freedom for constructing research studies. As noted earlier, the primary advantage of factorial studies is that they allow researchers to observe the influence of two (or more) variables acting and interacting simultaneously. Thus, factorial designs have an almost unlimited range of potential applications. In this section, however, we focus on three specific situations in which adding a second factor to an existing study answers a specific research question or solves a specific research problem.

Expanding and Replicating a Previous Study

Often, factorial designs are developed when researchers plan studies that are intended to build on previous research results. For example, a published report may compare a set of treatment conditions or demonstrate the effectiveness of a particular treatment by comparing the treatment condition with a control condition. The critical reader asks questions such as:

Would the same treatment effects be obtained if the treatments were administered under different conditions?

Would the treatment outcomes be changed if individuals with different characteristics had participated?

Developing a research study to answer these questions would involve a factorial design. Answering the first question, for example, requires administering the treatments (one factor) under a variety of different conditions (a second factor). The primary prediction for this research is to obtain an interaction between factors; that is, the researcher predicts that the effect of the treatments depends on the conditions under which they are administered. Similarly, the second question calls for a factorial design involving the treatments (factor one) and different types of participants (factor two). Again, the primary prediction is for an interaction.

Because current research tends to build on past research, factorial designs are fairly common and very useful. In a single study, a researcher can replicate and expand previous research. The replication involves repeating the previous study by using the same factor or independent variable exactly as it was used in the earlier study. The expansion involves adding a second factor in the form of new conditions or new participant characteristics to determine whether the previously reported effects can be generalized to new situations or new populations.

One example of adding a new factor to an existing study comes from research examining the perceived value of future rewards. In a typical study, people are asked to choose between a $1000 payment in 5 years and a smaller payment today. The general result is that the longer the $1000 payment is delayed, the smaller the amount people will accept in exchange today. For example, a person may be willing to settle for $500 today instead of waiting 5 years to receive $1000. However, the same person would settle for $200 today rather than wait 10 years for the $1000. This general phenomenon is known as delayed discounting because the value of the future payment is discounted based on how long it is delayed. Green, Fry, and Myerson (1994) questioned whether the relationship between delay and discounting depended on the age of the participants. They predicted that younger people would be more impulsive and unwilling to wait for a future reward. Older people, on the other hand, were expected to have more self-control and give greater value to future rewards. To answer this question, the researchers added age as a second factor. In the resulting two-factor study, the first factor simply repeated the standard discounting experiment by measuring the value given to a $1000 reward for seven different delay periods ranging from 0 years (immediate payment) to 25 years. The second factor consisted of three age groups, sixth graders: college students, and older adults. Notice that the primary prediction for this research study is an interaction between the delay period and age; younger people should show a quick drop in value as the delay increases and older people should discount more slowly. Figure 13.9 shows the structure of the research study.

LEARNING CHECK

A researcher has demonstrated that a new noncompetitive physical education program significantly improves self-esteem for children in a kindergarten program.

a. What additional information can be obtained by introducing participant gender as a second factor to the original research study?

b. What additional information can be obtained by adding participant age (third grade, fifth grade, and so on) to the original study?

Participant Age
(the New Factor)

	6th-grade students	College students	Older adults
No delay (immediate payment)			
50-month delay			
100-month delay			
150-month delay			
200-month delay			
250-month delay			
300-month delay			

Delay Period (the Original Factor)

The original study only used college students

FIGURE **13.9** Creating a New Research Study by Adding a Second Factor to an Existing Study

Green, Fry, and Myerson (1994) repeated a standard delayed discounting study by examining the value given to a future reward of $1000 for seven different delay periods and then extended the study by adding age as a second factor. The results showed that the effect of increasing the delay period (first factor) depends on the age of the participants (second factor), resulting in an interaction.

Reducing Variance in Between-Subjects Designs

In Chapter 10, we noted that individual differences such as age or gender can create serious problems for between-subjects research designs. One such problem is the simple fact that differences between participants can result in large variance for the scores within a treatment condition. Recall that large variance can make it difficult to establish any significant differences between treatment conditions (see p. 293). Often a researcher has reason to suspect that a specific participant characteristic such as age or gender is a major factor contributing to the variance of the scores. In this situation, it often is tempting to eliminate or reduce the influence of the specific characteristic by holding it constant or by restricting its range. For example, suppose that a researcher compares two treatment conditions using a separate group of children for each condition. Within each group, the children range in age from 6 to 14 years of age. The study is shown in Figure 13.10a. However, the researcher is concerned that the older children may have higher scores than the younger children simply because they are more mature. If the scores really are related to age, then there will be big individual differences and high variance within each group. In this situation, the researcher may be tempted to restrict the study by holding age constant (for example, using only 10-year-old participants). This will produce more homogeneous groups with less variance, but it will also limit the researcher's ability to generalize the results. Recall that limiting generalization reduces the external validity of the study. Fortunately, there is a relatively simple solution to this dilemma that allows the researcher to reduce variance within groups without sacrificing external validity. The solution involves using the specific variable as a second factor, thereby creating a two-factor study. For this example, the researcher could use age as a second factor to divide the participants into three groups within each treatment: a younger age group (6 to 8 years), a middle age group (9 to 11 years), and an older group (12 to 14 years). The result is the two-factor experiment shown in Figure 13.10b, with one factor consisting of the two treatments (I and II) and the second factor consisting of the three age groups (younger, middle, and older).

By creating six groups of participants instead of only two, the researcher has greatly reduced the individual differences (age differences) within each group, while still keeping the full range of ages from the original study. In the new, two-factor design, age differences still exist, but now they are differences between groups rather than variance within groups. The variance has been reduced without sacrificing external validity. Furthermore, the researcher has gained all of the other advantages that go with a two-factor design. In addition to examining how the different treatment conditions affect memory, the researcher can now examine how age (the new factor) is related to memory, and can determine whether there is any interaction between age and the treatment conditions.

LEARNING CHECK   Under what circumstances would a researcher reduce the variance of the scores by adding gender as a second factor in a between-subjects study comparing two treatments?

(a) A study comparing two treatments with large age differences among the participants in each group

Treatment I	Treatment II
A group of 12 participants ranging in age from 6 to 14 years old	A group of 12 participants ranging in age from 6 to 14 years old

(b) Using participant age as a second factor, the participants have been separated into smaller, more homogeneous groups. The smaller age differences within each group should reduce the variability of the scores.

	Treatment I	Treatment II
Younger (Six to Eight Years Old)	A group of four participants ranging in age from 6 to 8 years old	A group of four participants ranging in age from 6 to 8 years old
Middle (Nine to 11 Years Old)	A group of four participants ranging in age from 9 to 11 years old	A group of four participants ranging in age from 9 to 11 years old
Older (12 to 14 Years Old)	A group of four participants ranging in age from 12 to 14 years old	A group of four participants ranging in age from 12 to 14 years old

FIGURE **13.10** A Participant Characteristic (Age) Used as a Second Factor to Reduce the Variability of Scores in a Research Study

(a) Each treatment condition contains a wide range of ages, which probably produces large variability among the scores. (b) The participants have been separated into more homogeneous age groups, which should reduce the variability within each group.

Evaluating Order Effects in Within-Subjects Designs

In Chapter 11, we noted that order effects can be a serious problem for within-subjects research studies. Specifically, in a within-subjects design, each participant goes through a series of treatment conditions in a particular order. In this situation, it is possible that treatments that occur early in the order may influence a participant's scores for treatments that occur later in the order. Because order effects can alter and distort the true effects of a treatment condition, they are generally considered a confounding variable that should be eliminated from the study. In some circumstances, however, a researcher may want to investigate the order effects (where and how big they are). For example, a researcher may be specifically interested in how the order of treatments influences the effectiveness of treatments (is treatment I more effective if it comes before treatment II or after it?). Or a researcher simply may want to remove the order effects to obtain a clearer view of the data. In any of these situations, it is possible to create a research design that actually measures the order effects and separates them from the rest of the data.

Using Order of Treatments as a Second Factor

To measure and evaluate order effects, it is necessary to use counterbalancing (as discussed in Chapter 11). Remember that counterbalancing requires separate groups of participants with each group going through the set of treatments in a different order. The simplest example of this procedure is a within-subjects design comparing two treatments: I and II. The design is counterbalanced so that half of the participants begin with treatment I and then move to treatment II. The other half of the participants start with treatment II and then receive treatment II. The structure of this counterbalanced design can be presented as a matrix with the two treatment conditions defining the columns and the order of treatments defining the rows (Figure 13.11).

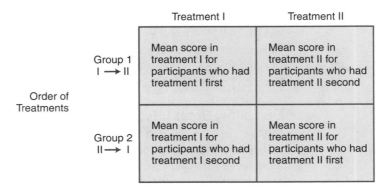

FIGURE **13.11** Order of Treatments Added as a Second Factor to a Within-Subjects Study

The original study uses a counterbalanced design to compare two treatment conditions. Thus, half of the participants have treatment I first, and half have treatment II first. Similarly, half of the participants have treatment I second, and half have treatment II second.

You should recognize the matrix structure in Figure 13.11 as a two-factor research design and an example of a mixed design. In particular, the two treatments form a within-subjects factor, and the two orders form a between-subjects factor. By using the order of treatments as a second factor, it is possible to evaluate any order effects that exist in the data. There are three possible outcomes that can occur, and each produces its own pattern of results.

1. *No order effects.* When there are no order effects, it does not matter if a treatment is presented first or second. An example of this type of result is shown in Figure 13.12. For these data, when treatment I is presented first (group 1), the mean is 20, and when treatment I is presented second (group 2), the mean is still 20. Similarly, the order of presentation has no effect on the mean for treatment II. As a result, the difference between treatments is 10 points for both groups of participants. Thus, the treatment effect (factor 1) does not depend on the order of treatments (factor 2). You should recognize this pattern as an example of data with no interaction. When there are no order effects, the data show a pattern with no interaction. It makes no difference whether a treatment is presented first or second; the mean is the same in either case.

2. *Symmetrical order effects.* When order effects exist, the scores in the second treatment are influenced by participation in the first treatment. For example, participation in one treatment may produce practice effects which lead to improved performance in the second treatment. An example of this situation is shown in Figure 13.13. Notice that the data now include a 5-point order effect. For both groups of participants, the mean score is raised by 5 points for the treatment that occurs second. For group 1 the order effect influences the scores in treatment II, and for group 2 the order effect influences scores in treatment I. Also notice that the order effect is symmetrical; that is, the second treatment always gets an extra 5 points, whether it is treatment I or treatment II.

    In this situation, the size of the treatment effect (I versus II) depends on the order of treatments. Thus, the effect of one factor depends on the other factor. You should recognize this as an example of interaction. When order effects exist, they show up in the two-factor analysis as an interaction between treatments and the order of treatments.

    For these data, the order effect is symmetrical and the symmetry of the order effect appears in the data as a symmetrical interaction. In the graph of the data, for example, the two lines cross exactly at the center. Also, the 5-point difference between the two groups in treatment I (left-hand side of the graph) is exactly equal to the 5-point difference between the groups in treatment II (right-hand side of the graph). This symmetry only exists in situations in which the order effects are symmetrical.

3. *Nonsymmetrical order effects.* Often, order effects are not symmetrical. For example, participation in different treatment conditions may produce different levels of fatigue or practice. This situation is shown

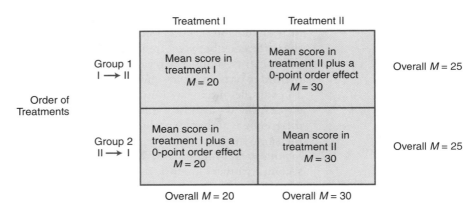

Treatment I   Treatment II

X ⟶ X + 0   Group 1
X ⟶ X + 0   Half the participants
X ⟶ X + 0   get treatment I first and
X ⟶ X + 0   treatment II second.

X + 0 ⟵ X   Group 2
X + 0 ⟵ X   Half the participants
X + 0 ⟵ X   get treatment II first and
X + 0 ⟵ X   treatment I second.

	Treatment I	Treatment II	
Group 1 I ⟶ II	Mean score in treatment I $M = 20$	Mean score in treatment II plus a 0-point order effect $M = 30$	Overall $M = 25$
Group 2 II ⟶ I	Mean score in treatment I plus a 0-point order effect $M = 20$	Mean score in treatment II $M = 30$	Overall $M = 25$
	Overall $M = 20$	Overall $M = 30$	

Order of Treatments

FIGURE 13.12 Treatment Effects and Order Effects Revealed in a Two-Factor Design Using Order of Treatment as a Second Factor

A 10-point difference between the two treatment conditions is assumed, with the mean score for treatment I equal to $M = 20$ and the mean score for treatment II equal to $M = 30$. It is also assumed that there are no order effects. Thus, participating in one treatment has no effect (0 points) on an individual's score in the following treatment. In the two-factor analysis, the treatment effect shows up as a 10-point main effect for the treatment factor, and the absence of any order effects is indicated by the absence of an interaction between treatments and order of treatments.

in Figure 13.14. Notice the following characteristics for the data in the figure:

a. The participants in group 1 received treatment I first. This treatment produces a relatively large, 10-point order effect. For these participants, the 10-point order effect increases the mean for treatment II by 10 points.

b. The participants in group 2 receive treatment II first. This treatment produces a relatively small, 5-point order effect that increases the mean for treatment I by 5 points.

Notice that the graph in Figure 13.14 shows an interaction, just as with symmetrical order effects. Again, the existence of an interaction in this analysis is an indication that order effects exist. For these data,

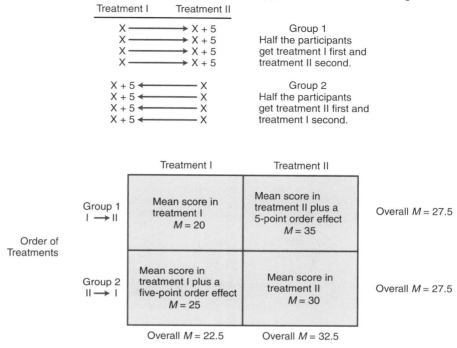

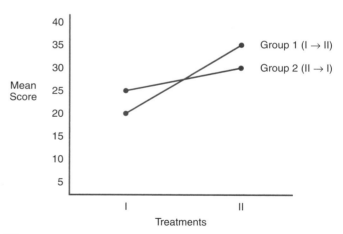

FIGURE 13.13 Symmetrical Order Effects Revealed in a Two-Factor Design Using Order of Treatments as a Second Factor

A 10-point difference between the two treatment conditions is assumed, with the mean score for treatment I equal to $M = 20$ and the mean score for treatment II equal to $M = 30$. There is also a symmetrical 5-point order effect. After participating in one treatment, the order effect adds 5 points to each participant's score in the second treatment. In this situation, the order effect appears as an interaction between treatments and the order of treatments.

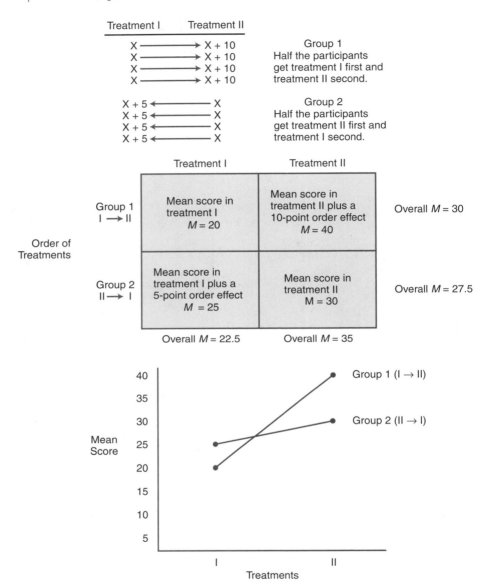

FIGURE **13.14** Nonsymmetrical Order Effects Revealed in a Two-Factor Design Using Order of Treatments as a Second Factor

A 10-point difference between the two treatment conditions is assumed, with the mean score for treatment I equal to $M = 20$ and the mean score for treatment II equal to $M = 30$. An asymmetrical order effect is added. After participating in treatment I. the order effect adds 10 points to each participant's score, and after participating in treatment II, the order effect adds 5 points to each participant's score. In this situation, the order effects appear as an interaction between treatments and order of treatments. Because the order effects are not symmetrical, the structure of the interaction is also not symmetrical.

however, the interaction is not symmetrical; in the graph, the two lines do not intersect at their midpoints. Also, the difference between groups in treatment I is much smaller than the difference in treatment II. In general, nonsymmetrical order effects produce a lopsided, or nonsymmetrical, interaction between treatments and orders as seen in Figure 13.14.

In the preceding examples, the order effects were clearly displayed in the data. In this artificial situation, we knew that order effects existed and how big they were. In an actual experiment, however, a researcher cannot see the order effects. However, as we have demonstrated in the three examples, using order of treatments as a second factor makes it possible to examine any order effects that exist in a set of data; their magnitude and nature are revealed in the interaction. Thus, researchers can observe the order effects in their data and separate them from the effects of the different treatments.

 **LEARNING CHECKS**

What does it mean to say that order effects are symmetrical or nonsymmetrical?

For each of the following possibilities, describe how order effects reveal themselves in a two-factor analysis when the order of treatments is added as a second factor.
a. No order effects.
b. Symmetrical order effects.
c. Nonsymmetrical order effects.

■ CHAPTER SUMMARY

To examine more complex, real-life situations, researchers often design research studies that include more than one independent variable or more than one quasi-independent variable. These designs are called factorial designs. Factorial designs are commonly described with a notation system that identifies not only the number of factors in the design but also the number of values or levels that exist for each factor. For example, a 2×3 factorial design is a two-factor design with two levels of the first factor and three levels of the second factor.

The results from a factorial design provide information about how each factor individually affects behavior (main effects) and how the factors jointly affect behavior (interaction). The value of a factorial design is that it allows a researcher to examine how unique combinations of factors acting together influence behavior. When the effects of a factor vary depending on the levels of another factor, it means that the two factors are combining to produce unique effects and that there is an interaction between the factors.

In factorial designs, it is possible to have a separate group for each of the conditions (a between-subjects design) and to have the same group of individuals participate in all of the different conditions (a within-subjects design). In addition, it is possible to construct a factorial design in which the factors are not manipulated but rather are quasi-independent variables. Finally, a factorial design can use any combination of factors to create a variety of mixed designs and combined research strategies. As a result, a factorial study can combine elements of experimental and nonexperimental or quasi-experimental strategies, and it can mix between-subjects and within-subjects designs within a single research study.

Although factorial designs can be used in a variety of situations, three specific applications were discussed: (1) Often, a new study builds on existing research by adding another factor to an earlier research study; (2) using a participant variable such as age or gender as a second factor can separate participants into more homogeneous groups and thereby reduce variance in a between-subjects design; and (3) when the order of treatments is used as a second factor in a counterbalanced within-subjects design, it is possible to measure and evaluate the order effects.

KEY WORDS

factor	interaction between factors,	mixed design
factorial design	or interaction	combined strategy
main effect		

EXERCISES

1. In addition to the key words, you should also be able to define the following terms:
   two-factor design
   single-factor design
   levels
   three-factor design
   higher-order factorial design
2. Suppose that a researcher finds a significant difference between two treatment conditions. What additional information might be obtained by adding participant gender as a second factor?
3. What is a main effect?
4. Explain why it is better to use a factorial design in research than to conduct two separate studies.
5. How many independent variables are there in a 4 × 2 × 2 factorial design?
6. How many main effects are there in a study examining the effects of treatment (behavioral versus psychoanalytic versus cognitive) and experience of the therapist (experienced versus not experienced) on depression?

7. Suppose a research conducts a two-factor study comparing two treatments (I and II) for males versus females. The structure of the study is shown in the following matrix.

	Treatment	
	I	II
Female		
Male		

a. If the results show that females have higher scores than males in treatment I and equivalent scores in treatment II, is it likely that there will be a main effect for gender? Is it likely that there will be an interaction?
b. If the results show that females have higher scores than males in treatment I and lower scores than males in treatment II, is it likely that there will be a main effect for gender? Is it likely that there will be an interaction?

8. Use the values in the following matrix to answer questions a, b, and c:

	Before Treatment	After Treatment	Overall
Males	$M = 20$	$M = 24$	$M = 22$
Females	$M = 22$	$M = 32$	$M = 27$
Overall	$M = 21$	$M = 28$	

   a. Which numbers are compared to evaluate the main effect for the treatment?
   b. Which numbers are compared to evaluate the main effect for gender?
   c. Which numbers are compared to evaluate the interaction?

9. The following matrix represents the results (the means) from a 2×2 factorial study. One mean is not given.

	A1	A2
B1	40	20
B2	30	

   a. What value for the missing mean would result in no main effect for factor A?
   b. What value for the missing mean would result in no main effect for factor B?
   c. What value for the missing mean would result in no interaction?

10. Examine the data in the following graph.

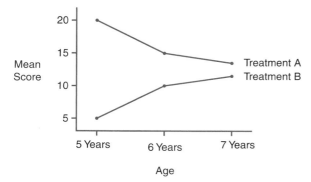

   a. Is there a main effect for the treatment factor?
   b. Is there a main effect for the age factor?
   c. Is there an interaction between age and the treatment?

11. Explain the issue of interdependence and independence of factors, and how it is related to interaction.

12. A researcher conducts a $2 \times 3 \times 2$ factorial study with 20 participants in each treatment condition.
   a. If the researcher uses an exclusively between-subjects design, how many individuals participate in the entire study?
   b. If the researcher uses an exclusively within-subjects design, how many individuals participate in the entire study?

13. Under what circumstances will the main effects in a factorial study not provide an accurate description of the results?

14. A researcher would like to compare two therapy techniques for treating depression in both adolescents and adults. Identify which factor is experimental and which is quasi-experimental.

15. Under what circumstances would adding gender as a second factor in a between-subjects study not reduce variability?

16. Suppose a researcher has demonstrated that a particular treatment is effective in reducing stress in adults. Describe some ways to add a second factor to expand these results.

LEARNING ACTIVITIES

1. Use PsycINFO or a similar database to locate a research study using a factorial design. (Note: You can try a subject term based on an area of interest, but the most direct path to finding factorial designs is to use a search term such as "2 × 2" or "2 × 3.") Once you find a factorial study, do the following:
   a. Identify each factor and the specific levels that are used for each factor.
   b. Specify whether each factor is an independent variable or a quasi-independent variable.
   c. Specify whether each factor is a between-subjects or a within-subjects factor.
   d. Describe the results of the study in terms of main effects and interactions (Which main effects were significant? Was the interaction significant?) Then describe the results of the study in terms of the variables studied.

2. In Figure 11.5, we show three combinations of main effects and interactions for a 2 × 2 factorial design. Using the same 2 × 2 structure, with factor A defining the rows and factor B defining the columns, create a set of means that produce each of the following patterns:
   a. A main effect for factors A and B, but no interaction.
   b. A main effect for factor A and an interaction, but no main effect for factor B.
   c. A main effect for both factors and an interaction.

WEB RESOURCES

Visit the Book Companion Website at **www.cengage.com/international** to access study tools including a glossary, flashcards, and web quizzing.

14

Statistical Analyses

CHAPTER OVERVIEW

In this chapter, we consider Step 8 of the research process: evaluating the data. Both descriptive and inferential statistics are described in detail. In addition, special statistical analyses for research are considered.

14.1 | THE ROLE OF STATISTICS IN THE RESEARCH PROCESS

The exception is single-subject research in which visual inspection is used in place of statistical techniques.

When the data collection phase of the research process is completed, a researcher typically is confronted with pages of data consisting of the scores, measurements, and observations recorded during the research study. The next step, Step 8 in the research process, is to use statistical methods to help make sense of the data. Statistical methods serve two principal purposes.

1. Statistics help organize and summarize the data so the researcher can see what happened in the study and communicate the results to others.
2. Statistics help the researcher answer the general questions that initiated the research by determining exactly what conclusions are justified based on the results.

These two general purposes correspond to the two general categories of statistical techniques: descriptive statistics and inferential statistics. **Descriptive statistics** are techniques that help describe a set of data. Examples of descriptive statistics include organizing a set of scores into a graph or a table and calculating a single value, such as the average score, that describes the entire set. The goal of descriptive statistics is to organize, summarize, and simplify data.

Inferential statistics, on the other hand, are methods that use the limited information from samples to answer general questions about populations. Recall from Chapter 5 that research questions concern a population, but research studies are conducted with relatively small samples. Although the sample is selected from the population and is intended to represent the population, there is no guarantee that a sample provides a perfectly accurate picture of the population. Thus, researchers must be cautious about assuming that the results obtained from a sample will generalize to the entire population. Inferential statistics help researchers determine when it is appropriate to generalize from a sample to a population.

DEFINITIONS

Descriptive statistics are methods that help researchers organize, summarize, and simplify the results obtained from research studies.

Inferential statistics are methods that use the results obtained from samples to help make generalizations about populations.

Planning Ahead

Although using statistics to evaluate research results appears as Step 8 in the research process, you should think about statistics long before you begin the research study. In particular, you should decide how you want to describe your results and exactly which descriptive statistics are needed. This task includes an evaluation of your planned measurement procedure to be sure that the scores you obtain are compatible with the statistics you plan to use. For example, if you intend to compute mean scores, you need to have numerical data. You also need to anticipate the inferential statistics you will use. This involves deciding exactly what kind of conclusion you would like to make and then ensuring that there is an appropriate inferential procedure to make your point.

In general, as soon as you begin to make decisions about how to define and measure the variables in your research study, you should also make decisions about the statistical analysis of your data. You should anticipate the appearance of your research data, plan the descriptive statistics that will allow you to present your data so that others can see and understand your results, and plan the inferential statistics that will allow you to interpret your results.

Statistics Terminology

Before we discuss descriptive and inferential statistical techniques, two additional terms should be introduced. The most commonly used descriptive technique is to compute one or two numerical values that summarize an entire set of data. When the set of data is a sample, the summary values are called **statistics.**

DEFINITION	A summary value that describes a sample is called a **statistic.** A common example of a statistic is the average score for a sample.

Sample statistics serve a dual purpose.

1. They describe or summarize the entire set of scores in the sample. For example, the average IQ score for a sample of 100 people provides a summary description of the intelligence level of the entire sample.
2. They provide information about the corresponding summary values for the entire population. For example, the average reading score for a sample of 25 first-grade students provides information about the general reading level for the entire population of first graders.

Once again, summary values computed for a sample are called statistics. The corresponding summary values for a population are called **parameters.** For example, if a sample of 20 students is selected from a high school with a total population of 1,148 students, then the average age for the students in the sample would be a statistic and the average age for the entire population would be a parameter.

DEFINITION	A summary value that describes a population is called a **parameter.** A common example of a parameter is the average score for a population.

Each statistic (computed for a sample) has a corresponding parameter (for the entire population). As we show later in this chapter, most inferential statistical techniques use sample statistics as the basis for drawing general conclusions about the corresponding population parameters.

 **LEARNING CHECKS**   Describe the two general purposes of statistics and the two corresponding general categories of statistical techniques.

Explain the difference between a statistic and a parameter.

14.2 | DESCRIPTIVE STATISTICS

As noted earlier, the general goal of descriptive statistics is to organize or summarize a set of scores. Two general techniques are used to accomplish this goal.

1. Organize the entire set of scores into a table or a graph that allows researchers (and others) to see the whole set of scores.
2. Compute one or two summary values (such as the average) that describe the entire group.

Each of these techniques is discussed in the following sections.

Frequency Distributions

One method of simplifying and organizing a set of scores is to group them into an organized display that shows the entire set. The display is called a **frequency distribution** and consists of a tabulation of the number of individuals in each category on the scale of measurement. Thus, a frequency distribution displays two sets of information:

1. The set of categories that make up the scale of measurement.
2. The number of individuals with scores in each of the categories.

Depending on the method used to display the scale of measurement and the frequencies, a frequency distribution can be a table or a graph. The advantage of a frequency distribution is that it allows a researcher to view the entire set of scores. The disadvantage is that constructing a frequency distribution without the aid of a computer can be somewhat tedious, especially with large sets of data.

Frequency Distribution Tables

A frequency distribution table consists of two columns of information. The first column presents the scale of measurement or simply lists the set of categories into which individuals have been assigned. The second column lists the frequency, or the number of individuals, located in each category. Table 14.1 is a frequency distribution table summarizing the scores from a 5-point quiz given to a class of $n = 15$ students. The first column lists the entire set of possible quiz scores (categories of measurement) in order from 5 to 0; it is headed X to indicate that these are the potential scores. The second column shows the frequency of occurrence for each score. In this example, one person had a perfect score of $X = 5$ on the quiz, three people had scores of $X = 4$, and so on.

Frequency Distribution Graphs

The same information that is presented in a frequency distribution table can be presented in a graph. The graph shows the scale of measurement (set of categories) along the horizontal axis and the frequencies on the vertical axis. Recall from Chapter 4 that there are four different scales of measurement: nominal, ordinal, interval, and ratio. When the measurement scale (scores) consists of numerical values (interval or ratio scale of measurement), there are two options for graphing the frequency distribution.

TABLE **14.1**
A Frequency Distribution Table

The table shows the distribution of scores from a 5-point quiz.

X	f
5	1
4	3
3	4
2	3
1	2
0	2

1. A **histogram** shows a bar above each score so that the height of the bar indicates the frequency of occurrence for that particular score. The bars for adjacent scores touch each other.
2. A **polygon** shows a point above each score so that the height of the point indicates the frequency. Straight lines connect the points, and additional straight lines are drawn down to the horizontal axis at each end to complete the figure.

Figure 14.1 shows two histograms and a polygon presenting the same data as Table 14.1. Figure 14.1a is a traditional histogram with a bar above each category. In Figure 14.1b, we modified the histogram slightly by changing each bar into a stack of blocks. The modification helps emphasize the concept of a frequency distribution. Each block represents one individual, and the graph shows how the individuals are distributed (piled up) along the scale of measurement. Finally, Figure 14.1c presents the same data in a polygon. Each of the graphs gives an organized picture of the entire set of scores so you can tell at a glance where the scores are located on the scale of measurement.

When the categories on the scale of measurement are not numerical values (nominal or ordinal scales), the frequency distribution is presented as a **bar graph.** A bar graph is like a histogram except that a space is left between adjacent bars. Figure 14.2 is a bar graph that presents a frequency distribution of academic majors in an introductory college course. Notice that the height of each bar indicates the frequency associated with that particular category. In this example, the class contains 10 psychology majors, 6 biology majors, and so on.

Frequency distributions, especially graphs, can be a very effective method for presenting information about a set of scores. The distribution shows whether the scores are clustered together or spread out across the scale. You can see at a glance if the scores are generally high or generally low; that is, where the distribution is centered. Also, it is easy to see if there are any extreme scores that are very different from the rest of the group. However, a frequency distribution is generally considered to be a preliminary method of statistical analysis. As a result, frequency distributions are rarely shown in

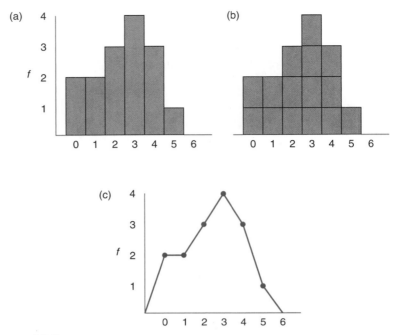

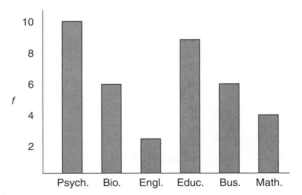

FIGURE **14.1** Frequency Distribution Graphs

The same set of scores is shown in a traditional histogram (a), in a modified histogram (b), and in a polygon (c). In the modified histogram (b), each score is represented by a block so there is no need for a vertical axis to show the frequency for each score.

FIGURE **14.2** A Bar Graph Showing the Frequency Distribution of Academic Majors in an Introductory Psychology Class

Notice the space between adjacent bars.

published research reports. Nonetheless, a frequency distribution graph is an excellent first step in examining a set of data. As soon as you finish data collection, constructing a frequency distribution graph gives you a clear picture of the results. In addition, a frequency distribution graph is probably the single best method for thinking about a set of data. Whenever you encounter the concept of a sample or a set of scores, we suggest that you visualize the scores in a frequency distribution graph. The image of a frequency distribution graph gives you a concrete representation of all the individual scores as well as the appearance of the entire set of data.

LEARNING CHECKS

What are the advantages and disadvantages of using a frequency distribution to organize data?

What type of data should be presented in a histogram, and what type of data should be presented in a bar graph?

Measures of Central Tendency

Although frequency distribution tables and graphs have the advantage of presenting a complete picture of a set of data, there are simpler methods for describing the scores in a sample. Perhaps the most commonly used descriptive statistic involves computing the average score for a set of data. In statistical terms, this process is called measuring **central tendency.** The purpose of measuring central tendency is to locate the center of the distribution of scores by finding a single score that represents the entire set. The goal is to find the average, or the most typical, score for the entire set.

DEFINITION

Central tendency is a statistical measure that identifies a single score that defines the center of a distribution. The goal of central tendency is to identify the value that is most typical or most representative of the entire group.

Measures of central tendency can be used to describe or summarize a group of individuals. For example, if a research report states that the children who participated in the study had an average IQ of 124, you should recognize that these children are definitely smarter than average (IQs average 100). In addition, measures of central tendency are the most commonly used measures for comparing two (or more) different sets of data. For example, a research report might state that the students who received special tutoring had exam scores that averaged 12 points higher than the scores of students who did not receive tutoring.

Although the concept of central tendency is fairly straightforward, a few concerns arise in implementing the concept. The goal is to use an objective, clearly defined procedure for determining the center of a set of scores so that other researchers will know exactly how the average score for a sample was computed and be able to duplicate the process. Unfortunately, no single procedure always works. As a result, researchers have developed three different procedures for measuring central tendency, each suited to a specific situation or type of data. The three measures of central tendency are the mean, the median, and the mode.

The Mean

When individual scores are numerical values obtained from an interval or a ratio scale of measurement, the **mean** is the most commonly used measure of central tendency. The mean is computed by adding the scores and dividing the sum by the number of individuals. Conceptually, the mean is the amount each individual would receive if the total were divided equally. In research reports, the convention is to use the letter *M* to represent a sample mean. The mean for a population is represented by the symbol μ, the Greek letter mu. As noted earlier, the mean is the most commonly used measure of central tendency. However, there are situations in which the mean does not provide a good measure of central tendency or in which it is impossible to compute a mean. Usually, these situations fall into one of the following categories.

- When a sample contains a few extreme scores—unusually high or unusually low values compared to the rest of the scores—the mean tends to be distorted by the extreme values so that it is not a good central, representative value. For example, one or two exceptionally large scores can raise the mean so that it is not located in the center of the distribution.
- Often, sample data consist of measurements from a nominal scale and are not numerical values. For example, a researcher might measure variables such as gender, occupation, academic major, or eye color for a sample of students. Because no numerical values are involved, it is impossible to compute a mean value for such data. Occasionally, nominal measurements are coded with numerical values. For example, a researcher may use the value 0 for a male and the value 1 for a female. In this situation, it is possible to compute a mean; however, the result is a meaningless number.

When it is impossible to compute a mean or when the mean does not produce a good representative value, there are two alternative measures of central tendency: the median and the mode.

The Median

The **median** is the score that divides a distribution in half, so that 50% of the individuals have scores that are less than or equal to the median. Usually, the median is used for data sets in which the mean does not provide a good representative value. In a distribution with a few extreme scores, for example, the extreme values can displace the mean so that it is not a central value. In this situation, the median often provides a better measure of central tendency. Thus, you can think of the median as a backup measure of central tendency that is used in situations in which the mean does not work well. Often, demographic data such as family income or prices of new single-family homes contain a few extreme values. In these situations, the median income or the median price is typically used to describe the average.

The Mode

The **mode** is the score or category with the greatest frequency. In a frequency distribution graph, the mode identifies the location of the peak (highest point) in the distribution. When the scores consist of classifications that are not numerical values (for example, measurements from a nominal scale of measurement), it is impossible to compute the mean or the median. In this case, the mode is the only available measure of central tendency. When the scores are numerical values, the mode is often reported along with the mean because it helps describe the shape of the distribution. Although a distribution of scores can have only one mean and only one median, it is possible to have multiple peaks and, therefore, multiple modes. A distribution with two distinct peaks is said to be **bimodal.** A distribution with more than two modes is **multimodal.**

DEFINITIONS

The **mean** is a measure of central tendency obtained by adding the individual scores, then dividing the sum by the number of scores. The mean is the arithmetic average.

The **median** measures central tendency by identifying the score that divides the distribution in half. If the scores are listed in order, 50% of the individuals have scores at or below the median.

The **mode** measures central tendency by identifying the most frequently occurring score in the distribution.

Examples demonstrating calculation of the mean, the median, and the mode are presented in Appendix B, p. 524.

LEARNING CHECKS

What is the purpose of measuring central tendency?

In which situations would it be best to use the mean as a measure of central tendency?

In which situations should you use an alternative method?

Describe a situation in which the median provides a better measure of central tendency than the mean.

Measures of Variability

Variability describes the spread of the scores in a distribution. When variability is small, it means that the scores are all clustered close together. Large variability means that there are big differences between individuals and the scores are spread across a wide range of values. As with central tendency, there are several different ways to measure or describe variability; however, the most common are the standard deviation and its associated measure, variance.

Standard Deviation and Variance

Whenever the mean is used as the measure of central tendency, the **standard deviation** is used as the measure of variability. Standard deviation uses the mean of the distribution as a reference point and measures variability by measuring the distance between each score and the mean. Conceptually, standard deviation measures the average distance from the mean. When the scores are clustered close to the mean, the standard deviation is small; when the scores are scattered widely around the mean, the standard deviation is large.

Although the concept of the standard deviation is fairly straightforward, its actual calculation is somewhat more complicated. Instead of simply computing the average distance from the mean, the calculation of standard deviation begins by computing the average *squared* distance from the mean. This average squared value is called **variance.** Although variance is not an intuitively meaningful concept, it is an important statistical measure, especially in the context of inferential statistics. In summary, the calculation of variance and standard deviation can be viewed as a series of steps.

1. For each score, measure the distance away from the mean. This distance is often called a *deviation*. For example, if the mean is 80 and you have a score of 84, then the distance (or deviation) is 4 points.

2. Square each of the distances and compute the average of the squared distances. This is variance. We should note, however, that the average squared distance for a sample is computed by dividing the sum of the squared distances by $n - 1$, where n is the number of scores in the sample. The value of $n - 1$ is called **degrees of freedom,** or *df.* Finding the average by dividing by $n - 1$ (instead of n) produces a variance for the sample that is an accurate and unbiased representation of the population variance.

3. Because the variance measures the average squared distance from the mean, simply take the square root to obtain the standard deviation. Thus, variance and standard deviation are directly related by a squaring or square root operation.

$$\text{Standard deviation} = \sqrt{\text{Variance}}$$

$$\text{Variance} = (\text{Standard deviation})^2$$

In statistics textbooks, the sample standard deviation is usually identified by the letter s, and the sample variance is s^2. In published reports, the sample standard deviation is identified as *SD*.

DEFINITIONS

Variability is a measure of the spread of scores in a distribution.

Variance measures variability by computing the average squared distance from the mean. First, measure the distance from the mean for each score, then square the distances and find the sum of the squared distances. Next, for a sample, the average squared distance is computed by dividing the sum of the squared distances by $n - 1$.

Standard deviation is the square root of the variance and provides a measure of variability by describing the average distance from the mean.

Because the standard deviation is a measure of distance, it is a fairly easy concept to understand. Therefore, the standard deviation is considered the best way to describe variability. Once again, standard deviation provides a measure of the standard distance from the mean. A small value for standard deviation indicates that the individual scores are clustered close to the mean and a large value indicates that the scores are spread out relatively far from the mean. You can also think of standard deviation as describing the distance between scores; a small standard deviation, for example, indicates that the differences, or distances, from one score to another are relatively small.

Variance, on the other hand, measures squared distance. Because squared distance is not a simple concept, variance is not usually used to describe variability. However, variance also provides a measure of distance. A small

14.2 Descriptive Statistics **405**

variance indicates that the scores are clustered close together; a large variance means that the scores are widely scattered.

Sample Variance and Degrees of Freedom

Although sample variance is described as measuring the average squared distance from the mean, the actual calculations involve dividing the sum of the squared distances by $n - 1$ (instead of dividing by n). As we noted, the value of $n - 1$ is called degrees of freedom (df). Dividing by $n - 1$ is a necessary adjustment to ensure that the sample variance provides an accurate representation of its population variance. Without the adjustment, the sample variance tends to underestimate the actual variance in the population. With the adjustment, the sample variance—on average—gives an accurate and unbiased picture of the population variance.

It is not critical to understand the concept of degrees of freedom; however, degrees of freedom (df) are encountered in nearly every situation in which statistics are computed or reported. In most cases, you should be able to find a relationship between the structure of the study and the value for degrees of freedom. For example, a research study with 20 participants has a sample variance with $df = 19$. The topic of degrees of freedom occurs again later in the context of hypothesis tests (section 15.4). Examples demonstrating the calculation of standard deviation and variance are presented in Appendix B, pp. 524–525.

LEARNING CHECKS

Describe the relationship between variance and standard deviation.
Describe the relationship between the standard deviation and the mean.

Describing Interval and Ratio Data (Numerical Scores)

Earlier in this chapter, we introduced the frequency distribution as the best method of visualizing a set of scores. When the scores are numerical values measured on an interval or a ratio scale, the mean and the standard deviation are the best methods of describing a set of scores. In fact, all three of these statistical concepts (distribution, mean, and standard deviation) are interrelated.

In a frequency distribution graph, the mean can be represented by a vertical line drawn through the center of the set of scores. By definition, the mean identifies the location of the center. In the same way, the standard deviation can be represented by two arrows that point out from the mean toward the opposite extremes of the frequency distribution. The two arrows should be the same length (equal to the standard deviation), and the length is usually about half the distance from the mean to the most extreme scores. Figure 14.3 shows a frequency distribution graph with the mean and standard deviation displayed as described. Notice that the standard deviation is shown as a distance from the mean and is intended to represent the standard distance. Some of the scores are closer to the mean, and some are farther away from the mean, but the arrows represent the standard or average distance. As a general rule, roughly 70% of the scores in a distribution are within one standard deviation of the mean and roughly 95% of the scores are within two standard deviations.

As you examine Figure 14.3, also notice that the values for the mean and the standard deviation provide information about the location of the scores in

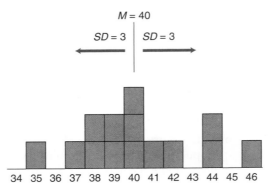

FIGURE **14.3** A Distribution of Scores with a Mean of $M = 40$ and a
Standard Deviation of $SD = 3$

Notice that the mean is shown with a vertical line positioned at a value of 40. The
standard deviation (standard distance from the mean) is shown with arrows that
extend three points above the mean and three points below the mean.

the distribution. Specifically, the value of the mean identifies the numerical
score in the center of the distribution, and the standard deviation specifies how
far the scores are distributed to the right and left of the mean. In Figure 14.3,
the mean is 40 and the standard deviation is 3. Thus, the mean is located at a
value of 40, and the arrows extend to 43 on the right and 37 on the left. For
this distribution, most of the scores are located between 37 and 43.

Figure 14.4a is a frequency distribution for a set of scores. This is the kind
of distribution you might prepare after collecting data in a research study. Just
by looking at the distribution, you should be able to make reasonably accurate
estimates of the mean and the standard deviation. Try it. For this set of scores,
the actual mean is 16.88, and the standard deviation is 2.23. How close were
your estimates?

In the literature the mean is identified by the letter M and the standard deviation is identified by SD. These two values are probably the most commonly
reported descriptive statistics, and they should provide enough information to
construct a good picture of the entire set of scores. For example, if a research
report describes a set of scores by stating that $M = 45$ and $SD = 6$, you should
be able to visualize (or sketch) a frequency distribution graph showing the set of
scores. Try it; your distribution should look like the graph in Figure 14.4b.

Describing Non-numerical Data from Nominal and Ordinal Scales of Measurement

Occasionally, the measurements or observations made by a researcher are not
numerical values. Instead, a researcher may simply classify participants by
placing them in separate nominal or ordinal categories. Examples of this kind
of measurement include:

- Classification of people by gender (male or female).
- Classification of attitude (agree or disagree).
- Classification of self-esteem (high, medium, or low).

(a)

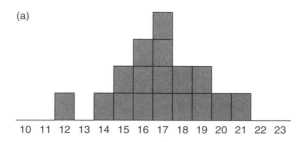

10 11 12 13 14 15 16 17 18 19 20 21 22 23

(b)

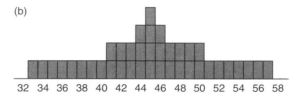

32   34   36   38   40   42   44   46   48   50   52   54   56   58

FIGURE **14.4** The Mean and Standard Deviation in Two Frequency Distributions

(a) A distribution of scores with a mean of $M = 16.88$ and a standard deviation of $SD = 2.23$.
(b) A distribution with a mean of $M = 45$ and a standard deviation of $SD = 6$.

In each case, the data do not consist of numerical values: there are no numbers with which to compute a mean or a standard deviation. In this case, the researcher must find some other method of describing the data.

One of the simplest ways to describe nominal and ordinal data is to report the proportion or percentage in each category. These values can be used to describe a single sample or to compare separate samples. For example, a report might describe a sample of voters by stating that 43% prefer candidate Green, 28% prefer candidate Brown, and 29% are undecided. A research report might compare two groups by stating that 80% of the 6-year-old children were able to successfully complete the task, but only 34% of the 4-year-olds were successful.

In addition to percentages and proportions, you also can use the mode as a measure of central tendency for data from a nominal scale. Remember, the mode simply identifies the most commonly occurring category and, therefore, describes the most typical member of a sample. For example, if the modal response to a survey question is "no opinion," you can probably conclude that the people surveyed do not care much about the issue. However, the concept of *distance between scores* is meaningless with non-numerical values and it is impossible to compute a meaningful measure of variability.

Using Graphs to Summarize Data

When a research study compares several different treatment conditions (or several different populations), it is common to use a graph to display the summary statistics for all the different groups being compared. The value of a graph is that it allows several different statistics to be displayed simultaneously so that an observer can easily see the differences (or similarities) between them. For example, it is possible to list the means from eight different treatment conditions, but it probably is easier to compare the eight means if they are all presented in a single picture.

The most common statistics to present in a graph are sample means, but it is possible to present sample medians or sample proportions. In each case, the graph is organized with the same basic structure.

1. The different groups or treatment conditions are listed on the horizontal axis. Usually, this involves the different levels of an independent variable or different values for a quasi-independent variable.
2. The values for the statistics are listed on the vertical axis. Usually, this involves values for the sample means that are being compared.

The graph can be constructed as either a **line graph** or a bar graph. Figure 14.5 shows each type of graph displaying the means from four different treatment conditions. To construct the line graph, we placed a point above each value on the horizontal axis (each treatment) so that the vertical position of the point corresponds to the mean for that treatment condition, and then connected the points by straight lines. The bar graph simply uses a bar above each of the treatment conditions so that the height of the bar corresponds to the mean for the treatment. By convention, line graphs are used when the values on the horizontal axis are measured on an interval or a ratio scale; bar graphs are used when the values are from a nominal or ordinal scale.

Similar graphs are used to display sample medians or sample proportions. Two examples are shown in Figure 14.6. The first graph shows the median incomes for three samples of 30-year-old men. The samples represent three different levels of education. The second graph shows the results from a study examining how preferences for wristwatch styles are related to age. Participants in three samples (representing three age groups) were asked whether they preferred a digital watch or a traditional analog watch. The graph shows the proportion preferring digital watches for each of the three samples.

Factorial research studies (Chapter 13) include two or more independent variables (or quasi-independent variables). For example, a researcher may want to examine the effects of heat and humidity on performance. For this study, both the temperature (variable 1) and the humidity (variable 2) would be manipulated, and performance would be evaluated under a variety of different temperature and humidity conditions. The structure of this type of experiment can be represented as a matrix, with one variable determining the rows and the second variable defining the columns. Each cell in the matrix corresponds to a specific combination of treatments. Figure 14.7 presents hypothetical data for the temperature and humidity experiment just described. The figure includes a matrix showing the mean level of performance for each treatment condition and demonstrates how the means would be displayed in a graph. As a general rule, graphs for two-factor studies are constructed by listing the values of one of the independent variables on the horizontal axis and listing the values for the dependent variable on the vertical axis. For this

(a)

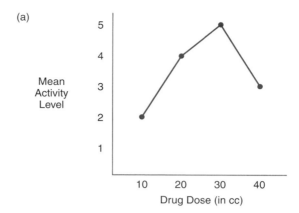

(b)

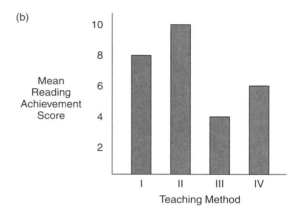

FIGURE **14.5** Presenting Means and Mean Differences in a Graph
(a) A line graph and (b) a bar graph showing treatment means obtained from a research study.

figure, we list temperature values on the horizontal axis and list values for the mean level of performance on the vertical axis. Then, a separate line is used to present the means for each level of the second independent variable. In this case, there is a separate line for each of the two levels of humidity. Notice that the top line presents the means in the top row of the data matrix and the bottom line shows the means from the bottom row. The result is a graph that displays all six means from the experiment, and allows comparison of means and mean differences.

LEARNING CHECK What techniques can be used to describe nominal and ordinal data?

(a)

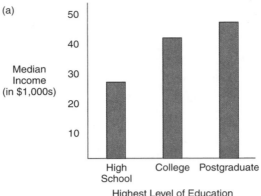

(b)

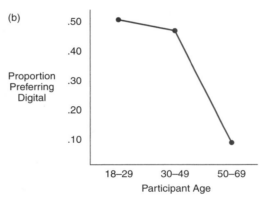

FIGURE **14.6** Graphs Showing (a) Medians and (b) Proportions

Correlations

Thus far, all of the statistics we have considered are intended to describe a group of scores and to permit a researcher to look for differences between groups. For example, a researcher interested in examining the relationship between self-esteem and task performance could conduct a differential study, selecting a sample of high self-esteem participants and a sample of low self-esteem participants (see Chapter 12, pp. 338–340). Each individual is given a task and performance is measured. An example of the data resulting from this type of study is shown in Table 14.2a. Notice that the researcher has two sets of scores. The mean would be computed for each set to describe the scores, and the difference between the two means would describe the relationship between self-esteem and performance.

An alternative research approach is to use a correlational design in which self-esteem and performance are measured for each participant (see Chapter 8). Instead of comparing two groups of scores, the researcher now has one group of participants with two scores for each individual. An example of the data that

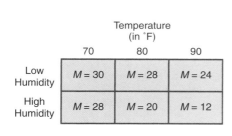

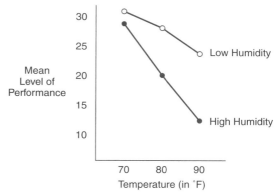

FIGURE **14.7** A Matrix and a Graph Showing the Means from a Two-Factor Study.

result from this type of study is shown in Table 14.2b. For this type of data, the researcher computes a **correlation** that measures and describes the relationship between the two variables. For this example, the correlation would measure and describe the relationship between self-esteem and performance.

The data for a correlation always consist of two scores for each individual. By convention, the scores are identified as X and Y and can be presented in a table or in a graph called a **scatter plot**. Figure 14.8 shows a scatter plot for the self-esteem and performance data in Table 14.2b. In the scatter plot, each individual is represented by a point in the graph; the horizontal position of the point corresponds to the value of X (self-esteem) and the vertical position is the value of Y (performance). A scatter plot can be a great aid in helping you see the nature of a relationship between two variables.

A correlation measures and describes three aspects of the relationship between two variables:

1. The direction of the relationship is described by the sign of the correlation. A positive correlation indicates that X and Y tend to change in the same direction. For a negative correlation, X and Y change in opposite directions.
2. The form of the relationship is determined by the type of correlation. The **Pearson correlation,** usually identified by the letter r, evaluates linear (straight line) relationships and is by far the most commonly used correlation. The Spearman correlation, identified by r_s, is simply the Pearson correlation applied to ordinal data (ranks). If the original scores are numerical values from an interval or ratio scale, it is possible to rank the scores and then compute a **Spearman correlation.** In this case, the Spearman correlation measures the degree to which the relationship is consistently one-directional, or monotonic.
3. The degree of consistency, or strength, of the relationship is described by the numerical value of the correlation. A correlation of 1.00 indicates a perfectly consistent relationship and a correlation of 0.00 indicates no consistent relationship whatsoever. Different degrees of relationship were discussed in Chapter 8 (see Figure 8.3 on p. 232).

TABLE 14.2

Two Different Strategies for Evaluating the Relationship between
Self-Esteem and Performance

One study (a) uses a nonexperimental strategy and evaluates the mean difference between two groups of participants. The other study (b) uses a correlational strategy, measuring two variables for each participant, and computing a correlation to evaluate the relationship between variables.

(a)

High Self-Esteem Group	Low Self-Esteem Group	
19	12	
23	14	
21	10	
24	17	←——————— Performance Scores
17	13	
18	20	
20	13	
22	11	
$M = 20.50$	$M = 13.75$	

(b)

Participant	Self-Esteem Scores	Performance Scores	
A	62	13	
B	84	20	
C	89	22	
D	73	16	←——————— Two Separate Scores
E	66	11	for Each Participant
F	75	18	
G	71	14	
H	80	21	

Finally, we should note that the sign of the correlation and the strength, or magnitude, of the correlation are independent. For example, correlations of $r = +0.85$ and $r = -0.85$ are equally strong, and Pearson correlations of $r = +1.00$ and $r = -1.00$ both indicate a perfect linear relationship.

DEFINITION   A **correlation** is a statistical value that measures and describes the direction and degree of relationship between two variables.

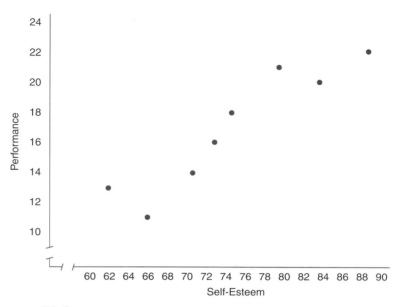

FIGURE **14.8** A Scatter Plot Showing the Data from Table 14.2b

The data show a strong, positive relationship between self-esteem and performance. The Pearson correlation is $r = 0.933$.

Examples demonstrating the calculation of the Pearson and Spearman correlations are presented in Appendix B, 525–528.

LEARNING CHECK

A researcher obtains a correlation of $r = -0.72$ between grade point average and amount of time spent watching television for a sample of college students. For this sample, who tends to get the better grades: the students who watch a lot of television or the students who watch only a little television? Explain your answer.

Regression

The Pearson correlation describes the linear relationship between two variables. Whenever a linear relationship exists, it is possible to compute the equation for the straight line that provides the best fit for the data points. The process of finding the linear equation is called **regression,** and the resulting equation is called the **regression equation.**

Figure 14.9 shows a scatter plot of X and Y values with a straight line drawn through the center of the data points. The straight line is valuable because it makes the relationship easier to see and it can be used for prediction. That is, for each value of X, the line provides a predicted value of Y.

All linear equations have the same general structure and can be expressed as

$$Y = bX + a$$

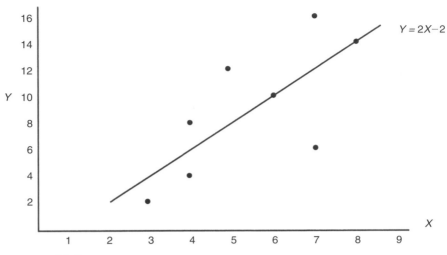

FIGURE 14.9 A Scatter Plot and Regression Line

For each value of X it is possible to calculate a Y value on the line that serves as a predicted value of Y.

The regression equation actually minimizes the total *squared* error between the actual Y values and the predicted Y values, and is often called the least squared error solution.

where b and a are fixed constants. The value of b is called the **slope constant** because it describes the slope of the line (how much Y changes when X is increased by 1 point). The value of a is called the **Y-intercept** because it is the point at which the line intersects the Y axis. The process of regression identifies the specific values for b and a that produce the most accurate predictions for Y. That is, regression identifies the specific equation that results in the smallest possible error between the predicted Y values on the line and the actual Y values in the data.

Often the regression equation is reported in standardized form, which means that the original X and Y scores were standardized, or transformed into z-scores, before the equation was computed. In standardized form the equation for predicting Y values becomes

$$z_Y = \beta z_X$$

where z_Y and z_X are the standardized values (z-scores) for X and Y, and the Greek letter beta (β) is the standardized slope constant. For linear regression using one variable (X) to predict one variable (Y), the value of beta is equal to the Pearson correlation between X and Y.

Unless there is a perfect linear relationship (a Pearson correlation of +1.00 or −1.00), there is some error between the predicted Y values and the actual Y values. The amount of error varies from point to point, but the average amount of error is directly related to the value of the Pearson correlation. For a correlation near 1.00 (plus or minus), the data points are clustered close to the line and the average error is small. For a correlation near zero, the data points are widely scattered around the line and the average error is large. The squared value of the correlation, r^2, describes the overall accuracy of the prediction. Specifically, r^2 equals the proportion of the Y-score variance that is predicted by the regression equation.

Multiple Regression

Occasionally, researchers try to get more accurate predictions by using more than one predictor variable. For example, using a student's high school grades and SAT scores to predict college performance should result in more accurate predictions than those obtained from only one of the two predictors. The process of finding the most accurate prediction equations with multiple predictors is called **multiple regression,** and the resulting equation is called the **multiple-regression equation.**

When two variables, X_1 and X_2, are used to predict Y, the general form of the multiple-regression equation is

$$Y = b_1 X_1 + b_2 X_2 + a$$

Multiple regression determines the specific values of a, b_1, and b_2, that produce the most accurate predictions. In standardized form, the equation becomes

$$z_Y = \beta_1 z_{X1} + \beta_2 z_{X2}$$

where z_Y, z_{X1}, and z_{X2}, are the standardized values (z-scores) for Y, X_1, and X_2, and the beta values are the slope constants.

Again, there usually is some error between the predicted Y values and the actual Y values in the data. In the same way that r^2 measures the proportion of variance that is predicted with one predictor variable, it is possible to compute a corresponding proportion for multiple regression. The symbol R^2 describes the proportion of the total variance of the Y scores that is accounted for by the regression equation. Occasionally, researchers use one predictor variable in the initial regression equation, and then add a second predictor to determine how much the prediction accuracy improves. In this situation, researchers often report a value for ΔR^2, which measures how much the value of R^2 changes (increases) when the second predictor variable is added.

DEFINITIONS

The statistical process of finding the linear equation that produces the most accurate predicted values for Y using one predictor variable (X) is called **regression.** When more than one predictor variable is used, the process is called **multiple regression.**

LEARNING CHECKS

A researcher computes a regression equation of $Y = 10X + 85$ for predicting IQ scores (Y) from student grade point averages (X). Based on this equation, what IQ would be predicted for a student with a grade point average of 3.50?

14.3 | INFERENTIAL STATISTICS

Although research questions typically concern an entire population, research studies typically involve a relatively small sample selected from the population (see Chapter 5, p. 138). For example, a researcher would like to know whether adolescents' social skills are influenced by their social experiences as infants. To answer this question, the researcher could select a sample of 25 adolescents, measure their social skills, and interview their parents to get a measure of their social experiences as infants. Notice that the researcher is relying on a specific group of 25 adolescents to provide an answer for a question about all adolescents. This creates a general problem for researchers. Does the sample accurately represent the population? If the researcher took a different sample, would different results be obtained? Addressing these questions is the purpose of inferential statistics.

The general goal of inferential statistics is to use the limited information from samples as the basis for reaching general conclusions about the populations from which the samples were obtained. Notice that this goal involves making a generalization or an inference from limited information (a sample) to a general conclusion (a population). The basic difficulty with this process is centered on the concept of **sampling error.** In simple terms, sampling error means that a sample does not provide a perfectly accurate picture of its population; that is, there is some discrepancy, or error, between the information available from a sample and the true situation that exists in the general population.

The concept of sampling error is illustrated in Figure 14.10. The figure shows a population of 1,000 college students and two samples, each with 5 students who were selected from the population. The figure also shows a set of parameters for the population and the corresponding statistics for the two samples. First, notice that none of the sample statistics are exactly equal to the population parameters. This is the fundamental idea behind sampling error; there is always some discrepancy between a sample statistic and the corresponding population parameter. Also note that the sample statistics differ from one sample to the other. This is another consequence of sampling error; each sample has its own individuals and its own scores, and each sample has its own statistics.

DEFINITION	**Sampling error** is the naturally occurring difference between a sample statistic and the corresponding population parameter.

The fundamental problem for inferential statistics is to differentiate between research results that represent real patterns or relationships, and those that result from sampling error. Figure 14.11 shows a prototypical research situation. In this case, the research study is examining the relationship between violence on television and aggressive behavior for preschool children. Two groups of children (two samples) are selected from the population. One sample watches television programs containing violence for 30 minutes, and the other sample watches nonviolent programs for 30 minutes. Both groups are then observed during a play period, and the researcher records the amount of aggression displayed by each child. The researcher calculates a sample mean (a statistic) for each group and compares the two sample means. In Figure 14.11, there is a 4-point difference between the two sample means. The problem for the researcher is to decide whether the 4-point difference was caused by the treatments (the different television programs) or is just a case of sampling error

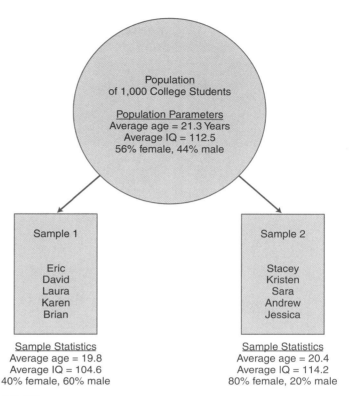

FIGURE 14.10 A Demonstration of Sampling Error

Two samples are selected from the same population. Notice that the sample statistics are different from one sample to another, and all of the sample statistics are different from the corresponding population parameters.

(like the differences that are shown in Figure 14.10). That is, does the 4-point difference provide convincing evidence that viewing television violence has an effect on behavior, or is it simply a result of chance? The purpose of inferential statistics is to help researchers answer this question.

Hypothesis Tests

In Chapter 1, we presented an overview of the research process, and we have followed the research process step-by-step throughout this book. Recall that the second step in the research process was to use your research idea to form a specific, testable hypothesis, which is a tentative statement describing the relationship between variables. The following steps involved planning and conducting a research study to determine whether the hypothesis is correct. Now, the data have been collected, and it is time to use the data to test the credibility of the original hypothesis.

As we have noted, the original research question and the hypothesis concern the population. The research results, however, come from a sample. Thus,

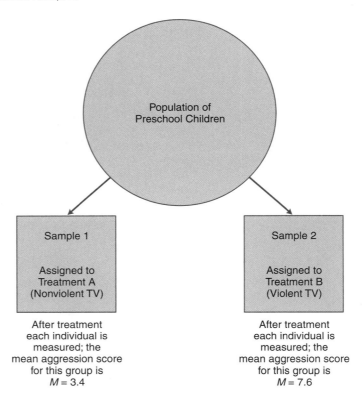

FIGURE **14.11** A Research Study Examining the Relationship between Television Violence and Aggressive Behavior for Preschool Children

Two groups of children (two samples) receive two different treatments and produce different means. The problem is to determine if the mean difference was caused by the treatments or is simply an example of sampling error (as in Figure 14.10).

the task of evaluating a research hypothesis involves using the information from samples as the basis for making general conclusions about populations. This is the task of inferential statistics. One of the most commonly used inferential procedures is the **hypothesis test.** In very general terms, a hypothesis test is a systematic procedure that determines whether the sample data provide convincing evidence to support the original research hypothesis.

A hypothesis test can be viewed as a technique to help ensure the internal validity of a research study. Recall in Chapter 6 (p. 170) that internal validity is threatened whenever there is an alternative explanation for the results obtained in a research study. Because it is always possible that the results observed in a sample are simply random variation caused by sampling error, it is always possible that pure chance (sampling error) is an alternative explanation. In Figure 14.11, for example, the 4-point difference between the two sample means could have been caused by the treatments, but it also could have been caused by chance.

The goal of a hypothesis test is to rule out chance as a plausible explanation for the results. The hypothesis test accomplishes this goal by first determining what kind of results can be reasonably expected from chance, then ensuring that the actual results are significantly different from those expected by chance.

DEFINITION	A **hypothesis test** is a statistical procedure that uses sample data to evaluate the credibility of a hypothesis about a population. A hypothesis test attempts to distinguish between two explanations for the sample data: (1) that the patterns in the data represent systematic relationships among variables in the population, and (2) that the patterns in the data were produced by random variation from chance or sampling error.

Although the details of a hypothesis test vary from one situation to another, the different tests all use the same basic logic and consist of the same basic elements. In this section, we introduce the five basic elements of a hypothesis test.

1. The Null Hypothesis

The **null hypothesis** is a statement about the population, or populations, being examined, and always says that there is no effect, no change, or no relationship. In general, the null hypothesis specifies what the population parameter(s) should be if nothing happened. In a study comparing two treatments, for example, the null hypothesis states that there is no difference between the treatments and the population mean difference is zero. In a study examining a correlation, the null hypothesis states that there is no relationship and the correlation for the population is zero. According to the null hypothesis, any patterns in the sample are nothing more than chance (sampling error). For the research situation shown in Figure 14.11, the null hypothesis states that the type of television program has no effect on behavior and, therefore, the 4-point difference between the two sample means is simply sampling error.

In Chapter 1 (p. 28), we introduced the idea of developing a good hypothesis as Step 2 in the research process. At that time, we noted that one characteristic of a good hypothesis is that it must make a positive statement about the existence of a relationship or the existence of a treatment effect. The null hypothesis is exactly the opposite of the research hypothesis. The research hypothesis says that the treatment does have an effect, and the null hypothesis says that the treatment has no effect. The goal of the research study is to gather enough evidence to demonstrate convincingly that the treatment really does have an effect. The purpose of the hypothesis test is to evaluate the evidence. The test determines whether the results of the research study are sufficient to reject the null hypothesis and justify a conclusion that the treatment has an effect.

2. The Sample Statistic

The data from the research study are used to compute the sample statistic (or statistics) corresponding to the parameter (or parameters) specified in the null hypothesis. For example, if the null hypothesis states that there is no difference between two population means, the sample statistic would be the difference between two sample means. Or, if the null hypothesis states that the population correlation is zero, the sample statistic would be the sample correlation obtained in the research study.

3. The Standard Error

Earlier, we introduced the concept of sampling error as the natural difference between a sample statistic and the corresponding parameter. Figure 14.10, for example, shows several sample means (statistics) that are all different from the corresponding population means (parameters). Some samples are representative of the population and produce statistics that are very similar to the population parameters. There also are always some extreme, unrepresentative samples whose statistics are very different from the population values. In most research situations, it is possible to calculate the average size of the sampling error; that is, the average difference between a statistic and a parameter. This average distance is called the **standard error.**

DEFINITION   **Standard error** is a measure of the average, or standard, distance between a sample statistic and the corresponding population parameter.

The advantage of computing the standard error is that it provides a measure of how much difference it is reasonable to expect between a statistic and a parameter. Notice that this distance is a measure of the natural discrepancy that occurs just by chance. Samples are intended to represent their populations but they are not expected to be perfect. Typically, there is some discrepancy between a sample statistic and the population parameter, and the standard error tells you how much discrepancy to expect.

4. The Test Statistic

A **test statistic** is a mathematical technique for comparing the sample statistic with the null hypothesis, using the standard error as a baseline. In many hypothesis tests, the test statistic is a ratio with the following structure:

$$\text{Test statistic} = \frac{\text{Sample statistic} - \text{Parameter from the null hypothesis}}{\text{Standard error}}$$

$$= \frac{\text{Actual difference between the data and the hypothesis}}{\text{Difference expected by chance}}$$

The null hypothesis states that the results of the research study represent nothing more than chance. If this is true, then the actual results (the numerator) and the chance results (the denominator) should be very similar, and the test statistic will have a value near 1.00. Thus, when the test statistic produces a value near 1.00, it is an indication that there is no treatment effect, no difference, or no relationship; that is, the results are consistent with the null hypothesis.

On the other hand, if there is a real treatment effect or a real relationship, the actual results should be noticeably bigger than those expected from chance. In this case, the test statistic should produce a value much larger than 1.00. Thus, a large value for a test statistic (much greater than 1.00) is an indication of a large discrepancy between the data and the hypothesis, and suggests that the null hypothesis should be rejected.

DEFINITION

In the context of a hypothesis test, a **test statistic** is a summary value that measures the degree to which the sample data are in accordance with the null hypothesis. Typically, a large value for the test statistic indicates a large discrepancy between the sample statistic and the parameter specified by the null hypothesis, and leads to rejecting the null hypothesis.

5. The Alpha Level (Level of Significance)

The final element in a hypothesis test is the **alpha level,** or **level of significance.** The alpha level provides a criterion for interpreting the test statistic. As we noted earlier, a test statistic with a value greater than 1.00 usually indicates that the obtained result is greater than would be expected from chance. How-ever, researchers typically demand research results that are not just greater than chance but *significantly* greater than chance. The alpha level provides a criterion for significance.

Remember, the goal of a hypothesis test is to rule out chance as a plausible explanation for the results. To achieve this, researchers determine which re-sults are reasonable to expect just by chance (without any treatment effect), and which results are extremely unlikely to be obtained by chance alone. The alpha level is a probability value that defines what is extremely unlikely. That is, the alpha level is the probability that the sample results would be obtained even if the null hypothesis were true. By convention, alpha levels are very small probabilities, usually .05, .01, or .001. An alpha level of .01, for example, means that a sample result is considered to be extremely unlikely to occur by chance (without any treatment effect) if it has a probability that is less than .01. Such a sample results in rejection of the null hypothesis and the conclusion that a real treatment effect does exist.

With rare exceptions, a value of .05 is the largest acceptable alpha level.

DEFINITION

The **alpha level,** or **level of significance,** for a hypothesis test is the maxi-mum probability that the research result was obtained simply by chance. A hypothesis test with an alpha level of .01, for example, means that the test demands that there is less than a 1% (.01) probability that the results are caused only by chance.

The following scenario provides a concrete example for the concept of an alpha level and the role it plays in a hypothesis test.

Suppose that I get a brand new coin from the bank. The null hypothesis says that there is nothing wrong with the coin, it is perfectly balanced and should produce 50% heads if it is tossed repeatedly. I decide to test the coin by counting the number of heads I obtain in a sample of 100 tosses, using an alpha level of .05.

According to the null hypothesis, I should get around 50 heads in a sample of 100 tosses. Remember, a sample is not expected to be perfect; there will be some sampling error, so I should not be surprised to obtain 47 heads or 52 heads in 100 tosses. However, it is very unlikely that I would obtain more than 60 heads. In fact, the probability of obtaining more than 60 heads in 100 tosses of a balanced coin is only 0.0228. Thus, any sample with more than 60 heads is very unlikely to occur if the null hypothesis is true (the probability is less than an alpha level of .05). Therefore, if I obtain a sample with more than 60 heads, my decision will be to reject the null hypothesis and conclude that the coin is not perfectly balanced.

 **LEARNING CHECK**

A researcher selects a sample of 25 college students and measures the amount of time it takes each student to type and send a scripted 16-word text message. The researcher also records each student's grade point average and intends to measure the correlation between texting speed and grade point average for the sample.

a. If there actually is no correlation between texting speed and grade point average for the general population of college students, would you expect the sample correlation to be exactly equal to zero? Explain why or why not.

b. No matter what value the researcher obtains for the sample correlation, what would the null hypothesis say about the corresponding correlation for the population?

Reporting Results from a Hypothesis Test

The goal of a hypothesis test is to establish that the results from a research study are very unlikely to have occurred by chance. "Very unlikely" is defined by the alpha level. When the results of a research study satisfy the criterion imposed by the alpha level, the results are said to be **significant,** or **statistically significant.** For example, when the difference between two sample means is so large that there is less than a 1% probability that the difference occurred by chance, it is said to be a significant difference at the .01 level of significance. Notice that a smaller level of significance means that you have more confidence in the result. A result that is significant at the .05 level means that there is a 5% risk that the result is just a result of chance. Significance at the .01 level, on the other hand, means that there is only a 1% probability that the result is caused by chance. If the research results do not satisfy the criterion established by the alpha level, the results are said to be not significant.

In the literature, significance levels are reported as p values. For example, a research paper may report a significant difference between two treatments with $p < .05$. The expression $p < .05$ simply means that there is less than a .05 probability that the result is caused by chance.

When statistics are done on a computer, the printouts usually report exact values for p. For example, a computer-based hypothesis test evaluating the mean difference between two treatments may report a significance level of $p = .028$. In this case, the computer has determined that there is a .028 probability that the mean difference could have occurred simply by chance or sampling error without any treatment effect. Based on this outcome and using an alpha level of .05, the researcher would:

- Reject the null hypothesis. In other words, the researcher rejects chance as a plausible explanation for the research results.
- Report a significant result with $p < .05$ or $p = .028$. In the past, research reports identified the probability of chance in relation to standard alpha levels. In this example, the exact probability of $p = .028$ is less than the standard alpha level of .05, so the researcher would report $p < .05$, indicating that it is very unlikely (probability less than .05) that the results can be explained by chance. More recent studies report the exact level of probability, in this case, $p = .028$. If the computer reported a value of $p = .067$, the researcher would have to conclude that the result is not statistically significant. Because the actual probability is larger than the standard value of .05, the researcher would accept chance as a plausible explanation for the research results, and report the result as not significant with $p > .05$.

DEFINITION

A **significant result,** or a **statistically significant result,** means that it is extremely unlikely that the research result was obtained simply by chance. A significant result is always accompanied by an alpha level that defines the maximum probability that the result is caused only by chance.

 **LEARNING CHECKS**

What is the goal of a hypothesis test?

What does it mean when a result is found to be significant at the .01 level?

Suppose that a researcher conducts a hypothesis test on a computer and obtains a reported value of $p = .03$.
a. With an alpha level of .05, does the researcher reject or fail to reject the null hypothesis?
b. With an alpha level of .01, does the researcher reject or fail to reject the null hypothesis?

Errors in Hypothesis Testing

Because a hypothesis test is an inferential process (using limited information to reach a general conclusion), there is always a possibility that the process will lead to an error. Specifically, a sample always provides limited and incomplete information about its population. In addition, some samples are not good representatives of the population and can provide misleading information. If a researcher is misled by the results from the sample, it is likely that the researcher will reach an incorrect conclusion. Two kinds of errors can be made in hypothesis testing.

Type I Errors

One possibility for error occurs when the sample data appear to show a significant effect but, in fact, there is no effect in the population. By chance, the researcher has selected an unusual or extreme sample. Because the sample appears to show that the treatment has an effect, the researcher incorrectly concludes that there is a significant effect. This kind of mistake is called a **Type I error.**

Note that the consequence of a Type I error is a false report. This is a serious mistake. Fortunately, the likelihood of a Type I error is very small, and the exact probability of this kind of mistake is known to everyone who sees the research report. Recall that a significant result means that the result is very unlikely to have occurred by chance. It does not mean that it is impossible for the result to have occurred by chance. In particular, a significant result is always accompanied by an alpha level or an exact p value (for example, $p < .01$ or $p = .006$). By reporting the p value, researchers are acknowledging the possibility that their result is caused by chance. In other words, the alpha level or the p value identifies the probability of a Type I error.

Type II Errors

The second possibility for error occurs when the sample data do not show a significant effect when, in fact, there is a real effect in the population. This often occurs when an effect is very small and does not produce sample data that are sufficiently extreme to reject the null hypothesis. In this case, the researcher concludes that there is no significant effect when a real effect actually exists. This is a **Type II error.**

The consequence of a Type II error is that a researcher fails to detect a real effect. Whenever research results do not show a significant effect, the researcher may choose to abandon the research project under the assumption that either there is no effect or the effect is too small to be of any consequence. On the other hand, the researcher may be convinced that an effect really exists but failed to show up in the current study. In this case, the researcher may choose to repeat the study, often using a larger sample, a stronger version of the treatment, or some other refinement that might increase the likelihood of obtaining a significant result.

DEFINITIONS

A **Type I error** occurs when a researcher finds evidence for a significant result when, in fact, there is no effect (no relationship) in the population. The error occurs because the researcher has, by chance, selected an extreme sample that appears to show the existence of an effect when there is none.

A **Type II error** occurs when sample data do not show evidence of a significant effect when, in fact, a real effect does exist in the population. This often occurs when the effect is so small that it does not show up in the sample.

Although Type I and Type II errors are mistakes, they are not foolish or careless mistakes in the sense that the researcher is overlooking something that should be perfectly obvious. In fact, these errors are the direct result of a careful evaluation of the research results. The problem is that the results are misleading. For example, in the general population there is no difference in average IQ between males and females. However, it is possible for a researcher to select a random sample of 25 females who have exceptionally high (or low) IQ scores. Note that the researcher is not deliberately seeking exceptional people and is not using a biased selection process. Instead, the exceptional women are selected purely by chance. As a result, the researcher finds that the women in the study have significantly higher IQs than the men. This result appears to provide clear evidence that the average IQ is not the same for men and women. Based on this result, the researcher is likely to conclude that a real difference exists and, thereby, make a Type I error.

 **LEARNING CHECKS** Describe the relationship between the alpha level and the likelihood of making a Type I error.

Describe the consequences of each type of error.

Factors that Influence the Outcome of a Hypothesis Test

There are several factors that help determine whether a hypothesis test will successfully reject the null hypothesis and conclude that there is a significant effect. When the test involves numerical scores that have been used to compute means or correlations, there are two factors that are particularly important:

1. The number of scores in the sample.
2. The variability of the scores, typically described by the sample variance.

The Number of Scores in the Sample

The key question for a hypothesis test is whether the sample data provide convincing evidence for a real mean difference between treatments or a real correlation between two variables. In general, results obtained from large samples are simply more convincing than results from small samples. For example, suppose a research study finds a 2-point mean difference between treatments using a sample of $n = 4$ participants in each treatment. Because there are only four people in each group, the sample means are considered to be relatively unstable. One new person in each group could change the means enough to erase the 2-point difference. Thus, the 2-point difference obtained for samples of $n = 4$ is not likely to be significant. On the other hand, suppose the study finds the same 2-point difference using samples of $n = 100$ participants. Now the sample means are quite stable; adding a few new people will not noticeably affect the means. As a result, the 2-point difference is viewed as solid evidence of a real difference between treatments and is likely to be statistically significant. In general, a mean difference or a correlation found with a large sample is more likely to be significant than the same result found with a small sample. The optimal sample size depends on a variety of factors including the expected size of the treatment effect and the size of the variance. However, increasing sample size always increases the chances for detecting a treatment effect if one exists. (Also see the discussion of sample size on pp. 141–142.)

The Size of the Variance

In simple terms, small variance means that the scores are clustered together with all of the individual scores close to each other and close to the mean. In this situation, any individual score that is selected is likely to be representative of the entire group. On the other hand, large variance means that the scores are widely scattered with relatively large distances between individual scores and the overall mean. When variance is large, it is easy to select an individual or a group of individuals whose scores are extreme and not representative. As a result, sample statistics are generally viewed as unreliable and unstable if the variance is high. With high variance, for example, adding one or two new people to a sample can drastically change the value of the mean. Remember, a few extreme scores can distort the mean (see p. 402) and extreme scores are common when the variance is high. In general, a sample mean difference or a correlation found with high variance is less convincing and less likely to be significant than the same result found with low variance.

The idea that large variance can obscure any meaningful patterns was first introduced in Chapter 10 (pp. 290–293) in the context of individual differences. Figure 14.12 reproduces Figures 10.3 and 10.4, which show the results from two research studies. Both studies use a between-subjects design (separate samples)

(a)

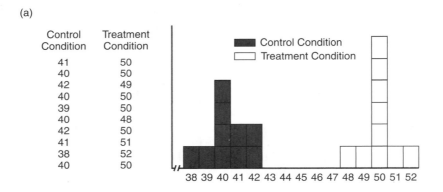

(b)

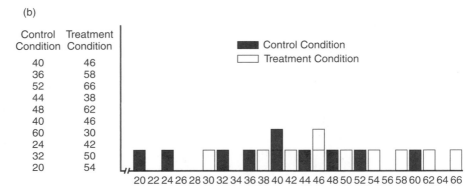

FIGURE **14.12** The Results from Two Research Studies Demonstrating the Role of Variance

(a) When the variance is small, the data show a clear mean difference between the two treatments. (b) With large variance, the mean difference between treatments is obscured.

to compare two treatment conditions, and both studies find a mean difference between treatments of approximately 10 points. In Figure 14.12a, there are small individual differences and small variance, and the 10-point mean difference between treatments is easy to see. In Figure 14.12b, however, the individual differences and variance are increased and the same 10-point difference is no longer visible.

The effect of large variance that is shown visually in Figure 14.12 is supported by the two hypothesis tests. The appropriate test for comparing two means from two separate samples is the independent-measures t test. For the data in Figure 14.12a (small variance), the test shows a statistically significant difference between the two sample means. In this case, it is very unlikely ($p < .001$) that the mean difference is caused by chance. For the data in Figure 14.12b (large variance), however, the test shows no significant mean difference. With the larger variance, there is a reasonable probability ($p = .084$) that the mean difference is simply the result of chance.

When the variance is small, the 10-point treatment effect is easy to see and is statistically significant (Figure 14.12a). However, the same 10-point treatment effect is obscured and is not significant when the variance is large (Figure 14.12b). Once again, the general point is that large variance reduces the likelihood of obtaining a statistically significant result.

Supplementing Hypothesis Tests with Measures of Effect Size

In the preceding section we noted that the outcome of a hypothesis test depends in part on the size of the sample. Specifically, increasing the sample size increases the likelihood of obtaining a significant result. As a result, a very small treatment effect can be statistically significant if the sample is large enough. Because a *significant* effect does not necessarily mean a *large* effect, many scientists have criticized hypothesis tests for providing inadequate or incomplete analyses of research results (Loftus, 1996; Hunter, 1997; Killeen, 2005). As a result, it is strongly recommended that researchers include an independent measure of **effect size** whenever they report a statistically significant effect (see the guidelines presented by Wilkinson & Task Force on Statistical Inference, 1999). The purpose for measuring and reporting effect size is to provide information about the absolute size of the treatment effect that is not influenced by outside factors such as sample size. Statisticians have developed several different methods for computing a standardized measure of effect size. We consider two examples that are representative of the most commonly used techniques for measuring and reporting effect size.

Measuring Effect Size with Cohen's d

Cohen (1961) recommended that the size of the mean difference between two treatments be standardized by measuring the mean difference in terms of the standard deviation. The resulting measure of effect size is defined as **Cohen's d** and is computed as

$$d = \frac{\text{Sample mean difference}}{\text{Sample standard deviation}}$$

For example, a value of $d = 2.00$ indicates that the mean difference is twice as big as the standard deviation. On the other hand, a value of $d = 0.5$ indicates that the mean difference is only half as large as the standard deviation. The concept of measuring effect size with Cohen's d is easier to understand if you visualize two frequency distributions corresponding to the scores from two different treatment conditions. In this context, Cohen's d corresponds to the amount of separation between the two distributions. For example, Figure 14.13a shows a situation in which Cohen's d is equal to 0.50. The distribution on the left corresponds to scores from treatment 1. Notice that we

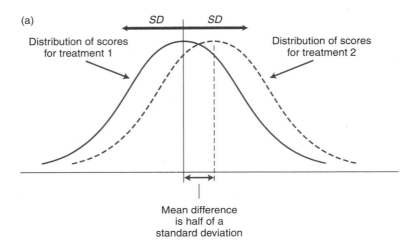

(a)

SD | *SD*

Distribution of scores for treatment 1

Distribution of scores for treatment 2

Mean difference
is half of a
standard deviation

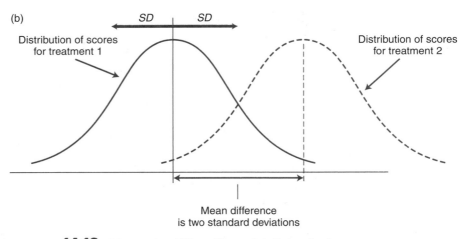

(b)

SD | *SD*

Distribution of scores for treatment 1

Distribution of scores for treatment 2

Mean difference
is two standard deviations

FIGURE **14.13** Measuring Effect Size with Cohen's *d*

Cohen's *d* measures the mean difference between two distributions in terms of the standard deviation. (a) The two distributions are separated by half of a standard deviation, $d = 0.50$. (b) The two distributions are separated by two standard deviations, $d = 2.00$.

have marked the location of the mean and indicated the size of the standard deviation for this distribution. The distribution on the right corresponds to scores from treatment 2. The two distributions are drawn so that the distance between means is equal to exactly half of the standard deviation; that is, Cohen's $d = 0.50$. For comparison, Figure 14.13b shows a situation for which Cohen's $d = 2.00$; that is, the two means are separated by two full standard deviations. Cohen (1988) also provided objective criteria for evaluating the size of an effect. These criteria are presented in Table 14.3. Finally, we should note that Cohen's d is used primarily to evaluate effect size in research situations comparing two treatment means.

We also should note that Cohen originally defined this measure of effect size in terms of the population mean difference and the population standard deviation. When sample values are used to estimate the population parameters the obtained value is more accurately called an estimated d and is sometimes named after one of the statisticians who first substituted sample values in Cohen's formula (for example, Glass's g or Hedges's g). Examples demonstrating the calculation of Cohen's d are presented in Appendix B, pp. 530–532.

Measuring Effect Size as a Percentage of Variance (r^2 and η^2)

When there is a consistent relationship between two variables, it is possible to predict whether a participant's score on one variable will be relatively high or relatively low if you know the participant's score on the second variable. For example, there is a consistent positive correlation between a child's IQ and the IQ of the child's mother. If you know that the mother has a relatively high IQ, you can predict that the child also has a relatively high IQ. In the same way, if there is a consistent difference between two treatment conditions, it is possible to predict whether a participant's score will be relatively high or relatively low if you know which treatment the participant receives. For example, suppose one group of participants receives an effective cholesterol-lowering medication and a second group receives an ineffective placebo. In this case, we can predict that people who receive the drug will have lower cholesterol levels than people who do not receive the drug.

The ability to predict differences forms the basis of another method of measuring effect size by computing the **percentage of variance accounted for**. This calculation involves measuring the percentage of variance for one variable that can be predicted by knowing a second variable. For example, the

TABLE **14.3**

Criteria for Evaluating Effect Size Using Cohen's d

Magnitude of d	Evaluation of Effect Size
$d = 0.2$	Small effect (mean difference around 0.2 standard deviation)
$d = 0.5$	Medium effect (mean difference around 0.5 standard deviation)
$d = 0.8$	Large effect (mean difference around 0.8 standard deviation)

participants in the cholesterol study all have different cholesterol levels. In statistical terms, their scores are variable. However, some of this variability can be predicted by knowing the treatment condition for each participant; individuals in the drug condition score lower than individuals in the no-drug condition. By measuring exactly how much of the variability is predictable, we can obtain a measure of how big the effect actually is. When the percentage of variance is measured for t tests (comparing two sample means) or for correlations, it is typically called r^2. When the percentage is measured for analysis of variance, or ANOVA, (comparing multiple sample means) it is usually called η^2 (the Greek letter eta squared). For a t test evaluating the difference between two sample means, the value of r^2 can be obtained directly from the t statistic and its degrees of freedom (df) by the following formula:

$$r^2 = \frac{t^2}{t^2 + df}$$

Examples demonstrating the calculation of r^2 and η^2 are presented in Appendix B, pp. 530, 532, and 534. Criteria for evaluating the size of a treatment effect using r^2 or η^2 are presented in Table 14.4 (Cohen, 1988). Effect size is most commonly measured with r^2 in research situations that compare two treatment means or for research evaluating relationships, such as a correlational study. Effect size is measured with η^2 for research studies that compare more than two treatment means.

LEARNING CHECK   If a researcher reports a significant mean difference between two treatments, what additional information would be provided by also reporting a measure of effect size such as Cohen's d or r^2?

Confidence Intervals

An alternative technique for measuring or describing the size of a treatment effect or the strength of a relationship is to compute a confidence interval. The concept of a confidence interval is based on the observation that sample statistics tend to provide reasonably accurate estimates of the corresponding population parameters. For example, if a sample is selected from a population, you

TABLE **14.4**
Criteria for Evaluating Effect Size Using r^2 or η^2
(Percentage of Variance Accounted for)

Magnitude of r^2 or η^2	Evaluation of Effect Size
r^2 or η^2 = 0.01	Small effect (around 1%)
r^2 or η^2 = 0.09	Medium effect (around 9%)
r^2 or η^2 = 0.25	Large effect (around 25% or more)

do not expect the sample mean to be exactly equal to the population mean, but the sample mean should give a good indication of the actual value for the population mean. Thus, a sample mean of $M = 85$ suggests that the population mean is probably around 85. Similarly, a sample correlation of $r = 0.64$ indicates that the population correlation is probably around 0.64.

The fact that sample statistics tend to be close to their population parameters means that we can use the sample values as estimators of the corresponding population values. A **confidence interval** involves estimating that an unknown population parameter is located within an interval, or range of values, around a known sample statistic. For example, if a sample is selected from an unknown population and the sample mean is found to be $M = 60$, then we can estimate that the population mean is around 60. We don't expect the population mean to be exactly equal to the sample mean but if the sample mean is $M = 60$, then the population mean should be near 60. For example, the actual population mean is likely to be within 5 points of $M = 60$; that is, within an interval from 55 to 65. It is even more likely that the population mean is within 10 points of $M = 60$, somewhere in an interval from 50 to 70. Notice that the likelihood of the estimate being correct depends on the width of the interval. If the sample has a mean of $M = 60$, it is almost guaranteed that the population mean has a value between 30 and 90 ($M = 60 \pm 30$ points).

DEFINITION	A **confidence interval** is a technique for estimating the magnitude of an unknown population value such as a mean difference or a correlation. The logic behind a confidence interval is that a sample statistic should provide a reasonably accurate estimate of the corresponding population parameter. Therefore, the value of the parameter should be located in an interval, or a range of values, centered around the sample statistic.

Researchers construct confidence intervals by creating a range of values on each side of a known sample statistic. The wider the range of values, the more confidence the researchers have that the interval actually contains the unknown population value. Notice that there is a tradeoff between the precision of the estimate and the confidence in the estimate. A very narrow interval provides a precise estimate but gives very little confidence. A wider interval gives more confidence but is less precise.

The width of a confidence interval is determined by two factors: the standard error for the sample statistic and the level of confidence desired by the researcher. Recall that the standard error provides a measure of the average, or standard distance between a sample statistic and the corresponding population parameter (p. 420). A small standard error means that all the possible sample statistics are within a small distance of the population parameter. As a result, the unknown population parameter is likely to be contained in a relatively narrow interval around the sample statistic. A large standard error, on the other hand, tends to produce a relatively wide interval. The second factor, level of confidence, is also directly related to the width of the confidence interval, so that increasing confidence produces an increase in interval width. Typically, a researcher selects a level of confidence, usually a large value such as 90% or 95%, and constructs a confidence interval. If the resulting interval provides a reasonable level of precision, the job is done and the researcher has a good estimate of the unknown parameter. However, if the interval is so wide that it fails to provide the desired level of precision, the researcher must make some compromise. In this case, the researcher can either lower the level of confidence to produce a narrower, more precise interval, or increase the sample size, which also produces a narrower, more precise interval.

Confidence intervals provide a good indication of how large a treatment effect actually is. For example, Anderson, Huston, Wright, and Collins (1988) report that high school students who regularly watched Sesame Street as children had better grades in high school than their peers who did not watch the program. Suppose that sample data show that a group of Sesame Street watchers has an average grade of $M = 93$ and a group of non-watchers has an average grade of $M = 85$. These sample data show an 8-point treatment effect (from $M = 85$ to $M = 93$) from watching Sesame Street, indicating that the true population mean difference is around 8 points. A confidence interval would provide additional information about the size of the treatment effect. For example, a 95% confidence interval showing that the true mean difference is between 7 and 9 points (8 ± 1) would indicate a fairly strong and consistent effect. On the other hand, a 95% confidence interval ranging from 2 to 14 points (8 ± 6) gives less certainty about the size and consistency of the effect.

Finally, we should note that confidence intervals, like hypothesis tests, are influenced by the size of the sample(s). In general, larger samples lead to smaller standard errors, which increase the likelihood of finding a significant result and decrease the width of confidence intervals. Because confidence intervals are influenced by sample size they do not provide an unqualified measure of absolute effect size and are not an adequate substitute for Cohen's d or r^2.

14.4 | EXAMPLES OF HYPOTHESIS TESTS

In this section, we discuss some of the different kinds of hypothesis tests that are used for different research situations. We present only a small selection of the many different tests that exist; however, those described here include most of the statistical tests needed for student research projects or class assignments. We classify the different types of hypothesis tests and briefly describe each one. Our goal is to help you determine which test is appropriate for a particular research situation and help you interpret the results of the test. This information should be sufficient if you use a computer to perform the hypothesis test.

If you perform the calculations yourself, you can consult Appendix B, where we present numerical examples for many different hypothesis tests. Or refer to a statistics textbook for a detailed description of each test. Appendix C contains step-by-step instructions for using the latest version of the SPSS computer program, now called PASW, to perform the tests in this section as well as to compute most of the descriptive statistics discussed earlier.

Comparing Groups of Scores: Statistical Tests for the Experimental, Quasi-Experimental, and Nonexperimental Research Strategies

In Chapter 6 (p. 165) we noted that the experimental, quasi-experimental, and nonexperimental research strategies all produce similar data and rely on similar statistical analyses. Specifically, all three strategies involve comparing different groups of scores. When the scores are numerical values (interval or ratio scales), this usually involves computing a mean score for each group and then comparing means. If the scores are non-numerical (ordinal or nominal scales), then we are comparing proportions or percentages. This section introduces the statistical hypothesis tests that are used for making comparisons and evaluating differences between groups of scores.

Tests for Mean Differences

In many research situations, the data are numerical scores, so it is possible to compute sample means. All of the hypothesis tests covered in this section use the means obtained from sample data as the basis for testing hypotheses about population means. The goal of each test is to determine whether the observed sample mean differences are more than would be expected by chance alone; that is, if the sample data provide enough evidence for the conclusion that some factor other than chance (for example, a treatment effect) has caused the means to be different.

Two-Group Between-Subjects Test

The **independent-measures *t* test** is the appropriate hypothesis test to compare the two means obtained from a two-group between-subjects research design (see p. 298). The two groups of participants may represent two different treatment conditions (for example, in an experimental research design) or two different populations (for example, in a nonexperimental design comparing males and females). The mean is calculated for each group, and the sample mean difference is used to test a hypothesis about the corresponding population mean difference. The null hypothesis states that the population mean difference is zero.

The *t* statistic is a ratio that directly compares the actual difference between the sample means with the amount of difference that would be expected if the null hypothesis were true. For example, a *t* statistic of $t = 3.00$ indicates that the obtained difference between sample means is three times greater than would be expected if there were no mean difference in the population. A large value for the *t* statistic (either positive or negative) indicates a significant difference. For an independent-measures *t* test the appropriate measure of effect size is either Cohen's *d* or the percentage of variance accounted for, as measured by r^2.

In a research report, the results of an independent-measures *t* test are reported in the following format:

$$t(28) = 4.00, p = .01, r^2 = 0.36$$

This report indicates that the researcher obtained a t statistic with a value of 4.00, which is very unlikely to have occurred by chance (probability equal to .01). The number in parentheses is the value of degrees of freedom (df) for the test. For this test, $df = (n_1 - 1) + (n_2 - 1)$ where n_1 is the number of participants in one group, and n_2 is the number in the second group. Finally, the measure of effect size, in this case r^2, is reported immediately after the p-value for the hypothesis test.

An example demonstrating the independent-measures t test is in Appendix B, pp. 528–530.

Two-Treatment Within-Subjects Test

The **repeated-measures t test** is the appropriate hypothesis test for a within-subjects research design comparing two treatment conditions (see p. 325). In this situation, the same group of participants is measured in two different treatment conditions. The sample mean is computed for each treatment condition and the sample mean difference is used to test a hypothesis about the corresponding population mean difference. The null hypothesis states that the population mean difference is zero.

Once again, the t statistic is a ratio comparing the obtained sample mean difference with the amount of difference that would be expected from chance alone without any treatment effect. As with the independent-measures t, a large value for the t statistic indicates a significant difference. For a repeated-measures t test the appropriate measure of effect size is either Cohen's d or the percentage of variance accounted for, as measured by r^2.

In a research report, the results of a repeated-measures t test are reported in the following format:

$$t(19) = 2.40, p = .04, d = 0.21$$

This report indicates that the researcher obtained a t statistic with a value of 2.40, which is very unlikely to have occurred by chance (probability equal to .04). The number in parentheses is the value of degrees of freedom (df) for the test. For this test, $df = n - 1$, where n is the number of participants in the study. For these data, Cohen's $d = 0.21$.

An example demonstrating the repeated-measures t test is in Appendix B, pp. 530–532.

Comparing More Than Two Levels of a Single Factor

When a research study obtains means from more than two groups or more than two treatment conditions, the appropriate hypothesis test is an analysis of variance, commonly referred to as an ANOVA. When the groups are defined by a single factor with more than two levels (such as three age groups or three temperature conditions), the test is called a **single-factor analysis of variance,** or a **one-way ANOVA** (see p. 299). The mean is computed for each group of participants or for each treatment condition, and the differences among the means from the sample data are used to evaluate a hypothesis about the differences among the corresponding population means. The null hypothesis states that there are no differences among the population means.

The test statistic for ANOVA is an *F*-ratio, which has the same basic structure as the *t* statistic. The numerator of the ratio measures the size of the obtained mean differences and the denominator measures how much difference is reasonable to expect between the sample means if the null hypothesis is true. However, both the numerator and denominator of the *F*-ratio are variances that provide an overall measure of the mean differences among several different sample means. The denominator of the *F*-ratio is often called the **error variance** because it measures mean differences that are not caused by the treatments but rather are simply the result of chance or error. A large *F*-ratio indicates that the sample mean differences are greater than would be expected if there were no corresponding mean differences in the population. The appropriate measure of effect size is η^2, which measures the percentage of variance accounted for by the treatment effect. In general, η^2 is computed by dividing the sum of squared deviations (*SS*) for the treatment by the sum of squared deviations for the error variance.

Note that the single-factor ANOVA can be used with data from either a between-subjects or a within-subjects design. However, the calculation of the error variance is different for the two designs, so you must specify which design is being used.

In a research report, the results of a single-factor ANOVA are reported as follows:

$$F(2, 36) = 5.00, p = .025, \eta^2 = 0.14$$

The report indicates that the researcher obtained an *F*-ratio with a value of 5.00, which is very unlikely to have occurred by chance (probability equal to .025). The two numbers in parentheses are the degrees of freedom (*df*) values for the *F*-ratio. The first of the two numbers is the degrees of freedom for the numerator of the *F*-ratio and is determined by $(k - 1)$, where *k* is the number of groups or treatment conditions being compared. The second number is the degrees of freedom for the error variance in the denominator of the *F*-ratio. For a between-subjects design, the error degrees of freedom is determined by $(n_1 - 1) + (n_2 - 1) + (n_3 - 1) + ...$ where n_1 is the number of participants in the first group, n_2 is the number in the second group, and so on. For a within-subjects design, the degrees of freedom for the error variance are determined by $(k - 1)$ times $(n - 1)$, where *k* is the number of treatment conditions and *n* is the number of participants. For this example, the value of η^2 indicates that the mean differences among treatment conditions account for 14% of the variance.

Post Hoc Tests

If an ANOVA finds significant mean differences for a research study comparing more than two levels of a factor, it usually is necessary to complete the analysis with a set of follow-up tests known as **post hoc tests** or simply as **post tests.** Post hoc tests are necessary because the original ANOVA simply establishes that mean differences exist, but does not identify exactly which means are significantly different and which are not. A study comparing three treatments, for example, produces three means and three mean differences. If the three means are $M_1 = 12$, $M_2 = 7$, and $M_3 = 5$, then the mean differences are:

$$M_1 - M_2 = 12 - 7 = 5 \text{ points}$$
$$M_1 - M_3 = 12 - 5 = 7 \text{ points}$$
$$M_2 - M_3 = 7 - 5 = 2 \text{ points}$$

A significant F-ratio from the original ANOVA indicates that at least one of these mean differences is large enough to be significant but it does not identify exactly which one(s). The purpose for post hoc tests is to determine exactly which means are significantly different. The general strategy for post hoc tests is to go back through the data and compare treatment means two at a time. With three means, for example, post hoc tests would compare M_1 versus M_2, then M_1 versus M_3, and finally M_2 versus M_3 to determine which mean differences are significant and which are not.

Although post hoc tests are designed to solve one problem, they unfortunately introduce another problem. Specifically, it usually requires several post hoc tests to determine exactly which means are different, and each test is conducted with its own alpha level and its own risk of a Type I error. If a researcher conducts three post hoc tests, each with $\alpha = .05$, then each of the three tests has a 5% risk of a Type I error. Although the probability for error does not simply add across the three tests, a 5% risk for the first test and a 5% risk for the second test and a 5% risk for the third test does accumulate to be an unacceptably large risk of a Type I error. To deal with this problem researchers and statisticians have developed several different procedures for conducting post hoc tests. Each has its own method for controlling the risk of a Type I error and each test has its own name. If you conduct an ANOVA on the SPSS computer program, for example, and you choose to do a post hoc test as part of the analysis, you will be given 15 different choices from which to select. All of the post hoc tests do essentially the same thing and all are legitimate alternatives. We suggest that you consult published research articles in your topic area to determine which post hoc tests are commonly used within that field.

Examples demonstrating the single-factor ANOVA (between-subjects and within-subjects) are in Appendix B, pp. 532–537.

Factorial Tests

When a research design includes more than one factor (a factorial design), you must use a hypothesis test to evaluate the significance of the mean differences (see Chapter 13, p. 372). The simplest case, a two-factor design, requires a **two-factor analysis of variance, or two-way ANOVA.** The two-factor ANOVA consists of three separate hypothesis tests. One test evaluates the main effects for the first factor, a second test evaluates the main effects for the second factor, and a third test evaluates the interaction. The significance of any one test has no relationship to the significance of any other test. The analysis also produces three separate values of η^2 to measure the effect size for each of the main effects and for the interaction.

The data from a two-factor design can be displayed as a matrix with the levels of one factor defining the rows and the levels of the second factor defining the columns. The mean is computed for each cell in the matrix, and the overall mean is computed for each row and for each column. The differences among the sample means are used to evaluate the three hypotheses about the differences among the corresponding population means. For all three tests, the null hypothesis states that there are no differences among the population means.

A variance is computed for the set of column means to measure the size of the mean differences for one factor. A second variance, called error variance, is computed to measure the magnitude of the sample mean differences that would be expected from chance if there are no population mean differences. The F-ratio evaluating the main effect for the factor is a ratio of the two variances. A large F-ratio indicates that the actual mean differences are greater than would be expected from chance alone, and there is a significant main effect for the factor. The main effect for the second factor is evaluated using the set of row means from the data matrix. The interaction is evaluated by computing a variance for the set of cell means, then subtracting the variance for the two main effects. The resulting variance is then compared with the error variance in an F-ratio to determine whether the mean differences from the interaction are significantly greater than would be expected from chance. A research report for a two-factor ANOVA includes three separate F-ratios and three separate values for η^2.

The two-factor ANOVA can be used with either a between-subjects or a within-subjects design; however, the calculation of the error variance is different for the two designs. An example of the two-factor ANOVA for between-subjects designs is given in Appendix B, pp. 538–542.

Comparing Proportions

A hypothesis test that uses sample means or sample correlations to evaluate hypotheses about the corresponding population values is known as a **parametric test.** In general, parametric tests rely on sample data consisting of numerical scores (so it is possible to compute means and variances) and they test hypotheses about population parameters (such as mean differences). In many research situations, however, the data are not numerical scores so it is impossible to compute sample means. Instead, the data consist of frequencies or proportions (see p. 406). In this situation it is still possible to determine whether there is a significant difference between groups using a **nonparametric test.** In general, nonparametric tests do not require numerical scores and do not involve hypotheses about specific population parameters. For example, a researcher may find that in a group of 50 young women diagnosed with an eating disorder, only 6 women (12%) have high self-esteem. By comparison, in a control group of 50 women who have no diagnosed disorder, 24 (48%) have high self-esteem. The data for this study are shown in Table 14.5. Note that the data can be organized in a matrix, with the levels of one variable (diagnosis) defining the rows and the levels of the second variable (self-esteem) defining the columns. The numbers in each cell of the matrix correspond to the frequency or number of individuals in that category. For the data in Table 14.5, for example, 26 women were classified as having no eating disorder and having low self-esteem. Although the data consist entirely of frequencies (or proportions), it is still possible to determine whether there is a significant difference between the two groups using a nonparametric test known as the **chi-square test for**

TABLE **14.5**
Research Data Consisting of Frequencies

The distribution of self-esteem for a group of 50 participants diagnosed with an eating disorder (bottom row) and a group of 50 participants who have no diagnosed disorder (top row).

	Self-Esteem		
	Low	High	
No Disorder	26	24	50
Diagnosed Disorder	44	6	50

independence. Note that Chi is a Greek letter (χ) and the symbol for chi-square is χ^2.

The rationale behind the chi-square test is that sample proportions, just like sample means, are not expected to provide perfectly accurate representations of their corresponding population values. Thus, there may be patterns in the sample proportions that do not accurately represent the actual proportions in the population. The question is whether the patterns observed in the sample data can be explained by chance or are caused by real patterns that exist in the population.

The null hypothesis for the chi-square test says that in the population, the proportions in one group are not different from the proportions in any other group. Note that the hypothesis does not involve any specific parameters such as the population means. Instead, the hypothesis states that the overall distribution for one group has the same shape (same proportions) as the overall distribution for the other group. The chi-square statistic is computed by first calculating a set of expected frequencies that represent an ideal sample that is in perfect agreement with the null hypothesis. These expected frequencies are then compared with the actual observed frequencies to determine the degree to which the sample fits the hypothesis. A large value for the chi-square statistic indicates a big discrepancy between the sample and the hypothesis, and suggests that the null hypothesis should be rejected. To determine whether the value obtained for the chi-square statistic is significantly large, you first must find the value of degrees of freedom (df), which is determined by

$$df = (C_1 - 1)(C_2 - 1)$$

where C_1 is the number of levels for the first variable and C_2 is the number of levels for the second variable.

The obtained chi-square value is then compared with the critical values obtained from the chi-square distribution with the appropriate degrees of freedom.

Effect size for a chi-square test for independence is measured by either a phi-coefficient (Φ), which is a measure of correlation or by Cramér's V, which is a modification of the phi-coefficient. The phi-coefficient is used when the data form a 2×2 matrix and can be computed directly from the obtained chi-square value and the sample size (n):

$$\Phi = \sqrt{\frac{\chi^2}{n}}$$

Cramér's V uses the same basic formula but incorporates a modified version of the degrees of freedom (df^*), which is the smaller of either the ($C_1 - 1$) or ($C_2 - 1$) values that are used to compute the df value for the chi-square test.

$$V = \sqrt{\frac{\chi^2}{n(df^*)}}$$

Note that the phi-coefficient and Cramér's V are both measures of correlation and occasionally are squared to produce a measure of effect size that is equivalent to the r^2 or η^2 values discussed earlier.

In a research report, the results from a chi-square test for independence are reported as follows:

$$\chi^2(3, n = 40) = 8.70, p = .02, V = 0.29$$

The report indicates that the researcher obtained a chi-square statistic with a value of 8.70, which is very unlikely to occur by chance (probability is equal to .02). The numbers in parentheses indicate that the chi-square statistic has degrees of freedom (df) equal to 3 and that there were 40 participants ($n = 40$) in the study.

An example demonstrating the chi-square test is in Appendix B, pp. 544–547.

Evaluating Relationships: Statistical Tests for the Correlational Research Strategy

In Chapter 6 (p. 161), we noted that the correlational research strategy does not involve comparing different groups of scores. Instead, a correlational study measures two different variables (two different scores) for each individual in a single group, then looks for patterns within the set of scores. If a correlational study produces numerical scores or ranks, the data are evaluated by computing a correlation. If the data consist of non-numerical classifications, then the statistical evaluation is usually a chi-square test.

Evaluating Correlations

Whenever a Pearson correlation or a Spearman correlation is computed for sample data, the sample correlation is not expected to be identical to the corresponding correlation for the whole population. In the same way that there is sampling error between a sample mean and a population mean, there also is sampling error between a sample correlation and the population correlation. Thus, a sample correlation (r) is expected to be representative of the population correlation, but it is not expected to be perfectly accurate. In particular, a nonzero correlation for a sample does not necessarily mean that there is a real nonzero correlation in the population. The problem for researchers is deciding whether a correlation obtained for a sample provides enough evidence to justify a conclusion that there is a corresponding correlation in the population.

The hypothesis test for a correlation begins with a null hypothesis stating that there is no correlation in the population; that is, that the population correlation is zero. The hypothesis test uses either a t statistic or an F-ratio. If a t statistic is used, the test computes a t value that is a ratio of the actual sample correlation and the magnitude of correlation that would be expected from chance. A large value of t indicates that the sample correlation is greater than would be expected if the population correlation is zero. If an F-ratio is used, it simply squares the t statistic ($F = t^2$). In a research report, the results of a test for the significance of a correlation are reported as follows:

$$r = 0.65, n = 40, p < .01$$

The report indicates that the sample correlation is $r = 0.65$ for a group of $n = 40$ participants, which is very unlikely to have occurred if the population correlation is zero (probability less than .01). Note that the report does not identify the exact test (t or F) that was used to evaluate the significance of the correlation. Also note that the report does not include a measure of effect size because the r value (or r^2) already measures effect size.

An example demonstrating the test for the significance of a correlation is presented in Appendix B, p. 543.

Evaluating Significance for a Regression Equation

As we noted, the data for a sample probably will produce a nonzero correlation even when there is no relationship whatsoever between the two variables in the population. Whenever a nonzero correlation is obtained, the data also produce a regression equation that can be used to make predictions. However, it is possible that both the correlation and the regression equation are meaningless, resulting entirely from sampling error and not representing any real relationship. In the same way that a hypothesis test evaluates the significance of a correlation (is it real or not?), it is possible to test the significance of a regression equation.

The hypothesis test for regression begins with a null hypothesis that can be phrased several different ways. In one form, the null hypothesis states that the regression equation does not predict a significant portion of the Y-score variance. This version of the null hypothesis says that the regression equation is based entirely on sampling error and does not represent any real relationship between X and Y. The predictions from the equation are no better than would be obtained by chance alone. A second version of the null hypothesis states that the slope constant in the equation is b = 0. Both versions are equivalent to saying that there is no relationship, either positive or negative, between X and Y. (If there is no positive trend or negative trend, all that remains is a horizontal line with a slope of zero.)

The hypothesis test is based on an F-ratio that compares the predicted variance, which is determined by r^2 or R^2, with the unpredicted, error variance which is determined by $(1 - r^2)$ or $(1 - R^2)$. A large value of F indicates that the predicted variance is greater than would be expected from chance alone.

Research reports of regression results should include the sample size, the values for b and/or β, the value of r^2 or R^2 (which describes effect size), and the level of significance (for example, $p < .01$). When variables are entered successively in a multiple regression equation, it is also customary to report the ΔR^2 values.

Evaluating Relationships for Non-numerical Scores

In a correlational study in which two variables are measured by simply classifying individuals into categories instead of obtaining two numerical scores for each person, the relationship can be evaluated using a chi-square test for independence. Earlier (p. 438), we introduced this test as a method for comparing proportions using an example that compared self-esteem scores (high and low) for two groups of women (one group with an eating disorder and one without). In that context, we focused on the difference between two groups. However, the same data can be viewed as representing a single group of participants with two scores for each participant; a self-esteem score and an eating disorder score. Viewed from this perspective, the chi-square test determines whether there is a significant relationship between eating disorders and self-esteem.

An example demonstrating the chi-square test for the significance of a relationship is presented in Appendix B, pp. 544–547.

LEARNING CHECK

The purpose of an independent-measures t test is to determine whether the mean difference obtained between two groups in a between-subjects study is greater than could reasonably be expected by chance. In other words, the test determines whether the data provide enough evidence to show that the mean difference was caused by something other than chance. Briefly describe the purpose of each of the following hypothesis tests:
a. single-factor ANOVA
b. test for the significance of a correlation
c. chi-square test for independence

14.5 | SPECIAL STATISTICS FOR RESEARCH

In addition to the traditional statistical techniques that are used for data analysis, several special mathematical procedures have been developed to help evaluate and interpret research results. Most of these special techniques address questions concerning measurement procedures, specifically the reliability of measurements. Recall from Chapter 4 that reliability refers to the stability or consistency of measurements. Specifically, reliability means that when the same individuals are measured under the same conditions, you should obtain nearly identical measurements.

Notice that reliability refers to the relationship between two sets of measurements. Often, the relationship is measured by computing a correlation.

However, there are situations in which a simple correlation may not be completely appropriate. To deal with these special situations, researchers have developed several techniques that produce an adjustment to the correlation or an alternative measure of relationship. In this section, we examine four statistical techniques for adjusting or correcting measures of reliability: the Spearman-Brown formula, the Kuder-Richardson formula 20, Cronbach's coefficient alpha, and Cohen's kappa.

The Spearman-Brown Formula

When a single variable is measured with a test that consists of multiple items, it is common to evaluate the internal consistency of the test by computing a measure of **split-half reliability.** The concept behind split-half reliability is that all the different items on the test measure the same variable and, therefore, the measurement obtained from each individual item should be related to every other item. Therefore, if you split the test items in half and compute a score for each half, then the score obtained from one half of the test should be related to the score obtained from the other half.

There are a number of ways to split a test in half. For a 20-item test, for example, you could compute one score for the first 10 items and a second score for the last 10 items. Alternatively, you could compute one score for the odd-numbered items and a second score for the even-numbered items. In any case, you obtain two scores for each participant, and you can compute a correlation to measure the degree of relationship between the scores. The higher the correlation is, the better the split-half reliability.

Although computing a correlation appears to be a straightforward method for measuring the relationship between two halves of a test, this technique has a problem. In particular, the two split-half scores obtained for each participant are based on only half of the test items. In general, the score obtained from half of a test is less reliable than the score obtained from the full test. (With a smaller number of items, there is a greater chance for error or chance to distort the participant's score.) Therefore, a measure of split-half reliability (based on half the test) tends to underestimate the true reliability of the full test. A number of procedures have been developed to correct this problem, but the most commonly used technique is the **Spearman-Brown formula.** The formula adjusts the simple correlation between halves as follows:

$$\text{Spearman-Brown } R = \frac{2r}{1+r}$$

where r is the simple correlation between the two halves of the test.

For a test consisting of 20 items, for example, each participant receives two scores with each score based on 10 items. If the split-half correlation between the two scores were $r = 0.80$, then the corrected correlation from the Spearman-Brown formula would be

$$R = \frac{2(0.80)}{1+0.80} = \frac{1.60}{1.80} = 0.89$$

Notice that the effect of the correction is to increase the size of the correlation to produce a better estimate of the true reliability for the full set of test items.

The Kuder-Richardson Formula 20

As we noted earlier, there are many different ways to split a test in half to obtain the two scores necessary to calculate a split-half reliability. Depending on how the test is split, you are likely to obtain different measures of reliability. To deal with this problem, Kuder and Richardson (1937) developed a formula that estimates the average of all the possible split-half correlations that can be obtained from all of the possible ways to split a test in half. The formula is the 20th and best one they tried and is, therefore, called the **Kuder-Richardson formula 20** (often shortened to **K-R 20**).

The K-R 20 is limited to tests in which each item has only two possible answers such as true/false, agree/disagree, or yes/no, and the two responses are assigned numerical values of 0 and 1. Each participant's score is the total, added over all the items. The Kuder-Richardson measure of reliability is obtained by

$$K - R\ 20 = \left(\frac{n}{n-1}\right)\left(\frac{SD^2 - \Sigma pq}{SD^2}\right)$$

The elements in the formula are defined as follows:

The letter n represents the number of items on the test.

SD is the standard deviation for the set of test scores.

For each item, p is the proportion of the participants whose response is coded 0 and q is the proportion of the participants whose response is coded 1 (note that $p + q = 1$ for each item).

Σpq is the sum of the p times q products for all items.

Again, the K-R 20 is intended to measure the average correlation from every possible way to split a test in half. Like a correlation, the formula produces values ranging from 0 to 1.00, with higher values indicating a higher degree of internal consistency or reliability.

Cronbach's Alpha

One limitation of the K-R 20 is that it can only be used for tests in which each item has only two response alternatives. Cronbach (1951) developed a modification of the K-R 20 that can be used when test items have more than two alternatives, such as a Likert scale that has five response choices (see p. 208). **Cronbach's alpha** has a structure similar to the K-R 20 and is computed as follows:

$$\text{Cronbach's alpha} = \left(\frac{n}{n-1}\right)\left(\frac{SD^2 - \Sigma\text{variance}}{SD^2}\right)$$

The elements in Cronbach's formula are identical to the elements in the K-R 20 except for Σvariance. To compute this new term, first calculate the variance of the scores for each item separately. With 20 participants, for example, you would compute the variance for the 20 scores obtained for item 1, and the variance for the 20 scores on item 2, and so on. Then add the variances across all the test items to obtain the value for Σvariance.

Like the K-R 20, Cronbach's alpha is intended to measure split-half reliability by estimating the average correlation that would be obtained by considering every possible way to split the test in half. Also like the K-R 20, Cronbach's alpha produces values between 0 and 1.00, with a higher value indicating a higher degree of internal consistency or reliability.

LEARNING CHECKS

For a test consisting of several items, explain why using a correlation to measure split-half reliability is likely to underestimate the true reliability of the test. (Note: This is the problem that the Spearman-Brown formula attempts to fix.)

Describe the problem with split-half reliability that the K-R 20 and Cronbach's alpha attempt to fix.

Cohen's Kappa

When measurements are obtained by behavioral observation, it is customary to evaluate the measurement procedure by determining inter-rater reliability (see p. 117). Inter-rater reliability is the degree of agreement between two observers who have independently observed and recorded behaviors at the same time. The simplest technique for determining inter-rater reliability is to compute the percentage of agreement as follows:

$$\text{Percent agreement} = \frac{\text{Number of observation in agreement}}{\text{Total number of observations}} \times 100$$

For example, if two observers agree on 46 out of 50 observations, their percent agreement is (46/50)100 = 92%.

The problem with a simple measure of percent agreement is that the value obtained can be inflated by chance. That is, the two observers may record the same observation simply by chance. As an extreme example, consider two individuals who are each tossing a coin. For each toss, they record whether the two coins agree. Note that in a series of coin tosses they will observe several agreements, but the agreements are just chance.

Cohen's kappa is a measure of agreement that attempts to correct for chance (Cohen, 1961). Cohen's kappa is computed as follows:

$$\text{Cohen's kappa} = \frac{PA - PC}{1 - PC}$$

The elements in the formula are defined as follows: *PA* is the observed percent agreement and *PC* is the percent agreement expected from chance.

We use the data in Table 14.6 to demonstrate the calculation of Cohen's kappa. The data show the recorded observations of two observers watching a child over 25 observation periods. For every observation period, each observer

TABLE **14.6**

Data That Can Be Used to Evaluate Inter-Rater Reliability Using Either the Percentage of Agreement or Cohen's Kappa

Two observers record behavior for the same individual over 25 observation periods and record whether they observe aggressive behavior during each period.

Observation Period	Observer 1	Observer 2	Agreement
1	Yes	Yes	Agree
2	Yes	Yes	Agree
3	Yes	No	Disagree
4	No	No	Agree
5	Yes	Yes	Agree
6	Yes	Yes	Agree
7	Yes	Yes	Agree
8	Yes	Yes	Agree
9	Yes	Yes	Agree
10	No	No	Agree
11	No	No	Agree
12	No	No	Agree
13	Yes	No	Disagree
14	Yes	Yes	Agree
15	Yes	Yes	Agree
16	Yes	Yes	Agree
17	Yes	Yes	Agree
18	No	Yes	Disagree
19	Yes	Yes	Agree
20	Yes	Yes	Agree
21	Yes	Yes	Agree
22	Yes	No	Disagree
23	Yes	Yes	Agree
24	Yes	Yes	Agree
25	Yes	Yes	Agree

records yes or no, indicating whether an example of aggressive behavior was observed. The number of agreements is obtained by counting the number of periods in which both observers record the same observation. For the data in Table 14.6, there are 21 agreements out of the 25 observation periods. Thus, the percent agreement is

$$PA = \frac{21}{25} = 84\%$$

To determine the percentage agreement expected from chance (*PC*), we must call on a basic law of probability. The law states:

> Given two separate events, A and B, with the probability of A equal to *p* and the probability of B equal to *q*, then the probability of A and B occurring together is equal to the product of *p* and *q*.

For example, if two coins are tossed simultaneously, the probability of each one coming up heads is 0.50 (*p* = *q* = 0.50). According to the rule, the probability that both coins will come up heads is *p* × *q* (0.50)(0.50) = 0.25.

Applying the probability rule to the data in Table 14.6, we can calculate the probability that both observers will say *yes* just by chance and the probability that both will say *no* just by chance. For the data in the table, the probability that observer 1 says *yes* is 20 out of 25, which equals 0.80. The probability that observer 2 says *yes* is 18 out of 25, or 0.72. According to the probability rule, the probability that both will say *yes* just by chance is

probability that both say *yes* = (0.80)(0.72) = 0.576 or 57.6%

Similarly, the probability that both will say *no* just by chance is

probability that both say *no* = (0.20)(0.28) = 0.056 or 5.6%

Combining these two values, we obtain an overall probability that the two observers will agree by chance:

$$PC = 57.6\% + 5.6\% = 63.2\%$$

The value for Cohen's kappa can now be computed as follows:

$$\text{Kappa} = \frac{PA - PC}{1 - PC} = \frac{84\% - 63.2\%}{1 - 63.2\%} = \frac{20.8\%}{36.8\%} = 56.5\%$$

Because there is a large probability that the two observers will agree by chance, correcting for chance dramatically reduces the true percentage of agreement from 84% without correction to 56.5% with Cohen's correction.

 **LEARNING CHECK** Briefly explain why the percentage of agreement between two observers is likely to overestimate the real degree of agreement. (Note: Cohen's kappa is intended to correct this problem.)

■ CHAPTER SUMMARY

This chapter examined the statistical techniques that researchers use to help describe and interpret the results from research studies. Statistical methods are classified into two broad categories: descriptive statistics, which are used to organize and summarize research results, and inferential statistics, which help researchers generalize the results from a sample to a population.

Descriptive statistical methods include constructing frequency distribution tables or graphs that provide an organized view of an entire set of scores. Commonly, a distribution of numerical scores is summarized by computing measures of central tendency and variability. The mean is the most commonly used measure of central tendency, but the median and the mode are available for situations in which the mean does not provide a good representative value. Variability is commonly described by the standard deviation, which is a measure of the average distance from the mean. Variance measures the average squared distance from the mean. The relationship between two variables can be measured and described by a correlation. The Pearson correlation measures the direction and degree of linear relationship for numerical scores, and the Spearman correlation measures the direction and degree of relationship for ordinal data (ranks). If numerical scores are converted to ranks, the Spearman correlation measures the degree to which the relationship is consistently one directional.

In behavioral science research, the most commonly used inferential statistical method is the hypothesis test. A hypothesis test begins with a null hypothesis, which states that there is no treatment effect or no relationship between variables for the population. According to the null hypothesis, any treatment effect or relationship that appears to exist in the sample data is really just chance or sampling error. The purpose of the hypothesis test is to rule out chance as a plausible explanation for the obtained results. A significant result is one that is very unlikely to have occurred by chance alone. The alpha level, or level of significance, defines the maximum probability that the results are caused by chance. Hypothesis tests evaluate the significance of mean differences, differences between proportions, and correlational relationships.

The final section of the chapter introduced special statistical procedures used to evaluate the reliability of measurements. Three techniques (the Spearman-Brown formula, the Kuder-Richardson formula 20, and Cronbach's alpha) are used to measure split-half reliability. All three techniques address the general problems resulting from the fact that split-half reliability is based on only half the test items. Cohen's kappa provides a measure of inter-rater reliability. Cohen's kappa is intended to correct for inter-rater agreements that are simply the result of chance.

KEY WORDS

descriptive statistics	central tendency	variability
inferential statistics	mean	variance
statistic	median	standard deviation
parameter	mode	correlation

regression
multiple regression
sampling error
hypothesis test
standard error

test statistic
alpha level, or level of
    significance
significant result, or statisti-
    cally significant result

Type I error
Type II error
confidence interval

EXERCISES

1. In addition to the key words, you should also
   be able to define each of the following terms:
   frequency distribution
   histogram
   polygon
   bar graph
   bimodal distribution
   multimodal distribution
   degrees of freedom, *df*
   line graph
   scatter plot
   Pearson correlation
   Spearman correlation
   regression equation
   slope constant
   Y-intercept
   multiple-regression equation
   null hypothesis
   effect size
   Cohen's *d*
   percentage of variance accounted for
      (r^2 or η^2)
   independent-measures *t* test
   repeated-measures *t* test
   single-factor analysis of variance or
      one-way ANOVA
   error variance
   post hoc tests or post tests
   two-factor analysis of variance or two-way
      ANOVA
   parametric test
   nonparametric test
   chi-square test for independence
   split-half reliability
   Spearman-Brown formula
   Kuder-Richardson formula 20, or K-R 20
   Cronbach's alpha
   Cohen's kappa

2. Explain why it is important to consider
   statistical analyses before you conduct a
   study and collect data.
3. Construct a frequency distribution
   histogram or polygon for the set of scores
   presented in the following frequency
   distribution table:

X	f
5	2
4	3
3	5
2	1
1	1

4. Statistical techniques are classified into two
   major categories: descriptive and inferential.
   Explain the basic purpose of the statistics in
   each category.
5. Define the term *sampling error*. Be sure to
   include the terms *statistic* and *parameter* in
   your definition.
6. In a distribution with a mean of 70
   a. If the distribution had a standard
      deviation of 4, would a score of 82 be
      considered an extreme value or an
      average score near the center of the
      distribution? (Hint: Use the mean and
      standard deviation to sketch a frequency
      distribution graph, then find the location
      for a score of 82.)
   b. If the distribution had a standard
      deviation of 20, would a score of 82 be
      considered an extreme value or an
      average score near the center of the
      distribution?

7. A national reading achievement test is standardized such that the mean score for the population of seventh-grade students is equal to 100. A researcher selects a sample of 25 seventh-grade students and enrolls them in a special reading course. After 6 weeks, the students in the sample take the standardized test. The mean for the sample is 112. Based solely on the sample mean, can the researcher conclude that the special training has an effect on reading achievement? Explain your answer. (Hint: If the course has no effect, how can you explain the 12-point difference between the sample mean and the population mean?)

8. Briefly explain what is meant when a researcher reports "a significant mean difference between two treatment conditions."

9. Identify the appropriate hypothesis test for each of the following research situations.

   a. A researcher conducts a cross-sectional developmental study to determine whether there is a significant difference in vocabulary skills between 8-year-old and 10-year-old children.

   b. A researcher determines that 8% of the males enrolled in Introductory Psychology have some form of color blindness, compared to only 2% of the females. Is there a significant relationship between color blindness and gender?

   c. A researcher records the daily sugar consumption and the activity level for each of 20 children enrolled in a summer camp program. The researcher would like to determine whether there is a significant relationship between sugar consumption and activity level.

   d. A researcher would like to determine whether a 4-week therapy program produces significant changes in behavior. A group of 25 participants is measured before therapy, at the end of therapy, and again 3 months after therapy.

   e. A researcher would like to determine whether a new program for teaching mathematics is significantly better than the old program. It is suspected that the new program will be very effective for small-group instruction but probably will not work well with large classes. The research study involves comparing four groups of students: a small class taught by the new method, a large class taught by the new method, a small class taught by the old method, and a large class taught by the old method.

10. Dr. Jones reports a significant result with $p < .05$, and Dr. Smith reports a significant result with $p < .01$. Who should be more confident that their result is real and not simply caused by chance? Explain your answer.

11. Each of the following special statistical techniques was developed to deal with a particular problem. In each case, identify the problem that the technique attempts to solve.
    The Spearman-Brown formula
    The Kuder-Richardson formula 20
    Cronbach's alpha
    Cohen's kappa

LEARNING ACTIVITIES

1. Make up a set of 10 scores such that the set of scores has a mean approximately equal to 30 and a standard deviation approximately equal to 5. (Hint: Sketch a frequency distribution graph similar to Figure 14.3. The graph should show a pile of 10 blocks centered at 30 with most of the blocks within one standard deviation and essentially all of the blocks within two standard deviations of the mean. Then list the scores as they appear in your sketch.) If you have access to SPSS or a similar data analysis

program, calculate the mean and standard deviation for your scores. (Note: Instructions for using the latest version of SPSS are contained in Appendix C.)

2. Make up a set of 10 pairs of scores (X and Y values) so that the Pearson correlation between X and Y is approximately $r = 0.70$. (Hint: Sketch a scatter plot similar to the one shown in Figure 14.8 showing a pattern that corresponds to a reasonably good, positive correlation. Then add numbers to both axes and read the X and Y values from your graph.) If you have access to SPSS or a similar data analysis program, calculate the Pearson correlation for your scores. (Note: Instructions for using the latest version of SPSS are contained in Appendix C.)

WEB RESOURCES

Visit the Book Companion Website at **www.cengage.com/international** to access study tools including a glossary, flashcards, and web quizzing.

15

Single-Subject Research Designs

CHAPTER OVERVIEW

Step 6 of the research process involves selecting a research design. In this chapter, we discuss in detail a unique type of experimental research: the single-subject design. The general characteristics of this design are discussed, as well as evaluation of the data it produces. Different types of single-subject designs are considered, followed by the general strengths and weaknesses of this type of design.

15.1 | INTRODUCTION

As the name implies, **single-subject designs** are experimental research designs that can be used with only one participant (or subject) in the entire research study. Single-subject designs are also commonly called **single-case designs.** We use the term *experimental* to describe these single-subject designs because the designs presented in this chapter allow researchers to identify relatively unambiguous cause-and-effect relationships between variables. Although these designs can be used with groups of participants, their particular advantage is that they provide researchers with an option for data collection and interpretation in situations in which a single individual is being treated, observed, and measured. This option is especially valuable when researchers want to obtain cause-and-effect answers in applied situations. For example, a clinician would like to demonstrate that a specific treatment actually causes a client to make changes in behavior, or a school psychologist would like to demonstrate that a counseling program really helps a student in academic difficulty.

DEFINITION

Single-subject designs, or **single-case designs,** are research designs that use the results from a single participant or subject to establish the existence of cause-and-effect relationships. To qualify as experiments, these designs must include manipulation of an independent variable and control of extraneous variables to prevent alternative explanations for the research results.

Historically, most single-subject designs were developed by behaviorists examining operant conditioning. The behavior of a single subject (usually a laboratory rat) was observed, and changes in behavior were noted while the researcher manipulated the stimulus or reinforcement conditions. Although clinicians have adopted the designs, their application is still largely behavioral, especially in the field of applied behavior analysis (previously called behavior modification). Despite this strong association with behaviorism, however, single-subject research is not tied directly to any single theoretical perspective and is available as a research tool for general application.

The goal of single-subject research, as with other experimental designs, is to identify cause-and-effect relationships between variables. In common application, this means demonstrating that a treatment (variable 1) implemented or manipulated by the researcher causes a change in the participant's responses (variable 2). Although single-subject studies are experimental, their general methodology incorporates elements of nonexperimental case studies and time-series designs (see Chapters 7 and 12, respectively). Like a case study, single-subject research focuses on a single individual, and allows a detailed description of the observations and experiences related to that unique individual. Like time-series research, the single-subject approach typically involves a series of observations made over time. Usually, a set of observations made before treatment is contrasted with a set of observations made during or after treatment. Although single-subject designs are similar to descriptive case studies and quasi-experimental time-series studies, the designs discussed in this chapter are capable of demonstrating cause-and-effect relationships and, therefore, are true experimental designs.

What is the goal of a single-subject research study?

Evaluating the Results from a Single-Subject Study

Unlike other experimental methods, the results of a single-subject design do not provide researchers with a set of scores from a group of subjects that can be used to compute means and variances, and conduct traditional tests for statistical significance. Instead, the presentation and interpretation of results from a single-subject experiment are based on visual inspection of a simple graph of the data. Figure 15.1, for example, shows hypothetical results from a study examining the effects of a behavior intervention program designed to treat the classroom-disruption behavior of a single student. The student's behavior (number of disruptions) was observed and recorded for 5 days prior to implementing the treatment. In the graph, each day's observation is recorded as a single point, with the series of days presented on the horizontal axis and the magnitude of the behavior (number of disruptions) on the vertical axis. The intervention program was implemented on day 6, and the student's behavior was recorded for 5 additional days while the program was being administered (days 6 through 10 on the graph). The vertical line in the graph between days 5 and 6 indicates when the treatment was started; the five points to the left of the line are before treatment and the five points to the right are during treatment. Also notice that the individual data points are connected by straight lines to help emphasize the pattern of behavior before treatment and the change in the pattern that occurred with treatment.

Because the results of a single-subject study do not involve any traditional statistical methods, researchers must rely on the visual inspection of a graph to convey the meaning of their results. The graph in Figure 15.1, for example, appears to indicate that a substantial change in behavior occurred when the treatment program was started. However, the graph by itself is not

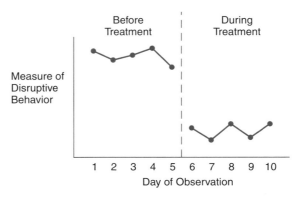

FIGURE **15.1** Data Obtained from a Single-Subject Research Study

a convincing demonstration that the treatment actually caused a change in behavior. In fact, there are two reasons for skepticism concerning the results.

1. The results as presented do not represent a true experiment because there is no control over extraneous variables. In particular, it is possible that factors other than the treatment are responsible for the apparent change in behavior. Variables outside the study such as the weather, changes in the student's family situation, or changes in the student's relationships with peers, may be responsible for causing the change in behavior. Because the study cannot measure or control all these potentially confounding variables, it is impossible to interpret the results as a clear, unambiguous demonstration of the treatment's effectiveness. To demonstrate a cause-and-effect relationship, single-subject designs must demonstrate convincingly that it is the treatment, not coincidental extraneous variables, causing the changes in behavior.

2. The second problem with interpreting results such as those shown in Figure 15.1 is that the apparent difference between the before-treatment observations and the after-treatment observations may simply be the result of chance. Notice that there is variability in the day-to-day observations; this variability is a natural part of behavior and measurement. Although the results appear to suggest a pattern of higher scores before treatment and lower scores after treatment, the "pattern" may be nothing more than normal variability. You may recognize this problem as the traditional question of statistical significance.

In a traditional group design (for example, a between-subjects or a within-subjects design), a researcher is able to obtain a precise measurement of how much difference is reasonable to expect by chance. A hypothesis test can then be used to determine whether the differences found in the data are significantly greater than the differences that are likely to occur by chance. In single-subject research, however, there is no group of scores that allows a researcher to calculate the patterns that are reasonable to occur by chance alone. Instead, a researcher must rely on the appearance of the graph to convince others that the treatment effect is significant. Hence, it is essential that the obtained data be unquestionably clear so that an observer can see the treatment effect by inspecting a graph of the results. (Guidelines for inspection of single-subject graphs are presented later in the chapter; see p. 460.)

LEARNING CHECK　What is the role of traditional statistics (means, variances, and hypothesis tests) in the evaluation of the results from a single-subject study?

15.2 | PHASES AND PHASE CHANGES

Before beginning discussion of specific single-subject experimental designs, we introduce and define the general concept of a **phase,** which is the basic building block used to construct most single-subject designs. A phase is a series of observations made under the same conditions. The results shown in Figure 15.1, for example, consist of two phases: The series of five observations before treatment constitutes one phase and the final five observations constitute a second phase (during treatment). In the terminology of single-subject research, observations made in the absence of a treatment are called **baseline observations,** and a series of baseline observations is called a **baseline phase.** Similarly, observations made during treatment are called **treatment observations,** and a series of treatment observations is called a **treatment phase.** By convention, a baseline phase is identified by the letter A, and a treatment phase is usually identified by the letter B. Designating different phases by different letters allows researchers to describe the sequence of phases in a study by using a sequence of letters. For example, the study producing the results shown in Figure 15.1 would be described as an AB design; that is, the study consists of a baseline phase (A) followed by a treatment phase (B).

DEFINITIONS	A **phase** is a series of observations of the same individual under the same conditions.

When no treatment is being administered, the observations are called **baseline observations.** A series of baseline observations is called a **baseline phase** and is identified by the letter A.

When a treatment is being administered, the observations are called **treatment observations.** A series of treatment observations is called a **treatment phase** and is identified by the letter B.

Although the letter B usually identifies the treatment phase of a single-subject study, there are situations in which other letters may be used. Specifically, when a study contains two or more distinct treatments, B identifies the first treatment condition, and C, D, and so on identify other treatments. Also, when a study contains modifications of a basic treatment, B identifies the basic treatment, and the different modifications are called B1, B2, and so on. Finally, when one phase involves administering two or more treatments simultaneously, the single phase can be identified by a pair of letters representing the two different treatments. Thus, a single-subject research design might be described as an A-B-B1-A-BC-C design. This letter sequence indicates that the researcher first made a series of baseline observations, and then implemented a treatment (B) while continuing to make observations. Next, the researcher tried a modification of the treatment (perhaps treatment B was not effective), followed by withdrawal of all treatment (back to baseline). Then, the original treatment (B) was administered in combination with a new treatment (C) and finally, treatment C was administered by itself.

Level, Trend, and Stability

The purpose of a phase within a single-subject experiment is to establish a clear picture of the participant's behavior under the specific conditions that define the phase. That is, the series of observations that make up the phase should show a clear pattern that describes the behavior. Ultimately, the researcher changes phases by implementing or withdrawing a treatment, and the goal is to show that the pattern of behavior changes from one phase to the next. Before it is possible to demonstrate a change in patterns, however, it is essential that the pattern within a phase be clearly established.

One way to define a pattern within a phase is in terms of the **level** of behavior. The term *level* simply refers to the magnitude of the participant's responses. If all of the observations within a phase indicate approximately the same magnitude, or level, of behavior, then the data have demonstrated a consistent or stable level of behavior within the phase. Figure 15.2a shows data demonstrating a stable level of behavior. Although there are minor differences in magnitude from one observation to another, the data points generally line up at the same level of magnitude. Notice that the concept of a stable level simply means that the data points within a phase tend to form a horizontal line on the graph.

An alternative way to define a pattern within a phase is in terms of a **trend.** The term *trend* refers to a consistent increase (or a consistent decrease) in the magnitude of behavior across the series of observations that make up the phase. Figure 15.2b shows data demonstrating a consistent or stable trend in behavior. Again, notice that the data points tend to form a relatively straight line, but now the line slopes upward to the right, indicating a consistent increase in the magnitude of behavior over time.

Thus, the pattern within a phase can be described in terms of level or trend. In either case, however, the critical factor is the consistency of the pattern. Remember that single-subject research does not use statistical analysis to

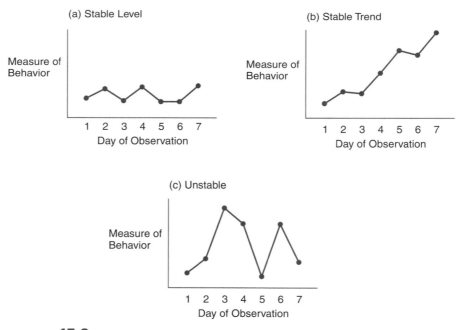

FIGURE **15.2** Three Patterns of Results for the Data from One Phase in a Single-Subject Research Study

(a) A stable level. (b) A stable trend. (c) Unstable data.

summarize or interpret the results, but depends on the visual appearance of the data in a graph. To establish that a treatment causes a change in behavior, for example, the graph must show a clear change in the pattern of behavior as the participant moves from a baseline phase to a treatment phase. Therefore, it is essential that the graph show a clear picture that establishes an unambiguous pattern (either a level or a trend) within each phase. In the terminology of single-subject research, the critical factor is the **stability** of the data. When the data points form a straight line with only minor deviations, the data are said to be stable, and the pattern is easy to see. Note that the data points do not have to form a perfectly straight line to be considered stable; some variability is allowed, but it should be relatively small.

On the other hand, if there are large differences (high variability) from one observation to the next, so that no obvious pattern emerges, the data are said to be unstable. Figure 15.2c shows unstable data. Unstable data are disastrous to the goals of single-subject research. When the data points vary wildly, it is impossible to define any pattern within a phase and, therefore, it is impossible to determine whether changing the phase (for example, implementing a treatment) produces any change in the pattern.

DEFINITIONS

A consistent **level** occurs when a series of measurements are all approximately the same magnitude. In a graph, the series of data points cluster around a horizontal line.

A consistent **trend** occurs when the differences from one measurement to the next are consistently in the same direction and are approximately of the same magnitude. In a graph the series of data points cluster around a sloping line.

The **stability** of a set of observations refers to the degree to which the observations show a pattern of consistent level or consistent trend. Stable data may show minor variations from a perfectly consistent pattern, but the variations should be relatively small and the linear pattern relatively clear.

 **LEARNING CHECK**   Why is it necessary to have a stable pattern within a phase?

Dealing With Unstable Data

Usually, behavior is fairly consistent over time, which means that a series of observations shows a consistent pattern (either a consistent level or consistent trend in behavior). Where data appear to be unstable, however, researchers can employ several techniques to help uncover a consistent pattern.

1. First, the researcher can simply wait; that is, keep making observations and hope that the data will stabilize and reveal a clear pattern. Occasionally, a participant reacts unpredictably to the novelty of being observed. When this happens, the first few days of observation are distorted by the participant's reactivity and may appear unstable. After several days, however, the novelty wears off and the participant returns to normal, consistent behavior.

2. A second method for stabilizing data is simply to average a set of two (or more) observations. Figure 15.3a shows a set of observations made over a 10-day period. Notice that the large, day-to-day differences produce a relatively unstable set of data. Figure 15.3b shows the same data after they have been smoothed by averaging over 2-day periods. To create Figure 15.3b, the first 2 days' observations were averaged to produce a single data point. Similarly, days three and four were averaged, and so on. Notice that the averaging process tends to reduce the variability of the data points and produces a more stable set of data in which the pattern of behavior is easier to see.

3. A final strategy for dealing with unstable data is to look for patterns within the inconsistency. For example, a researcher examining disruptive classroom behavior may find that a student exhibits very high levels of disruption on some days and very low levels on other days. Although the data appear to be very unstable, closer examination reveals that the high levels tend to occur on Mondays, Wednesdays, and Fridays, and the low levels are observed on Tuesdays and Thursdays. The obvious question is, "Why are Tuesdays and Thursdays different?" Checking the class schedule reveals that the student is in gym class immediately prior to the Tuesday/Thursday observation periods. Perhaps the exercise in gym allows the student to burn off excess energy and results in more subdued behavior. The researcher could try changing the time of observation to early morning to eliminate the influence of the gym class. Or the researcher could simply limit the data to observation made on the non-gym days. In general, unstable data may be caused by extraneous variables; it is often possible to stabilize the data by identifying and controlling them.

Length of a Phase

To establish a pattern (level or trend) within a phase and to determine the stability of the data within a phase, a phase must consist of a minimum of three observations. You may have noticed that the graphs in Figure 15.2 were constructed so that the first two data points are identical in all three graphs. In Figure 15.2a, the difference between the first two observations is simply minor variation that eventually becomes part of a consistent level. In Figure 15.2b, the difference

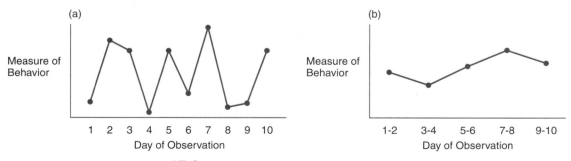

FIGURE **15.3** Stabilizing Data by Averaging over Successive Data Points
(a) The original unstable data. (b) The results of averaging over 2-day periods.

signifies the beginning of a consistent trend, and in Figure 15.2c, the difference between the two points is part of an unstable set of data. Our point is that the first two observations, by themselves, do not provide enough information to determine a pattern. Additional observations beyond the first two are essential to establish level, trend, and stability. Although three data points are the absolute minimum for determining a phase, typically five or six observations are necessary to determine a clear pattern. However, when high variability exists in the data points, additional observations should be made. In general, there is no single number that defines the optimal length for a phase. Instead, the length of a phase is determined by the number of data points needed to establish a clear and stable pattern in the data.

Changing Phases

After a researcher has obtained the necessary data points to establish a clear and stable pattern within a phase, it is possible to initiate a **phase change**. A phase change is essentially a manipulation of the independent variable and is accomplished by implementing a treatment, withdrawing a treatment, or changing a treatment. This process begins a new phase, during which the researcher collects a series of observations under a new set of conditions.

DEFINITION	A phase consists of a series of observations of the same individual under the same conditions. A **phase change** involves changing the conditions, usually by administering or stopping a treatment.

The purpose of a phase change is to demonstrate that adding a treatment (or removing a treatment) produces a noticeable change in behavior. This goal is accomplished when the data show a clear difference between the pattern that exists before the phase change and the pattern that exists after the phase change. For example, a dramatic drop in the level of behavior when the treatment is started (phase change) is evidence that the treatment has an effect on behavior.

Deciding When to Change Phases

As we have discussed, the primary factor determining when a new phase should be started is the emergence of a clear pattern within the preceding phase. However, there are several other factors that can influence the decision concerning when and if a phase change is appropriate.

The first consideration involves changing from a baseline phase to a treatment phase. When the data in a baseline phase show a trend indicating improvement in the client's behavior, a researcher should not intervene by introducing a treatment phase. There are two good reasons for this no-action strategy; one clinical and one experimental. From a clinical point of view, if the client is already showing improvement, the simplest and safest decision is to stand back and let the improvement run its course. The client's improvement indicates that there is no need for immediate intervention. From an experimental perspective, initiating a treatment when the participant is already showing a trend toward improvement can only result in ambiguous results. Specifically, if a treatment is started and the participant continues to improve, the researcher cannot determine whether the continued improvement is caused by the treatment or is simply the continuation of an established trend. Because the results cannot be interpreted as a clear demonstration of the treatment's effect, the experiment is compromised.

Another possibility is that the baseline data indicate a seriously high level of dangerous or threatening behavior. In this case, a researcher probably should not wait for the full set of five or six observations necessary to establish a clear pattern. Instead, the researcher/clinician has an ethical obligation to begin treatment immediately (after one or two observations). After the behavior is brought under control during a treatment phase, the researcher can consider resuming the experiment by changing back to a baseline (no-treatment) phase or by introducing a different treatment phase.

It also is possible that the data within a treatment phase can dictate a premature phase change. If, for example, a treatment appears to produce an immediate and severe deterioration in behavior, the researcher/clinician should stop, change, or modify the treatment immediately without waiting for a clear pattern to emerge.

In general, the decision to make a phase change is based on the participant's responses. If the responses establish a clear pattern, then a change is appropriate. If the responses indicate a serious problem, then a change is necessary. In either case, the step-by-step progress of the experiment is controlled by the participant and does not necessarily follow a predetermined plan developed by the researcher. This aspect of single-subject research creates a very flexible and adaptive research strategy that is particularly well suited to clinical application. We return to this point later when the strengths and weaknesses of single-subject designs are discussed in section 15.6.

LEARNING CHECKS

What is the primary factor that determines when it is time to change phases? What pattern of results is needed to provide convincing evidence that behavior changed when the phase was changed?

Visual Inspection Techniques

In very general terms, the goal of single-subject research is to demonstrate that manipulation of one variable (the treatment) causes a change in a second variable (the participant's behavior). More specifically, the goal is to demonstrate that the pattern of behavior established in a baseline phase changes to a different pattern when the researcher switches to a treatment phase. Because the interpretation of the experimental results depends entirely on the visual appearance of a graph, it is important that the change in pattern from baseline to treatment be easy to see when the results are presented in a graph. The most convincing results occur when the change in pattern is immediate and large.

Unfortunately, there are no absolute, objective standards for determining how much of a change in pattern is sufficient to provide a convincing demonstration of a treatment effect. The visual inspection of single-subject data is very much a subjective task, and different observers often interpret data in different ways (DeProspero & Cohen, 1979). Nonetheless, there are guidelines that focus attention on specific aspects of the data and help observers decide whether a phase change produced a real change in pattern. Kazdin (2003) has identified four specific characteristics of single-subject data that help determine whether there is a meaningful change between phases.

1. *Change in average level.* Although statistical means and variances are typically not computed for single-subject data, the average level of behavior during a phase provides a simple and understandable description of the behavior within the phase. Figure 15.4 shows hypothetical data from a single-subject design for which the average level for each phase is indicated by a dashed line. Notice that the data show clear differences in the average level from one phase to another. In general, large differences in the average level are a good indication that there is a real difference between phases.

2. *Immediate change in level.* Another indicator of a difference between phases is the initial response of the participant to the change. This involves comparing the last data point in one phase with the first data point in the following phase. A large difference between these two points is a good indication that the participant showed an immediate response to the addition (or removal) of the treatment. In Figure 15.4, for example, the data show a large difference between the final score in the first baseline phase and the first score in the first treatment phase. Apparently, the participant showed an immediate reaction when the treatment was introduced.

3. *Change in trend.* When the trend observed in one phase is noticeably different from the trend in the previous phase, it is a clear indication of a difference between phases. Figure 15.5 demonstrates changes in trend. Figure 15.5a shows a change from no trend (consistent level) to a clear, increasing trend. The data in Figure 15.5b are even more convincing. Here, the trends change direction from increasing to decreasing.

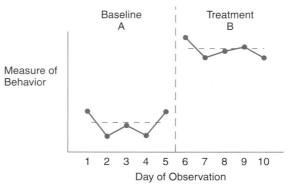

FIGURE **15.4** Data Showing a Change in Average Level from One Phase to the Next

The horizontal dashed lines in each phase correspond to the average level. A clear difference between averages is a good indication of a real difference between phases. Also note the large difference between the final point in the baseline phase and the first point in the treatment phase. This difference also indicates that the participant's behavior changed when the treatment was introduced.

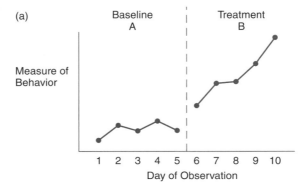

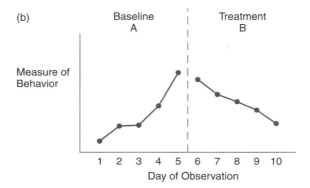

FIGURE **15.5** Two Examples of a Clear Change in Trend from One Phase to the Next

(a)   A clear change from no trend (consistent level) to an increasing trend.
(b)   A reversal in trend from increasing to decreasing.

Again, clear changes in trend are evidence of a real difference between phases.

4. *Latency of change.* The most convincing evidence for a difference between phases occurs when the data show a large, immediate change in pattern. A delay between the time the phase is changed and the time behavior begins to change undermines the credibility of a cause-and-effect explanation. Figure 15.6 shows two examples of a baseline-to-treatment phase change. In Figure 15.6a, the data show an immediate change in behavior when the treatment is introduced, providing clear evidence that the treatment is affecting behavior. In Figure 15.6b, however, there is no immediate change in behavior. Although there is an eventual change in behavior, it does not occur until several sessions after the treatment starts. In this case, the data do not provide unambiguous evidence that the treatment is causing the changes in behavior.

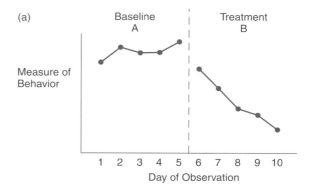

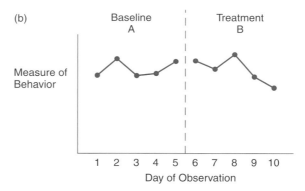

FIGURE **15.6** Latency of Change Affects Interpretation

(a) An immediate change in trend when treatment is introduced. This pattern provides good evidence that the treatment is influencing behavior. (b) The behavior remains at the baseline level for several days after the treatment is introduced. Although the behavior does eventually show a decreasing trend, it is not clear that the decrease occurs as a result of the treatment.

15.3 | THE ABAB REVERSAL DESIGN

We have introduced the concept of a phase as the basic building block of most single-subject experiments. A specific research design, therefore, consists of a sequence of phases that can be represented by a sequence of letters (for example, ABB1AC). Because each unique sequence of letters represents a unique experimental design, the number of potential designs is essentially unlimited. We address the issue of complex designs later in this section. For now, however, we focus on one design that is extremely common and probably accounts for the majority of single-subject research studies: the **ABAB design,** or **reversal design.**

As the letters indicate, the ABAB design consists of four phases: a baseline phase (A), followed by treatment (B), then a return to baseline (A), and finally a repitition of the treatment phase (B). The goal of the ABAB design is to demonstrate that the treatment causes a change in behavior by showing that:

- The pattern of behavior in each treatment phase is clearly different from the pattern in each baseline phase. This demonstration is necessary to establish a relationship between the treatment and the behavior.
- The changes in behavior from baseline to treatment and from treatment to baseline are the same for each of the phase-change points in the experiment. This demonstration is necessary to establish a causal relationship between treatment and behavior. That is, the results demonstrate that the researcher can cause the behavior to turn on and off simply by starting and stopping the treatment.

DEFINITION

An **ABAB design,** also known as a **reversal design,** is a single-subject experimental design consisting of four phases: a baseline phase, a treatment phase, a return-to-baseline phase, and a second treatment phase. The goal of the design is to demonstrate that the treatment causes changes in the participant's behavior.

The single-subject ABAB design is used in a variety of areas, including demonstrating the effectiveness of a treatment to improve social interaction in children with autism (Koegel, Vernon, & Koegel, 2009), a dietary treatment of OCD symptoms (Rucklidge, 2009), and a token economy to increase adherence to an exercise program to improve airway clearance for children with cystic fibrosis (Bernard, Cohen, & Moffett, 2009). In each case, the pattern of results obtained in the study is shown in Figure 15.7. Close examination of the graph reveals the elements that make it possible to infer a causal relationship between the treatments and the changes in behavior.

1. The first phase change (baseline to treatment) shows a clear change in the pattern of behavior. This first change by itself simply demonstrates that a behavior change accompanies the treatment. At this point, we cannot conclude that the treatment has caused the change in behavior, because some extraneous variable that changed coincidentally with the treatment might be responsible for changing the behavior. It is possible, for example, that on the same day that the treatment was first introduced, the participant woke up feeling much better after suffering with a cold for the previous week. If so, it could be that the change in behavior was caused by the change in health rather than the treatment.

2. The second phase change (treatment to baseline) shows the participant's behavior returning to the same level observed during the initial baseline phase. This component of the experiment is often called the *reversal,* or *return to baseline.* The reversal component is important because it begins to establish the causal relationship between the treatment and behavior. Although the participant's behavior may have been influenced by extraneous variables at the first phase change, it now appears more

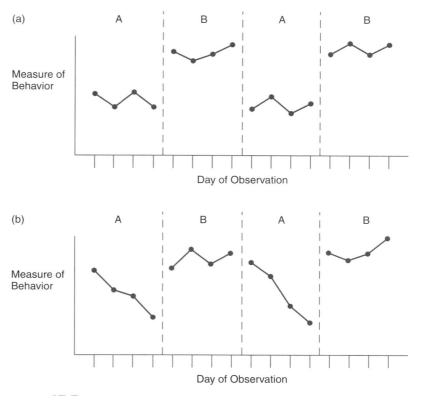

FIGURE **15.7** Two Examples of Optimal Results from an ABAB Reversal Design

(a) The data show a clear change in level when the treatment is introduced, a clear return to baseline when the treatment is withdrawn, and a clear replication of the treatment effect when the treatment is reintroduced. (b) A similar pattern, except that the treatment stops the baseline trend and restores behavior to a higher, more stable level.

likely that the treatment (not extraneous variables) is responsible for the change. Behavior changed when the treatment was introduced, and behavior reverted back to baseline when the treatment was withdrawn. During the return-to-baseline phase, it is not essential that behavior return to exactly the same level observed during the initial baseline. However, there must be a clear and immediate change toward the pattern established in the initial baseline phase.

3. The final phase change (baseline back to treatment) shows the same treatment effect that was observed in the initial phase change. This component of the experiment, the second AB in the sequence, provides a replication of the first AB. This replication clinches the argument for a causal interpretation of the results. By showing that behavior changes repeatedly when the treatment is implemented, the results minimize the

likelihood that a coincidence (extraneous variables) is responsible for the changes in behavior. Although it is possible that coincidence is responsible for the first change in behavior, it is very unlikely that another coincidence occurred the second time the treatment was introduced. By using replication, the ABAB design maximizes the likelihood that the observed changes in behavior are caused by the treatment.

In Figure 15.7(a) the data provide evidence for a cause-and-effect relationship by showing a change in level each time the treatment is introduced or withdrawn. It is also possible to demonstrate a cause-and-effect relationship by showing a change in trend. In Figure 15.7(b), for example, the decreasing trend is stopped when the treatment is introduced. Behavior returns to the baseline trend when the treatment is withdrawn, and the stable level returns when the treatment is reintroduced.

Although the ABAB design is typically used to show that a treatment does have an effect, it also can provide convincing evidence that a treatment is not effective. Craig and Kearns (1995) used an ABAB design to evaluate the effectiveness of acupuncture as a treatment for stuttering. Figure 15.8 shows the pattern of results obtained in the study. Notice that stuttering frequency remains at baseline levels throughout both of the treatment phases. These results provide a fairly strong demonstration that the acupuncture treatment has no effect on stuttering.

 **LEARNING CHECK** Identify the four phases that make up an ABAB (reversal) design, and describe how the participant's behavior is expected to change each time the phase is changed if the study is successful.

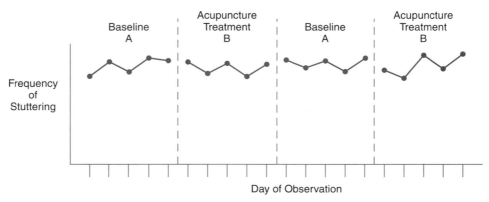

FIGURE **15.8** Hypothetical Data Similar to Results Obtained by Craig and Kearns (1995)

The graph shows results from an ABAB study in which the treatment clearly is not effective. The frequency of stuttering remains at baseline levels throughout the entire study. The data indicate that the acupuncture treatment has no effect.

Limitations of the ABAB Design

Like other experimental designs, the ABAB research design can establish, with good credibility, the existence of a cause-and-effect relationship between the manipulation of a treatment and corresponding changes in behavior. However, the credibility of this causal interpretation depends in large part on the reversal (return to baseline) that is a component of the design. Withdrawing treatment in the middle of the experiment can create some practical and ethical problems that can limit the application and success of this specific design.

The first issue related to the withdrawal of treatment focuses on the participant's response; withdrawing treatment may not result in a change in behavior. That is, although the researcher may return to baseline by removing the treatment, the participant's behavior may not return to baseline. From a purely clinical point of view this phenomenon is not a problem; in fact it is an excellent outcome. The clinician has implemented a treatment that has corrected a problem behavior, and when the treatment is removed, the correction continues. In simple terms, the client is cured. From an experimental perspective, however, the credibility of the treatment effect is seriously compromised if the participant's behavior does not respond to removal of the treatment. If a manipulation of the treatment fails to produce any response in the participant, the researcher is left with doubts about the treatment's effect. One obvious consequence of this problem is that an ABAB design is not appropriate for evaluating treatments that are expected to have a permanent or long-lasting effect.

Thus far, we have discussed the failure to return to baseline as an absolute, all-or-none phenomenon. Degrees of failure are also possible. That is, the participant may show some response to the withdrawal of treatment but not a complete or immediate return to the original baseline behavior. As long as there is some noticeable response when the treatment is removed, the experiment is not severely compromised. However, the degree of credibility generally depends on the degree of the response. Large responses that produce a pattern similar to the original baseline are more convincing than small responses. In addition, the final phase of the experiment (reintroducing the treatment) provides an opportunity to reestablish the credibility of the treatment effect. If the second application of the treatment produces another clear change in behavior, the problem of a less-than-perfect return to baseline becomes less critical.

A second problem with an ABAB design concerns the ethical question of withdrawing a successful treatment. The ABAB design asks a clinician to withdraw a treatment that has been shown to be effective. Furthermore, the treatment is withdrawn with the intention of having the client's behavior revert to its original problem condition. Although this reversal component is an integral part of the ABAB design, it appears to be contrary to good clinical practice. The ethical question is compounded by the practical problem of convincing the client, therapist, and family members to agree to stop treatment. Although this problem cannot be eliminated completely, two considerations help to minimize (or rationalize) its effect. First, everyone can be reassured that the withdrawal of treatment is a temporary event; the treatment will be returned. Second, the eventual withdrawal of treatment is often a practical necessity. Eventually, the client must be released to return to a normal life.

In this sense, the return-to-baseline phase can be viewed as a trial period to assess the permanence or long-term effectiveness of the treatment.

Explain why an ABAB reversal design is inappropriate for a treatment that has a permanent or long-lasting effect.

Variations on the ABAB Design: Creating More Complex Phase-Change Designs

Although researchers often begin a research study intending to use an ABAB design, circumstances that develop during the study may require adding new treatments or modifying the sequence of baseline and treatment phases. As a result, the exact sequence of baseline and treatment phases evolves during the course of the study creating an essentially unlimited number of potential designs. For example, a researcher may plan for an ABAB design but switch to a new treatment (C) when the participant fails to respond to the first treatment phase, thus creating a more complex phase-change design.

Although the number of potential phase sequences is unlimited, not every sequence qualifies as an experimental design. Remember, a true experiment should produce a reasonably unambiguous cause-and-effect explanation for the relationship between treatment and behavior. In single-subject research, the experiment must show a clear change in behavior when the treatment is introduced, and it must provide at least one replication of the change. These two criteria can produce some interesting consequences in a study with two or more different treatment phases. Consider the following example.

> Suppose that a researcher begins with the traditional baseline phase, and then moves to a specific treatment (B). However, the participant's responses indicate that the treatment has little or no effect, so the researcher modifies the treatment, creating a new phase (B1). Again, there is little or no response, so a completely different treatment (C) is started. Finally, the data show a clear change in pattern, indicating that treatment C may be effective. Thus far, the sequence of phases can be described as A-B-B1-C, and the pattern of results we have described is presented as a graph in Figure 15.9a. Although the data seem to suggest that treatment C has produced a change in behavior, there are several alternative explanations for the observed data.

- It is possible that the change in behavior is simply a coincidence caused by some extraneous variable that coincided with the beginning of treatment C.
- The change in behavior may be a delayed effect from one of the previous treatments (B or B1). That is, treatment B or B1 really was effective, but the effect did not become visible until several days after the treatment was administered.
- It is possible that the observed change is not the result of treatment C by itself. Instead, treatment C may be effective only when B and/or B1 precede it. That is, either treatment B or treatment B1 is a necessary catalyst that made the participant more receptive to treatment C.

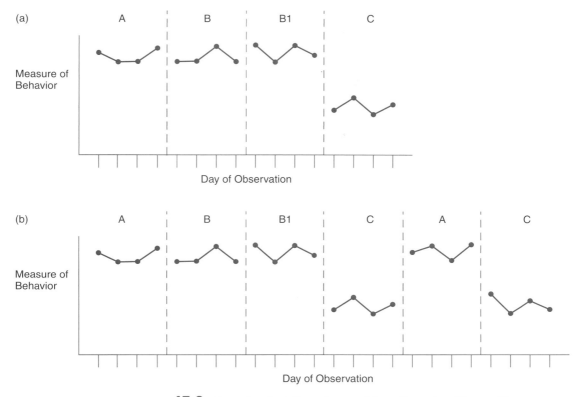

FIGURE **15.9** Hypothetical Data from a More Complex Phase-Change Design
(a) The first treatment B and its modification B1 appear to have no effect; however, treatment C produces a change in level.
(b) An extension of the study by addition of a return-to-baseline phase and a replication of treatment C.

To qualify as an experiment, the study must consider these alternatives and eventually produce one unambiguous explanation for the results. The problem for the researcher is to decide what to do next. One course of action is to begin a second baseline phase, hoping that the participant's behavior returns to baseline, then to try repeating treatment C. In symbols, the sequence of phases would become A-B-B1-C-A-C. If the observed behavior replicates the patterns seen in the original A and C phases (see Figure 15.9b), you can be reasonably confident that treatment C is causing the changes. Notice that the confidence in a cause-and-effect interpretation comes from the replication of the treatment effect. In this example, treatment C was shown to be effective when it was first administered, and the demonstration of effectiveness was repeated in the final phase of the study. On the other hand, failure to replicate the original effects of treatment C would suggest that this treatment by itself is not the causal agent. In this case, the study would need to be extended to evaluate the potential of a delayed effect from one of the preceding treatments or the potential of a catalyst effect. For example, the researcher could attempt another return to baseline followed by a B1-C sequence to determine whether the presence of treatment B1 is a necessary prerequisite for the effectiveness of treatment C.

Jones and Friman (1999) used a complex phase change design to evaluate the treatment of insect phobia for a 14-year-old boy named Mike whose academic performance was seriously disrupted by his fear of insects in the classroom. During a baseline phase (A), the researchers measured the number of math problems that Mike completed in a room containing three live crickets. Then, they started a graduated exposure treatment (B). This treatment was intended to gradually reduce fear by gradually increasing exposure to the feared object. The researchers constructed a hierarchy of 11 steps ranging from holding a jar of crickets (step 1) to holding a cricket in each hand for one minute (step 11). The treatment consisted of a 15- to 20-minute session in which Mike selected an initial exposure level and proceeded up the steps until he refused to continue. After five sessions, however, it became clear that the treatment had essentially no effect. At this point, the researchers added reinforcement to the exposure treatment by creating a new phase identified as BC (B for the exposure treatment and C for the added reinforcement). The reinforcement consisted of earning points that could be exchanged for videos, candy, toys, and other prizes. Adding the reinforcement produced a dramatic increase in performance. Following the BC phase, the researchers removed all treatment (back to baseline, A) for several sessions and then returned the treatment and reinforcement for a final phase. In symbols, this design can be described as A-B-BC-A-BC. Figure 15.10 shows data similar to the results obtained by Jones and Friman.

As you can see, a single-subject design can easily grow into a complex sequence of phases before a clear cause-and-effect relationship emerges. At any time during the study, the researcher's decision concerning the next phase is determined by the pattern of responses observed during the preceding phases.

LEARNING CHECK — In general, how does a phase-change design demonstrate that the treatment (rather than chance or coincidence) is responsible for changes in behavior?

15.4 | MULTIPLE-BASELINE DESIGNS

One basic problem with the single-subject designs considered thus far is the reversal, or return-to-baseline, component that is essential to provide a replication of the initial treatment effect. Specifically, reversal designs require that the participant's behavior revert to baseline as soon as the treatment is removed. In addition to the ethical dilemma created by withdrawing treatment, these studies are also limited to evaluation of treatments with only a temporary effect. The **multiple-baseline design** provides an alternative technique that eliminates the need for a return to baseline and therefore is particularly well suited for evaluating treatments with long-lasting or permanent effects.

A multiple-baseline design requires only one phase change—from baseline to treatment—and establishes the credibility of the treatment effect by replicating the phase change for a second participant or for a second behavior. The

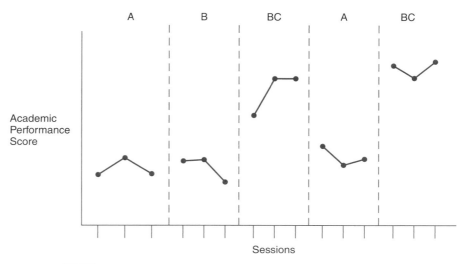

FIGURE **15.10** Hypothetical Data Similar to the Results Obtained by Jones and Friman (1999)

When a graduated exposure treatment (B) failed to cure an insect phobia by itself, reinforcement (C) was added to the treatment, creating a combined BC treatment.

general plan for a multiple-baseline study is shown in Figure 15.11. The figure shows hypothetical results for a study involving two different participants, both of whom are exhibiting the same problem behavior; the top half of the figure presents data for one participant and the bottom half shows the data for the second participant. Notice that the study begins with a baseline phase with simultaneous observations, beginning at the same time, for both participants. After a baseline pattern is established for both participants, the treatment phase is initiated for one participant only. Meanwhile, the baseline phase is continued for the second participant. Finally, the treatment phase is initiated for the second participant, but at a different time from that at which treatment is begun for the first participant. Thus, this study consists of simultaneous observations of two participants who experience two different baseline periods before the treatment is administered. When a multiple-baseline design uses two separate participants, it is called a **multiple-baseline across subjects.**

As we noted earlier, it also is possible to conduct a multiple-baseline study using two or more different behaviors for a single participant. The key to the single-subject version of the design is that the different behaviors are independent (one does not influence another) and can be treated separately by focusing a treatment on one behavior at a time. For example, a student may show disruptive behavior (speaking out and interrupting) and aggressive behavior (picking on other students). Each of these problem behaviors can be treated using a behavior modification program directed specifically at the problem behavior. Or a clinical client may have several different phobias, each of which can be treated with a specific desensitization program. Note that the same

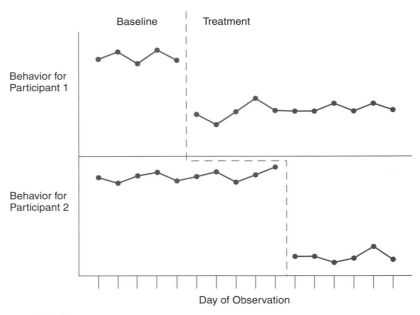

FIGURE **15.11** Hypothetical Data Showing the Results from a Multiple-Baseline Design

The baseline phase begins for two participants simultaneously but continues for one participant after the treatment phase has been started for the other participant.

treatment is used for each of the different behaviors. After clear baseline patterns are established for both behaviors, the treatment is started for one of the behaviors and baseline observations continue for the second behavior. After a short period, the treatment is started for the second behavior. The single-subject design follows exactly the same pattern that was shown in Figure 15.11; however, the top half of the figure now corresponds to one behavior and the bottom half represents the second behavior. This type of design, using two behaviors for a single participant, is called a **multiple-baseline across behaviors.**

Finally, the multiple-baseline design can be used to evaluate the treatment of one behavior that is exhibited in two different situations. For example, a child may exhibit disruptive behavior at school and at home. When it is possible to treat the two situations separately, we can begin baseline measurements for both situations simultaneously, then administer treatment at two different times for the two different situations. As before, the design follows the same pattern that was shown in Figure 15.11, however, the top half of the figure now corresponds to one situation and the bottom half represents the second situation. In this case, the design is called a **multiple-baseline across situations.**

A **multiple-baseline design** begins with two simultaneous baseline phases. A treatment phase is initiated for one of the baselines while baseline observations continue for the other. At a later time, the treatment is initiated for the second baseline.

When the initial baseline phases correspond to the same behavior for two separate participants, the design is called a **multiple-baseline across subjects.**

When the initial baseline phases correspond to two separate behaviors for the same participant, the design is called a **multiple-baseline across behaviors.**

When the initial baseline phases correspond to the same behavior in two separate situations, the design is called a **multiple-baseline across situations.**

Rationale for the Multiple-Baseline Design

The goal of a multiple-baseline design is to show that the treatment causes a change in behavior. The data in Figure 15.11 provide an ideal example of how this goal is accomplished. Notice that the following criteria for a successful multiple-baseline experiment are essentially identical to the criteria described earlier to define the success of an ABAB design.

- There is a clear and immediate change in the pattern of behavior when the researcher switches from a baseline to a treatment phase. This demonstration is necessary to establish a relationship between the treatment and the behavior; that is, a change in behavior accompanies the manipulation of the treatment.
- The design includes at least two demonstrations that behavior changes when the treatment is introduced. This replication is necessary to establish a causal relationship between treatment and behavior. It might be argued that the change observed when the treatment is first administered is simply a coincidental effect caused by extraneous variables. However, the fact that the change is replicated when the treatment is administered again at a different time undermines the coincidence argument.

For example, Ludwig and Geller (1991) used a multiple-baseline design to evaluate the effectiveness of a safe-driving program for pizza delivery drivers. The participants in this study were employees from three pizza stores. During an initial baseline phase, the authors observed safety-belt use for drivers at all three stores. After several weeks, a driver-safety program was initiated at one store. Three weeks later, the program was started at a second store. The third store served as a control, with no driver-safety program. Simplified results similar to those obtained in the study are presented in Figure 15.12. Notice that there is an immediate and substantial change in safety-belt use at both treatment stores when the treatment is initiated. Because the treatment and the accompanying change in behavior occur at different times for the two stores, the authors can be confident that it is the safety program and not some outside factor that is responsible for the change. The control store provides additional evidence that extraneous variables (for example, a police crackdown on seat-belt use) are not responsible for the changes in behavior.

LEARNING CHECK   Under what circumstances would you use a multiple-baseline design instead of an ABAB (reversal) design?

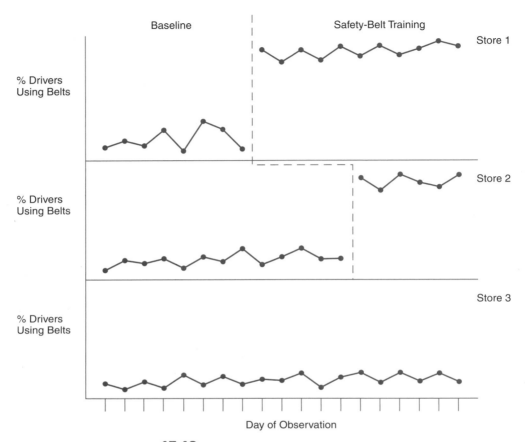

FIGURE **15.12** Data Showing a Multiple-Baseline Design with the Same Pattern of Results Obtained by Ludwig and Geller (1991)

The study evaluated the effectiveness of a safety-belt training program at three pizza shops. The training was started at two different times at two stores, and the third store served as a no-training control.

Strengths and Weaknesses of the Multiple-Baseline Design

The primary strength of the multiple-baseline design is that it eliminates the need for a reversal, or return-to-baseline, phase and, therefore, is well suited for evaluating treatment effects that are permanent or long-lasting. However, when this design is used with a single participant to examine two or more behaviors, it can be difficult to identify similar but independent behaviors. The risk is that a treatment applied to one behavior may generalize and produce changes in the second behavior. Once again, this problem illustrates a general conflict between clinical goals and experimental goals. From a clinical perspective, it is valuable for a single treatment to have a general effect; producing improvement in a variety of different problem behaviors. For the multiple-baseline experiment, however, it is essential that the treatment affect only the specific behavior to which it is applied. If both behaviors show a response to the initiation of treatment, the credibility of the treatment effect is undermined. That is, the observed changes may result from the treatment, or they may be caused by an outside variable that changes coincidentally with the treatment and affects both behaviors.

In addition, the clarity of the results can be compromised by individual differences between participants or between behaviors. In a multiple-baseline study across behaviors, for example, one behavior may show a large and immediate change, but the second behavior may show only a minor or gradual change when the treatment is introduced. When this happens, the pattern is different from one behavior to another and, therefore, creates doubts about the consistency of the treatment effect. The same problem can occur with research involving different participants with similar behavior problems. For example, Kercood and Grakovic (2009) examined the effects of color highlighting on mathematics performance for students with attention problems. The treatment consisted of giving the students colored highlighters to use while working on mathematics problems. The students were told that they could highlight important elements of each problem, color code problems according to the level of difficulty, or use the highlighters in any other way they wanted. For each of three student participants, the researchers recorded computational accuracy before and after the treatment. Somewhat simplified data similar to the research results are shown in Figure 15.13. Note that the first two participants show a clear increase in performance when they were given highlighters. For the third participant, however, there is so much variability in the pre-treatment scores that it is difficult to see any change when the treatment is administered. Again, the lack of consistency across participants creates some doubt about the consistency of the treatment effect.

LEARNING CHECK How does a multiple-baseline design rule out chance or coincidence as the explanation for changes in behavior that occur when the treatment is started?

15.5 | OTHER SINGLE-SUBJECT DESIGNS

The ABAB reversal design and the multiple-baseline designs are by far the most commonly used single-subject research designs. However, there are other examples of single-subject research that are designed to address specific research questions or are appropriate for specific research situations. In this section, we discuss three alternative single-subject designs.

Dismantling, or Component-Analysis, Design

When a treatment consists of several well-defined, distinct elements, it is possible to use a phase-change design to evaluate the extent to which each separate element contributes to the overall treatment effect. The general strategy is to use a series of phases, in which each phase adds or eliminates one component of the treatment. This type of design, in which a treatment

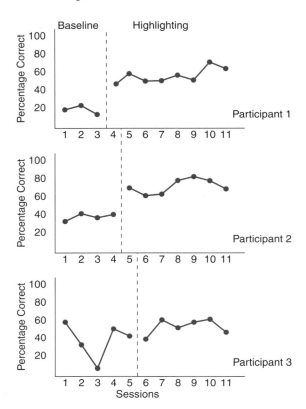

F I G U R E **15.13** Multiple-Baseline Data for Three Participants Showing Results Similar to Those Obtained by Kercood and Grakovic (2009)

For two of the three participants, there is a clear increase in mathematics performance when they are given highlighters. For participant 3, however, the large variability in the baseline data make the results far less convincing.

is broken down into its separate parts, is called a **dismantling design,** or a **component-analysis design.**

DEFINITION	A **dismantling design,** also called a **component-analysis design,** consists of a series of phases in which each phase adds or subtracts one component of a complex treatment to determine how each component contributes to the overall treatment effectiveness.

There are two general strategies for conducting a dismantling design. The first is to begin with a full-treatment phase (including all the different components), then remove components one by one to see whether the effectiveness of the treatment is reduced. The second strategy is to begin with a baseline phase, then add components one by one to see how each individual component contributes to the effectiveness of the total treatment package. The following example demonstrates this type of design.

Individuals with severe developmental disabilities or autism often have great difficulty communicating their needs and desires. Frustration from this inability to communicate often results in inappropriate behaviors such as aggression, self-injury, and tantrums. One method of treating this problem is functional communication training. This training typically involves two components: (1) training a communicative response (usually a sign or signal) to request a reinforcement, and (2) an intervention or punishment for the inappropriate behavior. Wacker et al. (1990) conducted a component-analysis study to evaluate the relative contribution of the two components. One participant in the study was identified as Bobby, a 7-year-old boy with autism who was nonverbal and also did not communicate with signs or gestures. The problem behavior for Bobby was hand biting; he bit his own hand several times an hour, often drawing blood. The total treatment package for Bobby consisted of two elements:

1. Reinforcement of signing. Bobby was trained to sign by touching his chin with one finger to indicate a request for play items. When he made this sign, he was given a selection of items.
2. Punishment for hand biting. The play items were immediately taken away when Bobby started biting his hand.

Simplified results similar to those obtained in the study are shown in Figure 15.14. We have eliminated other measures to show only the hand-biting data. Note that during the first phase, when the total treatment package is administered, hand biting stays near zero. During the next stage, signing is still reinforced but the punishment component is removed. When this component is eliminated, hand-biting behavior increases. In the third phase, the total treatment is returned, and hand biting drops back toward zero. In the next stage, Bobby is still punished for hand biting, but the reinforcement component

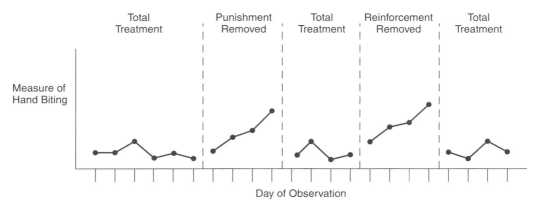

FIGURE 15.14 Simplified Data Showing Results from a Component-Analysis Design Similar to Those Obtained by Wacker et al. (1990)

The total treatment includes a punishment component and a reinforcement component. Note that when either component is removed from the treatment, hand-biting behavior increases.

is removed (signs are ignored). Once again, hand biting increases. Finally, the total package is administered again, and the problem behavior decreases toward zero. Using B to represent the reinforcement component and C for the punishment component, this study can be described in symbols as BC-B-BC-C-BC. The general conclusion from these data is that both treatment components are important; when either one is removed, behavior deteriorates.

The Changing-Criterion Design

Occasionally, a clinician or a researcher encounters a problem behavior that can be quantified into a set of different magnitudes or levels that are clearly defined and easily understood by both the client and the clinician. A good example is cigarette smoking, which can be quantified by the number of cigarettes smoked per day. In these situations, the treatment can involve a series of target levels or criteria that can be arbitrarily set and changed by the researcher. For example, a clinician might set a criterion of 20 cigarettes per day for the first week, then change the criterion to 10 cigarettes per day for the next 2 weeks, and continue lowering the criterion over the course of treatment. During treatment, the participant's behavior is continuously observed and recorded. If the behavior repeatedly and closely follows the criteria, the researcher can be reasonably confident that the criteria (treatment) are responsible for the observed changes in behavior. This type of research study is called a **changing-criterion design.**

DEFINITION	A **changing-criterion design** consists of a series of phases in which each phase is defined by a specific criterion that determines a target level of behavior. The criterion level is changed from one phase to the next. Evidence for a successful treatment effect is obtained when the participant's level of behavior changes in accordance with the changing criterion levels.

For example, Warnes and Allen (2005) used a changing-criterion design to evaluate biofeedback treatment of respiratory problems in an adolescent girl. The participant suffered from a disorder involving excessive muscle tension that partially closed her vocal cords when she inhaled, causing labored breathing and feelings of being choked. The treatment consisted of electromyographic biofeedback that presented the participant with a display of her current muscle tension. After two baseline sessions, the researchers set a criterion slightly below the baseline average and asked the participant to relax and try to lower her muscle tension below the criterion. If the participant successfully stayed at or below the criterion for three successive sessions, the criterion was lowered another 2 points. If two consecutive sessions were above the criterion, the criterion was raised by 1 point. Figure 15.15 shows data similar to the results obtained in the study. The criteria are shown as horizontal lines and the participant's actual level of muscle tension is shown as a series of dots connected by straight lines. Note that the participant's level of muscle tension follows the changing criterion levels, indicating that the criteria were effective in controlling behavior. Also note that the pattern of changing criteria is bidirectional (one increase in a series of decreasing criteria), and that the participant's behavior tracks the criteria in both directions.

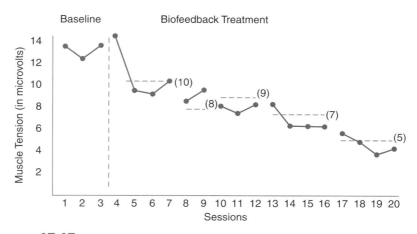

FIGURE **15.15** Data from a Changing-Criterion Design Showing Results Similar to Those Obtained by Warnes and Allen (2005)

Criteria levels are shown with dashed lines and numerical values. Three consecutive sessions at or below the criterion caused the criterion to be lowered by two points. Two consecutive sessions above the criterion caused the criterion to be raised by one point. Note that the participant's responses clearly track the changing criteria.

The most compelling evidence for a causal relationship between the treatment criteria and the participant's behavior occurs when the data consistently and closely track the criteria levels. As the discrepancy between the data and the criteria increases, the argument for a cause-and-effect interpretation becomes weaker. One specific problem for a changing-criterion design is to demonstrate that the behavior is tracking the criteria levels and not simply showing a general trend. To deal with this problem, researchers often incorporate one or more backward steps into the series of criteria and vary the duration of the criteria phases. These changes produce a nonlinear sequence of criteria that is clearly distinct from a general linear trend.

 **LEARNING CHECK**   Under what circumstances is a changing-criterion design an appropriate method for evaluating the effectiveness of a treatment?

The Alternating-Treatments Design

Each of the single-subject designs discussed thus far has involved comparisons between phases, and a phase has been defined by a specific block of time. The responses within one time block are grouped together to create a pattern that is then compared with the pattern within another time block. These designs require that each treatment condition (or baseline condition) be administered continuously for an extended period. The **alternating-treatments design,** on the other hand, allows a researcher to switch back and forth between treatments without waiting for a long series of observations to reveal a level, trend, or stability in the data. This type of design is also called a **discrete-trials design** because each trial or data point can be a separate, individual treatment condition.

The procedure for an alternating-treatments design involves using a random process to determine which of two treatment conditions will be administered for each observation. Thus, the series of observations corresponds to a randomly alternating series of treatment conditions. The basic requirements for an alternating treatments design are as follows:

1. It must be possible for the researcher or clinician to switch randomly between treatment conditions.
2. The participant's behavior must show an immediate response to the treatment being administered. There is no time for a response to evolve over a series of observations.

The conditions can be different treatments or treatment versus no-treatment.

DEFINITION   In an **alternating-treatments design,** also called a **discrete-trials design,** two (or more) treatment conditions are randomly alternated from one observation to the next. The result is a series of observations that represent a corresponding series of alternating treatment conditions.

The data from an alternating-treatments study are grouped by treatment conditions rather than grouped into blocks of time. In a graph of the results, a line is used to connect all the data points from one condition. A separate line is used for each separate condition. The following example presents a demonstration of an alternating-treatments study and shows how the results are presented in a graph.

Ryan and Hemmes (2005) used an alternating-treatments design to examine how homework assignments are related to learning. The participants were college students enrolled in an advanced undergraduate psychology course, which included required reading, a homework assignment, and a quiz for each textbook chapter. Each student alternated between two treatment conditions: 1. A points condition, for which homework was required and could earn up to 5 points toward the student's final grade, and 2. A no-points condition, for which the homework submission was not required and did not count toward the final grade. For both conditions, students were told that the homework was designed to help them prepare for the chapter quiz, students were encouraged to complete the homework, and students were told that they would receive written feedback for all completed assignments. As expected, nearly 100% of the students submitted homework for the required condition and typically less than 25% submitted homework when it was optional. The interesting variable, however, was the quiz grade obtained for each homework condition. The researchers present data for each of the 19 individual participants and show results averaged across the entire class. All of the graphs show the same basic pattern, which is displayed in Figure 15.16. Note that the quiz grades are consistently higher in the points condition (solid line) than in the no-points condition (dashed line). Clearly, student learning benefits if homework assignments are completed, especially when the assignments are directly related to course material.

One advantage of the alternating-treatments design is that it allows a fairly rapid comparison of two different treatments. This strategy can be useful in situations in which a clinician has two (or more) treatment options but is

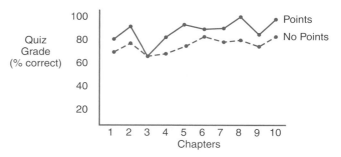

FIGURE **15.16** Data from an Alternating-Treatments Design Showing Results Similar to Those Obtained by Ryan and Hemmes (2005)
The solid line shows a typical student's performance on chapter quizzes when homework was required and added points to the student's grade. The dashed line shows performance when homework was optional and did not contribute to the grade.

unsure which is better for a particular client. With an alternating-treatments design, differences between treatments emerge after a relatively short series of observations, and the clinician can then switch to the more effective treatment. Although alternating between treatments is often done on a daily basis, this design also permits rapid alternation between conditions. For example, a clinician could divide a 1-hour session into a series of 5-minute observation periods, and then alternate between a warm and friendly attitude versus a cold and aloof attitude from one period to another while observing the patient's response. Finally, the alternating-treatments design can be used to compare different treatment techniques in situations in which alternation between therapists or treatment conditions occurs naturally. In a school or residential program, for example, a client may routinely encounter two or more different counselors or supervisors. In this situation, the two counselors may adopt different treatment strategies. For example, one counselor may be sympathetic to tantrums whereas a second counselor simply ignores the outbursts. Although this type of study is inherently confounded (different counselors are confounded with different strategies), the results may provide some insight into determining which strategy is more effective in dealing with the problem behavior.

LEARNING CHECK   Is an alternating-treatments design effective if one or both of the treatments has a permanent or long-lasting effect? Explain why or why not.

15.6 | GENERAL STRENGTHS AND WEAKNESSES OF SINGLE-SUBJECT DESIGNS

There are three fundamental differences between single-subject designs and traditional group designs.

1. The first and most obvious distinction is that single-subject research is conducted with only one participant or occasionally a very small group.

2. Single-subject research also tends to be much more flexible than a traditional group study. A single-subject design can be modified or completely changed in the middle of a study without seriously affecting the integrity of the design, and there is no need to standardize treatment conditions across a large set of different participants.

3. Single-subject designs require continuous assessment. In a traditional group design, an individual subject typically is observed and measured only once or twice. A single-subject design, however, normally involves a series of 10 to 20 observations for each individual.

As a consequence of these differences, single-subject designs have some advantages and some disadvantages in comparison with group designs. In this section, we identify and discuss the general strengths and weaknesses of single-subject research, beginning with the strengths.

Advantages of Single-Subject Designs

The primary strength of single-subject designs is that they allow researchers to establish cause-and-effect relationships between treatments and behaviors using only a single participant. This simple fact makes it possible to integrate experimental research into applied clinical practice. As we noted in Chapters 7 and 10, the demands and restrictions of traditional group experiments are often at odds with conducting research in natural settings such as a clinic with real clients. As a result, clinicians tend to prefer alternative strategies such as case studies or quasi-experimental research. However, these alternative strategies do not permit clinicians to establish causal relations between the treatments they use and the resulting behaviors. As a result, clinical psychologists are often left in the unenviable position of using treatments that have not been scientifically demonstrated to be effective. Single-subject designs provide a solution to this dilemma. By employing single-subject designs, a clinician who typically works with individual clients or small groups can conduct experimental research and practice therapy simultaneously without seriously compromising either activity. By recording and graphing observations during the course of treatment, a clinician can demonstrate a cause-and-effect relationship between a treatment and a client's behavior. This scientific demonstration is an important part of establishing accountability in the field of clinical psychology. That is, clinicians should be able to demonstrate unambiguously that the treatments they use are effective.

A second major advantage of single-subject designs comes from their flexibility. Although a researcher may begin a single-subject experiment with a preconceived plan for the design, the ultimate development of the design depends on the participant's responses. If a participant fails to respond to treatment, for example, the researcher is free to modify the treatment or change to a new treatment without compromising the experiment. Once again, this characteristic of single-subject research makes these designs extremely well suited to clinical research. In routine clinical practice, a therapist monitors a client's responses and makes clinical decisions based on those responses. This same flexibility is an integral part of most single-subject research. That is, the clinical decision to begin a new treatment and the experimental decision to begin a new phase are both determined by observing the participant's response to the current treatment or current phase. In addition, single-subject designs allow a clinician/researcher to individualize treatment to meet the needs of a specific client. Because these designs typically employ only one participant, there is no need to standardize a treatment across a group of individuals with different needs, different problems, and different responses.

In summary, the real strength of single-subject designs is that they make experimental clinical research compatible with routine clinical practice. These designs combine the clinical advantages of case study research with the rigor of a true experiment. In particular, single-subject research allows for the detailed description and individualized treatment of a single participant, and allows a clinician/researcher to establish the existence of a cause-and-effect relationship between the treatment and the participant's responses.

Disadvantages of Single-Subject Designs

Earlier, we noted that one of the strengths of a single-subject design is that it can establish the presence of a cause-and-effect relationship using only one participant. At the same time, however, a weakness of these designs is that the relationship is demonstrated only for one participant. This simple fact leaves researchers with some question as to whether the relationship can or should be generalized to other individuals. You should recognize this problem as the general concern of external validity. However, the problem of limited external validity is mitigated by the fact that single-subject research seldom exists in isolation. Usually, the researcher or clinician has observed the treatment effect in multiple cases before one individual case is selected for the single-subject research project. Also, the relationship between the treatment and outcome is commonly demonstrated in other nonexperimental research such as case studies or quasi-experimental studies. These other studies provide support for generalizing the treatment effect (external validity), and the single-subject study demonstrates the causal nature of the effect (internal validity).

A second potential weakness of single-subject designs comes from the requirement for multiple, continuous observations. If the observations can be made unobtrusively, without constantly interrupting or distracting the participant, there is little cause for concern. However, if the participant is aware that observations are continuously being made, this awareness may result in reactivity or sensitization that could affect the participant's responses (see Chapter 6). As a result, there is some risk that the participant's behavior may be affected not only by the treatment conditions but also by the assessment procedures. In experimental terminology, the continuous assessment can be a threat to internal validity.

Another concern for single-subject designs is the absence of statistical controls. With traditional group designs, researchers can use standard inferential statistical techniques to quantify the likelihood that the results show a real treatment effect versus the likelihood that the results simply reflect chance behavior. Single-subject designs, on the other hand, rely on the visual effect of a graph to convince others that the treatment effects are real. Problems can arise if there is any ambiguity at all in the graphed results. One observer, for example, may see clear indications of a treatment effect, whereas other observers may not. On the positive side, reliance on graphed results helps ensure that researchers report only results that are substantial; that is, the treatment effects must be sufficiently large that they are obvious to a casual observer when presented in a graph. Researchers often make a distinction between **statistical significance** and **practical significance** or **clinical significance**. Practical significance means that the treatment effect is substantial and large enough to have practical application. A **statistically significant** result, on the other hand, simply means that the observed effect, whether large or small, is very unlikely to have occurred by chance. Using this terminology, the results from a single-subject study tend to have practical significance, although they typically are not evaluated in terms of statistical significance.

The reliance on a graph to establish the significance of results places additional restrictions on the application of single-subject designs. Specifically, the treatment effects must be large and immediate to produce a convincing graph. Treatments that produce small effects or effects that are slow to develop can generate ambiguous graphs and, therefore, are unlikely to appear in published reports. As a result, single-subject research is likely to fail to detect such effects. From a research perspective, this tendency is unfortunate because many real treatments are overlooked. From a clinician's point of view, however, this aspect of single-subject research simply means that marginally effective treatments are weeded out and only those treatments that are truly effective are reported.

 **LEARNING CHECK**   Briefly explain why a clinical psychologist might prefer doing research with a single-subject design instead of traditional group design.

■ CHAPTER SUMMARY

In this chapter, we examined the characteristics of single-subject designs. The general goal of single-subject research, like other experimental designs, is to establish the existence of a cause-and-effect relationship between variables. The defining characteristic of a single-subject study is that it can be used with a single individual, by testing or observing the individual before and during or after the treatment is implemented by the researcher.

The basic building block of most single-subject designs is the phase, a series of observations all made under the same conditions. Observations are made in a baseline phase (that is, in the absence of a treatment) and in a treatment phase (that is, during treatment). The series of observations that make up any phase should show a clear pattern that describes the behavior. The pattern within a phase can be described in terms of level or trend, but in either case, the critical factor is the consistency or stability of the pattern. Ultimately, the researcher changes phases by implementing or withdrawing a treatment. The purpose for a phase change is to demonstrate that adding or removing a treatment produces a noticeable change in the pattern of behavior from one phase to the next.

Unlike other experimental designs, the results of a single-subject design are not evaluated with traditional tests for statistical significance. Instead, researchers must rely on graphs to convey the meaning of their results. The graph must show a clear change in behavior when the treatment is introduced. Also, the change in behavior must be replicated at least one more time to demonstrate that the first change was not a result of coincidence or chance.

Because the interpretation of the results depends entirely on the visual appearance of a graph, it is important that the change in pattern from baseline to treatment be easy to see when the results are presented in a graph. Visual inspection of single-subject data is, unfortunately, a very subjective task. However, four specific characteristics help determine whether there is meaningful change between phases: (1) change in the average level of behavior, (2) immediate change in level of behavior, (3) change in trend of behavior, and (4) latency of change in behavior.

Different types of single-subject designs were discussed, including the ABAB reversal design as well as more complex phase-change designs, variations of the multiple-baseline design, and other, less common single-subject designs. The primary advantage of single-subject designs is that they allow cause-and-effect relationships to be established with a single participant. In addition, the flexibility of these designs makes them well suited for clinical and other applied research. The primary disadvantage of single-subject research is that the results may be unique to the specific individual examined in the study.

KEY WORDS

single-subject designs, or
   single-case designs
phase
baseline observations
baseline phase
treatment observations
treatment phase
level
trend

stability
phase change
ABAB design, or reversal
   design
multiple-baseline design
multiple-baseline across
   subjects
multiple-baseline across
   behaviors

multiple-baseline across
   situations
dismantling design, or
   component-analysis
   design
changing-criterion design
alternating-treatments
   design, or discrete-trials
   design

EXERCISES

1. In addition to the key words, you should also be able to define the following terms: statistical significance, or statistically significant
practical significance or clinical significance
2. Describe the similarity between single-subject designs, case studies, and time-series designs.

3. Explain why single-subject designs are often preferred to traditional group designs for clinical research.
4. Describe how extraneous variables can threaten the internal validity of the results presented in Figure 15.1.
5. Describe how the level and trend of behavior can be used to define a pattern of

behavior in a graph showing the data from one phase of a single-subject design.

6. Describe the major difference between single-subject designs and other experimental designs.

7. Describe the three techniques that can be used to reveal a consistent pattern of behavior in situations in which the data appear to be unstable.

8. What is the purpose of a phase change?

9. Describe how changes in level and trend can each be used to evaluate data in a single-subject design.

10. Describe the advantages of the multiple-baseline design over the ABAB design.

11. Describe how the multiple-baseline design can be used to evaluate the treatment of one behavior in two participants.

12. Describe the importance of the reversal phase in the ABAB design.

13. Describe the strengths and weaknesses of the ABAB design.

14. Describe the strengths and weaknesses of the multiple-baseline design.

15. Describe the purpose of a dismantling design.

16. Describe the strengths and weaknesses of the changing-criterion design.

17. Describe the general strengths and weaknesses of single-subject designs.

18. Describe the strengths and weaknesses of the alternating-treatments design.

LEARNING ACTIVITIES

1. Draw a graph for an ABAB research design showing the data that would be obtained from a treatment with a permanent or long-lasting effect. Explain why the data you have drawn are not considered to be clear evidence for a cause-and-effect relationship between the treatment and the behavior.

2. Suppose that a complex therapy procedure contains one component that has absolutely no effect on behavior.
   a. Explain how a dismantling design could be used to demonstrate that the component has no effect.
   b. Draw a graph showing data that demonstrate that the component has no effect.

3. Suppose a researcher uses a multiple-baseline design to evaluate a therapy to treat two different problem behaviors for the same individual. Draw a graph showing the data that would be obtained if the therapy affected both behaviors simultaneously, even though the therapy was directed at only one behavior. Explain why the data you have drawn would not be considered to be clear evidence for a cause-and-effect relationship between the therapy and the behaviors.

WEB RESOURCES

Visit the Book Companion Website at **www .cengage.com/international** to access study tools including a glossary, flashcards, and web quizzing.

16

An Introduction to APA-Style Research Reports

CHAPTER OVERVIEW

In this chapter, we consider Step 9 of the research process: preparing a research report. A few general elements of APA style are considered. In addition, the details of the contents of each part of the research report are provided. Finally, the processes of submitting a manuscript for publication and writing a research proposal are discussed.

16.1 | THE GOAL OF A RESEARCH REPORT

Preparing a **research report** is Step 9 in the overall research process (see Chapter 1, p. 34). When the study is completed and the data are in and analyzed, it is time to share your work with others who are interested in the topic. Ideally, this means preparing a written report for future publication in a scientific journal. Perhaps your report will be presented as a poster or paper at a professional conference. Possibly, your report will be simply a classroom project to fulfill a course requirement. In any case, the research report fulfills one of the basic tenets of scientific investigation: science is public. Thus, your research is not finished until you have made it available to the rest of the scientific community.

The basic purpose of a good research report is to provide three kinds of information about the research study.

1. *What was done.* The report should describe in some detail the step-by-step process you followed to complete the research project.
2. *What was found.* The report should contain an objective description of the outcome. Typically, this involves the measurements that were taken, and the statistical summary and interpretation of those measurements.
3. *How your research study is related to other knowledge in the area.* As we noted in Chapter 2, a good research study does not stand alone, but rather grows out of an existing body of knowledge and adds to that body of knowledge. The research report should show the connections between the present study and past knowledge.

Although the prospect of writing an entire research report may appear overwhelming at first glance, several factors make this task more manageable. First, throughout the research process you have read and consulted many journal articles, each of which can be viewed as a good model of how your report should look. Second, if you have kept notes or maintained a journal of your research, you have an excellent foundation for preparing a formal report. Simply noting what background literature you consulted, how you used each journal article, how you obtained a sample for your study, what was done to individuals in your study, what each subject or participant actually did, and so on, should give you a very complete outline for the written report. Finally, you should realize that a research report is a very structured document. It is subdivided into separate, well-defined segments, and each segment has a specified content. You simply need to describe your own study, piece by piece, in each segment.

Although several styles exist for the preparation of research reports in various disciplines, in the following sections of this chapter, we examine the formal style and structure that have become the generally accepted convention for writing research reports in the behavioral sciences. This style and structure have evolved over the years, and the current guidelines are presented in the ***Publication Manual of the American Psychological Association*** (6th edition, 2010; henceforth referred to as the *Publication Manual*). The writing style developed by the American Psychological Association (known commonly as

If you are already familiar with the guidelines presented in the 5th edition *PM*, you can access information about what's new in the 6th edition, along with other information about the 6th edition *PM* at www.apastyle.org.

The 1st printing of the 6th edition *PM* has multiple errors. Check the copyright page (unnumbered p. iv) to determine which printing you are using. Lists of errors can be found at http://supp.apa.org/style/pubman-reprint-corrections-for-2e.pdf and corrected sample papers can be found at http://www.apastyle.org/manual/related/sample-experiment-paper-1.pdf.

APA style) is used by many publications throughout the behavioral sciences, however, it is not universal. If you are planning to submit a manuscript to a specific journal to be considered for publication, you should consult the journal's Instructions to Authors for specific information on style and submission requirements. Incidentally, you probably will find that writing a research report is very different from any other writing you have done.

We should also note that this chapter is only a brief summary of some of the more important aspects of APA format and style; for final answers you should consult the *Publication Manual* itself. In addition, to assist you with learning APA format and style, APA has also published a workbook, *Mastering APA Style: Student's Workbook and Training Guide 6e* and a pocket guide, *Concise Rules of APA Style*.

DEFINITION   A **research report** is a written description of a research study that includes a clear statement of the purpose of the research, a review of the relevant background literature that led to the research study, a description of the methods used to conduct the research, a summary of the research results, and a discussion and interpretation of the results.

 **LEARNING CHECK**   What is the purpose of a research report?

16.2 | GENERAL APA GUIDELINES FOR WRITING STYLE AND FORMAT

Appendix D contains an example of a complete research report manuscript. Portions of the manuscript appear as figures in this chapter.

Although your research report may eventually be published in a professionally formatted, two- or three-column journal, everyone must start with a typed or word-processed manuscript. The *Publication Manual* provides detailed information on the proper method of preparing a manuscript to be submitted for publication. The methods it presents are generally accepted and appropriate for most scientific writing. The goal of the *Publication Manual* is to establish a standardized style and format for scientific reports so that readers will know exactly where to find specific information within a report and will not be distracted by tangential topics or personalized writing styles.

Some Elements of Writing Style

A research report is not the same as creative writing. You are not trying to amuse, entertain, challenge, confuse, or surprise your reader. Instead, the goal is to provide a simple, straightforward description and explanation of your research study. The *Publication Manual* contains hundreds of guidelines and suggestions to help create a clear and precise manuscript, and we do not attempt to repeat all of them here. Because we present only a selected portion of the general guidelines, you would be wise to consult the *Publication Manual* directly when you actually write a research report. In addition, you can access some of its information, along with helpful tutorials, at www.apastyle.org. In the meantime, this discussion of four general elements of style will help you get a good start.

Impersonal Style

A research report is different from other types of literature and should be written in an objective style. Your goal is to provide a clear and concise report of the research study and its results. Avoid distracting the reader with literary devices such as alliteration, rhyming, deliberate ambiguity, or abrupt changes in topic. You should avoid colloquial expressions such as "once in a blue moon" (in place of "rarely"), and jargon such as "left-winger" (in place of "politically liberal"). You may use personal pronouns to describe what you did as a researcher, "I instructed the participants," but keep in mind that you are writing a research report, not a personal journal.

Verb Tense

When describing or discussing past events that occurred at a specific time, use the past tense (for example, "They demonstrated"). If the event did not occur at a specific time or is continuing into the present, use the present perfect tense ("Several studies have demonstrated"). This applies to the presentation of background material and previous research that is used to introduce your study and to the description of the methods used to conduct the study. When you present your results, always use the past tense ("the scores increased"). After you have described the study and presented the results, switch to the present tense to discuss the results and your conclusions ("the data suggest").

Reducing Biased Language

Scientific writing should be free of implied or irrelevant evaluation of groups. Therefore, when describing or discussing characteristics of participants, avoid implying bias against people on the basis of gender, sexual orientation, racial or ethnic group, disability, or age. The *Publication Manual* gives three guidelines for avoiding biased language. First, describe people with a level of specificity that is accurate. For example, when describing ethnic groups, instead of general terms such as Asian American or Hispanic American, use Korean American or Mexican American. Second, be sensitive to labels; call people what they prefer to be called. For example, "people diagnosed with schizophrenia" and "older adults" are currently preferred to "schizophrenics" and "the elderly." In addition, for example, Black and African American are preferred to the older terms Negro and Afro-American. And keep in mind that over time, preferences change. Third, acknowledge people's participation in your study. For example, instead of "the participants were run in the study," write "the students completed the survey," or "participants completed the study." The *Publication Manual* provides the details of these guidelines as well as further information about avoiding biased language.

Citations

Throughout your manuscript, you will cite the published research of other scientists. Other research results are cited as background for your hypothesis, to establish a basis for any claims or facts you assert, and to credit those who prepared the foundation for your own work. Recall from Section 4.4 that using someone else's ideas or words as your own is **plagiarism,** a serious breach of ethics. See Chapter 3 (pp. 96–98) for further discussion and examples of plagiarism. Whenever you assert a fact that may not be common knowledge or refer to a previous research finding, you must provide a **citation** that identifies your source. Citation of a source means that you read the cited work. The APA convention for a citation requires that you identify the author(s) and the year of publication. Although there are a variety of methods for accomplishing this goal, two formats are commonly used for citation:

1. State a fact or make a claim in the text; then cite your source in parentheses within the same sentence. In this case, the author(s) last name(s) and the date of publication appear outside the body of the sentence (that is, contained within parentheses). For example:

   It has been demonstrated that immediate recall is extremely limited for 5-year-old children (Jones, 2008).
   Previous research has shown that response to an auditory stimulus is much faster than response to a visual stimulus (Smith & Jones, 2009).

2. You may want to use the source as the subject of your sentence. In this case, the author(s) name(s) appear within the body of the sentence and only the year of publication is noted in parentheses. For example:

   In a related study, Jones (2008) found that...
   Smith and Jones (2009) found that...

With multiple authors, note that an ampersand (the symbol "&") is used before the last author's name when you cite your source in parentheses. Also note that the word "and" is used before the last author's name when your source is the subject of your sentence. A few additional commonly used citation rules include the following:

1. When a publication has one or two authors, you cite all the author's last names and the date every time you refer to this item in your text.
2. When a publication has three to five authors, you cite all of the author's last names and the date the first time you refer to this item in your text. In subsequent citations, you only include the first author's last name followed by "et al." and the date. For example:

First time cited in text:

   It has been found that word recall decreases as a function of age (Jones, Smith, & Brown, 2002).

Or

   In a related study, Jones, Smith, and Brown (2002) found that...

Subsequent times cited in text:

   It has also been found that word recognition decreases as a function of age (Jones et al., 2002).

Or

   Jones et al. (2002) found that...

3. When a publication has six or more authors, you only include the first author's last name followed by "et al." and the date for the first and subsequent citations.

4. When you are citing more than one publication within the same parentheses, you list them in alphabetical order by the first authors' last names and separate the items with a semicolon. For example,

Several studies (Jones, Smith, & Brown, 2002; Smith & Jones, 2009) found that...

In any case, the citation should provide enough information for the reader to find the complete reference in your list of references at the end of the paper. Note that the APA convention for a citation requires that you identify only the author(s) and the year of publication. Specifically, you do not include the authors' first names, the name of the institution where the research was done, the title of the article, the name of the journal, or the volume number and pages. In addition, APA conventions allow you to simplify subsequent citations if a particular publication has already been cited within the same paper. See Table 16.1 for a summary of the rules and some examples of citations.

It also is customary to distinguish between citations of empirical results and citations of theory or interpretation. To report an empirical result, for example, you could use:

Jones (2008) demonstrated...

To cite a theory or speculation, for example, you might use:

Jones (2008) argued...

DEFINITION A **citation** identifies the author(s) and the year of publication of the source of a specific fact or idea mentioned in a research report. The citation provides enough information for a reader to locate the full reference in the list of references at the end of the report.

As a general rule, be conservative about the references you include in a research report, especially a report of an empirical study. References should

TABLE **16.1**
Examples of Original and Subsequent Citations

Number of Authors	First Time in Text	Subsequent Times in Text	First Time in Parentheses	Subsequent Times in Parentheses
1	Jones (2008)	Jones (2008)	(Jones, 2008)	(Jones, 2008)
2	Smith and Jones (2009)	Smith and Jones (2009)	(Smith & Jones, 2009)	(Smith & Jones, 2009)
3-5	Jones, Smith, and Brown (2002)	Jones et al. (2002)	(Jones, Smith, & Brown, 2002)	(Jones et al., 2002)
6 or more	Jones et al. (2007)	Jones et al. (2007)	(Jones et al., 2007)	(Jones et al., 2007)

all be directly relevant to the study that you are presenting. Your goal is to describe and explain your study, not to provide readers with a complete literature review that summarizes every publication that may be remotely related. Select only those references that are truly useful and contribute to your arguments.

As a general rule, it is better to paraphrase a point using your own words than to quote directly from another work. There are rare occasions when direct quotations can be useful, but they should be used only when it is necessary to preserve the whole essence of the original statements. Thus, quotations should be used sparingly. When directly quoting from another work, in addition to identifying the author(s) and year of publication, you must also provide a page number (or paragraph number in the case of online sources without page numbers). For short quotations, fewer than 40 words, the quotation is embedded in the text with quotation marks at both ends. For example,

> Resenhoeft, Villa, and Wiseman (2008) report that participants judged a model without a visible tattoo as "more attractive, athletic, and intelligent than the same model shown with a tattoo" (p. 594).

Quotations of 40 or more words are presented as an indented block, separate from the other text, and without any quotation marks. For example,

> Fontes (2004) offers several recommendations to help protect the confidentiality and safety of individuals participating in studies investigating violence against women and girls, including the following:
>> Interviewers should be trained to terminate or change the subject of discussion if the interview is interrupted by anyone. Researchers can have a questionnaire on a less sensitive topic in women's health (e.g., menstruation or eating habits) to "switch to" if they are interrupted. Researchers should forewarn respondents that they will switch to this other topic if the interview is interrupted. (p. 155)

But remember that, whenever you paraphrase someone else's work or use direct quotations, you need to provide a citation to give them credit.

LEARNING CHECK   What is the *Publication Manual* and what is its purpose?

Guidelines for Typing or Word Processing

The general APA guidelines require that a manuscript be double-spaced (with the exception that tables and figures may be single-spaced) with at least a 1" margin on all sides (8½ × 11" page). In addition, the text should have a straight left-hand margin but an uneven or ragged right-hand margin without hyphenation (breaking words at the ends of lines). Indent the first line of each paragraph five to seven spaces; indentation should be consistent throughout the manuscript. For APA publications, the preferred typeface is 12-point Times New Roman. This uniform format serves several purposes. First, it ensures a lot of blank space on every page to allow editors, reviewers, or professors to make comments or corrections. In addition, uniform spacing makes it possible for editors to estimate the length of a printed article from the number of pages in a manuscript.

Manuscript Pages

In addition to the body of the manuscript (the basic text that describes the research study), a research report consists of several other parts that are necessary to form a complete manuscript. In section 16.3, we discuss each of these parts in much more detail, but, for now, note that they are organized in the following order, with each part starting on its own separate page:

Title Page: Title, author's name and affiliation, and the author note. Page 1.

Abstract: A brief summary of the research report. Page 2.

Text: This is the body of the research report (containing four sections: introduction, method, results, and discussion) beginning on page 3.

References: Listed together, starting on a new page.

Tables: Each table starts on a new page.

Figures: Each figure starts on a new page and includes a caption on the same page.

Appendices (if any): Each appendix starts on a new page.

16.3 | THE ELEMENTS OF AN APA-STYLE RESEARCH REPORT

In the previous section, we identified the components of a complete manuscript. In this section, we look in more detail at the contents of each part, dividing the body of the manuscript into additional subsections that make up the majority of a research report.

Title Page

The **title page** is the first page of the manuscript and contains, in order from top to bottom of the page, the running head and page number (1), the title of the paper, the author names (byline) and affiliations, and author note.

Running Head and Page Number

The first line of the title page is the running head and the page number 1. The **running head** is a complete, but abbreviated, title that contains a maximum of 50 characters, including spaces and punctuation. On the title page, the running head begins at the left margin with the phrase, Running head: followed by the abbreviated title, all in capital letters. The page number appears at the right margin. An example of a running head and page number on a title page would appear as follows:

Running head: SCHOOL SIZE AND CYBERBULLYING   1

The running head (without the phrase *Running head* typed out) and page number run consecutively on every page of the manuscript. An example of a running head and page number on all subsequent pages after the title page would appear as follows:

SCHOOL SIZE AND CYBERBULLYING   2

The pages are numbered consecutively, starting with the title page, so that the manuscript can be reassembled if the pages become mixed, and to allow editors and reviewers to refer to specific items by their page number. To have the running head and page number appear on each page of the manuscript, generate them using headers in a word-processing program. Do not manually type this information in on each page. In a published article, the running head appears at the top of the pages to identify the article for the readers.

Title

The title, typed in upper and lower case letters, is positioned in the upper half of the page centered between the left and right margins. It is recommended that a title be no more than 12 words in length. The title should be a concise statement that describes your study as accurately and completely as possible. It should identify the main variables or theories, and the relationships being investigated. Keep in mind that the words used in the title are often the basis for indexing and referencing your paper. Also remember that the title gives the first impression of your paper and often determines whether an individual reads the rest of the article. (Recall that in section 2.4, we discussed using the title of an article as a first basis for deciding whether or not to read the rest of the article.) Following are some general guidelines for writing a title:

1. Avoid unnecessary words. It is tempting to begin your title with "A study of" or "The relationship between." However, these phrases usually do not add any useful information and can be deleted with no negative consequences.
2. If possible, the first word in the title should be of special relevance or importance to the content of the paper. If your main topic concerns gender stereotypes, try to begin your title with "Gender stereotypes." Again, your title gives the first impression of the article and the first few words provide the first impression of the title.
3. Avoid cute or catchy titles. For example, newspaper headlines often use catchy phrases to attract the reader's attention. However, this type of title is usually not appropriate for a research study because it typically does not provide the reader with much information about the content of the article.

Author Name(s) (Byline) and Affiliation

Immediately following the title, centered on the next double-spaced lines, are the author's name(s), followed by the institution(s) where each researcher was when the research was conducted (without the words *by* or *from*). If there are multiple authors, the order of the names is usually significant; the first author listed is typically the individual who made the primary contribution to the

---

To set up the running head, in Microsoft Word, click View on the toolbar and select Header and Footer. On the Header and Footer toolbar, click File and select Page Setup. The popup box contains a checkbox for "different first page." Check that box to have the words *Running head:* followed by the abbreviated title, all in capital letters, appear in the header on the title page, and only the abbreviated title, all in capital letters (without the words *Running head*) appear in the header on all subsequent pages of the manuscript.

research, and the remaining authors are listed in descending order of their contributions.

The **author note** is placed on the title page, several lines below the title, byline, and affiliation. The words Author Note are centered on one line with the paragraphs comprising the author note beginning on the next double-spaced line. Typically the author note contains four paragraphs, each paragraph starting with an indent, that provide details about the authors, including:

- Departmental affiliation.
- Changes in affiliation (if any) since the time that the research was conducted.
- Acknowledgements of sources of financial support for the research (if any), and recognition of others who contributed or assisted with the study (if any). Disclosure of special circumstances (if any).
- Identification of a contact person if a reader wants further information.

You may have noticed that individual identification (such as your name) appears only on the title page. This allows editors to create a completely anonymous manuscript by simply removing the title page. The anonymous manuscript can then be forwarded to reviewers who will not be influenced by the author's reputation but can give an unbiased review based solely on the quality of the research study. Many journals are now requesting that manuscripts be submitted electronically.

A title page from an APA-style manuscript, illustrating all of these elements, is shown in Figure 16.1. The complete manuscript is in Appendix D.

Throughout this chapter, we use a series of figures to illustrate different parts of a manuscript. The figures present portions of an edited adaptation of a research manuscript prepared by undergraduate student Danielle Gentile as part of a course requirement at The College at Brockport, State University of New York. A complete copy of the edited manuscript appears in Appendix D.

DEFINITIONS

The **title page** is the first page of a research report manuscript and contains the running head and page number (1), the title of the paper, the author names (byline) and affiliations, and the author note.

A **running head** is an abbreviated title for a research report containing a maximum of 50 characters and is printed on every page of the manuscript, flush left, on the same line as the page number, which is printed at the right margin. The running head appears at the top of the pages if the manuscript becomes a published article.

LEARNING CHECK

Describe where the running head appears in a manuscript and what purpose it serves.

Abstract

The **abstract** is a concise summary of the paper that focuses on what was done and what was found. The abstract appears alone on page 2 of the manuscript. The word Abstract is centered at the top of page 2, and the one-paragraph summary starts on the next double-spaced line with no paragraph indentation. Although the abstract appears on page 2 of your manuscript, the abstract typically is written last, after the rest of the paper is done. It is considered the most

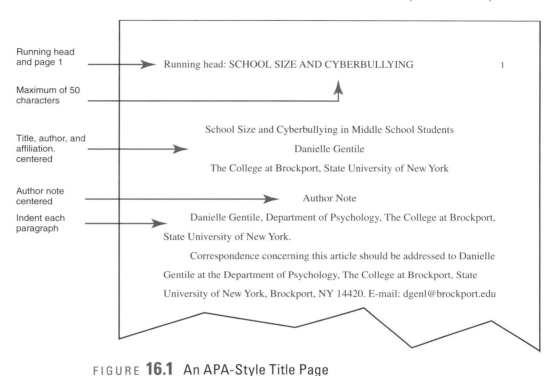

FIGURE **16.1** An APA-Style Title Page

important section of a research report. With the possible exception of the title, the abstract is the section that most people read and use to decide whether to seek out and read the entire article. (In section 2.4, we discussed using the abstract of an article as a second screening device, after the title, for deciding whether to read the rest of the article.)

For most journals the word limit for an abstract ranges from 150 to 250 words. It should be a self-contained summary that does not add to or evaluate the body of the paper. The abstract of an empirical study should include the following elements, not necessarily in this order.

1. A one-sentence statement of the problem or research question
2. A brief description of the subjects or participants (identifying how many and any relevant characteristics)
3. A brief description of the research method and procedures
4. A report of the results
5. A statement about the conclusions or implications

The abstract of an APA-style manuscript is shown in Figure 16.2. The complete manuscript is in Appendix D.

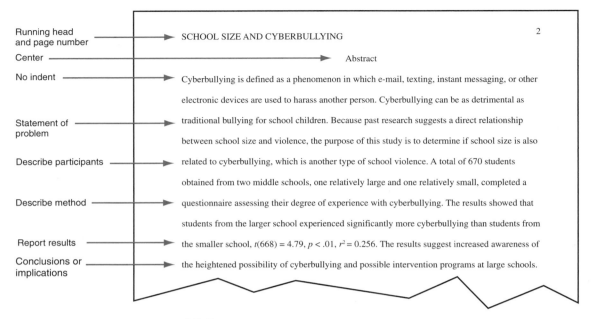

FIGURE **16.2** An APA-Style Abstract

DEFINITION The **abstract** is a brief summary of the research study totaling between 150 to 250 words. The abstract focuses on what was done and what was found in the study.

LEARNING CHECK Describe the elements of an abstract.

Introduction

The first major section of the body or text of a research report is the introduction. The **introduction** provides the background and orientation that introduces the reader to your research study. The introduction should identify the question or problem that your study addresses, and explain why the problem is important; it should explain how you arrived at the question from the previous research in the area; it should identify the hypotheses and how they relate to the research design; and it should explain the implications of the study. A good introduction should address these issues in a few pages. The introduction begins on page 3 of your manuscript. It is identified by centering the title of the article (exactly as it appears on the title page) at the top of the page. The first paragraph of the introduction begins with a paragraph indentation on the next double-spaced line. An introduction typically consists of the following four parts, not necessarily in this order (the parts are not labeled).

1. Typically, this section begins with a general introduction to the topic of the paper. In a few sentences or paragraphs, describe the issue investigated and why this problem is important and deserves new research.
2. Next is a review of the relevant literature. You do not need to review and discuss everything that has been published in the area, only the articles that are directly relevant to your research question. Discuss only relevant sections of previous work. Identify and cite the important points along the way, but do not provide detailed descriptions. The literature review should not be an article-by-article description of one study after another; instead, the articles should be presented in an integrated manner. Taken together, your literature review should provide a rationale for your study. Remember, you are taking your readers down a logical path that leads to your research question.
3. Ultimately, the introduction reaches the specific problem, hypothesis, or question that the research study addresses. State the problem or purpose of your study, and clearly define the relevant variables. The review of the literature should lead directly to the purpose of or the rationale for your study.
4. Describe the research strategy that was used to evaluate your hypothesis or to obtain an answer to your research question. Briefly outline the methodology used for the study (the details of which are provided in the next section of the report, the method section). At this point, simply provide a snapshot of how the study was conducted so the reader is prepared for the upcoming details. Also explain how the research strategy provides the information necessary to address your hypothesis or research question.

If the introduction is well written, your readers will finish the final paragraphs with a clear understanding of the problem you intend to address, the rationale that led to the problem, and a basic understanding of how you answered the problem. Figure 16.3 shows portions of the introduction of an APA-style manuscript. The complete introduction and the rest of the manuscript are in Appendix D.

DEFINITION	The **introduction** is the first major section of text in a research report. The introduction presents a logical development of the research question, including a review of the relevant background literature, a statement of the research question or hypothesis, and a brief description of the methods used to answer the question or test the hypothesis.

LEARNING CHECK	Describe the major elements of the introduction for an empirical research report.

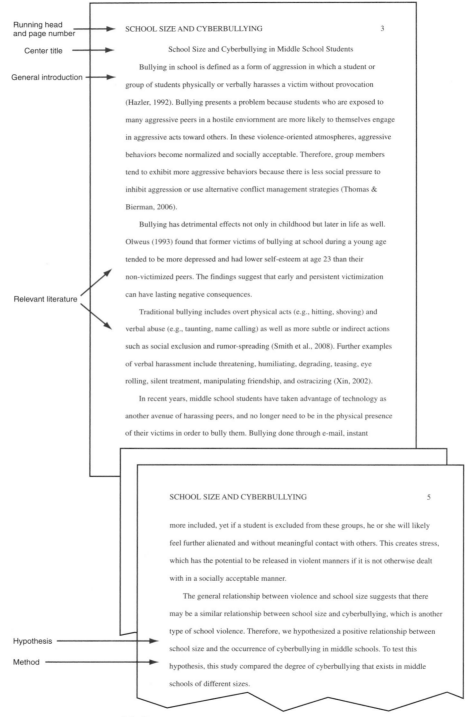

FIGURE **16.3** Excerpts from an APA-Style Introduction

Method

The second major section of the body or the text of a research report is the method section. The **method section** provides a relatively detailed description of exactly how the variables were defined and measured and how the research study was conducted. Other researchers should be able to read your method section and obtain enough information to determine whether your research strategy adequately addresses the question you hope to answer. It also allows other researchers to duplicate all of the essential elements of your research study. The method section immediately follows the introduction. Do not start a new page. Instead, after the last line of the introduction, on the next double-spaced line, type the word Method, centered and in boldface. Usually, a method section is divided into two subsections: Subjects or Participants, and Procedure. Each subsection heading is presented at the left margin in boldface with uppercase and lowercase letters.

The first major subsection of the method section is either the **subjects subsection** (for nonhumans) or the **participants subsection** (for humans). This subsection describes the sample that participated in the study. For nonhumans, describe (1) the number of animals used in the study, (2) their genus, species, and strain, (3) the supplier, (4) how the animals were housed and handled, and (5) their specific characteristics, including sex, weight, and age. For humans, it is customary to report (1) the number of participants, (2) eligibility and exclusion criteria, (3) basic demographic characteristics of the group, including age, gender and ethnicity, and (4) any other characteristics relevant to the study (for example, IQ or psychopathology diagnosis).

The second major subsection of the method section is the procedure subsection. The **procedure subsection** provides a description of the step-by-step process used to complete the study. Include (1) a description of selection procedures, (2) the settings and locations in which data were collected, (3) any payments made to participants, (4) ethical standards met and safety-monitoring procedures, (5) any methods used to divide or assign participants into groups or conditions and how many individuals were in each condition, (6) a description of instructions given to participants, (7) the research design, (8) any experimental manipulation or intervention, and (9) any apparatus or materials that were used.

If portions of your study are complex or require detailed description, additional subsections can be added. One example is entitled either Apparatus or Materials. This subsection describes any apparatus (equipment) or materials (questionnaires and the like) used in the study. Occasionally, both subsections are included in a research report. In an **apparatus subsection,** common items such as chairs, tables, and stopwatches are mentioned without a lot of detail. The more specialized the equipment, the more detail is needed. For custom-made equipment, a figure or picture is required as well. For studies that use questionnaires, a common additional subsection is a **materials subsection.** The materials subsection includes identification of the variables and how they were operationalized; that is, how they were defined and measured. Each questionnaire used in the study requires a description, a citation, and an explanation of its function in the study (what it was used to measure). Also include information on the instrument's psychometric properties (evidence of reliability and

The term *operationalized* is an example of jargon, meaning "operationally defined" (see p. 105).

validity). For a new questionnaire that you developed for the purposes of your study, it is also necessary to provide a copy of the measure in an appendix.

Figure 16.4 shows portions of the method section of an APA-style manuscript. The complete method section and the rest of the manuscript are in Appendix D. Notice that the sample manuscript uses two subsections.

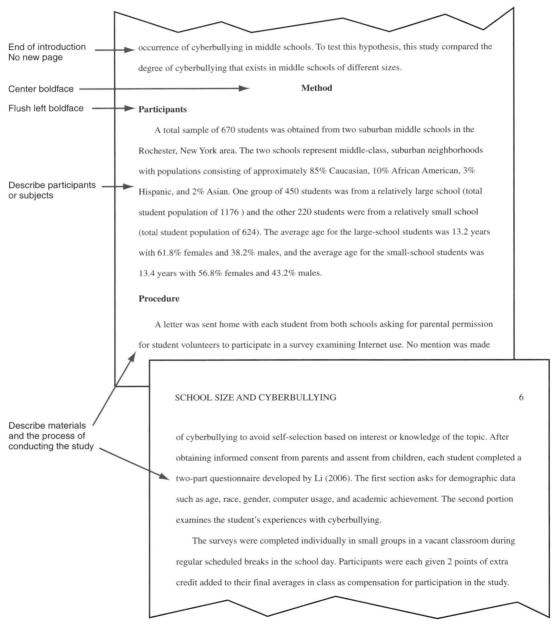

FIGURE **16.4** An APA-Style Method Section

| **DEFINITION** | The **method section** of a research report describes how the study was conducted including information about the subjects or participants, and the procedures used. |

|  **LEARNING CHECK** | Identify the two major subsections of the method section and describe the contents of each. |

Results

The third major section of the body or text of the research report is the results section. The **results section** presents a summary of the data and the statistical analyses. The results section immediately follows the method section. Do not start a new page. Instead, after the last line of the method section, on the next double-spaced line, type Results, centered and in boldface. The first paragraph in the results section is indented and begins on the next double-spaced line.

The results section simply provides a complete and unbiased reporting of the findings, just the facts, with no discussion of the findings. Usually, a results section begins with a statement of the primary outcome of the study, followed by the basic descriptive statistics (usually means and standard deviations), then the inferential statistics (usually the results of hypothesis tests), and finally the measures of effect size. If the study was relatively complex, it may be best to summarize the data in a table or a figure. However, with only a few means and inferential tests, it usually is more practical to report the results as text. Note that figures and tables are not included in the results section but are placed at the end of the manuscript. Figures and tables are numbered (for example, Table 1 or Figure 1), and are referred to by number in the text.

Reports of statistical significance should be made in a statement that identifies (1) the type of test used, (2) the degrees of freedom, (3) the outcome of the test, (4) the level of significance, and (5) the size and direction of the effect. When reporting the level of significance, you are encouraged to use the exact probability value (as provided by most computer programs), or you may use a traditional alpha level (.05, .01, .001) as a point of reference. For example, a report using an exact probability might state "The results indicated a significant mean difference between groups, $F(1, 36) = 4.37$, $p = .006$, $\eta^2 = 0.12$." With a traditional alpha level, the same result would be reported as "The results indicated a significant mean difference between groups, $F(1, 36) = 4.37$, $p < .01$, $\eta^2 = 0.12$." Figure 16.5 shows portions of the results section of an APA-style manuscript. The complete results section and the rest of the manuscript are in Appendix D.

> Statistical tests of significance and measures of effect size are discussed in Chapter 14.

| **DEFINITION** | The **results section** of a research report presents a summary of the data and the statistical analysis. |

Discussion

The fourth and final major section of the body or text of a research report is the discussion section. In the **discussion section,** you offer interpretation, evaluation, and discussion of the implications of your findings. The discussion

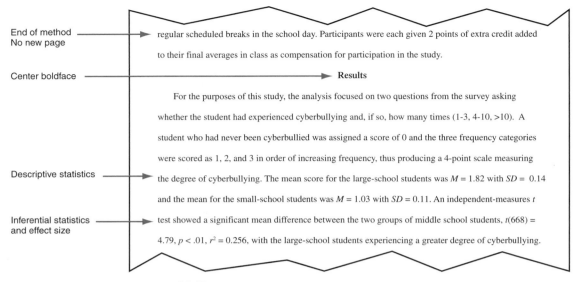

End of method
No new page

regular scheduled breaks in the school day. Participants were each given 2 points of extra credit added

to their final averages in class as compensation for participation in the study.

Center boldface

Results

For the purposes of this study, the analysis focused on two questions from the survey asking

whether the student had experienced cyberbullying and, if so, how many times (1-3, 4-10, >10). A

student who had never been cyberbullied was assigned a score of 0 and the three frequency categories

were scored as 1, 2, and 3 in order of increasing frequency, thus producing a 4-point scale measuring

Descriptive statistics

the degree of cyberbullying. The mean score for the large-school students was $M = 1.82$ with $SD = 0.14$

and the mean for the small-school students was $M = 1.03$ with $SD = 0.11$. An independent-measures t

Inferential statistics
and effect size

test showed a significant mean difference between the two groups of middle school students, $t(668) =$

$4.79, p < .01, r^2 = 0.256$, with the large-school students experiencing a greater degree of cyberbullying.

FIGURE **16.5** An APA-Style Results Section

section immediately follows the results section. Do not start a new page; instead, after the last line of the results section, on the next double-spaced line, type Discussion, centered and in boldface. The first paragraph of the discussion section is indented and begins on the next double-spaced line.

The discussion section should begin with a restatement of the hypothesis. (Recall that your hypothesis is first presented at the end of the introduction.) Next, briefly restate your major results, and indicate how they either support or fail to support your primary hypothesis. Note that the results are described in a sentence format without repeating all the numerical statistics that appear in the results section. Next, relate your results to the work of others, explaining how your outcome fits into the existing structure of knowledge of the area. It is also common to identify any limitations of the research, especially factors that affect the generalization of the results.

It can be helpful to think of the discussion section as a mirror image of the introduction. Remember, the introduction moved from general to specific, using items from the literature to focus on a specific hypothesis. Now, in the discussion section, you begin with a specific hypothesis (your outcome) and relate it back to the existing literature. Do not simply repeat statements from the introduction, but you may find it useful to mention some of the same references you used earlier to make new points relating your results to the other work.

In the last paragraphs of the discussion section, you may reach beyond the actual results and begin to consider their implications and/or applications. This corresponds to Step 10 in the research process, refining or reformulating a research idea (see Chapter 1, p. 35). Your results may support or challenge existing theories, suggest changes in practical, day-to-day interactions, or indicate new interpretations of previous research results. Any of these is an appropriate topic for a discussion section, and each can lead to new ideas for future research.

If your results support your original hypothesis, it is now possible to test the boundaries of your findings by extending the research to new environments or different populations. If the research results do not support your hypothesis, then more research is needed to find out why. It is common, at the end of the discussion section, to pose problems that remain unsolved as the result of the findings of the study. This never-ending process of asking questions, gathering evidence, and asking new questions is part of the general scientific method. The answer to a research question is always open to challenge. Figure 16.6 shows portions of the discussion section of an APA-style manuscript. The complete discussion section and the rest of the manuscript are in Appendix D.

DEFINITION

The **discussion section** of a research report restates the hypothesis, summarizes the results, and then presents a discussion of the interpretation, implications, and possible applications of the results.

LEARNING CHECK

For each of the following, identify the section of a research report that would probably contain the desired information:

How many individuals participated in the study and what are their characteristics?

Why was the study done?

Did the study use any questionnaires or unusual measurement techniques?

Did the study produce a statistically significant result?

What are the implications of the results and how might they be applied?

References

Beginning on a new page, with the centered title, References, the **reference section** provides complete information about each item cited in the manuscript. Notice that there is a precise one-to-one relationship between the items listed in the references and the items cited in the paper. Each item cited must appear in the references, and each item in the references must have been cited in the body of the report. The references are listed alphabetically by the last name of the first author. One-author entries precede multiple-author entries beginning with the same first author. References with the same author or authors in the same order are listed chronologically from oldest to most recent publication date. Figure 16.7 shows the first page of the reference section of an APA-style manuscript. The complete reference section and the rest of the manuscript are in Appendix D.

DEFINITION

The **reference section** of a research report is a listing of complete references for all sources of information cited in the report, organized alphabetically by the last name of the first author.

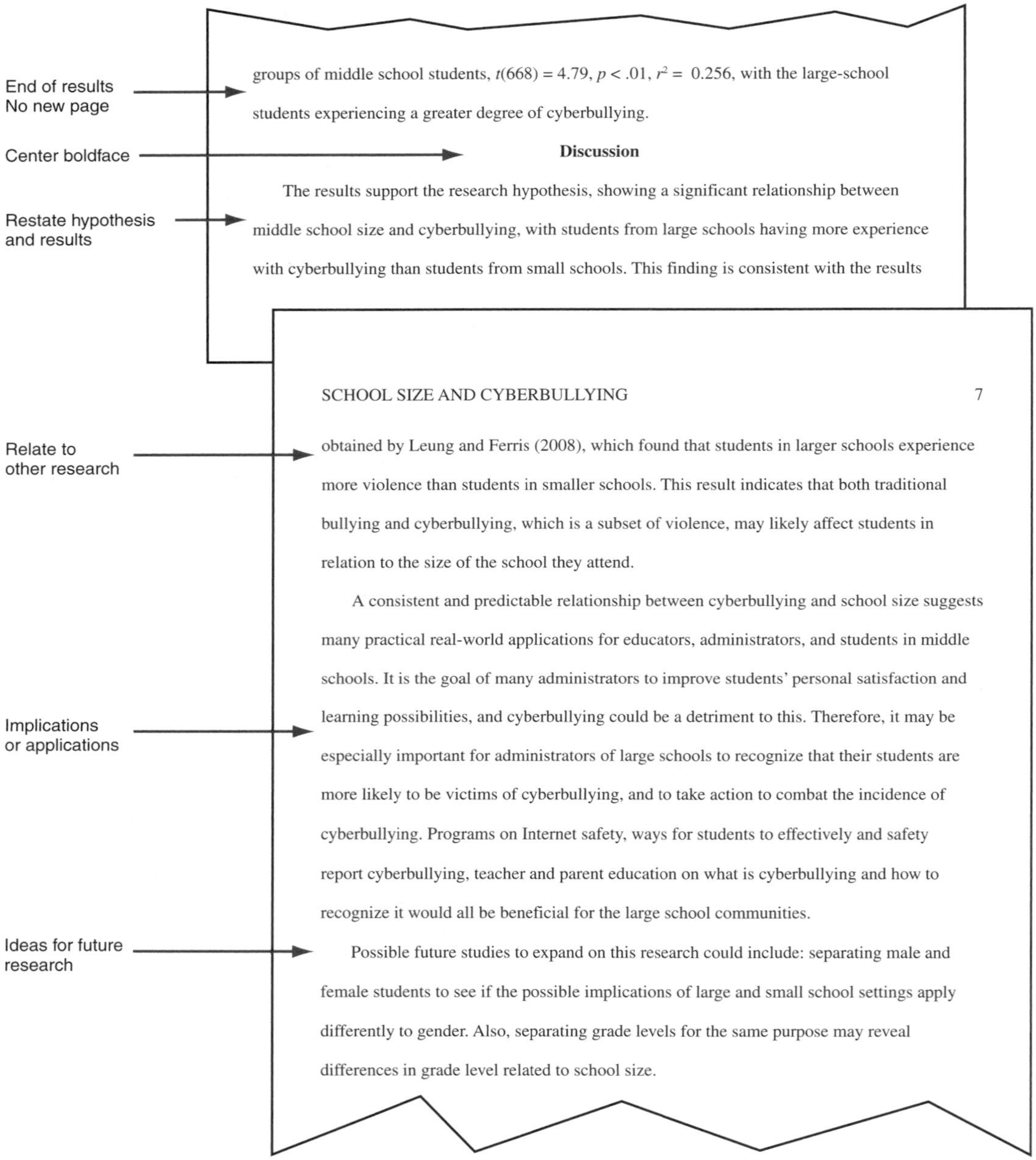

End of results
No new page →

Center boldface →

Restate hypothesis
and results →

Relate to
other research →

Implications
or applications →

Ideas for future
research →

groups of middle school students, $t(668) = 4.79$, $p < .01$, $r^2 = 0.256$, with the large-school

students experiencing a greater degree of cyberbullying.

Discussion

The results support the research hypothesis, showing a significant relationship between

middle school size and cyberbullying, with students from large schools having more experience

with cyberbullying than students from small schools. This finding is consistent with the results

SCHOOL SIZE AND CYBERBULLYING   7

obtained by Leung and Ferris (2008), which found that students in larger schools experience

more violence than students in smaller schools. This result indicates that both traditional

bullying and cyberbullying, which is a subset of violence, may likely affect students in

relation to the size of the school they attend.

A consistent and predictable relationship between cyberbullying and school size suggests

many practical real-world applications for educators, administrators, and students in middle

schools. It is the goal of many administrators to improve students' personal satisfaction and

learning possibilities, and cyberbullying could be a detriment to this. Therefore, it may be

especially important for administrators of large schools to recognize that their students are

more likely to be victims of cyberbullying, and to take action to combat the incidence of

cyberbullying. Programs on Internet safety, ways for students to effectively and safety

report cyberbullying, teacher and parent education on what is cyberbullying and how to

recognize it would all be beneficial for the large school communities.

Possible future studies to expand on this research could include: separating male and

female students to see if the possible implications of large and small school settings apply

differently to gender. Also, separating grade levels for the same purpose may reveal

differences in grade level related to school size.

FIGURE **16.6** An APA-Style Discussion Section

Table 16.2 presents examples of proper formatting of the most commonly used types of references. Note that the *Publication Manual* provides formats for more than 100 types and variations of referenced works. As a general rule, direct readers as closely as possible to a persistent link for the source used. Many publishers now identify individual publications with a unique digital

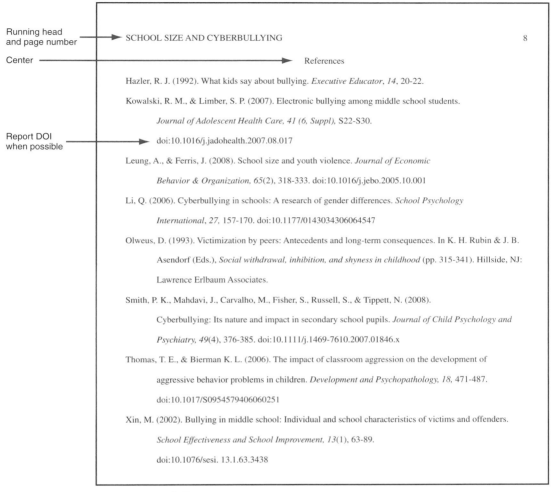

FIGURE **16.7** An APA-Style References Section

object identifier (DOI) that provides continuous access to the item. When a DOI is available, it is recommended that you include it for both print and electronic sources. DOIs are typically located at the top of the first page of a journal article, or in the Detailed Record of PsycINFO. All DOIs begin with the number 10. If no DOI is available, provide the homepage URL of the journal or the book. In general it is no longer necessary to include database information or retrieval dates unless the material may change over time.

Tables and Figures

The final sections of the manuscript present any tables and figures used to illustrate points or present results. As a general rule, tables and figures supplement the text; they should not duplicate information that has already been presented in text form, and they should not be completely independent of the

TABLE **16.2**
Common Reference Formats and Examples

Journal Article with DOI Assigned

Begin with the author's last name and initials, followed by the year of publication in parentheses. With multiple authors, list each author's last name and initials, with authors separated by commas. An ampersand (&) is used instead of the word *and* before the final author. Then list the title of the journal article, the name of the journal (in italics), volume number (in italics), and the pages for the article. End with the digital object identifier (DOI) as a unique identifier of and link to the item. Note that no database name (e.g., PsycArticles) or URL is needed when a DOI is available.

Example

McNall, L. A., & Roch, S. G. (2007). Effects of electronic monitoring types on perceptions of procedural justice, interpersonal justice, and privacy. *Journal of Applied Social Psychology, 37,* 658–682. doi:10.1111/j.1559-1816.2007.00179.x

Journal Article without DOI

Begin with the author's last name and initials, followed by the year of publication in parentheses. Then list the title of the journal article, the name of the journal (in italics), volume number (in italics), and the pages for the article. If a URL is available, provide it.

Examples

Mazur, J. E. (2007). Choice in a successive-encounters procedure and hyperbolic decay of reinforcement. *Journal of the Experimental Analysis of Behavior, 88,* 73–86. Retrieved from http://seab.envmed.rochester.edu/jeab/articles/2007/jeab-88-01-0073.pdf

Miller, R. J. (2007). Another slant on the oblique effect in drawings and paintings. *Empirical Studies of the Arts, 25,* 41–61.

Entire Book, Print Version

Begin with the author's last name and initials; if there are multiple authors, list them exactly as in a journal article. Follow with the book title (in italics), the city and state of the publisher, and the name of the publisher.

Example

Gravetter, F. J., & Forzano, L. B. (2012). *Research methods for the behavioral sciences* (4th ed.). Belmont, CA: Wadsworth.

Book Chapter

This reference consists of two parts: a reference for the chapter and a reference for the edited book. The reference for the chapter or article consists of the author's (or authors') name listed exactly as in a journal article, the year of publication in parentheses, and the title of the chapter or article. The reference for the edited book begins with the word *In*, followed by the name (or names) of the editor (initials first, then last name) followed by (Ed.) for a single editor or (Eds.) for multiple editors. Then list the name of the book (in italics), the page numbers of the article or chapter, the city and state of the publisher, and the name of the publisher. If electronic version of book chapter is available, include the DOI or URL.

Example

Gillespie, J. F. (2003). Social competency, adolescence. In T. P. Gullotta & M. Bloom (Eds.), *Encyclopedia of primary prevention and health promotion* (pp. 1004–1009). New York, NY: Kluwer Academic/Plenum.

text. Instead, any table or figure should be mentioned in the text by number, and the text should point out some of the more important aspects of the figure or table.

Tables, formatted according to APA specifications, are each typed separately on a new page. The table number and title, respectively, are displayed at the top of the page, each at the left margin. The title or header for the table should describe what information is included in the table. The title is printed in italics. Three types of notes may appear below the table and are used to provide further explanation for elements of the table. *General notes* refer to the entire table and begin with *Note* (italic and followed by a period). *Specific notes* refer to items in the table that have been identified with superscript, lowercase letters (for example, [a], [b]) and each note begins with the corresponding letter (superscript and lowercase). *Probability notes* identify the level of significance for statistics reported in the table that have been identified with one or more asterisks (for example, $*p < .05$, $**p < .01$). Tables may be printed either single- or double-spaced, to enhance readability.

The figures are included next, prepared according to APA specifications, each on a new page, as final artwork or photographs. A figure number and caption is placed directly below the figure. The caption is a concise explanation of the figure and serves as the figure title. The word *Figure* and the number appears at the left margin in italics. Only the "F" in Figure is capitalized, and the figure number is followed by a period. The figure caption immediately follows on the same line.

Appendix

An **appendix** may be included as a means of presenting detailed information that is useful but would interrupt the flow of text if it were presented in the body of the paper. Examples of items that might be presented in an appendix are a copy of a questionnaire, a computer program, a detailed description of an unusual or complex piece of equipment, and detailed instructions to participants. Appendices each start on a new page with the centered title, Appendix, and are identified by consecutive letters (A, B, C, and so on) if there is more than one (for example, Appendix A).

Table 16.3 lists, in order, the parts of a complete research report. For each part, we have identified the APA formatting issues to be considered, in a checklist format.

Conference Presentations: Papers and Posters

Thus far our discussion has focused on preparing a written research report for future publication in a scientific journal. An alternative way to prepare a research report, and hence make your research available to the rest of the scientific community, is to present it as a paper or poster at a professional conference. Typically, this kind of research report consists of two phases: first, a written summary or abstract is submitted to the conference organizers for approval, and second, the actual oral presentation or poster is made.

Typically a paper presentation at a conference is a 1-hour session during which several researchers each present their research in a related area. An oral presentation at a conference does not simply mean that you read aloud your written research report. Instead, you simplify your research to present orally to an audience, avoiding picky details. This typically includes preparing a PowerPoint presentation with slides that provide information on each of the elements of an APA-style research report, including: an introduction to your topic area, purpose or rationale for the study, and hypothesis, methodology,

TABLE **16.3**
APA Format Checklist

Overall

- Double-spaced lines
- 1″ margins on all sides
- Straight left-hand margin, with uneven, or ragged, right-hand margin, without hyphenation
- Indent first line of each paragraph five to seven spaces.
- Typeface should be 12-point Times New Roman.
- Running head (positioned flush left) and page number (positioned flush right corner) on every page

Title Page

- Running head and page number
  - Top of title page
  - Type the words Running head: (including the colon) flush left followed by the running head all in capitals.
  - Running head is a maximum of 50 characters, including spaces and punctuation.
  - Across from the running head, on the same line, flush right, type the page number. For the title page, the page number is 1.
- A few lines down from running head, in the upper half of the page, centered, type the title.
  - The title is no more than 12 words in length.
- Centered on the next available double-spaced lines, type author name(s) (byline) and affiliation(s).
- A few lines down, centered, type the words *Author Note*.
- On the following lines, type the author note consisting of two to four paragraphs (affiliation; changes of affiliation, if any; acknowledgments, if any; and person to contact), each paragraph starting with an indent.

Abstract

- Running head and page number
  - Running head, flush left, in all capitals, appears in the header on its own (without the words Running head) for all remaining pages of the manuscript.
  - Page 2 (flush right)
- Centered, type the word *Abstract*.

- On the next double-spaced line, begin typing the abstract.
- One paragraph, no indent
- Between 150 and 250 words

Introduction

- Begins on page 3
- Centered, type the title of paper.
- Text begins on the next double-spaced line.

Method

- Begins immediately following the end of the introduction on the next available double-spaced line (do not begin a new page)
- Centered, boldfaced, type the word *Method*.
- Text begins on the next double-spaced line.
- Common subsection headings include: participants or subjects, and procedure.
- Type subsection headings flush left in boldface with upper and lowercase letters.

Results

- Begins immediately following the end of the method section on the next available double-spaced line (do not begin a new page)
- Centered, boldfaced, type the word *Results*.
- Text begins on the next double-spaced line.

Discussion

- Begins immediately following the end of the results section on the next available double-spaced line (do not begin a new page)
- Centered, boldfaced, type the word *Discussion*.
- Text begins on the next double-spaced line.

References

- Begins on a new page
- Centered, type the word *References*.
- Entries begin on the next double-spaced line.
- Entries listed in alphabetical order by first author's last name

TABLE **16.3**
APA Format Checklist—Cont'd

- For multiple works by the same first author, list one-author entries first in chronological order (earliest first), followed by multiple-author entries, listed alphabetically by second author's last name
- Entry formats (see Table 16.2)
- Hanging indents for each entry

Table

- Each begins on a new page
- Top, flush left margin, type the word *Table* and the number. On the next available double-spaced line (in italics) type the table title. On the following lines include the table in APA format
- May be single- or double-spaced

Figures

- Each on its own page
- Identified with figure number (type the word *Figure* and the number in italics, followed by a period) and caption, directly below the figure.

Appendices

- Each begins on new page
- Centered, type the word *Appendix*.
- Text begins on the next double-spaced line.
- Multiple appendices are identified by consecutive letters, A, B, C, and so on; for example, *Appendix A*.

results, and conclusions. For an oral presentation you are given a strict time limit (commonly between 10 and 20 minutes). You should practice your presentation, with your slides, until you are comfortable sticking to that time limit. You should also prepare a summary of your presentation and bring copies of this summary for distribution to those who are interested.

Typically a poster session at a conference is a large room filled with rows of bulletin boards, where individual researchers are given space to display their research for an hour or two. Each researcher stands by his or her poster as attendees walk by to look and ask questions. Although poster presentations are very common at conferences, the *Publication Manual* provides no guidelines for their preparation. Therefore, there are big differences from one to another. When a poster is accepted for presentation, you receive some guidelines from the organization for preparation. In addition, Szuchman (2011) provides some helpful hints for preparing posters. All posters should be easy to read at a distance of approximately 3 feet. For example, text should be no smaller than 24 points, with headings and poster title being even larger, and a font that is easy to read, such as Arial or Times New Roman. Your poster should be laid out in an organized, logical way, with as few words as possible, so that a reader can figure out the rationale of your study, based on a very brief introduction, the purpose or hypothesis of your study, the method, the results and the conclusions, within 1 to 2 minutes. Use bulleted lists, tables, and graphs. Mounting each page of your poster on a colored board backing or sparingly using colored text for titles and headings is common, as is having professionally produced glossy vinyl posters that can simply be unrolled. For a poster you are given a strict space limit (commonly 4 feet high by 6 feet wide). You should ensure that you keep your poster within the space limitation for the conference. You should also bring pushpins for mounting your poster, as well as copies of a summary of your poster for distribution to those who are interested.

16.4 | SUBMITTING A MANUSCRIPT FOR PUBLICATION

After you have prepared your research report, you are ready to submit the manuscript for publication in a scientific journal. Recall that communicating your research to the scientific community makes your finding public, which is necessary in the realm of science. The *Publication Manual* provides detailed information for preparation and submission of a manuscript for publication and you can access a checklist for manuscript submission in section 8.07 of the *Publication Manual* or at www.apa.org/journals/authors/manuscript_check .html. However, the following three steps will help you get a good start.

1. First, select a journal that is appropriate for the topic of your research report. Most journals focus on a few special topics. A journal's website describes what kinds of manuscripts are appropriate for that journal (Figure 16.8). In addition, there are a few journals that exclusively

---

Author Guidelines

Instructions for Authors for the American Journal Health Behavior (http://www.ajhb.org). After 33 years of printing hard copies, the journal is going green and as of January 2010, the journal will be totally online.

Only electronic submissions are accepted. Use the **Author Submit** *link to submit manuscripts for review which can be found at* http://www.ajhb.org.

PHILOSOPHY OF THE JOURNAL

The American Journal of Health Behavior (ISSN 1087-3244) is the official journal of the American Academy of Health Behavior (http://www.aahb.org/). The Journal seeks to improve the approach of health education, health promotion, and other multidisciplinary health efforts by fostering a better understanding of the multidimensional nature of both individuals and social systems as they relate to health behaviors.

JOURNAL OBJECTIVE

To provide a comprehensive understanding of the impact of personal attributes, personality characterstics, behavior patterns, social structure, and processess on health maintenance, health restoration, and health improvement; to disseminate knowledge of holistic, multidisciplinary approaches to designing and implimenting effective health programs; and to showcase health behavior analysis skills that have been proven to affect health improvement and recovery.

FIGURE **16.8** Author Information on Content for the *American Journal of Health Behavior* from the Journal's Website, www.ajhb.org/submission/ guidelines.htm

The same website also contains instructions for manuscript preparation and submission.

publish undergraduate research papers. *Psi Chi Journal of Undergraduate Research* and *Modern Psychological Studies* are such journals.

2. Consult the journal's Instructions to Authors for specific submission requirements. Instructions to authors are typically found on the journal's website. Be sure to identify whether the manuscript is to be submitted electronically (and if so, in what format) or if a hard copy is to be mailed (and if so, be sure to include the number of additional photocopies required by the journal). Instructions for submitting manuscripts for all APA journals can be found at www.apa.org/pubs/authors/instructions.aspx

3. Enclose a cover letter to the journal editor along with the manuscript. Detailed information concerning the contents of the cover letter can be founded in section 8.03 of the *Publication Manual.*

When a manuscript is received by a journal editor, the editor usually informs the author of its receipt and distributes copies of the manuscript to reviewers. The reviewers are selected on the basis of their expertise in the research area of your manuscript. Reviewers provide the editor with an evaluation of the manuscript, but, ultimately, the editor makes the decision to accept it, reject it, or request its revision. Note that most manuscripts are rejected for publication; only the best of the best get published.

16.5 | WRITING A RESEARCH PROPOSAL

Although we have identified writing a research report as Step 9 in the research process, researchers often do some writing earlier. Before conducting a study, many researchers write a research proposal. A **research proposal** is basically a plan for a new study. As outlined in the research process (see Chapter 1), before data are collected, you must (1) find a research idea, (2) form a hypothesis and a prediction, (3) define and choose your measures, (4) identify and select the individuals for your study, (5) select a research strategy, (6) select a research design, and make a plan for analyzing and interpreting the data (discussed in Chapter 14). A research proposal is a written report that addresses these points.

Why Write a Research Proposal?

Research proposals are commonly used in the following situations.

- Researchers submit research proposals to government and local funding agencies to obtain financial support for their research.
- Researchers develop proposals for their own use to help develop and refine their thinking, and to remind themselves to attend to details they might otherwise overlook.
- Undergraduate honors thesis students and graduate students submit proposals to their thesis and dissertation committees for approval.
- Undergraduate students are asked to write research proposals for the purposes of research methods classes (even when they are not required to conduct the actual study).

In each case, the research proposal is evaluated, feedback is provided, and suggestions for modification are made. Like the research report, the basic purpose of a good research proposal is to provide three kinds of information about the research study.

1. *What will be done.* The proposal should describe in some detail the step-by-step process you will follow to complete the research project.
2. *What may be found.* The proposal should contain an objective description of the possible outcomes. Typically, this involves a description of the measurements that will be taken and the statistical methods that will be used to summarize and interpret those measurements.
3. *How your planned research study is related to other knowledge in the area.* The research proposal should show the connections between the planned study and past knowledge.

DEFINITION	A **research proposal** is a written report presenting the plan and underlying rationale of a future research study. A proposal includes a review of the relevant background literature, an explanation of how the proposed study is related to other knowledge in the area, a description of how the planned research will be conducted, and a description of the possible results.

LEARNING CHECK	Explain why it can be useful to write a research proposal before conducting the actual research study.

How to Write a Research Proposal

Writing a research proposal is very much like writing a research report. First, the general APA style guidelines discussed in section 16.2 are identical, with the exception of verb tense. In a research proposal, always use the future tense when you describe your study. You will need to do this (1) at the end of the introduction when you introduce your study (for example, "The purpose of this study will be"); (2) in the method section (for example, "The participants will be" or "Participants will complete"); and (3) in the results/discussion (for example, "It is expected that the scores will increase"). In a research proposal, unlike in a research report, the study has not been conducted yet and, therefore, it does not make sense to refer to it in the past tense.

Second, the content of each part of the manuscript body discussed in section 16.3 is identical, with these exceptions.

1. An abstract is optional in a research proposal.
2. The literature review in the introduction is typically more extensive than the review in a research report.
3. The results and discussion sections are typically replaced either by a combined Results/Discussion section, or a section entitled Expected Results and Statistical Analysis or Data Analysis and Expected Results. Regardless of its heading, this final section of the body of the research proposal should describe (1) how the data will be collected and

analyzed, (2) the expected or anticipated results, (3) other plausible outcomes, and (4) implications of the expected results.

 **LEARNING CHECK** | Describe the similarities and differences between a research proposal and a research report.

■ CHAPTER SUMMARY

Your research is not finished until you have made it available to the rest of the scientific community. Therefore, when the study is completed and the data are in and analyzed, it is time to prepare a research report (Step 9 in the overall research process). Briefly, a research report describes what was done, what was found, and how your research study is related to other knowledge in the area.

The current guidelines for the formal style and structure that are the convention for research reports in the behavioral sciences are presented in the *Publication Manual of the American Psychological Association* (6th edition, 2010). The *Publication Manual* provides detailed information on properly preparing a manuscript to be submitted for publication.

Although the *Publication Manual* contains hundreds of guidelines and suggestions for creating a clear, precisely written manuscript, four elements of writing style help you get a good start: using an impersonal writing style, past-tense verbs, unbiased language, and appropriate citations. We also describe elements of format, including general guidelines for word processing, and order of manuscript pages.

The contents of each part of a research report are described in detail. Submitting a manuscript for publication and writing a research proposal are briefly discussed as well.

KEY WORDS

research report	abstract	discussion section
citation	introduction	reference section
title page	method section	research proposal
running head	results section	

EXERCISES

1. In addition to the key words, you should also be able to define each of the following terms:
   Publication Manual of the American Psychological Association
   plagiarism
   author note

   subjects subsection
   participants subsection
   procedure subsection
   apparatus subsection
   materials subsection
   appendix

2. What information appears on the title page of a research manuscript?

3. To learn why a particular research study was done, which section of the research manuscript should you read?

4. Which section of a research manuscript is usually written last? Why?

5. Which section of a research manuscript usually contains most of the citations? Why?

6. In 1994, Steven Schmidt published a research report demonstrating that humor has a positive effect on human memory. Write a sentence that presents this result as a statement of fact that cites the 1994 publication.

7. To find out if the results of the study have any practical applications, which section of the research manuscript should you read?

8. Which section of the research report provides step-by-step instructions for replicating the study?

LEARNING ACTIVITIES

1. Following is a list of some of the journals published by the APA. Select a journal that sounds interesting to you, and locate it in your library or in a full-text database such as PsycArticles. Check a recent issue of the journal and find a report of an empirical study. Once you have found your study, do the following.

   a. Provide a complete reference for the study using APA format (see Table 16.2).

   b. Find a statement of the hypothesis or the purpose for the research study. Which section of the article usually contains this information?

   c. See if the author(s) includes a suggestion for future research or identifies a limitation of the current study that might be corrected in future research. Which section of the article usually contains such a suggestion?

   d. Find out how many individuals participated in the study and describe their characteristics (age, gender, and so on). Where is this information located in the report?

   American Psychologist; Behavioral Neuroscience; Developmental Psychology; Journal of Abnormal Psychology; Journal of Applied Psychology; Journal of Comparative Psychology; Journal of Consulting and Clinical Psychology; Journal of Counseling Psychology; Journal of Educational Psychology; Journal of Experimental Psychology: Animal Behavior Processes; Journal of Experimental Psychology: Applied; Journal of Experimental Psychology: General; Journal of Experimental Psychology: Human Perception and Performance; Journal of Experimental Psychology: Learning, Memory, and Cognition; Journal of Family Psychology; Journal of Personality and Social Psychology; Neuropsychology; Personality Disorders; Professional Psychology; Psychological Assessment; Psychological Bulletin; Psychological Review; Psychology and Aging; Psychology, Public Policy, and Law; Psychology of Addictive Behaviors; Psychology of Violence.

2. Psychology journals and medical journals tend to use different formats for citations.

   a. Locate a report in a medical journal such as *Lancet* or the *American Journal of Drug and Alcohol Abuse*, and describe how the references are cited in the text.

   b. Check another category of journal (such as economics, philosophy, or sports) and describe the format they use for citations.

WEB RESOURCES

Visit the Book Companion Website at **www .cengage.com/international** to access study tools including a glossary, flashcards, and web quizzing. You will also find a link to

Statistics and Research Methods Workshops. For this chapter, we suggest you look at the following workshop:

APA Style

A

Random Number Table and Instruction

In the text, we often discuss using a process such as a coin toss to randomly select participants from a population or to randomly assign participants to groups. Instead of tossing a coin, many researchers prefer to use a table of random numbers. A table of random numbers is simply a huge list of randomly generated digits (0 to 9) grouped into five-digit sequences and organized into rows and columns. A table of random numbers is included on p. 521 (RAND, 2001).

The process of using a table of random numbers is demonstrated in the following two examples.

Example A

For this example, we use the table of random numbers to randomly select a sample of 20 individuals from a population of 197 people. Each individual in the population is assigned a number from 1 to 197. The goal is to randomly pick a set of 20 numbers between 1 and 197 to identify the 20 individuals in the sample. To use the random number table, follow these steps.

1. Because you want to generate numbers from 001 to 197, limit the selections to three-digit numbers. However, each column consists of five-digit values; therefore, you need to decide how to identify three digits within each group. For example, you can use the first three digits, the middle three digits, the last three digits, or some other three-digit sequence.

2. Begin in a random spot; close your eyes and place your finger or a pen anywhere in the table. If your pen falls on one of the digits, you are ready to begin. Otherwise, try again.

3. The number on which your pen falls determines the first value. For example, if you have decided to use the final three digits in each sequence, and your pen lands on the 4 in the number 14225 in row 19, column 3, then the first number to consider is 225.

4. Numbers outside the range of the population are skipped. In our example, any value greater than 197 is outside the range. Therefore, 225 is not a usable number and is skipped.

5. The next number is determined by continuing down the column of numbers. In our example, 479, 940, and 157 are the next three numbers to consider. The first two are outside our range and are skipped. However, 157 is usable, and the participant numbered 157 is selected for the sample.

6. Continue down the column of numbers until you have selected the designated number of participants. If you are sampling without replacement, skip any number that has already been selected. When you cannot go any further down a column, go to the top of the next column.

Example B

For this example, we use the table of random numbers to assign participants to four different treatment conditions. Each treatment condition is assigned a number from 1 to 4 and the participants are organized sequentially (first, second, third, and so on). The goal is to randomly pick a number between 1 and 4 to determine the treatment condition for each of the participants. To use the random number table, follow these steps.

1. Because you want to generate numbers from 1 to 4, limit the selections to one-digit numbers. Decide how to identify one digit within each group of five digits. For example, you can use the first digit, the second digit, the third digit, and so on.

2. Begin in a random spot; close your eyes and place your finger or a pen anywhere in the table. If your pen falls on one of the digits, you are ready to begin. Otherwise, try again.

3. The number on which your pen falls determines the first value. For example, if you have decided to use the first digit in each sequence, and your pen lands on the 4 in the number 14225 in row 19, column 3, then the first number to consider is 1.

4. Numbers outside the range are skipped. In our example, the range is values from 1 to 4. Therefore, the value 1 is a usable number. The first participant is assigned to treatment condition 1.

5. The next number to consider is determined by continuing down the column of numbers. In our example, numbers 6, 2, and 8 are the next three numbers to consider. The first and third numbers are outside our range and are skipped. However, 2 is a usable value, and the second participant is assigned to treatment condition 2.

6. Continue down the column of numbers until you have selected a treatment condition for each participant. When you cannot go any further down a column, go to the top of the next column.

A portion of a table of random numbers (from RAND Corporation, 2001) follows.

TABLE **A1**
A Page of Random Numbers

Row/Col	(1)	(2)	(3)	(4)	(5)	(6)	(7)	(8)	(9)	(10)
00000	10097	32533	76520	13586	34673	54876	80959	09117	39292	74945
00001	37542	04805	64894	74296	24805	24037	20636	10402	00822	91665
00002	08422	68953	19645	09303	23209	02560	15953	34764	35080	33606
00003	99019	02529	09376	70715	38311	31165	88676	74397	04436	27659
00004	12807	99970	80157	36147	64032	36653	98951	16877	12171	76833
00005	66065	74717	34072	76850	36697	36170	65813	39885	11199	29170
00006	31060	10805	45571	82406	35303	42614	86799	07439	23403	09732
00007	85269	77602	02051	65692	68665	74818	73053	85247	18623	88579
00008	63573	32135	05325	47048	90553	57548	28468	28709	83491	25624
00009	73796	45753	03529	64778	35808	34282	60935	20344	35273	88435
00010	98520	17767	14905	68607	22109	40558	60970	93433	50500	73998
00011	11805	05431	39808	27732	50725	68248	29405	24201	52775	67851
00012	83452	99634	06288	98083	13746	70078	18475	40610	68711	77817
00013	88685	40200	86507	58401	36766	67951	90364	76493	29609	11062
00014	99594	67348	87517	64969	91826	08928	93785	61368	23478	34113
00015	65481	17674	17468	50950	58047	76974	73039	57186	40218	16544
00016	80124	35635	17727	08015	45318	22374	21115	78253	14385	53763
00017	74350	99817	77402	77214	43236	00210	45421	64237	96286	02655
00018	69916	26803	66252	29148	36936	87203	76621	13990	94400	56418
00019	09893	20505	14225	68514	46427	56788	96297	78822	54382	14598
00020	91499	14523	68479	27686	46162	83554	94750	89923	37089	20048
00021	80336	94598	26940	36858	70297	34135	53140	33340	42050	82341
00022	44104	81949	85157	47954	32979	26575	57600	40881	22222	06413
00023	12550	73742	11100	02040	12860	74697	96644	89439	28707	25815
00024	63606	49329	16505	34484	40219	52563	43651	77082	07207	31790

Continued

TABLE **A1**

A Page of Random Numbers—cont'd

Row/Col	(1)	(2)	(3)	(4)	(5)	(6)	(7)	(8)	(9)	(10)
00025	61196	90446	26457	47774	51924	33729	65394	59593	42582	60527
00026	15474	45266	95270	79953	59367	83848	82396	10118	33211	59466
00027	94557	28573	67897	54387	54622	44431	91190	42592	92927	45973
00028	42481	16213	97344	08721	16868	48767	03071	12059	25701	46670
00029	23523	78317	73208	89837	68935	91416	26252	29663	05522	82562
00030	04493	52494	75246	33824	45862	51025	61962	79335	65337	12472
00031	00549	97654	64051	88159	96119	63896	54692	82391	23287	29529
00032	35963	15307	26898	09354	38351	35462	77974	50024	90103	39333
00033	59808	08391	45427	26842	83609	49700	13021	24892	78565	20106
00034	46058	85236	01390	92286	77281	44077	93910	83647	70617	42941
00035	32179	00597	87379	25241	05567	07007	86743	17157	85394	11838
00036	69234	61406	20117	45204	15956	60000	18743	92423	97118	96338
00037	19565	41430	01758	75379	40419	21585	66674	36806	84962	85207
00038	45155	14938	19476	07246	43667	94543	59047	90033	20826	69541
00039	94864	31994	36168	10851	34888	81553	01540	35456	05014	51176
00040	98086	24826	45240	28404	44999	08896	39094	73407	35441	31880
00041	33185	16232	41941	50949	89435	48581	88695	41994	37548	73043
00042	80951	00406	96382	70774	20151	23387	25016	25298	94624	61171
00043	79752	49140	71961	28296	69861	02591	74852	20539	00387	59579
00044	18633	32537	98145	06571	31010	24674	05455	61427	77938	91936
00045	74029	43902	77557	32270	97790	17119	52527	58021	80814	51748
00046	54178	45611	80993	37143	05335	12969	56127	19255	36040	90324
00047	11664	49883	52079	84827	59381	71539	09973	33440	88461	23356
00048	48324	77928	31249	64710	02295	36870	32307	57546	15020	09994
00049	69074	94138	87637	91976	35584	04401	10518	21616	01848	76938

RAND. (2001). *A million random digits with 100,000 normal deviates.* Santa Monica, CA: RAND. Copyright RAND 2001 (RAND/ MR-1418). (Originally published by The Free Press, Glencoe, IL, 1995.)

B

Statistics Demonstrations and Statistical Tables

DESCRIPTIVE STATISTICS

THE MEAN

To compute the mean, you first find the sum of the scores (represented by ΣX) and then divide by the number of scores (represented by n).

Scores: 4, 2, 1, 5, 2, 2, 3, 4, 3, 2, 3, 1

$\Sigma X = 32$ and $n = 12$. The mean is $M = 32/12 = 2.67$.

THE MEDIAN

To compute the median, you first list the scores in order. With an odd number of scores, the median is the middle value. With an even number of scores, the median is the average of the middle two scores.

Scores: 4, 2, 1, 5, 2, 2, 3, 4, 3, 2, 3, 1

Listed in order: 1, 1, 2, 2, 2, 2, 3, 3, 3, 4, 4, 5

The middle two scores are 2 and 3. The median is 2.5.

THE MODE

The mode is simply the most frequently occurring score.

Scores: 4, 2, 1, 5, 2, 2, 3, 4, 3, 2, 3, 1

There are more scores of $X = 2$ than any other value. The mode is 2.

VARIANCE AND *SS* (SUM OF SQUARED DEVIATIONS)

Variance is the average squared distance from the mean and is usually identified with the symbol s^2. The calculation of variance involves two steps:

Step 1:

Compute the distance from the mean, or the deviation, for each score, then square each distance, then add the squared distances. The result is called *SS*, or the sum of the squared deviations.

Score	Distance from M	Squared Distance	
5	1	1	For these scores:
6	2	4	$n = 5$, $\Sigma X = 20$,
1	3	9	and $M = 20/5 = 4$.
5	1	1	
3	1	1	
		16 = SS (The sum of the squared deviations)	

Note: The value for *SS* can also be completed using a computational formula:

$$SS = \Sigma X^2 - \frac{(\Sigma X)^2}{n}$$

For these scores:

X	X²	
5	25	$\Sigma X = 20$
6	36	$\Sigma X^2 = 96$
1	1	
5	25	
3	9	
20	96	

$$SS = 96 - \frac{(20)^2}{5}$$
$$= 96 - 80$$
$$= 16$$

Step 2:

Variance is obtained by dividing SS (the sum of squared deviations) by $n - 1$. Note that the value of $n - 1$ is also called degrees of freedom or simply *df*.

For the scores we have been using,

$$\text{Variance} = s^2 = \frac{SS}{n-1} = \frac{16}{4} = 4$$

STANDARD DEVIATION (*SD*)

Standard deviation is the square root of the variance and measures the standard distance from the mean.

In the demonstration of variance we computed a variance of 4 for a set of $n = 5$ scores. For these scores, the standard deviation is

$$SD = \sqrt{4} = 2.$$

PEARSON CORRELATION AND REGRESSION

The Pearson correlation measures and describes the direction and degree of linear relationship between two variables. The data consist of two measurements (two different variables) for each individual in the sample. The process of regression determines the equation for the best fitting straight line for the X and Y data points. The following data will be used to demonstrate the calculation of the Pearson correlation and the regression equation. Note that the two variables are labeled X and Y, and that we have already computed the sum of squared deviations (SS) for the X values and for the Y values.

X	Y	
3	1	For the X scores, $M_X = 2$ and $SS = 10$
4	2	
0	5	For the Y scores, $M_Y = 4$ and $SS = 40$
2	3	
1	9	

In addition to the *SS* for the *X* scores and *SS* for the *Y* scores, the calculation of the Pearson correlation requires the sum or the products of the deviations, or *SP*. The value of *SP* can be computed directly by:

1. For each individual, find the distance from the mean for the *X* score and the distance from the mean for the *Y* score including the sign (+/ −) for each distance.
2. Multiply the two distances to obtain the product for each individual.
3. Add the products.

This process is demonstrated as follows:

X	Y	Distance for X	Distance for Y	Products
3	1	1	−3	−3
4	2	2	−2	−4
0	5	−2	1	−2
2	3	0	−1	0
1	9	−1	5	−5
				−14 = SP

Note: The value for *SP* can also be found using a computational formula:

$$SP = \Sigma XY - \frac{(\Sigma X)(\Sigma Y)}{n}$$

For these data,

X	Y	XY
3	1	3
4	2	8
0	5	0
2	3	6
1	9	9
		26 = ΣXY

$$SP = 26 - \frac{(10)(20)}{5}$$
$$= 26 - 40$$
$$= -14$$

The Pearson correlation, identified by the letter *r*, can now be computed as follows:

$$r = \frac{SP}{\sqrt{(SS \text{ for } X)(SS \text{ for } Y)}}$$

For our data,

$$r = \frac{-14}{\sqrt{(10)(40)}} = \frac{-14}{\sqrt{400}} = -0.70$$

The regression equation has the general form, $Y = bX + a$, where

$$b = r \frac{s_Y}{s_X} \text{ or } b = \frac{SP}{SS_X} \text{ and } a = M_Y - bM_X$$

where r is the Pearson correlation, s_X is the standard deviation for the X scores, and s_Y is the standard deviation for the Y scores.

For these data, $b = \dfrac{-14}{10} = -1.4$ and $a = 4 - 1.4(2) = 1.2$

The regression equation is $Y = -1.4X + 1.2$

SPEARMAN CORRELATION

The Spearman correlation measures and describes the degree of relationship between two variables that have been measured on an ordinal scale (ranks). This correlation also can be used to measure the degree of monotonic (one-directional) relationship between two variables measured on an interval or ratio scale (numerical scores) by first ranking the numerical values and then computing the Spearman correlation for the ranks. The Spearman correlation is computed by simply applying the Pearson correlation formula to ordinal data (ranks). The following data are used to demonstrate the calculation of the Spearman correlation. Notice that we begin with numerical scores from an interval or ratio scale.

The first step is to transform the numerical values into ranks. First rank the X values: the smallest score gets a rank of 1, the next smallest gets a 2, and so on. Then rank the Y values.

	Original Scores			*Ranks*	
Person	X	Y	*Person*	X	Y
A	3	1	A	4	1
B	4	2	B	5	2
C	0	5	C	1	4
D	2	3	D	3	3
E	1	9	E	2	5

Then, use the Pearson correlation for the ranks.

For the X ranks, $\Sigma X = 15$, $M = 3$ and $SS = 10$
For the Y ranks, $\Sigma Y = 15$, $M = 3$ and $SS = 10$

Multiplying the X rank times the Y rank for each person produces 4, 10, 4, 9, and 10. These values add to $\Sigma XY = 37$, and the computational formula for SP produces

$$SP = \Sigma XY - \frac{(\Sigma X)(\Sigma Y)}{N} = 37 - \frac{(15)(15)}{5} = 37 - 45 = -8$$

Finally, the Spearman correlation, identified by the symbol r_S, is:

$$r_S = \frac{SP}{\sqrt{(SS \text{ for } X)(SS \text{ for } Y)}} = \frac{-8}{\sqrt{(10)(10)}} = -0.80$$

The Spearman correlation can also be computed using a special formula that works only when the scores have already been converted to ranks. We introduce and demonstrate the special formula using the same ranked data that were used to demonstrate the Spearman correlation.

The special Spearman formula is:

$$r_S = 1.00 - \frac{6\Sigma D^2}{n(n^2 - 1)}$$
where D is the difference between the X rank and the Y rank for each individual.

For these data, the ranks, the D values, and the D^2 values are as follows:

Person	X	Y	D	D²
A	4	1	3	9
B	5	2	3	9
C	1	4	3	9
D	3	3	0	0
E	2	5	3	9

$$36 = \Sigma D^2$$

Using the special formula, we obtain:

$$r_S = 1.00 - \frac{6\Sigma D^2}{n(n^2 - 1)} = 1.00 - \frac{6(36)}{5(24)}$$
$$= 1.00 - 1.80$$
$$= -0.80$$

Note that this is exactly the same value we obtained for the Spearman correlation using the regular Pearson formula.

INFERENTIAL STATISTICS

INDEPENDENT-MEASURES t TEST

The independent-measures t test is a hypothesis test used to evaluate the mean difference between two separate groups. The test involves computing a t statistic (as is demonstrated) and then consulting a statistical table to determine whether the obtained value of t is large enough to indicate a significant mean difference. The following sample data are used to demonstrate the independent-measures t test. Note that each group is described by the number of scores (n), the mean (M), the sum of squared deviations (SS), and the degrees of freedom ($df = n - 1$):

Group 1	Group 2
$n_1 = 10$	$n_2 = 5$
$M_1 = 44$	$M_2 = 40$
$SS_1 = 280$	$SS_2 = 110$
$df_1 = 9$	$df_2 = 4$

The calculation of the t statistic involves three steps:

Step 1:

Pool the two sample variances.

$$\text{pooled variance} = s_p^2 = \frac{SS_1 + SS_2}{df_1 + df_2} = \frac{280 + 110}{9 + 4} = \frac{390}{13} = 30$$

The pooled variance can also be obtained using the df value and the variance (or squared standard deviation) for each of the two samples. The formula is as follows:

$$\text{pooled variance} = \frac{df_1(s_1^2) + df_2(s_2^2)}{df_1 + df_2}$$

This alternative formula is especially useful when you are dealing with summarized data, such as the printout from a computer program.

Step 2:

Compute the standard error (denominator of the t statistic).

$$\text{standard error} = \sqrt{\frac{s_p^2}{n_1} + \frac{s_p^2}{n_2}} = \sqrt{\frac{30}{10} + \frac{30}{5}} = \sqrt{3 + 6} = \sqrt{9} = 3$$

Step 3:

Compute the t statistic.

$$t = \frac{M_1 - M_2}{\text{Standard error}} = \frac{44 - 40}{3} = \frac{4}{3} = 1.33$$

You must consult a t distribution table to determine whether the obtained t statistic ($t = 1.33$) is large enough to indicate a significant difference. The t statistic has degrees of freedom equal to the sum of the df values for the two groups.

$$df \text{ for the } t \text{ statistic} = df_1 + df_2$$

For these data, $df = 9 + 4 = 13$. The t distribution table shows that a minimum value of $t = 2.160$ is needed for significance with an alpha level of .05. Our t value does not meet this criterion, so we must conclude that there is no significant difference between the two means.

Effect Size for the Independent-Measures t Test

It is customary to report a measure of effect size along with the results from a hypothesis test. For the independent-measures t test, effect size can be measured with Cohen's d or r^2. Cohen's d is a standardized measure of mean difference that is computed by:

$$d = \frac{\text{Mean difference}}{\text{Standard deviation}}$$

For the independent-measures t, the standard deviation is obtained by taking the square root of the pooled variance. Using the data from the previous demonstration:

$$d = \frac{M_1 - M_2}{\sqrt{s_p^2}} = \frac{44 - 40}{\sqrt{30}} = \frac{4}{5.48} = 0.73$$

The proportion of variance accounted for is represented by r^2 and is computed by:

$$r^2 = \frac{t^2}{t^2 + df}$$

For the data from the independent-measures t demonstration, we obtained $t = 1.33$ with $df = 13$. For these data:

$$r^2 = \frac{(1.33)^2}{(1.33)^2 + 13} = \frac{1.77}{14.77} = 0.12$$

REPEATED-MEASURES t TEST

The repeated-measures t test is a hypothesis test used to evaluate the mean difference between two sets of scores obtained from a single group of participants. The test involves computing a t statistic (as is demonstrated) and then consulting a statistical table to determine whether the obtained value of t is large enough to indicate a significant mean difference. The following sample data are used to demonstrate the repeated-measures t test. Notice that we have computed the difference between the first and second score for each participant by subtracting the first score from the second. Note that the signs (+/−) are important.

Participant	Score in Condition 1	Score in Condition 2	Difference
A	20	22	+2
B	24	23	−1
C	18	24	+6
D	21	24	+3
E	26	28	+2
F	19	25	+6

The calculation of the t statistic involves three steps.

Step 1:

Compute the mean and the variance for the set of difference scores. For these data, there are $n = 6$ difference scores with a mean of $M = 3.00$ and a variance of $s^2 = 7.2$.

Step 2:

Compute the standard error (denominator of the t statistic).

$$\text{standard error} = \sqrt{\frac{s^2}{n}} = \sqrt{\frac{7.2}{6}} = \sqrt{1.20} = 1.10$$

Step 3:

Compute the t statistic.

$$t = \frac{M}{\text{Standard error}} = \frac{3.00}{1.10} = 2.73$$

You must consult a t distribution table to determine whether the obtained t statistic ($t = 2.73$) is large enough to indicate a significant difference. The t statistic has degrees of freedom equal to $n - 1$.

For these data, $df = 5$. The t distribution table shows that a minimum value of $t = 2.571$ is needed for significance with an alpha level of .05. Our t value exceeds this criterion, so we conclude that there is a significant mean difference between the two treatment conditions.

Effect Size for the Repeated-Measures t Test

As with the independent-measures test, effect size can be measured with either Cohen's d or r^2. Cohen's d is a standardized measure of mean difference that is computed by:

$$d = \frac{\text{Mean difference}}{\text{Standard deviation}}$$

For the repeated-measures t, the standard deviation is simply the square root of the variance. Using the data from the previous demonstration:

$$d = \frac{M}{\sqrt{s^2}} = \frac{3}{\sqrt{7.2}} = \frac{3}{2.68} = 1.12$$

The proportion of variance accounted for is represented by r^2 and is computed by:

$$r^2 = \frac{t^2}{t^2 + df}$$

For the data from the repeated-measures t demonstration, we obtained $t = 2.73$ with $df = 5$. For these data:

$$r^2 = \frac{(2.73)^2}{(2.73)^2 + 5} = \frac{7.45}{12.45} = 0.60$$

SINGLE-FACTOR ANALYSIS OF VARIANCE (INDEPENDENT MEASURES)

The single-factor analysis of variance is a hypothesis test used to evaluate the mean differences among two or more separate groups when the groups are defined by separate values of the same variable or factor. The test involves computing an F-ratio (as is demonstrated) and then consulting a statistical table to determine whether the value obtained for the F-ratio is large enough to indicate significant mean differences. The following sample data are used to demonstrate the single-factor analysis of variance. Note that each group is described by the number of scores (n), the mean (M), the sum of squared deviations (SS), and the degrees of freedom ($df = n - 1$). Also note that we have computed ΣX and ΣX^2 for the entire set of $N = 15$ scores.

Treatment 1 Group 1	Treatment 2 Group 2	Treatment 3 Group 3	Totals
0	1	2	$N = 15$
2	5	5	
1	2	6	$\Sigma X = 60$
5	4	9	
2	8	8	$\Sigma X^2 = 354$
$n = 5$	$n = 5$	$n = 5$	
$M = 2$	$M = 4$	$M = 6$	
$SS = 14$	$SS = 30$	$SS = 30$	
$df = 4$	$df = 4$	$df = 4$	

The *F*-ratio for the analysis is a ratio of two variances:

$$F = \frac{\text{Variance between treatments}}{\text{Variance within treatments}}$$

Where each variance is computed as:

$$\text{Variance} = \frac{SS}{df}$$

The *SS* values and the *df* values for the two variances are obtained by an analysis process that first computes *SS* and *df* for the total set of scores, then separates the total into the two components: between treatments and within treatments. The analysis for *SS* and *df* can be pictured as follows:

We demonstrate the analysis of variance in three steps: First, analyzing the *SS* values, then analyzing the *df* values, and finally using the *SS* and *df* values to compute the two variances and the *F*-ratio.

Step 1:

Analysis of the *SS* (sum of squared deviations).

Using the computational formula, *SS* for the total set of scores is:

$$SS \text{ total} = \Sigma X^2 - \frac{(\Sigma X)^2}{n}$$
$$= 354 - \frac{(60)^2}{15}$$
$$= 354 - 240$$
$$= 114$$

The value for *SS* within treatments is obtained directly from the *SS* values that were computed inside each treatment.

$$SS \text{ within treatments} = \Sigma SS = 14 + 30 + 30 = 74$$

Finally, the value for *SS* between treatments is obtained by subtraction.

$$SS \text{ between treatments} = SS \text{ total} - SS \text{ within treatments}$$
$$= 114 - 74$$
$$= 40$$

Step 2:

Analysis of *df* (degrees of freedom).
Degrees of freedom for the total set of scores is simply:

$$df \text{ total} = N - 1 = 14$$

The value for *df* within treatments is obtained directly from the *df* values that were computed inside each treatment.

$$df \text{ within treatments} = \Sigma df = 4 + 4 + 4 = 12$$

Finally, the value for *df* between treatments is obtained by subtraction.

$$Df \text{ between treatments} = df \text{ total} - df \text{ within treatments}$$

$$= 14 - 12$$

$$= 2$$

Step 3:

Compute the two variances and the *F*-ratio.

$$\text{Variance between treatments} = \frac{SS \text{ between}}{df \text{ between}} = \frac{40}{2} = 20$$

$$\text{Variance within treatments} = \frac{SS \text{ within}}{df \text{ within}} = \frac{74}{12} = 6.17$$

For these data, the *F*-ratio is:

$$F = \frac{\text{Variance between treatments}}{\text{Variance within treatments}} = \frac{20.00}{6.17} = 3.24$$

You must consult an *F* distribution table to determine whether the obtained *F*-ratio, ($F = 3.24$), is large enough to indicate a significant difference. The *F*-ratio has two values for degrees of freedom, one for the variance in the numerator and one for the denominator. For our example, the *F*-ratio has *df* = 2 for the numerator and *df* = 12 for the denominator. Together, the *F*-ratio has *df* = 2, 12.

The *F* distribution table shows that a minimum value of $F = 3.88$ is needed for significance with an alpha level of .05. Our *F*-ratio does not meet this criterion, so we must conclude that the mean differences among the three groups are not significant.

Measuring Effect Size for the Single-Factor Independent-Measures ANOVA

For analysis of variance it is customary to measure effect size with η^2 (the Greek letter *eta* squared), which measures the percentage of variance accounted for by the mean differences. For the independent-measures analysis we just completed, η^2 is computed as:

$$\eta^2 = \frac{SS \text{ between treatments}}{SS \text{ total}} = \frac{40}{114} = 0.35$$

SINGLE-FACTOR ANALYSIS OF VARIANCE (REPEATED-MEASURES)

The repeated-measures analysis of variance serves exactly the same purpose as the independent-measures analysis in the previous demonstration. However, the repeated-measures analysis is used when the different sets of scores are all obtained from a single group of participants. To demonstrate the single-factor, repeated-measures analysis of variance, we use the same scores that were used for the independent-measures demonstration. Notice that the data are now presented as scores from one group of participants, with each individual measured three times. Also note that we have computed the mean score for each of the five participants.

Participant	Treatment 1	Treatment 2	Treatment 3	Participant Means	Total
A	0	1	2	$M = 1$	$N = 15$
B	2	5	5	$M = 4$	$\Sigma X = 60$
C	1	2	6	$M = 3$	$\Sigma X^2 = 354$
D	5	4	9	$M = 6$	
E	2	8	8	$M = 6$	
	$n = 5$	$n = 5$	$n = 5$		
	$M = 2$	$M = 4$	$M = 6$		
	$SS = 14$	$SS = 30$	$SS = 30$		
	$df = 4$	$df = 4$	$df = 4$		

Most of the repeated-measures analysis uses exactly the same computations that were used for the independent-measures analysis of variance. With repeated measures, however, we can use the participant means to measure the magnitude of the individual differences, and then subtract these differences from the denominator before computing a final F-ratio. Thus, the F-ratio for the repeated-measures analysis has the following structure:

$$F = \frac{\text{Variance between treatments}}{\text{Error variance (individual differences removed)}}$$

Each variance is computed as:

$$\text{Variance} = \frac{SS}{df}$$

The *SS* values and the *df* values for the two variances are obtained by a two-stage analysis. The first stage is identical to the independent-measures analysis and can be pictured as follows:

The second stage analyzes the within-treatment components by measuring and subtracting out the differences between subjects.

The first stage of this analysis is identical to the independent-measures analysis in the previous demonstration and produces exactly the same values.

SS total = 114   *df* total = 14

SS between treatments = 40   *df* between treatments = 2

SS within treatments = 74   *df* within treatments = 12

The second stage involves computing *SS* and *df* between subjects and then subtracting these values from the corresponding *SS* and *df* within treatments. The results provide the *SS* and *df* for the error variance in the denominator of the *F*-ratio.

Using the symbol *k* to represent the number of treatment conditions, the *SS* between subjects can be computed as follows:

$$SS \text{ between subjects} = k(SS \text{ for the participant means})$$

First, we compute *SS* for the set of means. The means and squared means are presented in the following table and the computational formula is used to obtain *SS*.

X	X²		
1	1	$\Sigma X = 20$	
4	16		
3	9	$\Sigma X^2 = 98$	
6	36		
6	36		
20	98		

$$SS = 98 - \frac{(20)^2}{5}$$
$$= 98 - 80$$
$$= 18$$

For these data we have $k = 3$ treatments, so:

$$SS \text{ between subjects} = 3(18) = 54$$

With a group of $n = 5$ participants:

$$df \text{ between subjects} = n - 1 = 4$$

Completing the second stage of the analysis, we obtain:

$$SS \text{ error} = SS \text{ within treatments} - SS \text{ between subjects}$$
$$= 74 - 54$$
$$= 20$$

$$df \text{ error} = df \text{ within treatments} - df \text{ between subjects}$$
$$= 12 - 4$$
$$= 8$$

Finally, the two variances and the F-ratio are:

$$\text{Variance between treatments} = \frac{SS \text{ between treatments}}{df \text{ between treatments}} = \frac{40}{2} = 20$$

$$\text{Error variance} = \frac{SS \text{ error}}{df \text{ error}} = \frac{20}{8} = 2.50$$

For these data, the F-ratio is:

$$F = \frac{\text{Variance between treatments}}{\text{Error variance}} = \frac{20.00}{2.50} = 8.00$$

You must consult an F distribution table to determine whether the obtained F-ratio ($F = 8.00$) is large enough to indicate a significant difference. The F-ratio has two values for degrees of freedom, one for the variance in the numerator and one for the denominator. For our example, the F-ratio has $df = 2$ for the numerator and $df = 8$ for the denominator. Together, the F-ratio has $df = 2, 8$.

The F distribution table shows that a minimum value of $F = 4.46$ is needed for significance with an alpha level of .05, and a minimum value of 8.65 is needed with an alpha level of .01. Our F-ratio ($F = 8.00$) is large enough to conclude that there are significant differences at the .05 level of significance.

Measuring Effect Size for the Single-Factor Repeated-Measures ANOVA

For a repeated-measures analysis of variance it is customary to remove the variance accounted for by the individual differences before computing η^2 (the Greek letter *eta* squared), which measures the percentage of variance accounted for by the mean differences. For the repeated-measures analysis we just completed, η^2 is computed as:

$$\eta^2 = \frac{SS \text{ between treatments}}{SS \text{ total} - SS \text{ between subjects}} = \frac{40}{114 - 54} = \frac{40}{60} = 0.67$$

TWO-FACTOR ANALYSIS OF VARIANCE (INDEPENDENT MEASURES)

The two-factor analysis of variance is a hypothesis test used to evaluate the mean differences in a research study with two factors. The different groups in the study can be represented as cells in a matrix, with the levels of one factor determining the rows and the levels of the second factor determining the columns. The test involves computing three separate F-ratios: One to evaluate the main effects of the first factor, one to evaluate the main effects of the second factor, and one to evaluate the interaction. The following sample data are used to demonstrate the two-factor analysis of variance. Note that each group is described by the number of scores (n), the mean (M), the sum of squared deviations (SS), and the degrees of freedom ($df = n - 1$). Also note that we have computed the overall mean for each row in the matrix (each level of factor A) and the overall mean for each column (each level of factor B). Finally, note that we have computed ΣX and ΣX^2 for the entire set of $N = 30$ scores.

Factor B

	B1	B2	B3	
A1	$n = 5$ $M = 10$ $SS = 400$ $df = 4$	$n = 5$ $M = 20$ $SS = 500$ $df = 4$	$n = 5$ $M = 30$ $SS = 400$ $df = 4$	$M = 20$
A2	$n = 5$ $M = 10$ $SS = 300$ $df = 4$	$n = 5$ $M = 10$ $SS = 300$ $df = 4$	$n = 5$ $M = 10$ $SS = 500$ $df = 4$	$M = 10$
	$M = 10$	$M = 15$	$M = 20$	

Factor A

Overall
$N = 30$
$\Sigma X = 450$
$\Sigma X^2 = 10{,}900$

  The two-factor analysis of variance can be viewed as a two-stage process. The first stage is identical to the single-factor analysis of variance with each cell of the matrix considered as a separate treatment condition. In this stage, we first compute SS and df for the total set of scores, then separate the total into the two components: between treatments and within treatments. This stage of the analysis for SS and df can be pictured as follows:

Total SS → Between-Treatments SS, Within-Treatments SS

Total df → Between-Treatments df, Within-Treatments df

In the second stage of the analysis, the values for *SS* and *df* between treatments are further analyzed into the main effect for factor A, the main effect for factor B, and the interaction. This stage can be pictured as follows:

We demonstrate the two-factor analysis of variance in three steps: The first two steps correspond to the two stages of the analysis and the third step will involve computing the variances and the *F*-ratios.

Step 1:

Analyze the total *SS* and *df* values into a between treatments component and a within treatments component.

SS total measures the *SS* for the entire set of $N = 30$ scores. Using the computational formula, *SS* for the total set of scores is:

$$SS \text{ total} = \Sigma X^2 - \frac{(\Sigma X)^2}{n}$$
$$= 10{,}900 - \frac{(450)^2}{30}$$
$$= 10{,}900 - 6750$$
$$= 4150$$

The value for *SS* within treatments is obtained directly from the *SS* values that were computed inside each treatment (each cell of the matrix).

$$SS \text{ within treatments} = \Sigma SS = 400 + 500 + 400 + 300 + 300 + 500$$
$$= 2400$$

Finally, the value for *SS* between treatments is obtained by subtraction.

$$SS \text{ between treatments} = SS \text{ total} - SS \text{ within treatments}$$
$$= 4150 - 2400$$
$$= 1750$$

Degrees of freedom for the total set of scores is simply:

$$df \text{ total} = N - 1 = 29$$

The value for *df* within treatments is obtained directly from the *df* values that were computed inside each treatment (each cell of the matrix).

$$df \text{ within treatments} = \Sigma df = 4 + 4 + 4 + 4 + 4 + 4 = 24$$

Finally, the value for *df* between treatments is obtained by subtraction.

$$df \text{ between treatments} = df \text{ total} - df \text{ within treatments}$$
$$= 29 - 24$$
$$= 5$$

Step 2:

Split the between-treatments *SS* and *df* values into three separate components that correspond to the main effect for factor A, the main effect for factor B, and the interaction.

The *SS* for factor A can be computed using the overall means for A1 and A2 (the means for the two rows). Each of these means was computed from a set of 15 scores (three groups, each with $n = 5$), so the *SS* for factor A can be computed as follows:

$$SS \text{ factor A} = 15(SS \text{ for the A1 and A2 means})$$

The first step is to compute *SS* for the set of means. The means and squared means are presented in the following table and the computational formula is used to obtain *SS*.

X	X²		
20	400	$\Sigma X = 30$	$SS = 500 - \dfrac{(30)^2}{2}$
10	100		$= 500 - 450$
30	500	$\Sigma X^2 = 500$	$= 50$

Multiplying by 15 gives us:

$$SS \text{ factor A} = 15(50) = 750$$

The *SS* for factor B can be found using the means for B1, B2, and B3. Each of these means is based on 10 scores (2 groups, each with $n = 5$), so the *SS* for factor B can be computed as follows:

$$SS \text{ factor B} = 10(SS \text{ for the B1, B2, and B3 means})$$

The first step is to compute *SS* for the set of means. The means and squared means are presented in the following table and the computational formula is used to obtain *SS*.

X	X²		
10	100	$\Sigma X = 45$	$SS = 725 - \dfrac{(45)^2}{3}$
15	225		$= 725 - 675$
20	400	$\Sigma X^2 = 725$	$= 50$
45	725		

Multiplying by 10 gives us:

$$SS \text{ factor A} = 10(50) = 500$$

Finally, we compute SS for the interaction by subtraction:

$$SS \text{ interaction} = SS \text{ between treatments} - SS \text{ factor A} - SS \text{ factor B}$$
$$= 1750 - 750 - 500 = 500$$

There were only 2 means for factor A, so:

$$df \text{ factor A} = 2 - 1 = 1$$

There were 3 means for factor B, so:

$$df \text{ factor B} = 3 - 1 = 2$$

df for the interaction is found by subtraction:

$$df \text{ interaction} = df \text{ between treatments} - df \text{ factor A} - df \text{ factor B}$$
$$= 5 - 1 - 2 = 2$$

Step 3:

Compute the variances and the F-ratios.

$$\text{Variance for factor A} = \frac{SS \text{ for factor A}}{df \text{ for factor A}} = \frac{750}{1} = 750$$

$$\text{Variance for factor B} = \frac{SS \text{ for factor B}}{df \text{ for factor B}} = \frac{500}{2} = 250$$

$$\text{Variance for the interaction} = \frac{SS \text{ for the interaction}}{df \text{ for the interaction}} = \frac{500}{2} = 250$$

The variance within treatments will be the denominator for each F-ratio:

$$\text{Variance within treatments} = \frac{SS \text{ within treatments}}{df \text{ within treatments}} = \frac{2400}{24} = 100$$

Finally, the three F-ratios are:

$$F\text{-ratio for factor A} = \frac{\text{Variance for factor A}}{\text{Variance within treatments}} = \frac{750}{100} = 7.50$$

$$F\text{-ratio for factor B} = \frac{\text{Variance for factor B}}{\text{Variance within treatments}} = \frac{250}{100} = 2.50$$

$$F\text{-ratio for the interaction} = \frac{\text{Variance for the interaction}}{\text{Variance within treatments}} = \frac{250}{100} = 2.50$$

You must consult an F distribution table to determine whether the obtained F-ratios are large enough to indicate significant differences. Each F-ratio has two values for degrees of freedom: one for the variance in the numerator and one for the denominator. For our example, the *F*-ratio for factor A has $df = 1$ for the numerator and $df = 24$ for the denominator. With $df = 1, 24$, the *F* distribution table shows that a minimum value of $F = 4.26$ is needed for significance with an alpha level of .05, and a value of $F = 7.82$ for an alpha level of .01. Our *F*-ratio exceeds the .05 value (but not the .01 value), so we conclude that the mean difference between the two levels of factor A is significant at the .05 level of significance. That is, the main effect for factor A is significant.

The *F*-ratios for factor B and for the interaction both have $df = 2, 24$. For these degrees of freedom, the *F* distribution table shows that a minimum value of $F = 3.40$ is needed for significance with an alpha level of .05. Both of our *F*-ratios fail to meet this criterion, so we must conclude that there is no significant main effect for factor B and no significant interaction between factors.

MEASURES OF EFFECT SIZE FOR A TWO-FACTOR ANALYSIS OF VARIANCE

In addition to reporting the statistical significance of mean differences, it is also recommended that you provide a report of the size of the mean differences. Following a two-factor analysis of variance, the common technique for measuring effect size is to compute the proportion of variance accounted for by the mean differences in both main effects and in the interaction. The resulting values are each called η^2 (the Greek letter eta squared). For a two-factor analysis of variance it is customary to remove the variance accounted for by other main effects and interactions before computing η^2 for any specific main effect or interaction. With a repeated-measures two-factor design, it is also customary to remove the variance accounted for by the individual differences before computing any η^2 values. In each case, the η^2 values are computed using only the variance for the specific effect being evaluated and the variance for the error term (denominator of the F-ratio).

We demonstrate the calculation of the η^2 values using the data from the previous demonstration of the two-factor analysis of variance. For factor A:

$$\eta^2 = \frac{SS \text{ for factor A}}{SS \text{ for factor A} + SS \text{ for the the error term}}$$

For the data from the two-factor demonstration, this value is:

$$\eta^2 = \frac{750}{750 + 2400} = 0.238$$

Similarly, the η^2 for factor B is computed by:

$$\eta^2 = \frac{SS \text{ for factor B}}{SS \text{ for factor B} + SS \text{ for the error term}}$$

$$= \frac{500}{500 + 2400} = 0.17$$

Finally, the η^2 for the interaction is computed by:

$$\eta^2 = \frac{SS \text{ for the interaction}}{SS \text{ for the interaction} + SS \text{ for the error term}}$$

$$= \frac{500}{500 + 2400} = 0.17$$

For a within-subjects analysis, the calculation of the error term changes somewhat but the equations for the η^2 values are identical to those used for the between-subjects analysis.

SIGNIFICANCE OF A CORRELATION

The significance test for a correlation is used to determine whether a sample correlation is sufficiently large to justify concluding that there is a real, non-zero correlation in the population. To demonstrate the test for significance of a correlation, we assume that a researcher has obtained a correlation of $r = +0.41$ for a sample of $n = 25$ individuals.

The significance test is based on a t statistic that is computed as follows:

$$t = \frac{r}{\sqrt{\dfrac{(1-r^2)}{df}}}$$

where the degrees of freedom are $df = n - 2$.

Note: If all the terms in the t formula are squared, the calculation produces an F-ratio with degrees of freedom determined by $df = 1, n - 2$.

For the sample in this demonstration, $r = 0.41$, $r^2 = 0.17$, and $df = 23$. With these values:

$$t = \frac{0.41}{\sqrt{\dfrac{(1-0.17)}{23}}} = 2.16$$

You must consult a t distribution table to determine whether the obtained t statistic is large enough to indicate a significant correlation. With $df = 23$, the table shows that a minimum value of $t = 2.069$ is needed to be significant with an alpha level of .05. Our sample exceeds this criterion, so we can conclude that there is a significant correlation between the two variables.

SIGNIFICANCE OF A REGRESSION EQUATION (ANALYSIS OF REGRESSION)

The significance test for regression is used to determine whether the regression equation predicts a significant proportion of the variance for the Y scores. Alternatively, the test determines whether the slope constant (or constants) in the equation is significantly different from zero. To demonstrate the test for significance, we assume that a researcher has computed a regression equation with

$k = 2$ predictor variables and obtained $R^2 = 0.30$ for a sample of $n = 25$ individuals.

The analysis of regression is similar to an analysis of variance and produces an F-ratio that compares the predicted variance (numerator) with the unpredicted error variance (denominator). The general structure of the analysis for SS and for df values is as follows:

| Total SS | | Total df $(n-1)$ | |
| Predicted SS R^2 | Error SS $(1-R^2)$ | Predicted df k | Error df $n-(k+1)$ |

For the sample in this demonstration, $R^2 = 0.30$, $n = 25$, and $k = 2$. The predicted variance and the error variance are:

$$\text{Predicted variance} = \frac{\text{Predicted } SS}{\text{Predicted } df} = \frac{R^2}{k} = \frac{0.30}{2} = 0.15$$

$$\text{Error variance} = \frac{\text{Error } SS}{\text{Error } df} = \frac{(1-R^2)}{n-(k+1)} = \frac{0.70}{22} = 0.032$$

With these values:

$$F = \frac{\text{Predicted variance}}{\text{Error variance}} = \frac{0.15}{0.032} = 4.69$$

You must consult an F distribution table to determine whether the obtained F-ratio is large enough to indicate a significant regression equation. With $df = 2, 22$, the table shows that a minimum value of $F = 3.44$ is needed to be significant with an alpha level of .05. Our sample exceeds this criterion, so we can conclude that the regression equation is significant.

CHI-SQUARE TEST FOR INDEPENDENCE

The chi-square test for independence is a hypothesis test that is used to evaluate the relationship between two variables measured on nominal or ordinal scales, or the difference in proportions between separate groups of participants. The following data are used to demonstrate the chi-square test for independence. The data represent a frequency distribution for a sample of 200 people. Each person is classified on two different variables: Personality (introvert or extrovert) and favorite color (red, yellow, green, or blue). The number in each cell is the number of individuals with the corresponding personality and color preference. For example, 10 people were classified as Introverts and selected Red as their favorite color. The frequency values found in the data are called *observed frequencies*, or f_O values.

Favorite Color

	Red	Yellow	Green	Blue	Total
Introvert	10	3	15	22	50
Extrovert	90	17	25	18	150
Total	100	20	40	40	

For these data, the null hypothesis can be stated in two versions:

1. There is no relationship between personality and color preference.
2. The distribution of color preferences (the set of proportions) is the same for introverts and extroverts.

Step 1:

The first step in the chi-square test is to compute a hypothetical set of frequencies that represent how the sample would appear if it were in perfect accord with the null hypothesis. The hypothetical frequencies are called *expected frequencies* or f_E values. For each cell in the matrix, the expected frequency can be computed by:

$$f_E = \frac{\text{(row total)(column total)}}{\text{total number}}$$

For example, the upper left-hand cell in the matrix is in the first row (with a total of 50) and in the first column (with a total of 100). The total number of participants in the entire study is 200, so this cell would have an expected frequency of:

$$f_E = \frac{(50)(100)}{200} = 25$$

The complete set of expected frequencies is shown in the following matrix.

Favorite Color

	Red	Yellow	Green	Blue	Total
Introvert	25	5	10	10	50
Extrovert	75	15	30	30	150
Total	100	20	40	40	

Step 2:

The second step in the chi-square test is to compute the value of chi-square (χ^2), which provides a measure of how well the observed frequencies (the data) fit the expected frequencies (the hypothesis). The formula for chi-square is:

$$\chi^2 = \Sigma \frac{(f_O - f_E)^2}{f_E}$$

The step-by-step calculation for our data is shown in the following table:

1. For each cell in the matrix, find the difference between the expected and the observed frequency.
2. Square the difference.
3. Divide the squared difference by the expected frequency.
4. Add the resulting values for each category.

f_O	f_E	$(f_O - f_E)$	$(f_O - f_E)^2$	$(f_O - f_E)^2/f_E$
10	25	15	225	9.00
3	5	2	4	0.80
15	10	5	25	2.50
22	10	12	144	14.40
90	75	15	225	3.00
17	15	2	4	0.27
25	30	5	25	0.83
18	30	12	144	4.80

$$35.60 = \chi^2$$

You must consult a chi-square distribution table to determine whether the obtained chi-square value ($\chi^2 = 35.60$) is large enough to be statistically significant. The chi-square statistic has degrees of freedom given by:

$$df = (C_1 - 1)(C_2 - 1)$$

C_1 is the number of categories for the first variable and C_2 is the number of categories for the second variable. For our data:

$$df = (2 - 1)(4 - 1) = 3$$

With $df = 3$, the table shows that a minimum value of $\chi^2 = 11.34$ is needed for significance with an alpha level of .01. Our data exceed this criterion, so, depending on which version of the null hypothesis was used, we can conclude either there is a significant relationship between personality and color preference or the distribution of color preferences for introverts is significantly different from the distribution for extroverts.

Effect Size for the Chi-Square Test for Independence

When there are exactly two categories for each variable the data can be displayed as a 2×2 matrix and the effect size can be measured with a correlation known as a phi-coefficient. The phi-coefficient can be computed directly from the value obtained for chi-square as follows:

$$\Phi = \sqrt{\frac{\chi^2}{n}}$$

With more than two categories for either variable, effect size is measured with a modification of the phi-coefficient known as Cramér's V. Cramér's V uses the same basic formula as the phi-coefficient but incorporates a modified version of the degrees of freedom (df^*), which is the smaller of either the $(C_1 - 1)$ or $(C_2 - 1)$ values that are used to compute the df value for the chi-square test. For the data in the previous chi-square example, we obtained $\chi^2 = 35.60$ for a sample of $n = 200$ participants with 2 categories for personality and 4 categories for color. For these data, Cramér's V is:

$$V = \sqrt{\frac{\chi^2}{n(df^*)}} = \sqrt{\frac{35.60}{200(1)}} = \sqrt{0.178} = 0.422$$

STATISTICAL TABLES

TABLE **B.1**
The *t* Distribution

Table entries are the minimum values of *t* that are necessary for a *t* statistic to be significant at the alpha level specified. To be significant, a calculated *t* statistic must be greater than or equal to the value in the table.

	Alpha Level for a Directional (One-Tailed) Test					
	0.25	0.10	0.05	0.025	0.01	0.005
	Alpha Level for a Nondirectional (Two-Tailed) Test					
df	0.50	0.20	0.10	0.05	0.002	0.01
1	1.000	3.078	6.314	12.706	31.821	63.657
2	0.816	1.886	2.920	4.303	6.965	9.925
3	0.765	1.638	2.353	3.182	4.541	5.841
4	0.741	1.533	2.132	2.776	3.747	4.604
5	0.727	1.476	2.015	2.571	3.365	4.032
6	0.718	1.440	1.943	2.447	3.143	3.707
7	0.711	1.415	1.895	2.365	2.998	3.499
8	0.706	1.397	1.860	2.306	2.896	3.355
9	0.703	1.383	1.833	2.262	2.821	3.250
10	0.700	1.372	1.812	2.228	2.764	3.169
11	0.697	1.363	1.796	2.201	2.718	3.106
12	0.695	1.356	1.782	2.179	2.681	3.055
13	0.694	1.350	1.771	2.160	2.650	3.012
14	0.692	1.345	1.761	2.145	2.624	2.977
15	0.691	1.341	1.753	2.131	2.602	2.947
16	0.690	1.337	1.746	2.120	2.583	2.921
17	0.689	1.333	1.740	2.110	2.567	2.898
18	0.688	1.330	1.734	2.101	2.552	2.878
19	0.688	1.328	1.729	2.093	2.539	2.861
20	0.687	1.325	1.725	2.086	2.528	2.845
21	0.686	1.323	1.721	2.080	2.518	2.831
22	0.686	1.321	1.717	2.074	2.508	2.819
23	0.685	1.319	1.714	2.069	2.500	2.807
24	0.685	1.318	1.711	2.064	2.492	2.797
25	0.684	1.316	1.708	2.060	2.485	2.787
26	0.684	1.315	1.706	2.056	2.479	2.779
27	0.684	1.314	1.703	2.052	2.473	2.771
28	0.683	1.313	1.701	2.048	2.467	2.763
29	0.683	1.311	1.699	2.045	2.462	2.756
30	0.683	1.310	1.697	2.042	2.457	2.750
40	0.681	1.303	1.684	2.021	2.423	2.704
60	0.679	1.296	1.671	2.000	2.390	2.660
120	0.677	1.289	1.658	1.980	2.358	2.617
∞	0.674	1.282	1.645	1.960	2.326	2.576

Table III of R. A. Fisher and F. Yates, *Statistical Tables for Biological, Agricultural and Medical Research*, 6th ed. London: Longman Group Ltd., 1974 (previously published by Oliver and Boyd Ltd., Edinburgh). Copyright © 1963 R.A. Fisher and Pearson Education Ltd.

TABLE **B.2**
The *F* Distribution

Table entries lightface type are the minimum values that are necessary for a *F*-ratio to be significant at an alpha level of 0.05. Boldface entries are the minimum vales that are necessary for an *F*-ratio to be significant at an alpha level of 0.01. To be significant, a calculated *F*-ratio must be greater than or equal to the value in the table.

Degrees of
Freedom:
Denominator   Degrees of Freedom: Numerator

	1	2	3	4	5	6	7	8	9	10	11	12	14	16	20
1	161	200	216	225	230	234	237	239	241	242	243	244	245	246	248
	4052	**4999**	**5403**	**5625**	**5764**	**5859**	**5928**	**5981**	**6022**	**6056**	**6082**	**6106**	**6142**	**6169**	**6208**
2	18.51	19.00	19.16	19.25	19.30	19.33	19.36	19.37	19.38	19.39	19.40	19.41	19.42	19.43	19.44
	98.49	**99.00**	**99.17**	**99.25**	**99.30**	**99.33**	**99.34**	**99.36**	**99.38**	**99.40**	**99.41**	**99.42**	**99.43**	**99.44**	**99.45**
3	10.13	9.55	9.28	9.12	9.01	8.94	8.88	8.84	8.81	8.78	8.76	8.74	8.71	8.69	8.66
	34.12	**30.92**	**29.46**	**28.71**	**28.24**	**27.91**	**27.67**	**27.49**	**27.34**	**27.23**	**27.13**	**27.05**	**26.92**	**26.83**	**26.69**
4	7.71	6.94	6.59	6.39	6.26	6.16	6.09	6.04	6.00	5.96	5.93	5.91	5.87	5.84	5.80
	21.20	**18.00**	**16.69**	**15.98**	**15.52**	**15.21**	**14.98**	**14.80**	**14.66**	**14.54**	**14.45**	**14.37**	**14.24**	**14.15**	**14.02**
5	6.61	5.79	5.41	5.19	5.05	4.95	4.88	4.82	4.78	4.74	4.70	4.68	4.64	4.60	4.56
	16.26	**13.27**	**12.06**	**11.39**	**10.97**	**10.67**	**10.45**	**10.27**	**10.15**	**10.05**	**9.96**	**9.89**	**9.77**	**9.68**	**9.55**
6	5.99	5.14	4.76	4.53	4.39	4.28	4.21	4.15	4.10	4.06	4.03	4.00	3.96	3.92	3.87
	13.74	**10.92**	**9.78**	**9.15**	**8.75**	**8.47**	**8.26**	**8.10**	**7.98**	**7.87**	**7.79**	**7.72**	**7.60**	**7.52**	**7.39**
7	5.59	4.47	4.35	4.12	3.97	3.87	3.79	3.73	3.68	3.63	3.60	3.57	3.52	3.49	3.44
	12.25	**9.55**	**8.45**	**7.85**	**7.46**	**7.19**	**7.00**	**6.84**	**6.71**	**6.62**	**6.54**	**6.47**	**6.35**	**6.27**	**6.15**
8	5.32	4.46	4.07	3.84	3.69	3.58	3.50	3.44	3.39	3.34	3.31	3.28	3.23	3.20	3.15
	11.26	**8.65**	**7.59**	**7.01**	**6.63**	**6.37**	**6.19**	**6.03**	**5.91**	**5.82**	**5.74**	**5.67**	**5.56**	**5.48**	**5.36**
9	5.12	4.26	3.86	3.63	3.48	3.37	3.29	3.23	3.18	3.13	3.10	3.07	3.02	2.98	2.93
	10.56	**8.02**	**6.99**	**6.42**	**6.06**	**5.80**	**5.62**	**5.47**	**5.35**	**5.26**	**5.18**	**5.11**	**5.00**	**4.92**	**4.80**
10	4.96	4.10	3.71	3.48	3.33	3.22	3.14	3.07	3.02	2.97	2.94	2.91	2.86	2.82	2.77
	10.04	**7.56**	**6.55**	**5.99**	**5.64**	**5.39**	**5.21**	**5.06**	**4.95**	**4.85**	**4.78**	**4.71**	**4.60**	**4.52**	**4.41**
11	4.84	3.98	3.59	3.36	3.20	3.09	3.01	2.95	2.90	2.86	2.82	2.79	2.74	2.70	2.65
	9.65	**7.20**	**6.22**	**5.67**	**5.32**	**5.07**	**4.88**	**4.74**	**4.63**	**4.54**	**4.46**	**4.40**	**4.29**	**4.21**	**4.10**
12	4.75	3.88	3.49	3.26	3.11	3.00	2.92	2.85	2.80	2.76	2.72	2.69	2.64	2.60	2.54
	9.33	**6.93**	**5.95**	**5.41**	**5.06**	**4.82**	**4.65**	**4.50**	**4.39**	**4.30**	**4.22**	**4.16**	**4.05**	**3.98**	**3.86**
13	4.67	3.80	3.41	3.18	3.02	2.92	2.84	2.77	2.72	2.67	2.63	2.60	2.55	2.51	2.46
	9.07	**6.70**	**5.74**	**5.20**	**4.86**	**4.62**	**4.44**	**4.30**	**4.19**	**4.10**	**4.02**	**3.96**	**3.85**	**3.78**	**3.67**
14	4.60	3.74	3.34	3.11	2.96	2.85	2.77	2.70	2.65	2.60	2.56	2.53	2.48	2.44	2.39
	8.86	**6.51**	**5.56**	**5.03**	**4.69**	**4.46**	**4.28**	**4.14**	**4.03**	**3.94**	**3.86**	**3.80**	**3.70**	**3.62**	**3.51**
15	4.54	3.68	3.29	3.06	2.90	2.79	2.70	2.64	2.59	2.55	2.51	2.48	2.43	2.39	2.33
	8.68	**6.36**	**5.42**	**4.89**	**4.56**	**4.32**	**4.14**	**4.00**	**3.89**	**3.80**	**3.73**	**3.67**	**3.56**	**3.48**	**3.36**
16	4.49	3.63	3.24	3.01	2.85	2.74	2.66	2.59	2.54	2.49	2.45	2.42	2.37	2.33	2.28
	8.53	**6.23**	**5.29**	**4.77**	**4.44**	**4.20**	**4.03**	**3.89**	**3.78**	**3.69**	**3.61**	**3.55**	**3.45**	**3.37**	**3.25**
17	4.45	3.59	3.20	2.96	2.81	2.70	2.62	2.55	2.50	2.45	2.41	2.38	2.33	2.29	2.23
	8.40	**6.11**	**5.18**	**4.67**	**4.34**	**4.10**	**3.93**	**3.79**	**3.68**	**3.59**	**3.52**	**3.45**	**3.35**	**3.27**	**3.16**

Continued

TABLE **B.2**
The *F* Distribution—cont'd

Degrees of Freedom: Denominator						Degrees of Freedom: Numerator								
	1	2	3	4	5	6	7	8	9	10	11	12	14	16	20
18	4.41	3.55	3.16	2.93	2.77	2.66	2.58	2.51	2.46	2.41	2.37	2.34	2.29	2.25	2.19
	8.28	**6.01**	**5.09**	**4.58**	**4.25**	**4.01**	**3.85**	**3.71**	**3.60**	**3.51**	**3.44**	**3.37**	**3.27**	**3.19**	**3.07**
19	4.38	3.52	3.13	2.90	2.74	2.63	2.55	2.48	2.43	2.38	2.34	2.31	2.26	2.21	2.15
	8.18	**5.93**	**5.01**	**4.50**	**4.17**	**3.94**	**3.77**	**3.63**	**3.52**	**3.43**	**3.36**	**3.30**	**3.19**	**3.12**	**3.00**
20	4.35	3.49	3.10	2.87	2.71	2.60	2.52	2.45	2.40	2.35	2.31	2.28	2.23	2.18	2.12
	8.10	**5.85**	**4.94**	**4.43**	**4.10**	**3.87**	**3.71**	**3.56**	**3.45**	**3.37**	**3.30**	**3.23**	**3.13**	**3.05**	**2.94**
21	4.32	3.47	3.07	2.84	2.68	2.57	2.49	2.42	2.37	2.32	2.28	2.25	2.20	2.15	2.09
	8.02	**5.78**	**4.87**	**4.37**	**4.04**	**3.81**	**3.65**	**3.51**	**3.40**	**3.31**	**3.24**	**3.17**	**3.07**	**2.99**	**2.88**
22	4.30	3.44	3.05	2.82	2.66	2.55	2.47	2.40	2.35	2.30	2.26	2.23	2.18	2.13	2.07
	7.94	**5.72**	**4.82**	**4.31**	**3.99**	**3.76**	**3.59**	**3.45**	**3.35**	**3.26**	**3.18**	**3.12**	**3.02**	**2.94**	**2.83**
23	4.28	3.42	3.03	2.80	2.64	2.53	2.45	2.38	2.32	2.28	2.24	2.20	2.14	2.10	2.04
	7.88	**5.66**	**4.76**	**4.26**	**3.94**	**3.71**	**3.54**	**3.41**	**3.30**	**3.21**	**3.14**	**3.07**	**2.97**	**2.89**	**2.78**
24	4.26	3.40	3.01	2.78	2.62	2.51	2.43	2.36	2.30	2.26	2.22	2.18	2.13	2.09	2.02
	7.82	**5.61**	**4.72**	**4.22**	**3.90**	**3.67**	**3.50**	**3.36**	**3.25**	**3.17**	**3.09**	**3.03**	**2.93**	**2.85**	**2.74**
25	4.24	3.38	2.99	2.76	2.60	2.49	2.41	2.34	2.28	2.24	2.20	2.16	2.11	2.06	2.00
	7.77	**5.57**	**4.68**	**4.18**	**3.86**	**3.63**	**3.46**	**3.32**	**3.21**	**3.13**	**3.05**	**2.99**	**2.89**	**2.81**	**2.70**
26	4.22	3.37	2.98	2.74	2.59	2.47	2.39	2.32	2.27	2.22	2.18	2.15	2.10	2.05	1.99
	7.72	**5.53**	**4.64**	**4.14**	**3.82**	**3.59**	**3.42**	**3.29**	**3.17**	**3.09**	**3.02**	**2.96**	**2.86**	**2.77**	**2.66**
27	4.21	3.35	2.96	2.73	2.57	2.46	2.37	2.30	2.25	2.20	2.16	2.13	2.08	2.03	1.97
	7.68	**5.49**	**4.60**	**4.11**	**3.79**	**3.56**	**3.39**	**3.26**	**3.14**	**3.06**	**2.98**	**2.93**	**2.83**	**2.74**	**2.63**
28	4.20	3.34	2.95	2.71	2.56	2.44	2.36	2.29	2.24	2.19	2.15	2.12	2.06	2.02	1.96
	7.64	**5.45**	**4.57**	**4.07**	**3.76**	**3.53**	**3.36**	**3.23**	**3.11**	**3.03**	**2.95**	**2.90**	**2.80**	**2.71**	**2.60**
29	4.18	3.33	2.93	2.70	2.54	2.43	2.35	2.28	2.22	2.18	2.14	2.10	2.05	2.00	1.94
	7.60	**5.42**	**4.54**	**4.04**	**3.73**	**3.50**	**3.33**	**3.20**	**3.08**	**3.00**	**2.92**	**2.87**	**2.77**	**2.68**	**2.57**
30	4.17	3.32	2.92	2.69	2.53	2.42	2.34	2.27	2.21	2.16	2.12	2.09	2.04	1.99	1.93
	7.56	**5.39**	**4.51**	**4.02**	**3.70**	**3.47**	**3.30**	**3.17**	**3.06**	**2.98**	**2.90**	**2.84**	**2.74**	**2.66**	**2.55**
32	4.15	3.30	2.90	2.67	2.51	2.40	2.32	2.25	2.19	2.14	2.10	2.07	2.02	1.97	1.91
	7.50	**5.34**	**4.46**	**3.97**	**3.66**	**3.42**	**3.25**	**3.12**	**3.01**	**2.94**	**2.86**	**2.80**	**2.70**	**2.62**	**2.51**
34	4.13	3.28	2.88	2.65	2.49	2.38	2.30	2.23	2.17	2.12	2.08	2.05	2.00	1.95	1.89
	7.44	**5.29**	**4.42**	**3.93**	**3.61**	**3.38**	**3.21**	**3.08**	**2.97**	**2.89**	**2.82**	**2.76**	**2.66**	**2.58**	**2.47**
36	4.11	3.26	2.86	2.63	2.48	2.36	2.28	2.21	2.15	2.10	2.06	2.03	1.98	1.93	1.87
	7.39	**5.25**	**4.38**	**3.89**	**3.58**	**3.35**	**3.18**	**3.04**	**2.94**	**2.86**	**2.78**	**2.72**	**2.62**	**2.54**	**2.43**
38	4.10	3.25	2.85	2.62	2.46	2.35	2.26	2.19	2.14	2.09	2.05	2.02	1.96	1.92	1.85
	7.35	**5.21**	**4.34**	**3.86**	**3.54**	**3.32**	**3.15**	**3.02**	**2.91**	**2.82**	**2.75**	**2.69**	**2.59**	**2.51**	**2.40**
40	4.08	3.23	2.84	2.61	2.45	2.34	2.25	2.18	2.12	2.07	2.04	2.00	1.95	1.90	1.84
	7.31	**5.18**	**4.31**	**3.83**	**3.51**	**3.29**	**3.12**	**2.99**	**2.88**	**2.80**	**2.73**	**2.66**	**2.56**	**2.49**	**2.37**
42	4.07	3.22	2.83	2.59	2.44	2.32	2.24	2.17	2.11	2.06	2.02	1.99	2.5	1.89	1.82
	7.27	**5.15**	**4.29**	**3.80**	**3.49**	**3.26**	**3.10**	**2.96**	**2.86**	**2.77**	**2.70**	**2.64**	**2.54**	**2.46**	**2.35**
44	4.06	3.21	2.82	2.58	2.43	2.31	2.23	2.16	2.10	2.05	2.01	1.98	1.92	1.88	1.81
	7.24	**5.12**	**4.26**	**3.78**	**3.46**	**3.24**	**3.07**	**2.94**	**2.84**	**2.75**	**2.68**	**2.62**	**2.52**	**2.44**	**2.32**

TABLE **B.2**
The *F* Distribution—cont'd

Degrees of Freedom: Denominator	Degrees of Freedom: Numerator														
	1	2	3	4	5	6	7	8	9	10	11	12	14	16	20
46	4.05	3.20	2.81	2.57	2.42	2.30	2.22	2.14	2.09	2.04	2.00	1.97	1.91	1.87	1.80
	7.21	5.10	4.24	3.76	3.44	3.22	3.05	2.92	2.82	2.73	2.66	2.60	2.50	2.42	2.30
48	4.04	3.19	2.80	2.56	2.41	2.30	2.21	2.14	2.08	2.03	1.99	1.96	1.90	1.86	1.79
	7.19	5.08	4.22	3.74	3.42	3.20	3.04	2.90	2.80	2.71	2.64	2.58	2.48	2.40	2.28
50	4.03	3.18	2.79	2.56	2.40	2.29	2.20	2.13	2.07	2.02	1.98	1.95	1.90	1.85	1.78
	7.17	5.06	4.20	3.72	3.41	3.18	3.02	2.88	2.78	2.70	2.62	2.56	2.46	2.39	2.26
55	4.02	3.17	2.78	2.54	2.38	2.27	2.18	2.11	2.05	2.00	1.97	1.93	1.88	1.83	1.76
	7.12	5.01	4.16	3.68	3.37	3.15	2.98	2.85	2.75	2.66	2.59	2.53	2.43	2.35	2.23
60	4.00	3.15	2.76	2.52	2.37	2.25	2.17	2.10	2.04	1.99	1.95	1.92	1.86	1.81	1.75
	7.08	4.98	4.13	3.65	3.34	3.12	2.95	2.82	2.72	2.63	2.56	250	2.40	2.32	2.20
65	3.99	3.14	2.75	2.51	2.36	2.24	2.15	2.08	2.02	1.98	1.94	1.90	1.85	1.80	1.73
	7.04	4.95	4.10	3.62	3.31	3.09	2.93	2.79	2.70	2.61	2.54	2.47	2.37	2.30	2.18
70	3.98	3.13	2.74	2.50	2.35	2.23	2.14	2.07	2.01	1.97	1.93	1.89	1.84	1.79	1.72
	7.01	4.92	4.08	3.60	3.29	3.07	2.91	2.77	2.67	2.59	2.51	2.45	2.35	2.28	2.15
80	3.96	3.11	2.72	2.48	2.33	2.21	2.12	2.05	1.99	1.95	1.91	1.88	1.82	1.77	1.70
	6.96	4.88	4.04	3.56	3.25	3.04	2.87	2.74	2.64	2.55	2.48	2.41	2.32	2.24	2.11
100	3.94	3.09	2.70	2.46	2.30	2.19	2.10	2.03	1.97	1.92	1.88	1.85	1.79	1.75	1.68
	6.90	4.82	3.98	3.51	3.20	2.99	2.82	2.69	2.59	2.51	2.43	2.36	2.26	2.19	2.06
125	3.92	3.07	2.68	2.44	2.29	2.17	2.08	2.01	1.95	1.90	1.86	1.83	1.77	1.72	1.65
	6.84	4.78	3.94	3.47	3.17	2.95	2.79	2.65	2.56	2.47	2.40	2.33	2.23	2.15	2.03
150	3.91	3.06	2.67	2.43	2.27	2.16	2.07	2.00	1.94	1.89	1.85	1.82	1.76	1.71	1.64
	6.81	4.75	3.91	3.44	3.14	2.92	2.76	2.62	2.53	2.44	2.37	2.30	2.20	2.12	2.00
200	3.89	3.04	2.65	2.41	2.26	2.14	2.05	1.98	1.92	1.87	1.83	1.80	1.74	1.69	1.62
	6.76	4.71	3.88	3.41	3.11	2.90	2.73	2.60	2.50	2.41	2.34	2.28	2.17	2.09	1.97
400	3.86	3.02	2.62	2.39	2.23	2.12	2.03	1.96	1.90	1.85	1.81	1.78	1.72	1.67	1.60
	6.70	4.66	3.83	3.36	3.06	2.85	2.69	2.55	2.46	2.37	2.29	2.23	2.12	2.04	1.92
1000	3.85	3.00	2.61	2.38	2.22	2.10	2.02	1.95	1.89	1.84	1.80	1.76	1.70	1.65	1.58
	6.66	4.62	3.80	3.34	3.04	2.82	2.66	2.53	2.43	2.34	2.26	2.20	2.09	2.01	1.89
∞	3.84	2.99	2.60	2.37	2.21	2.09	2.01	1.94	1.88	1.83	1.79	1.75	1.69	1.64	1.57
	6.64	4.60	3.78	3.32	3.02	2.80	2.64	2.51	2.41	2.32	2.24	2.18	2.07	1.99	1.87

Table A14 of *Statistical Methods*, 7th ed., by George W. Snedecor and William G. Cochran. Copyright © 1980 by the Iowa State University Press. Used with permission.

TABLE **B.3**
The Chi-Square Distribution

Table entries are the minimum values of chi-square (χ^2) that are necessary for a chi-square statistic to be significant at the alpha level specified. To be significant, a calculated χ^2 statistic must be greater than or equal to the value in the table.

df	Proportion in Critical Region				
	0.10	0.05	0.025	0.01	0.005
1	2.71	3.84	5.02	6.63	7.88
2	4.61	5.99	7.38	9.21	10.60
3	6.25	7.81	9.35	11.34	12.84
4	7.78	9.49	11.14	13.28	14.86
5	9.24	11.07	12.83	15.09	16.75
6	10.64	12.59	14.45	16.81	18.55
7	12.02	14.07	16.01	18.48	20.28
8	13.36	15.51	17.53	20.09	21.96
9	14.68	16.92	19.02	21.67	23.59
10	15.99	18.31	20.48	23.21	25.19
11	17.28	19.68	21.92	24.72	26.76
12	18.55	21.03	23.34	26.22	28.30
13	19.81	22.36	24.74	27.69	29.82
14	21.06	23.68	26.12	29.14	31.32
15	22.31	25.00	27.49	30.58	32.80
16	23.54	26.30	28.85	32.00	34.27
17	24.77	27.59	30.19	33.41	35.72
18	25.99	28.87	31.53	34.81	37.16
19	27.20	30.14	32.85	36.19	38.58
20	28.41	31.41	34.17	37.57	40.00
21	29.62	32.67	35.48	38.93	41.40
22	30.81	33.92	36.78	40.29	42.80
23	32.01	35.17	38.08	41.64	44.18
24	33.20	36.42	39.36	42.98	45.56
25	34.38	37.65	40.65	44.31	46.93
26	35.56	38.89	41.92	45.64	48.29
27	36.74	40.11	43.19	46.96	49.64
28	37.92	41.34	44.46	48.28	50.99
29	39.09	42.56	45.72	49.59	52.34
30	40.26	43.77	46.98	50.89	53.67
40	51.81	55.76	59.34	63.69	66.77
50	63.17	67.50	71.42	76.15	79.49
60	74.40	79.08	83.30	88.38	91.95
70	85.53	90.53	95.02	100.42	104.22
80	96.58	101.88	106.63	112.33	116.32
90	107.56	113.14	118.14	124.12	128.30
100	118.50	124.34	129.56	135.81	140.17

C

Instructions for Using SPSS

The Statistical Package for the Social Sciences (SPSS) is a computer program that performs statistical calculations and is widely available on college campuses. The program is updated regularly and the current version is also known as Predictive Analysis SoftWare (PASW) Statistics 17. SPSS consists of two basic components: a data matrix and a set of statistical commands.

The **data matrix** is a huge matrix of numbered rows and columns. To begin any analysis, you must type your data into the matrix. Typically, the scores are entered into columns of the matrix. Before scores are entered, each of the columns is labeled "var." After scores are entered, the first column becomes var00001, the second column becomes var00002, and so on. To enter data into the matrix, the **Data View** tab must be set at the bottom left of the screen. If you want to assign a name to a column (instead of using var00001), click on the **Variable View** tab at the bottom of the data matrix. You will get a description of each variable in the matrix, including a box for the name. You may type in a new name using up to eight lower-case characters (no spaces, no hyphens). Click the **Data View** tab to go back to the data matrix.

The **statistical commands** are listed in menus that are made available by clicking on the **Analyze** box that is located on the tool bar at the top of the screen. When you select a statistical command, SPSS typically asks you to identify exactly where the scores are located and exactly what other options you want to use. This is accomplished by identifying the column(s) in the data matrix that contain the needed information. Typically, you are presented with a display similar to the following figure. On the left is a box that lists all of the columns in the data matrix that contain information. In this example, we have typed values into columns 1, 2, 3, and 4. On the right is an empty box that is waiting for you to identify the correct column. For example, suppose that you wanted to do a statistical calculation using the scores in column 3. You should highlight var00003 by clicking on it in the left-hand box, then click the arrow to move the column label into the right hand box. (If you make a mistake, you can highlight the variable in the right-hand box and the arrow will reverse so that you can move the variable back to the left-hand box.)

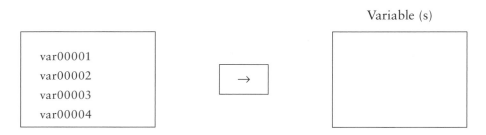

Variable (s)

Following is a set of basic statistical operations that can be performed with SPSS. This is only a partial listing of the many statistical computations that SPSS can do, but it should cover most of the statistics that would be needed in an introductory research methods course.

FREQUENCY DISTRIBUTIONS

A frequency distribution is an organized tabulation showing how many individuals have scores in each category on the scale of measurement. A frequency distribution can be presented either as a table or a graph.

A FREQUENCY DISTRIBUTION TABLE
Data Entry
1.   Enter all the scores in one column of the data matrix, probably var00001.

Data Analysis
1.   Click **Analyze** on the tool bar.
2.   Select **Descriptive Statistics.**
3.   Select **Frequencies.**
4.   Highlight the column label for the set of scores (var0001) in the left box.
5.   Click the arrow to move the column label into the **Variable** box.
6.   Be sure that the option to **Display Frequency Table** is selected.
7.   Click **OK.**

Output
The frequency distribution table lists the score values in a column from smallest to largest, with the percentage and cumulative percentage also listed for each score. Score values that do not occur (zero frequency) are not included in the table, and the program does not group scores into class intervals (all values are listed).

A FREQUENCY DISTRIBUTION HISTOGRAM OR BAR GRAPH
Data Entry
1.   Enter all the scores in one column of the data matrix, probably var00001.

Data Analysis

1. Click **Analyze** on the tool bar.
2. Select **Descriptive Statistics**.
3. Select **Frequencies**.
4. Highlight the column label for the set of scores (var00001) in the left box.
5. Click the arrow to move the column label into the **Variable** box.
6. Click **Charts**.
7. Select either **Bar Graph** or **Histogram**.
8. Click **Continue**.
9. Click **OK**.

Output

SPSS displays a frequency distribution table and a graph (Figure C.1). Note that the program often produces a histogram that groups the scores in unpredictable intervals. A bar graph usually produces a clearer picture of the actual frequency associated with each score.

Example: The following set of scores produce a frequency distribution (either a table or a graph) showing that three people had scores of $X = 1$, five people had $X = 2$, six people had $X = 3$, four had $X = 4$, and two had $X = 5$.

Scores: 1, 2, 4, 2, 3, 3, 5, 1, 3, 4, 2, 4, 3, 2, 4, 3, 1, 3, 2, 5

The bar graph from the computer printout for this example is shown in Figure C.1.

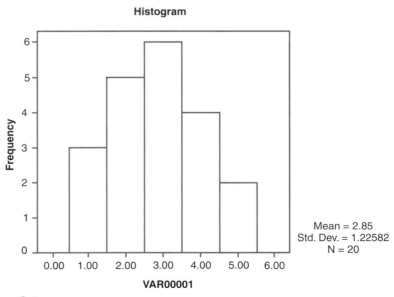

FIGURE **C.1**

A Frequency Distribution Histogram from SPSS

MEANS AND STANDARD DEVIATIONS

The mean and standard deviation are probably the two most commonly used statistics for describing a set of scores. The mean describes the center of the set of scores and the standard deviation describes how the scores are scattered around the mean. In simple terms, the standard deviation provides a measure of the average distance from the mean.

Data Entry

1. Enter all of the scores in one column of the data matrix, probably var00001.

Data Analysis

1. Click **Analyze** on the tool bar.
2. Select **Descriptive Statistics**.
3. Select **Descriptives**.
4. Highlight the column label for the set of scores (var00001) in the left box.
5. Click the arrow to move the column label into the **Variable** box.
6. Click **OK**.

Output

SPSS produces a summary table listing the number of scores (N), the minimum score, the maximum score, the mean, and the standard deviation (Figure C.2). Note that SPSS computes the *sample* standard deviation using $n - 1$. If your scores are intended to be a population, you must multiply the sample standard deviation by the square root of $(n - 1)/n$ to obtain the population standard deviation.

Note: You can also obtain the mean and standard deviation for a sample if you use SPSS to display the scores in a frequency distribution histogram (see the preceding section on frequency distributions). The mean and standard deviation are displayed beside the graph.

Example: The following scores produce a mean of $M = 2.85$ and a standard deviation of $SD = 1.23$.

Scores: 1, 2, 4, 2, 3, 3, 5, 1, 3, 4, 2, 4, 3, 2, 4, 3, 1, 3, 2, 5

The computer printout for this example is shown in Figure C.2.

Descriptive Statistics

	N	Minimum	Maximum	Mean	Std. Deviation
VAR00001	20	1.00	5.00	2.8500	1.22582
Valid N (listwise)	20				

FIGURE **C.2**

Descriptive Statistics from SPSS

THE INDEPENDENT-MEASURES *t* TEST

The independent-measures *t* test is used to compare two means from a between-subjects research design: that is, the test evaluates the mean difference between two separate samples that represent two separate treatment conditions or two separate populations. A *significant difference* indicates that there appears to be a consistent, systematic difference between the two treatments and that the obtained mean difference is very unlikely ($p < .05$) to have occurred by chance alone. The significance is determined by the p value that is reported as part of the computer output.

Data Entry

1. The scores are entered in what is called a *stacked format,* which means that all the scores from *both samples* are entered in one column of the data matrix (probably var00001).
2. Values are then entered into a second column (var00002) to designate the sample or treatment condition corresponding to each of the scores. For example, enter a 1 beside each score from sample #1 and enter a 2 beside each score from sample #2.

Data Analysis

1. Click **Analyze** on the tool bar.
2. Select **Compare Means**.
3. Click on **Independent-Samples T Test**.
4. Highlight the column label for the set of scores (var00001) in the left box.
5. Click the arrow to move the column label into the **Test Variable** box.
6. Highlight the column label containing the sample numbers (var00002) in the left box.
7. Click the arrow to move the column label into the **Group Variable** box.
8. Click on **Define Groups.**
9. Click on the button for **Use Specific Values** and enter a 1 in the box for Group 1 and a 2 in the box for Group 2.
10. Click **Continue.**
11. Click **OK.**

Output

SPSS produces a summary table showing the number of scores, the mean, the standard deviation, and the standard error for each of the two samples (Figure C.3). SPSS also conducts a test for homogeneity of variance, using Levene's test. Homogeneity of variance is an assumption for the *t* test and requires that the two populations from which the samples were obtained have equal variances. This test should *not* be significant (you do not want the two variances to be different), so you want the reported **Sig.** value to be greater than .05. Next, the results of the hypothesis test are presented using two different assumptions; we focus on the top row, where equal variances are assumed. [If Levene's test is significant (the Sig value is less than .05), then use the values in the bottom row.] The test results include the calculated t value, the degrees of freedom, the level of significance (probability of a Type I error), and the size of the mean difference. Finally, the output includes a report of the standard error for the mean difference and a 95% confidence interval that provides a range of values estimating how much difference exists between the two treatment conditions.

The output also includes the information necessary to compute measures of effect size. The values for t and df can be used to calculate r^2. The sample mean difference and the two sample standard deviations can be used to compute Cohen's d (see Appendix B, p. 530).

Example: The following two samples produce a t statistic of $t = 3.834$, with degrees of freedom equal to $df = 6$, and a significance level of $p = 0.009$ with Cohen's $d = 2.71$ and $r^2 = 0.710$. The computer printout for this example is shown in Figure C.3.

Treatment 1 (Sample 1)	Treatment 2 (Sample 2)
3	12
5	10
7	8
1	14

Group Statistics

	VAR00002	N	Mean	Std. Deviation	Std. Error Mean
VAR00001	1.00	4	4.0000	2.58199	1.29099
	2.00	4	11.0000	2.58199	1.29099

Independent Samples Test

		t-test for Equality of Mean				
		t	df	Sig. (2-tailed)	Mean Difference	Std. Error Difference
VAR00001	Equal variances assumed	-3.834	6	.009	-7.00000	1.82574
	Equal variances not assumed	-3.834	6.000	.009	-7.00000	1.82574

FIGURE **C.3**   An Independent Samples t Test Printout from SPSS

The portions of the printout showing Levine's test and the confidence interval have been deleted to conserve space.

THE REPEATED-MEASURES *t* TEST

The repeated-measures *t* test is used to compare two means from a within-subjects research design: that is, the test evaluates the mean difference between two treatment conditions in which the same set of individuals is measured in both treatments. A *significant difference* indicates that there appears to be a consistent, systematic difference between the two treatments and that the obtained mean difference is very unlikely ($p < .05$) to have occurred by chance alone. The significance is determined by the p value that is reported as part of the computer output.

Data Entry

1. Enter the data into two columns (var00001 and var00002) in the data matrix with the first score for each participant in the first column and the second score in the second column.

Data Analysis

1. Click **Analyze** on the tool bar.
2. Select **Compare Means.**
3. Click on **Paired-Samples T Test.**
4. Highlight the label for the first data column in the left box and then click on the arrow to move the label into the **Variable 1** area of the **Paired Variables** box.
5. Highlight the label for the second data column in the left box and click on the arrow to move the label into the **Variable 2** area of the **Paired Variables** box.
6. Click **OK.**

Output

SPSS produces a summary table showing descriptive statistics for each of the two sets of scores, and a table showing the correlation between the first and second scores. Finally, SPSS conducts the *t* test for the difference scores. The output shows the mean difference, the standard deviation and the standard error for the difference scores, as well as the value for *t*, the value for *df*, and the level of significance (Figure C.4). The output also includes a 95% confidence interval that provides a range of values estimating how much difference exists between the two treatment conditions.

The output includes the information necessary to compute measures of effect size. The values for *t* and *df* can be used to calculate r^2. The mean and the standard deviation for the difference scores can be used to compute Cohen's *d* (see Appendix B, p. 531).

Note: If you have already computed the difference score for each participant (instead of pairs of scores), you can do the repeated-measures *t* test by entering the difference scores in one column and selecting the **One-Sample T Test** option. Click **Analyze** on the tool bar, select **Compare Means,** and click on **One-Sample T Test.** Move the column label for the set of difference scores into the **Test Variable** box, and enter a value of zero in the **Test Value** box.

Example: The following data show a mean difference of five points between the two treatments and produce $t = 2.50$, with $df = 3$, and a significance level of $p = 0.088$ with Cohen's $d = 1.25$ and $r^2 = 0.676$. The computer printout for this example is shown in Figure C.4.

Participant	First Treatment	Second Treatment	Difference
A	19	12	−7
B	35	36	+1
C	20	13	−7
D	31	24	−7

SINGLE-FACTOR, INDEPENDENT-MEASURES ANALYSIS OF VARIANCE (ANOVA)

The single-factor, independent-measures ANOVA is used to compare the means from a between-subjects research study using two or more separate samples to compare two or more separate treatment conditions or populations. A significant difference indicates that there appears to be a consistent, systematic difference between at least two of the treatments and that the obtained mean differences are very unlikely ($p < .05$) to have occurred by chance alone. The significance is determined by the p value that is reported as part of the computer output.

Paired Samples Statistics

		Mean	N	Std. Deviation	Std. Error Mean
Pair 1	VAR00001	26.2500	4	7.97392	3.98696
	VAR00002	21.2500	4	11.23610	5.61805

Paired Samples Test

	Paired Differences					Sig. (2-tailed)
	Mean	Std. Deviation	Std. Error Mean	t	df	
Pair 1 VAR00001 - VAR00002	5.00000	4.00000	2.00000	2.500	3	.088

FIGURE **C.4**   An SPSS Printout for a Paired Samples t Test

The table showing the correlation and a portion of the printout showing the confidence interval have been deleted to conserve space.

Data Entry

1. The scores are entered in a *stacked format* in the data matrix, which means that all the scores from all of the different treatments are entered in a single column (var00001).
2. In a second column (var00002), enter a number to designate the treatment condition for each score. For example, enter a 1 beside each score from the first treatment, enter a 2 beside each score from the second treatment, and so on.

Data Analysis

1. Click **Analyze** on the tool bar.
2. Select **Compare Means.**
3. Click on **One-Way ANOVA.**
4. Highlight the column label for the scores (var00001) in the left box.
5. Click the arrow to move the column label into the **Dependent List** box.
6. Highlight the column label for the treatment numbers in the left box.
7. Click the arrow to move the column label into the **Factor** box.
8. If you want to conduct post hoc tests to determine exactly which means are different, click on the **Post Hoc** box, select a test, and click **Continue.**
9. Click on the **Options** box and select **Descriptives** if you want descriptive statistics for each sample, then click **Continue.**
10. Click **OK.**

Output

If you select the **Descriptives** Option, SPSS produces a table showing descriptive statistics for each of the samples along with a summary table showing the results from the analysis of variance (Figure C.5). Also note that the Between-Groups and Total Sum of Squares values in the summary table can be used to compute η^2 to measure effect size (see Appendix B, p. 534).

Example: For the following data, the first treatment has $M = 1.00$ with $SD = 1.73$, the second treatment has $M = 5.00$ with $SD = 2.24$, and the third treatment has $M = 6.00$ with $SD = 1.87$. The analysis produces an F-ratio of $F = 9.13$, with $df = 2, 12$, and a significance level of $p = 0.004$ with $\eta^2 = 0.603$. The computer printout for this example is shown in Figure C.5.

First Treatment	Second Treatment	Third Treatment
0	6	6
4	8	5
0	5	9
1	4	4
0	2	6

Descriptives

VAR00001

	N	Mean	Std. Deviation	Std. Error	95% Confidence Interval for Mean	
					Lower Bound	Upper Bound
1.00	5	1.0000	1.73205	.77460	−1.1506	3.1506
2.00	5	5.0000	2.23607	1.00000	2.2236	7.7764
3.00	5	6.0000	1.87083	.83666	3.6771	8.3229
Total	15	4.0000	2.87849	.74322	2.4059	5.5941

ANOVA

VAR00001

	Sum of Squares	df	Mean Square	F	Sig.
Between Groups	70.000	2	35.000	9.130	.004
Within Groups	46.000	12	3.833		
Total	116.000	14			

FIGURE **C.5**   An SPSS Printout for a Single-Factor Independent-Measures ANOVA

SINGLE-FACTOR, REPEATED-MEASURES ANOVA

The single-factor, repeated-measures ANOVA is used to compare the means from a within-subjects research study using one sample to compare two or more separate treatment conditions (each individual is measured in each of the treatment conditions). A *significant difference* indicates that there appears to be a consistent, systematic difference between at least two of the treatments and that the obtained mean differences are very unlikely ($p < .05$) to have occurred by chance alone. The significance is determined by the p value that is reported as part of the computer output.

Data Entry

1. Enter the scores for each treatment condition in a separate column, with the scores for each individual in the same row. All the scores for the first treatment go in var00001, the second treatment scores in var00002, and so on.

Data Analysis

1. Click **Analyze** on the tool bar.
2. Select **General Linear Model**.
3. Click on **Repeated Measures**.
4. SPSS presents a box titled **Repeated-Measures Define Factors**. Within the box, the Within-Subjects Factor Name should already contain **Factor1**. If not, type in Factor 1.
5. Enter the **Number of Levels** (number of different treatment conditions) in the next box.

6. Click on Add.
7. Click Define.
8. One by one, move the column labels for your treatment conditions into the Within-Subjects Variables box. (Highlight the column label on the left and click the arrow to move it into the box.)
9. If you want to conduct post hoc tests to determine exactly which means are different, click on the Post Hoc box, select a test, and click Continue.
10. Click on the Options and select Descriptives if you want descriptive statistics for each treatment, then click Continue.
11. Click OK.

Output

If you select the Descriptives Option, SPSS produces a table showing the mean and standard deviation for each treatment condition. The rest of the Output is relatively complex and includes a lot of statistical information that goes well beyond the scope of this book. However, if you focus on the table showing Test of Within-Subjects Effects, the top line of the factor1 box and the top line of the Error(factor1) box shows the sum of squares, the degrees of freedom, and the mean square for the numerator and denominator of the F-ratio, as well as the value of the F-ratio and the level of significance (Figure C.6). The two Sum of Squares values that are used in the calculation of the F-ratio are also the values needed to compute η^2 to measure effect size (see Appendix B, p. 537).

   Example: For the following data, the first treatment has $M = 5.00$ with $SD = 1.87$, the second treatment has $M = 4.00$ with $SD = 1.58$, and the third treatment has $M = 3.00$ with $SD = 1.58$. The analysis produces an F-ratio of $F = 10.00$, with $df = 2, 8$, and a significance level of $p = 0.007$ with $\eta^2 = 0.714$. Part of the computer printout for this example is shown in Figure C.6.

Tests of Within-Subjects Effects

Measure: MEASURE_1

Source		Type III Sum of Squares	df	Mean Square	F	Sig.
factor1	Sphericity Assumed	10.000	2	5.000	10.000	.007
	Greenhouse-Geisser	10.000	1.000	10.000	10.000	.034
	Huynh-Feldt	10.000	1.000	10.000	10.000	.034
	Lower-bound	10.000	1.000	10.000	10.000	.034
Error(factor1)	Sphericity Assumed	4.000	8	.500		
	Greenhouse-Geisser	4.000	4.000	1.000		
	Huynh-Feldt	4.000	4.000	1.000		
	Lower-bound	4.000	4.000	1.000		

FIGURE **C.6**   Part of the SPSS Printout for a Single-Factor Repeated-Measures ANOVA
The top line for "factor1" and the top line for "Error(factor1)" contain the relevant portions of the analysis.

Participant	First Treatment	Second Treatment	Third Treatment
A	5	4	3
B	3	2	1
C	4	3	2
D	5	6	4
E	8	5	5

TWO-FACTOR, INDEPENDENT-MEASURES ANOVA

The two-factor, independent-measures ANOVA is used to compare the means from a between-subjects research study using two independent variables (or quasi-independent variables). The structure of a two-factor study can be represented as a matrix with the levels of one independent variable defining the rows and the levels of the second independent variable defining the columns. Each cell in the matrix corresponds to a unique treatment condition, and there is a separate sample for each cell. The two-factor ANOVA consists of three separate tests for mean differences: (1) The main effect for the first factor consists of the mean differences between the rows of the matrix; (2) the main effect for the second factor consists of the mean differences between the columns of the matrix; (3) the interaction consists of any additional mean differences that are not accounted for by the two main effects. For each of the three tests, a *significant difference* indicates that there appears to be a consistent, systematic difference between at least two of the treatments and that the obtained mean differences are very unlikely ($p < .05$) to have occurred by chance alone. The significance is determined by the p value that is reported as part of the computer output.

Data Entry

1. The scores are entered into the SPSS data matrix in a *stacked format*, which means that all the scores from all the different treatment conditions are entered in a single column (var00001).
2. In a second column (var00002) enter a number to designate the level of factor A for each score. If factor A defines the rows of the data matrix, enter a 1 beside each score from the first row, enter a 2 beside each score from the second row, and so on.
3. In a third column (var00003) enter a number to designate the level of factor B for each score. If factor B defines the columns of the data matrix, enter a 1 beside each score from the first column, enter a 2 beside each score from the second column, and so on.

Data Analysis

1. Click **Analyze** on the tool bar.
2. Select **General Linear Model**.
3. Click on **Univariant**.
4. Highlight the column label for the scores (var00001) in the left box.

5. Click the arrow to move the column label into the **Dependent Variable** box.
6. One by one, highlight the two column labels for the two factors (var0002 and var003) and click the arrow to move the labels into the **Fixed Factors** box.
7. If you want to conduct post hoc tests to determine exactly which means are different, click on the **Post Hoc** box, select a test, and click **Continue**.
8. Click on **Options** and select **Descriptives** if you want descriptive statistics for each sample, then click **Continue**.
9. Click **OK**.

Output

If you select the **Descriptives** Option, SPSS produces a table showing the means and standard deviations for each treatment condition. The results of the ANOVA are shown in a summary table in which each factor is identified by its column label (Figure C.7). Note that the summary table includes some extra values, such as *Corrected Model* and *Intercept,* that are beyond the scope of this text. Effect size for each main effect and for the interaction is measured with an η^2 value that is calculated using the Sum of Squares values in the output (see Appendix B, p. 542).

Example: The following data produce an *F*-ratio for the main effect of factor A of $F = 8.167$ with $df = 1, 24$ and a significance level of $p = 0.009$ with $\eta^2 = 0.254$. The *F*-ratio for the main effect of factor B is $F = 3.167$ with $df = 2, 24$ and a significance level of $p = 0.060$ (not significant) with $\eta^2 = 0.209$. The A $\times$ B interaction has $F = 1.167$ with $df = 2, 24$ and a significance level of $p = 0.328$ (not significant) with $\eta^2 = 0.089$. The means and standard deviations are shown with the individual samples. The computer printout for this example is shown in Figure C.7.

		Factor B		
		B1	B2	B3
	A1	3	1	5
		1	4	5
		1	8	9
		6	6	2
		4	6	4
		$M = 3$	$M = 5$	$M = 5$
Factor A		$SD = 2.12$	$SD = 2.24$	$SD = 2.54$
	A2	0	3	0
		2	8	0
		0	3	0
		0	3	5
		3	3	0
		$M = 1$	$M = 4$	$M = 1$
		$SD = 1.41$	$SD = 2.24$	$SD = 2.24$

Tests of Between-Subjects Effects

Dependent Variable: VAR00001

Source	Type III Sum of Squares	df	Mean Square	F	Sig.
Corrected Model	84.167[a]	5	16.833	3.367	.019
Intercept	300.833	1	300.833	60.167	.000
VAR00002	40.833	1	40.833	8.167	.009
VAR00003	31.667	2	15.833	3.167	.060
VAR00002 * VAR00003	11.667	2	5.833	1.167	.328
Error	120.000	24	5.000		
Total	505.000	30			
Corrected Total	204.167	29			

a. R Squared = .412 (Adjusted R Squared = .290)

FIGURE **C.7** Part of the Printout for a Two-Factor Independent-Measures ANOVA

Relevant information about the two main effects, the interaction, and the error term is contained in the middle four lines of the table titled "Tests of Between-Subjects Effects."

TWO-FACTOR MIXED DESIGN ANOVA (ONE BETWEEN-SUBJECTS FACTOR AND ONE WITHIN-SUBJECTS FACTOR)

The mixed design two-factor ANOVA is used to compare the means from a research study using one between-subjects factor (with a different sample for each level) and one within-subjects factor (with the same sample participating in every level). The structure of the mixed design can be represented as a matrix with the levels of the between-subjects factor defining the rows and the levels of the within-subjects factor defining the columns. The two-factor ANOVA consists of three separate tests for mean differences:

1. The main effect for the between-subjects factor consists of the mean differences between the rows of the matrix (note that there is a separate sample for each row).
2. The main effect for the within-subjects factor consists of the mean differences between the columns of the matrix (note that the same individuals are tested in the first column and in the second column, and so on).
3. The interaction consists of any additional mean differences that are not accounted for by the two main effects (note that the interaction is also considered to be a within-subjects test).

For each of the three tests, a significant difference indicates that there appears to be a consistent, systematic difference between at least two of the treatments and that the obtained mean differences are very unlikely ($p < .05$) to have occurred by chance alone. The significance is determined by the p value that is reported as part of the computer output.

Data Entry

1. All of the scores for each level of the within-subjects factor go into a separate column of the data matrix, with the scores for each participant in the same row. For the data in the following example, all the scores from the "quiet" condition are entered in order into one column (var00001), the scores from the "moderate" condition are entered in a second column (var00002), and the scores from the "loud" condition are entered into var00003.
2. An additional column is then used to identify the levels of the between-subjects factor. For the data in the following example, in a fourth column (var00004) enter a 1 for each of the three males and a 2 for each of the three females.

Data Analysis

1. Click Analyze on the tool bar.
2. Select General Linear Model.
3. Click on Repeated Measures.
4. SPSS presents a box titled Repeated-Measures Define Factors. Within the box, the Within-Subjects Factor Name should already contain Factor1. If not, type in Factor1.
5. Enter the Number of Levels (number of treatment conditions for the within-subjects factor) in the next box.
6. Click on Add.
7. Click Define.
8. One by one, move the column labels for your within-subjects treatment conditions into the Within-Subjects Variables box. (Highlight the column label on the left and click the arrow to move it into the box.)
9. Move the column label for the column containing the levels of your between-subjects factor into the Between-Subjects Factor(s) box. (Highlight the column label on the left and click the arrow to move it into the box.)
10. If you want to conduct post hoc tests to determine exactly which means are different, click on the Post Hoc box, select a test, and click Continue.
11. Click on Options and select Descriptives if you want descriptive statistics for each treatment combination, then click Continue.
12. Click OK.

Output

If you select the Descriptives Option, the output includes a table with the mean and standard deviation for each treatment condition. Near the bottom of the output you will find a box labeled Tests of Within-Subjects Effects (Figure C.8) which contains the F-ratios, df values, and significance levels for the main effect of the within-subjects factor and the interaction (use the top row labeled Sphericity Assumed for each). Finally, the box labeled Tests of Between-Subjects Effects contains the F-ratio, df values, and significance level for the main effect of the between-subjects factor (use the middle row labeled with the variable name).

Tests of Within-Subjects Effects

Measure: MEASURE_1

Source		Type III Sum of Squares	df	Mean Square	F	Sig.
factor1	Sphericity Assumed	52.000	2	26.000	78.000	.000
	Greenhouse-Geisser	52.000	1.000	52.000	78.000	.001
	Huynh-Feldt	52.000	1.333	39.000	78.000	.000
	Lower-bound	52.000	1.000	52.000	78.000	.001
factor 1 * VAR00004	Sphericity Assumed	12.000	2	6.000	18.000	.001
	Greenhouse-Geisser	12.000	1.000	12.000	18.000	.013
	Huynh-Feldt	12.000	1.333	9.000	18.000	.006
	Lower-bound	12.000	1.000	12.000	18.000	.013
Error(factor1)	Sphericity Assumed	2.667	8	.333		
	Greenhouse-Geisser	2.667	4.000	.667		
	Huynh-Feldt	2.667	5.333	.500		
	Lower-bound	2.667	4.000	.667		

Tests of Between-Subjects Effects

Measure: MEASURE_1
Transformed Variable: Average

Source	Type III Sum of Squares	df	Mean Square	F	Sig.
Intercept	242.000	1	242.000	55.846	.002
VAR00004	18.000	1	18.000	4.154	.111
Error	17.333	4	4.333		

FIGURE **C.8** Portions of the SPSS Printout for a Mixed Design Two-Factor ANOVA

The top line in each of the three sections of the within-subjects table shows relevant information for the main effect, interaction, and error term for the within-subjects factor. The between-subjects table shows the main effect and error term for the between-subjects factor.

Effect size for each main effect and for the interaction is measured with an η^2 value that is calculated using the Sum of Squares values in the output. For each specific treatment effect, the η^2 value is computed as

$$\eta^2 \text{ for the treatment effect} = \frac{SS_{treatment}}{SS_{treatment} + SS_{error}}$$

The η^2 value for the main effect for the within-subjects factor and the interaction use the error Sum of Squares from the Tests-of-Within-Subjects-Effects box in the output, and η^2 for the main effect of the between-subjects factor uses the error Sum of Squares from the Tests-of-Between-Subjects-Effects box.

Example: The following data represent a mixed design, two-factor study. The between-subjects factor is gender (male/female) with two separate samples, a group of three males and a group of three females. The within-subjects factor is the level of background noise (quiet/moderate/loud). Note that each of the two samples is tested in all three of the noise conditions. For the main effect for gender, the ANOVA produces $F = 4.154$ with $df = 1, 4$ and $p = 0.111$ (not significant) with $\eta^2 = 0.509$. The main effect for background noise produces $F = 78.00$ with $df = 2, 8$ and a significance level of $p = 0.00$ (reported as $p < .001$) with $\eta^2 = 0.951$. The interaction produces $F = 18.00$ with $df = 2, 8$ and a significance level of $p = 0.001$ with $\eta^2 = 0.818$. The computer printout for this example is shown in Figure C.8.

			Background Noise	
	Participant	Quiet	Moderate	Loud
Males	A	1	3	1
	B	2	3	2
	C	3	6	3
Females	D	3	7	1
	E	4	7	2
	F	5	10	3

The means and standard deviations for the different treatment conditions are as follows:

	Quiet	Moderate	Loud
Males	$M = 2.00$	$M = 4.00$	$M = 2.00$
	$SD = 1.00$	$SD = 1.73$	$SD = 1.00$
Females	$M = 4.00$	$M = 8.00$	$M = 2.00$
	$SD = 1.00$	$SD = 1.73$	$SD = 1.00$

THE PEARSON CORRELATION

The Pearson correlation measures and describes the direction and degree of linear relationship between two variables. The data are numerical scores, with two separate scores, representing two different variables, for each individual. The two scores are identified as X and Y. A positive correlation indicates that X and Y tend to vary in the same direction (as X increases, Y also increases), and a negative correlation indicates that X and Y vary in opposite directions (as X increases, Y decreases). A correlation of 1.00 (or −1.00) indicates that the data points fit perfectly on a straight line. A correlation of 0.00 indicates that there is no linear relationship whatsoever. Values between 0 and 1.00, indicate intermediate degrees of relationship. It is also possible to evaluate the statistical significance of a correlation by determining the probability that the sample correlation was obtained, just by chance, from a population in which there is a zero correlation.

Data Entry

1. The data are entered into two columns in the data matrix, one for the X values (var00001) and one for the Y values (var00002), with the two scores for each individual in the same row.

Data Analysis

1. Click **Analyze** on the tool bar.
2. Select **Correlate**.
3. Click on **Bivariate**.
4. One by one move the labels for the two data columns into the **Variables** box. (Highlight each label and click the arrow to move it into the box.)
5. The **Pearson** box should be checked, but you can click the **Spearman** box if you want to compute a Spearman correlation (SPSS converts the scores to ranks).
6. Click **OK**.

Output

SPSS produces a correlation matrix showing all the possible correlations (Figure C.9). You want the correlation of X and Y, which is contained in the upper right corner (or the lower left). The output includes the significance level (p value) for the correlation. Effect size, r^2, is obtained by simply squaring the correlation.

Example: The following data produce a Pearson correlation of 0.535 with a significance level of $p = 0.216$ (not significant) and $r^2 = 0.286$. The computer printout for this example is shown in Figure C.9.

X	Y
3	6
5	9
2	12
1	8
5	13
4	10
6	14

Correlations

		VAR00001	VAR00002
VAR00001	Pearson Correlation	1	.535
	Sig. (2-tailed)		.216
	N	7	7
VAR00002	Pearson Correlation	.535	1
	Sig. (2-tailed)	.216	
	N	7	7

FIGURE **C.9** An SPSS Printout for the Pearson Correlation

REGRESSION WITH ONE OR TWO PREDICTOR VARIABLES

With one predictor variable, regression produces the equation for the best fitting straight line for a set of X and Y data points. The data for regression are the same as would be used for a Pearson correlation. It is also possible to evaluate the statistical significance of the regression equation by determining the probability that the equation would be obtained if the sample was selected from a population in which there is no relationship between X and Y (the Pearson correlation is zero).

With two predictor variables, multiple regression produces the best fitting linear equation of the form: $Y = b_1X_1 + b_2X_2 + a$. Again, it is possible to evaluate the statistical significance of the multiple regression equation by determining the probability that the equation would be obtained if the sample was selected from a population in which X_1 and X_2 have no relationship with Y.

Data Entry

1. With one predictor variable (X), you enter the X values in one column (var00001) and the Y values in a second column (var00002) of the SPSS data editor. With two predictors (X_1 and X_2), enter the X_1 values in one column, X_2 in a second column, and Y in a third column.

Data Analysis

1. Click **Analyze** on the tool bar, select **Regression**, and click on **Linear**.
2. In the left-hand box, highlight the column label for the Y values, then click the arrow to move the column label into the **Dependent Variable** box.
3. For one predictor variable, highlight the column label for the X values and click the arrow to move it into the **Independent Variable(s)** box. For two predictor variables, highlight the X_1 and X_2 column labels, one at a time, and click the arrow to move them into the **Independent Variable(s)** box.
4. Click **OK**.

Output

The printout includes a table that simply lists the predictor variables that were entered into the regression equation. A second table (Model Summary) presents the values for R, R^2, and the standard error of estimate. R^2 is the customary measure of effect size, or the strength of the regression equation. Note: for a single predictor, R is simply the Pearson correlation between X and Y (Figure C.10). The third table (ANOVA) presents the analysis of regression evaluating the significance of the regression equation, including the F-ratio and the level of significance. The final table, summarizes the unstandardized and the standardized coefficients for the regression equation. For one predictor, the table shows the values for the constant (a) and the coefficient (b). For two predictors, the table shows the constant a and the two coefficients b_1 and b_2 (Figure C.11). The standardized coefficients are the beta values. For one predictor, beta is simply the Pearson correlation between X and Y. Finally, the

Model Summary

Model	R	R Square	Adjusted R Square	Std. Error of the Estimate
1	.535[a]	.286	.143	2.65684

a. Predictors: (Constant), VAR00001

ANOVA[b]

Model		Sum of Squares	df	Mean Square	F	Sig.
1	Regression	14.134	1	14.134	2.002	.216[a]
	Residual	35.294	5	7.059		
	Total	49.429	6			

a. Predictors: (Constant), VAR00001
b. Dependent Variable: VAR00002

Coefficients[a]

Model		Unstandardized Coefficients		Standardized Coefficients	t	Sig.
		B	Std. Error	Beta		
1	(Constant)	7.118	2.454		2.901	.034
	VAR00001	.853	.603	.535	1.415	.216

a. Dependent Variable: VAR00002

FIGURE **C.10** An SPSS Printout for Regression With One Predictor Variable

table uses a t statistic to evaluate the significance of each predictor variable. For one predictor variable, this is identical to the significance of the regression equation and you should find that the t value is equal to the square root of the F-ratio from the analysis of regression. For two predictor variables, the t values measure the significance of the contribution of each variable beyond what is already predicted by the other variable.

Example for one predictor: The same data that were used to demonstrate the Pearson correlation produce a regression equation of $Y = 0.853X + 7.118$. The equation is not significant with $p = .216$ (which is identical to the significance level obtained for the correlation), and has $R^2 = 0.286$. The computer printout for this example is shown in Figure C.10.

Example for two predictors: The following data add a second predictor (X_2) to the same X and Y values that were used for the single predictor regression example (the original X values are now labeled X_1). The data produce a multiple regression equation of $Y = 1.288X_1 + .445X_2 + 0.168$. The equation is significant with $p = .030$ and has $R^2 = 0.827$. Each of the predictor variables makes a significant contribution (ΔR^2) beyond the prediction of the other variable alone (the additional contribution of X_1 is significant with $p = .022$ and the additional contribution of X_2 is significant with $p = .024$). The com-

Model Summary

Model	R	R Square	Adjusted R Square	Std. Error of the Estimate
1	.910[a]	.827	.741	1.46007

a. Predictors: (Constant), VAR00002, VAR00001

ANOVA[b]

Model		Sum of Squares	df	Mean Square	F	Sig.
1	Regression	40.901	2	20.451	9.593	.030[a]
	Residual	8.527	4	2.132		
	Total	49.429	6			

a. Predictors: (Constant), VAR00002, VAR00001
b. Dependent Variable: VAR00003

Coefficients[a]

Model		Unstandardized Coefficients		Standardized Coefficients	t	Sig.
		B	Std. Error	Beta		
1	(Constant)	.168	2.380		.070	.947
	VAR00001	1.288	.353	.807	3.645	.022
	VAR00002	.445	.125	.785	3.543	.024

a. Dependent Variable: VAR00003

FIGURE **C.11** An SPSS Printout for Regression with Two Predictor Variables
Note that the first table of the printout is not shown.

puter printout for this example is shown in Figure C.11. The values in the ANOVA table evaluate the significance of the overall equation and the values in the Coefficients table evaluate the significant of the contribution of each predictor.

X_1	X_2	Y
3	5	6
5	6	9
2	18	12
1	16	8
5	10	13
4	14	10
6	15	14

THE CHI-SQUARE TEST FOR INDEPENDENCE

The chi-square test for independence evaluates the relationship between two variables. Instead of measuring numerical scores, each individual is simply classified into a category for each of the two variables; for example, each individual could be classified by gender (male/female) and by personality (introvert/extrovert). The data are usually organized in a matrix with the categories of one variable defining the rows and the categories of the second variable defining the columns. The actual data (called *observed frequencies*) consist of the number of individuals from the sample who are in each cell of the matrix; for example, how many introverted males, how many introverted females, how many extroverted males, and how many extroverted females.

Suppose for example, that you are using a chi-square test to examine the relationship between gender and self-esteem for a sample of $n = 50$ students (see the following example). Each student is classified as male or female, and each student is classified as high, medium, or low in terms of self-esteem. Note that the data are organized in a matrix with two rows and three columns.

Data Entry

1. Enter all of the observed frequencies into one column in the data matrix (var00001).
2. In a second column (var00002), enter a number designating the row from which the observed frequency was obtained. For the data in the following example, enter a 1 beside each observed frequency for the males and enter a 2 beside each frequency for the females.
3. In a third column (var00003), enter a number designating the column from which the observed frequency was obtained. For the data in the example, enter a 1 beside each observed frequency for high self-esteem, enter a 2 beside each frequency for medium, and enter a 3 beside each frequency for low.
4. Click **Data** on the tool bar.
5. Select the **weigh cases** option.
6. Click the **weigh cases by** option.
7. Move the label for the column containing the observed frequencies (var00001) into the **Frequency Variable** box. (Highlight the column label and click the arrow to move it into the box.)
8. Click **OK**.

Data Analysis

1. Click **Analyze** on the tool bar.
2. Select **Descriptive Statistics**.
3. Click on **Crosstabs**.
4. Move the label for the column containing the rows (var00002) into the **Rows** box. (Highlight the label and click the arrow to move it into the box.)
5. Move the label for the column containing the columns (var00003) into the **Columns** box. (Highlight the label and click the arrow to move it into the box.)
6. Click on **Statistics**.

VAR00002 * VAR00003 Cross-tabulation

Count

		VAR00003			Total
		1.00	2.00	3.00	
VAR00002	1.00	10	6	4	20
	2.00	8	12	10	30
Total		18	18	14	50

Chi-Square Tests

	Value	df	Asymp. Sig. (2-sided)
Pearson Chi-Square	2.910ᵃ	2	.233
Likelihood Ratio	2.904	2	.234
Linear-by-Linear Association	2.495	1	.114
N of Valid Cases	50		

ᵃ 0 cells (.0%) have expected count less than 5. The minimum expected count is 5.60.

FIGURE **C.12**   An SPSS Printout for Chi-Square

The top row of the chi-square tests table shows the results of the chi-square test.

7. Select **Chi-Square.**
8. Click **Continue.**
9. Click **OK.**

Output

The Output includes a cross-tabulation table showing the matrix of observed frequencies, and a table of chi-square tests in which you should focus on the **Pearson Chi-Square** (Figure C.12). The table includes the calculated chi-square value, the degrees of freedom, and the level of significance (p value). A measure of effect size (either ϕ for a 2×2 data matrix, or Cramér's V) can be calculated using the value obtained for chi-square, the sample size, and the number of rows and columns in the data matrix (see Appendix B, p. 546).

Example: The following data represent the observed frequencies for a sample of 50 students who have been classified by gender (male/female) and by self-esteem (high, medium, low). The data produce a chi-square statistic of 2.91 with $df = 2$ and a significance level of $p = 0.233$ (no significant relationship) with Cramér's $V = 0.241$. The computer printout for this example is shown in Figure C.12.

Self-Esteem

	High	Medium	Low
Males	10	6	4
Females	8	12	10

D

Sample APA-Style Research Report Manuscript for Publication

This appendix presents an example of a complete APA-style research report manuscript using the current guidelines presented in the *Publication Manual of the American Psychological Association* (6th edition, 2010). The manuscript is an edited version of a of a research manuscript prepared by undergraduate student Danielle Gentile as part of a course requirement at The College at Brockport, State University of New York. The intent of this example is to demonstrate the appearance of manuscript pages as well as the content of each section of an APA-style research report. Portions of the manuscript are presented as figures and discussed in the text in Chapter 16.

School Size and Cyberbullying in Middle School Students

Danielle Gentile

The College at Brockport, State University of New York

Author Note

Danielle Gentile, Department of Psychology, The College at Brockport, State University of New York.

Correspondence concerning this article should be addressed to Danielle Gentile at the Department of Psychology, The College at Brockport, State University of New York, Brockport, NY 14420.

E-mail: dgenl@brockport.edu

SCHOOL SIZE AND CYBERBULLYING   2

Abstract

Cyberbullying is defined as a phenomenon in which e-mail, texting, instant messaging, or other electronic devices are used to harass another person. Cyberbullying can be as detrimental as traditional bullying for school children. Because past research suggests a direct relationship between school size and violence, the purpose of this study is to determine if school size is also related to cyberbullying, which is another type of school violence. A total of 670 students obtained from two middle schools, one relatively large and one relatively small, completed a questionnaire assessing their degree of experience with cyberbullying. The results showed that students from the larger school experienced significantly more cyberbullying than students from the smaller school, $t(668) = 4.79$, $p < .01$, $r^2 = 0.256$. The results suggest increased awareness of the heightened possibility of cyberbullying and possible intervention programs at large schools.

SCHOOL SIZE AND CYBERBULLYING   3

School Size and Cyberbullying in Middle School Students

Bullying in school is defined as a form of aggression in which a student or group of students physically or verbally harasses a victim without provocation (Hazler, 1992). Bullying presents a problem because students who are exposed to many aggressive peers in a hostile environment are more likely themselves to engage in aggressive acts towards others. In these violence oriented atmospheres, aggressive behaviors become normalized and socially acceptable. Therefore, group members tend to exhibit more aggressive behaviors because there is less social pressure to inhibit aggression or use alternative conflict management strategies (Thomas & Bierman, 2006).

Bullying has detrimental effects not only in childhood but later in life as well. Olweus (1993) found that former victims of bullying at school during a young age tended to be more depressed and had lower self-esteem at age 23 than their non-victimized peers. The findings suggest that early and persistent victimization can have lasting negative consequences.

Traditional bullying includes overt physical acts (e.g., hitting, shoving) and verbal abuse (e.g., taunting, name calling) as well as more subtle or indirect actions such as social exclusion and rumor-spreading (Smith et al., 2008). Further examples of verbal harassment include threatening, humiliating, degrading, teasing, eye rolling, silent treatment, manipulating friendship, and ostracizing (Xin, 2002).

SCHOOL SIZE AND CYBERBULLYING   4

In recent years, middle school students have taken advantage of technology as another avenue of harassing peers, and no longer need to be in the physical presence of their victims in order to bully them. Bullying done through e-mail, instant messaging, in chat rooms, on web sites, and through text and picture messaging to cell phones has been defined as cyberbullying or electronic bullying (Kowalski & Limber, 2007).

Cyberbullying presents a more difficult challenge for teachers, parents, and administrators than traditional bullying because adults often are unaware that it is even happening (Li, 2006). Furthermore, many victims who experience cyberbullying do not know who the perpetrator is, making it impossible to take action against the attacker. Victims often have no way of knowing whether the perpetrator is an individual or group of individuals, leading to further anxiety. Children may wonder if each person they meet could potentially be the perpetrator (Kowalski & Limber, 2007). Further complicating the management of cyberbulllying is the fact that much of it occurs outside of school premises. Some schools have tried to combat the issue by banning mobile phones and Internet use, but only 20% of students studied reported that this is an effective way to stop cyberbullying (Smith et al., 2008).

Previous research on school violence may provide some clues concerning the variables that are related to cyberbullying. For example, Leung and Ferris (2008) found a significant relationship between youth violence and school size, with a tendency for larger schools to have more violent acts than smaller schools. After controlling for other variables which could affect violence such as family situation, friends and peers, it was found that schools in excess of 2000 students were 22 percent more likely than smaller schools to have students who engage in serious violence. The authors suggest that large school size increases feelings of alienation and isolation in students because the number of interactions with strangers rather than friends is increased. In order to combat the feeling of isolation, students form groups in which they can feel more included, yet if a student is excluded from these groups, he or she will likely feel further alienated and without meaningful contact with others. This creates stress, which has the potential to be released in violent manners if it is not otherwise dealt with in a socially acceptable manner.

The general relationship between violence and school size suggests that there may be a similar relationship between school size and cyberbullying, which is another type of school violence. Therefore, we hypothesized a positive relationship between school size and the occurrence of cyberbullying in middle schools. To test this hypothesis, this study compared the degree of cyberbullying that exists in middle schools of different sizes.

Method

Participants

A total sample of 670 students was obtained from two suburban middle schools in the Rochester, New York area. The two schools represent middle-class, suburban neighborhoods with populations consisting of approximately 85% Caucasian, 10% African American, 3% Hispanic, and 2% Asian. One group of 450 students was from a relatively large school (total student population of 1176) and the other 220 students were from a relatively small school (total student population of 624). The average age for the large-school students was 13.2 years with 61.8% females and 38.2% males, and the average age for the small-school students was 13.4 years with 56.8% females and 43.2% males.

Procedure

A letter was sent home with each student from both schools asking for parental permission for student volunteers to participate in a survey examining internet use. No mention was made of cyberbulling to avoid self-selection based on interest or knowledge of the topic. After obtaining informed consent from parents and assent from children, each student completed a two-part questionnaire developed by Li (2006). The first section asks for demographic data such as age, race, gender, computer usage, and academic achievement. The second portion examines the student's experiences with cyberbullying. The surveys were completed individually in small groups in a vacant classroom during regular scheduled breaks in the school day. Participants were each given 2 points of extra credit added to their final averages in class as compensation for participation in the study.

Results

For purposes of this study, the analysis focused on two questions from the survey asking whether the student had experienced cyberbullying and, if so, how many times (1-3, 4-10, >10). A student who had never been cyberbullied was assigned a score of 0 and the three frequency categories were scored as 1, 2, and 3 in order of increasing frequency, thus producing a 4-point scale measuring the degree of cyberbullying. The mean score for the large-school students was $M = 1.82$ with $SD = 0.14$ and the mean for the small-school students was $M = 1.03$ with $SD = 0.11$. An independent-measures t test showed a significant mean difference between the two groups of middle school students, $t(668) = 4.79$, $p < .01$, $r^2 = 0.256$, with the large-school students experiencing a greater degree of cyberbullying.

Discussion

The results support the research hypothesis, showing a significant relationship between middle school size and cyberbullying, with students from large schools having more experience with cyberbullying than students from small schools. This

SCHOOL SIZE AND CYBERBULLYING   8

finding is consistent with the results obtained by Leung and Ferris (2008), which found that students in larger schools experience more violence than students in smaller schools. This result indicates that both traditional bullying and cyberbullying, which is a subset of violence, may likely affect students in relation to the size of the school they attend.

A consistent and predictable relationship between cyberbullying and school size suggests many practical real-world applications for educators, administrators, and students in middle schools. It is the goal of many administrators to improve student's personal satisfaction and learning possibilities, and cyberbullying could be a detriment to this. Therefore, it may be especially important for administrators of large schools to recognize that their students are more likely to be victims of cyberbullying, and to take action to combat the incidence of cyberbullying. Programs on Internet safety, ways for students to effectively and safely report cyberbullying, teacher and parent education on what is cyberbullying and how to recognize it would all be beneficial for large school communities.

Possible future studies to expand on this research could include: separating male and female students to see if the possible implications of large and small school settings apply differently to gender. Also, separating grade levels for the same purpose may reveal differences in grade level related to school size.

SCHOOL SIZE AND CYBERBULLYING   9

References

Hazler, R. J. (1992). What kids say about bullying. *Executive Educator, 14,*
   20-22.

Kowalski, R. M., & Limber, S. P. (2007). Electronic bullying among middle
   school students. *Journal of Adolescent Health Care, 41 (6, Suppl),*
   S22-S30. doi:10.1016/j.jadohealth.2007.08.017

Leung, A., & Ferris, J. (2008). School size and youth violence. *Journal of
   Economic Behavior & Organization, 65*(2), 318-333. doi:10.1016/
   j.jebo.2005.10.001

Li, Q. (2006). Cyberbullying in schools: A research of gender differences. *School
   Psychology International, 27,* 157-170. doi:10.1177/0143034306064547

Olweus, D. (1993). Victimization by peers: Antecedents and long-term
   consequences. In K. H. Rubin & J. B. Asendorf (Eds.), *Social withdrawal,
   inhibition, and shyness in childhood* (pp. 315-341). Hillside, NJ: Lawrence
   Erlbaum Associates.

Smith, P. K., Mahdavi, J., Carvalho, M., Fisher, S., Russell, S., & Tippett, N.
   (2008). Cyberbullying: Its nature and impact in secondary school pupils.
   Journal of Child Psychology and Psychiatry, 49 (4), 376-385. doi:10.1111/
   j.1469-7610.2007.01846.x

Thomas, T. E., & Bierman K. L. (2006). The impact of classroom aggression on the development of aggressive behavior problems in children. *Development and Psychopathology, 18,* 471-487. doi:10.1017/S0954579406060251

Xin, M. (2002) Bullying in middle school: Individual and school characteristics of victims and offenders. *School Effectiveness and School Improvement, 13* (1), 63-89. doi:10.1076/sesi.13.1.63.3438

GLOSSARY

ABAB design   A single-subject experimental design consisting of four phases: a baseline phase, a treatment phase, a return-to-baseline phase, and a second treatment phase. Also known as a reversal design.

Abstract   A brief summary of a research study, usually totaling no more than 150 to 250 words.

Accessible population   The easily available segment of a target population. Researchers typically select their samples from this type of population.

Accuracy (of measurement)   The degree to which a measure conforms to the established standard.

Active deception   The intentional presentation of misinformation about a study to its participants. The most common form of active deception is misleading participants about the specific purpose of the study. Also known as commission.

Alpha level   In a hypothesis test, the criterion for statistical significance that defines the maximum probability that the research result was obtained simply by chance. Also known as level of significance.

Alternating-treatments design   A single-subject design in which two (or more) treatment conditions are randomly alternated from one observation

to the next. Also known as a discrete-trials design.

Anchors   On a rating scale question, the verbal labels that identify the opposite extremes and establish the endpoints of the scale.

Anonymity   The practice of ensuring that an individual's name is not directly associated with the information or measurements obtained from that individual. Keeping records anonymous is a way to preserve the confidentiality of research participants.

APA Ethics Code   A common set of principles and standards on which psychologists build their professional and scientific work. This code is intended to provide specific standards that cover most situations encountered by psychologists. Its primary goal is the welfare and protection of the individuals and groups with whom psychologists work.

Apparatus subsection   In a research report, the portion of the method section that describes any equipment used in the study.

Appendix   The section of a research report that presents detailed information that is useful but would interrupt the flow of information if presented in the body of the paper.

Applied research   Research studies that are intended to answer practical questions or solve practical problems.

Apprehensive subject role   In a study, a participant's tendency to respond in a socially desirable fashion rather than truthfully.

Archival research   Looking at historical records (archives) to measure behaviors or events that occurred in the past.

Argument   In the rational method, a set of premise statements that are logically combined to yield a conclusion.

Artifact   In the context of a research study, an external factor that could influence or distort measures. Artifacts threaten the validity of the measurement, as well as both internal and external validity.

Assessment sensitization   *See* sensitization.

Assignment bias   A threat to internal validity that occurs when the process used to assign different participants to different treatments produces groups of individuals with noticeably different characteristics.

Author note   The section of a research report that provides details about the authors. It is placed on the title page below the title, byline, and affiliation,.

Bar graph   A frequency distribution graph in which a vertical bar indicates the frequency of each score from a nominal or ordinal scale of measurement.

589

Baseline observations In a single-subject research study, observations or measurements made while no treatment is being administered.

Baseline phase In a single-subject research study, a series of baseline observations identified by the letter A.

Basic research Research studies that are intended to answer theoretical questions or gather knowledge simply for the sake of new knowledge.

Behavior categories Categories of behavior to be observed (such as group play, play alone, aggression, social interaction). A set of behavior categories and a list of exactly which behaviors count as examples of each are developed before observation begins.

Behavioral measure A measurement obtained by the direct observation of an individual's behavior.

Behavioral observation Direct observation and systematic recording of behaviors.

Belmont Report A summary of the basic ethical principles for protecting humans in research published in 1979 by the National Commission for the Protection of Human Subjects in Biomedical and Behavioral Research. Today's federal regulations for protecting human participants are based on the Belmont Report.

Between-subjects design A research design in which each of the different groups of scores is obtained from a separate group of participants. Also known as an independent-measures design.

Between-subjects experimental design An experimental design using a separate, independent group of individuals for each treatment condition being compared. Also known as an independent-measures experimental design.

Biased sample A sample with characteristics different from those of the population.

Bimodal distribution In a frequency distribution graph, a distribution of scores with two modes or two distinct peaks.

Carryover effects Changes in the scores observed in one treatment condition that are caused by the lingering aftereffects of a specific earlier treatment condition.

Case history A case study that does not include a treatment or intervention.

Case study design An in-depth study and detailed description of a single individual (or a very small group). A case study may involve an intervention or treatment administered by the researcher.

Ceiling effect The clustering of scores at the high end of a measurement scale, allowing little or no possibility of increases in value; a type of range effect.

Central tendency A statistical measure that identifies a single score that defines the center of a distribution. It provides a representative value for the entire group.

Changing-criterion design A single-subject design consisting of a series of phases, each phase defined by a specific criterion that determines a target level of behavior. The criterion level is changed from one phase to the next.

Chi-square test for independence A hypothesis test that evaluates the statistical significance of the differences between proportions for two or more groups of participants.

Citation An identification of the author(s) and year of publication for the source of a specific fact or idea mentioned in a research report.

Clinical equipoise The ethical issue requiring clinicians to provide the best possible treatment for their patients, thus limiting research to studies that compare equally preferred treatments.

Clinical significance *See* practical significance.

Cluster sampling A probability sampling technique involving random selection of groups instead of individuals from a population.

Coefficient of determination, r^2 The squared value of a correlation that measures the percentage of variability in one variable, which is determined or predicted by its relationship with the other variable.

Cohen's *d* A standard measure of effect size computed by dividing the sample mean difference by the sample standard deviation.

Cohen's kappa A calculation that corrects for chance agreement when interrater reliability is measured.

Cohort effects Differences between age groups that are caused by characteristics or experiences other than age. Also called generation effect.

Cohorts Individuals who were born at roughly the same time and grew up under similar circumstances.

Combined strategy A factorial study that combines two different research strategies, such as experimental and nonexperimental or quasi-experimental, in the same factorial design.

Commission *See* active deception.

Common Rule The Code of Federal Regulations, Title 45, Part 46 (1991), which is based on the principles of the Belmont Report and provides a common set of federal regulations for protecting human participants. It is used by review boards.

Compensatory equalization A threat to internal validity that occurs when an untreated group demands to receive a treatment that is the same as or equivalent to the treatment received by another group in the research study.

Compensatory rivalry A threat to internal validity that occurs when an untreated group learns about special treatment received by another group, then works extra hard to show they can perform just as well as that group.

Complete counterbalancing In within-subjects designs, using a separate group of participants for every possible order of the treatment conditions. With *n* different treatment conditions, there are *n*! (*n* factorial) different orders.

Component-analysis design *See* dismantling design.

Concurrent validity The type of validity demonstrated when scores obtained from a new measure are directly related to scores obtained from a more established measure of the same variable.

Confederate A person who pretends to be a participant in a research study but actually is working for the researcher to create a false environment.

Confidence interval A range of values, centered around a sample statistic, used to estimate the magnitude of an unknown population value such as a mean difference or a correlation. The width of the interval is directly related to the degree of confidence in its accuracy.

Confidentiality The practice of keeping strictly secret and private the information or measurements obtained from an individual during a research study. APA ethical guidelines require researchers to ensure the confidentiality of their research participants.

Confounding variable An extraneous variable (usually unmonitored) that is allowed to change systematically along with the two variables being studied. In the context of an experiment, an extraneous variable that changes systematically along with the independent variable *and* has the potential to influence the dependent variable. A confounding variable provides an alternative explanation for the observed relationship and, therefore, is a threat to internal validity.

Consent form A written statement by the researcher containing all of the elements of informed consent and a line for the participant's signature. The consent form is provided before the study so that potential participants have all the information they need to make an informed decision regarding participation.

Constructs Hypothetical attributes or mechanisms that help explain and predict behavior in a theory. Also known as hypothetical constructs.

Construct validity The type of validity demonstrated when scores obtained from a measurement behave exactly the same as the variable itself. Construct validity is based on many research studies and grows gradually as each new study contributes more evidence.

Content analysis Using the techniques of behavioral observation to measure the occurrence of specific events in literature, movies, television programs, or similar media that present replicas of behaviors.

Contrast effect An example of a carryover effect in which the perception of a treatment condition is influenced by its contrast with the previous treatment.

Contrived observation Observation in settings arranged specifically to facilitate the occurrence of specific behaviors. Also known as structured observation.

Control group In a research study, a condition that involves no treatment or a placebo treatment.

Convenience sampling A nonprobability sampling method involving selection of individuals on the basis of their availability and willingness to respond; that is, because they are easy to get. Occasionally called accidental sampling or haphazard sampling.

Convergent validity The type of validity demonstrated by a strong relationship between the scores obtained from two different methods of measuring the same construct.

Correlation A statistical value that measures and describes the direction and degree of relationship between two variables. The sign (+/–) indicates the direction of the relationship. The numerical value (0.0 to 1.0) indicates the strength or consistency of the relationship. The type (Pearson or Spearman) indicates the form of the relationship. Also known as correlation coefficient.

Correlation coefficient *See* correlation.

Correlational research strategy A general approach to research that involves measuring two or more variables for each individual to describe the relationship between the variables. The measurements are reviewed to identify any patterns of relationship that exist between the variables and to measure the strength of the relationship; however, no attempt is made to explain the relationship.

Counterbalancing In a within-subjects design, a procedure to minimize threats from order effects and time-related factors by changing the order in which treatment conditions are administered from one participant to another so that the treatment conditions are matched with respect to time. The goal is to use every possible order of treatments with an equal number of individuals participating in each sequence.

Criterion variable In a correlational study, a researcher often is interested in the relationship between two variables to use knowledge about one variable to help predict or explain the second variable. In this situation, the second variable (being explained or predicted) is called the criterion variable.

Cronbach's alpha A generalization of the Kuder-Richardson formula that estimates the average of all possible split-half reliability correlations when each test item has more than two responses.

Cross-sectional developmental research design A developmental design comparing different groups of individuals, each group representing a different age.

Curvilinear relationship In a graph showing the changing values of two variables, a pattern in which the data points tend to cluster around a curved line.

Database A computerized cross-referencing tool that focuses on an individual topic area (such as psychology); used for searching the literature for articles relevant to a topic.

Debriefing A postexperimental explanation of the purpose of the study. A debriefing is given after a participant completes a study, especially if deception was used.

Deception The purposeful withholding of information or misleading of participants about a study. There are two forms of deception: passive and active.

Deduction The use of a general statement as the basis for reaching a conclusion about specific examples. Also known as deductive reasoning.

Deductive reasoning *See* deduction.

Degrees of freedom The value $n - 1$ when the variance is computed for a sample of n scores. In general, the number of independent elements when a sample statistic is computed.

Demand characteristics Any potential cues or features of a study that (1) suggest to the participants what the purpose and hypothesis are, and (2) influence the participants to respond or behave in a certain way. Demand characteristics are artifacts and can threaten the validity of the measurement, as well as both internal and external validity.

Dependent variable In an experiment, the variable that is observed for changes to assess the effects of manipulating the independent variable. In nonexperiments and quasi-experiments the dependent variable is the variable that is measured to obtain the scores within each group. The dependent variable is typically a behavior or a response measured in each treatment condition.

Descriptive research strategy A general approach to research that involves measuring a variable or set of variables as they exist naturally to produce a description of individual variables as they exist within a specific group, but does not attempt to describe or explain relationships between variables.

Descriptive statistics Statistical methods used to organize, summarize, and simplify the results obtained from research studies.

Desynchrony Lack of agreement between two measures.

Developmental research designs Non-experimental research designs used to examine the relationship between age and other variables.

Differential attrition A threat to internal validity that occurs when attrition in one group is systematically different from the attrition in another group.

Differential effects In a research study, time-related threats to internal validity that affect the groups differently. For example, differential history effects, differential instrumentation effects, differential maturation, differential testing, and differential regression.

Differential research design A non-experimental research design that compares preexisting groups rather than randomly assigning individuals to groups. Usually, the groups are defined by a participant characteristic such as gender, race, or personality.

Diffusion A threat to internal validity that occurs when a treatment effect spreads from the treatment group to the control group, usually from participants talking to each other.

Directionality problem Demonstrating that changes in one variable tend to be accompanied by changes in another variable simply establishes that the two variables are related. The remaining problem is to determine which variable is the cause and which is the effect.

Discrete-trials design *See* alternating-treatments design.

Discussion section The portion of a research report that restates the hypothesis, summarizes the results, and presents a discussion of the interpretation, implications, and possible applications of the results.

Dismantling design A single-subject design consisting of a series of phases in which each phase adds or subtracts one component of a complex treatment. Also known as component-analysis design.

Divergent validity A type of validity demonstrated by using two different methods to measure two different constructs. Convergent validity then must be shown for each of the two constructs. Finally, there should be little or no relationship between the scores obtained for the two different constructs when they are measured by the same method.

Double-blind research A research study in which both the researcher and the participants are unaware of the predicted outcome for any specific participant.

Duration method In behavioral observation, a technique for converting observations into numerical scores; involves recording how much time an individual spends engaged in a specific behavior during a fixed-time observation period.

Effect size The measured magnitude of a treatment effect or relationship that is not influenced by factors such as sample size.

Empirical method A method of acquiring knowledge in which observation and direct sensory experience are used to obtain knowledge. Also known as empiricism.

Empiricism *See* empirical method.

Error variance A variance computed to measure the magnitude of differences that would be expected if the null hypothesis is true and there are no population mean differences. The denominator of the F-ratio computed in an analysis of variance.

Ethics The study of proper action.

Event sampling A technique of behavioral observation that involves observing and recording one specific event or behavior during the first interval, then shifting to a different event or behavior during the second interval, and so on for the full series of intervals.

Experiment A study that attempts to show that changes in one variable are directly responsible for causing changes in a second variable. Also known as a true experiment.

Experimental group The treatment condition in an experiment.

Experimental realism In simulation research, the extent to which the psychological aspects of the research environment duplicate the real-world environment that is being simulated.

Experimental research strategy A research strategy that attempts to establish the existence of a cause-and-effect relationship between two variables by manipulating one variable while measuring the second variable and controlling all other variables.

Experimenter bias The influence on the findings of a study from the experimenter's expectations about the study.

Experimenter bias is a type of artifact and threatens the validity of the measurement, as well as both internal and external validity.

External validity The extent to which we can generalize the results of a research study to people, settings, times, measures, and characteristics other than those used in that study.

Extraneous variable Any variable that exists within a study other than the variables being studied. In an experiment, any variable other than the independent and dependent variables.

Face validity An unscientific form of validity that concerns whether a measure superficially appears to measure what it claims to measure.

Factor A variable that differentiates a set of groups or conditions being compared in a research study. In an experimental design, a factor is an independent variable.

Factorial design A research design that includes two or more factors.

Faithful subject role In a study, a participant's attempt to follow experimental instructions to the letter and to avoid acting on the basis of any suspicions about the purpose of the experiment.

Fatigue A threat to internal validity that occurs when prior participation in a treatment condition or measurement procedure tires the participants and influences their performance on subsequent measurements; an example of a testing effect or an order effect.

Field Any research setting that the participant or subject perceives as a natural environment.

Field study An experiment conducted in a setting that the participant or subject perceives as a natural environment.

Floor effect The clustering of scores at the low end of a measurement scale, allowing little or no possibility of decreases in value; a type of range effect.

Fraud The explicit efforts of a researcher to falsify and misrepresent data. Fraud is unethical.

Frequency distribution An organized display of a set of scores that shows how many scores are located in each category on the scale of measurement.

Frequency method In behavioral observation, a technique for converting observations into numerical scores that involves counting the instances of each specific behavior that occur during a fixed-time observation period.

Generation effects *See* cohort effects.

Good subject role In a study, a participant's tendency to respond in a way that is expected to corroborate the investigator's hypothesis.

Habituation In behavioral observation, repeated exposure of participants to the observer's presence until it is no longer a novel stimulus.

Higher-order factorial design A factorial research design with more than two factors.

Histogram A frequency distribution graph in which a vertical bar indicates the frequency of each score from an interval or ratio scale of measurement.

History A threat to internal validity from any outside event that influences the participants' scores in one treatment differently than in another treatment.

Hypothesis A statement that provides a tentative description or explanation for the relationship between variables.

Hypothesis test An inferential statistical procedure that uses sample data to evaluate the credibility of a hypothesis about a population. A hypothesis test determines whether research results are statistically significant.

Hypothetical constructs *See* constructs.

Idiographic approach The study of individuals, in contrast to the study of groups.

Independent-measures design *See* between-subjects design.

Independent-measures experimental design *See* between-subjects experimental design.

Independent-measures *t* test In a between-subjects design, a hypothesis test that evaluates the statistical significance of the mean difference between two separate groups of participants.

Independent variable In an experiment, the variable manipulated by the researcher. In behavioral research, the independent variable usually consists of two or more treatment conditions to which participants are exposed.

Individual differences Characteristics that differ from one participant to another.

Individual sampling A technique of behavioral observation involving identifying one participant to be observed during the first interval, then shifting attention to a different individual for the second interval, and so on.

Induction The use of a relatively small set of specific observations as the basis for forming a general statement about a larger set of possible observations. Also known as inductive reasoning.

Inductive reasoning *See* induction.

Inferential statistics Statistical methods used to determine when it is appropriate to generalize the results from a sample to an entire population.

Informed consent The ethical principle requiring the investigator to provide all available information about a study so that a participant can make a rational, informed decision regarding whether to participate in the study.

Institutional Animal Care and Use Committee (IACUC) A committee that examines all proposed research with respect to its treatment of nonhuman subjects. IACUC approval must be obtained prior to conducting any research with nonhuman subjects.

Institutional Review Board (IRB) A committee that examines all proposed research with respect to its treatment of human participants. IRB approval must be obtained prior to conducting any research with human participants.

Instrumental bias *See* instrumentation.

Instrumental decay *See* instrumentation.

Instrumentation A threat to internal validity from changes in the measurement instrument that occur during the time a research study is being conducted. Also known as instrumental bias or instrumental decay.

Interaction *See* interaction between factors.

Interaction between factors In a factorial design, whenever one factor modifies the effects of a second factor. If the mean differences between the treatment conditions are explained by the main effects, then the factors are independent and there is no interaction. Also, when the effects of one factor depend on the different levels of a second factor. Indicated by the existence of nonparallel (converging or crossing)

lines in a graph showing the means for a two-factor design. Also known as interaction.

Internal validity The extent to which a research study produces a single, unambiguous explanation for the relationship between two variables.

Inter-rater reliability The degree of agreement between two observers who simultaneously record measurements of a behavior.

Interrupted time-series design A quasi-experimental research design consisting of a series of observations before and after an event. The event is not a treatment or an experience created or manipulated by the researcher.

Interval method In behavioral observation, a technique for converting observations into numerical scores; involves dividing the observation period into a series of intervals, recording whether or not a specific behavior occurs during each interval, and then counting the number of intervals in which the behavior occurred.

Interval scale A scale of measurement in which the categories are organized sequentially and all categories are the same size. The zero point of an interval scale is arbitrary and does not indicate a total absence of the variable being measured.

Interviewer bias The influence of the researcher verbally asking participants questions on the participants' natural responses.

Introduction The first major section of a research report, which presents a logical development of the research question including a review of the relevant background literature, a statement of the research question or hypothesis, and a brief description of the methods used to answer the question or test the hypothesis.

Kuder-Richardson formula 20 (K-R 20) A formula for computing split-half reliability that uses one split-half correlation to estimate the average of all possible split-half correlations when each test item has only two responses.

Laboratory A research setting that is obviously devoted to the discipline of science. It can be any room or space that the subject or participant perceives as artificial.

Latin square An $n \times n$ matrix in which each of n different items appears exactly once in each column and exactly once in each row. Used to identify sequences of treatment conditions for partial counterbalancing.

Law of large numbers In the field of statistics, the principle that states that the larger the sample size, the more likely it is that values obtained from the sample are similar to the actual values for the population.

Level In a single-subject research study, the overall magnitude for a series of observations. A consistent level occurs when measurements in a series are all approximately the same magnitude.

Level of significance See alpha level.

Levels In an experiment, the different values of the independent variable selected to create and define the treatment conditions. In other research studies, the different values of a factor.

Likert scale A rating scale presented as a horizontal line divided into categories so that participants can circle a number or mark an X at the location corresponding to their response.

Linear relationship In a graph showing the changing values of two variables, a pattern in which the data points tend to cluster around a straight line.

Line graph A display in which points connected by straight lines show several different means obtained from different groups or treatment conditions. Also used to show different medians, proportions, or other sample statistics.

Literature search The process of gaining a general familiarity with the current research conducted in a subject area, and finding a small set of journal articles that serve as the basis for a research idea and provide the justification or foundation for new research.

Longitudinal developmental research design A developmental research design that examines development by making a series of observations or measurements over time. Typically, a group of individuals who are all the same age is measured at different points in time.

Main effect In a factorial study, the mean differences among the levels of one factor.

Manipulation In an experiment, identifying the specific values of the independent variable to be examined

and then creating treatment conditions corresponding to each of these values. The researcher then manipulates the variable by changing from one condition to another.

Manipulation check In an experiment, an additional measure used to assess how the participants perceived and interpreted the manipulation and/or to assess the direct effect of the manipulation.

Matched-subjects design A research design comparing separate groups of individuals in which each individual in one group is matched with a participant in each of the other groups. The matching is done so that the matched individuals are equivalent with respect to a variable that the researcher considers to be relevant to the study.

Matching The assignment of individuals to groups so that a specific variable is balanced or matched across the groups.

Materials subsection In a research report, the portion of the method section that describes any questionnaires used in the study.

Maturation A threat to internal validity from any physiological or psychological changes that occur in a participant during the time that research study is being conducted and that can influence the participant's scores.

Mean A measure of central tendency obtained by adding the individual scores and dividing the sum by the number of scores.

Median A measure of central tendency that identifies the score that divides the distribution in half so that 50% of the individuals have scores at or below the median.

Method of authority A method of acquiring knowledge in which a person relies on information or answers from an expert in the subject area.

Method of faith A variant of the method of authority in which people have unquestioning trust in the authority figure and, therefore, accept information from the authority without doubt or challenge.

Method of intuition A method of acquiring knowledge in which information is accepted on the basis of a hunch or "gut feeling."

Method of tenacity A method of acquiring knowledge in which

information is accepted as true because it has always been believed or because superstition supports it.

Method section The section of a research report that describes how the study was conducted, including information about the subjects or participants and the procedures used.

Methods of acquiring knowledge The variety of ways in which a person can know things or discover answers to questions.

Mixed design A factorial study that combines two different research designs, such as between-subjects and within-subjects, in the same factorial design.

Mode A measure of central tendency that identifies the most frequently occurring score in the distribution.

Monotonic relationship A consistently one-directional relationship between two variables. As one variable increases, the other variable also tends to increase or tends to decrease. The relationship can be either linear or curvilinear.

Multimodal distribution In a frequency distribution graph, a distribution of scores with more than two modes or distinct peaks.

Multiple-baseline across behaviors A multiple-baseline design in which the initial baseline phases correspond to two separate behaviors for the same participant.

Multiple-baseline across situations A multiple-baseline design in which the initial baseline phases correspond to the same behavior in two separate situations.

Multiple-baseline across subjects A multiple-baseline design in which the initial baseline phases correspond to the same behavior for two separate participants.

Multiple-baseline design A single-subject design that begins with two simultaneous baseline phases, then initiates a treatment for one baseline, and, at a later time, initiates the treatment for the second baseline.

Multiple regression A statistical technique used for studying multivariate relationships. The statistical process of finding the linear equation that produces the most accurate predicted values for Y using more than one predictor variable.

Multiple-regression equation The resulting equation from a multiple regression analysis.

Multiple-treatment interference A threat to external validity that occurs when participants are exposed to more than one treatment and their responses are affected by an earlier treatment.

Mundane realism In simulation research, the extent to which the superficial, usually physical, characteristics of the research environment duplicate the real-world environment that is being simulated.

National Research Act A set of regulations for the protection of human participants in research, mandated by Congress in 1974.

Naturalistic observation A type of observation in which a researcher observes behavior in a natural setting as unobtrusively as possible. Also known as nonparticipant observation.

Negative relationship A relationship in which the two variables or measurements tend to change together in opposite directions.

Negativistic subject role In a study, a participant's tendency to respond in a way that is expected to refute the investigator's hypothesis.

Nominal scale A scale of measurement in which the categories represent qualitative differences in the variable being measured. The categories have different names but are not related to each other in any systematic way.

Nomothetic approach The study of groups in contrast to the study of individuals.

Nonequivalent control group design A research design in which the researcher does not randomly assign individuals to groups but rather uses preexisting groups, with one group serving in the treatment condition and another group serving in the control condition.

Nonequivalent group design A research study in which the different groups of participants are formed under circumstances that do not permit the researcher to control the assignment of individuals to groups and the groups of participants are, therefore, considered nonequivalent.

Nonexperimental research strategy A research strategy that attempts to demonstrate a relationship between two variables by comparing different groups of scores, but makes little or no attempt to minimize threats to internal validity or to explain the relationship.

Nonparametric test A hypothesis test that does not require numerical scores and does not involve a hypothesis about specific population parameters. The chi-square test for independence is an example of a nonparametric test.

Nonparticipant observation *See* naturalistic observation.

Nonprobability sampling A method of sampling in which the population is not completely known, individual probabilities cannot be known, and the selection is based on factors such as common sense or ease with an effort to maintain representativeness and avoid bias.

Nonresponse bias In survey research involving mailed surveys, individuals who return the survey are not usually representative of the entire group who received the survey. Nonresponse bias is a threat to external validity.

No-treatment control group In an experiment, a group or condition in which the participants do not receive the treatment being evaluated.

Novelty effect A threat to external validity that occurs when individuals participating in a research study (a novel situation) perceive and respond differently than they would in the normal, real world.

Null hypothesis In a hypothesis test, a statement about the population(s) or treatments being studied that says there is no change, no effect, no difference, or no relationship.

Nuremberg Code A set of 10 guidelines for the ethical treatment of human participants in research. The Nuremberg Code, developed from the Nuremberg Trials in 1947, laid the groundwork for the current ethical standards for medical and psychological research.

Observational research design Descriptive research in which the researcher observes and systematically records the behavior of individuals to describe the behavior.

Omission *See* passive deception.

One-group pretest-posttest design A nonexperimental design involving one measurement before treatment and one measurement after treatment for a single group of participants.

One-way ANOVA *See* single-factor analysis of variance.

Operational definition A procedure for measuring and defining a construct. An operational definition specifies a measurement procedure (a set of operations) for measuring an external, observable behavior and uses the resulting measurements as a definition and a measurement of the hypothetical construct.

Order effects Whenever individuals participate in a series of treatment conditions and experience a series of measurements, their behavior or performance at any point in the series may be influenced by experience that occurred earlier in the sequence. Order effects include carryover effects and progressive error. Also known as testing effects

Ordinal scale A scale of measurement on which the categories have different names and are organized sequentially (for example, first, second, third).

Parallel-forms reliability The type of reliability established by comparing scores obtained by using two alternate versions of a measuring instrument to measure the same individuals and calculating a correlation between the two sets of scores.

Parameter A summary value that describes a population.

Parametric test A hypothesis test that uses sample means or sample correlations to evaluate a hypothesis about the corresponding population. Parametric tests rely on sample data consisting of numerical scores.

Partial counterbalancing A system of counterbalancing that ensures that each treatment condition occurs first for one group of participants, second for one group, third for one group, and so on, but does not require that every possible order of treatment conditions be used.

Participant attrition The loss of participants that occurs during the course of a research study conducted over time. Attrition can be a threat to internal validity. Also known as participant mortality.

Participant mortality *See* participant attrition.

Participant observation A type of observation in which the researcher engages in the same activities as the people being observed in order to observe and record their behavior.

Participants   Humans who take part in a research study.

Participants subsection   In a research report, the portion of the method section that describes the humans who participated in the study.

Passive deception   The intentional withholding or omitting of information whereby participants are not told some information about the study. Also known as omission.

Pearson correlation   A correlation used to evaluate linear (straight-line) relationships.

Peer review   The editorial process that many articles undergo when a researcher submits a research report for publication. In a typical peer-review process, the editor of the journal and a few experts in the field of research review the paper in extreme detail. The reviewers critically scrutinize every aspect of the research with the primary purpose of evaluating the quality of the study and its contribution to scientific knowledge. Reviewers are also likely to detect anything suspect about the research or the findings.

Percentage of variance accounted for (r^2 or η^2)   The percentage of variance for one variable that can be predicted using the known values for a second variable.

Phase   In a single-subject research design, a series of observations of the same individual under the same conditions.

Phase change   In a single-subjects research study, a change in the conditions from one phase to another, usually involving administering or stopping a treatment.

Physiological measure   Measurement obtained by recording a physiological activity such as heart rate.

Placebo   An ineffective, inert substitute for a treatment or medication.

Placebo control group   A group or condition in which the participants receive a placebo instead of the actual treatment.

Placebo effect   A participant's response to an inert medication or treatment that has no real effect on the body; occurs simply because the individual thinks the placebo is effective.

Plagiarism   Presenting someone else's ideas or words as one's own. Plagiarism is unethical.

Polygon   A frequency distribution graph in which a series of points connected by straight lines indicates the frequency of each score from an interval or ratio scale of measurement.

Population   The entire set of individuals of interest to a researcher. Although the entire population usually does not participate in a research study, the results from the study will be generalized to the entire population. Also known as target population.

Positive relationship   A relationship in which the two variables or measurements tend to change together in the same direction.

Post hoc tests or post tests   Follow-up hypothesis tests done after an analysis of variance to determine exactly which mean differences are significant.

Posttest-only nonequivalent control group design   A nonexperimental design in which one group is observed (measured) after receiving a treatment, and a second, nonequivalent group is measured at the same time but receives no treatment.

Practical significance   In a research study, a result or treatment effect that is large enough to have value in a practical application. Also known as clinical significance.

Practice   A threat to internal validity that occurs when prior participation in a treatment condition or measurement procedure provides participants with additional skills that influence their performance on subsequent measurements. An example of a testing effect or an order effect.

Predictive validity   The type of validity demonstrated when scores obtained from a measure accurately predict behavior according to a theory.

Predictor variable   In a correlational study, a researcher often is interested in the relationship between two variables to use knowledge about one variable to help predict or explain the second variable. In this situation, the first variable is called the predictor variable.

Premise statements   Sentences used in logical reasoning that describe facts or assumptions.

Pre–post designs   Quasi-experimental and nonexperimental designs consisting of a series of observations made over time. The goal is to evaluate the effect of an intervening treatment or event by comparing observations made before versus after the treatment.

Pretest–posttest nonequivalent control group design   A quasi-experimental research design comparing two nonequivalent groups; one group is measured twice, once before treatment is administered and once after. The other group is measured at the same two times but receives no treatment.

Pretest sensitization   *See* sensitization.

Primary source   A firsthand report of observations or research results written by the individual(s) who actually conducted the research and made the observations.

Probability sampling   A sampling method in which the entire population is known, each individual in the population has a specifiable probability of selection, and sampling is done using a random process based on the probabilities.

Procedure subsection   In a research report, the portion of the method section that describes the step-by-step process used to complete the study.

Progressive error   In a research study, changes in the scores observed in one treatment condition that are related to general experience in a research study over time, but not to a specific treatment or treatments. Common kinds of progressive error are practice effects and fatigue.

Proportionate random sampling   *See* proportionate stratified random sampling.

Proportionate stratified random sampling   A probability sampling technique that involves identifying specific subgroups to be included, determining what proportion of the population corresponds to each subgroup, and randomly selecting individuals so that the proportion for each subgroup in the sample exactly matches the corresponding proportion in the population. Also known as proportionate random sampling.

Pseudoscience   A set of ideas based on nonscientific theory, faith, and belief.

PsycArticles   A computerized database for searching the psychological literature that contains the full text of the original publication.

PsycInfo   A computerized database for searching the psychology literature for articles relevant to a research topic.

PsycInfo provides abstracts or summaries for each publication.

Publication Manual of the American Psychological Association A manual that describes conventions for style and structure of written research reports in the behavioral sciences.

Qualitative research Research that is based on observations that are summarized and interpreted in a narrative report.

Quantitative research Research that is based on measuring variables for individual participants or subjects to obtain scores, usually numerical values, that are submitted to statistical analyses for summary and interpretation.

Quasi-experimental research strategy A research strategy that attempts to limit threats to internal validity and produce cause-and-effect conclusions (like an experiment), but lacks one of the critical components—either manipulation or control—that is necessary for a true experiment. Typically compares groups or conditions that are defined with a nonmanipulated variable.

Quasi-independent variable In a quasi-experimental or nonexperimental research study, the variable that differentiates the groups or conditions being compared. Similar to the independent variable in an experiment.

Quota sampling A nonprobability sampling method; a type of convenience sampling involving identifying specific subgroups to be included in the sample and then establishing quotas for individuals to be sampled from each group.

Random assignment A procedure in which a random process is used to assign participants to treatment conditions.

Randomization The use of a random process to help avoid a systematic relationship between two variables. The intent is to disrupt any systematic relationship that might exist between extraneous variables and the independent variable.

Random process A procedure that produces one outcome from a set of possible outcomes. The outcome must be unpredictable each time, and the process must guarantee that each of the possible outcomes is equally likely to occur.

Range effect The clustering of scores at one end of a measurement scale. Ceiling effects and floor effects are types of range effects.

Rationalism *See* rational method.

Rational method A method of acquiring knowledge that involves seeking answers by the use of logical reasoning. Also known as rationalism.

Ratio scale A scale of measurement in which the categories are sequentially organized, all categories are the same size, and the zero point is absolute or nonarbitrary, and indicates a complete absence of the variable being measured.

Reactivity Participants' modification of their natural behavior in response to the fact that they are participating in a research study or the knowledge that they are being measured. Reactivity is an artifact and can threaten the validity of the measurement, as well as both internal and external validity.

Reference section The section of a research report that lists complete references for all sources of information cited in the report, organized alphabetically by the last name of the first author.

Refutable hypothesis A hypothesis that can be demonstrated to be false. That is, the hypothesis allows the possibility that the outcome will differ from the prediction.

Regression A statistical technique used for predicting one variable from another. The statistical process of finding the linear equation that produces the most accurate predicted values for Y using one predictor variable, X.

Regression equation The equation from a regression analysis.

Regression toward the mean *See* statistical regression.

Reliability The degree of stability or consistency of measurements. If the same individuals are measured under the same conditions, a reliable measurement procedure will produce identical (or nearly identical) measurements.

Repeated-measures design *See* within-subjects design.

Repeated-measures experimental design *See* within-subjects experimental design.

Repeated-measures *t* test In a within-subjects or matched-subjects design, a

hypothesis test that evaluates the statistical significance of the mean difference between two sets of scores obtained from the same group of participants.

Replication Repetition of a research study with the same basic procedures used in the original study. The intent of replication is to test the validity of the original study. Either the replication will support the original study by duplicating the original results, or it will cast doubt on the original study by demonstrating that the original result is not easily repeated.

Representativeness The extent to which the characteristics of the sample accurately reflect the characteristics of the population.

Representative sample A sample with the same characteristics as the population.

Research design A general plan for implementing a research strategy. A research design specifies whether the study will involve groups or individual subjects, will make comparisons within a group or between groups, or specifies how many variables will be included in the study.

Research ethics The responsibility of researchers to be honest and respectful to all individuals who may be affected by their research studies or their reports of the studies' results. Researchers are usually governed by a set of ethical guidelines that assist them to make proper decisions and choose proper actions. In psychological research, the American Psychological Association (APA) maintains a set of ethical principles for research.

Research procedure The exact, step-by-step description of a specific research study.

Research proposal A written report presenting the plan and underlying rationale for a future research study. A proposal includes a review of the relevant background literature, an explanation of how the proposed study is related to other knowledge in the area, a description of how the planned research will be conducted, and a description of the possible results.

Research report A written description of a research study that includes a clear statement of the purpose of the research, a review of the relevant background literature that led to the research study, a description of the methods used to conduct the research, a summary of the research results, and a discussion and interpretation of the results.

Research strategy A general approach to research determined by the kind of question that the research study hopes to answer.

Resentful demoralization A threat to internal validity that occurs when an untreated group learns of special treatment given to another group, and becomes less productive and less motivated because they resent the other group's expected superiority.

Response set On a rating-scale question, a participant's tendency to answer all (or most) of the questions the same way.

Restricted random assignment A random process for assigning individuals to groups that has a limitation to ensure predetermined characteristics (such as equal size) for the separate groups.

Results section The section of a research report that presents a summary of the data and the statistical analysis.

Reversal design *See* ABAB design.

Running head The abbreviated title of a research report containing a maximum of 50 characters that appears on the title page and at the top of every page of the manuscript. It also appears at the top of the pages in a published article.

Sample A set of individuals selected from a population, usually intended to represent the population in a research study.

Sampling The process of selecting individuals to participate in a research study.

Sampling bias *See* selection bias.

Sampling error The naturally occurring difference between a sample statistic and the corresponding population parameter.

Sampling methods The variety of ways of selecting individuals to participate in a research study. Also known as sampling techniques or sampling procedures.

Sampling procedures *See* sampling methods.

Sampling techniques *See* sampling methods.

Scale of measurement The set of categories used for classification of individuals. The four types of measurement scales are nominal, ordinal, interval, and ratio.

Scatter plot A graph that shows the data from a correlational study. The two scores for each individual appear as a single point in the graph with the vertical position of the point corresponding to one score and the horizontal position corresponding to the other.

Scientific method A method of acquiring knowledge that uses observations to develop a hypothesis, then uses the hypothesis to make logical predictions that can be empirically tested by making additional, systematic observations. Typically, the new observations lead to a new hypothesis, and the cycle continues.

Secondary source A description or summary of another person's work, written by someone who did not participate in the research or observations discussed.

Selection bias When participants or subjects are selected in a manner that increases the probability of obtaining a biased sample. A threat to external validity that occurs when the selection process produces a sample with characteristics that are different from those in the population. Also known as sampling bias.

Self-report measure A measurement obtained by asking a participant to describe his or her own attitude, opinion, or behavior.

Semantic differential A type of rating scale question that presents pairs of bipolar adjectives (such as happy—sad, boring—exciting) and asks each participant to identify the location between the two adjectives that best describes a particular individual.

Sensitization A threat to external validity that occurs when the assessment procedure alters participants so that they react differently to treatment than they would in the real world when the treatment is used without assessment. Also known as assessment sensitization or pretest sensitization.

Significant result *See* statistically significant result.

Simple random sampling A probability sampling technique in which each individual in the population has an equal and independent chance of selection.

Simulation In an experiment, the creation of conditions that simulate or closely duplicate the natural environment in which the behaviors being examined would normally occur.

Single-blind research A research study in which the researcher does not know the predicted outcome for any specific participant.

Single-case designs *See* single-subject designs.

Single-factor analysis of variance A hypothesis test that evaluates the statistical significance of the mean differences among two or more sets of scores obtained from a single-factor multiple-group design. Also known as one-way ANOVA.

Single-factor design A research study with one independent variable or one quasi-independent variable.

Single-factor multiple-group design A research design comparing more than two groups of participants (or groups of scores) representing more than two levels of the same factor.

Single-factor two-group design A research design comparing two groups of participants or two groups of scores representing two levels of a factor. Also known as the two-group design.

Single-subject designs Experimental research designs that use the results from a single participant or subject to establish the existence of a cause-and-effect relationship. Also known as single-case designs.

Slope constant In the linear equation $Y = bX + a$, b describes the slope of the line (how much Y changes when X is increased by 1 point).

Spearman-Brown formula A formula for computing split-half reliability that corrects for the fact that individual scores are based on only half of the total test items.

Spearman correlation A correlation used with ordinal data or to evaluate monotonic relationships.

Split-half reliability A measure of reliability obtained by splitting the items on a questionnaire or test in half, computing a separate score for each half, and then measuring the degree of consistency between the two scores for a group of participants.

Stability The degree to which a series of observations shows a consistent level or trend.

Standard deviation A measure of variability that describes the average distance from the mean; obtained by taking the square root of the variance.

Standard error A measure of the average or standard distance between a sample statistic and the corresponding population parameter.

Statistic A summary value that describes a sample.

Statistically significant result In a research study, a result that is extremely unlikely (as defined by an alpha level, or level of significance) to have occurred simply by chance. Also known as a significant result.

Statistical regression A statistical phenomenon in which extreme scores (high or low) on a first measurement tend to be less extreme on a second measurement; considered a threat to internal validity because changes in participants' scores could be caused by regression rather than by the treatments. Also known as regression toward the mean.

Statistical significance In a research study, a result or treatment effect that is large enough to be extremely unlikely to have occurred simply by chance.

Statistical significance of a correlation In a correlational study, the correlation in the sample is large enough that it is very unlikely to have been produced by random variation, but rather represents a real relationship in the population.

Stratified random sampling A probability sampling technique that involves identifying specific subgroups to be included in the sample and then selecting equal random samples from each pre-identified subgroup.

Structured observation *See* contrived observation.

Subject role behavior *See* subject roles.

Subject roles The different ways that participants respond to experimental cues based on whatever they judge to be appropriate in the situation. Also known as subject role behavior.

Subjects Nonhumans who take part in a research study.

Subjects subsection In a research report, the portion of the method section that describes the nonhumans who participated in the study.

Subject words Terms used to identify and describe the variables in a study. Subject words are used to direct a search in a database.

Survey research design A research study that uses a survey to obtain a description of a particular group of individuals.

Systematic sampling A probability sampling technique in which a sample is obtained by selecting every nth participant from a list containing the total population after a random starting point.

Target population A group defined by a researcher's specific interests; see also population.

Testable hypothesis A hypothesis for which all of the variables, events, and individuals are real and can be defined and observed.

Testing effects A threat to internal validity that occurs when participants are exposed to more than one treatment and their responses are affected by participation in an earlier treatment. Examples of testing effects include fatigue and practice. Also known as order effects.

Test-retest reliability The type of reliability established by comparing the scores obtained from two successive measurements of the same individuals and calculating a correlation between the two sets of scores.

Test statistic A summary value computed in a hypothesis test to measure the degree to which the sample data are in accord with the null hypothesis.

Theories In the behavioral sciences, statements about the mechanisms underlying a particular behavior.

Third-variable problem The possibility that two variables appear to be related when, in fact, they are both influenced by a third variable that causes them to vary together.

Threat to external validity Any characteristic of a study that limits the ability to generalize the results.

Threat to internal validity Any factor that allows for an alternative explanation for the results of a study.

Threat to validity Any component of a research study that introduces questions or raises doubts about the quality of the research process or the accuracy of the research results.

Three-factor design A research study involving three independent or quasi-independent variables.

Time-related variables Environmental or participant variables that change over time. A threat to the internal validity of studies that compare measures of the same individuals taken at different times.

Time sampling A technique of behavioral observation that involves observing for one interval, then pausing during the next interval to record all the observations. The sequence of observe-record-observe-record is continued through the series of intervals.

Time-series design A quasi-experimental research design consisting of a series of observations before a treatment or event and a series of observations after the treatment or event. A treatment is a manipulation administered by the researcher and an event is an outside occurrence that is not controlled or manipulated by the researcher.

Title A concise statement of the content of a paper that identifies the main variables being investigated.

Title page The first page of a research report manuscript; contains the running head and page number, the title of the paper, the author names and affiliations, and the author note.

Treatment condition In an experiment, a situation or environment characterized by one specific value of the manipulated variable. An experiment contains two or more treatment conditions that differ according to values of the manipulated variable.

Treatment observations In a single-subject research study, observations or measurements made while a treatment is being administered.

Treatment phase In a single-subject research study, a series of treatment observations identified by the letter B.

Trend In a single-subject research study, a consistent difference in direction and magnitude from one measurement to the next in a series.

True experiment *See* experiment.

Two-factor ANOVA *See* two-way analysis of variance.

Two-factor design A research study involving two independent or quasi-independent variables.

Two-group design *See* single-factor two-group design.

Two-way analysis of variance A hypothesis test that evaluates the statistical significance of the mean differences (both main effects and interaction) obtained in a two-factor research study. Also known as two-factor ANOVA.

Type I error The conclusion, based on a hypothesis test, that a result is statistically significant when, in fact, there is no effect (no relationship) in the population.

Type II error The conclusion, based on a hypothesis test, that a result is not statistically significant when, in fact, a real effect or relationship does exist in the population.

Validity (of a measurement procedure) The degree to which the measurement process measures the variable it claims to measure.

Validity (of a research study) The degree to which the study accurately answers the question it was intended to answer.

Variability A measure of the size of the spread of scores in a distribution.

Variables Characteristics or conditions that change or have different values for different individuals.

Variance A measure of variability obtained by computing the average squared distance from the mean.

Variance within groups *See* variance within treatments.

Variance within treatments A measure of the differences between scores for a group of individuals who have all received the same treatment. The intent is to measure naturally occurring differences that have not been caused by a treatment effect. Also known as variance within groups.

Volunteer bias A threat to external validity that occurs because volunteers are not perfectly representative of the general population.

Within-subjects design A research design in which the different groups of scores are all obtained from the same group of participants. Also known as repeated-measures design.

Within-subjects experimental design An experimental design in which the same group of individuals participates in all of the different treatment conditions. Also known as a repeated-measures experimental design.

Y-intercept In the linear equation $Y = bX + a$, a, the Y-intercept, is the point at which the line intersects the Y-axis.

REFERENCES

Allport, G. W. (1961). *Pattern and growth in personality.* New York: Holt, Reinhart, and Winston.

American Psychological Association. (1973). Ethical principles in the conduct of research with human participants. *American Psychologist, 28,* 79–80. doi:10.1037/h0038067

American Psychological Association. (1996). *Guidelines for the ethical conduct in the care and use of animals.* Retrieved from http://www.apa.org/science/rcr/guide-lines.pdf

American Psychological Association. (2001). *Publication manual of the American Psychological Association* (5th ed.). Washington, DC: APA.

American Psychological Association. (2002). Ethical principles of psychologists and code of conduct. *American Psychologist, 57,* 1060–1073. Retrieved from http:// www.apa.org/ethics/code2002.html

American Psychological Association. (2007). *APA style guide to electronic references.* Retrieved from http:// www.apastyle.org/elecref.html

Anderson, D. R., Huston, A. C., Wright, J. C., & Collins, P. A. (1998). Initial findings on the long term impact of Sesame Street and educational television for children: The recontact study. In R. Noll & M. Price (Eds.), *A communication cornucopia: Markle Foundation essays on information policy* (pp. 279–296). Washington, DC: Brookings Institution.

Aronson, E., & Carlsmith, J. M. (1968). Experimentation in social psychology. In G. Lindzey & E. Aronson (Eds.), *Handbook of social psychology* (2nd ed., Vol. 2, pp. 1–79). Reading, MA: Addison-Wesley.

Asch, S. (1956). Studies of independence and conformity: A minority of one against a unanimous majority. *Psychological Monographs, 76*(9, Whole No. 416).

Badenhausen, K., Ozanian, M. K., & Settimi, C. (Eds.). (2010). The business of baseball. Retrieved September 8, 2010, from http://www.forbes.com.

Bahrick, H. P., & Hall, L. K. (1991). Lifetime maintenance of high school mathematics content. *Journal of Experimental Psychology: General, 120,* 20–33. doi:10.1037/0096-3445.120.1.20

Baldwin, E. (1993). The case for animal research in psychology. *Journal of Social Issues, 49,* 121–131.

Baltes, P. B., & Schaie, K. W. (1974). The myth of the twilight years. *Psychology Today, 8,* 35–40.

Barnard, N. D., & Kaufman, S. R. (1997). Animal research is wasteful and misleading. *Scientific American, 276,* 80–82.

Baumrind, D. (1985). Research using intentional deception: Ethical issues revisited. *American Psychologist, 40,* 165–174. doi:10.1037/0003-066X.40.2.165

Bernard, R. S., Cohen, L. L., & Moffett. K. (2009). A token economy for exercise adherence in pediatric cystic fibrosis: A single-subject analysis. *Journal of Pediatric Psychology, 34,* 354-365. doi:10.1093/jpepsy/jsn101

Bhattacharjee, Y. (Ed.). (2008). Memorable. *Science, 322,* 1765-1765.

Bordens, K. S., & Horowitz, I. A. (1983). Information processing in joined and severed trials. *Journal of Applied Social Psychology, 13,* 351–370.

Botting, J. H., & Morrison, A. R. (1997). Animal research is vital to medicine. *Scientific American, 276,* 83–85.

Bouhuys, A. L., Bloem, G. M., & Groothuis, T. G. G. (1995). Induction of depressed and elated mood by music influences the perception of facial emotional expressions in healthy subjects. *Journal of Affective Disorders, 33,* 215–226. doi:10.1016/0165-0327(94)00092-N

Bowd, A. J., & Shapiro, K. D. (1993). The case against animal research in psychology. *Journal of Social Issues, 49,* 133–142.

Brennan, K. A., & Morris, K. A. (1997). Attachment styles, self-esteem, and patterns of seeking feedback from romantic partners. *Personality and Social Psychology Bulletin, 23,* 23-31. doi:10.1177/0146167297231003

Broadhead, W. E., Kaplan, B. H., James, S. A., Wagner, E. H., Schoenbach, V. I., Grimson, R., Heyden, S., Tibblin, G., & Gehlbach, S. H. (1983). The epidemiologic evidence for a relationship between social support and health. *American Journal of Epidemiology, 117,* 521–537.

Bryan, J. H., & Test, M. A. (1967). Models and helping: Naturalistic studies in aiding behavior. *Journal of Personality and Social Psychology, 6,* 400–407. doi:10.1037/h0024826

Camara, W., & Echternacht, G. (2000). *The SAT I and high school grades: Utility in predicting success in college* (College Board Report No. RN-10). New York: College Entrance Examination Board.

Campbell, D. T., & Fiske, D. W. (1959). Convergent and discriminant validation by the multitrait-multimethod matrix. *Psychological Bulletin, 56,* 81-105. doi:10.1037/h0046016

Campbell, D. T., & Stanley, J. C. (1963). *Experimental and quasi-experimental designs for research.* Chicago: Rand McNally.

Cialdini, R. B., Reno, R. R., & Kallgren, C. A. (1990). A focus theory of normative conduct: Recycling the concept of norms to reduce littering in public places. *Journal of Personality and Social Psychology, 58,* 1015–1026. doi:10.1037/0022-3514.58.6.1015

Clark, D. M., & Tessdale, J. D. (1985). Constraints on the effects of mood on memory. *Journal of Personality and Social Psychology, 48,* 1595-1608. doi:10.1037/0022-3514.48.6.1595

Cohen, J. (1960). A coefficient of agreement for nominal scales. *Educational and Psychological Measurement, 20,* 37–46. doi:10.1177/001316446002000104

Cohen, J. (1988). *Statistical power analysis for the behavioral sciences* (2nd ed.). New York: Academic Press.

Cohn, E. J., & Rotton, J. (2000). Weather, disorderly conduct, and assaults: From social contact to social avoidance. *Environment and Behavior, 32,* 651–673. doi: 10.1177/00139160021972720

Collins, R. L., Elliott, M. N., Berry, S. H., Kanouse, D. E., Kunkel, D., Hunter, S. B., & Miu, A. (2004). Watching sex on television predicts adolescent initiation of sexual behavior. *Pediatrics, 114,* e280–289.

Collins, R. L., & Ellickson, P. L. (2004). Integrating four theories of adolescent smoking. *Substance Use & Misuse, 39,* 179–209. doi:10.1081/JA-120028487

Crafts, L. W., & Gilbert, R. W. (1934). The effect of punishment during learning upon retention. *Journal of Experimental Psychology, 17,* 73–84. doi:10.1037/h0072744

Craig, A. R., & Kearns, M. (1995). Results of a traditional acupuncture intervention for stuttering. *Journal of Speech & Hearing Research, 38,* 572–578.

Craik, F. I. M., & Lockhart, R. S. (1972). Levels of processing: A framework for memory research. *Journal of Verbal Learning and Verbal Behavior, 11,* 671–684. doi: 10.1016/S0022-5371(72)80001-X

Cronbach, L. J. (1951). Coefficient alpha and the internal structure of tests. *Psychometrika, 16,* 297–334. doi:10.1007/BF02310555

DeGoede, K. M., Ashton-Miller, J. A., Liao, J. M., & Alexander, N. B. (2001). How quickly can healthy adults move their hands to intercept an approaching object? Age and gender effects. *Journals of Gerontology: Series A: Biological Sciences and Medical Sciences, 56,* 584–588.

DeProspero, A., & Cohen, S. (1979). Inconsistent visual analyses of intrasubject data. *Journal of Applied Behavior Analysis, 12,* 573–579. doi:10.1901/jaba.1979.12-573

Dillman, D. A., Clark, J. R., & Sinclair, M. A. (1995). How prenotice letters, stamped return envelopes, and reminder postcards affect mailback responses rates for census questionnaires. *Survey Methodology, 21,* 1-7.

Dillman, D. A., Smyth, J. D., & Christian, L. M. (2009). *Internet, mail, and mixed-mode surveys: The tailored design method.* Hoboken, NJ: John Wiley & Sons, Inc.

Downs, D. S., & Abwender, D. (2002). Neuropsychological impairment in soccer athletes. *Journal of Sports Medicine and Physical Fitness, 42,* 103–107.

Eysenck, H. J. (1999). *Intelligence: A new look.* New Brunswick, NJ: Transaction.

Dunn, C. M., & Chadwick, G. (1999). *Protecting study volunteers in research: A manual for investigative sites.* Boston: CenterWatch.

Feeney, J. A. (2004). Transfer of attachment from parents to romantic partners: Effects of individual and relationship variables. *Journal of Family Studies, 10,* 220-238.

Ferguson, E. D., & Schmitt, S. (1988). Gender linked stereotypes and motivation affect performance in the prisoner's dilemma game. *Perceptual and Motor Skills, 66,* 703–714.

Feshbach, S., & Singer, R. (1971). *Television and aggression.* San Francisco: Jossey-Bass.

Fisher, C. B., & Fyrberg, D. (1994). Participant partners: College students weigh the costs and benefits of deceptive research. *American Psychologist, 49,* 417–425. doi:10.1037/0003-066X.49.5.417

Fontes, L. A. (2004). Ethics in violence against women research: The sensitive, the dangerous, and the overlooked. *Ethics and Behavior, 14,* 141-174. doi:10.1207/s15327019eb1402

Fossey, D. (1983). *Gorillas in the mist.* Boston: Houghton Mifflin Company.

Freedman, R., Coombs, L. C., & Chang, M. (1974). Trends in family size preferences and practice of family planning: Taiwan, 1965–1970. *Studies in Family Planning, 3,* 281-296.

Gillespie, J. F. (1999). The why, what, how and when of effective faculty use of Institutional Review Boards. In G. Chastain, & R. E. Landrum (Eds.), *Protecting human subjects* (pp. 157–177). Washington, DC: APA.

Gluck, J. P., & Bell, J. (2003). Ethical issues in the use of animals in biomedical and psychopharmacological research. *Psychopharmacology, 171,* 6–12. doi:10.1007/s00213-003-1478-y

Goldie, J., Schwartz, L., McConnachie, A., & Morrison, J. (2001). Impact of a new course on students' potential behavior on encountering ethical dilemmas. *Medical Education, Special Issue, 35,* 295–302. doi:10.1046/j.1365-2923.2001.00872.x

Goodall, J. (1971). *In the shadow of man.* Boston: Houghton Mifflin.

Goodall, J. (1986). *The chimpanzees of Gombe: Patterns of behavior.* Cambridge, MA: Harvard University Press.

Green, L., Fry, A. F., & Myerson, J. (1994). Discounting of delayed rewards: A life-span comparison. *Psychological Science, 5,* 33–36. doi:10.1111/j.1467-9280.1994.tb00610.x

Hallam, S., Price, J., & Katsarou, G. (2002). The effects of background music on primary school pupils' task performance. *Educational Studies, 28,* 111–122. doi:10.1080/03055690220124551

Haney, C., Banks, C., & Zimbardo, P. (1973). Interpersonal dynamics in a simulated prison. *International Journal of Criminology and Penology, 1*, 69–97.

Harmon, T. M., Nelson, R. O., & Hayes, S. C. (1980). Self-monitoring of mood versus activity by depressed clients. *Journal of Consulting and Clinical Psychology, 48*, 30–38. doi:10.1037/0022-006X.48.1.30

Herbert, J. D., Lilienfeld, S. O., Lohr, J. M., Montgomery, R. W., O'Donohue, W. T., Rosen, G. M., & Tolin, D. F. (2000). Science and pseudoscience in the development of eye movement desensitization and reprocessing: Implications for clinical psychology. Clinical Psychology Review, 20, 945-971. doi:10.1016/S0272-7358(99)00017-3

Holmes, D. S. (1976a). Debriefing after psychological experiments I: Effectiveness of post-deception dehoaxing. *American Psychologist, 31*, 858–867. doi:10.1037/0003-066X.31.12.858

Holmes, D. S. (1976b). Debriefing after psychological experiments II: Effectiveness of post-deception desensitizing. *American Psychologist, 31*, 868–875. doi:10.1037/0003-066X.31.12.868

Horn, J. L., & Donaldson, G. (1976). On the myth of intellectual decline in adulthood. *American Psychologist, 31*, 701–719. doi:10.1037/0003-066X.31.10.701

Hornstein, H. A., Fisch, E., & Holmes, M. (1968). Influence of a model's feeling about his behavior and his relevance as a comparison on other observers' helping behavior. *Journal of Personality and Social Psychology, 10*, 222–226. doi:10.1037/h0026568

Huck, S. W., & Sandler, H. M. (1979). *Rival hypotheses: Alternative explanations of data based conclusions.* New York: Harper & Row.

Hughes, C., Cutting, A. L., & Dunn, J. (2001). Acting nasty in the face of failure? Longitudinal observations of "hard-to-manage" children playing a rigged competitive game with a friend. *Journal of Abnormal Child Psychology, 25*, 403–416. doi:10.1023/A:1010495319182

Hughes, C., Oksanen, H., Taylor, A., Jackson, J., Murray, L., Caspi, A., & Moffitt, T. E. (2002). "I'm gonna beat you!" SNAP!: An observational paradigm for assessing young children's disruptive behaviour in competitive play. *Journal of Child Psychology & Psychiatry & Allied Disciplines, 43*, 507–516. doi:10.1111/1469-7610.00041

Hunter, J. E. (1997). Needed: A ban on the significance test. *Psychological Science, 8*, 3–7. doi:10.1111/j.1467-9280.1997.tb00534.x

Ijuin, M., Homma, A., Mimura, M., Kitamura, S., Kawai, Y., Imai, Y., & Gondo, Y. (2008). Validation of the 7-minute screen for the detection of early-stage Alzheimer's disease. *Dementia and Geriatric Cognitive Disorders, 25*, 248-255. doi:10.1159/000115972

James, J. M., & Bolstein, R. (1992). Large monetary incentives and their effect on mail survey response rates. *Public Opinion Quarterly, 56*, 442–453. doi:10.1086/269336

Jeffres, L. W. (1997). *Mass media effects* (2nd ed.). Prospect Heights, IL: Waveland.

Jones, J. H. (1981). *Bad blood: The Tuskegee syphilis experiment.* New York: Free Press.

Jones, K. M., & Friman, P. C. (1999). A case study of behavioral assessment and treatment of insect phobia. *Journal of Applied Behavior Analysis, 32*, 95–98. doi:10.1901/jaba.1999.32-95

Jones, J. T., Pelham, B. W., Carvallo, M., & Mirenberg, M. C. (2004). How do I love thee, let me count the Js: Implicit egotism and interpersonal attraction. *Journal of Personality and Social Behavior, 87*, 665–683. doi:10.1037/0022-3514.87.5.665

Kamin, L. J. (1974). *The science and politics of IQ.* Potomac, MD: Lawrence Erlbaum.

Kassin, S. M., & Kiechel, K. (1996). The social psychology of false confessions: Compliance, internalization, and confabulation. *Psychological Science, 7*, 125–128. doi:10.1111/j.1467-9280.1996.tb00344.x

Katz, J. (1972). *Experimentation with human beings.* New York: Russell Sage Foundation.

Kazdin, A. E. (2003). *Research design in clinical psychology* (4th ed.). Boston: Allyn and Bacon.

Kent, R. N., Wilson, G. T., & Nelson, R. (1972). Effects of false heart-rate feedback on avoidance behavior: An investigation of "cognitive desensitization." *Behavior Therapy, 3*, 1–6. doi:10.1016/S0005-7894(72)80046-7

Kercood, S., & Grskovic, J. A. (2009). The effects of highlighting on the math computation performance and off-task behavior of students with attention problems. *Education & Treatment of Children, 32*, 231-241.

Killeen, P. R. (2005). An alternative to null-hypothesis significance tests. *Psychological Science, 16*, 345–353. doi:10.1111/j.0956-7976.2005.01538.x

Kling, K. C., Hyde, J. S., Showers, C. J., & Buswell, B. N. (1999). Gender differences in self-esteem: A meta-analysis. *Psychological Bulletin, 125*, 470–500. doi:10.1037/0033-2909.125.4.470

Klohnen, E. C., & Luo, S. (2003). Interpersonal attraction and personality: What is attractive-self similarity, ideal similarity, complementarity, or attachment security? *Journal of Personality and Social Psychology, 83*, 709–722. doi:10.1037/0022-3514.85.4.709

Koegel, R. L., Vernon, T. W., & Koegel, L. K. (2009). Improving social initiations in young children with autism using reinforcers with embedded social interactions. *Journal of Autism and Developmental Disorders, 39*, 1240-1251. doi:10.1007/s10803-009-0732-5

Kuder, G. F., & Richardson, M. W. (1937). The theory of estimation of test reliability. *Psychometrika, 2*, 151–160. doi:10.1007/BF02288391

Kuo, M., Adlaf, E. M., Lee, H., Gliksman, L., Demers, A., & Wechsler, H. (2002). More Canadian students drink but American students drink more: Comparing college alcohol use in two countries. *Addiction, 97*, 1583–1592. doi:10.1046/j.1360-0443.2002.00240.x

La Vaque, T. J., & Rossiter, T. (2001). The ethical use of placebo controls in clinical research: The declaration of Helsinki. *Psychophysiology & Biofeedback, 26*, 23–37. doi: 10.1023/A:1009563504319

Li, C., Pentz, M. A., & Chou, C. (2002). Parental substance use as a modifier of adolescent substance use risk. *Addiction, 97*, 1537–1550. doi:10.1046/j.1360-0443.2002.00238.x

Liguori, A., & Robinson, J. H. (2001). Caffeine antagonism of alcohol-induced driving impairment. *Drug and Alcohol Dependence, 63*, 123–129. doi:10.1016/S0376-8716(00)00196-4

Likert, R. (1932). A technique for the measurement of attitudes. *Archives of Psychology* (No. 140), 55.

Lilienfeld, S. O., Lynn, S. J., & Lohr, J. M. (2003). Science and pseudoscience in clinical psychology: initial thoughts, reflections, and considerations. In S. O. Lilienfeld, S. J. Lynn, & J. M. Lohr (Eds.), *Science and pseudoscience in clinical psychology* (pp. 1-11). New York: The Guilford Press.

Loftus, G. R. (1996). Psychology will be a much better science when we change the way we analyze data. *Current Directions in Psychological Science, 5,* 161-171. doi:10.1111/1467-8721.ep11512376

Loftus, E. F., & Palmer, J. C. (1974). Reconstruction of automobile destruction: An example of the interaction between language and memory. *Journal of Verbal Learning & Verbal Behavior, 13,* 585-589. doi:10.1016/S0022-5371(74)80011-3

Logue, A. W. (1991). *The psychology of eating and drinking: An introduction* (2nd ed.). New York: W. H. Freeman and Company.

Lord, F. M. (1953). On the statistical treatment of football numbers. *American Psychologist, 8,* 750-751. doi:10.1037/h0063675

Ludwig, T. D., & Geller, E. S. (1991). Improving the driving practices of pizza deliverers: Response generalization and moderating effects of driving history. *Journal of Applied Behavior Analysis, 24,* 31–44. doi:10.1901/jaba.1991.24-31

Maloney, D. M. (1984). *Protection of human research subjects: A practical guide to federal laws and regulations.* New York: Plenum Press.

McClelland, D. C. (1958). Risk taking in children with high and low need for achievement. In J. W. Atkinson (Ed.), *Motives in fantasy, action, and society* (pp. 306–321). New York: Van Nostrand.

McKenna, K. Y., & Bargh, J. A. (2000). Plan 9 from cyberspace: The implications of the Internet for personality and social psychology. *Personality and Social Psychology Review, 4,* 57-75. doi:10.1207/S15327957PSPR0401_6

McMahon, S. R., Rimsza, M. E., & Bay, R. C. (1997). Patients can dose liquid medication accurately. *Pediatrics, 100,* 330–333.

Melton, G. B., Levine, R. J., Koocher, G. P., Rosenthal, R., & Thompson, W. C. (1988). Community consultation in socially sensitive research: Lessons from clinical trials in treatments for AIDS. *American Psychologist, 43,* 573–581. doi:10.1037/0003-066X.43.7.573

Milgram, S. (1963). Behavioral study of obedience. *Journal of Abnormal and Social Psychology, 67,* 371–378. doi:10.1037/h0040525

Mitchell, M. L., Jolley, J. M., & O'Shea, R. P. (2007). *Writing for psychology* (2nd ed.). Belmont, CA: Thomson Wadsworth.

Mitchell, K. J., Wolak, J., & Finkelhor, D. (2007). Trends in youth reports of sexual solicitations, harassment and unwanted exposure to pornography on the internet. *Journal of Adolescent Health, 40,* 116–126. doi:10.1016/j.jadohealth.2006.05.021

Myers, A., & Hansen, C. (2006). *Experimental psychology* (6th ed.). Belmont, CA: Wadsworth.

National Commission for the Protection of Human Subjects in Biomedical and Behavioral Research (1979). *Ethical principles and guidelines for the protection of human subjects of research.* Retrieved from http://www.hhs.gov/ohrp/humansubjects/guidance/belmont.htm

National Research Council. (1996). *Guide for the care and use of laboratory animals.* Washington, DC: National Academy Press.

Ng, D. M., & Jeffery, R. W. (2003). Relationships between perceived stress and health behaviors in a sample of working adults. *Health Psychology, 22,* 638–642. doi:10.1037/0278-6133.22.6.638

Nicks, S. D., Korn, J. H., & Mainieri, T. (1997). The rise and fall of deception in social psychology and personality research. *Ethics and Behavior, 7,* 69–77. doi:10.1207/s15327019eb0701

Norman, G. (2010). Likert scales, levels of measurement and the "laws" of statistics. Retrieved from http://www.springerlink.com/content/p111562668125341/

Office of Laboratory Animal Welfare. (2002). *Public health service policy on humans and use of laboratory animals.* Retrieved from http://grants.nih.gov/grants/olaw/references/phspol.htm

O'Hara, R., Brooks, J. O., Friedman, L., Schroder, C. M., Morgan, K. S., & Kraemer, H. C. (2007). Long-term effects of mnemonic training in community-dwelling older adults. *Journal of Psychiatric Research, 4,* 585–590. doi:10.1016/j.jpsychires.2006.04.010

Oppenheimer, L. (2006). The belief in a just world and subjective perceptions of society: A developmental perspective. *Journal of Adolescence, 29,* 655–669. doi:10.1016/j.adolescence.2005.08.014

Orne, M. T. (1962). On the social psychology of the psychological experiment: With particular reference to demand characteristics and their implications. *American Psychologist, 17,* 776–783. doi:10.1037/h0043424

Page, R. M., Hammermeister, J. J., & Scanlan, A. (2000). Everybody's not doing it: Misperceptions of college students' sexual activity. *American Journal of Health Behavior, 24,* 387–394.

Piliavin, I. M., Rodin, J., & Piliavin, J. A. (1969). Good samaritanism: An underground phenomenon. *Journal of Personality and Social Psychology, 13,* 289–299. doi:10.1037/h0028433

Piliavin, J. A., & Piliavin, I. (1972). Effects of blood on reactions to a victim. *Journal of Personality and Social Psychology, 23,* 353–361. doi:10.1037/h0033166

Pope, H. G., Ionescu-Pioggia, M., & Pope, K. W. (2001). Drug use and life style among college undergraduates: A 30-year longitudinal study. *American Journal of Psychiatry, Special Issue, 158,* 1519–1521. doi:10.1176/appi.ajp.158.9.1519

Posner, R. A. (2007). *The little book of plagiarism.* New York: Pantheon Books.

Posner, M. I., & Badgaiyan, R. D. (1998). Attention and neural networks. In R. W. Parks & D. S. Levine (Eds.), *Fundamentals of neural network modeling: Neuropsychology and cognitive neuroscience* (pp. 61–76). Cambridge, MA: The MIT Press.

Quirin, M., Kazén, M., & Kuhl, J. (2009). When nonsense sounds happy or helpless: The implicit positive and negative affect test (IPANAT). *Journal of Personality and Social Psychology, 97,* 500-516. doi:10.1037/a0016063

Rahe, R. H., & Arthur, R. J. (1978). Life change and illness studies: Past history and future directions. *Journal of Human Stress, 4,* 3–15.

Ray, W. J. (2000). *Methods: Toward a science of behavior and experience* (6th ed.). Bellmont, CA: Wadsworth.

Rea, L. M., & Parker, R. A. (2005). *Designing and conducting survey research: A comprehensive guide.* San Francisco: Jossey-Bass.

Reich, W. T. (Ed.). (1995). *Encyclopedia of bioethics: Revised edition* (vol. 3). New York: Simon & Schuster.

Ring, K., Wallston, K., & Corey, M. (1970). Mode of debriefing as a factor affecting subjective reaction to a Milgram-type obedience experiment: An ethical inquiry. *Representative Research in Social Psychology (University of North Carolina, Department of Psychology), 1,* 67–88.

Romanov, L. (2006). *Car carma.* Toronto: InsuranceHotline. com.

Rosenhan, D. L. (1973). On being sane in insane places. *Science, 179,* 250–258.

Rosenthal, R., & Fode, K. L. (1963). The effect of experimenter bias on the performance of the albino rat. *Behavioral Science, 8,* 183–189.

Rosenthal, R., & Rosnow, R. (1975). *The volunteer subject.* New York: John Wiley & Sons.

Rosnow, R., & Rosenthal, R. (1997). *People studying people: Artifacts and ethics in behavioral research.* New York: W. H. Freeman & Company.

Rosnow, R. L., & Rosnow, M. (2006). *Writing papers in psychology: A student guide to research papers, essays, proposals, posters, and handouts* (7th ed.). Belmont, CA: Thomson Wadsworth.

Rubin, Z. (1985). Deceiving ourselves about deception. Comment on Smith and Richardson's "Amelioration of deception and harm in psychological research." *Journal of Personality and Social Psychology, 48,* 252–253. doi:10.1037/0022-3514.48.1.252

Rucklidge, J. J. (2009). Successful treatment of OCD with a micronutrient formula following partial response to cognitive behavioral therapy (CBT): A case study. *Journal of Anxiety Disorders, 23,* 836-840. doi:10.1016/j.janxdis.2009.02.012

Ryan, C. S., & Hemmes, N. S. (2005). Effects of the contingency for homework submission on homework submission and quiz performance in a college course. *Journal of Applied Behavior Analysis, 38,* 79-88. doi:10.1901/jaba.2005.123-03

Sales, B. D., & Folkman, S. (2000). *Ethics in research with human participants.* Washington, DC: APA.

Schmidt, S. R. (1994). Effects of humor on sentence memory. *Journal of Experimental Psychology: Learning, Memory, & Cognition, 20,* 953–967. doi:10.1037/0278-7393.20.4.953

Scoville, W. B., & Milner, B. (1957). Loss of recent memory after bilateral hippocampal lesions. *Journal of Neurology, Neurosurgery, and Psychiatry, 20,* 11–21. doi:10.1136/jnnp.20.1.11

Sears, D. (1986). College sophomores in the laboratory: Influences of a narrow data base on social psychology's view of human nature. *Journal of Personality and Social Psychology, 51,* 515–530. doi:10.1037/0022-3514.51.3.515

Shanahan, F. (1984, October). *BAT overview and preliminary results of selected subtests.* Paper presented at the annual meeting of the Human Factors in Aviation Screening and Performance Prediction Sub-Technical Advisory Group of the Human Factors Engineering Technical Advisory Group, San Antonio, TX.

Shapiro, A. K., & Morris, L. A. (1978). The placebo effect in medical and psychological therapies. In S. L. Garfield & A. E. Bergin (Eds.), *Handbook of psychotherapy and behavior change: An empirical analysis* (2nd ed.). (pp. 369–410). New York: Wiley.

Shrauger, J. S. (1972). Self-esteem and reactions to being observed by others. *Journal of Personality and Social Psychology, 23,* 192–200. doi:10.1037/h0033046

Siegel, J. M. (1990). Stressful life events and use of physician services among the elderly: The moderating role of pet ownership. *Journal of Personality and Social Psychology, 58,* 1081–1086. doi:10.1037/0022-3514.58.6.1081

Skjoeveland, O. (2001). Effects of street parks on social interactions among neighbors. *Journal of Architectural and Planning Research, Special Issue, 18,* 131–147.

Smith, S. S., & Richardson, D. (1983). Amelioration of deception and harm in psychological research: The important role of debriefing. *Journal of Personality and Social Psychology, 44,* 1075–1082. doi:10.1037/0022-3514.44.5.1075

Stanley, B., Sieber, J., & Melton, G. (1996). *Research ethics: A psychological approach.* Lincoln, NE: University of Nebraska Press.

Stephens, R., Atkins, J., & Kingston, A. (2009). Swearing as a response to pain. *NeuroReport: For Rapid Communication of Neuroscience Research, 20,* 1056-1060. doi:10.1097/WNR.0b013e32832e64b1

Strack, F., Martin, L. L., & Stepper, S. (1988). Inhibiting and facilitating conditions of the human smile: A nonobtrusive test of the facial feedback hypothesis. *Journal of Personality and Social Psychology, 54,* 768–777. doi:10.1037/0022-3514.54.5.768

Sun, Y. (2001). Family environment and adolescents' well-being before and after parents' marital disruption: A longitudinal analysis. *Journal of Marriage and Family, 63,* 697–713. doi:10.1111/j.1741-3737.2001.00697.x

Szuchman, L. T. (2008). *Writing with style: APA style made easy* (4th ed.). Belmont, CA: Thomson Wadsworth.

Teasdale, J. D., & Fogarty, S. J. (1979). Differential effects of induced mood on retrieval of pleasant and unpleasant events from episodic memory. *Journal of Abnormal Psychology, 88,* 248–257. doi:10.1037/0021-843X.88.3.248

Thigpen, C. H., & Cleckley, H. M. (1954). A case of multiple personality. *Journal of Abnormal and Social Psychology, 49,* 135–151.

Thigpen, C. H., & Cleckley, H. M. (1957). *Three faces of Eve.* New York: McGraw-Hill.

Thompson, T., Webber, K., & Montgomery, I. (2002). Persistence and persistence of worriers and non-worriers following success and failure feedback. *Personality & Individual Differences, 33,* 837–848. doi:10.1016/S0191-8869(01)00076-9

Tomer, J. F. (1987). Productivity through intra-firm cooperation: A behavioral economic analysis. *Journal of Behavioral Economics, 16,* 83–95.

Trockel, M. T., Barnes, M. D., & Egget, D. L. (2000). Health-related variables and academic performance among first-year college students: Implications for sleep and other behaviors. *Journal of American College Health, 49,* 125-131.

Tversky, A., & Kahneman, D. (1973). Availability: A heuristic for judging frequency and probability. *Cognitive Psychology, 5,* 207–232. doi:10.1016/0010-0285(73)90033-9

Tyson, G. A., Schlachter, A., & Cooper, S. (1988). Game playing strategy as an indicator of racial prejudice among South African students. *Journal of Social Psychology, 128,* 473–485.

Valins, S., & Ray, A. A. (1967). Effects of cognitive desensitization on avoidance behavior. *Journal of Personality and Social Psychology, 7*, 345–350. doi:10.1037/h0025239

Van Tilburg, M. A. L., & Vingerhoets, A. (2002). The effects of alcohol on mood induced by an emotional film: A study among women. *Journal of Psychosomatic Research, 53*, 805–809. doi:10.1016/S0022-3999(02)00325-2

Wacker, D. P., Steege, M. W., Northup, J., Sasso, G., Berg, W., Reimers, T., Cooper, L., Cigrand, K., & Donn, L. (1990). A component analysis of functional communication training across three topographies of severe behavior problems. *Journal of Applied Behavior Analysis, 23*, 417–429. doi:10.1901/jaba.1990.23-417

Wager, T. D., & Smith, E. E. (2003). Neuroimaging studies of working memory: A meta-analysis. *Cognitive, Affective & Behavioral Neuroscience, 3*, 255–274. doi:10.3758/CABN.3.4.255

Wager, T. D., Rilling, J. K., Smith, E. E., Sokolik, A., Casey, K. L., Davidson, R. J., Kosslyn, S. M., Rose, R. M., & Cohen, J. D. (2004). Placebo-induced changes in fMRI in the anticipation and experience of pain. *Science, 303*, 1162–1167.

Warnes, E., & Allen, K. D. (2005) Biofeedback treatment of paradoxical vocal fold motion and respiratory distress in an adolescent girl. *Journal of Applied Behavior Analysis, 38*, 529-532. doi:10.1901/jaba.2005.26-05

Weber, S. J., & Cook, T. D. (1972). Subject effects in laboratory research: An examination of subject roles, demand characteristics, and valid inferences. *Psychological Bulletin, 77*, 273–295. doi:10.1037/h0032351

Wilkinson, L., & Task Force on Statistical Inference. (1999). Statistical methods in psychology journals. *American Psychologist, 54*, 594–604. doi:10.1037/0003-066X.54.8.594

Wolak, J., Mitchell, K. J., & Finkelhor, D. (2002). Close online relationships in a national sample of adolescents. *Adolescence, 37*, 441–455.

Wolosin, R., Sherman, S., & Mynat, C. (1972). Perceived social influence in a conformity situation. *Journal of Personality and Social Psychology, 23*, 184–191. doi:10.1037/h0033041

Wood, W., Wong, F. Y., & Chachere, J. G. (1991). Effects of television violence on viewers' aggression in unconstrained social-interaction. *Psychological Bulletin, 109*, 371–383. doi: 10.1037/0033-2909.109.3.371

Wright, K. B. (2005). Researching Internet-based populations: Advantages and disadvantages of online survey research, online questionnaire authoring software packages, and Web survey services. *Journal of Computer-Mediated Communication, 10*(3), article 11. Retrieved from: http://jcmc.indiana.edu/vol10/issue3/wright.html

Young, S. N. (2002). The ethics of placebo in clinical psychopharmacology: The urgent need for consistent regulation. *Journal of Psychiatry & Neuroscience, 27*, 319–321.

NAME INDEX

SUBJECT INDEX